The Things Which My Father Saw

The Things Which My Father Saw

Approaches to Lehi's Dream and Nephi's Vision

*edited by Daniel L. Belnap,
Gaye Strathearn,
and Stanley A. Johnson*

**THE 40TH ANNUAL
BRIGHAM YOUNG UNIVERSITY
SIDNEY B. SPERRY SYMPOSIUM**

The Sperry Symposium is sponsored annually by Brigham Young University and the Church Educational System in honor of Sidney B. Sperry. In the course of his forty-five-year career as a religious educator, Dr. Sperry earned a reputation for outstanding teaching and scholarship. The symposium seeks to perpetuate his memory by fostering continuing research on gospel topics.

Copublished by the Religious Studies Center, Brigham Young University, Provo, Utah, and Deseret Book Company, Salt Lake City, Utah.

© 2011 Brigham Young University

All rights reserved.

Any uses of this material beyond those allowed by the exemptions in U.S. copyright law, such as section 107, "Fair Use," and section 108, "Library Copying," require the written permission of the publisher, Religious Studies Center, 167 HGB, Brigham Young University, Provo, Utah 84602. The views expressed herein are the responsibility of the authors and do not necessarily represent the position of Brigham Young University or the Religious Studies Center.

DESERET BOOK is a registered trademark of Deseret Book Company.

Visit us at DeseretBook.com

Library of Congress Cataloging-in-Publication Data
Sperry Symposium (40th : 2011 : Brigham Young University)
   The things which my father saw : approaches to Lehi's dream and Nephi's vision / edited by Daniel L. Belnap, Gaye Strathearn, and Stanley A. Johnson ; the 40th Annual Brigham Young University Sidney B. Sperry Symposium.
   p. cm.
   Summary: The 2011 Sperry Symposium volume explores the rich symbolism of Lehi's dream and Nephi's vision, placing such symbols as the mists of darkness, the great and spacious building, and the church of the Lamb of God in the context of the last days.
   Includes bibliographical references and index.
   ISBN 978-1-60908-738-8 (hardbound : alk. paper)
   1. Lehi's dream—Congresses. 2. Book of Mormon. Nephi, 1st—Congresses. 3. Lehi (Book of Mormon figure)—Congresses. I. Belnap, Daniel, editor. II. Strathearn, Gaye, editor. III. Johnson, Stanley A. (Stanley Alan), 1950– , editor. IV. Title.
   BX8627.S64 2011
   289.3'22—dc23   2011017588

Printed in the United States of America
Publishers Printing, Salt Lake City, UT

10 9 8 7 6 5 4 3 2

Contents

Preface vii

1. The Power of Inspired Invitations
   Russell T. Osguthorpe 1

2. The Double Nature of God's Saving Work:
   The Plan of Salvation and Salvation History
   Heather Hardy 15

3. The Church of the Lamb of God
   Casey Paul Griffiths 37

4. Lehi's Dream and Nephi's Vision as Apocalyptic Literature
   Jared M. Halverson 53

5. Nephi's Vision and the Loss and Restoration of
   Plain and Precious Truths
   Lori Driggs 70

6. Lehi Dreamed a Dream:
   The Report of Lehi's Dream in Its Biblical Context
   Dana M. Pike 92

7. "The Presence of the Lord"
   Jennifer C. Lane 119

8. The Strait and Narrow Path:
   The Covenant Path of Discipleship Leading to the Tree of Life
   Aaron Schade 135

9. The Doctrine of Christ in 2 Nephi 31–32 as an Approach to the
   Vision of the Tree of Life
   Jared T. Parker 161

10. Lehi's Dream as a Template for Understanding
    Each Act of Nephi's Vision
    Amy Easton-Flake 179

11. Prophetic Perspectives:
    How Lehi and Nephi Applied the Lessons of Lehi's Dream
    Grant Hardy 199

12. "Even as Our Father Lehi Saw":
    Lehi's Dream as Nephite Cultural Narrative
    Daniel L. Belnap 214

13. *Not Partaking of the Fruit:*
    Its Generational Consequences and Its Remedy
    Matthew L. Bowen 240

14. "Delivered by the Power of God": Nephi's Vision of America's Birth
    Kenneth L. Alford 264

15. What Nephi's Vision Teaches
    about the Bible and the Book of Mormon
    Frank F. Judd Jr. 282

16. Illuminating a Darkened World
    Seth J. King 300

17. Bitter and Sweet: Dual Dimensions of the Tree of Life
    C. Robert Line 318

18. Sacrifice and Condescension:
    Types and Shadows for Latter-day Living
    D. Mick Smith 330

19. "It Filled My Soul with Exceedingly Great Joy":
    Lehi's Vision of Teaching and Learning
    Charles Swift 347

20. Lehi's Dream and Nephi's Vision as Used by Church Leaders
    Mary Jane Woodger and Michelle Vanegas Brodrick 374

    Index 393

Preface

In January 2007, President Boyd K. Packer addressed the student body of Brigham Young University using Lehi's dream as his theme. In his presentation, he challenged the listener to find meaning in the dream: "You may think that Lehi's dream or vision has no special meaning for you, but it does. You are in it; all of us are in it. Nephi said that all scripture is likened a unto us, that it might be for our profit and learning" (1 Nephi 19:23). Lehi's dream or vision of the iron rod has in it everything a Latter-day Saint needs to understand the test of life."[1]

This invitation reveals the importance of both the dream and Nephi's subsequent vision. The importance is further emphasized by the amount of space, almost one-half of the entire book of 1 Nephi (almost 20 percent of the total among of Nephi's writings), that Nephi devotes to the two experiences.

Coming as it did at the beginning of the wilderness journey, a journey fraught with unknown perils, with no apparent understanding as to how long the journey would be, and without even a promise that they would return to the lands of their inheritance in Jerusalem, the dream reflects Lehi's fears, as both a father and a leader, that his people would become lost, physically and spiritually. Though highly symbolic, it gave him and his people assurances from the Lord. Yet the symbolism in the dream is such that those who read of it today can sympathize with Lehi's plight. Lehi's dream speaks to all of us who find ourselves, at times, battling the dark and dreary trials of mortality. Thus the dream exemplifies our own struggle to return to our Heavenly Father and also guides us through this stage of the plan of salvation. As Elder L. Tom Perry pointed out in the October 1995 general conference, "This dream or vision of the tree of life, symbolically presented, provides us with much knowledge about life and the course we should follow."[2]

One individual who was clearly struck by the power of the dream was Lehi's son Nephi, who, upon hearing his father recount the particulars of the dream, desired to have a similar revelatory experience. Like another young man being raised to become prophet, Nephi desired to "see, and hear, and know these things, by the power of the Holy Ghost," knowing that to the one who diligently sought for such, "the mysteries of God [would] be unfolded unto them" (1 Nephi 10:17, 19). Though Nephi did in fact see the symbolic elements that his father did, the manner in which he experienced them was strikingly different.

Nephi became a witness and recorder to one of the most detailed visionary discourses on Christ's ministry, both in the Old World and the New; the ensuing apostasy following Christ's death and resurrection; and the eventual Restoration of the gospel, culminating in the fulfilling of the Father's covenant with his children on this earth. Yet, as vast as this historical revelatory panorama was, Nephi understood the individualized nature of his vision as witnessed by his conversation with his brothers as he applied his vision to their experience (see 1 Nephi 15) and provided a scriptural example of President Packer's invitation to find ourselves in the dream.

Since the coming forth of the Book of Mormon, the dream and the vision has resonated in the Latter-day Saint spiritual imagination, reflected in song and artwork, fulfilling President Packer's observation. In this vein, this volume presents twenty studies on Lehi's dream and Nephi's vision that provide insights into the ancient setting, the meaning of the symbols, and their gospel application. The papers were delivered at the 40th Annual Sidney B. Sperry Symposium held at Brigham Young University. The keynote address of Russell T. Osguthorpe, Sunday School general president for The Church of Jesus Christ of Latter-day Saints, opens our volume with insights into teaching and learning and sets the tone for what we hope is an invitation inherent in each paper—that the reader may come to realize that they too "are in it."

We express our appreciation to the contributors of the volume and the work that they have done as represented in the volume. We also thank our reviewers who, through their comments and insights, blessed both the authors and us as the committee. Finally, we also thank Robert L. Millet, R. Devan Jensen, Brent R. Nordgren, Joany O. Pinegar, Jessica Arnold, Heidi Bishop, Jake Frandsen, Matt Larsen, Art Morrill, Jonathon Owen, Rosie Ricks, Nyssa Silvester, and Jeff Wade at the Religious Studies Center at Brigham Young University and our colleagues at Deseret Book for the time and effort that they gave to bring forth this volume. To all those mentioned, we recognize how integral each individual was to the quality of this volume—thank you.

Daniel L. Belnap
Stanley A. Johnson
Patty A. Smith
Gaye Strathearn
Thomas A. Valletta
2011 Sperry Symposium
Committee

Notes

1. Boyd K. Packer, "Lehi's Dream and You," *Ensign*, August 2010, 22.
2. Tom L. Perry, "If Ye Are Prepared Ye Shall Not Fear," *Ensign*, November 1995, 35.

1

The Power of Inspired Invitations

Russell T. Osguthorpe

When I was called as the Sunday School general president in March of 2009, President Thomas S. Monson welcomed me into his office in his uniquely warm way. He looked at me as if he were sizing me up and said, "You've got broad shoulders—that's good!" Then Elder Russell M. Nelson greeted me with equal warmth, and the three of us sat down to talk. President Monson reviewed my bio sheet and made a few comments on it. Then he issued the call to serve in the Sunday School. He told the story of Lucy Gertsch, his Sunday School teacher when he was a young boy, and shared his own conviction of the importance of learning and teaching in the Church. His purpose, I believe, was to build my confidence—to help prepare me for the responsibilities that lay ahead.

A calling is a particular kind of invitation. In fact, a calling includes several invitations. In my case, President Monson's secretary *invited* me to accept an appointment to see him. Then President Monson *invited* me into his office and *invited* me to accept this assignment. Following my visit with President Monson, Elder Nelson *invited* me to his office, where he instructed me on

---

Russell T. Osguthorpe is Sunday School general president of The Church of Jesus Christ of Latter-day Saints, a professor of instructional psychology and technology, and director of the Center for Teaching and Learning at Brigham Young University.

my duties in this new calling. He *invited* me to learn my duty. At every point in the process, I could exercise my own agency to accept or reject the invitation offered to me. I could have turned down the secretary or decided not to keep the appointment or even turned down the call. The decision always rested with me, the one receiving the invitation.

The act of inviting is central to the gospel of Jesus Christ. Invitations occur not only with callings but are woven into the fabric of our daily lives as members of the restored Church. Until recently, I had never considered the central role of invitation in Lehi's vision. One of the most powerful scenes in the dream—a dream in which all scenes are powerful—is the image of Lehi immediately after he tastes the fruit of the tree of life. What is his first thought once he knows how desirable the fruit is? He wants his family to partake. So he begins looking for them afar off. He sees his wife and Sam and Nephi, and he notices that they seem unsure of where to go: "At the head thereof I beheld your mother Sariah, and Sam, and Nephi; and they stood as if they knew not whither they should go. And it came to pass that I beckoned unto them; and I also did say unto them with a loud voice that they should come unto me, and partake of the fruit, which was desirable above all other fruit. And it came to pass that they did come unto me and partake of the fruit also" (1 Nephi 8:14–16).

There are multiple layers and types of invitations in Lehi's dream. At the very beginning of the vision, Lehi sees the Savior, "and it came to pass that he spake unto me, and bade me follow him" (1 Nephi 8:6). We no longer use the verb *bid* to mean *ask* or *invite*. We would not say, "He bade me come to dinner." If we examine the former use of the word, however, we see that it was a special kind of invitation. It meant to "entreat" or "beg" or "pray" the person to come.[1] To *entreat* means to "ask with earnestness." It is not a casual form of invitation. It is heartfelt, just as when Ruth said to Naomi, "Intreat me not to leave thee" (Ruth 1:16).

Then Lehi sees the tree of life. He is attracted to the tree as soon as he sees it because in this case he knows that it is an answer to his prayer. It is an invitation by the Spirit: "And after I had traveled for the space of many hours in darkness, I began to pray unto the Lord that he would have mercy on me, according to the multitude of his tender mercies. . . . And it came to pass that I beheld a tree, whose fruit was desirable to make one happy" (1 Nephi 8:8, 10).

Invitations emerge throughout Lehi's vision—the first, a direct invitation to Lehi from the Savior; the second, an inaudible invitation of the Spirit; and the third, a direct invitation from Lehi to his family. When Lehi invited Sariah, Sam, and Nephi to come and partake, his earnestness was evident. He first beckoned them—meaning he motioned to them with his hand—and then he called to them in a loud voice. He wanted them to taste the fruit that he had tasted. He wanted them to experience the love of God as he had experienced it.

Throughout the scriptures, the Lord says, "Come unto me" (John 6:65; 3 Nephi 9:14; 12:19, 23; 27:20; 12:20, 24; Alma 5:16, 34, 35; Ether 4:13, 18; 12:27). These are the very words that Lehi uses when he invites his family to partake of the fruit: "And I also did say unto them with a loud voice that they should *come unto me*" (1 Nephi 8:15; emphasis added). Lehi is the loving father who invites his children to come unto him, just as we are constantly being invited to come unto God.

Why are invitations so central to the gospel? Because invitations are based on agency, and moral agency is a foundational doctrine. When Lehi saw Sariah, Sam, and Nephi, they were standing at the head of the river—a river that represented the very "depths of hell" (1 Nephi 12:16). Lehi wanted to protect them from the filth in that river. He wanted them to partake of the love of God as he had. The way to help them do that was to *invite* them to come and partake. They came and partook, but Laman and Lemuel did not. Laman and Lemuel received the same invitation from the same loving father. But they rejected the invitation. The scriptures do not provide any detail about the nature of their rejection. We don't know if they were belligerent or if they simply turned away and ignored their father. But it really doesn't matter whether their resistance was passive or aggressive. They chose to distance themselves from their family and from God. Rather than accepting an inspired, loving invitation, they accepted the deceptive invitation of the adversary—they fell into temptation.

Invitation and Temptation

An inspired invitation is one that comes from God—an invitation to do good or to be good: "But behold, that which is of God inviteth and enticeth to do good continually; wherefore, every thing which inviteth and enticeth to do good, and to love God, and to serve him, is inspired of God" (Moroni 7:13).

A deceptive invitation comes from the adversary—an invitation to do evil or be evil: "For the devil is an enemy unto God, and fighteth against him continually, and inviteth and enticeth to sin, and to do that which is evil continually" (Moroni 7:12).

The table below contrasts inspired invitation with temptation. As the table shows, the motive for inspired invitations is always love. The Lord invites us to come unto him because he loves us. Lehi invited his family to partake of the fruit because he loved them. Temptation, on the other hand, is always motivated by selfishness. From the time of the Council in Heaven until now, the adversary has wanted all the glory for himself. He is *never* trying to help those he tempts; he is trying only to hurt them.

	Invitation versus temptation	
	Inspired invitation	Temptation
Motive	Love	Selfishness
Action	Entreat	Coerce
Result	Agency and love	Addiction

How do the actions of inspired invitation and temptation differ? To *invite* means to *entreat*. An invitation is an act of love. Lehi wanted with all of his heart to have each member of his family partake of the fruit. He wanted them to "grow up unto the Lord" (Helaman 3:21). Satan and all of his followers, however, use coercion to accomplish their ends. Temptation is an act of manipulation and coercion—an attempt to cause unsuspecting victims to turn on themselves, to do something that somewhere inside they know will destroy them. The Lord has told us that in the last days, "conspiring men" (D&C 89:4) will try to lead us astray in every way imaginable. And the motives of these conspiring individuals are usually quite obvious—to satisfy their own selfish desires.

The table also contrasts the results of invitations with those of temptations. The most common result of yielding to temptation is addiction to something: drugs, sex, pornography, gambling—the list goes on and on. And some addictions, when they spin out of control, literally lead to physical death. All such addictions, however, can lead to spiritual death—moving away from God, as did Laman and Lemuel in Lehi's dream.

The results of accepting an inspired invitation are vastly different than the results of yielding to a temptation. This is the key to understanding why invitation, as a principle of the gospel, is so central to our eternal well-being. Accepting an invitation from God—whether that invitation comes directly from him through the Spirit or from one of his servants—has positive consequences, both immediate and eternal. Each time a person accepts an inspired invitation, that person's power to exercise his or her moral agency increases. Agency is a gift from God that permits us to follow his will. Every time we heed his invitation to "come follow me," our internal power to choose the good increases. We draw near unto him, and so he draws near unto us (see D&C 88:63). The closer we draw unto him, the more we want to follow his will for us in the future.

A young child does not need to experience an electrical shock to learn that it's dangerous to insert metal objects into an outlet. With instruction—in this case, firm invitation—the child can gain self-control. The child's power increases to choose the good thing. By accepting the parent's invitation, which is given out of love and concern for the child, the child's interest in making the wrong choice subsides. So it is with all of our choices. When we accept the invitation to pray often, we eventually do not need to work to make it happen. Rather, we come to a point where we never want to miss praying. We draw near unto God, and he draws near unto us. Our will gradually becomes more in tune with his will—all because of our desire to accept his invitations.

The culmination of accepting inspired invitations is increased capacity to love. This is so closely aligned with one's capacity to exercise moral agency that the two almost merge. But I like to think of them separately, simply because it is a constant reminder of the importance of both agency and charity in our lives. When children grow up with parents who love them, the children are more likely to become loving parents themselves. But when children experience neglect and abuse, their capacity to love is damaged. Unless they receive the help they need, they may continue to suffer in their adult years.

By accepting Lehi's inspired invitation to come unto him and partake of the fruit, Sariah, Sam, and Nephi experienced not only an increase of God's love but also an increase in their own capacity to love. Every time we accept an inspired invitation, we grow in our ability to express love.

While serving as a mission president, I usually asked each new missionary in our first interview, "Is there anything I should know about you that would help me serve you better as a mission president?" One missionary said, "Well, yes. I probably should tell you that I've never spoken with anyone except my family." I thought he was simply telling me that he was quiet, something I had already noticed. But no, he was telling me that he had never spoken with anyone outside his own home.

I asked, "So, what did you do at school when the teacher called on you?"

He said, "They knew that I wouldn't say anything, so they never called on me."

"How about friends? Did you have any friends you talked with?"

"No, I didn't have any friends, just my family—they were the only ones I ever talked to."

"How did you ever get up the courage to come on a mission?" I asked.

"I don't know. I've always wanted to serve a mission; so when the call came, I accepted it."

I was actually quite astonished. I wondered how this missionary could ever succeed if he was unable to speak to strangers, since that would be his focus every day for the next two years. I found myself praying for him often. One day I called to see how he was doing. I asked, "How many times in one day does someone say to you, 'Hey, you should talk more. You're a missionary!'" He responded, "Maybe twenty or thirty times." I said, "I've got something I want you to try. I want you to do just two things: speak up, and speak first." I explained that people would no longer see him as overly quiet if he could raise his speaking volume and then speak before his companion spoke. He would not need to dominate the conversation—just do those two things.

Several months later, I had the privilege of watching him teach an investigator. At this point in his mission—about one year into his service—he was no longer perceived as being too quiet. He was confident and convincing. He had accepted his call as a missionary, even though he knew it would be the greatest challenge he would ever face. And then he eagerly followed the counsel he received. Because of that, the Lord blessed him to love the people. When you were around him, it was easy to feel the love he had for those he served. The more he accepted the invitations that came to him, the greater was his capacity to love others.

Therefore, What?

There is great power in giving and receiving inspired invitations. The power is divine. Lehi accepted the Lord's invitation to follow him. Lehi prayed to receive the tender mercies of the Lord, and the Lord showed him the tree of life. Lehi then invited his family to receive these same tender mercies. Some of his family accepted the invitation while others did not. Agency and love were at play every step of the way. Agency and love were the foundational motives for the invitations, and they were the ultimate results of the actions. Sariah, Sam, and Nephi came closer to the Lord, accepted his invitations, and gave their wills to him. Their capacity to make righteous choices grew continually. Laman and Lemuel rejected the invitation of their father, yielded to temptation, distanced themselves from God, and gradually reaped the whirlwind of destruction (see Proverbs 1:27).

The implication for those who *receive* invitations is clear: be wise servants in discerning an inspired invitation from one that is deceptive—follow the whisperings of the Spirit and don't yield to temptation. However, once we know that an invitation is one we should accept, *how* exactly do we accept it? Consider callings, for example. While serving in a bishopric, I once extended a call to a faithful sister to serve as a Primary teacher. She paused and then said, "I would be happy to accept that call at any other time, but I am going in for jaw surgery this coming week, and my mouth will be wired shut for several months. Perhaps I could continue to serve in the library until I can talk again."

The bishopric was unaware of her surgery and felt fine about postponing the call. She was willing but not able. On another occasion, I went to the home of an older couple in the ward to issue a call to the sister, a faithful and devoted member of the Church. I rang the doorbell, and then I had a distinct impression not to issue the calling. I wasn't sure what to say to the sister as we began our conversation. Then I said, "I intended to call you to serve in the Primary, but I feel that this would not be the correct calling for you right now." She began to cry and then responded, "I have served in the Primary for more than twenty years, but I just can't do it right now. My health is just not good enough." I assured her that she was not turning down the call, because the call was not being issued. In essence, I withdrew the invitation I had intended to give.

Both of these sisters were totally willing, but their physical conditions did not permit them to serve in certain ways at that particular time. But what about someone who *is* physically and mentally able but who rejects the calling? This is a serious mistake. While serving as a stake president in a BYU married stake, I became concerned about the number of brethren who consistently failed to do their home teaching. As I counseled with the elders quorum presidents, I said, "I'm concerned about those who are not being visited, but I'm actually much more concerned about those who month after month fail to carry out their priesthood duty."

Although the home teachers may not have viewed it this way, they were falling short of the covenants they had made to visit those they had been assigned to home teach. I explained to the quorum presidents that when anyone fails to keep a covenant, he or she loses something—something dies inside that person (see D&C 5:27). And when that pattern continues for a sustained period of time, the person's faith can diminish unless he "humble[s] himself... and keep[s the] commandments" (D&C 5:28). Passively resisting an inspired invitation is dangerous. When Laman and Lemuel resisted their father's invitation to partake of the fruit, they might have done it without any anger at all, but their decision to resist was still just as catastrophic. Covenants come to us by invitation, and it is our privilege and duty to make and keep them.

After my great-great-grandparents immigrated from England to Pennsylvania, the missionaries called upon them, taught them the gospel, and invited them to be baptized. Their history indicates that when they heard the gospel and received the invitation to join the Church, they "accepted it gladly." Soon after their baptism, they also accepted the invitation to cross the plains and settle in Utah. This is how we want to accept inspired invitations—with gladness, wholeheartedly. We can accept a calling in this way. We can also reject a calling. Or we can even accept with reluctance. The scriptures teach us that accepting with reluctance and giving our gift of service without real intent is the same as if we had not given the service at all (see Moroni 7:8). So when a calling comes—when any inspired invitation comes to us—we need to accept it gladly and carry out our duties with real intent.

What about the implications for those who *give* invitations? There are many types of inspired invitations one might offer. In fact, the variance of invitations is as wide as the variance among the individuals receiving the invitations. To be inspired, an invitation has to meet the unique needs of a certain individual. The invitation needs to be what the Lord knows that person needs.

Missionaries give invitations to their investigators. Teachers give invitations to their students. Parents give invitations to their children. We give invitations to those we believe will accept our invitations. When we invite, we are hoping the one receiving our invitation will accept. An inspired invitation can never be selfishly given. It always has to be based on love for the one receiving the invitation.

Missionaries want their investigators to accept their invitation to be baptized. Teachers want their students to accept their invitation to learn and live the gospel. Parents want their children to accept their invitation to not "fight and quarrel one with another" (Mosiah 4:14). This means that the process of giving the invitation may be as important as the invitation itself. Parents may feel inspired to invite one of their children to do something, but unless the parents deliver the invitation in the right way, the child may not accept it. And, of course, even if they do deliver the invitation in exactly the right way, the child may still choose to reject it. So the stakes are high when we are giving invitations. We need to make certain that the invitation we are giving is the one the Lord would have that person receive and that we give it in the best possible way.

In the missionary training video *District 2*, a companionship tries to commit a man to be baptized. The invitation is a good one. But the missionaries become frustrated when the man resists, and they then begin to apply pressure. Following the encounter, the missionaries realize that they could have done better. They resolve to improve their process of giving this sort of invitation in the future. Another set of missionaries offers the same invitation but in a very different way. In this scene, there is no pressure. The whole focus is on the needs of the couple considering baptism. It is the same invitation, but it is given in a very different way.

Matthew O. Richardson shared with me an experience he had in the grocery store. As he was shopping, he noticed a mother who was losing her patience with her two children. One of the children kept hitting the other. The exasperated mother took the hand of her child and began hitting it while saying, "We do not hit; we do not hit!" This was a good invitation, but it was not given in a good way.

There is an infinite variety in types of invitations, as well as in the ways those invitations can be given. One invitation can inspire, while another invitation can comfort. An invitation can strengthen, heal, or instruct. Invitations can come in the form of correction. As Elder Neal A. Maxwell said, "Be grateful for people in your lives who love you enough to correct you."[2] Invitations can cause us to work, study, pray, or participate in "wholesome recreational activities"—one of my favorite phrases in the proclamation on the family.[3] Invitations can heal: "Have ye any that are sick among you? . . . Bring them hither and I will heal them" (3 Nephi 17:7). Invitations can testify: "Then saith he to Thomas,

Reach hither thy finger, and behold my hands; and reach hither thy hand, and thrust it into my side: and be not faithless, but believing" (John 20:27).

Invitations and the Restoration

The Restoration itself began with an invitation, and it led to an endless series of additional invitations. A single verse of scripture in James was invitational for young Joseph—so powerful that he went to the grove to pray. His petition to the Lord was then answered with an invitation, in this case an invitation of what *not* to do: "I was answered that I must join none of them" (Joseph Smith—History 1:19). Later Moroni told Joseph that God had a "work for [him] to do" (v. 33).

Think of it: the Restoration of the gospel of Jesus Christ depended on invitations being received and followed. If Joseph had not been inspired by the invitation of James, he may not have sought an answer to his question. If he had not accepted the invitation of Moroni to go to a hill, retrieve the plates, and translate them through the gift and power of God, he would not have received the blessings of doing so. The Lord would have found a different person to restore the gospel—a person who would accept his invitations. We have the blessing of being able to study the Book of Mormon and Lehi's vision because of invitations.

But the Restoration not only began with invitations being offered and accepted—invitations are at the heart of the gospel today as well. The Restoration began with Joseph, but it did not end with him. We are all participants in the ongoing restoration. Many glorious wonders continue to be revealed to the prophets. One of those wonders is "The Family: A Proclamation to the World." This document is filled with invitations to husbands and wives, mothers and fathers, individuals, and "citizens and officers of government everywhere."[4] Invitations have always been and will continue to be central to the Restoration.

In the words that the Prophet Joseph wrote to John Wentworth in 1842, "The truth of God will go forth boldly, nobly, and independent."[5] Those prophetic words are reaffirmed every day, and the reaffirmations come most often through invitations being offered and accepted.

Missionaries throughout the world are extending invitations to read the Book of Mormon, attend Church meetings, and be baptized and confirmed. In fact, as we learn in *Preach My Gospel*, without some form of invitation or commitment being extended, the missionaries have not taught an actual lesson. Invitation is an essential part of learning and teaching. My firm belief is that every time any individual learns a truth of the gospel of Jesus Christ, the truth of God is going forth "boldly, nobly, and independent." Yet missionaries and newly baptized members are not the only ones who are helping the truth of God go forth. Help comes from anyone who accepts the invitation to learn and then teaches the truths of the restored gospel.

Inspired invitations are powerful because they always have blessings attached to them. Speaking to those who are less active, President Dieter F. Uchtdorf has said, "The Church needs you; we need you. It is always the right time to walk in His way. It is never too late." He also said, "I testify that the Lord will bless your life, endow you with knowledge and joy beyond comprehension."[6]

President Monson has invited us all to reach out and rescue those who have become less active in the Church. Just as Lehi invited his family to come and partake of the fruit, President Monson continues to invite us to invite our less-active neighbors to come back.[7]

During the past year, we have experienced the miracle of rescue in our own family. My wife's brother Steve has been less active for most of his life. I will recount his experience in his own words:

> I made some very poor choices in my life that led to my inactivity in the Church when I was in high school. I also married outside the Church, and my wife was not interested. I had been inactive for fifty years.
>
> My first wife passed away, and I had no plans to remarry.
>
> Then Brooke entered my life. Ours is a great love story and the beginning of my transformation. Brooke has always been active in the Church, so it wasn't long before I was drawn into meeting and associating with members of our ward.
>
> Two years ago Brooke and I attended Women's Conference at BYU. We were seated in the second row from the podium on the floor of the Marriott Center. When President Monson came into the center, the audience stood and spontaneously began singing "We Thank Thee, O God, for a Prophet." It was a stirring moment. As he was standing at the podium looking out over the 22,000 people assembled and singing, he looked directly at me for a moment with a

look on his face that said to me, "Why don't you come join us?" I was simply overwhelmed.

So Steve was invited back into activity in the Church by his wife, by President Monson, by the Spirit, and also by many in his ward and extended family. Invitations were the key. His bishop invited him to prepare to be ordained a priest in the Aaronic Priesthood and then later invited him to receive the Melchizedek Priesthood. Not long after that, he received his patriarchal blessing and called to tell me what a wonderful experience it was. One invitation after another—some direct invitations to do something, others indirect invitations of example that caused him to change.

So I ask myself the following questions: Am I open to the invitations that I need to receive? Am I in tune so that I can understand each invitation and act on it? Am I sensitive enough to the needs of those around me that I can invite them as the Savior would invite them? These are pretty tall orders, but they are absolutely essential to my own progress, as well as to the progress of those around me. When I'm reading the scriptures, can I listen to the Spirit as Joseph did? Can I exercise the faith to go and do as he did? Can I receive and give invitations in my marriage that will strengthen rather than weaken the relationship? Can I receive inspired invitations from my children and give them the invitations they need? Can I give invitations in ways that will help and never in ways that will hurt? Are my invitations to others based on love rather than on my own selfish desires?

As I mentioned earlier, the first verse of Lehi's vision was the invitation he received from the Savior to follow him. The final verse that Nephi recounts is a reflection of Lehi's disappointment that Laman and Lemuel rejected his invitation. He first says, "And Laman and Lemuel partook not of the fruit, said my father" (1 Nephi 8:35). Nephi then explains in verse 36 how fearful Lehi was that Laman and Lemuel would be cut off from the presence of the Lord because of their unwillingness to accept the invitation to partake of the fruit. In the next verse, Lehi exhorts Laman and Lemuel "with all the feeling of a tender parent" (1 Nephi 8:37). Inspired invitations like those of Lehi are always given in love. After preaching the truths of the gospel to his sons, Lehi's parting invitation was for his sons to follow his invitation and keep the commandments: "And after he had preached unto them, and also prophesied unto them of many things, he bade them to keep the commandments of the Lord; and he did cease speaking unto them" (1 Nephi 8:38).

Lehi loved his sons enough to invite them again and again. They did not return to the Lord in this life, but my brother-in-law Steve has shown that it's possible to come back even after fifty years of inactivity. One never knows which invitation will finally be accepted, so we should never stop inviting.

In a pre–general conference training meeting for General Authorities and Area Seventies, President Monson spoke on the importance of "the rescue"—helping people like Steve come back into activity. President Monson was particularly powerful in his remarks that day. At one point he looked across the audience of Church leaders seated in front of him and asked, "Brethren, when was the last time you rescued someone?" His question was as powerful an invitation as I had ever received. A prophet of God—the only one on earth who is authorized to exercise all priesthood keys—was asking me when I last rescued someone.

His invitation hit me hard. I had actually been trying to help someone close to me return to activity. I had invited him to attend general conference, even though he was not attending any other Church meetings. So, during the break, I called him on the phone to see if he was still planning to come. He assured me that he was. He came, but he has not yet returned to full activity in the Church. On one occasion, after he had turned down one of my invitations, I asked him if he wanted me to stop inviting him. He said, "No, you can still invite me. When you invite me, I start thinking of some of the things I miss in the Church." I said, "Good, keep thinking about all of the things you miss."

President Monson's invitation to rescue someone is a prophetic invitation. It has already led to the reactivation of thousands of Church members. I once attended a multistake leadership meeting in which the Area Seventy reported that over four hundred prospective elders in those stakes had returned to activity during the previous year. There are still so many who would be blessed by coming back.

So, in the spirit of President Monson's invitation, I ask, "When was the last time you gave an inspired invitation?" Every inspired invitation helps rescue someone from something. An invitation might rescue someone from ignorance, from doubt, or from discouragement. It might rescue someone from making a poor decision. It might help someone set a righteous goal. If we invite in the right way—in the way the Savior would invite—those who receive the invitation and act on it will come closer to him, and their lives will improve.

Every week in classrooms throughout the Church, members old and young hope to be edified by deepening their knowledge of the restored gospel of Jesus Christ. Every week, teachers have the privilege of extending invitations to those they teach. The invitations are often woven into the very verses of scripture they are reviewing in class. But the teacher needs to recognize the invitation and help others in the class receive and act on it. These scriptural invitations come from the Lord and from his prophets. They are inspired invitations. And each person in the class will understand the invitation and act on it differently based upon his or her unique needs. Our role as teachers is to make certain that we help class members see and understand these inspired invitations.

My prayer is that we will reach out to those around us who need us—that we will receive and give inspired invitations. I pray that our invitations will be given "with all the feeling of a tender parent," as Lehi's invitations were given to his family. I pray that those who receive our invitations will respond as Sariah, Sam, and Nephi did. I know that as we give inspired invitations, the Savior himself will carry our words into the hearts of those we love. He lives. He is our Redeemer. He will never stop inviting us to come unto him.

Notes

1. *Oxford English Dictionary*, 2nd ed., "bade."
2. Neal A. Maxwell, "Remember How Merciful the Lord Hath Been," *Ensign*, May 2004, 44–46.
3. "The Family: A Proclamation to the World," *Ensign*, November 1995, 102.
4. "The Family: A Proclamation to the World," 102.
5. *History of the Church of Jesus Christ of Latter-day Saints*, ed. B. H. Roberts, 2nd ed. rev. (Salt Lake City: Deseret Book, 1957), 4:540.
6. Dieter F. Uchtdorf, "The Way of the Disciple," *Ensign*, May 2009, 75–78.
7. See Thomas S. Monson, "Stand in Your Appointed Place," *Ensign*, May 2003, 54–57.

2

The Double Nature of God's Saving Work: The Plan of Salvation and Salvation History

Heather Hardy

While tarrying in the valley of Lemuel, Lehi instructed his family members on their individual spiritual well-being by relating his dream of a tree laden with precious fruit, as recorded in 1 Nephi 8. Two chapters later, in the same address, he prophesied additionally of the Lord's future redemptive acts on behalf of collective Israel. Nephi received a vision of his own, reported in 1 Nephi 11–14, which integrated these two distinct aspects of salvation by elaborating on the Lord's redemption of both individuals and entire peoples. Over the ensuing decades, Lehi, Nephi, and Nephi's brother Jacob pondered the implications of this double nature of God's saving work, studying scriptural precedents and receiving new revelations. Their insights—expanding on Lehi's wilderness address—serve as both the thematic underpinning of Nephi's small plates and the theological foundation of the Lehite understanding of salvation.

Heather Hardy earned an MBA from Brigham Young University and worked for several years in university administration at Yale and BYU before leaving the workforce to raise children and pursue a life of learning.

Lehi's Wilderness Address as Differentiating
Two Aspects of Salvation

Whenever considering Lehi's dream, readers should keep in mind that 1 Nephi 8 was only the first half of the prophet's address to his family in the valley of Lemuel. Despite the fact that Nephi concludes this chapter with the words "After he had preached unto them, . . . he did cease speaking unto them" (1 Nephi 8:38), when the account resumes after a brief editorial interlude (1 Nephi 9), Lehi is still talking. As Nephi reports, "After my father had made an end of speaking the words of his dream, and also of exhorting [Laman and Lemuel] to all diligence, he spake unto them concerning the Jews" (1 Nephi 10:2). Subsequent textual evidence confirms a continuation of Lehi's speaking. For example, when Nephi expresses his desire to see, hear, and know his father's teachings for himself, he mentions both "the things which [Lehi] saw in a vision, and also the things which he spake by the power of the Holy Ghost" (1 Nephi 10:17). In describing his own vision, Nephi includes elements not only from Lehi's dream but also from his prophecies. Later, when Laman and Lemuel seek clarification of difficult elements "concerning the things which [Lehi] had spoken unto them" (1 Nephi 15:2), their questions address the meaning of the allegory of the olive tree (from 1 Nephi 10) as well as of Lehi's dream of the tree (from 1 Nephi 8; see 1 Nephi 15:7–36). It is within a single discourse, then, that Lehi teaches his children about obtaining the fruit desirable above all others (see 1 Nephi 8:2–38) and also about the coming of a Messiah, the scattering of Israel, and the ministering of the Holy Ghost to the Gentiles (see 1 Nephi 10:2–14).

The balanced structure of Lehi's wilderness teachings similarly suggests an intended unity in his account of the dream in 1 Nephi 8 and his discussion of the destiny of the house of Israel in 1 Nephi 10. Both segments include an allegory (8:4–35; 10:12–14), prophecies (8:38; 10:3–15), and some level of interpretation (8:36; 10:4, 13, 15). Each allegory focuses on a particular fruit-bearing tree. The first, the allegory of the tree of life,[1] came to Lehi as an original revelation and reflects his concerns about the well-being of family members as they traveled in the wilderness. It depicts individuals responding to the offer of sustenance inherent in an exquisite tree whose fruit is "desirable to make one happy" (1 Nephi 8:10). The second, the allegory of the olive tree, was apparently derived from Lehi's study of the prophet Zenos's writings on the brass plates since both compare the house of Israel to an olive tree whose branches are broken off, dispersed, and eventually gathered together again (see 1 Nephi 5:10, 21; see also Jacob 5). Lehi's reading of Zenos is supplemented by new revelation that seems to have been prompted by his concern for the well-being of the house of Israel in light of Jerusalem's pending destruction (see 1 Nephi 10:2–3). Significantly, these are the only two allegories included in the Book of Mormon, and Lehi adopts each in turn as the conceptual foundation for a distinct aspect of salvation.

By his own admission, Nephi substantially abridges Lehi's teachings in both 1 Nephi 8 and 10, explicitly to save room on the plates and avoid redundancy (8:29–30, 38; 10:8, 15). He indicates that a more comprehensive version of his father's wilderness address is preserved "in mine other book" (1 Nephi 10:15), and he seems to presume, erroneously as it turns out, that his readers will have access to both accounts. Here, in the small plates, Nephi's editing initially de-emphasizes the unity of Lehi's discourse; instead of combining the two segments into a single literary unit, Nephi deliberately separates them by inserting an extended editorial comment in the middle (1 Nephi 9).[2] The disconnection invites readers to consider the thematic link between the two portions of Lehi's teachings.

Nephi has previously articulated a strong editorial priority for his second record, the account we are reading in 1 and 2 Nephi: "And it mattereth not to me that I am particular to give a full account of all the things of my father, for they cannot be written upon these plates, for I desire the room that I may write of the things of God. For *the fulness of mine intent* is that I may persuade men to come unto the God of Abraham, and the God of Isaac, and the God of Jacob, and be saved" (1 Nephi 6:3–4; emphasis added). If this focus on salvation is indeed the "fulness" of Nephi's intent, and if the capacity of the small plates is indeed limited, we should expect that everything that Nephi includes in these writings can be readily understood as encouraging his readers to believe in God's saving power and respond accordingly.

In Nephi's telling here, Lehi does, in fact, open each half of his discourse with the subject of salvation. Regarding the dream, Lehi reports, "And behold, because of the thing which I have seen, I have reason to rejoice in the Lord because of Nephi and also of Sam; for I have reason to suppose that they, and also many of their seed, will be saved" (1 Nephi 8:3). Later, in speaking of the future of the Jews, Lehi again begins his remarks in salvific terms, prophesying first of their eventual deliverance from Babylon, that "they should return again, yea, even be brought back out of captivity" (1 Nephi 10:3). Note here that these passages—abbreviated as they are—seem to be describing very different concepts of salvation: the first concerning the spiritual well-being of individuals, and the latter, the temporal redemption of an entire people. The contours of these distinct but complementary concepts of salvation will become clearer as we proceed through Nephi's small plates.

Lehi introduces the plan of salvation (1 Nephi 8). At this point, we turn to Lehi's dream in 1 Nephi 8. The elements of the allegory are familiar enough: a beautiful tree, a rod of iron, a river, mists of darkness, and a great and spacious building. An angel will reveal their meanings to Nephi in his subsequent vision (see 1 Nephi 11:21–25, 36; 12:16–18), and Nephi will emend some of his father's details when he responds to Laman's and Lemuel's questions, describing an awful gulf of filthiness and a flaming fire ascending up forever (see 1 Nephi 15:26–30). Decades later, he will again return to the symbols of Lehi's dream, finally identifying the "strait and narrow path" and how it is that one can "press forward" thereon (see 1 Nephi 8:20, 21, 24, 30; 2 Nephi 31:9, 18–20; 33:9).

In keeping with the salvific theme of Lehi's brief introduction, the thing to note here about the dream is that the people clinging to the rod or arriving at the tree or jeering from the great and spacious building are all making personal choices and are being rewarded or punished as individuals. Although the invitation to come to the tree is offered to all, the actual partaking (or rejecting) of the fruit is performed individually. And while "great was the multitude that did enter into that strange building" (1 Nephi 8:33), the people have all self-selected; the edifice represents a collective of individuals and not a nation or people such as the Gentiles or the Babylonians.

Lehi is particularly concerned about his eldest sons' choices and the gravity of their consequences: "But behold, Laman and Lemuel, I fear exceedingly because of you," he tells them twice, "lest [you] should be cast off from the presence of the Lord" (1 Nephi 8:4, 36). This last comment is the only part of Lehi's interpretation of the allegory that Nephi provides us, and it suggests two things. First, the offer of a blessing (the fruit of the tree) is an oppositional one that ultimately separates those who choose to accept it from those who do not. Once the offer is extended, there is no neutral response; it culminates in either salvation or judgment. Second, although the allegory's focus is on nourishment, albeit of a remarkable kind, the reality it addresses has a spiritual significance far beyond the typical dailiness of such concerns. While Lehi acknowledges the import and urgency of the risk of being cast off from the Lord's presence, it is Nephi who will later make explicit that this dissociation will last "forever and ever," having "no end" (1 Nephi 15:30).

From the allegory, we can outline the concept of salvation that Lehi is presenting here: It is available to individuals as a matter of personal decision and action. It is something that must be pursued and persisted in. It has been planned in advance—there is a clearly defined goal and a particular path to follow for its attainment. The path is punctuated by perils; it is possible to be diverted along the way, to become confused, to wander off, and even to enjoy the blessing and then be ashamed. It is possible to request assistance and receive guidance. Others can either aid in the endeavor (by inviting and encouraging one's progress) or detract from it (by presenting distractions or mocking the journey). The nature of salvation itself is not precisely defined. It is represented as deliverance from darkness, fatigue, and weariness with the world, and it somehow constitutes what is happy, sweet, pure, and desirable in superlative ways.

Although familiar to Latter-day Saints, this complex of ideas would have been very new to Lehi and his family, who would have been accustomed to thinking of both the conditions and rewards of salvation in the context of the house of Israel, covenants, and the material blessings of prosperity, political security, and tenure in the promised land. While an allegory is an effective vehicle for rendering a new complex of ideas both accessible and memorable, it is a less than optimal foundation for establishing doctrine; and in this regard, we sorely miss the preaching and prophesying that Lehi added by way of interpretation (see 1 Nephi 8:38) and that Nephi chose to omit at this point from his record. The doctrine will be provided later, an understanding of salvation that we will label here as the *plan of salvation*.

When we as Latter-day Saints speak of the plan of salvation, we generally mean God's design—in its grandest scope—for the well-being of his children as individuals, from premortal existence through the three degrees of glory, sealed together in eternal family units. There is little evidence that the Nephites knew of the two extreme ends of the plan (even for Joseph Smith, a full understanding of this was revealed only gradually). Nevertheless, beginning with Lehi's allegory of the tree in 1 Nephi 8, the Book of Mormon clearly teaches that mortality is a time of testing, that all people will eventually be returned to the presence of God in a resurrected state to be judged of their actions during the days of their probation, and that, while in mortality, individuals can choose to come to Christ, repent of their sins, and be saved from eternal captivity to the devil through the Atonement regardless of ethnicity, gender, or social station.[3] Although only the intermediate events of God's plan, from mortality through judgment, were revealed to Lehi and his family, they were sufficient to instruct them (along with Nephi's readers) in knowing how, as individuals, "to come unto . . . God . . . and be saved" (1 Nephi 6:4).

Lehi introduces salvation history (1 Nephi 10). Lehi preaches about a different aspect of salvation in 1 Nephi 10. He begins by prophesying of the return of the Jerusalem exiles from their captivity in Babylon, and he then predicts that God will again intervene in Israel's history at a very specific time and place: "Yea, even six hundred years from the time that my father left Jerusalem, a prophet would the Lord God raise up among the Jews—even a Messiah, or, in other words, a Savior of the world" (1 Nephi 10:4). Although Lehi is alluding here to a well-known prophecy from Moses (see Deuteronomy 18:15, 18), the specificity of his teaching regarding both the timing and identity of this prophet is communicated as new revelation. Lehi has searched the scriptures and found additional corroborating witnesses, and he goes on to affirm "how great a number [of the prophets] had testified of these things, concerning this Messiah" (1 Nephi 10:5). Nephi will later quote several of them from their writings on the brass plates (see 1 Nephi 19:8–17).

Lehi returns to speaking of the Jews and their relationship to both the Gentiles and also to "remnants of the house of Israel" (1 Nephi 10:14). He again provides a conceptual framework by way of an allegory—this time borrowed from the brass plates rather than of his own devising—comparing the future history of these various peoples (including his own descendants) to an olive tree with branches that are broken off and then grafted back in. Throughout these prophecies, he is always speaking of large groups. Clearly, the Jews and the Gentiles are made up of individuals who make personal decisions regarding the gospel, but in Lehi's discussion of salvation here, they are always treated by God as corporate entities.

In this part of his discourse, Lehi presents salvation as large-scale events in which God himself enters into the arena of human activity to judge or deliver entire peoples. We will use the term *salvation history* to designate these historical actions of corporate salvation, a term long used by biblical scholars to denote God's redemptive activity in the human sphere.[4] In contrast to either spiritual concepts of redemption or secular accounts of history, salvation history refers to the sum of those occasions in which God intervenes in human affairs to work out his divine purposes through this-worldly events. Promised blessings are typically both temporal and collective in nature, including land, prosperity, posterity, and political security. Before 600 BC, salvation history was the standard way of reflecting on God's relationship with his people.

Within this theological construct, it is understood that God reveals himself to Israel particularly through "saving acts" that simultaneously offer salvation to the righteous and judgment upon the wicked. These acts include such historical events as the Exodus, the offering of the Mosaic covenant, and the establishment of the children of Israel in the land of Canaan.

In keeping with this tradition, Lehi prophesies in 1 Nephi 10 that the Jews will be restored from captivity only to be scattered again, the Lehites will be led to their own land of promise, and the Gentiles will receive a witness of the Holy Ghost and, eventually, the fulness of the gospel. In Nephi's overarching intention to persuade all men to come unto God and be saved (see 1 Nephi 6:4), the term "men" applies as much to these corporate groups as to individuals, just as "saved" applies to the groups' receipt of such collective blessings as their restoration as a nation, their tenure in a land of promise, and their blessing of having the presence of God in the midst of their community. Although a serious concern with the corporate salvation of the house of Israel is lost from the bulk of the Nephite record after the demise of the first generation that migrated from Jerusalem, it is restored to prominence in the prophecies of the resurrected Jesus as recorded in 3 Nephi 16:4–20 and 20:10–26:5. Salvation history is never thereafter far from the Nephite record keepers' minds as they recognize (and direct) their own writings as a vehicle of both salvation and judgment to the Jews, Gentiles, and Lehites of latter days.[5]

Nephi's Vision as Integrating and Elaborating on Lehi's Two Aspects of Salvation

At the conclusion of Nephi's presentation of Lehi's wilderness address, Nephi has not made it obvious for his readers how the allegories of the two trees (which, in turn, represent the plan of salvation and salvation history) fit together thematically or otherwise. In Nephi's telling, the meaning was apparently unclear to him on first hearing as well, since his initial response was to inquire of the Lord to "see, and hear, and know of these things" (1 Nephi 10:17). It seems here that this desire was not so much for the spiritual encounter he ultimately received as it was for a comprehensive understanding of his father's teachings. Nephi affirms the unfolding of God's mysteries to those who diligently seek for it (see 1 Nephi 10:19); and, once he has been carried away in the Spirit, his request, somewhat surprisingly, is to know the interpretation of the allegory of the tree rather than to taste of the precious fruit (see 1 Nephi 11:10–11). In reporting his own vision, Nephi will forge a conceptual unity between the two aspects of salvation that he has to this point kept separated.[6]

We need to keep in mind that the meaning of Lehi's dream is only half of what Nephi sought to understand after listening to his father's teachings.[7] In the vision he receives, Nephi is first offered a clear identification of elements from the dream in plan of salvation terms: the tree and the fountain represent the love of God, the iron rod is the word of God, the river is the depths of hell, the mists of darkness are temptations of the devil, and the large and spacious building is the pride of the children of men (see 1 Nephi 11:25; 12:16–18). But Nephi's angelic guide goes on to interpret these same symbols in salvation history terms as well, now identifying the tree as the tree of life from the Garden of Eden (thus linking a saving act with individual salvation, a topic Lehi will return to in 2 Nephi 2:15–23); the spacious building represents those who persecute the Apostles, and later the Lehites who, in their folly, war against each other (see 1 Nephi 11:35–36; 12:18–19); and the mists are identified as precursors to the judgments that will befall Lehi's descendants before both the calamities preceding Christ's Nephite visitation and their subsequent annihilation (see 1 Nephi 12:4, 17, 19).

While interspersing interpretative commentary on Lehi's dream from 1 Nephi 8, the presentation of the vision follows the outline provided by Lehi's prophecies from 1 Nephi 10. Nephi first witnesses the mortal coming and baptism of the Messiah (see 1 Nephi 11:14–27; see also 10:4, 9–10), with an explicit reference to Lehi's account: "I looked and beheld the Redeemer of the world, of whom my father had spoken; and I also beheld the prophet who should prepare the way before him" (1 Nephi 11:27; see also 10:5, 7). Immediately before this disclosure, the angel reveals to Nephi that Jesus Christ is the centerpiece of both portions of Lehi's teachings by identifying the tree of the precious fruit with "the Lamb of God" (1 Nephi 11:21; see also 1 Nephi 10:10).

Like his father before him, Nephi also "[speaks] much concerning the Gentiles, and also concerning the house of Israel" (1 Nephi 10:12). Although he makes no explicit reference in his vision to the allegory of the olive tree, he does provide further interpretation of it by mentioning both the judgment and scattering of Israel and by describing in detail his own family's future in the land of promise (see 1 Nephi 12:1–23; 13:39; see also 10:13). Where Lehi prophesies that "after the Gentiles had received the fulness of the Gospel, the natural branches of the olive tree, or the remnants of the house of Israel, should be grafted in, or come to the knowledge of the true Messiah" (1 Nephi 10:14), Nephi provides an explanation of the prophecy in terms of future saving acts: the Lord will manifest himself in the flesh to both the Jews and the Lehites; both of these peoples will record accounts of the Lord's ministry, and then through these accounts (and through the Holy Ghost) the Lord will manifest himself to the Gentiles.[8] Once in the possession of the Gentiles, the records of the Jews and the Lehites "shall be established in one" and "shall make known to all kindreds, tongues, and people, that the Lamb of God is the Son of the Eternal Father, and the Savior of the world" (1 Nephi 13:40–41). Nephi describes how, in the latter days, the salvation of the house of Israel and the salvation of the Gentiles will be intertwined. God's favors will be shown to each in turn so that salvation may ultimately be offered to the entire world (see 1 Nephi 13:42; 14:7).

Additional Development of Lehi's Two Aspects of Salvation

When Nephi takes up the task of presenting the two aspects of God's saving work to his readers, he begins, as he tells us Lehi did, by relating the two allegories in 1 Nephi 8 and 10, thus rendering accessible the broad contours of the plan of salvation and salvation history. In recounting the remainder of Lehi's teachings in the valley of Lemuel, Nephi additionally presents to his readers what is presumably familiar to them from Israel's scriptures (allusions to specific passages, a prophecy of the Jews returning from exile, an understanding of God's saving acts on Israel's behalf, and so forth). Only then does he introduce the innovative prophecies and doctrines that have been gradually unfolded to his family.

Regarding salvation history, Lehi and his sons find much prophetic collaboration for their own revelations in the brass plates, which is hardly surprising since revealing such acts before they occur is one of the primary responsibilities of Israel's prophets (see Amos 3:7). Lehi, as we have seen, alludes to Moses's teachings in Deuteronomy 18 regarding the coming of the Messiah (see 1 Nephi 10:4). Nephi quotes this verse (see 1 Nephi 22:20–21),[9] as well as passages from Zenock, Neum, and Zenos (see 1 Nephi 19:10–12). Most of the cited scriptures provide support for new prophecies regarding God's future dealings with Israel (see 1 Nephi 15:20; 19:22–24; 2 Nephi 6:4–5; 25:7–8). Lehi borrows his allegory of the olive tree in 1 Nephi 10 from Zenos, and he quotes an extensive passage from Joseph of Egypt in 2 Nephi 3. Nephi includes most of Isaiah's chapters 2–14, 29, 48–49 verbatim, along with dozens of individual verses and distinctive phrases;[10] and Jacob quotes Isaiah 49:22–52:2 in 2 Nephi 6–8 and later includes Zenos's entire allegory in Jacob 5. In all cases, their incorporation of the words of brass plates' prophets is careful, deliberate, and nuanced, supporting their own revelations and demonstrating the great value they placed on these records.

The many citations likewise confirm that for Lehi and his sons salvation history was a familiar means of understanding God's saving acts in the context of Israel and her covenants. In contrast, the relative scarcity of prophetic corroboration for Lehi's plan of salvation teachings (Lehi refers to Genesis 3:4–5, 23–24 and Isaiah 14:12 in 2 Nephi 2; Jacob and Nephi both quote Isaiah 55:1 at 2 Nephi 9:50 and 26:25 respectively) demonstrates just how original this doctrine was for Lehi's family. Nephi admits to his brothers that Lehi "truly spake many great things . . . which were hard to be understood, save a man should inquire of the Lord" (1 Nephi 15:3). He, Jacob, and Lehi do inquire and are repeatedly blessed with divine instruction.

The varied but unquestionably authoritative nature of the inspiration the three of them receive confirm its truth value, as they appeal to visions (see 1 Nephi 8:2; 11:1; 2 Nephi 1:4; 2:3; 4:23, 25), the voice of the Lord (see 1 Nephi 13:33–37; 14:3, 7; 2 Nephi 1:20; 9:16, 23; 10:7–19; 2 Nephi 28:30–29:14; 31:11–15), angelic communication (see 1 Nephi 11–14; 19:8–10, 2 Nephi 6:9, 11; 10:3), and the instruction of the Spirit (see 1 Nephi 10:17; 15:12; 2 Nephi 1:6; 4:12; 25:11; Jacob 4:15). As Nephi reflects upon this learning process, he expresses deep satisfaction with all that he has come to know: "For my soul delighteth in the scriptures, and my heart pondereth them, and writeth them for the learning and the profit of my children. Behold, my soul delighteth in the things of the Lord; and my heart pondereth continually upon the things which I have seen and heard" (2 Nephi 4:15–16).

The expanded understanding of Lehi and his sons is expressed in seven additional discourses, six reported by Nephi and the seventh added by Jacob in his own writings. All of these writings focus on the nature of salvation, and each incorporates both the plan of salvation and salvation history, the two aspects Lehi first introduced in his teachings in the valley of Lemuel.[11] The content of these eight salvation-focused discourses can be categorized as follows:

The Double Nature of God's Saving Work as Presented in the Small Plates		
	Plan of Salvation	Salvation History
Lehi's Preaching in the Valley of Lemuel	1 Nephi 8	1 Nephi 10
Introductory Allegory	*Tree of Life*	*Olive Tree*
Nephi's Vision	1 Nephi 11:21–25, 36; 12:9–10, 16–18; 13:36–37, 40; 14:3–4, 7	1 Nephi 11–14
Nephi's Response to Laman and Lemuel	1 Nephi 15:21–36	1 Nephi 15:7–20
Nephi's Appeal to the Brass Plates	1 Nephi 22:30–31	1 Nephi 19–22:29
Lehi's Final Words	2 Nephi 2	2 Nephi 1, 3
Jacob's Discourse	2 Nephi 9	2 Nephi 6–8, 10
Nephi's Concluding Discourse	2 Nephi 31–32	2 Nephi 25–30
Jacob's Quotation and Interpretation of Zenos's Allegory of the Olive Tree	Jacob 6	Jacob 4–5

We see here the inclusion of two sermons each from Lehi and Jacob as well as four from Nephi himself. Evidently, it is important to Nephi to confirm that these doctrines of salvation were independently affirmed by multiple teachers. Elsewhere he explains this commitment to the Deuteronomic law of witnesses: "I will send their words forth unto my children to prove unto them that my words are true. Wherefore, by the words of three, God hath said, I will establish my word." Although Nephi is explicitly referring here to the revelations of Isaiah and Jacob, Lehi's testimony certainly applies as well.

He concludes, "Nevertheless, God sendeth more witnesses, and he proveth all his words" (2 Nephi 11:3; see also Deuteronomy 19:15).

Note the consistency of how all of the eight above-listed discourses address both the plan of salvation and salvation history, even if only for a few verses. Sometimes the two aspects of salvation are thoroughly integrated, as in Nephi's vision; at other times they are balanced but clearly divided, as in Nephi's response to Laman's and Lemuel's questions or in Lehi's final words; and sometimes one aspect or another is emphasized, as in Nephi's appeal to the brass plates. But both aspects of salvation are always included.

Also note that in contrast to Lehi's opening discourse, which presents the plan of salvation first, subsequent iterations always begin with salvation history. This may simply reflect the words as they were originally uttered, but the consistency of the presentation suggests that it may have been Nephi's intention generally to begin with more familiar, scripture-based teachings before moving on to newly revealed tenets. Regardless, there is a significant development of both detailed prophecy and plain-spoken doctrine as Nephi progresses through his reporting of these discourses, beginning with the allegories that distinguish the two aspects of salvation in 1 Nephi 8 and 10, and culminating in his own teachings at 2 Nephi 25–32 which specify the role that Lehi's posterity will play in the coming forth of a salvific book in the latter days and then finally enumerate conditions for attaining individual salvation.

There are dozens of examples of how Lehi, Nephi, and Jacob clarify and integrate the concepts of the plan of salvation and salvation history in their discourses, either by means of explicit instruction or by such indirect strategies as scriptural allusion and recontextualization, wordplay, and the juxtaposition of prophecies. By way of illustration, we will consider a few examples from each of these founding Nephite prophets. First, we will see how Lehi deftly recontextualizes salvation history prophecies from the brass plates in plan of salvation terms, followed by the observation of Jacob's clever use of wordplay to highlight connections between the two aspects of salvation. Then we will consider Nephi's most significant integration of the plan of salvation and salvation history as we trace the development of his teachings about the Atonement of Jesus Christ over the course of his writings, concluding with his return to Lehi's wilderness teachings in declaring how it is that individuals can "come unto the God of Abraham, and the God of Isaac, and the God of Jacob, and be saved" (1 Nephi 6:4).

Lehi's recontextualization of salvation history prophecies in plan of salvation terms. Nephi opens his account of Lehi's final words to his family with a paraphrase of the blessings they have thus far received. Lehi's first quoted words report another revelation: "For, behold, . . . I have seen a vision, in which I know that Jerusalem is destroyed" (2 Nephi 1:4), and he continues to prophesy about the welfare of his posterity in their new land of promise. Later, when he shifts to admonishment, he elaborates on a passage from Isaiah:[12]

Isaiah 52:1–2	2 Nephi 1:13–14
Awake, awake, put on thy strength, O Zion; put on thy beautiful garments, O Jerusalem, the holy city; for henceforth there shall no more come into thee the uncircumcised and unclean. *Shake thyself from the dust; arise,* and sit down, O Jerusalem; *loose thyself from the bands of thy neck,* O *captive* daughter of Zion.	O that ye would *awake; awake* from a deep sleep, yea, even from the sleep of hell, and *shake off the awful chains by which ye are bound,* which are the chains which bind the children of men, that they are carried away *captive* down to the eternal gulf of misery and woe. Awake! and *arise from the dust.*

Note the similarity in theme and distinctive wording here: both passages cluster the exhortations to *awake* and *shake oneself* or *arise from the dust* in the context of the chains or bands of captivity. But where Isaiah is foreseeing the deliverance of Jerusalem from Babylonian captivity through the perspective of salvation history, Lehi recontextualizes the prophecy in plan of salvation terms for his wayward sons. Both the placement of his words and its revised message are emotionally devastating. After praising God for the land of liberty to which he has brought them, Lehi indicates that Laman and Lemuel are already in captivity, not politically or temporally but rather with the chains of hell, which will bring them finally to captivity in the "eternal gulf of misery and woe." Lehi takes the same words that Isaiah has used to proclaim deliverance and instead warns of destruction.

Later in the discourse, after giving his most complete description of the plan of salvation, Lehi again conflates the two aspects of salvation by recontextualizing a critical text from the brass plates. Consider his application of the famous conclusion of the Lord's covenant with the children of Israel just prior to their entry into Canaan: "I have set before you *life and death*, blessing and cursing: *therefore choose life*, that both thou and thy seed may live" (Deuteronomy 30:19; emphasis added). Although Moses is speaking here to the people collectively in a salvation history mode, Lehi's adaptation at 2 Nephi 2:27–28 will again shift to a plan of salvation context (including a corresponding shift from mortal "life" to "eternal life"): "Wherefore, men are free . . . to choose *liberty and eternal life*, through the great Mediator of all men, or to choose *captivity and death*, according to the captivity and power of the devil. . . . And now, my sons, I would that ye should look to the great Mediator, and hearken unto his great commandments; and be faithful unto his words, and *choose eternal life*."

Jacob's use of wordplay to highlight connections between salvation history and the plan of salvation. For a second example of a particular strategy for integrating salvation history and the plan of salvation, we will consider Jacob's use of several instances of wordplay in 2 Nephi 9. Several chapters earlier, following the general pattern, Jacob opens this discourse with a discussion of salvation history that appeals to both established scripture and new revelation (see 2 Nephi 6:4, 8–9). After interspersing his own commentary with a lengthy quotation from Isaiah, Jacob makes a transition in 2 Nephi 9 to a discussion of the plan of salvation by first identifying and then manipulating an ambiguity.

"For I know that ye have searched much, many of you, *to know of things to come*," Jacob tells his listeners. In keeping with the salvation history emphasis of the discourse so far, he continues by relating a prophecy with which his audience is by now very familiar: "I know that ye know that in the body [the Lord] shall show himself unto those at Jerusalem, from whence we came" (2 Nephi 9:4–5). But in between these two comments, and camouflaged by his use of similar rhetoric, Jacob inserts an apparent non sequitur: "I know that ye know that our flesh must waste away and die; nevertheless, in our bodies we shall see God." The ambiguity Jacob is playing off here is the particular content of the "things to come." Is it the salvation history proclamation of the coming of the Son of God or the plan of salvation inevitability of postmortal judgment? Jacob's presentation suggests both and also implies a connection between the two events, not just because they share the rather generic connections of Nephite interest and futurity but also because they each involve the literal witnessing of God.

As he moves on to a comprehensive articulation of how it is that "in our bodies we shall see God," Jacob continues to manipulate ambiguities to his advantage by applying plan of salvation meanings to familiar salvation history concepts. One of his most clever wordplays in this regard is his use of the salvation history term "restoration." As 2 Nephi 9 opens, Jacob's theme has been the dual nature of this concept for Israel's future when, in the latter days, "they shall be restored to the true church and fold of God" and also "established in all their lands of promise" (v. 2). But in short order he has applied both of these aspects—a spiritual sense as well as a physical one—to resurrection itself, in which hell and paradise will each deliver up the spirits they contain and the grave will deliver up its captive bodies so that "the bodies and the spirits of men will be *restored* one to the other" (vv. 12–13). Later, Jacob tries yet another permutation, this time comparing a plan of salvation sense of united, resurrected bodies being "*restored* to that God who gave them breath" (v. 26; emphasis added) with a salvation history sense of his distant posterity as a group being "*restored*" to God by coming to "the true knowledge of their Redeemer" (2 Nephi 10:2; emphasis added).

Nephi's presentation of the Atonement of Christ as the ultimate integration of salvation history and the plan of salvation. Absolutely the most significant integration of salvation history and the plan of salvation in the small plates is its prophetic declaration of the person and mission of Jesus Christ. He is the central figure in each aspect of salvation, and we will consider in turn how his coming into the world constitutes a saving act for entire peoples, and also how it provides the necessary mediation for the eternal deliverance of individual souls. Indeed, he is the only "way" or "name" given whereby man can be saved (see 2 Nephi 9:41; 25:20; 31:21), either collectively or individually.

Lehi begins his prophesying of the coming of Christ in 1 Nephi 10 in terms of salvation history. He is the prophet to be raised up among the Jews (see v. 4). He will provide redemption for the sins of the world as "the Lamb of God," that is, in the ritual terms of the Mosaic law, as a scapegoat for the collective (v. 10). Nephi expands the understanding of the Messiah's coming as a saving act when he makes clear from his own vision that Christ will manifest himself in turn to the Jews, the Lehites, and the Gentiles. In each case, the divine manifestation will cause division among an entire people, resulting in both judgment and salvation.

Thus Nephi reports that when the Holy One of Israel comes in the flesh among the Jews, he will minister in power and great glory, performing mighty miracles, healing the sick, and casting out devils (see 1 Nephi 11:28, 31). These gracious actions in themselves offer deliverance for their recipients and are sufficient evidence for those who observe them to know that he is their God. Nephi assures us that those at Jerusalem who believe in Christ will be saved in the kingdom of God (see 2 Nephi 25:13), but the vast majority will stiffen their necks against him, judge him to be a thing of naught, and cast him out from among them (see 2 Nephi 10:5; 1 Nephi 19:9; 11:28). In their rejection of Jesus, the Jews will collectively bring down the judgments of God upon themselves, or, as Zenos prophesied, "they shall be scourged by all people, *because* they crucify the God of Israel, and turn their hearts aside, rejecting signs and wonders, and the power and glory of the God of Israel" (1 Nephi 19:13; emphasis added; see also 2 Nephi 6:10; 10:6; 25:12).

Nephi asserts that Jesus' postmortal manifestation to the Lehites will also constitute a saving act. In this case, the division of the people will precede his coming. The wicked who kill those prophets and Saints that testify of Christ will be destroyed in the great and terrible judgments preceding his visitation (see 1 Nephi 12:4–5; 2 Nephi 26:3–6), but to those who believe in the prophecies and wait patiently for his coming, "the Son of righteousness shall appear unto them, and he shall heal them, and they shall have peace with him" (2 Nephi 26:9). Again, these are momentous events that will be experienced by multitudes, all together, in historical time.

Both Lehi and Nephi describe the manifestation of Jesus Christ to the Gentiles, a manifestation which will not take the bodily form that it does for the Jews and Lehites.[13] Rather, Lehi prophesies that after the Messiah has risen from the dead, he will make himself known to the Gentiles by the Holy Ghost and then, in the latter days, will offer to them "the fulness of the Gospel" (see 1 Nephi 10:11, 14). Nephi explains that the Lamb of God will "manifest himself unto them in word, and also in power, in very deed," such that "if the Gentiles repent it shall be well with them; . . . [but] whoso repenteth not must perish" (1 Nephi 14:1, 5).

Jesus' coming into the world also provides the necessary mediation for the eternal deliverance of individual souls in accordance with the plan of salvation. Lehi, Nephi, and Jacob each attest that the mortal mission of Jesus Christ will culminate in his making intercession with the Father for all of the children of men. According to Lehi, "redemption cometh in and through the Holy Messiah," who "offereth himself a sacrifice for sin" (2 Nephi 2:6, 7). Nephi indicates that he will be "lifted up upon the cross and slain for the sins of the world" (1 Nephi 11:33). Jacob clarifies that God will raise all men from physical death by the power of Christ's Resurrection, while those who have faith in the Redeemer can also be saved from spiritual death by the power of his Atonement (see 2 Nephi 9:10–16; 10:25). It is finally in 2 Nephi 31 that Nephi presents the "doctrine of Christ" (2 Nephi 31:2), indicating with plainness and precision how it is that individuals can come unto Christ and be so saved.

Nephi's return to Lehi's wilderness teachings in his concluding discourse. In delivering this culminating message, Nephi returns to both halves of Lehi's teachings in the valley of Lemuel, as well as to his own sweeping angelic vision from 1 Nephi 11–14. In doing so, he brings the fulness of his gospel understanding back to its foundational origins, subtly testifying of just how much salvific truth the Lord has revealed to his family. He opens his concluding remarks by inviting readers to return with him to those early teachings, recalling first the Messiah's baptism foretold by Lehi in 1 Nephi 10 but not commented on since his own vision in 1 Nephi 11: "I would that ye should remember that I have spoken unto you concerning that prophet which the Lord showed unto me, that should *baptize the Lamb of God*, which *should take away the sins of the world*" (2 Nephi 31:4; emphasis added).

Although referencing his own experience here ("I have spoken . . . concerning that prophet which the Lord showed unto *me*," see also vv. 8, 17), Nephi acknowledges the dependency of his vision upon his father's prior prophecy by employing Lehi's words in describing John the Baptist: "After he had baptized the Messiah with water, he should behold and bear record that he had *baptized the Lamb of God*, who *should take away the sins of the world*" (1 Nephi 10:10; emphasis added). The latter phrase appears only in these two verses in the small plates, and although the designation of Jesus as the "Lamb of God" is a key phrase in Nephi's vision, employed there more than two dozen times, it too has not been mentioned since in Nephi's writings. The fact that he now employs it again several times in quick succession (see 2 Nephi 31:4–6) provides strong support for the intentionality of the allusion here to earlier teachings.

As Nephi continues with his meditation on Jesus' baptism, he will also incorporate three distinctive, though as yet undefined, elements from Lehi's dream in 1 Nephi 8: the invitation from the man in a white robe to "follow me" (see v. 6; 2 Nephi 31:10, 12–13), the strait and narrow path (see v. 20; 2 Nephi 31:18, 19),[14] and the necessity for travelers to the tree to continue "pressing forward" (see vv. 21, 24; 2 Nephi 31:20). He begins by posing a question: "And now, if the Lamb of God, he being holy, should have need to be baptized by water, to fulfil all righteousness, O then, how much more need have we, being unholy, to be baptized, yea, even by water?" (2 Nephi 31:5). Drawing on insights from his father's dream, Nephi responds that one of the purposes of Christ's baptism was to show humankind the way to salvation: "It showeth unto the children of men the *straitness of the path*, and the *narrowness* of the gate by which they should enter, he having set the example before them. And he said unto the children of men, 'Follow thou me'" (2 Nephi 31:9–10; emphasis added).

Appealing to what may be his most remarkable revelation of all, Nephi reports crucial information to his readers, defining the conditions of their individual salvation. Instead of claiming the Spirit, a vision, or even an angelic guide as his authority (as he and his family members have done in the past to support their developing understanding of salvation), Nephi instead relates a scripturally unprecedented exchange between the Father and the Son, whose voices come to him in turn, in essence enacting a saving covenant as they unfold the principles and ordinances of the gospel:

> The Father: "Repent ye, repent ye, and be baptized in the name of my Beloved Son."
>
> The Son: "He that is baptized in my name, to him will the Father give the Holy Ghost, like unto me; wherefore, follow me, and do the things which ye have seen me do."
>
> The Son: "After ye have repented of your sins, and witnessed unto the Father that ye are willing to keep my commandments, by the baptism of water, and have received the baptism of fire and of the Holy Ghost, . . . and after this should deny me, it would have been better for you that ye had not known me."
>
> The Father: "Yea, the words of my Beloved are true and faithful. He that endureth to the end, the same shall be saved" (see 2 Nephi 31:11, 12, 14, 15).

Interspersed with these statements is a running commentary in which Nephi highlights Jesus' plan of salvation role as exemplar and encourages his readers to follow both the actions and commandments of Christ. Nephi expresses this encouragement in terms from Lehi's dream, concluding with a final promise from the Father:

> And now, my beloved brethren, after ye have gotten into this *strait and narrow path*, I would ask if all is done? Behold, I say unto you, Nay; for ye have not come thus far save it were by *the word of Christ* with unshaken faith in him, relying wholly upon the merits of him who is mighty to save.
>
> Wherefore, ye must *press forward* with a steadfastness in Christ, having a perfect brightness of hope, and a love of God and all men. Wherefore, if ye shall *press forward*, feasting upon *the word of Christ*, and endure to the end, behold, thus saith the Father: Ye shall have eternal life. (2 Nephi 31:19–20; emphasis added).

The return of a few key phrases reminds us of Lehi's description of those who were pressing forward, "holding fast to the rod of iron" (1 Nephi 8:30), a rod later interpreted as "the word of God" (1 Nephi 11:25).

The Fulness of the Gospel

In 1 Nephi 6:4, Nephi states that his intention in writing the book that is itself to become a saving act in latter days is to "persuade men to come unto the God of Abraham, and the God of Isaac, and the God of Jacob, and be saved." We have seen how he has carefully devised his own contribution to that record by using his father Lehi's distinction in 1 Nephi 8 and 10 between the two aspects of God's saving work: the plan of salvation, for the eternal deliverance of individuals from death, hell, and captivity to the devil; and salvation history, the divine intervention in human affairs which delivers entire peoples from physical destruction and captivity, both to their enemies and to ignorance.

In addition to these two aspects of salvation, the phrase "the fulness of the Gospel" was also introduced by Lehi in his foundational discourse in the valley of Lemuel (1 Nephi 10:14). Nephi clarifies the concept in 1 Nephi 15:13–14, emphasizing that this fulness will come unto the Gentiles in the latter days, confirming Israel's covenant relationship with God, testifying of the Redeemer of the world, and instructing all humankind in "the very points of his doctrine, that they may know how to come unto him and be saved." It may be that the integration of the plan of salvation and salvation history found in Nephi's record can be profitably understood as constituting this fulness of the gospel—the summation of the tidings of great joy declaring that God has prepared a way to deliver humankind from bondage, whether spiritual or temporal, individual or collective.

Notes

1. Lehi himself never refers to the tree in his dream as the tree of life. This identification was added by Nephi at 1 Nephi 11:25.

2. Nephi does seem to be aware of the parallel nature of the two sections of Lehi's discourse even though he chooses not to highlight it at this point. This is evidenced in his conclusion of both sections with a reference to being "cast off" from the presence of God (see 1 Nephi 8:36–37; 10:21) and also with a comment that the preceding preaching occurred while Lehi "dwelt in a tent, in the valley of Lemuel" (1 Nephi 9:1; 10:16).

3. Many of the great sermons included by Mormon and Moroni deal precisely with this theme, including King Benjamin's discourse (see Mosiah 2–6); Abinadi's prophesying (see Mosiah 12–17); Alma's sermons and teachings to his sons (see Alma 5, 7, 36–42), Alma's and Amulek's preaching (see Alma 9–13; 32–34); Samuel the Lamanite's prophesying (see Helaman 13–15); and Mormon's sermon on faith, hope, and charity (see Moroni 7); see also Mormon's lamentation at Helaman 12 and Moroni's exhortation at Moroni 10.

4. The term *salvation history* was popularized in the nineteenth century by J. C. von Hofmann as *heilsgeschichte*. For summaries of its widespread usage, see H. G. Reventlow, *Problems of Old Testament Theology in the Twentieth Century* (Philadelphia: Fortress, 1985), 87–110; Gerald G. O'Collins, "Salvation," in *The Anchor Bible Dictionary*, ed. David Noel Freedman (New York: Doubleday, 1992), 5:907–914; and John Ruemann, "Salvation History," in *The Encyclopedia of Christianity*, ed. Erwin Fahlbusch and others (Grand Rapids, MI: Eerdmans; Leiden: Brill, 1999–2008), 4:832–36.

5. For Mormon's and Moroni's commitment to the concept of salvation history, see 3 Nephi 29–30; Mormon 3:17–22; 5:8–24; 7:1–10; Ether 2:11–12; 4:8–19; 12:22–29; title page.

6. Previous authors have noted connections between Lehi's dream at 1 Nephi 8 and Nephi's vision of 1 Nephi 11–14, but they have not recognized that Lehi's prophecies at 1 Nephi 10 were part of his original explication of his dream and that Nephi's vision picks up elements from both chapters. See John W. Welch, "Connections Between the Visions of Lehi and Nephi," in *Pressing Forward with the Book of Mormon: The FARMS Updates of the 1990s*, ed. John W. Welch and Melvin J. Thorne (Provo, UT: FARMS, 1999), 49–53; and in more detail in Corbin T. Volluz, "Lehi's Dream of the Tree of Life: Springboard to Prophecy," *Journal of Book of Mormon Studies* 2, no. 2 (1993): 14–38.

7. Or perhaps only a third, since there is textual evidence to suggest that Nephi's vision also includes details from the vision Lehi received at the time of his prophetic call. Common notable details not identified in 1 Nephi 10 include the vision of one "descending out of heaven" (1 Nephi 1:9; 11:7; 12:6), the Messiah's twelve followers (see 1 Nephi 1:10; 11:29; 12:7); and the book presented by one of the twelve (see 1 Nephi 1:11; 14:20–23).

8. Interestingly enough, in Nephi's telling it is the Gentiles who are to be grafted in to Israel ("numbered among the house of Israel," 1 Nephi 14:2) and not the other way around, as suggested by the allegory at 1 Nephi 10:14. Another slight discrepancy is that in Nephi's reporting of the words of the Lord, the latter-day Gentiles are to receive "much of my gospel" (1 Nephi 13:34) rather than "the fulness of the Gospel" spoken of in 1 Nephi 10:14.

9. Nephi seems to be applying Deuteronomy 18:18–19 here to the Lord's Second Coming rather than to his mortal ministry. Jesus Christ applies the same prophecy to his Nephite ministry at 3 Nephi 20:23–26, equating the term "raise up" with his own Resurrection. In all three cases, though, the scripture is recognized as being fulfilled in the person of Jesus Christ.

10. For a preliminary list of these phrasal quotations and allusions, see the footnotes for 1 Nephi 22 and 2 Nephi 25–30 in Grant Hardy, ed., *The Book of Mormon: A Reader's Edition* (Urbana, IL: University of Illinois Press, 2005).

11. Several decades ago, Bruce W. Jorgensen suggested that typology might provide a unified reading of the Book of Mormon based on Lehi's dream, but his short article did not allow for sustained analysis along these lines, and as he himself admitted, because the dream was not a historical event, it was therefore "not properly a type or figure." More recently, Steven L. Olsen has proposed that Mormon patterned his historical narrative on Nephi's vision, but the correspondence between Nephi's prophecies and their fulfillment in later history seems natural enough both in terms of chronology and major events. I believe there is another continuity between the small plates and Mormon's abridgment of the large plates in the way the theological breakthrough realized by Lehi and Nephi with regard to salvation is explored and elaborated on by later Nephite prophets. See Bruce W. Jorgensen, "The Dark Way to the Tree: Typological Unity in the Book of Mormon," in *Literature of Belief: Sacred Scripture and Religious Experience*, ed. Neal E. Lambert (Provo, UT: Religious Studies Center, Brigham Young University, 1981), 217–32; and Steven L. Olsen, "Prophecy and History: Structuring the Abridgments of the Nephite Records," *Journal of Book of Mormon Studies* 15, no. 1 (2006): 18–29.

12. Lehi actually seems to be combining two Isaiah passages here in his expansion, both of which feature the keyword "dust." In addition to alluding to Isaiah 52:1–2, Lehi also clusters the following distinctive phrases from Isaiah 29: "deep sleep" (2 Nephi 1:13; Isaiah 29:10), coming out of the dust (see 2 Nephi 1:14, 21, 23; Isaiah 29:4) and "out of obscurity" (2 Nephi 1:23; Isaiah 29:18), although there is little thematic overlap. Nephi will quote Isaiah 29:3–24 in 2 Nephi 26–27.

13. The resurrected Jesus Christ confirms to the Nephites that his mission to manifest himself directly (either by his voice or by his physical presence) applies only to the house of Israel. The Gentiles, in contrast, are to receive the testimony of Israel and the witness of the Holy Ghost (see 3 Nephi 15:19–16:3).

14. Jacob also alludes to the strait and narrow path at 2 Nephi 9:23, 41, where he introduces the notion of a gate which may or may not have been an element in either Lehi's dream or his subsequent interpretation of the dream. Mormon, in an apparent allusion to Lehi, makes mention of "the gate of heaven" as well as of laying hold on "the word of God" and walking "a strait and narrow course across that everlasting gulf of misery" (Helaman 3:28–29). A "strait" or "narrow" gate is mentioned in 2 Nephi 31:9, 17–19; 33:9; and Jacob 6:11.

3

The Church of the Lamb of God

Casey Paul Griffiths

As one who gloried in plainness (see 2 Nephi 33:6), Nephi loved to paint his revelations in black and white, using contrasts to teach principles. This view of things was also favored by the Lord and his messengers, who in the final portion of Nephi's vision presented him with a stark contrast: "There are save two churches only; the one is the church of the Lamb of God, and the other is the church of the devil; wherefore, whoso belongeth not to the church of the Lamb of God belongeth to that great church, which is the mother of abominations" (1 Nephi 14:10). Thus far, almost all modern commentary on this portion of the vision has sought to discover the identity of the church of the devil. This is a worthy pursuit, because prophets have stressed that one of the main purposes of the Book of Mormon is to expose the enemies of Christ.[1] Just as instructive, however, can be an examination of the brief but powerful glimpse Nephi gives us of the role of the church of the Lamb in the latter days. Understanding Nephi's vision of this church can help readers understand the role and place of the followers of Christ in the tumultuous

---

Casey Paul Griffiths is a teacher at Jordan Seminary in Sandy, Utah.

events of the last days and provide them with a hope that the righteous, with the Lord's help, will eventually overcome the power of the adversary.

The Church of the Lamb of God

The phrase "church of the Lamb of God" never appears in the Book of Mormon outside of 1 Nephi 14. The phrase does not appear in any other book of scripture. While details are scattered throughout Nephi's vision, the main body of his description of the church of the Lamb of God is contained mainly in three verses:

> And it came to pass that I beheld the church of the Lamb of God, and its numbers were few, because of the wickedness and abominations of the whore who sat upon many waters; nevertheless, I beheld that the church of the Lamb, who were the saints of God, were also upon all the face of the earth; and their dominions upon the face of the earth were small, because of the wickedness of the great whore whom I saw.
>
> And it came to pass that I beheld that the great mother of abominations did gather together multitudes upon the face of all the earth, among all the nations of the Gentiles, to fight against the Lamb of God.
>
> And it came to pass that I, Nephi, beheld the power of the Lamb of God, that it descended upon the saints of the church of the Lamb, and upon the covenant people of the Lord, who were scattered upon all the face of the earth; and they were armed with righteousness and with the power of God in great glory. (1 Nephi 14:12–14)

These brief words offer a remarkable vision of the organization of God's followers during the end times.

Before diving into Nephi's description of the church of the Lamb of God, however, some fundamental questions must be asked. Is his description literal or figurative? Depending on which lens we choose to examine the passage, different interpretations may emerge. For example, Stephen E. Robinson, in his exposition on the great and abominable church of Nephi's vision, notes that the vision often shifts from a *historical* explanation of the events to a *typological* exposition on the battles between good and evil in the last days.[2]

Saying that the vision is *historical* in nature means that Nephi was describing actual future events. There can be no doubt as to the historical nature of Nephi's vision. Prophecy is sometimes referred to as history in reverse, and Nephi describes in clear detail the flow of history from his time into our own. Several events such as the ministry of the Savior in the Old and New Worlds, the destruction of the Nephites, and the discovery and settlement of America are clear examples of historical events that Nephi saw.

Typology, on the other hand, refers to the symbolic principles of the vision. When Nephi's writings are examined through this lens, the vision becomes involved in themes and becomes a work of apocalyptic literature, similar to the book of Revelation. Instead of trying to identify the exact identity of every person, place, or organization in the vision, the reader is asked to instead see the grand themes of the plan of salvation. This kind of scriptural writing is meant to remind us of the struggles between good and evil that have happened throughout the earth's existence. Describing how this kind of literature functions, Robinson wrote: "Apocalyptic literature is dualistic. Since it deals with types, everything boils down to opposing principles: love and hate, good and evil, light and dark. There are no gray areas in apocalyptic writing."[3]

Nephi's vision can be read both ways. In one sense, it is an extraordinary description of the key historical events that lead to the Restoration of the gospel and the Second Coming of the Savior. In another sense, it is a profound exposition of how the forces of good and evil operate among the peoples of the earth. Examining Nephi's prophecy of the church of the Lamb of God through these two lenses provides some interesting insights into the accuracy and meaning of Nephi's prophecy. Accordingly, we shall consider first the historical implications of the vision, then what the typological implications may be.

Historical Context

In a strictly historical sense, the church of the Lamb of God referred to in Nephi's vision is The Church of Jesus Christ of Latter-day Saints. Multiple prophets and apostles have identified the modern Church as such. President George Albert Smith stated, "This is our Father's work. This is the Church of the Lamb of God."[4] Presenting the Latter-day Saints as the only true Church of God, however, has sometimes led to acrimony from members of other faiths. In a world largely content with the attitude of "God doesn't care which church you go to on Sunday as long as you show up," the declaration of the existence of one true church sometimes gives the impression that Latter-day Saints assume an air of superiority over devoted members of other faiths. Yet the doctrine of one true church is an area where the Saints can give little ground, since the Savior himself declared it to be "the only true and living church upon the face of the whole earth" (D&C 1:30).

President Boyd K. Packer summarized the importance of this doctrine when he taught, "Good conduct without the ordinances of the gospel will neither redeem nor exalt mankind; covenants and the ordinances are essential. We are required to teach the doctrines, even the unpopular ones. Yield on this doctrine, and you cannot justify the Restoration. The doctrine is true; it is logical. The opposite is not. . . . We did not invent the doctrine of the only true church. It came from the Lord. Whatever perception others have of us, however presumptuous we appear to be, whatever criticism is directed to us, we must teach it to all who will listen."[5] Similarly, Nephi's declaration that "there are save two churches only" (1 Nephi 14:10), the church of the Lamb and the church of the devil, may not be too popular with other faiths, but it is, as President Packer stated, both logical and true.

Before Church members become too convinced that they are superior, however, it should be noted that the next part of that statement was "with which I, the Lord, am well pleased, speaking unto the church collectively and not individually." Individual acceptance of truth can be measured only on an individual basis, but there can be no doubt that the only church that fully conforms to the doctrines and practices which Christ set forth in ancient and modern revelation is The Church of Jesus Christ of Latter-day Saints.

With this in mind, Nephi's vision of the church of the Lamb of God paints an illustrative picture of what the members of the true Church may expect in the last days. Among the most illuminating points of the vision are the following:

- The Church's numbers were few and its dominions small (see 1 Nephi 14:12).
- The Church's members were scattered upon all the face of the earth (see 1 Nephi 14:12, 14).
- Nephi saw the power of the Lamb descend upon the Saints of the Church and beheld that they were armed with righteousness and the power of God in great glory (see 1 Nephi 14:14).

These few phrases together give a marvelous description of the place and function of the Church in the last days. Further, modern Church history shows the accuracy of this description. Consider each point separately:

Its numbers were few. In recent years much attention has been devoted to the rapid growth of the Church. Among the most famous predictions of Mormon growth was Rodney Stark's 1984 study entitled "The Rise of a New World Faith."[6] Stark predicted an astonishing growth rate for the Church over the next century. His low estimate was that there would be 64 million Latter-day Saints by 2080, and his high estimate predicted that there would be 267 million members by that time![7] Stark's prediction was met with both applause and derision. Some called his projections unrealistic; yet when Stark compared his study with the actual growth of the Church in 2003, he noted that Church growth had exceeded his high estimate. Stark concluded, "Granted, there are seventy-seven more years to go. But, so far, so good."[8]

While Church growth statistics are a remarkable testament to the power and vitality of Mormonism as well as the Lord's prophecy that the little stone of Daniel's vision would "roll forth, until it has filled the whole earth" (D&C 65:2), Nephi's vision brings our heads down out of the clouds a little bit. By noting that Church members were "few" and that the dominions of the Church were "small," Nephi puts the role of the Church into proper perspective. Even if Stark's most optimistic predictions are fulfilled, the members of the Church will remain a tiny minority among the people of the earth. To illustrate, if Stark's high estimate is met, there will be 267,452,000 members by 2080. At the same time, the earth's total population is projected to have grown to over 8.5 billion by then, which means that the Saints would still only make up just over 3 percent of the world's total population.[9]

Nephi's words become even more poignant when it is recognized that the majority of the Saints are, with some exceptions, minority members where they live. In Utah, Church members may be 68 percent of the total population, but in the eastern United States Church members are on average less than 1 percent of the total population and are usually one out of several hundred. In a European country, Church members are usually less than one in a thousand, and in a place like India, where the Church is still in its infancy, the percentage of Church members in the total population is less than .0006, or one in several hundred thousand![10] When the number of less-active members is brought into account, congregations may be even smaller. These statistics are not cited to be pessimistic, but to show just how rare and exceptional it is to find an active, faithful Latter-day Saint among the people of the world anywhere.

Given the tumultuous trends of the last century, it may be difficult for anyone who is not a prophet to make any kinds of predictions about the future growth of the Church. What Nephi's vision tells us more about is the role that the Saints will play in the last days. One Latter-day Saint scholar has noted that even if Church membership increased overnight to a billion members, Church membership would still only be one person in every six, a status that would still match Nephi's wording of "few."[11] President Joseph Fielding Smith captured the spirit of Nephi's description when he noted, "While it may be said . . . that we are but handful in comparison with . . . the world, yet we may be compared with the leaven of which the Savior spoke, which will eventually leaven [or lift] the whole world."[12]

Nephi also gave an explicit reason why the members the church of the Lamb were few: "because of the wickedness and abominations of the whore who sat upon many waters." From a prophetic view, obstacles to Church growth come directly from the followers of the adversary. Demographic trends and issues with the public perceptions of the Saints are only symptoms of a larger battle raging for the souls of men. According to Nephi, the Church should never look to be the largest or most powerful organization, at least in worldly measures. Nephi informed us that the Saints would always be the underdogs until the coming of the Savior.

Scattered upon all the face of the earth. Nephi's assertion that the Saints of the church of the Lamb would be scattered upon all the face of the earth is even more remarkable when looked at through a historical lens. Just over half a century ago, Mormonism could still be considered a regional faith based largely in the Intermountain West. In the latter half of the twentieth century, Church membership grew explosively outside of the West and in many regions of the world. In 1955 only 11 percent of the Church's population resided outside the United States. That figure had increased to 21 percent by 1977, and to 51 percent by 1999.[13] As of 2009, roughly 56 percent of the members of the Church lived outside the United States, a remarkable feat by any measure.[14] Presently the frontiers of Mormonism have spread beyond the borders of the United States and into all nations. In our time, the histories of the Saints in cities such as Tokyo, Johannesburg, Santiago, and Warsaw are taking their places alongside the histories of the Saints in Palmyra, Kirtland, and Nauvoo.[15] Nephi's vision fits alongside Joseph Smith's prophecy that "this Church will fill North and South America, it will fill the world."[16] The calling of General Authorities and spread of the priesthood worldwide are fulfillments of the Savior's words that "every man shall hear the fulness of the gospel in his own tongue, and his own language, through those who are ordained unto this power, by the administration of the Comforter, shed forth upon them for the revelation of Jesus Christ" (D&C 90:11).

While the international growth of the Church is remarkable, there are still frontiers to conquer. Over 44 percent of the membership of the Church is in the United States, and over 85 percent of the membership of the Church is in the Western Hemisphere.[17] Some regions have no access to the message of the gospel at all. There is still much work to do before the restored gospel has, in Joseph Smith's words, "penetrated every continent, visited every clime, swept every country, and sounded in every ear."[18]

They were armed with righteousness and with the power of God in great glory. The last of the three items might be the most difficult to find any tangible measures for. There are positive signs that point toward an increase in righteousness among the members of the Church in all nations. One positive sign of the increase in the righteousness of the Saints is the rise in the number of stakes in the Church. As an ecclesiastical unit of the Church, a stake can be formed only when a certain number of priesthood holders and faithful members are present, fulfilling callings, and carrying out duties. In 1955 there were 224 stakes, with only one outside of the United States or Canada.[19] As of 2009 there were 2,818 stakes, 1,380 of which were outside of the United States,[20] an astounding figure that indicates a strengthening corps of priesthood and auxiliary leaders who are moving forward the work of the Church.

Another indication of increased righteousness may be found in the dramatic increase in temple construction during the last half of the twentieth century. In the first century of the Restoration, seven temples were built. Now, eighty years into the second century, over one hundred and twenty-six more temples have been constructed. In fulfillment of Nephi's prophecy of the Saints being scattered upon all the face of the earth, over sixty of these temples have been built in international areas.[21] The increase in the number of temples brings an immeasurable increase in the power of Christ on the earth. President George Q. Cannon taught, "Every foundation stone that is laid for a temple, and every temple completed according to the order of the Lord has revealed for His Holy Priesthood, lessens the power of Satan on the earth and increases the power of God and Godliness."[22] In addition, there are more members meeting the standards for temple worthiness, and the privilege of temple attendance helps Saints to develop greater spiritual strength. Part of the promise given in the dedicatory prayer of the Kirtland Temple, given by Joseph Smith, promised that the Lord's servants would leave the temple "armed with thy power, and that thy name may be upon them, and thy glory round about them" (D&C 109:22).

Despite the wonderful growth of the Church, we must at the same time recognize that the real strength of the Church comes in more intangible measures. President Packer warned: "We have done very well at distributing the *authority* of the priesthood. We have priesthood authority planted nearly everywhere. We have quorums of elders and high priests worldwide. But distributing the *authority* of the priesthood has raced, I think, ahead of distributing the *power* of the priesthood. The priesthood does not have the strength that it should have and will not have until the *power* of the priesthood is firmly fixed in the families as it should be."[23] President Packer reminds us that the *number* of priesthood holders, temples, members, and other factors, does not necessarily tell us if we have received the *power* which Nephi prophesied the Church would receive.

While statistical figures can provide a measurable way of verifying the accuracy of Nephi's prophecy, the real strength of the church of the Lamb is measured in personal testimonies and lives changed. President Gordon B. Hinckley recalled meeting a naval officer from Asia who had joined the Church. The officer came from a non-Christian home and had converted during his training in the United States. When President Hinckley inquired about what would happen to the officer when he returned home, the officer replied: "My family will be disappointed. I suppose they will cast me out. They will regard me as dead. As for my future and my career, all opportunity may be foreclosed against me." When President Hinckley asked why the officer was willing to pay such a price to join the Church, the officer's eyes grew teary and he replied, "It's true, isn't it?"[24] This same story, told a thousand times over about different people in the varied cultures and nations of the world, speaks of the righteousness Nephi saw the Saints armed with.

Typological Context

While Nephi's vision presents a compelling view of the Church when looked at historically, there is also value in examining Nephi's description as a typology. For example, it is clear from Nephi's descriptions in 1 Nephi 13 and 14 that no single historical organization quite fits the profile of the great and abominable church. The church of the devil is a type, designed to represent the work of the adversary among all people, nations, and societies in the world. Elder Bruce R. McConkie wrote, "The church of the devil is every evil and worldly organization on earth. It is all of the systems, both Christian and non-Christian, that have perverted the pure and perfect gospel: it is all of the governments and powers that have run counter to divine will. . . . It is the man of sin speaking in churches, orating in legislative halls, and commanding the armies of men."[25] Taken typologically, the church of the devil is a powerful symbol for the influence of evil in all its manifestations.

What, then, are typological implications for the church of the Lamb of God? If we apply Elder McConkie's logic in both directions, the pavilion under which the church of the Lamb resides must be enlarged to include "every thing which inviteth to do good, and to persuade to believe in Christ" (Moroni 7:16). Membership in the church of the Lamb in this context expands beyond denominational lines to include all who genuinely strive to do good according to the light they have been given. The Savior expressed this idea in the Doctrine and Covenants when he proclaimed, "This is Zion—the pure in heart; therefore, let Zion rejoice, while all the wicked shall mourn" (D&C 97:21).

This interpretation should not be taken to contradict the statements shared earlier which identified the church of the Lamb with the Latter-day Saints. An important contribution the revelations of the Restoration make to Christian theology is the authoritative declaration that all people are judged by two standards: "according to their works, [and] according to the desire of their hearts" (D&C 137:9). This allows us to recognize righteous individuals outside of our own faith who will stand in opposition to the work of the church of the devil. By this standard there are members of all faiths who may reside within the church of the Lamb of God, and there may be people on the rolls of the Latter-day Saints who reside in the church of the devil. By this standard, membership in the church of the Lamb is based on the desires of your heart, not just on which church you attend.[26]

Looking at the church of the Lamb in this context does not diminish the importance of the role of the restored Church in any sense. In some ways, it may increase the importance of the role the Church plays in the last days. The scriptures testify that the restored Church will act as a shield to protect the righteous of all creeds as violence and wickedness increase in the earth. As the trials that precede the Lord's coming become more severe, many people who choose to abstain from the violence will look to the Saints for refuge. The Savior revealed that in that day *"every man* that will not take his sword against his neighbor must needs flee unto Zion for safety. And there shall be gathered unto it out of every nation under heaven; and it shall be the only people that shall not be at war one with another" (D&C 45:68–69; emphasis added).[27] The Prophet Joseph Smith warned, "The time is soon coming, when no man will have any peace but in Zion and her stakes."[28]

While the typological viewpoint might allow us to feel better about our friends of other faiths, it also raises some disturbing implications, since we still have to deal with Nephi's revelation that the church of the Lamb will be small and scattered but armed with righteousness. Saying that the righteous in the last days will be small is unsettling because most of us want to feel that generally most people are good and seek to do right. This may not be the case in the days just before the Savior's coming.

Just before describing the final struggles between the two churches, the Savior prophesied of a "great and a marvelous work among the children of men; a work which shall be everlasting, either on the one hand or on the other—either to the convincing of them unto peace and life eternal, or unto the deliverance of them to the hardness of their hearts and the blindness of their minds unto their being brought down into captivity, and also into destruction, both temporally and spiritually" (1 Nephi 14:7). Other prophets have testified that the gray area between the righteous and the wicked will continue to recede until there is none left. A proclamation issued in 1845 by the Quorum of the Twelve Apostles prophesied of this outcome: "As this work progresses in its onward course, and becomes more and more an object of political and religious interest and excitement, no king, ruler, or subject, no community or individual, will stand *neutral*. All will at length be influenced by one spirit or the other; and will take sides either for or against the kingdom of God, and the fulfillment of the prophets, in the great restoration and return of his long dispersed covenant people."[29]

Though the 1845 proclamation speaks in stark terms of the division before the end times, it also proclaims that righteous individuals of other faiths will play a role in the triumph of the church of the Lamb, continuing, "Some will act the part of the venerable Jethro, the father-in-law of Moses, or the noble Cyrus; and will aid and bless the people of God; or like Ruth, the Moabitess. . . . You will, therefore, either be led by the good Spirit to cast in your lot, and to take a lively interest with the Saints of the Most High, and the covenant people of the Lord, or on the other hand, you will become their inveterate enemy, and oppose them by every means in your power."[30] A typological view of the church of the Lamb allows us to include the modern day Cyruses who will stand with the Saints in defense of righteousness. Scripture paints dark days for the Saints as the end draws near, but it does not leave them without allies in their struggles.

The Triumph of the Lamb

Both historically and typologically, Nephi's vision depicts the members of the church of the Lamb of God as a relatively small band, besieged by the church of the devil on all sides. Although the vision presents the righteous with a realistic picture of the difficulties they will face in the last days, it is also meant to present a light at the end of the tunnel. While the Saints of the church of the Lamb and the covenant people of the Lord are arming themselves with righteousness, their enemies will begin to tear themselves apart from the inside. Nephi described the beginning of "wars and rumors of wars among all the nations which belonged to the mother of abominations," and his angelic guide informed him that "the wrath of God is poured out upon the mother of harlots" (1 Nephi 14:16–17). While the dismemberment of the church of the devil will wreak havoc among the nations, it may also open doors for the gospel to spread as well. The messenger informed Nephi that at the time that the wrath of God is poured out upon the great and abominable church, "the work of the Father shall commence, in preparing the way for the fulfilling of his covenants, which he hath made to his people who are of the house of Israel" (1 Nephi 14:17).

This passage may have several different meanings. During his ministry on the American continent, the Savior that taught when his words spoken among the Nephites (meaning the Book of Mormon) would come forth among the Gentiles, it would be the sign that the great work of the Father had begun (see 3 Nephi 21:1–4). If we take the commencement of the "work of the Father" to be all the events surrounding the Restoration, beginning with the religious forerunners to Joseph Smith and the early laborers of the gospel, we may take heart in knowing that the seeds of the fall of Babylon were laid long ago and continue to grow as we draw nearer to the Second Coming. There can be no doubt that the number of wars and their severity has increased exponentially since the Church has been restored to the earth. However, the wars in and of themselves have opened doors for the gospel to spread among the nations. The most rapid increase in Church membership came in the decades following the world wars of the first half of the twentieth century. Those tragic events, taken in a millennial context, may be a manifestation of the Lord's promise that "with the sword and by bloodshed the inhabitants of the earth shall mourn" (D&C 87:6). While war is a tragedy, it also drives men to Christ. C. S. Lewis wryly commented that one of Satan's best weapons, contented worldliness, is rendered useless during these times because "in wartime not even a human can believe that he is going to live forever."[31] While the church of the devil exists to oppose the church of the Lamb, the Lord has a way of using tragedy to bring us to repentance and into the fold of God.

Another interpretation of what is meant by the commencement of the Father's work is found in a discourse the Savior gave during his ministry among the Nephites. The Savior prophesied of the building of the New Jerusalem, a millennial event. After this had come to pass, the Savior foretold that "then shall the work of the Father *commence* at that day, even when this gospel shall be preached among the remnant of this people, . . . yea, even the tribes which have been lost, which the Father hath led away out of Jerusalem" (3 Nephi 21: 26; emphasis added). The Savior continues, "Yea, the work shall *commence* among all the dispersed of my people, with the Father to prepare the way whereby they may come unto me, that they may call upon the Father in my name. Yea, and then shall the work *commence*, with the Father among all nations in preparing the way whereby his people may be gathered home to the land of their inheritance" (3 Nephi 21:27–28; emphasis added).

Why does the Savior say that the work will commence *after* an event which has yet to occur, namely the building of the New Jerusalem? After all, hasn't the gospel been on earth in its fullness since the days of Joseph Smith? What the Savior is saying in no way diminishes the work of Church members in our day, but it may indicate that the labors of the Saints prior to the building of the New Jerusalem will only act as a prologue to the work to be performed in the great millennial day. In the last days, the Lord promised that "righteousness and truth will I cause to sweep the earth as with a flood" (Moses 7:62), a rising tide finally reaching its peak in the Millennium. At that time the members of the restored Church of Jesus Christ will finally join with the pure in heart of all faiths who stood by their side during the last days in embracing the fullness of the gospel of Jesus Christ. President Joseph Fielding Smith wrote, "The gospel will be taught far more intensely and with greater power during the millennium, *until all the inhabitants of the earth shall embrace it.*"[32] President Brigham Young prophesied of this great millennial day when he declared, "To accomplish this work there will have to be not only one temple but thousands of them, and thousands and tens of thousands of men and women will go into those temples and officiate for people who have lived as far back as the Lord shall reveal."[33] Continuing on this theme, Elder McConkie wrote, "We expect to see the day when temples will dot the earth, each one a house of the Lord; each one built in the mountains of the Lord; each one a sacred sanctuary to which Israel and the Gentiles shall gather to receive the blessings of Abraham, Isaac, and Jacob. Perhaps they will number in the hundreds, or even in the thousands, before the Lord returns."[34]

Nephi's Vision and the Followers of the Lamb

Looked at from any angle, Nephi's vision of the church of the Lamb of God assures us that Satan will seek desperately to destroy or hinder the followers of God in the last days. We still live in a troubled world where the devil holds sway. The Saints and their allies have faced intolerance, violence, and opposition in the past and will again in the future. Elder McConkie wrote, "Our persecutions and difficulties have scarcely begun. We saw mobbing and murders and martyrdom as the foundations of the work were laid in the United States. These same things, with greater intensity, shall yet fall upon the faithful in all nations."[35] Along with the spiritual triumphs, we may anticipate that the persecutions and trials that followed the Saints in America will be repeated in Latin America, Africa, Asia, Europe, and everywhere the Church grows and spreads. The gulf between the righteous and the wicked will continue to widen. However, in spite of the dark days ahead, the scriptures assure us of better things to come.

Nephi's vision of the church of the Lamb ended rather abruptly. He was assured that the church of the devil would meet its demise and that the church of the Lamb would take part in the commencement of the Father's work, but the things that came after these events were not shown. Instead, his guide showed him that the Apostle John would write the remainder of the vision. But his glimpse of future events was enough to sustain Nephi. Later in his life, Nephi would write of the millennial time after the work of the Father had commenced and the church of the Lamb had triumphed over its foes. Whether he had seen it in another vision, or had extrapolated from what he had previously been told, Nephi assured us of a future day when, "because of the righteousness of his [the Lord's] people, Satan has no power; wherefore, he cannot be loosed for the space of many years; for he hath no power over the hearts of the people, for they dwell in righteousness, and the Holy One of Israel reigneth" (1 Nephi 22:26).

In our day Nephi's vision of the church of the Lamb reminds us that though the righteous may be facing an overwhelming flood of wickedness, there is no need to fear. The faithful may be few and scattered, but the power of the Lord is with them. We can rest assured that the church of the Lamb, "armed with righteousness and with the power of God in great glory" (1 Nephi 14:14), will eventually triumph over all of its foes. Nephi reminds us that no matter how dark our times may become, there is a sure hand protecting the faithful and guiding them to safety. Viewed as a historical prophecy, Nephi provides us with a healthy reminder that though the Church may be relatively small, it will play a critical role in the salvation of men in the last days. Viewed as typology, Nephi reminds us that strength lies not in numbers but in purity. Both views speak to the truth taught by another Book of Mormon prophet, "that by small and simple things are great things brought to pass; and small means in many instances doth confound the wise. And the Lord God doth work by means to bring about his great and eternal purposes; and by very small means the Lord doth confound the wise" (Alma 37:6).

Notes

1. Ezra Taft Benson, "The Book of Mormon Is the Word of God," *Ensign*, January 1988, 3.

2. Stephen E. Robinson, "Warring against the Saints of God," *Ensign*, January 1988, 34.

3. Robinson, "Warring against the Saints of God," 37.

4. George Albert Smith, in Conference Report, October 1949, 9.

5. Boyd K. Packer, "The Only True Church," *Ensign*, October 1985, 82.
6. Rodney Stark, "The Rise of a New World Faith," *Review of Religious Research* 26, no. 1 (September 1984): 18–27.
7. Rodney Stark, *The Rise of Mormonism*, ed. Reid L. Neilson (New York: Columbia University Press, 2005), 22.
8. Stark, *Rise of Mormonism*, 146. The 2010 *Church Almanac* cites Church membership as of January 1, 2009, to be 13,508,509, which places actual membership in the middle of Stark's estimates for where Church membership would be in 2010, with a high estimate of 15,564,000 and a low estimate of 10,190,000. *2010 Church Almanac* (Salt Lake City: *Deseret News*, 2010).
9. Department of Economic and Social Affairs, Population Division, *World Population to 2300: Proceedings of the United Nations Expert Meeting on World Population in 2300* (New York: United Nations, 2004), 4, http://www.un.org/esa/population/publications/longrange2/WorldPop2300final.
10. All statistics taken from the *2010 Church Almanac*. To offer a few examples, Church membership in New York State is .4 percent of the total population, or 1 in 257. In a Western European country like Germany, membership is .05%, or 1 in 2,193. In India, Church membership is .0006, or 1 in 153,918.
11. Joseph Fielding McConkie, *Answers: Straightforward Answers to Gospel Questions* (Salt Lake City: Deseret Book, 1998), 119–20.
12. Joseph Fielding Smith, in Conference Report, October 1968, 123, quoted in Boyd K. Packer, "The Power of the Priesthood," *Ensign*, May 2010, 7.
13. Victor L. Ludlow, "The Internationalization of the Church," in *Out of Obscurity: The LDS Church in the Twentieth Century* (Salt Lake City: Deseret Book), 2000.
14. This figure was calculated by statistics taken from the *Deseret News 2010 Church Almanac*, 4–5.
15. Reid L. Neilson, "A Recommissioning of Latter-day Saint Historians," in *Global Mormonism*, ed. Reid L. Neilson (Provo, UT: Religious Studies Center, Brigham Young University, 2008), xi–xv.
16. Wilford Woodruff, *The Discourses of Wilford Woodruff*, ed. G. Homer Durham (Salt Lake City: Bookcraft, 1990), 38–39.
17. Calculated from statistics in *Deseret News 2010 Church Almanac*, 4–5.
18. *History of the Church of Jesus Christ of Latter-day Saints*, ed. B. H. Roberts, 2nd ed. rev. (Salt Lake City, Deseret Book, 1976), 4:540.
19. Ludlow, *Out of Obscurity*, 216-17.
20. *Deseret News 2010 Church Almanac*, 4, 185.
21. From information taken from http://lds.org/church/temples/around-the-world/list?lang=eng.
22. George Q. Cannon, *Gospel Truth: Discourses and Writings of President George Q. Cannon*, ed. Jerreld L. Newquist (Salt Lake City: Deseret Book, 1974), 111.
23. Boyd K. Packer, "The Power of the Priesthood," *Ensign*, May 2010, 6.
24. Gordon B. Hinckley, "The True Strength of the Church," *Ensign*, July 1973, 48.
25. Bruce R. McConkie, *The Millennial Messiah: The Second Coming of the Son of Man* (Salt Lake City: Deseret Book, 1982), 54–55. Elder McConkie's views regarding the identity of the church of the devil have long been a lively topic of discussion. Several

accounts of controversy on this topic may be found in Joseph Fielding McConkie, *The Bruce R. McConkie Story: Reflections of a Son* (Salt Lake: Deseret Book, 2003), 182–94; and Gregory A. Prince and Wm. Robert Wright, *David O. McKay and the Rise of Modern Mormonism* (Salt Lake City: University of Utah Press, 2005), 49–52, 122. Elder McConkie's views here are taken from his latest writings and, I believe, represent the most accurate account of his views on the subject.

26. Robinson, "Warring against the Saints of God," 37.

27. Doctrine and Covenants 45:68 designates these people as being among the wicked. In speaking of members of other faiths on the earth during the Millennium, Joseph Smith taught, "There will be wicked men on the earth during the thousand years." *Teachings of the Prophet Joseph Smith*, comp., Joseph Fielding Smith (Salt Lake City: Deseret Book, 1976), 268–69. President Joseph Fielding Smith interpreted the Prophet's use of *wicked* in the context of D&C 84:49–53 as referring to those who have not received the ordinances. See Joseph Fielding Smith, *Doctrines of Salvation*, comp. Bruce R. McConkie (Salt Lake City: Bookcraft, 1956), 3:63–64. I would assume that the use of *wicked* in section 45 is also used in this sense, at least in terms of those who refuse to commit violence.

28. Joseph Smith, *Teachings of the Prophet Joseph Smith*, 161.

29. James R. Clark, ed., *Messages of the First Presidency* (Salt Lake City: Bookcraft, 1965), 1:257.

30. Clark, *Messages of the First Presidency*, 1:257.

31. C. S. Lewis, *The Joyful Christian* (New York: Touchstone, 1996), 148–49.

32. Joseph Fielding Smith, *Doctrines of Salvation*, 3:64; emphasis in original.

33. Brigham Young, in *Journal of Discourses* (London: Latter-day Saints' Book Depot, 1856), 3:372.

34. McConkie, *Millennial Messiah*, 277.

35. McConkie, *Millennial Messiah*, 55.

4

Lehi's Dream and Nephi's Vision as Apocalyptic Literature

Jared M. Halverson

Like the parables of Jesus, the visions of Ezekiel, or the revelation of John, the symbolism of Lehi's dream begs elucidation. A tree and a river, a building and a rod, mists of darkness and wandering multitudes—each element leaves inquisitive readers with a desire that echoes Nephi's—"to know the interpretation thereof" (1 Nephi 11:11). Even the dulled spiritual senses of Laman and Lemuel were roused in wonder until the usually apathetic brothers asked Nephi a question that paralleled his own, "What meaneth this thing which our father saw in a dream?" (1 Nephi 15:21). The dream's imagery elicited fascination, and understandably so, for "the closed door will always impel the curious to peek behind it."[1]

Of course, how wide that door will swing open—and how much is recognized within—largely depends on the readiness of the one looking inside. In Nephi's case, an eager learner found a generous teacher, and a series of Spirit-given, angel-directed visions unfolded, which now fill over ten pages of text (see 1 Nephi 11–14). Laman and Lemuel, on the other hand, received from Nephi a scant sixteen verses (see 1 Nephi 15:21–36), which consisted mostly of

---

Jared M. Halverson is director of the Nashville Tennessee Institute of Religion.

exhortation rather than explanation, and that only after considerable effort on Nephi's part to prepare his brothers to be taught.[2]

Mere length, however, is only one difference between the two successive interpretations of Lehi's dream. Far more significant is the interpretive methodology employed. In either case, the lens through which the dream's elements are interpreted casts the dream in a different light and links it to a distinct literary genre.[3] Nephi gives his brothers a straightforward image-to-object explanation, casting Lehi's dream as parable.[4] In contrast, the angel shows Nephi the interpretation in terms of salvation history, casting Lehi's dream as apocalypse.[5]

Ironically, our understanding of Lehi's dream tends to reflect the straightforward explanation given to Laman and Lemuel more than the apocalyptic interpretation that Nephi received. The allegorical approach is fitting and beneficial; however, when we limit ourselves to an "image-to-*object*" method of interpretation, we miss the richness of the "image-to-*event*" approach the angel employed. We find personal application, but we miss the panoramic, historical interpretation that Nephi was blessed to obtain. Surely we hope to mirror Nephi's spiritual aptitude more than that of his brothers. This requires us to ask what we can learn from the angel's message and method that we cannot gain from the answers offered to Laman and Lemuel, and how the details in the second narrative inform our understanding of the first.[6] In the following pages I argue that the evidence for and the benefits of an apocalyptic reading of these narratives are compelling. By recognizing Lehi's dream and Nephi's vision as paired pieces of apocalyptic literature—complete with the historical narrative, eschatology, and dualism typical of that genre—readers may be better able to place themselves, both temporally and spiritually, within its prophetic framework.[7]

Lehi's Dream as History

While parables may find fulfillment in history,[8] it is in apocalyptic literature that history plays a starring role. Its message is typically couched in historical terms from the start, and its purpose is to guide its readers through—and prepare them for—an unfolding panorama of future events. Thus, while parable is primarily *story* (with personal application possible in any age), apocalypse is more often *history* (with specific fulfillment in the final age). Lehi's dream fits within both genres and is therefore similarly suited for both ageless personal application (what Nephi hoped for his brothers) and specific historical fulfillment (what Nephi learned for himself). The differences appear in the manner of interpreting the dream's elements. In Laman and Lemuel's case, it was as though they had a painting of the dream to which Nephi attached labels identifying its constituent parts—each image representing an ageless spiritual reality. In Nephi's experience, as history proceeded to unfold, it was as if he was seeing each of the dream's elements take shape before his eyes—each image representing a time-bound historical event.

Unlike Lehi's dream, then, Nephi's vision contains, in the words of one scholar, "a literal dimension. Nephi sees relevant future events as they would transpire in real space and time and as they would involve real people," each of which is meant to explain an element of his father's dream.[9] He first witnessed the condescension of God as shown by the birth of his Only Begotten Son, and in doing so he saw, as it were, the tree of life bud, blossom, and bear fruit (see 1 Nephi 11:13–22). Next he beheld the ministries of Christ, John the Baptist, and the Twelve Apostles and, in essence, saw the iron rod form beside the tree and stretch out into the field beyond (see 1 Nephi 11:24–31). He then was shown the Crucifixion of Christ and the persecution of the early Church, and thus the great and spacious building began taking shape in the distance (see 1 Nephi 11:32–36). Shifting his gaze from the Old World to the New, Nephi saw "wars, and rumors of wars, and great slaughters with the sword among [his] people" (1 Nephi 12:2). Though interrupted by the ministry of Christ among his descendants, violence eventually erupted again, and consequently mists of darkness began to veil the rod and shroud the tree, filthy water began bubbling up like a river from hell, and the building he had seen earlier loomed ever larger and more sinister (see 1 Nephi 12:2–23). Time continued its onward march, and Nephi observed the deepening apostasy and the corruption of Christianity until, peering through the suffocating mists, he perceived in that great and spacious building the unmistakable trappings of a great and abominable church (see 1 Nephi 13:1–9). By then, each of the dream's elements had appeared and the field had been populated with people whose actions were divided no longer into the four distinct groups Lehi had described, but rather into the two possible directions their actions were taking them, either toward the tree or away from it, inspired by either the church of the Lamb of God or by the church of the devil. The battle between these two opposing forces continued and intensified (see

1 Nephi 13–14), and after a hint of their eventual end, the curtain closed on the apocalyptic vision of Nephi.

Image	Object (allegorical approach)	Event (historical approach)
Tree of life	Love of God (see 1 Nephi 11:22)	Birth of Christ (see 1 Nephi 11:13–22)
Rod of iron	Word of God (see 1 Nephi 11:25; 15:24)	Ministry of Christ and his Apostles (see 1 Nephi 11:24–31)
Great and spacious building	Pride of the world (see 1 Nephi 11:36); vain imaginations (see 1 Nephi 12:18)	Crucifixion, persecution (see 1 Nephi 11:32–36); apostasy (see 1 Nephi 13:1–9)
Mists of darkness	Temptations of the devil (see 1 Nephi 12:17)	Wars and wickedness among Nephites and Lamanites (see 1 Nephi 12:2–23); continued apostasy (see 1 Nephi 13:27–28)
River of water	Depths of hell (see 1 Nephi 12:16)	Destruction of the wicked (see 1 Nephi 12:15; 14:3–4)

Apocalyptic Literature

The use of a narrative history like that of Nephi's vision is one of the distinguishing features of the apocalyptic genre. The word *apocalypse* comes from the Greek noun *apokalypsis*, meaning "revelation" or "disclosure," and what is usually being revealed is the hand of God in the events of history, especially during times when history does not appear to be going God's way. During such periods, the focus of scripture becomes increasingly eschatological, in hopes that today's trials will be eclipsed by hope for tomorrow. This explains the preoccupation of apocalyptic writers with the end times—for instance, Daniel during the Babylonian exile or John during the Roman persecution—as each looked forward longingly to the day when "God shall wipe away all tears from their eyes" (Revelation 7:17; 21:4).

Both the writings of Daniel and the book of Revelation typify the apocalyptic genre, which is generally defined as "a genre of revelatory literature with a narrative framework, in which a revelation is mediated by an otherworldly being to a human recipient, disclosing a transcendent reality which is both temporal, insofar as it envisages eschatological salvation, and spatial insofar as it involves another, supernatural world."[10] Scholars have further clarified that in apocalyptic literature these "transcendent realities" are revealed by means of "visions and otherworldly journeys, supplemented by discourse or dialogue and occasionally by a heavenly book. The constant element is the presence of an angel who interprets the vision or serves as guide on the otherworldly journey. This figure indicates that the revelation is not intelligible without supernatural aid. . . . [Therefore,] the disposition of the seer before the revelation and his reaction to it typically emphasize human helplessness in the face of the supernatural."[11]

The classic illustration of the genre is the book which gives it its name, the Apocalypse of John, also known as the book of Revelation. In the book's first verse are found almost all of the characteristic elements of the genre. It is a revelation in the form of prophetic narrative, is "sent and signified . . . by [God's] angel unto his servant John," and describes "things which must shortly come to pass" (Revelation 1:1).

Judged by the scholarly definition and the example of Revelation, 1 Nephi 11–14 qualifies for the title "The Apocalypse of Nephi."[12] His vision takes the form of narrative (unfolding several thousand years of history), is mediated by otherworldly beings (at first the Spirit of the Lord and subsequently an angel), and is unintelligible without divine assistance (the revelation only occurs after Nephi has recognized his dependence on heaven's help [see 1 Nephi 10:17–11:6]). Perhaps even more significantly, Lehi's dream fits the description of apocalyptic literature as well. It too is in narrative form (the story of various groups' movements toward or away from the tree of life), Lehi is guided by an otherworldly being (the man dressed in a white robe), and he is only able to see the object of his journey when he begins "to pray unto the Lord that he would have mercy on [him]" (1 Nephi 8:8). Thus Lehi's dream may likewise be termed "The Apocalypse of Lehi."

Apocalyptic Literature	Revelation of John	Lehi's Dream	Nephi's Vision
Narrative framework	Narrative of the earth's seven thousand years	Narrative of various person's journeys to the tree of life	Narrative of history from Jesus' day to latter days

Apocalyptic Literature	Revelation of John	Lehi's Dream	Nephi's Vision
Revelation	"The Revelation of Jesus Christ" (Revelation 1:1)	"I have dreamed a dream; or, in other words, I have seen a vision" (1 Nephi 8:2)	Series of visions (see 1 Nephi 11–14)
Otherworldly being	"Sent and signified it by his angel" (Revelation 1:1)	"A man . . . dressed in a white robe" (1 Nephi 8:5)	The Spirit of the Lord; later an angel (see 1 Nephi 11:11, 14)
Human recipient	"Unto his servant John" (Revelation 1:1)	Lehi	Nephi
Transcendent reality	"Things which must shortly come to pass" (Revelation 1:1)	The individual—coming unto Christ	The history of the world—coming unto Christ

Spatial versus Temporal Dimensions

As shown, the apocalyptic nature of Lehi's dream is not derived merely from its explanatory association with Nephi's vision; it is apocalyptic in its own right. In other words, it is not simply the springboard for Nephi's apocalyptic vision but rather the first half of an apocalyptic whole. And when coupled, the two accounts do together what neither version can accomplish singlehandedly: they provide both the spatial and temporal dimensions at which apocalyptic literature aims. Lehi's dream is *spatial*, dealing with a supernatural world and our journey through spiritual darkness to God's brilliant tree of life. Nephi's vision is *temporal*, foretelling the onward march of history and the role of God within it. Stated differently, Lehi's dream is *vertical*, describing our spiritual journey heavenward, toward the love of God, while Nephi's vision is *horizontal*, chronicling humanity's historical journey forward, toward the end of time.[13]

That Lehi's dream and Nephi's vision would together point both forward and upward is particularly significant. The book of Revelation—the most famous Christian apocalypse—likewise does both, though the heavenly journey found in chapter 4 is heavily overshadowed by the temporal narration of the opening of the seven seals. Yet among Jewish apocalypses, only the apocryphal *Apocalypse of Abraham* combines the two,[14] making the tandem apocalypses of Lehi and Nephi a particularly rare and valuable gem. As one expert explains, "When consideration is given to the perennial tension between temporal and spatial definitions of salvation (e.g., mythic versus epic views of reality in antiquity and historical versus existential views today), the juxtaposition of temporal and spatial axes within ancient apocalypses seems conceptually fitting."[15]

In other words, when the ancients asked if meaning was to be found in myths (spatial/vertical) or in epics (historical/horizontal), or when people today wonder if salvation is spiritual or temporal—that is, whether it is found beyond this world (spatial/vertical) or within it (historical/horizontal)—apocalyptic literature answers yes! No wonder Nephi would later call his father's dream "a representation of things both temporal and spiritual" (1 Nephi 15:32). Together, the visions of Lehi and Nephi offer what some have considered mutually exclusive eschatologies—one "with the goal of the individual in existential terms" and the other with "the goal of history in cosmological terms."[16] They show that God is at work both in history and in the human heart. That he functions within time as well as outside of it. That not only can we be saved, but the world in which we live can be saved as well. In short, the apocalyptic contribution of this prophetic father and son shows not only what we must do to arrive at the tree of life but also what God is doing to take history in the same divine direction. They dramatize not only one's path to salvation but also the plan of salvation itself.

Apocalyptic Literature	
Lehi's Dream	Nephi's Vision
Heavenly journey	Chronological narrative
Mystical	Historical
Spiritual	Temporal
Spatial	Sequential
Vertical (upward)	Horizontal (forward)
Mythic	Epic
Existential	Cosmological

Prophetic versus Apocalyptic Eschatology

In addition to combining the spatial and temporal aspects of apocalyptic literature, Lehi's dream and Nephi's vision also reflect the genre's continuum between "prophetic eschatology" and "apocalyptic eschatology."[17] In both cases, eschatology "refers to a time in the future when the course of history will be changed to such an extent that one can speak of an entirely new state of reality."[18] The difference lies in how one arrives at that future state. Prophetic eschatology emphasizes personal and communal repentance and righteousness, which brings about deliverance and prosperity in this life. According to this view, present problems are largely due to one's own wickedness and therefore increased holiness will result in future blessings. Book of Mormon prophets reflect this outlook each time they repeat the promise "Inasmuch as ye shall keep my commandments ye shall prosper in the land" (2 Nephi 1:20; see also 1 Nephi 2:20; 2 Nephi 1:9; 4:4; Jarom 1:9; Omni 1:6; Mosiah 1:7; 2:22, 31; Alma 9:13; 36:1, 30; 37:13; 38:1; 48:15, 25; 50:20).

Apocalyptic eschatology, meanwhile, draws a picture of present conditions that is far more difficult to correct. Human reform alone will be insufficient to effect the needed change, and thus God will have to intervene in the course of history to preserve his people and bring about their redemption. In this view, evil is largely an outer enemy, one that God alone can overcome, doing so with cataclysmic events meant to alter the world order. Thus the scriptures—Bible, Book of Mormon, and Doctrine and Covenants alike—speak of a new heaven and a new earth (see Isaiah 65:17; 2 Peter 3:13; Revelation 21:1; Ether 13:9; D&C 29:23–24).

The eschatologies presented in Lehi's dream and Nephi's vision are, respectively, prophetic and apocalyptic.[19] In his dream, Lehi focused on the personal actions that would bring individuals to the tree; "whose fruit was desirable to make one happy" (1 Nephi 8:10): his own prayers, which brought him out of the "dark and dreary wilderness" (v. 4); his family members' heeding him when he beckoned them to come unto him (vv. 14–15); the multitudes' desire to "obtain the path" (v. 21); and the willingness of still others to "[hold] fast to the rod of iron" as it led through the mists of darkness (v. 30).[20] In each case, these individuals held the keys to their own deliverance—prayer was rewarded with prosperity, listening with learning, seeking with obtaining, and endurance with triumph. Apocalyptic literature always has "a hortatory aspect,"[21] and each of these descriptions was in fact an admonition. Moreover, by addressing his dream specifically to Laman and Lemuel,[22] exhorting them to hearken at the end of the story, preaching and prophesying unto them "of many things," and bidding them obey (vv. 37–38), Lehi placed an immediate solution squarely into the hands of his murmuring sons. Yes, in their journey from Jerusalem they too were wandering through what seemed "a dark and dreary wilderness," all because a white-robed man—in this case their father—had bade them follow. But if they would only "pray unto the Lord" and ask for "his tender mercies," the darkness would disappear, the field of opportunity would appear, and they too would gain access to a source of "exceedingly great joy" (vv. 4–12). No wonder Nephi's later words to his brothers were likewise more invitation than explanation. Keeping to the prophetic eschatology of his father, he "exhort[ed] them with all the energies of [his] soul, and with all the faculty which [he] possessed" to give heed, to remember, and to obey (1 Nephi 15:25).

Nephi certainly could have given them much more than that, having just descended from his own series of panoramic visions. But the message he received had been couched in different terms—characterized by apocalyptic, rather than prophetic, eschatology. The dream that Laman and Lemuel had heard was "intimate, symbolic, and salvific. Nephi's vision [was] collective, historic, and eschatological."[23] Compared to what Nephi saw, the problem of wandering multitudes was only a minor problem, one largely resolvable "in house." The real drama was a cosmological struggle between good and evil, one that the righteous could win only if "the power of the Lamb of God . . . descended upon the saints of the church of the Lamb, and upon the covenant people of the Lord" (1 Nephi 14:14). God himself would have to intervene for his people to gain an eventual victory and, throughout Nephi's vision, he does.[24] In the discovery of America, the independence of the United States, and the Restoration of the gospel, the Lord is a principal player, at work backstage until "the time cometh that he shall manifest himself unto all nations" (1 Nephi 13:42). Unlike Lehi's dream, which focuses on individual choice rather than divine intervention, Nephi's vision portrays a God at work in the world, "manifest[ing] himself . . . in word, and also in power, in very deed" (1 Nephi 14:1). For Lehi the plea was "Come and partake"; for Nephi it was "Thy kingdom come."

Dualism

Whether spatial or temporal in its narrative or prophetic or apocalyptic in its eschatology, apocalyptic literature typically conveys its message in strongly dualistic terms. In the spatial/temporal dichotomy, whether moving upward through space or forward through time, one is leaving a baser, more worldly reality for a higher, more heavenly one. The latter (prophetic/apocalyptic) portrays the struggle as being between righteousness and wickedness in this life or between the forces of good and evil at the end of times. Thus the apocalyptic work itself reflects the context in which it was written: the turmoil unleashed by two opposing forces, and the choice between them that must be made.

It is in clarifying this choice—and forcing it upon us—that dualism in apocalyptic literature makes its greatest contribution.[25] Middle ground is effectively eliminated, leaving readers no longer able to "halt . . . between two opinions" (1 Kings 18:21). Thus, in works like the book of Revelation, it is not only the "lukewarm" Laodiceans that are challenged to choose between hot and cold (see Revelation 3:15–16); each reader is presented with the same clear choice, with both options depicted in graphic, dualistic terms. The decision the book of Revelation forces upon its readers is summarized eloquently by one author:

> Will it be war or peace? Repentance or continued wickedness? Hatred or love? Vengeance or forgiveness? Zion or Babylon? Apostasy or Restoration? Destruction or salvation? The plowshare or the sword? Ultimately the decision is that to which John devotes the entire book of Revelation. Will it be the grasping dragon or the sacrificing Lamb? The devouring beast or the growing man child offering his gentle iron rod? The bride clothed in the sun or the whore appareled in her trappings? The harvest joy of the whitened fields or the despair of the grapes of wrath?[26]

This tendency to juxtapose opposing elements is also present in Lehi's dream, and to an even greater extent, in Nephi's vision. In Lehi's case, the "dark and dreary wilderness" gives way to the white and desirable fruit (1 Nephi 8:4–12). The great and spacious building is placed in opposition to the tree of life. And beside the river of filthy water is an iron rod that "extend[s] along [its] bank" (1 Nephi 8:19), the two possibilities running literally and symbolically in parallel. Wherever one might be along the path, both the turbulence of the dirty water and the stability of the iron rod are choices within easy reach.

Similarly, Nephi's vision foretells a drama of good versus evil presented in stark dualistic opposition: the "multitudes of the earth . . . gathered together to fight against the apostles of the Lamb" (1 Nephi 11:34); "the power of God" upon one group of Gentiles and "the wrath of God" upon those who "gathered together against them" (1 Nephi 13:18); the loss of "plain and precious things" from the "book of the Lamb of God" and the coming forth of "other books . . . by the power of the Lamb" to restore those truths that were lost (1 Nephi 13:26–40). Throughout his vision, Nephi sees the righteous and the wicked divided, in one way or another, by "a great and a terrible gulf" (1 Nephi 12:18; see also 1 Nephi 15:28–30), too wide to be bridged by indecision. All would have to choose one side of that gulf or the other, for, as foretold in the vision, the continuous work of God would be "everlasting, either on the one hand or on the other," with "peace and life eternal" fixed opposite captivity and destruction (1 Nephi 14:7).

The dualism in Nephi's vision becomes most pronounced as the narrative shifts from specific images and events to the opposing powers behind those elements. In a dramatic declaration, Nephi's angelic guide presents a cosmology in which all things are subsumed into two competing camps. "There are save two churches only," he affirms; "the one is the church of the Lamb of God, and the other is the church of the devil." A classic example of dualism, there is no middle ground, "wherefore, whoso belongeth not to the church of the Lamb of God belongeth to that great church, which is the mother of abominations; and she is the whore of all the earth" (1 Nephi 14:10). Black or white. Good or evil. No places of neutrality in which to hide. The church of the devil would exist "among all nations, kindreds, tongues, and people," and so would the church of the Lamb; though its numbers would be smaller, it too would be "upon all the face of the earth" (1 Nephi 14:11–12). Lest we limit this "church" to a single ecclesiastical entity, Nephi later refers to it in terms that clearly show its symbolic, archetypal nature.[27] Therefore, rather than symbolizing a specific religious organization per se, the great and abominable church consists of anyone "that fighteth against Zion, both Jew and Gentile, both bond and free, both male and female, . . . for they are they who are the whore of all the earth." As with the earlier verse, this one also ends in a definite duality in which two—and only two—options exist: "For they who are not for me are against me, saith our God" (2 Nephi 10:16).

Throughout Nephi's vision, the church of the devil is decidedly against the church of the Lamb. It is the moving force behind the mists of darkness, the river of filth, and the great and spacious building, which, like the church it represents, was similarly "filled with people, both old and young, both male and female" (1 Nephi 8:27). In opposition to the forces of righteousness, it "slayeth the saints of God," it "pervert[s] the right ways of the Lord," and it "fight[s] against the Lamb of God" wherever it may be (1 Nephi 13:5, 27; 14:13). As Nephi learned, "the devil . . . [is] the founder of it," and the desires of those who belong to its ranks center on worldliness and materialism ("gold, and silver, and silks, and scarlets, and fine-twined linen, and all manner of precious clothing"), the lusts of the flesh ("harlots"), and pride ("the praise of the world") (1 Nephi 13:6–9). In this respect, its tactics mirror the adversary's three original temptations of Christ (see Matthew 4:1–11) as well as the downfalls of the three kings of united Israel.[28] Indeed, the church of the devil is as old as the church of the Lamb it opposes.

Parallels to the Book of Revelation

With its historical narrative, its apocalyptic eschatology, and its dualistic juxtaposition of good and evil, the Apocalypse of Nephi is strikingly similar to the Apocalypse of John, the archetype of the apocalyptic genre. The threefold desires of the great and abominable church parallel the images of Babylon that populate the book of Revelation, where John likewise paints pictures of an enemy that influences through pride and power (the beasts in Revelation 13), worldliness and materialism (the merchant city in Revelation 18), and the lusts of the flesh (the great whore in Revelation 17). Both apocalypses personify the kingdom of the devil as "the mother of harlots" (1 Nephi 14:17; Revelation 17:5), who sits "upon many waters" (1 Nephi 14:11; Revelation 17:1) and fights against the people of God (see 1 Nephi 14:13; Revelation 13:7). She brings mists of darkness out of the chaos of war (see 1 Nephi 12:2–5; Revelation 9:1–11) and causes her victims to stumble, either by "pervert[ing] the right ways of the Lord" (1 Nephi 13:27) or, stated more symbolically, by making them "drunk with the wine of her fornication" (Revelation 17:2). Nevertheless, the kingdom of the devil falls—whether as Babylon (see Revelation 18:2) or the great and spacious building (see 1 Nephi 11:36)—and Satan is cast into the bottomless pit (see Revelation 20:1–3), which he and his followers had dug for others (see 1 Nephi 14:3). At that time, only the faithful Saints remain, dressed in white robes of righteousness (see 1 Nephi 12:10–11; Revelation 7:13–15; 19:8), having overcome the world. It is then their blessing to enjoy the living water and the tree of life (see 1 Nephi 11:25; Revelation 22:1–2).

The shift from wickedness to righteousness in each account centers on the battle over revealed truth. In John's account, he sees a beast bearing the name of blasphemy, worshipped by the wicked and at war with the Saints. Elsewhere called "the false prophet" (see Revelation 16:13; 19:20; 20:10), this beast—as a counterfeit Christ—has "two horns *like a lamb*" but speaks "as a dragon," bent on "deceiv[ing] them that dwell on the earth" by means of "miracles," "great wonders," and signs "from heaven" (Revelation 13:11–14; emphasis added). Of note is the fact that each element in this description of the beast bears a religious connotation, giving context to the battle between good and evil that John describes.[29] Therefore, it is only fitting that John would counter his depiction of "another beast" (Revelation 13:11) with the promise of "another angel," one who would have "the everlasting gospel to preach unto them that dwell on the earth" (Revelation 14:6).

Similarly, much of Nephi's vision of the great and abominable church centers on its efforts to deceive by "tak[ing] away from the gospel of the Lamb many parts which are plain and most precious; and also many covenants of the Lord" (1 Nephi 13:26). Nephi saw the book that contained the gospel of the Lamb, but devoid of the plain and precious parts that had been removed by the great and abominable church, "an exceedingly great many [would] stumble, yea, insomuch that Satan [would have] great power over them" (1 Nephi 13:28–30). Nevertheless, just as the angel did in John's revelation, God would restore those truths that had been lost, bringing forth "other books . . . by the power of the Lamb" to "make known the plain and precious things which [had] been taken away" (1 Nephi 13:39–40).

Though striking, these parallels between the Apocalypses of Nephi and John should not come as a surprise, for the one was a prelude to the other. In concluding his vision, Nephi foresaw his New Testament counterpart, "one of the twelve apostles of the Lamb" who would "see and write the remainder of these things" (1 Nephi 14:20–21). And though Nephi was forbidden to write the rest of what would be contained in Revelation, it was nevertheless part of what he saw in vision (see 1 Nephi 14:24–25). John and Nephi bore tandem testimonies of what God would do in the last days.

Application in Apocalypse

Speaking of the vision of the tree of life to students at Brigham Young University, President Boyd K. Packer affirmed, "You may think that Lehi's dream or vision has no special meaning for you, but it does. You are in it; *all of us are in it*."³⁰ Depending on our approach to the dream, we may see ourselves "in it" symbolically, as in Lehi's version, or historically, as in Nephi's account, but in either case, for us "this story is reality," as an earlier General Authority declared.³¹ In truth, we simultaneously appear in both genres, since our spiritual journey to the tree of life takes place within the temporal framework of Nephi's eschatological vision. Our individual quest to partake of the fruit is therefore inseparable from the Lord's plans to establish his kingdom. In both cases, we are players on the stage of salvation history, enticed by two opposing forces in the drama's decisive final scenes.

By contrast, readers typically place themselves within Lehi's dream alone, without positioning that dream in Nephi's prophetic chronology. Unfortunately, by separating the two accounts, we miss the eschatology and duality inherent in the apocalyptic narrative. If, on the other hand, we maintain a sense of both chronology and duality in our reading of Lehi's dream (projecting Nephi's interpretive framework onto the elements his father saw), the account becomes something like a cosmic chess match between God and the adversary, each player attempting to win us to his side. The contest begins as God beckons us to an incomparable tree bearing love and life. In opposition, Satan sends forth a river of filth bent on sweeping us up in its current. Sensing our danger, the Lord counters by marking a path that leads safely to the tree of life (and out of the river's reach), only to find the adversary conjuring a spacious structure filled with mocking masses—a mirage of materialism to lure us from the path of safety. In response, the Lord erects an iron rod designed to anchor us to the path, a guardrail meant to rouse us from our wanderings. Yet Satan, undeterred, either conceals that rod in mists of obscurity or removes whole sections ("plain and precious parts") under cover of darkness, hoping to blur the boundary between journeying safely and wandering lost. Within this apocalyptic framework, both the individual and society itself are marching forward, pulled between the poles of righteousness and wickedness—the tree of life and the great and spacious building, the church of the Lamb and the church of the devil.

In the end, choosing Christ and coming unto him becomes the message of both narratives and constitutes what President Packer called "the central message of the Book of Mormon."³² In Lehi's dream, Christ is "the source of eternal life, [and] the living evidence of divine love." In Nephi's vision, he is "the means whereby God will fulfill his covenant with the house of Israel and indeed the entire family of man."[33] In either version—or better said, through a combination of the two—we see the purposes assigned these narratives by Nephi: that all might "come to the knowledge of their Redeemer and the very points of his doctrine, that they may know how to come unto him and be saved" (1 Nephi 15:14).

Notes

1. S. Michael Wilcox, *Who Shall Be Able to Stand? Finding Personal Meaning in the Book of Revelation* (Salt Lake City: Deseret Book, 2003), 7.

2. To further illustrate the difference in depth between the two explanations, consider the fact that while Nephi needed only one verse apiece to clarify the tree and rod symbols for his brothers (see 1 Nephi 15:22, 24), the angel led Nephi through a trio of visions and forced him to wrestle with a question he could not at first answer. Only then did the angel confirm the explanation that Nephi was finally able to deduce (see 1 Nephi 11:8–25). Along the way, Nephi saw the mother of Jesus and the birth of Christ and came to understand the condescension of God, all by way of answers to his question about the tree.

3. Similarly, Steven L. Olsen wrote, "While Lehi's and Nephi's experiences both center on the plan of salvation, they represent, for the most part, different literary genres. Lehi's dream is largely allegorical, while Nephi's vision is largely a historical narrative." "The Centrality of Nephi's Vision," *Religious Educator* 11, no. 2 (2010): 52.

4. The parabolic approach seems most common in treatments of Lehi's dream. In essence, we see it as the story of a spiritual journey (much like the parables of the prodigal son or the good Samaritan). Or we see it as a quest for what is most desirable (like the parable of the pearl of great price) or as a choice between good and evil (like the parable of the wheat and tares). For an insightful parallel between Lehi's dream and the parable of the sower, centering on the four different groups of people presented in each narrative, see Jeffrey R. Holland, *Christ and the New Covenant* (Salt Lake City: Deseret Book, 1997), 161–62.

5. Viewing Lehi's dream as apocalyptic literature fits well within the framework of "visionary literature" proposed for the dream by Charles Swift in his article, "Lehi's Vision of the Tree of Life: Understanding the Dream as Visionary Literature," *Journal of Book of Mormon Studies* 14, no. 2 (2005): 52–63.

6. For pedagogical insights relating to the angel's methodology, see David A. Bednar, "Seek Learning by Faith," *Religious Educator* 7, no. 3 (2006): 4.

7. Richard Dilworth Rust has written, "The impact of *what* the Book of Mormon says often is created through *how* it is said." *Feasting on the Word: The Literary Testimony of the Book of Mormon* (Salt Lake City: Deseret Book; Provo, UT: FARMS, 1997), 2. Eric D. Huntsman cites this statement in his own discussion of genre theory, affirming, "A major literary concern when we read a passage of scripture is to identify what

kind of writing the passage is and how this genre affects how we read it." "Teaching through Exegesis: Helping Students Ask Questions of the Text," *Religious Educator* 6, no. 1 (2005): 114.

8. This is especially true when the parable or allegory in question is viewed through the expanded lens of the Restoration, with its emphasis on the establishment of the kingdom of God in the last days. For example, section 86 of the Doctrine and Covenants clearly places Christ's parable of the wheat and tares in the context of the Apostasy, the latter-day gathering, and the Final Judgment. Joseph Smith saw similar historical fulfillment in the parables of the kingdom found in Matthew 13, which trace the destiny of the kingdom of God from the Savior's time "even unto the end of the world." See *History of the Church of Jesus Christ of Latter-day Saints*, ed. B. H. Roberts, 2nd ed. rev. (Salt Lake City: Deseret Book, 1976), 2:264–72. For a discussion of Joseph Smith's historical view of the parables of the kingdom, especially the parable of the sower, see Jared M. Halverson, "Of Soils and Souls: The Parable of the Sower," *Religious Educator* 9, no. 3 (2008): 32–36. The allegory of the olive tree in Jacob 5 is likewise steeped in history, chronicling—in advance—the Lord's ongoing efforts to redeem his people. In each of these cases, timeless truths double as concrete historical developments. They are as much about prophecy as they are about principles.

9. Olsen, "Nephi's Vision," 53. See also Corbin T. Volluz, "Lehi's Dream of the Tree of Life: Springboard to Prophecy," *Journal of Book of Mormon Studies* 2, no. 2 (Fall 1993): 14–38.

10. John J. Collins, *The Apocalyptic Imagination: An Introduction to Jewish Apocalyptic Literature*, 2nd ed. (Grand Rapids, MI: Eerdmans, 1998), 5; see also Paul D. Hanson, "Apocalypses and Apocalypticism," in *The Anchor Bible Dictionary*, ed. David Noel Freedman (New York: Doubleday, 1992), 1:279.

11. Collins, *Apocalyptic Imagination*, 5–6.

12. Eric D. Huntsman refers to the "Apocalypse of Nephi" in "Teaching through Exegesis," 120. Stephen E. Robinson also categorizes Nephi's vision as apocalyptic literature in "Nephi's 'Great and Abominable Church,'" *Journal of Book of Mormon Studies* 7, no. 1 (1998): 34–36.

13. "Nephi's historic-prophetic perspective extended beyond a cyclical view to a linear and teleological view of history as he elaborated broader themes in the divine plan." Roy A. Prete, "God in History? Nephi's Answer," *Journal of Book of Mormon Studies* 14, no. 2 (2005): 37.

14. See Collins, *Apocalyptic Imagination*, 6.

15. Hanson, "Apocalypses and Apocalypticism," 279.

16. Hans Schwarz, "Eschatology," in Donald W. Musser and Joseph L. Price, eds., *A New Handbook of Christian Theology* (Nashville: Abingdon Press, 1992), 158.

17. See Hanson, "Apocalypses and Apocalypticism," 281.

18. David L. Petersen, "Eschatology," in *The Anchor Bible Dictionary*, 2:575.

19. Another way to consider these two distinct perspectives is by associating the prophetic view and the apocalyptic view with what scholars have differentiated, respectively, as the Old Testament hope for blessings in this life and the New Testament expectation for the coming of the kingdom of God.

20. For an excellent summary of the various means by which one may reach the tree of life, see Matthew O. Richardson, "Vision, Voice, Path, and Rod: Coming to Partake of the Fulness," in *The Fulness of the Gospel: Foundational Teachings from the Book of Mormon* (Salt Lake City: Deseret Book, 2003), 26–38.

21. Collins, *Apocalyptic Imagination*, 6.

22. When relating the dream, Lehi refers to Laman and Lemuel with the second-person "you" (see 1 Nephi 8:4). He refers to Nephi and Sam using the third-person "they" (see 1 Nephi 8:3).

23. John W. Welch, "Connections between the Visions of Lehi and Nephi," *Insights*, July 1993, 2.

24. Roy A. Prete has written, "As a truly great prophet with an unusually clear view of future developments, Nephi provides a vast sweep of God's role in human affairs for the accomplishment of divine purposes." "God in History," 37.

25. In words well suited to the history portrayed in apocalyptic literature, Frederic Farrar wrote that "the object of Prophecy in all ages has been moral warning infinitely more than even the vaguest chronological indication, since to the voice of Prophecy as to the eye of God all Time is but one eternal Present." Frederic W. Farrar, *The Life of Christ* (Salt Lake City: Bookcraft, 1999), 542.

26. Wilcox, *Who Shall Be Able to Stand?*, 215.

27. For a discussion of the great and abominable church in both historical and typological terms, see Robinson, "Nephi's Great and Abominable Church," 32–39.

28. In Christ's temptations in the wilderness, changing stones into bread was a temptation of the lusts of the flesh, casting himself down from the temple was a temptation of pride, and being offered the kingdoms of the earth was a temptation of worldliness and materialism. In ancient Israel, King Saul fell to a sin of pride, King David fell to the lusts of the flesh, and King Solomon fell to worldliness and materialism. Satan may alter his tactics, but he still uses the same three types of temptation. The desires of the great and abominable church are still the same.

29. See Wilcox, *Who Shall Be Able to Stand?*, 188–90.

30. Boyd K. Packer, "Lehi's Dream and You," in *Brigham Young University 2006–2007 Speeches* (Provo, UT: Brigham Young University), 258; emphasis added.

31. William Grant Bangerter, "Coming through the Mists," *Ensign*, May 1984, 28.

32. Boyd K. Packer, "The Things of My Soul," *Ensign*, May 1986, 61.

33. Holland, *Christ and the New Covenant*, 162.

5

Nephi's Vision and the Loss and Restoration of Plain and Precious Truths

Lori Driggs

In the great vision of the ancient American prophet Nephi, he describes the coming forth of a record of the Jews, the Bible, which contains "the covenants of the Lord" and "many of the prophecies of the holy prophets" (1 Nephi 13:23). Of this book Nephi declares, "When it proceeded forth from the mouth of a Jew it contained the fulness of the gospel of the Lord," but "there are many plain and precious things taken away from the book" (vv. 24, 28). How were the plain and precious truths lost from the Bible? What factors may have influenced or brought about the loss of these truths? Which plain and precious truths were brought forth to us again through the record of Nephi? This study will examine (1) factors that may have caused truth to be lost from the Bible, (2) truths Nephi considered plain and precious enough to include in the Book of Mormon, and (3) the significance of the loss and restoration of plain and precious truth for us today. Much of the discussion regarding the Bible will center on the texts of the New Testament, focusing on textual changes made before approximately fifth century AD.

Lori Driggs has a master of arts degree in biblical studies from Iliff School of Theology in Denver.

As we begin our discussion, let us first consider some of the teachings set forth by Nephi in his vision regarding this topic. It is clear from Nephi's vision that the book—the Bible—initially "proceeded forth from the mouth of a Jew" and that when "these things [went] forth from the Jews" they went forth "in purity" (1 Nephi 13:24–25). He further announces that the truths originally "go forth by the hand of the twelve apostles of the Lamb, from the Jews unto the Gentiles." After the truths are disseminated by the hand of the twelve Apostles, a "great and abominable church, which is most abominable above all other churches," is formed, which takes "away from the gospel of the Lamb many parts which are plain and most precious, and also many covenants of the Lord" (v. 26).[1]

It is interesting to note Nephi's wording about how the plain and precious truths were lost from the Jewish record, known to us as the Bible. He says, "Thou seest that after the book hath gone forth *through the hands* of the great and abominable church, that there are many plain and precious things taken away from the book, which is the book of the Lamb of God" (1 Nephi 13:28; emphasis added). This seems to imply a passage of time, through the hands of many people and influences.[2]

The Loss of Plain and Precious Truth Defined

It may be helpful, before we launch into a discussion of factors contributing to the loss of truth in the Bible, to be clear about how truth may be lost. What exactly does it mean to "lose" truth from the Bible? The first and most obvious way is to have truth removed—in whole or in part—or changed in the biblical text. Nephi provides us with a second definition of how truth may be lost from the Bible when, at the end of his vision, he says that the truths originally proceeding forth from the mouth of a Jew "were plain and pure, and most precious and easy to the understanding of all men" (1 Nephi 14:23). We may understand from this, as it relates to the loss of plain and precious truth, that unless truths are written plainly and purely in a clear and understandable way, important gospel truths may be lost because they may not be recognized or readily comprehended. In some cases, precious truth may still be found in the Bible, at least in part, but they are no longer plain to our understanding without the Book of Mormon and other revelation brought to us by the Lord's prophets. Examples of such doctrines include the Fall, the Atonement, the Resurrection, the scattering and gathering of Israel, agency, justice, mercy, and baptism for the dead, to name a few.

In 2 Nephi 25:4, after Nephi has recorded several chapters from the book of Isaiah, Nephi makes the following statement before he begins to clarify for us the doctrines Isaiah has just taught us. Nephi says, "I shall prophesy according to the plainness which hath been with me from the time that I came out from Jerusalem with my father; for behold, my soul delighteth in plainness unto my people, that they may learn." Why had "plainness" been with Nephi since the time he came out from Jerusalem? The answer seems obvious. It was at that time Nephi received his great vision and saw how many people would stumble because of the plain and precious truths lost from the Bible. After seeing this happen to the Bible and after being taught the significance of the restoration of plain and precious truth, is it any wonder that Nephi's soul "delighteth in plainness"? (2 Nephi 31:3).

Something more may be said here of the import of plainness in the word of God. The word of God is of immeasurable worth in bringing us to Christ. In their visions, both Lehi and Nephi saw a rod of iron leading to the tree of life, or Christ. It was by clinging to this rod that multitudes were enabled to come to Christ. Nephi tells us the rod of iron "was the word of God; and whoso would hearken unto the word of God, and would hold fast unto it, they would never perish; neither could the temptations and the fiery darts of the adversary overpower them unto blindness, to lead them away to destruction" (1 Nephi 15:24). In very deed, we will not and cannot come to Christ without his word.

After all the things Nephi saw and was taught by the Spirit of the Lord, Nephi's soul delighted in plainness in the word of God, "for after this manner doth the Lord God work among the children of men. For the Lord God giveth light unto the understanding; for he speaketh unto men according to their language, unto their understanding" (2 Nephi 31:3).

Factors Influencing or Causing the Loss of Plain and Precious Truths

With greater clarity regarding what it means to lose truth from the Bible, we may now begin to examine what caused it to be lost. As mentioned before, this occurred over time, and the causes were multifaceted. Although it is not possible to consider everything here that caused the loss of plain and precious truth from the Bible, we can at least briefly discuss some factors that were particularly influential. Only four areas will be covered in this paper: early manuscripts, copyists and scribes, theological differences within Christianity, and translation.

Early manuscripts. A foundational concept to consider is the nature of ancient texts. In the first century, manuscripts were very different than those we have today. The biblical canon had not yet been established, and individual books of the Bible were written on separate scrolls made of papyrus or parchment (that is, the book of Luke would be on one scroll and 1 Peter on another, and so forth). It was not until the end of the first century or the beginning of the second century that the codex, an early version of today's page, began to be used.[3] Finally, by the fourth century, the production of codices was sufficiently developed to contain a complete collection of Christian scripture.[4] This development at long last provided a stable and tangible means by which a Christian canon could be established, an event that occurred in about fifth century AD.[5] Thus the lack of an authoritative canon and the manner in which records were kept facilitated the loss of plain and precious truth from the Bible. This should become more clear as we continue our discussion.

Early copyists and scribes. Ancient copyists exerted an enormous influence over the integrity of the biblical texts. In early centuries, copies of the scriptures could only be painstakingly reproduced by hand, since the printing press had not yet been invented.[6] This automatically guaranteed inaccuracy in the biblical text, because human error is a likely companion of any human endeavor.

According to Bruce M. Metzger and Bart D. Ehrman, the earliest biblical manuscripts were more likely to contain a greater number of variations than texts made later, because the copyists were members of assorted congregations who were literate but untrained. Textual errors were then easily perpetuated, they continue, when additional copies were made from an already erroneous manuscript.[7] Furthermore, copies of biblical texts were often made quickly and with little revision in those early centuries, especially during early periods when the Christian Church was a persecuted, poor, and uneducated body.[8]

In the third and fourth centuries, professionally trained scribes began to emerge within the Christian Church.[9] By the fourth century, too, Christianity became the church officially recognized by the government, and biblical texts began to be reproduced in places called scriptoriums.[10] Metzger and Ehrman describe the scriptorium as a workroom where several trained scribes copied a biblical text slowly while a lector or reader read it aloud. In a place such as this, they say, errors easily occurred through momentary inattention caused by fatigue or noise, distraction from dipping one's pen in the inkwell, or not hearing the reader clearly. Moreover, they tell us, textual inaccuracies resulted from words that were pronounced the same but spelled differently, as in the English *there* and *their*.[11] In subsequent years, trained monks began to replicate biblical texts.

Errors of the mind, hand, eye, and hearing all contributed to the degeneration of textual accuracy. These types of mistakes include carelessly repeating words, confusing similar letters, misunderstanding abbreviations or contractions, and not distinguishing correctly between a spoken vowel or a diphthong.[12] The arduous and fatiguing nature of copying a text, the cramped body position, and the drudgery of the task would also have made errors more likely.[13]

When we consider the foregoing research, it is not hard to imagine the changes that could evolve in ancient biblical manuscripts over centuries of transmission by the hand of copyists prone to human error. At this point we may consider another significant reason for the loss of truth in a once pure and plain Jewish record. It may be found in the controversies raging within Christianity during the early centuries of the Christian era.

Theological differences within Christianity. We would do well to first return to the Book of Mormon record to begin our discussion of theological differences within Christianity. In Nephi's great vision, he saw that after the crucifixion of the Son of God "the multitudes of the earth . . . were gathered together to fight against the apostles of the Lamb" and that "the house of Israel hath gathered together to fight against the twelve apostles of the Lamb" (1 Nephi 11:34–35). The Apostles had been chosen by Jesus and given authority to act in his name. Nephi describes the receipt of apostolic authority in his vision, saying, "I also saw and bear record that the Holy Ghost fell upon twelve . . . ; and they were ordained of God, and chosen" (1 Nephi 12:7; see also Luke 6:13; Acts 1:15–26).[14] The fight against the Apostles continued until all of them were gone. With the demise of the Apostles, the authority given them by Jesus to act in his name was lost as well.

In addition to the loss of authorized leadership, revelation from God ceased, because the multitudes of the earth and the house of Israel had rejected Christ and his Apostles. In the preface to his great vision, Nephi provides us with important information regarding some qualifying factors for receiving revelation. After hearing his father's vision and the words his father spoke by the power of the Holy Ghost, Nephi observes that his father received "the power of the Holy Ghost . . . by faith on the Son of God" (1 Nephi 10:17). Nephi then declares that he (Nephi) likewise "was desirous also that I might see, and hear, and know of these things, by the power of the Holy Ghost, which is the gift of God unto all those who diligently seek him, as well in times of old as in the time that he should manifest himself unto the children of men. For he is the same yesterday, to-day, and forever. . . . For he that diligently seeketh shall find; and the mysteries of God shall be unfolded unto them, by the power of the Holy Ghost, . . . as well in times of old as in times to come" (1 Nephi 10:17–19). In these verses Nephi identifies essential elements in the receipt of revelation: faith in Jesus Christ, the gift and power of the Holy Ghost, desire to know truth, and diligence in seeking Christ.

Unfortunately, ancient peoples lacked these necessary precursors for revelation, as evidenced by their willful rejection of Christ and his Apostles. Revelation, therefore, was lost. As a result, many of those professing Christianity began to embrace or incorporate other philosophies and ideologies into their belief systems, thus seeking to effect a compromise between Christianity and their sometimes hostile environment. Such an occurrence was a concern of Church leaders even during the time of the original twelve Apostles (see Colossians 2:8; Hebrews 13:9; 2 Corinthians 11:3). This led to tremendous diversity among the theological beliefs of Christians themselves. The stability of core doctrines began to disintegrate, and single ideas or doctrines came to be interpreted very differently. This in turn caused divisiveness and controversy among Christians, resulting in the rise of various factions within Christianity, each determined that they were correct in their views. To make matters worse, with the lack of an established and authoritative biblical canon and the means by which to regulate it, when these diverse groups obtained a scroll of biblical text, they could intentionally or unintentionally modify or adapt it to their own beliefs. Plain and precious truths could thus easily be altered, made unclear, or be taken completely from a given text.[15]

One very significant theological issue, which caused a great deal of disputation among Christians of the first five centuries, had to do with views about Jesus Christ, also known as Christology. We get a sense of the diversities and contentions raging within Christianity when we read Ehrman's summary of the Christological differences existing during this early period:

> In the second and third centuries there were, of course, Christians who believed in only one God; others, however, claimed that there were two Gods; yet others subscribed to 30, or 365, or more. Some Christians accepted the Hebrew Scriptures as a revelation of the one true God, the sacred possession of all believers; others claimed that the Scriptures had been inspired by an evil deity. Some Christians believed that God had created the world and was soon going to redeem it; others said that God neither had created the world nor had ever had any dealings with it. Some Christians believed that Christ was somehow both a man and God; others said that he was a man, but not God; others claimed that he was God, but not a man; others insisted that he was a man who had been temporarily inhabited by God. Some Christians believed that Christ's death had brought about the salvation of the world; others claimed that his death had no bearing on salvation; yet others alleged that he had never even died.[16]

Factions within Christianity struggled for centuries for supremacy over the others. Eventually, orthodox Christians won and established a biblical canon they considered authoritative.[17] Until then, however, biblical texts were more subject to alteration, whether intentional or unintentional.

Translation. Last, but certainly not least, we need to examine the effect of translation in the loss of truth from the Bible. A translator's skill directly impacted the quality of the resulting text. This is evident in the Septuagint, where a close examination of the different books reveals that some of the translators were not as competent as others.[18] Augustine, a theologian born in the mid-fourth century, complained about copies made by those not knowing Greek well: "In the early times of the faith when anyone found a Greek codex, and he thought that he had some facility in both languages, he attempted to translate it."[19] He further grieved that "many translators are deceived by ambiguity in the original language which they do not understand, so that they transfer meaning to something completely alien to the writer's intention."[20]

When one considers translation, it is important to keep in mind that a translator's own cultural and theological views are likely to influence the resulting translation. Indeed, passages of ancient biblical texts could only be translated as the translators themselves understood them.[21] One modern scholar observes that theology may advise and sway the interpretation of a language, and the lexicon and syntax of a given text may be adjusted to favor a particular theological view.[22] One can imagine the impact this could have on the translation of a given text, especially during a time of apostasy, contention, and controversy.

Summary and reflections. It is easy to see from the foregoing discussion that anciently the field was ripe for a loss of truth that was plain and precious to our understanding of God and his ways. Truths were lost from the Bible through human frailty, disparity among Christians, and by poor or hurriedly made translations. In addition, people were left without the Lord's authorized leadership and revelation because they had willfully rejected Christ and his Apostles. They no longer received divine guidance to help them deal with their ever-changing society and environment, and to help them combat worldly philosophies and ideologies. Furthermore, there was no standardized biblical text until about fifth century AD, which facilitated the changing of biblical texts to reflect particular religious preferences.

In contrast to the Bible's development is the coming forth of the Book of Mormon. It, too, came forth in a day when religious controversy raged (see Joseph Smith—History 1:5–9). In the case of the Book of Mormon, however, the Lord's protection, guidance, and power were very involved. It was "written . . . by the spirit of prophecy and of revelation—written and sealed up, and hid up unto the Lord, that [it] might not be destroyed" or tampered with over the centuries (title page of the Book of Mormon; see also 1 Nephi 13:35). The Lord prepared "means for the interpretation thereof" (Mormon 9:34), and limited his translators to one person: Joseph Smith, the prophet called of God to restore the Church of Jesus Christ once again upon the earth. The effect of human frailty on the Book of Mormon was and is minimized because the Lord's grace "is sufficient for the meek, that [the Gentiles] shall take no advantage of [the writers'] weakness" in writing (Ether 12:26). The Book of Mormon truly "[came] forth unto the Gentiles, by the gift and power of the

Lamb," and contains "[the Lord's] gospel . . . and [his] rock and [his] salvation" (1 Nephi 13:35–36).

Variations in Early Biblical Texts Influencing the Loss of Plain and Precious Truths

A consideration of the types of variations that have been found in early biblical texts can also be instructive in understanding plain and precious truths taken from the Bible. Several types of variants have been found in ancient biblical texts, but only three will be considered here in any depth: omission, theological changes, and ancient punctuation and writing style. These three are chosen because they are considered to be more theologically significant for the purposes of this study.

Omission. As heretofore mentioned, many corruptions of biblical manuscripts were due to the frailties of human nature, as was the case with many textual omissions. Frequently words, phrases, and even paragraphs were unintentionally omitted from ancient manuscripts. This could occur, for example, when words having similar spellings caused the scribe's eye to skip from one place to another in the text. When this happened, all the words in between were omitted.[23] An example of how this could affect a text is found in John 17:15 of one manuscript, when the scribe wrote, "I do not pray that you take them from the [world, but that you keep them from the] evil one."[24] Omissions in manuscripts also came about when portions of a text were intentionally shortened because early Christians found them objectionable.[25]

Latter-day Saints understand, for example, that material was removed from the writings of Moses. The Lord explained to him, "And in a day when the children of men shall esteem my words as naught and take many of them from the book which thou shalt write, behold, I will raise up another like unto thee; and they shall be had again among the children of men—among as many as shall believe" (Moses 1:41). One possible omission from the Bible may be a prophecy of Joseph of Egypt found in Joseph Smith Translation, Genesis 50:24–38 and 2 Nephi 3.[26] This prophecy contains important truths regarding the raising up of a Messiah, the scattering and gathering of Israel, and the coming forth of a great work of salvation in the latter days through a seer called Joseph. This seer, according to the prophecy, would be given power to bring forth the word of the Lord "unto the confounding of false doctrines, and laying down of contentions, and establishing peace" among Joseph of

Egypt's seed (Joseph Smith Translation, Genesis 50:31). Fortunately for us, the Lord restored this plain and precious truth through the great latter day seer named Joseph Smith.

Theological changes. As previously discussed, in early centuries there was considerable diversity and disputation among those professing Christianity. In contemplating how this could affect the transmission and translation of ancient biblical manuscripts, we should remember that scribes working with these documents were human beings with thoughts and feelings of their own with regard to religious dogma and controversies of their day. Ehrman notes that theological changes in the text are to be expected from this period, when both the text and theology were constantly changing and when the church lacked an authoritative and fixed biblical canon.[27]

In Nephi's vision, he saw that plain and precious truths were taken from the Jewish record by some who did it "that they might pervert the right ways of the Lord, that they might blind the eyes and harden the hearts of the children of men" (1 Nephi 13:27). Other plain and precious truths may have been lost simply by having passed "through the hands of the great and abominable church" (v. 28). As a result, "an exceedingly great many do stumble, yea, insomuch that Satan hath great power over them" (v. 29).

Modern scholars agree that changes were deliberately made to ancient biblical texts. Ehrman claims that scribes altered passages so they would be less vulnerable to abuse by those with opposing theological views. He proposes that this was particularly true of orthodox Christians regarding Christological passages.[28] Keith Elliott and Ian Moir agree that ancient scribes were instructed by ecclesiastical personnel, especially within orthodoxy, to change the texts to hinder opponents from using them to their ends.[29] They further note that in certain passages referring to Christology, the manuscripts are obscure and susceptible to textual variants.[30] Indeed, ancient biblical manuscripts frequently show the greatest variations in those passages referring specifically to the words, actions, and statements of Jesus.[31] According to Ehrman, however, despite some deliberate changes occurring in the biblical texts for theological reasons, most changes were not motivated by theology but were instead the result of human error.[32]

Ancient punctuation and writing style. The last reason that will be discussed here regarding the loss of plain and precious truth in the Bible is that of ancient writing style and punctuation. The earliest biblical manuscripts were different from modern manuscripts, in that there were no spaces between words, and no distinctions made between small and capital letters. Furthermore, until about the eighth century, very little punctuation was used.

Metzger and Ehrman provide an example of how this could affect the reading of a text. If we were to read GODISNOWHERE, those of us who believe in God would likely read it very differently than one who is an atheist. An atheist would likely read, "God is nowhere," and a believer in God would be more inclined to read, "God is now here."[33] While the nature of the Greek language does not often allow for obscurity of this kind because of word ending requirements, occasional misrepresentations could still have occurred from this style of writing.[34]

We may see how punctuation affects the clarity of written truth in the King James Version of the Bible by using an illustration supplied by Elder James E. Talmage. In John 8:58 we read, "Verily, verily, I say unto you, Before Abraham was, I am." Elder Talmage explains that the Hebrew *Ehyeh*, meaning *I Am*, is related by definition and derivation to the term *Yahveh* or *Jehovah*.[35] He then tells us that a more correct rendering of this declaration would be, "Before Abraham, was I AM." In other words, it would be the same as though Christ had said, "Before Abraham, was I, Jehovah."[36]

Summary and reflections. As these variations suggest, many corruptions of the biblical text were likely the result of human frailty. This is to be expected, given the lack of technology and the methods for record keeping during this era. Such changes were inevitable.

Some alterations, on the other hand, were deliberate. Although we cannot know the motivations of all those who calculated such modifications, evidence suggests that some did so to support their own views and foil those of the opposition. Nephi saw in his vision that the desires of the great and abominable church were riches, harlots, and "the praise of the world" (see 1 Nephi 13:6–9). In addition, they sought to "pervert the right ways of the Lord" to lead others astray (v. 27). Contrast this with countless prophets and peoples of the Book of Mormon, exemplified by Nephi. He affirms that "the fulness of mine intent [in keeping this record] is that I may persuade men to come unto the God of Abraham, and the God of Isaac, and the God of Jacob, and be saved. Wherefore, the things which are pleasing unto the world I do not write, but the things which are pleasing unto God and unto those who are not of the world" (1 Nephi 6:4–5).

With regard to Christology, we may thank the Book of Mormon for providing us with greater clarification regarding Jesus Christ, and we may be assured that the Lord has not left us with a deficit on this topic. In his vision, Nephi saw and bore testimony of Jesus, the Lamb of God and Son of the Eternal Father, and recorded Jesus' great ministries on two continents (see 1 Nephi 11–13). The Book of Mormon contains several other accounts of those who actually saw Jesus.[37] Indeed, the entire Book of Mormon is an amazing witness for Jesus Christ and is replete with teachings about his nature, his character, his Atonement, his gospel, and his plan for the salvation of the human race.

Truths Nephi Considered Plain and Precious

We now come to one of the most important reasons for this study: the truths Nephi considered plain and precious. Nephi saw many great things in vision and received much instruction at the Lord's hand (see 1 Nephi 18:3; 2 Nephi 4:23–25). Nevertheless, he was limited in what he could preserve for us. What were truths Nephi considered plain and precious enough to write on the few pages allotted to him in the Book of Mormon? While some of Nephi's chapters are faith-promoting narrative accounts of his own experiences and those of his family, the majority contain an elaboration of the truths described in overview form through his great vision.[38] These plain and precious truths Nephi saw fit to include in the Book of Mormon may be categorized into three areas in which his "soul delighteth." In 2 Nephi 11, he states that (1) "my soul delighteth in proving unto my people the truth of the coming of Christ," (2) "my soul delighteth in the covenants of the Lord which he hath made to our fathers," and (3) "my soul delighteth in his grace, and in his justice, and power, and mercy in the great and eternal plan of deliverance from death" and "in proving unto my people that save Christ should come all men must perish" (2 Nephi 11:4–6). While the plain and precious truths Nephi included in the Book of Mormon will be discussed as separate areas for ease of presentation, the truths in these areas are inseparably connected and overlap each other. In expounding these truths, Nephi uses the teachings and prophecies of four different witnesses: Lehi, Jacob, Isaiah, and himself.

Area 1. The truth of the coming of Christ. Nephi devotes the first chapter of his great vision to his witness of the coming of Christ (see 1 Nephi 11). In it, he saw a virgin, "the mother of the Son of God," who was "bearing a child in her arms," even the "Lamb of God, . . . the Son of the Eternal Father" (1 Nephi 11:18, 20–21). Nephi beheld "that he went forth ministering unto the people, in power and great glory," and that in the course of his ministry "angels [descended] upon the children of men; and they did minister unto them" (1 Nephi 11:28, 30). Multitudes of people "were healed by the power of the Lamb of God; and the devils and unclean spirits were cast out" (1 Nephi 11:28, 31). Nephi further saw that "the Son of the everlasting God was judged of the world" and "was lifted up upon the cross and slain for the sins of the world" (1 Nephi 11:32–33). Later, Nephi "saw the heavens open, and the Lamb of God descending out of heaven; and he came down and showed himself" in resurrected form unto the people of the Americas (1 Nephi 12:6). At least two of these events in this portion of Nephi's vision are not recorded in the Bible: (1) the ministering of angels among children of men during the Savior's mortal ministry (see 1 Nephi 12:5-11), seemingly similar to what occurred among the Nephites (see 3 Nephi 17:24; 19:14–15), and (2) Christ's ministry on the American continent (see 1 Nephi 12:5-11).

Nephi determined to send forth in his writings the words of three other witnesses "to prove . . . that my words are true. Wherefore, by the words of three, God hath said, I will establish my word. Nevertheless, God sendeth more witnesses, and he proveth all his words" (2 Nephi 11:3).[39] Although there are witnesses of Christ's coming in the Bible, Nephi surely added the precious words of these witnesses to the Book of Mormon because God commanded him to provide further proof of the reality of Christ and his ministry (see 2 Nephi 33:11). These additional witnesses also attest to the divinity of Jesus Christ, a fact which some question in our day.

One witness Nephi provides us is through a vision of his father, Lehi, who saw the Lord "descending out of the midst of heaven" and said his "luster was above that of the sun at noon-day" (1 Nephi 1:9). The second witness Nephi imparts is that of his brother Jacob, who "beheld that in the fulness of time [the Redeemer] cometh to bring salvation unto men" (2 Nephi 2:3). Nephi's third witness is Isaiah, the great prophet, who saw "the Lord sitting upon a throne, high and lifted up" (2 Nephi 16:1).

Area 2. The covenants of the Lord. In his vision, Nephi was told that "many covenants" were taken away from the Jewish record by the great and abominable church (1 Nephi 13:26). His explanations of the covenants of the Lord and their fulfillment are extensive in his writings, and may be touched on only summarily here. Within this category we may include prophecies of the coming of the Messiah and his great ministries, the establishment of a great nation on the land of promise, the restoration of the gospel of the Lamb to the Gentiles, the state of wickedness and apostasy and the workings of the devil in the latter days when knowledge of the Lord and his gospel is restored, the scattering and gathering of the house of Israel in general, the scattering and gathering of the Jews, the scattering and gathering of the seed of Nephi and his brethren, the coming forth of the Book of Mormon and other books containing the words of Christ, the second coming and restoration of the house of Israel to the lands of their inheritance, and the millennial day of peace and rejoicing when the Lord will dwell with his people. While many of these truths are found scattered throughout the Bible, nowhere in holy writ are they found as plainly and fully expounded as in Nephi's writings.

Before Nephi even records his vision, he says that "to proceed with mine account, I must speak somewhat of the things of my father" (1 Nephi 10:1). He does so to prepare our minds and hearts, to make his account more clear to us. One thing he speaks "somewhat" of is the coming of the Savior and his forerunner, John the Baptist. This readies us for his discussion of seeing in vision the Messiah and his ministry in mortality and in the Americas. Another preparatory prophecy he provides us is an abbreviated version of the scattering of the house of Israel and their gathering through coming to "the knowledge of the true Messiah, their Lord and their Redeemer" (1 Nephi 10:14). By providing us with this information, Nephi can be assured that when the angel asks him in vision, "Rememberest thou the covenants of the Father unto the house of Israel?" (1 Nephi 14:8), Nephi can know that not only does he know, but also that we, his readers, know "somewhat" of the covenants of the Lord. Before this point in his record, Nephi had not spoken much of these things. He does so now to increase the plainness of his writing, to prepare us for that which is to come in his vision.

To further augment the plainness with which he records his plain and precious truths, his vision then becomes a framework by which we may organize the truths he shares with us in subsequent pages of his record. This enables us to more fully comprehend the Lord and his great work among the children of men. In like manner, Lehi's dream does the same for Nephi's vision. Moreover, Nephi provides us with examples in his vision of how we may organize the details of his (Nephi's) vision in accordance with what Lehi saw in his dream.

Area 3. The great and eternal plan of deliverance. The truths discussed in the two previous areas may also be included here, of course, because all the doings of the Lord are according to his great and eternal plan of deliverance. For ease of discussion, however, in this section we will discuss what Nephi has included of the teachings and prophecies of Lehi and Jacob regarding the grace, justice, power, and mercy of the Holy Messiah. As mentioned earlier, one of Nephi's delights is in "proving . . . that save Christ should come all men must perish" (2 Nephi 11:6).

This Christ, our Savior, "offereth himself a sacrifice for sin, to answer the ends of the law, unto all those who have a broken heart and a contrite spirit," on an earth with opposition and "things to act and things to be acted upon" (2 Nephi 2:7, 14). He thus enables us to overcome the effects of the Fall and achieve a state of righteousness, holiness, and joy through our choices (see 2 Nephi 2:11, 16, 25–26). Because Christ has redeemed "the children of men from the fall, . . . they have become free forever, knowing good from evil; to act for themselves and not to be acted upon. . . . And they are free to choose liberty and eternal life, through the great Mediator of all men, or to choose captivity and death, according to the captivity and power of the devil" (2 Nephi 2:26–27). Through the infinite Atonement of the Holy Messiah, the way has been prepared for our deliverance from "the death of the body, and also the death of the spirit" (2 Nephi 9:10). "For behold," we are told, "[the Holy Messiah] offereth himself a sacrifice for sin, to answer the ends of the law, unto all those who have a broken heart and a contrite spirit; and unto none else can the ends of the law be answered. Wherefore, how great the importance to make these things known unto the inhabitants of the earth, that they may know that there is no flesh that can dwell in the presence of God, save it be through the merits, and mercy, and grace of the Holy Messiah, who layeth down his life according to the flesh, and taketh it again by the power of the Spirit, that he may bring to pass the resurrection of the dead" (2 Nephi 2:7–8). While the Bible may contain a smattering of these precious truths, it does not explain them as plainly and as beautifully as does the record of Nephi and subsequent pages of the Book of Mormon.

Summary and reflections: The plain and precious truths Nephi includes in the Book of Mormon, then, instruct us about three things touching on his vision. The first attests to the coming of the Messiah, his ministries, and his crucifixion. Secondly, we are provided with instruction regarding the covenants of the Lord with his people, and their ancient, modern, and future fulfillment. And last, but certainly not least, he provides us with enlightenment about the grace, justice, and mercy of the Lord, and of his power to deliver us from spiritual and physical death.

Key messages found in the plain and precious truths Nephi recorded may best be described by passages he has chosen to include in his writings. He tells us "for we labor diligently to write, and to persuade our children, and also our brethren, to believe in Christ, and to be reconciled to God; for we know that it is by grace that we are saved, after all we can do" (2 Nephi 25:23). We are told, through the words of Jacob recorded in Nephi's writings, "And now . . . seeing that our merciful God has given us so great knowledge concerning these things, let us remember him, and lay aside our sins, and not hang down our heads, for we are not cast off," individually or collectively, spiritually or physically (2 Nephi 10:20). Therefore, "come . . . every one that thirsteth, come ye to the waters; and he that hath no money, come buy and eat; yea, come buy wine and milk without money and without price . . . oh then . . . come unto the Lord, the Holy One. Remember that . . . the way for man is narrow, but it lieth in a straight course before him, and the keeper of the gate is the Holy One of Israel . . . and there is none other way save it be by the gate; for he cannot be deceived, for the Lord God is his name. And whoso knocketh, to him will he open" (2 Nephi 9:50, 41–42).

The Lord Hath All Power unto the Fulfilling of All His Words

We are now in a position to examine the significance of the loss and restoration of plain and precious truth. We know that many plain and precious truths have been lost from the Bible, just as Nephi saw in his vision hundreds of years before it actually happened. So what place should the Bible have in our lives? With the alterations it has suffered over the centuries, is its study still worth our time and effort? The answer is a resounding "Of course!" It is still one of the greatest witnesses we have of the Lord and his truths. The Prophet Joseph Smith taught, "We believe the Bible to be the word of God as far as it is translated correctly" (Articles of Faith 1:8). Nephi proclaims that the "covenants of the Lord" and the "prophecies of the holy prophets" contained in the Bible "are of great worth unto the Gentiles" (1 Nephi 13:23). And so they are.

In spite of plain and precious truth lost from the Bible, it has still been a tremendous instrument in the hands of the Lord. It paved the way for the First Vision and the restoration of the gospel of Jesus Christ in its fullness, complete with authority, revelation, and authorized leadership. It has blessed millions of lives all over the world.

The Bible is not enough, however, because it lacks truths we need to know for our salvation. The Lord in his wisdom knew that plain and precious truths would be lost from the Bible through translation, transmission, and deliberate alteration of the text, and he had already prepared a means to restore the truths. Before Nephi records his great vision, he testifies, "The Lord knoweth all things from the beginning; wherefore, he prepareth a way to accomplish all his works among the children of men; for behold, he hath all power unto the fulfilling of all his words" (1 Nephi 9:6). In his vision, Nephi declares, "Neither will the Lord God suffer that the Gentiles shall forever remain in that awful state of blindness, which thou beholdest they are in, because of the plain and most precious parts of the gospel of the Lamb which have been kept back by that abominable church" (1 Nephi 13:32). Eventually, "after the Gentiles do stumble exceedingly, because of the most plain and precious parts of the gospel of the Lamb which have been kept back by that abominable church," the Lord "will be merciful unto the Gentiles" and "bring forth unto them, in [his] power, much of [his] gospel, which shall be plain and precious" (1 Nephi 13:34). Nephi continues, "For, behold, saith the Lamb: I will manifest myself unto thy seed, that they shall write many things which I shall minister unto them, which shall be plain and precious" (1 Nephi 13:35). Those things would then "be hid up, to come forth unto the Gentiles, by the gift and power of the Lamb" (1 Nephi 13:35).

Nephi's writings provide for us many plain and precious truths we need to have in our day, ones that are either not available, are not fully clear, or are not complete in our surviving biblical record. His record supplies us with plain and pure instruction of invaluable truth, and goes a long way in fulfilling the purpose of the Book of Mormon, "which is to show unto the remnant of the House of Israel what great things the Lord hath done for their fathers; and that they may know the covenants of the Lord, that they are not cast off forever—And also to [convince] the Jew and the Gentile that Jesus is the Christ, the Eternal God, manifesting himself unto all nations" (title page).

In his great vision, Nephi sees both the Book of Mormon and the Bible, as we already know. He tells us that "these last records, which thou hast seen among the Gentiles, shall establish the truth of the first, which are of the twelve apostles of the Lamb, and shall make known the plain and precious things which have been taken away from them" (1 Nephi 13:40).[40] Then "the words of the Lamb shall be made known in the records of [Nephi's] seed, as well as in the records of the twelve apostles of the Lamb; wherefore they both shall be established in one; for there is one God and one Shepherd over all the earth" (1 Nephi 13:41).

Through the Lord's wisdom, foreknowledge, and power, the fact that plain and precious truths have been lost from the Bible is now largely inconsequential for sincere seekers of truth (see Moroni 10:3–5). Why? Because the Lord has once again provided us with those plain and precious truths through Nephi, and through the entire Book of Mormon: Another Testament of Jesus Christ, in an unadulterated and magnificent and saving form. Today is the day when the record of the Jews (the Bible) and the record of Nephi's seed (the Book of Mormon) have grown together, established as one, "unto the confounding of false doctrines and laying down of contentions, and establishing peace" (2 Nephi 3:12).

Notes

1. For the purposes of this paper, the "great and abominable church" will not be defined as any one organization or entity. In Nephi's vision, an angel described the "great and abominable church" as the "church of the devil" (1 Nephi 14:10), and may include (1) those who fight against the Lord and his servants, and (2) those that bind, yoke, or lead others into captivity (see 1 Nephi 13:5). Binding, yoking, and captivity may be defined as being either physical or spiritual in nature. I take full responsibility for this definition; it is not considered to be an official declaration of doctrine for The Church of Jesus Christ of Latter-day Saints. It is also not intended to be a personal crimination against any person, group, or entity but rather an expression that the definition of "great and abominable church" must not be too narrow in scope. For a discussion on this topic, see Stephen E. Robinson, "Nephi's 'Great and Abominable Church,'" *Journal of Book of Mormon Studies* 7, no. 1 (1998): 32–39.

2. By definition the word *through* means "in one side and out the other side of; from end to end," "in the midst of; among," or "completely to an end; to a conclusion." *Webster's New World Dictionary of the American Language* (New York: Simon and

Schuster, 1980). Through the definition we can better see that the loss of plain and precious truths from the Bible happened over process of time and through the hands of many people and influences.

3. Bruce M. Metzger, *The Canon of the New Testament: Its Origin, Development, and Significance* (Oxford: Clarendon Press, 1987), 108–9.

4. Harry Y. Gamble, *The New Testament Canon: Its Making and Meaning* (Philadelphia: Fortress Press, 1985), 67.

5. Gamble, *New Testament Canon*, 67; see also Metzger, *Canon of the New Testament*, 238.

6. The printing press was not developed until approximately 1450 by Johannes Gutenberg. See Bruce M. Metzger and Bart D. Ehrman, *The Text of the New Testament: Its Transmission, Corruption, and Restoration* (New York: Oxford University Press, 2005), 137; see also Sir Frederic Kenyon, *Our Bible and the Ancient Manuscripts* (New York: Harper and Brothers, 1958), 50.

7. Metzger and Ehrman, *Text of the New Testament*, 275.

8. Kenyon, *Our Bible and the Ancient Manuscripts*, 50.

9. Bart D. Ehrman, *Misquoting Jesus: The Story Behind Who Changed the Bible and Why* (New York: HarperSanFrancisco, 2005), 51. In his endnotes, Ehrman expands on this by saying, "By professional I mean scribes who were specially trained and/or paid to copy texts as part of their vocation. At a later period, monks in monasteries were typically trained, but not paid; I would include them among the ranks of professional scribes."

10. Metzger and Ehrman, *Text of the New Testament*, 25.

11. Metzger and Ehrman, *Text of the New Testament*, 25, 27.

12. Kenyon, *Our Bible and the Ancient Manuscripts*, 50–51; also Metzger and Ehrman, *The Text of the New Testament*, 255, 257. A diphthong may be defined as a complex vowel sound made by moving from one vowel sound to another within one syllable. Examples include (ai) as in *guide*, (ou) as in *round*, and (oi) as in *noise*.

13. Metzger and Ehrman, *Text of the New Testament*, 27. The Septuagint, an influential Greek translation of the Hebrew scriptures highly valued by early Christians, is a great example of human error in the transmission of a text. Origen, a scholar born late in the second century, was aware that by his time the Septuagint text had become substantially corrupted through scribal transmission, and varied substantially from the Hebrew and other Greek texts of his time. In an attempt to rectify this situation, he created a text called the Hexapla. The Hexapla was the Old Testament text arranged in six columns. It contained a Hebrew text, a Greek transliteration of the Hebrew text, and four distinct Greek versions. See Justo L. Gonzalez, *The Story of Christianity*, vol. 1: *The Early Church to the Dawn of the Reformation* (New York: HarperSanFrancisco, 1984, 78). To the Hexapla, Origen added a system of markings to indicate omissions, additions, and other variations within the texts. Gonzalez, *Story of Christianity*, 78. Unfortunately, in creating the Hexapla, Origen unknowingly only added to the chaos of the original Septuagint text, because when portions of the Hexapla were later copied by scribes, they misunderstood the many critical symbols used by Origen, and other texts were confused with the original Septuagint text. Bruce M. Metzger, "Versions, Ancient," in *The Interpreter's Dictionary of the Bible* (Nashville: Abingdon Press, 1962), 4:751. Note: A transliteration is to write or spell words using the corresponding letters of another alphabet.

14. This refers to the disciples chosen by Jesus Christ during his ministry in the Americas, but because God is "the same yesterday, today, and forever" the same would have been true of the Apostles chosen during Christ's mortal ministry, as well as today (1 Nephi 10:18).

15. Marcion, an early Christian leader labeled a heretic by those of the orthodox persuasion, can provide an example of this. He created his own biblical canon and adapted it to his own beliefs. He believed that Jehovah of the Old Testament was a god different from and inferior to the Supreme God the Father of the New Testament, for whom Christ was messenger. Whereas Jehovah was a revengeful and capricious God of justice, the Supreme God of the New Testament was a loving, forgiving, and good God. Therefore, in creating his canon he discarded the entire Old Testament, vehemently believing that it was incompatible with the New Testament, and that their teachings contradicted each other. He was convinced that the twelve Apostles misinterpreted and misrepresented Christ's teachings, and that Paul was the only one who truly understood Christ. Because of these beliefs, he included the epistles of Paul and the book of Luke in his canon, but only after purging them of all references to the Old Testament. He removed from the book of Luke and the epistles anything that was not in agreement with his views, including most of Luke 1–4 and numerous portions of Luke's final chapters (among which were the nativity, Jesus' genealogy, his temptation and baptism, and his resurrection). According to Metzger, Marcion's canon was the most prevalent and well-received New Testament text in the second century, and it influenced even non-Marcionite copies of Luke and Paul, at least to some degree. The information from this endnote is taken from Metzger, *Canon of the New Testament*, 91–94, 97.

16. Bart D. Ehrman, *The Orthodox Corruption of Scripture: The Effect of Early Christological Controversies on the Text of the New Testament* (New York: Oxford University Press, 1993), 3.

17. For a discussion of some of these issues, see Gaye Strathearn, "*Sōma Sēma*: The Influence of 'The Body Is a Tomb' in Early Christian Debates and the New Testament," in *The Life and Teachings of the New Testament Apostles: From the Day of Pentecost through the Apocalypse*, ed. Richard Neitzel Holzapfel and Thomas A. Wayment (Salt Lake City: Deseret Book, 2010), 276–98.

18. Sir Lancelot C. L. Brenton, *The Septuagint Version: Greek and English* (Grand Rapids, MI: Zondervan, 1980), iii. According to the LDS Bible Dictionary, most of the Old Testament quotations used in the New Testament are taken from the Septuagint (see "Septuagint," 771).

19. Saint Augustine, *On Christian Doctrine*, trans. D. W. Robertson Jr. (Upper Saddle River, NJ: Prentice-Hall, 1997), 44.

20. Saint Augustine, *On Christian Doctrine*, 45.

21. Brenton, *Septuagint Version*, iii.

22. Chrys C. Caragounis, *The Development of Greek and the New Testament: Morphology, Syntax, Phonology, and Textual Transmission* (Tubingen, Germany: Mohr Siebeck, 2004), 234. By understanding this about the translation process, one can more easily comprehend the need for God's involvement in the translation of his word. The Book of Mormon prophet Jacob has this to say: "Behold, great and marvelous are the works of the Lord. How unsearchable are the depths of the mysteries of him; and it is

impossible that man should find out all his ways. And no man knoweth of his ways save it be revealed unto him; wherefore, brethren, despise not the revelations of God. . . . Wherefore, . . . seek not to counsel the Lord, but to take counsel from his hand" (Jacob 4:8, 10). In other words (as this pertains to the translation process), for a translation to say what the Lord truly would have it say requires God's help through revelation.

    23. Keith Elliott and Ian Moir, *Manuscripts and the Text of the New Testament: An Introduction for English Readers* (Edinburgh, Scotland: T & T Clark, 1995), 2, 46.

    24. Metzger and Ehrman, *Text of the New Testament*, 253. The bracketed section indicates words omitted from the verse by the scribe.

    25. Elliott and Moir, *Manuscripts and the Text of the New Testament*, 39.

    26. For a discussion of the types of changes found in the Joseph Smith Translation, see Scott H. Faulring, Kent P. Jackson, and Robert J. Matthews, eds., *Joseph Smith's New Translation of the Bible: Original Manuscripts* (Provo, UT: Religious Studies Center, Brigham Young University, 2004), 8–11.

    27. Ehrman, *Orthodox Corruption of Scripture*, 277.

    28. Ehrman, *Orthodox Corruption of Scripture*, 4.

    29. Biblical texts were also altered by those not of the orthodox persuasion. One such example is the Hebrew text. With the destruction of the Jewish State in AD 70, the scriptures became *the* means by which Jews could retain their sense of national and religious awareness, and defend themselves against Christians who charged them with doctoring the texts. Kenyon, *Our Bible and the Ancient Manuscripts*, 74–75. Jews were compelled to renew their studies of the text in every detail, Kenyon proposes, and felt a vital need to interpret the text according to their own traditions. As Jews sought to explain and interpret every nuance of meaning, he continues, gradually over the centuries a semblance of an authorized text began to emerge, which eventually culminated in the formation of a fixed and standardized text called the Masoretic Text. Kenyon, *Our Bible and the Ancient Manuscripts*, 75–76. The Masoretes, the Jews who created the Masoretic Text, accumulated vast amounts of traditional learning, which they embellished and arranged in the margins on all sides of the manuscripts and devised a system of symbols to transmit the pronunciation of the text. Kenyon, *Our Bible and the Ancient Manuscripts*, 76–77; see also Gary D. Pratico and Miles V. Van Pelt, *Basics of Biblical Hebrew Grammar* (Grand Rapids, MI: Zondervan, 2001), 402. Underlying the system of pronunciation was a very complicated set of grammatical rules, portions of which were developed by them, which made the Hebrew grammar significantly different from the Hebrew of the first century, or from the time the Septuagint or Old Testament books were written. Kenyon, *Our Bible and the Ancient Manuscripts*, 77–78. Early Jewish scribes were also skilled in interpreting and explaining the law, and in places they changed the wording of the scriptures to be more reverential and doctrinal, as they saw it. Kenyon, *Our Bible and the Ancient Manuscripts*, 76. Note: Both ancient and modern scholars consider(ed) the Masoretic Text to be authoritative.

    30. Elliott and Moir, *Manuscripts and the Text of the New Testament*, 3, 73. John 1:1–17 is a great example of a Christological passage made more obscure, and therefore less plain, through textual changes (compare the passage in the Joseph Smith Translation, LDS Bible appendix).

    31. Elliott and Moir, *Manuscripts and the Text of the New Testament*, 3.

    32. Ehrman, *Misquoting Jesus*, 55.

33. Metzger and Ehrman, *Text of the New Testament*, 22.
34. Metzger and Ehrman, *Text of the New Testament*, 22–23.
35. James E. Talmage, *Jesus the Christ* (Salt Lake City: Deseret Book, 1974), 36.
36. Talmage, *Jesus the Christ*, 37.
37. Other actual eyewitnesses of Jesus Christ, as recorded in the Book of Mormon, include—but are not limited to—Mormon (see Mormon 1:15); Moroni (see Ether 12:39); Lehi (see 1 Nephi 1:8–9); Jacob (see 2 Nephi 2:3–4); the brother of Jared (see Ether 3:6–13, 17); Lamoni (see Alma 19:13); and 2500-plus people in the land Bountiful (see 3 Nephi 11–28).
38. These faith-promoting narratives Nephi included are also plain and precious truths Nephi was commanded to write in his record (see 1 Nephi 19:3), but since our focus at this time is primarily on Nephi's great vision, the narratives will not be included in this discussion.
39. It seems likely this is also the reason Nephi included multiple witnesses in the rest of his writings. These witnesses include, other than the ones already mentioned, Joseph of Egypt, Zenock, Neum, and Zenos (see 1 Nephi 19:10; 2 Nephi 3:3–24).
40. Nephi includes in "these last records" (1 Nephi 13:40) both the Book of Mormon and "other books" which "came forth by the power of the Lamb" (see 1 Nephi 13:39).

6

Lehi Dreamed a Dream: The Report of Lehi's Dream in Its Biblical Context

Dana M. Pike

"Behold, I have dreamed a dream," Lehi announced to his family one morning in the valley of Lemuel in northwestern Arabia (1 Nephi 8:2; see also 9:1; 10:16). This dream and its subsequent interpretation (given in vision to Nephi) provide a powerful Christ-centered foundation for the whole Book of Mormon.[1] Of course, Lehi's dream of his family, a tree, and its fruit was not the first revelatory dream he had received. Nephi indicates that his father, Lehi, had written an account of his own prophetic ministry that included "many things which he saw in visions and in dreams" (1 Nephi 1:16). The Lord had already communicated his will to Lehi through dreams on such important points as the command to leave Jerusalem (see 1 Nephi 2:1–2)[2] and to have his sons return to Jerusalem to retrieve the scripture record on the brass plates (see 1 Nephi 3:2). However, we do not have reports of these dreams, only references to them.

The account of Lehi's dream in 1 Nephi 8 has great significance in the Book of Mormon as a whole due to its length and detail, its warning about the spiritual status of Lehi's family, and its focus on the beauty and power

---

Dana M. Pike is a professor of ancient scripture at Brigham Young University.

of Christ's Atonement. These features, combined with this dream's prominent location early in the Book of Mormon, raise intriguing questions about dreams and revelation. Is it significant that this major revelation came to Lehi in a dream? Were dreams a legitimate and frequent means of revelation in ancient Israel? Is the report of Lehi's dream in 1 Nephi 8 similar to reports of revelatory dreams in the Bible? If so, how can understanding biblical dream reports help us better appreciate the account of Lehi's dream, his family's reactions to it, and the role it plays in the greater whole of the Book of Mormon?

Surprising as it may seem, such questions have not been discussed in previous Latter-day Saint studies on the report of Lehi's dream. Besides providing general commentary on Lehi's dream in 1 Nephi 8,[3] authors have studied it from a literary perspective,[4] emphasized the doctrinal aspects of its symbolism,[5] and tried to connect the symbolism with Arabian desert traditions[6] and even ancient Egyptian symbolism.[7] However, I am unaware of any analysis of Lehi's dream in the context of biblical and other ancient Near Eastern dream reports (the Near East is essentially the same region as the Middle East), although Lehi and his family had lived in the vicinity of Jerusalem and were presumably familiar with revelatory dream reports in their biblical tradition as well as inspired dreams claimed by their Israelite contemporaries.

My thesis is that understanding the scriptural and cultural context of Israelite dream reports and interpretations as preserved in the Bible provides a richer and more insightful understanding of Lehi's dream (and his son Nephi's corollary interpretive vision), both by way of general background as well as specific insights. To demonstrate this, I provide introductory comments on the report of Lehi's dream, a general introduction to dream reports and interpretations in ancient Near Eastern texts, and a review of the biblical accounts of dreams, followed by an analysis of the report of Lehi's dream in its biblical context. (Space constraints do not allow for a specific, focused analysis of Nephi's report of his vision in this paper.)

Preliminary Considerations regarding the Report of Lehi's Dream

The following four general observations on Nephi's report of Lehi's dream highlight important considerations for this study.

1. *The source of our information.* We are entirely dependent on what Nephi included on his small set of plates for the report of Lehi's dream in 1 Nephi 8. Nephi's report of his father's dream is presented as what Lehi shared with his

family after he experienced his dream (see 1 Nephi 8:2; 9:1). Beyond Nephi's mere memory of that occasion, he presumably retrieved information when writing his account from his father's written record, from what he (Nephi) had already transferred from his father's record to his large set of plates, or from both (see 1 Nephi 1:17; 19:1–2).[8] Recall that Nephi made his large set of plates about ten years after leaving Jerusalem (see 1 Nephi 19:1–2) but did not make his smaller plates, from which we get 1 Nephi, until about thirty years after his family left Jerusalem (see 2 Nephi 5:28–31). Nephi was thus quite dependent upon his father's and his own previous records for details he provided in relating Lehi's dream (see 1 Nephi 8) and his own vision (see 1 Nephi 11–14).

This is illustrated by the fact that Nephi began his report of Lehi's dream by quoting from his father's record, indicated by the first-person phrasing: "I [Lehi] have dreamed. . . . I did go forth. . . . I saw" (1 Nephi 8:2, 11, 21). This is the family-focused portion of the dream account, in which, once getting to the tree and eating of the fruit, Lehi looks for and calls to his wife and sons. However, Nephi later paraphrased in his own words what his father originally reported, using the third person: "Now I, Nephi, do not speak all the words of my father. But, to be short in writing, behold, he saw other multitudes" (vv. 29–30; see also vv. 31–33; these verses summarize the more universal view of many groups of people Lehi had seen in his dream). Thus the account of Lehi's dream is available *to us* only as a combination of quotation and paraphrase and only as it existed in Nephi's own record.

2. *Dreams and visions.* A second preliminary consideration is that Lehi's claim, "Behold, I have dreamed a dream; or, in other words, I have seen a vision" (v. 2; also v. 36), reflects an overlap in terminology that is also apparent in the Bible, wherein the terms *dream* and *vision* sometimes occur in parallel (see Isaiah 29:7: "as a dream of a night vision;" see also Job 4:13; Daniel 7:1–2). "Dream and vision are essentially related," and "the two phenomena are difficult to disentangle;"[9] it is thus evident that "the ancients equated dreams with visions."[10] In Israel and the greater ancient Near East, dreams and visions were considered similar, legitimate forms of visual revelation that the recipient experienced internally. Ancient people were less interested in whether the recipient was asleep or awake and more concerned about the reality of what was seen or heard. Thus, functionally, the only real difference between revelatory dreams and visions was that sleeping dreamers were less aware of their

external surroundings (contrast the awake Nephi and his vision in 1 Nephi 11:1).[11] This view of dreams and visions as related phenomena on a spectrum of revelatory modes helps explain why Lehi's wife, Sariah, when concerned that her sons might not return from a mission motivated by an inspired dream (1 Nephi 3:2), exasperatedly, and probably derisively, complained that Lehi was "a visionary man," a title he positively affirmed (1 Nephi 5:1–4; see also 2:11).[12]

3. *Cognate objects.* Lehi's expression "I have dreamed a dream" (1 Nephi 3:2; 8:2) may sound awkward in English, but it is an example of the use of a cognate accusative or cognate object that occurs in Hebrew and some other Semitic languages. In this construction, the verb and the object are derived from the same lexical root.[13] Other examples of this feature in scripture include Genesis 37:5 ("Joseph dreamed a dream"), 1 Samuel 1:11 ("And [Hannah] vowed a vow"), 1 Nephi 14:7 ("I will work a great and a marvelous work"), and 2 Nephi 5:15 ("I did teach my people to build buildings"). The fact that this grammatical construction occurs in the Bible in connection with dream reports provides an interesting link to the report of Lehi's dream.

4. *Lehi's dream and Nephi's vision.* A final preliminary consideration is the scope of Lehi's dream in relation to Nephi's vision. Although some have claimed that Lehi dreamed essentially what Nephi later saw in his vision,[14] it appears that Nephi actually envisioned things that went well beyond what Lehi had seen, even taking into account that Nephi did not include "all the words of [his] father" in reporting Lehi's dream (1 Nephi 8:29; see also 8:36; 9:1; 10:2, 15). For example, Nephi in his vision specifically requested of the Spirit of the Lord "to know the interpretation" of the tree (1 Nephi 11:11). What was shown to Nephi in response to his desire to understand the symbolism of the tree—the mortal ministry and sacrifice of God the Son (1 Nephi 11:11–36)—does not seem to have been shown to Lehi (otherwise why would Nephi have asked?), nor does it fit the style of Lehi's dream. Nephi's report of Lehi's dream presents it as a spiritual allegory, while Nephi's account of his own vision has a chronological, God-in-history orientation to it.[15] Thus, although the content of Lehi's dream and Nephi's vision overlap, there are differences in content and style, further emphasizing the need for a divinely given interpretation of the symbolism in Lehi's dream. With these several considerations in mind, we can now review general evidence for dream reports in the ancient Near East.

Ancient Near Eastern Dream Reports[16]

As far as we know, human beings have always dreamed. Influenced by Sigmund Freud (1856–1939), Western society for over a century has typically viewed dreams "as manifestations of the subconscious. What we have not resolved, what we are unwilling to admit, and even what we dare not recognize while awake—all find expression while we are sleeping."[17] Thus, for people in modern Western society, neurophysiology and our personal psychological state inform our view of dreams, their origins, and their meanings. However, this was not the view of people in the ancient Near East. They believed that many if not all dreams came as communications from external sources—gods sent pleasant dreams as well as warnings and judgments; demons sent nightmares.[18] Dreams in the ancient Near Eastern were thus seen as functioning to "impart knowledge; dispense healing or infirmity; or convey divine sanction or the reverse, divine punishment."[19]

Dreaming as a form of divine communication was so significant that examples of regular, everyday-type dreams, "in all their fantastic variety," were collected and catalogued into what we now call "dream books."[20] Evidence for this practice exists from ancient Mesopotamia, Egypt, Ugarit, and the Hittite empire. As was the case in other forms of divination (attempts to know the future),[21] ancient Near Eastern scholars produced lists of these dream elements and their expected outcomes with a standard protasis-apodosis structure (if . . . then . . .). These dream precedents along with their previously observed outcomes were viewed as a means to discern the fate of someone who received a similar divine communication in a similar dream. For example, a few lines from the so-called Chester Beatty "Dream Book," an Egyptian text dating to the reign of Ramses II (1297–1213 BC), read:

If a man see himself in a dream: . . .

    Eating the flesh of a donkey. Good. It means his promotion. . . .

    Looking through a window. Good. The hearing of his cry by his god. . . .

    Seeing a large cat. Good. It means a large harvest will occur for him. . . .

    Drinking warm beer. BAD. It means suppurating illness infects him. . . .

    Eating a filleted catfish. BAD. His seizure by a crocodile. . . .

Bitten by a snake. BAD. It means the occurrence of a quarrel against him.²²

Although the operative principles behind such interpretations are not always evident to us (why was dreaming about eating donkey flesh a good omen?),²³ these lists of dreams and their outcomes (as well as other divinatory lists of observed phenomena) exhibit an underlying effort to organize the world and its competing forces, and thus to better know the future and to counteract demonic influences.²⁴

Apart from dream catalogues, actual reports of individuals' dreams in the ancient Near East occur in royal inscriptions, literary texts, and letters, as well as in myths and epics. These dream reports were produced using the standard literary conventions of their time and culture to express in writing the content of the dream.²⁵ Although the available textual evidence of dream accounts from the Semitic peoples living in Syria and Canaan is much sparser, these reports and interpretations show evidence of early Mesopotamian influences.²⁶

For some time now, scholars have classified these written ancient Near Eastern dream reports as representing either *message* or *symbolic* dreams.²⁷ According to this typology, a message dream is one in which a divine being visits a person and delivers a spoken message. One well-known example is preserved in the Ugaritic tablets, in the poetic narration of a presumably epic king, Keret.²⁸ Through disease, accidents, and other tragedies, Keret's family was all destroyed. Lamenting the loss of his progeny one night, he fell asleep and the great West Semitic god, El, appeared to him in a dream (notice the parallelism in this text).

> As he [Keret] wept he fell asleep;
> as he cried slumber (came).
> Sleep overpowered him and he lay down;
> slumber, and he curled up.
> And in his dream El came down,
> in his vision the Father of Man,
> and he drew near, asking Keret:
> "What ails Keret that he weeps,
> the gracious one, heir of El, that he groans?" . . .
> ["It is s]ons I would beget,
> descendants I would multiply!"

> And Bull, his father, El re[plied]:
> "[Desist] from weeping, Keret,
> from crying, gracious one, heir of El.
> Wash yourself and rouge yourself;
> Wash your [han]ds to the elbow,
> [your] finge[rs] up to the shoulder." . . .

At this point El further instructs Keret to offer sacrifices and then to attack another kingdom, demanding the king's daughter for his wife. She will bear him a son to rule after him.

> Keret awoke, and (it was) a dream,
> the servant of El [awoke] and (it was) a vision.
> He washed himself and rouged himself,
> he washed his hands to the elbow,
> his fingers to the shoulder.[29]

The epic tells that after waking Keret did all that he had been instructed to do in El's message to him and everything came to pass just as Keret had dreamed.

A well-known biblical example of a message dream is the one Solomon received at Gibeon, narrated in 1 Kings 3:5–15. Shortly after securing the throne in Jerusalem, Solomon "went to Gibeon to sacrifice there; for that was the great high place" (v. 4; he had not yet built the temple in Jerusalem[30]). While there, "the LORD appeared to Solomon in a dream by night: and God said, Ask what I shall give thee" (v. 5). Solomon requested wisdom and "an understanding heart" (v. 9). Jehovah promised to grant him this, as well as "riches, and honour" (v. 13). These two classic examples of message dream reports (Keret's and Solomon's) portray a divine being conveying a message to the dreamer. There is no symbolic imagery requiring interpretation.

A symbolic dream, on the other hand, is one in which the dreamer sees visual images that convey a message about the future, but the symbolism in the dream requires interpretation after awakening. Reports of symbolic dreams are typically followed by an interpretation announced by someone other than the dreamer. For example, the Mesopotamian epic hero Gilgamesh dreamed that "there were stars in the sky for me. And (something) like a sky-bolt of Anu kept falling upon me! I tried to lift it up, but it was too heavy for me."

After awakening, he related this and the rest of his dream to his mother. She provided an interpretation of its symbolism.[31]

Genesis 41 contains a biblical example of a symbolic dream report in which the Egyptian Pharaoh dreamed he saw seven thin cows eating seven fat cows and then seven scrawny tassels of grain consuming seven plump tassels (see vv. 1–8). Joseph announced the same interpretation for these parallel dreams: seven years of plenty in Egypt would be followed by seven years of famine (see vv. 14–32).

However, all ancient Near Eastern dream reports do not fit so neatly into these two categories—message and symbolic dreams—and this schema overemphasizes a conceptual distinction between symbolic and nonsymbolic dream revelations that does not seem to have been important to ancient Near Eastern peoples.[32] The dream report in Genesis 28:11–16 illustrates this situation. Jacob "dreamed, and behold a ladder [or stairway] set up on the earth, and the top of it reached to heaven: and behold the angels of God ascending and descending on it. And, behold, the LORD stood above it, and said. . . ." The rest of the dream account relates Jehovah's promises to Jacob. Although the emphasis in the report is definitely on the Lord's appearance and message to Jacob, not on the symbolism of what he saw, this dream report demonstrates the lack of precision in designating dreams as either message or symbolic, since it combines both symbolism and spoken message. Nevertheless, I employ the standard designations—message and symbolic dreams—in this introductory survey.

Like other ancient Near Eastern forms of divination (attempts to learn the future), ancient Near Eastern dream reports regularly display various types of linguistic and literary wordplay, and sometimes even visual or orthographic punning based on the use of particular hieroglyphs or cuneiform signs.[33] Words, and even the forms in which they were written, were considered by the ancients to be "vehicles of power." Thus, punning and other types of wordplay in dream reports and their interpretations were thought to "limit that power by restricting the parameters of a dream's interpretation. The dream [could not] now mean anything, but only one thing."[34] Professional diviners and dream interpreters thus skillfully exhibited their power in controlling the interpretation of dreams that were written as text, thus avoiding potential future calamity.

Although such activity may seem odd, one scholar has rightly observed that, "while the process of dreaming certainly appears to be universal, the process of interpreting dreams is not, . . . the exegetical approach to dreams appears to be thoroughly grounded in, and determined by, the specific cultural and ontological frameworks of the interpreter."[35] Thus, ancient Near Eastern peoples sought legitimate, accurate, limiting interpretations of their symbol-laden dreams in order to determine the will of the gods and to avert danger.[36] To forget one's dream could be perilous, because without a correctly remembered dream one could not obtain the appropriate dream interpretation. Without an authentic interpretation, one could not prepare for or attempt to alter one's fate, if need be.[37] This is illustrated by the anxiety of the imprisoned Egyptian officials who said to Joseph, "We have dreamed a dream, and there is no interpreter of it" (Genesis 40:8).[38]

Biblical Dream Reports

Biblical dream reports and interpretations exhibit both similarities and differences with their counterparts in other ancient Near Eastern texts.[39]

The Hebrew noun *halom* is translated *dream* and is cognate with the same word in other northwest Semitic languages.[40] It designates every type of dream, from divine ones to nightmares. The Old Testament indicates that revelatory dreams were received by such well-known individuals as Jacob (see Genesis 28:12; 31:10–11), Joseph (see Genesis 37:5–10), Solomon (see 1 Kings 3:5–15), Job (see Job 7:14), and Daniel (see Daniel 7:1).[41] Accounts of dreams received by non-Israelites include the dreams of two Egyptian officials (see Genesis 40:5–8), an Egyptian Pharaoh (see Genesis 41), a Midianite soldier (see Judges 7:13–15), and Babylonian king Nebuchadnezzar (see Daniel 2; 4). These dreams functioned to relay divine approval and important knowledge of the future.[42]

As with other ancient Near Eastern dream literature, the Bible preserves reports of what are commonly labeled message dreams (such as Solomon's in 1 Kings 3) and symbolic dreams (such as Pharaoh's in Genesis 41). And as noted above, some dream reports (such as Jacob's in Genesis 28) do not fit so neatly into this general schema.

Interestingly, the majority of symbolic dreams in the Bible as it has come down to us were given to non-Israelites.[43] Other than young Joseph's dreams recounted in Genesis 37, which indicated that his family would eventually bow down to him, and Daniel's dream of four beasts and "the Ancient of days" (Daniel 7:22),[44] the other symbolic dreams reported in the Bible were received by imprisoned Egyptian officials (see Genesis 40), an

Egyptian Pharaoh (see Genesis 41), a Midianite soldier (see Judges 7), and King Nebuchadnezzar (see Daniel 2; 4). In the case of the dreams given to the Egyptians and the Babylonian king, Joseph and Daniel respectively were the interpreters. These symbolic dreams (except Judges 7:13–14, in which the Midianite's dream was immediately understood by his companion) served to demonstrate, among other things, that God-inspired Israelites had the necessary spiritual connections to interpret dreams accurately when others could not, and thus to emphasize the reality and superiority of Jehovah (see Genesis 40:8; Daniel 2:28).[45]

Biblical evidence indicates that Israelites, like other ancient Near Eastern peoples, believed that many if not all dreams came as communications from an external source. The Bible "only recounts dreams of religious value: messages sent by God."[46] There are no catalogs of dreams and dream omens preserved in the Bible (nor among Israelite inscriptions). Although dreams among other ancient Near Easterners originated with various deities and demons, the Bible, not surprisingly, indicates dreams originated with Jehovah, the true God, whether the dreams were sent to Israelites or non-Israelites. Job even attributed his nightmares to Jehovah (see Job 7:14).

However, in parallel with some ancient Near Eastern texts, certain biblical evidence suggests Israelites also had what they considered to be "ordinary dreams."[47] Passages that refer to these include Job 20:8 ("He shall fly away as a dream, and shall not be found") and Isaiah 29:7–8 ("the multitude of all the nations that fight against Ariel . . . shall be as a dream of a night vision, . . . even be as when an hungry man dreameth, and, behold, he eateth; but he awaketh, and his soul is empty").[48] At the very least, such passages illustrate that some dreams seemed fleeting and of no real substance to some Israelites (compare Jacob 7:26).[49]

The biblical narrative does make clear that Jehovah utilized dreams, whether they involved spoken instructions or more enigmatic symbolism, as one legitimate means of communicating with ancient Israelites. This was in addition to other accepted modes of revelation such as visions, divine appearances, prophecy, the Urim and Thummim, and casting lots.[50] For example, Jehovah instructed Aaron and Miriam that "if there be a prophet among you, I the Lord will make myself known unto him in a vision, and will speak unto him in a dream" (Numbers 12:6). Additionally, Elihu reminded Job that "God speaketh . . . in a dream, in a vision of the night, when deep sleep falleth upon men.... Then he openeth the ears of [speaks to] men, and sealeth their instruction" (Job 33:14–16). And on the night before his death, when a desperate Saul "enquired of the Lord, the Lord answered him not, neither by dreams, nor by Urim, nor by prophets" (1 Samuel 28:6)—all these modes of revelation are presented as legitimate but unavailable to Saul.

As with other modes of legitimate revelation, however, some Israelites falsely claimed to have received revelatory dreams. For example, the prophet Jeremiah, a contemporary of Lehi, warned the people of Jerusalem about false prophets who spoke in the name of Jehovah, but who "commit[ted] adultery, and walk[ed] in lies" (Jeremiah 23:14). Of them the Lord said, "I have not sent these prophets.... I have heard what the prophets said, that prophesy lies in my name, saying, I have dreamed, I have dreamed.... Behold, I am against them that prophesy false dreams, saith the Lord, ... and cause my people to err by their lies" (Jeremiah 23:21, 25, 32; see also 29:8–9). Moreover, Deuteronomy explicitly indicates that if "a prophet, or a dreamer of dreams" encouraged the Israelites to pursue other deities in addition to Jehovah, the Israelites should not only ignore him but also "put [him] to death" (Deuteronomy 13:1, 5).[51] In these passages, Jehovah was not speaking against authentic revelation by means of dreams, just against the false claims of false prophets.[52] Joel's prophecy supports this view, emphasizing that the Lord would continue to employ dreams as a legitimate form of divine communication in the future: "I [Jehovah] will pour out my spirit upon all flesh; and your sons and your daughters shall prophesy, your old men shall dream dreams, your young men shall see visions" (Joel 2:28). In light of the content of Jeremiah 23 and Deuteronomy 13, one wonders how aware Lehi's family was of these false prophets in Jerusalem and how this may have influenced the family's views of Lehi and his claims of revelatory dreams.

Turning now to some literary considerations, analysis reveals four consistent elements in the biblical reports of symbolic dreams: (1) an introduction, including the announcement that a dream has been received; (2) a description of the dream's contents; (3) an interpretation of the dream by someone else, found at variable distances from the dream report and not properly part of it; and (4) the realization of the events symbolized in the dream.[53] These features are clearly evident, for example, in the dream reports of Pharaoh's officials and of Pharaoh himself and in Joseph's interpretation of their dreams (see Genesis 40–41).

Another feature of symbolic dream reports in the Bible is the use of language that invites readers or listeners into the "living picture" that is being related by the dreamer.[54] One way this is accomplished is by the repeated use of the Hebrew particle *hinneh*, "behold," employed by a speaker or narrator to emphasize and draw attention to what occurs in the dream report.[55] For example, *hinneh* occurs six times in the seven verses containing the Pharaoh's dreams about cows and grain (see Genesis 41:1–7). This emphatic injunction thus encourages readers to look along with the person receiving the dream as it is narrated in the Bible.

As in other ancient Near Eastern dream texts, punning and other wordplay is evident in the biblical reports, although much of this is lost in translation.[56] A classic example occurs in Genesis 40. Angered with his chief cupbearer ("butler" in the KJV[57]) and baker, the Pharaoh imprisoned them in the same facility in which Joseph was being held. The two officials each dreamed a dream; Joseph interpreted both of them, saying to each, "Within three days shall Pharaoh lift up thine head" (Genesis 40:13, 19). So, on "the third day . . . [Pharaoh] made a feast . . . and he lifted up the head of the chief butler [cupbearer] and of the chief baker among his servants. And he restored the chief butler unto his butlership again; and he gave the cup into Pharaoh's hand: but he hanged the chief baker: as Joseph had interpreted to them" (Genesis 40:20–22). Thus, with biblical punning, one official's head "was lifted up" through exoneration and one by hanging.[58]

Another example of wordplay in biblical dream reports is the use of word clusters, concentrations of key words for emphasis.[59] The report of the Pharaoh's parallel dreams of cows and grain provides an example of such word clusters. The Hebrew word *sheba'*, "seven," occurs seven times in the narration of Pharaoh's dreams (see Genesis 41:1–7) and six more times in Pharaoh's telling of his dream to Joseph (see vv. 18–24). This word then occurs ten more times in the report of Joseph's interpretation of Pharaoh's dreams (see vv. 25–31). This concentration of the word "seven" serves to emphasize the interpretation that a complete cycle of seven years of agricultural plenty would be followed by a full cycle of famine.[60]

The last consideration in this section emphasizes the rhetorical value of dream reports. One scholar has correctly observed that biblical and other ancient Near Eastern dream reports "can [also] serve non-literary functions by contributing to the authority, ideology, and persuasiveness of the text."[61]

This is evident, for example, in the book of Daniel. Daniel 2 narrates Daniel's interpretation of King Nebuchadnezzar's dream, in which Nebuchadnezzar saw a great human image, segments of which were composed of different metals, that was ultimately smashed by a "stone . . . cut out of the mountain without hands" (Daniel 2:45). Significantly, the report of Daniel's interpretation of this dream begins with him verbalizing the claim that "wisdom and might are [God's]. . . . He removeth kings, and setteth up kings: he giveth wisdom unto the wise. . . . He revealeth the deep and secret things. . . . The light dwelleth with him" (Daniel 2:20–22). This overriding theme of God's superior knowledge and power, articulated in Daniel's interpretation of the Babylonian king's dream, provides a significant ideological, or theological, perspective that is emphasized throughout the rest of the book.

This review of biblical symbolic dream reports and their interpretations provides a context in which to now examine the report of Lehi's dream.

Lehi's Dream Report in Its Biblical Context

In light of the above overview, the account of Lehi's dream in 1 Nephi 8 definitely shares features and characteristics with dream reports in its greater ancient Near Eastern and, more specifically, biblical context. I will now highlight seven of these shared features before concluding.

1. *Symbolic dream reports and their introductions.* As reported by Nephi, Lehi's dream was a symbolic one. Interestingly, the claim to have "dreamed a dream" occurs in the Bible only in relation to symbolic dreams, such as those of Joseph (see Genesis 37:5–9) and the Pharaoh (see Genesis 41:15).[62] Nephi's report of Lehi's introduction—"Behold, I have dreamed a dream" (1 Nephi 8:2)—thus matches the phrasing that introduces biblical symbolic dream reports.

2. *Disturbing nature of symbolic dreams.* Just as the Pharaoh's "spirit was troubled" when he awoke from his symbolic dreams about cows and tassels of grain (Genesis 41:8), so Nebuchadnezzar's "spirit was troubled" and he was "afraid" when he awoke from his enigmatic dreams about a human figure made of various metals and about a great tree (Daniel 2:1–3; 4:5).

A different form of this feature is included in the report of Lehi's dream. Nephi quotes Lehi as saying that his dream caused him to fear for his sons Laman and Lemuel because in his dream they would not join the family at the tree (1 Nephi 8:4, 35–36). Lehi was thus troubled about certain sons, not about general conditions. Lehi's response demonstrates the degree to which he accepted his dream as a real manifestation of current and future truths. This aspect is similar to the "troubling" that was the outcome of several biblical dream accounts.

3. *Narrative structure.* Consistent with the four-point narrative structure outlined in the previous section, Nephi's account first opens with Lehi's announcement that he had "dreamed a dream" (1 Nephi 8:2). This phrase serves to introduce his symbolic dream and is followed by a description of the dream's contents, which appears to be partly quoted from Lehi and partly paraphrased by Nephi (see vv. 5–35).

The third point in the biblical narration of dream reports involves someone other than the dreamer announcing the interpretation of the dream after gaining it through revelation. As recounted in 1 Nephi 8, Lehi narrated his dream but provided neither interpretation nor explanation. Later, Nephi learned the interpretation of his father's dream in a God-given vision, which also included further specific knowledge (as indicated above). Interestingly, however, Nephi does *not* recount that he informed *his father*—the one who had dreamed the dream—of his vision and the interpretation he (Nephi) was given. Rather, Nephi relates that he answered his brothers' questions about their father's dream based on what he (Nephi) had learned in his vision (see 1 Nephi 15:1–7, 21–30). However, the first thing Nephi reports after the conclusion of his vision is that "after I, Nephi, had been carried away in the spirit, and seen all these things, I returned to the tent of my father" (1 Nephi 15:1). It is plausible that this is when he informed Lehi of his vision and shared his interpretation, presuming he would have done so before discussing his vision with his brothers.

This variation from the biblical pattern of another person interpreting the dream for the dreamer may be due to Nephi's choice to emphasize his sharing of interpretive knowledge with his less spiritually enlightened brothers. Significantly, however, the pattern in the Book of Mormon of someone receiving a symbolic dream and someone else announcing its meaning is consistent with the biblical pattern.

The fourth point in the narrative structure involves the realization of the events portrayed in the dream. The report of Lehi's dream includes this feature, especially in regard to his expressed fears about his sons Laman and Lemuel (see 1 Nephi 8:4, 36) because they would not partake of the fruit (see

1 Nephi 8:17–18, 35). As related in Nephi's own narrative and in the account of the generations that came after him, these fears were fully realized.

4. *Invitation for others to see.* Another common feature in biblical symbolic dream reports (mentioned above) is the use of the Hebrew emphatic particle, *hinneh*, "behold," to encourage readers and listeners to see along with the dreamer what they had experienced. However, *behold* occurs only a few times in 1 Nephi 8, as Lehi relates that he had dreamed a dream (four times in vv. 2–4). Nephi does not recount that Lehi spoke this word in sharing his dream with his family.[63]

Nevertheless, an alternative expression does serve to invite readers to see what Lehi saw. This is the repeated verbal form *beheld*, which in English looks similar to *behold*, but which is not a translation of the Hebrew particle *hinneh*, "behold." The English word *beheld* in 1 Nephi 8 is probably a translation of the common Hebrew verb *ra'ah*, "to see." This is often the case in the King James Version (e.g., Genesis 12:14; 48:8). The verb *beheld* occurs eleven times in Nephi's first person quotation of his father's earlier account of his dream (see 1 Nephi 8:2–28). Although this pattern differs in detail from biblical dream accounts, it is functionally similar. By emphasizing that "I [Lehi] beheld," or in other words, that "I [Lehi] saw [a field, a river, a tree, fruit, etc.]," the report of Lehi's dream not only narrates what he saw, but also invites us to enter his image-rich experience by seeing along with him.

5. *Wordplay.* As indicated above, most ancient Near Eastern reports of symbolic dreams, including those in the Bible, occur in a narrative context and demonstrate some sort of wordplay. Such wordplay provides keys to interpreting essential features of the dream and serves to connect the dream and its interpretation to the narrative[64] but is often lost in translation. This makes it challenging to ascertain the degree to which Nephi's report of Lehi's dream fits this category, since we only have the text as translated by Joseph Smith. However, one feature that is quite evident in 1 Nephi 8 is key-word clusters (reviewed above).

In the thirty-two verses that recount Lehi's dream (see 1 Nephi 8:4–35), the word *tree* occurs nine times (it also occurs nine times in chapter 11 in Nephi's report of his vision). The word *fruit* occurs in the report of Lehi's dream eighteen times (but, interestingly, only three times in Nephi's vision report, once in chapter 11 and twice in chapter 15). These word clusters emphasize the significance of the tree and its fruit in Lehi's dream. No other symbols in Lehi's dream are mentioned this often. Given the focus of the dream, it may seem obvious that the words *tree* and *fruit* are so frequently used. However, there is no inherent reason for these terms to occur more than a few times. It is the repetition of the words, over and over again, that heightens our awareness of the significance of these symbols. Accordingly, Lehi's dream affirms that nothing is more important than associating with the tree and internalizing its fruit.

Furthermore, as one scholar has observed regarding biblical word clusters, "the frequency with which we hear these words is more than literary embellishment; it is the thread that ties the dream to its interpretation."[65] Thus the similarly frequent occurrence of *tree* in both Lehi's dream and the early part of Nephi's vision report demonstrates and emphasizes the integrated interpretive role of Nephi's experience in relation to Lehi's dream.

Another example of wordplay in connection with Lehi's dream report involves the noun *seed*. The Hebrew word *zera'* ("seed") designates both seeds that are planted in the ground (e.g., Genesis 1:11; Isaiah 5:10) as well as human seed or offspring (e.g., Genesis 15:3; Exodus 32:13). The word *seed* occurs eight times in 1 Nephi 2–7 with this latter meaning, progeny. Nephi only reports the use of the word *seed* once in connection with Lehi's dream (1 Nephi 8:3), when, based on his dream, Lehi assumes that Nephi, Sam, "and many of their seed" would be saved. However, Lehi expressed grave concern about Laman and Lemuel, who were also his "seed."

Using the botanical usage, Nephi reports in 1 Nephi 8:1 that just before Lehi's dream his family "gathered together all manner of seeds of every kind, both of grain . . . and also of the seeds of fruit." Although *seed* with this botanical meaning does not occur again in 1 Nephi 8, the multiple occurrences of the terms *tree* and *fruit* in the account of Lehi's dream imply the notion of seeds. Lehi's dream account is thus connected to its narrative context in 1 Nephi by its concern for seed, human and otherwise.

Additionally, tying the report of Lehi's dream to its interpretation, the word *seed*, designating descendants, occurs thirty-three times in the account of Nephi's vision, primarily in 1 Nephi 12–13 (in reference to the future seed of Nephi and his brothers). So, while Lehi and his family took "seeds" with them on their journey to their new home (see 1 Nephi 8:1; 16:11; 18:6, 24), the Book of Mormon is primarily concerned with reporting the activity of Lehi and Sariah's "seed" in relation to Jesus's gospel.[66]

Thus the recurrence of key words highlighting major symbols in the reports of Lehi's dream and Nephi's vision link these two accounts and serve to emphasize primary themes narrated throughout the Book of Mormon: division and rebellion among Lehi and Sariah's seed and the absolute need to internalize the power of Christ's Atonement, symbolized by eating fruit from a particular tree.

6. *Rhetorical value.* As observed above, "dream account[s] can serve nonliterary functions by contributing to the authority, ideology, and persuasiveness of the text."[67] This can definitely be seen in the Book of Mormon. For example, the fact that Nephi and Sam joined their parents at the tree in the report of Lehi's dream, while Laman and Lemuel did not, foreshadows not only division in the family, but the superior role Nephi would play as a religious and political leader and historian among those of his family who, like himself, faithfully followed Lehi's prophetic direction. This development has parallels with Joseph's experiences, in which his own dreams when young (see Genesis 37) were fulfilled through his subsequent political rise to power in Egypt and his superior position within his own family (see Genesis 39–50).[68] In reality, Nephi's transition from spiritual heir-apparent to religious and political leader of his people had already been realized by the time Nephi produced the account of Lehi's dream on his small set of plates. Thus Lehi's dream, as reported by Nephi, serves to foreshadow and substantiate social and political developments among Lehi and Sariah's posterity.[69]

Additionally, as already observed, the Christ-centered nature of the Book of Mormon flows in large measure from this foundational combined dream and vision in its early chapters. The interrelated accounts of Lehi's dream and Nephi's vision authoritatively set the ideological or theological tone for all that follows, rhetorically strengthening the persuasiveness of later uses of tree and fruit symbolism (particularly in the teachings of Jacob and Alma) and of later prophetic invitations to come to Christ and live.

On a broader scale, by including the account of his father's dream, Nephi may have sought to ascribe increased persuasiveness and scriptural authority to his own record through its parallel with the biblical account, which begins with a tree of life in Eden and the eating of fruit, albeit from a different tree (see Genesis 2:9; 3:22, 24). In the report of his own vision, Nephi refers to the tree seen by Lehi in his dream as a "tree of life" (1 Nephi 11:25; 15:22, 28).[70] And later in the Book of Mormon the phrase "tree of life" is employed to hearken back to the tree in Lehi's dream by Lehi himself (see 2 Nephi 2:15) and also by Alma, who seems to refer to both Eden's tree of life and the tree in Lehi's dream (e.g., Alma 5:34, 62; 12:21, 23, 26).[71]

7. *Interpretation of symbolic dreams.* The tree with its fruit is the conceptual center point in the account of Lehi's dream; everything happens in relation to it. However, in harmony with biblical reports of symbolic dreams, the symbolism of the tree and its fruit is *not* explained to Lehi in his dream. In fact, during his own vision Nephi indicated to the Spirit of the Lord that he wanted to understand the interpretation of the meaning of the tree (1 Nephi 11:9–11),[72] and his brothers later specifically asked Nephi, "What meaneth this thing which our father saw in a dream? What meaneth the tree which he saw?" (1 Nephi 15:21).

It may be hard to imagine that Lehi and Nephi did not initially understand what the tree and fruit and other symbols in Lehi's dream represented. Presumably they discussed some possibilities. But the symbolic dream was a revelation from God, and as such it required a divine interpretation to accurately understand the message God intended to communicate. It was not wise to merely guess at what visual revelation was intended to convey. Similarly, the dreams reported in Genesis 41 (given to the Pharaoh) and Daniel 2 (given to Nebuchadnezzar) had come from Israel's God, and their interpretations were dependent upon specific revelation from him.

Such biblical combinations of dreams plus interpretations function as prophecy.[73] As Joseph said to the Pharaoh, "God hath shewed Pharaoh what he is about to do" (Genesis 41:25). So, likewise, the combination of Lehi's dream plus Nephi's interpretive vision in the Book of Mormon can be viewed as a great prophecy. But before Lehi and his family could fully appreciate this, Lehi's dream needed an inspired, authoritative interpretation.

Complicating the issue of their understanding Lehi's dream is the fact that many of the images in the dream report have multiple symbolic meanings. Trees, for example, are used in the Old Testament to symbolize abundant life (see Psalm 1:3), contented peace (see Micah 4:4), majesty and strength (see Ezekiel 31:3–5; Daniel 4:10–11), protection (see Ezekiel 31:6), longevity (see Isaiah 65:22), a righteous person who endures faithfully (see Jeremiah 17:7–8), and sins like pride and arrogance (see Isaiah 2:13; Zecheriah 11:2). Additionally, wisdom and righteousness are described as "a tree of life" to those who possess them (see Proverbs 3:18; 11:30). And Lehi himself was familiar with the use of an olive tree to symbolically represent the house of Israel (see 1 Nephi 10:12, 14).

First Nephi, therefore, portrays Nephi authoritatively relating through his vision experience the one true interpretation of the tree and the other symbols in his father's dream. Nephi's report of his vision permanently establishes the interpretation of Lehi's dream and its symbols, such that those reading his account to this day do not venture alternative views on the symbolism.

Conclusion

Nephi's report of Lehi's dream shares many similarities with biblical and other ancient Near Eastern reports of symbolic dreams. Understanding these similarities heightens our awareness of important aspects of Lehi's dream and its integration into and function within the text of 1 Nephi. These parallels range from such basic similarities as the fact that both Lehi's dream and symbolic biblical dreams are introduced with the expression "dreamed a dream," to more complex relationships evident in the narrative structuring of dream reports, the use of word clusters and other wordplay, and the rhetorical function they serve in their greater context.[74] Nephi's report of Lehi's dream is certainly compatible with its biblical Israelite context.

As mentioned, the Bible affirms that Jehovah sometimes chose vivid and richly symbolic dreams to reveal knowledge about his plans and to demonstrate his power to ancient people. The symbolic dreams given to Joseph, the Egyptian Pharaoh, Nebuchadnezzar, and Daniel convey via their enigmatic symbolism large-scale future developments, both national and family focused. The dream given to Lehi is no different. Its symbolic but compact representation of the future announces knowledge and truths that play out in the Book of Mormon and beyond. The report of Lehi's dream also serves to further reinforce the legitimate prophetic role of Lehi, to whom the Lord had made himself known through dreams (see Numbers 12:6).

Nephi's account of Lehi's grand dream of a tree and its fruit contains a power to instruct that goes beyond mere words, as it conveys a universal picture of personal salvation in a fallen world, connected more specifically to history through the interpretive vision given to Nephi. The fact that no other message or symbolic dream reports are included in the Book of Mormon after Lehi's dream and Nephi's visionary interpretation of it gives Lehi's dream a powerful position and influential status.[75] Our reading of the whole Book of

Mormon is significantly impacted by the authoritative presentation of doctrinal truths revealed through Lehi's dream and Nephi's interpretive vision. And all of this grows out of Lehi's matter-of-fact statement one morning, "Behold, I have dreamed a dream" (1 Nephi 8:2).

Notes

I thank my student assistants Angela Belle Wagner and Courtney Dotson for helping with research on this paper. I also thank my colleague Daniel L. Belnap and my wife, Jane Allis-Pike, for providing feedback on earlier drafts of this paper. Note that I have usually rendered Hebrew words according to the "general purpose" transliteration scheme found in The SBL Handbook of Style *(Peabody, MA: Hendrickson, 1999), 28.*

    1. Jeffrey R. Holland's statement about 1 Nephi 8 in *Christ and the New Covenant* (Salt Lake City: Deseret Book, 1997), 162, is often cited as support for this view: "At the very outset of the Book of Mormon, in its first fully developed allegory, Christ is portrayed as the source of eternal life and joy, the living evidence of divine love, and the means whereby God will fulfill his covenant with the house of Israel and indeed the entire family of man, returning them to all their eternal promises."

    2. Compare the similar dream revelations in Ether 9:3 ("the Lord warned Omer in a dream that he should depart out of the land") and Matthew 2:13 ("the angel of the Lord appeareth to Joseph in a dream, saying, Arise, and take the young child and his mother, and flee into Egypt;" see also Matthew 2:19–20).

    3. See, for example, George Reynolds and Janne M. Sjodahl, *Commentary on the Book of Mormon* (Salt Lake City: Deseret Book, 1955), 1:60–65; and Joseph Fielding McConkie and Robert L. Millet, *Doctrinal Commentary on the Book of Mormon* (Salt Lake City: Bookcraft, 1987), 1:54–61. Kent P. Jackson, "The Tree of Life and the Ministry of Christ (1 Nephi 8–11, 15)," in vol. 7 of *Studies in Scripture* (Salt Lake City: Deseret Book, 1987), 34–43, focuses primarily on 1 Nephi 11, saying little about chapter 8.

    4. Charles Swift, "Lehi's Vision of the Tree of Life: Understanding the Dream as Visionary Literature," *Journal of Book of Mormon Studies* 14, no. 2 (2005): 52–63. See also the format of this chapter as understood by Donald W. Parry, *The Book of Mormon Text Reformatted according to Parallelistic Patterns* (Provo, UT: FARMS, 1992), 12–15. James T. Duke, *The Literary Masterpiece Called the Book of Mormon* (Springville, UT: Cedar Fort, 2004), 70–72, adds nothing new to the discussion.

    5. See, for example, Susan Easton Black, "Behold, I Have Dreamed a Dream," in *The Book of Mormon: First Nephi, the Doctrinal Foundation*, ed. Monte S. Nyman and Charles D. Tate Jr. (Provo, UT: Religious Studies Center, Brigham Young University, 1988): 113–24, and Dennis L. Largey, "Lehi[1]'s Dream," in *Book of Mormon Reference Companion*, ed. Dennis L. Largey (Salt Lake City: Deseret Book, 2003), 516–18.

    6. See, for example, Hugh Nibley, *Lehi in the Desert; The World of the Jaredites; There Were Jaredites*, vol. 5, *The Collected Works of Hugh Nibley* (Salt Lake City: Deseret Book, 1988), 43–46; and more recently S. Kent Brown, "Lehi[1], journey of, to the promised

land," in *Book of Mormon Reference Companion*, ed. Dennis L. Largey (Salt Lake City: Deseret Book, 2003), 515, with further bibliography.

7. See C. Wilfred Griggs, "The Book of Mormon as an Ancient Book," *BYU Studies* 22, no. 3 (1982): 259–78, especially 274–78.

8. See S. Kent Brown's discussion of this in "Lehi, book of," in *Book of Mormon Reference Companion*, 511.

9. Ann Jeffers, *Magic and Divination in Ancient Palestine and Syria* (New York: Brill, 1996), 128 and 125.

10. Scott B. Noegel, *Nocturnal Ciphers: The Allusive Language of Dreams in the Ancient Near East* (New Haven, CT: American Oriental Society, 2007), 264–65. He further claims that we should at least think of dreams and visions "existing side by side on a continuum of mantic [divinatory] experiences." See similarly Frances Flannery-Dailey, *Dreamers, Scribes, and Priests: Jewish Dreams in the Hellenistic and Roman Eras* (Boston: Brill, 2004), 2, who observes that "the ancients placed dreams and visions along a thickly inhabited spectrum of hypnagogic phenomena." See also M. Ottosson, "*halom*," in *Theological Dictionary of the Old Testament*, ed. by G. Johannes Botterweck and Helmer Ringgren (Grand Rapids, MI: Eerdmans, 1980), 4:427.

11. Bruce R. McConkie, "Dreams," in *Mormon Doctrine*, 2nd ed. (Salt Lake City: Bookcraft, 1966), 208, states that "all inspired dreams are visions, but all visions are not dreams; . . . it is only when the vision occurs during sleep that it is termed a dream." See also Gerald N. Lund's discussion of dreams and visions and other more or less direct forms of revelation in *Hearing the Voice of the Lord* (Salt Lake City: Deseret Book, 2010), 30–42. Lund views, as I do, various types of revelation on a spectrum or continuum.

12. See Matthew Roper, "Scripture Update: Lehi as a Visionary Man," in *Insights* 27, no. 4 (2007): 2–3, who discusses the probable negative sense in which Sariah, and earlier her older sons, had used this phrase in reference to Lehi. Roper bases his assessment on passages in the book of Jeremiah, a contemporary of Lehi.

13. A number of Latter-day Saint authors have commented on this Hebraic feature in the Book of Mormon. See, for example, M. Deloy Pack, "Hebraisms," in *Book of Mormon Reference Companion*, 322–23; and John Tvedtnes, "The Hebrew Background of the Book of Mormon," in *Rediscovering the Book of Mormon*, ed. John L. Sorenson and Melvin J. Thorne (Salt Lake City: Deseret Book, 1991), 80–81.

14. See McConkie and Millet, *Doctrinal Commentary*, 56, who, writing in reference to Lehi's dream, state that they "will draw upon Nephi's account of the same vision (given in its entirety in 1 Nephi 11–14)."

15. See, for example, the observations in Steven L. Olsen, "Prophecy and History: Structuring the Abridgment of the Nephite Records," *Journal of Book of Mormon Studies* 15, no. 1 (2006): 24–25, on the content and stylistic nature of Lehi's dream, which he describes as "an allegorical representation of salvation," and Nephi's vision, which he describes as "a literal representation of the plan of salvation . . . [representing] God's redemptive work as it unfolds in real-world spatial, temporal, and human contexts." Contrast Duke, *Literary Masterpiece*, 70, who claims, incorrectly in my view, that "the Dream of Lehi, and Nephi's interpretation of that dream, is another wonderful example of an allegory (1 Nephi 8–15)." On the content of the dream and vision, see also John W. Welch, "Connections between the Visions of Lehi and Nephi," in John W. Welch and

Melvin J. Thorne, eds., *Pressing Forward with the Book of Mormon* (Provo, UT: FARMS, 1999), 49–53. Welch, while pointing out the many connecting similarities between Lehi's dream and Nephi's vision, observes that, "the two visions are very different in character. Lehi's dream is intimate, symbolic, and salvific; Nephi's vision is collective, historic, and eschatological" (49). Welch also states that, "Nephi's vision is not a mere rerun of the Lehi's. The second clearly develops each element of the first, from different perspectives and for different purposes" (52).

16. The foundation of modern research on dreams in the ancient Near East is the study by A. Leo Oppenheim, *The Interpretation of Dreams in the Ancient Near East: With a Translation of the Assyrian Dream Book* (Philadelphia: American Philosophical Society, 1956). Oppenheim actually based his categorization of dreams on the Hellenistic author Artemidorus of Daldis (second century AD). Many major and minor publications on dreams have followed Oppenheim's general assessment. Due to the scope and nature of this study, I cite only a few of the more recent books on the topic, assuming interested readers will consult the bibliographies therein for further citations and for a broader perspective.

17. Shaul Bar, *A Letter That Has Not Been Read: Dreams in the Hebrew Bible* (Cincinnati: Hebrew Union College, 2001), 1. I thank Fred Woods for bringing this book to my attention; unfortunately, it has received rather mixed reviews. See also S. A. L. Butler, *Mesopotamian Conceptions of Dreams and Dream Rituals* (Münster: Ugarit-Verlag, 1998), 13–14; and Flannery-Dailey, *Dreamers, Scribes, and Priests*, 1.

18. See, for example, Oppenheim, *The Interpretation of Dreams*, 237; and Butler, *Mesopotamian Conceptions of Dreams and Dream Rituals*, 14–15, 23, 73. Butler and Oppenheim write as if they accept that ancient Near Eastern peoples thought all dreams came from external sources. However, Ottosson, "halom," in *Theological Dictionary*, 4:424, claims that "certain dreams were considered to derive not from divine revelation but from the psychological state of the dreamer." Commenting on the religious orientation of dreams in ancient texts, Kelly Bulkeley, *Dreaming in the World's Religions: A Comparative History* (New York: New York University Press, 2008), 3–4, makes the interesting observation that "dreaming has always been regarded as a religious phenomenon. Throughout history, in cultures worldwide, people have seen their dreams first and foremost as religiously meaningful experiences.... As a matter of historical fact, ... dreams have played a powerful, complex, and dynamic role in the world's religious and spiritual traditions."

19. Flannery-Dailey, *Dreamers, Scribes, and Priests*, 35.

20. Jean-Marie Husser, *Dreams and Dream Narratives in the Biblical World*, trans. Jill M. Munro (Sheffield, England: Sheffield Academic Press, 1999), 18. See also Butler, *Mesopotamian Conceptions of Dreams*, 19, 97–101. Dream omens are much better attested from Mesopotamia than from Egypt. The remains of only one poorly preserved text represent a so-called dream book from Ugarit. See, for example, Dennis Pardee, "Ugaritic Dream Omens (1.93)," in *Context of Scripture*, ed. William W. Hallo and K. Lawson Younger (Boston: Brill, 2003), 1:293–94.

21. Divination was the ritual practice of "divining" or attempting to learn the future by observing natural phenomena thought to contain clues as to what the gods had decreed. Mesopotamian diviners, for example, observed and catalogued such things as

anomalies on the livers and other internal organs of sacrificial animals, irregular heavenly and meteorological manifestations, dreams, and the births of disfigured humans and animals. Such divinatory practices were forbidden according to the Israelite Mosaic law (see Deuteronomy 18:10; Isaiah 47:13).

22. Robert K. Ritner, "Dream Oracles (1.33)," in *Context of Scripture*, 1:53–54. Husser, *Dreams and Dream Narratives*, 59, accurately observes that while "dream interpretation is, however, well attested [in Egypt], . . . it is not an integral part of a divinatory system [as in Mesopotamia]; . . . rather it seems to be related to magic."

23. Husser, *Dreams and Dream Narratives*, 33, 68.

24. Noegel, *Nocturnal Ciphers*, 43.

25. For example, Oppenheim, *The Interpretation of Dreams*, 186–87, 206, observed that most ancient Near Eastern dream reports or narratives, not surprisingly, consist of two major aspects: (1) the setting of the dream, which information typically brackets or frames the dream report, and (2) the content of the dream. Also, the dreamer's response to the dream is often included. Oppenheim is cited by Bar, *A Letter That Has Not Been Read*, 218–19, who concludes at the end of his book that Oppenheim's observation was correct. Of course, genre and other factors impacted the use of stereotypical features in such reports.

26. Husser, *Dreams and Dream Narratives*, 73–74, provides a brief survey of the relevant texts from Ugarit and the first millennium Aramaic kingdoms. See also Noegel, *Nocturnal Ciphers*, 107–112.

27. See, for example, the discussion of these designations by Husser, *Dreams and Dream Narratives*, 23–24, 99–100; and Noegel, *Nocturnal Ciphers*, 6–8.

28. The remains of ancient Ugarit are located near the Mediterranean coast of Syria. King Keret's name is also written Kirta.

29. N. Wyatt, *Religious Texts from Ugarit: The Words of Ilimilku and His Colleagues* (Sheffield, England: Sheffield Academic Press, 1998), 183–86, 198. The text is KTU 1.14.

30. Gibeon is about six miles northwest of Jerusalem. Second Chronicles 1:3–6 indicates that the Mosaic tabernacle was then in Gibeon, even though David had brought the Ark of the Covenant into Jerusalem.

31. Stephanie Dalley, *Myths from Mesopotamia* (New York: Oxford, 1989), 57–58. This text is found on tablet one of the Gilgamesh epic.

32. For this reason Scott Noegel, *Nocturnal Ciphers*, 274–76, designates any dreams that required interpretation as "enigmatic," and he calls for a new and conceptually different terminology. See Oppenheim's preliminary use of the term *enigmatic* in *The Interpretation of Dreams*, 206.

33. See Noegel, *Nocturnal Ciphers*, 11–32, 89–91.

34. Noegel, *Nocturnal Ciphers*, 40; see also 45, 105–6. Additionally, Noegel observes that "similes and metaphors served 'magicians' long before they served poets" (90).

35. Noegel, *Nocturnal Ciphers*, 253.

36. Husser, *Dreams and Dream Narratives*, 29.

37. See, for example, Noegel, *Nocturnal Ciphers*, 46–50. His similar comments on Egyptian enigmatic dreams are found on pages 92–93.

38. Due to space limitations and a lack of relevancy for studying 1 Nephi 8, I have included no comments on the ancient practice of incubation. Incubation involved sleeping

at a temple or other sacred space, often in conjunction with other ritual activity, with the express intent of receiving a revelatory dream (all are reported to have been message dreams). For a summary of this practice throughout the ancient Near East, see Husser, *Dreams and Dream Narratives*, 46–50, 69–71, 172–76. I have also not included specific comments on the interesting evidence regarding dreams and interpretations in the Mari texts. On this material, see Jack Sasson, "Mari Dreams," *Journal of the American Oriental Society* 103 no. 1 (1983): 283–93; and Noegel, *Nocturnal Ciphers*, 83–86.

39. Ann K. Guinan, "Divination," in *Context of Scripture*, 1:422, asserts, citing Oppenheim and others for support, that "strong parallels do connect Mesopotamian and biblical accounts of dream interpretation." It is worth noting that there are no extant Israelite inscriptions that recount dream reports, interpretations, or omens.

40. See, for example, the summary comments in Ottosson, "*halom*," in *Theological Dictionary*, 4:427; Husser, *Dreams and Dream Narratives*, 88; and Flannery-Dailey, *Dreamers, Scribes, and Priests*, 46.

41. In the New Testament, reports of dreams occur in relation to Joseph, husband of Mary (Matthew 1:20; 2:13, 19–22), the wise men (Matthew 2:12), and probably Paul ("a vision appeared to Paul in the night;" Acts 16:9).

42. Flannery-Dailey, *Dreamers, Scribes, and Priests*, 53, notes that in the Bible "the [dream] function of healing is seriously attenuated," in contrast to dreams in the general ancient Near East.

43. Oppenheim, *The Interpretation of Dreams*, 207, 209, claimed that all biblical symbolic dreams were given to non-Israelites, but based on Genesis 37 and Daniel 7 (see below), I disagree.

44. For discussions of these symbolic, or enigmatic, dreams in the Bible, see Husser, *Dreams and Dream Narratives*, 106–22; and Noegel, *Nocturnal Ciphers*, 116–180. Husser, *Dreams and Dream Narratives*, 121–22, dismisses Daniel 7 as a symbolic dream, preferring to see it as a vision "presented as a dream." However, Noegel, *Nocturnal Ciphers*, 163–76, treats Daniel 7 as a symbolic enigmatic dream report, as do I.

45. Lehi and his family would have had no knowledge of Daniel's experiences, since these occurred after they had left Jerusalem, but I assume that Lehi and his family would have had some knowledge of Joseph and his dream experiences nearly a millennium earlier, at least after (if not before) the family obtained the brass plates. See 1 Nephi 5:10–11, 14. Of course, no extant copy of Genesis dates to Lehi's time, nor does Nephi mention in 1 Nephi anything about Joseph's dreams and interpretations, so we cannot be completely certain what was available to them. However, Nephi does mention the "five books of Moses" (1 Nephi 5:11).

46. Husser, *Dreams and Dream Narratives*, 101.

47. See, for example, Husser, *Dreams and Dream Narratives*, 102. In "Dreams, Visions," in *Dictionary of Biblical Imagery*, ed. by Leland Ryken, James C. Wilhoit, and Tremper Longman III (Downers Grove, IL: InterVarsity, 1998), 217, it is claimed that "all dreams in antiquity were not necessarily considered divine, but with few exceptions . . . ordinary dreams and nightmares play little or no part in the plot of most biblical narratives".

48. See also Ecclesiastes 5:3, 7.

49. Contrast the views in note 47 with Noegel, *Nocturnal Ciphers*, 120, who claims without qualification that "we should not be surprised to find that the Israelites also shared the Mesopotamian conception of dreams as divine messages."

50. For a brief discussion of the legitimate revelatory mode of casting lots, see Richard Neitzel Holzapfel, Dana M. Pike, and David Rolph Seely, *Jehovah and the World of the Old Testament* (Salt Lake City: Deseret Book, 2009), 157.

51. There are minor differences in the versification of the King James Bible and the traditional Hebrew Bible in this and several other passages cited in this paper. In all such cases, I have given only the English citation.

52. See, for example, Noegel, *Nocturnal Ciphers*, 186–87; and Flannery-Dailey, *Dreamers, Scribes, and Priests*, 50–51, who agree with this analysis, against Husser, *Dreams and Dream Narratives*, 139–42, who sees conveyed in Jeremiah 23 and related passages a preference by prophets such as Jeremiah for visions instead of dreams. Flannery-Dailey even suggests that Jeremiah 31:26 may refer to a dream Jeremiah experienced.

The challenge of false dreamers and prophets clearly continued into the Israelites' post-exilic period. Almost a century after Jeremiah, Zechariah proclaimed, "for the idols have spoken vanity, and the diviners have seen a lie, and have told false dreams; they comfort in vain: therefore they went their way as a flock, they were troubled, because there was no shepherd" (Zechariah 10:2). Such biblical passages reinforce the notion that receiving revelatory dreams was a part of legitimate prophetic activity, so much so that even false prophets feigned the experience.

53. Husser, *Dreams and Dream Narratives*, 106–7; and Flannery-Dailey, *Dreamers, Scribes, and Priests*, 39–41. This arrangement is not so different from the stereotypical features in the reports of ancient Near Eastern symbolic dreams, as discussed by Oppenheim, and cited in note 25, above.

54. Husser, *Dreams and Dream Narratives*, 107.

55. Of course, *hinneh* occurs many times in the Hebrew Bible outside dream reports. Such attestations are usually in narrated speech, similar to the narration of someone announcing a dream. Thus, while *hinneh* frequently occurs in biblical dream reports, it is not unique to them.

56. See the analysis of Noegel, *Nocturnal Ciphers*, 113–82.

57. The KJV rendered the Hebrew noun *mashqeh* in Genesis 40 and 41 as "butler," but the word is usually, and more accurately, rendered as "cupbearer" in modern English translations.

58. It is not clear from the Hebrew verb *t-l-h* whether hanging by the neck or impaling—hanging on a wooden stake—is intended here (some commentators also suggest beheading). See Noegel, *Nocturnal Ciphers*, 129–32, for a discussion of the dream reports in Genesis 40, including further examples of wordplay therein.

59. As with the occurrence of the emphatic particle *hinneh*, punning and word clusters are not unique to biblical dream reports, but are certainly well attested within them.

60. See, for example, Noegel, *Nocturnal Ciphers*, 132–34, for a discussion of this passage. Noegel observes that the report of Joseph's interpretation includes wordplay between *sheba'*, "seven," and *saba'*, "abundance, plenty," in Genesis 41:29: "there come seven [*sheba'*] years of great plenty [*saba'*] throughout all the land." In addition to sounding similar, the consonants of these two words look the same when written.

61. Noegel, *Nocturnal Ciphers*, 257.

62. Husser, *Dreams and Dream Narratives*, 89, makes this easily verified observation. There are only eight occurrences of the phrase in the Bible (see Genesis 37, 40–41; Judges 7; Daniel 2). The dreams Joseph received when he was still in Canaan (see Genesis 37:1–10) were symbolic but not really enigmatic, since his brothers and father clearly understand the implication of their symbolism. In this case, no specific interpretation is provided, although the truthfulness of these dreams is verified in the subsequent narration.

63. The word *behold* does occur in 1 Nephi 8:14, in the phrase, "I looked to behold," but this is a variant of the verb *beheld*, and not a possible occurrence of the Hebrew particle, *hinneh*, "behold." Nephi, in introducing his paraphrase (8:30), does employ this latter term, "but, to be short in writing, behold, he saw."

64. See Noegel, *Nocturnal Ciphers*, throughout.

65. Noegel, *Nocturnal Ciphers*, 170.

66. Susan Easton Black, "Behold, I Have Dreamed a Dream," 113–14, makes a partial form of this observation. Further highlighting the occurrence of the concept and word *seed* in the dream and vision is the fact that *seed* does not occur in the intervening chapters, 1 Nephi 9–10, which contain Nephi's comments about his metal plates and his report of some of his father's prophecies about the Messiah.

67. Noegel, *Nocturnal Ciphers*, 257.

68. See Husser, *Dreams and Dream Narratives*, 114, for comments on Joseph's situation.

69. Another possible rhetorical feature in 1 Nephi that I do not discuss in the body of this paper is the possibility that Nephi, especially after his own vision (11–14), considered himself an analogue to his ancestor Joseph, an interpreter of other people's dreams. If so, one wonders if this impacted the extent of Lehi's dream that Nephi reported in his account in proportion to his own vision.

70. Not only does the corollary between the Edenic tree of life and the tree Lehi saw in his dream increase the authority of Nephi's text, the fact that the Lord prohibited Adam and Eve from further access to the tree of life (see Genesis 3:22–24; Moses 4:28–31), allows Lehi's dream and Nephi's visions to illustrate the way back to the tree of life, the fruit of which will allow its worthy partakers to live with Christ and his Father. Additionally, the fact that Adam and Eve had to exit the garden after eating fruit from a tree has at least a loose correlation to Lehi and his family leaving their home and his dreaming about a tree of life.

71. See for example Alma 5:34, in which Alma quotes the Lord as saying, "Come unto me and ye shall partake of the fruit of the tree of life; yea, ye shall eat and drink of the bread and the waters of life freely." This sounds a lot like what Nephi learned in vision: "[the rod led to] the fountain of living waters, or to the tree of life; which waters are a representation of the love of God; and . . . the tree of life was a representation of the love of God" (1 Nephi 11:25). Likewise, Alma's counsel in Alma 5:62, "Come and be baptized unto repentance, that ye also may be partakers of the fruit of the tree of life," sounds more in harmony with the symbols in Lehi's dream than the tree in Eden.

72. Elsewhere the symbols in Lehi's dream were just explained to Nephi in his vision (e.g., 1 Nephi 12:16–18).

73. See the comments of Husser, *Dreams and Dream Narratives*, 110, on this topic. Frances Flannery, "Dream and Vision Reports," in *The Eerdmans Dictionary of Early Judaism*, ed. John J. Collins and Daniel C. Harlow (Grand Rapids, MI: Eerdmans, 2010), 550, relates that this view of considering dreams and their authoritative interpretations as prophecy continued through the Jewish Second Temple period, but that Rabbinic authors viewed them in much lower regard.

74. Recognizing these features also reinforces our understanding of the impact that Israelite cultural practices, as evidenced in the biblical dream reports, had on Lehi and his family. We would not expect them to have developed their own unique literary styles and cultural practices within weeks of leaving Jerusalem, and it appears that they were still heavily influenced decades later when the account of Lehi's dream was written by Nephi on his "small" set of plates.

75. The only other occurrences of the word *dream* in the Book of Mormon as we have it are found in reference to Lehi's dream (1 Nephi 10:2; 15:21); in Nephi's quotation of Isaiah (2 Nephi 27:3); in Jacob's description of his people's lives passing as "a dream" (Jacob 7:26); in the separate and presumably chronologically earlier dream of the Jaredite Omer (Ether 9:3); and in Korihor's claim to the Nephite high priest Giddonah that the Nephite leaders "have brought them [the Nephites] to believe, by their traditions and their dreams and their whims and their visions and their pretended mysteries," that they would offend God if they lived differently (Alma 30:28). It is not clear from this statement whether Korihor makes specific reference to the founding dream and vision experiences of Lehi and Nephi, to an ongoing tradition of prophetic dreams and visions that is not represented in our Book of Mormon, or to both. I think the last option is the most likely.

7

"The Presence of the Lord"

Jennifer C. Lane

Lehi's dream in 1 Nephi 8 has been interpreted in many rich and helpful ways. Most commonly we see it through the lens of Nephi's vision in 1 Nephi 11 or Nephi's explanation to his brothers in 1 Nephi 15, but this paper explores the insights we can gain by seeing the dream of the tree of life through the conceptual framework expressed by Lehi's comments. A careful study of Lehi's response to his dream can help us see what it means not only to him but also to all of us more universally.

At the end of his narrative, Lehi gives us an interpretive tool to read the significance of our relationship to the tree. After he recounts his vision, Lehi expresses fear that Laman and Lemuel "should be cast off from the presence of the Lord" (1 Nephi 8:36). Lehi's interpretation of his dream is framed by two central concepts or terms: being "cast off" and "the presence of the Lord." This interpretation suggests a bifurcation of existence into two conceptual categories—being in the presence of the Lord and being separated from the Lord.

We have a number of resources to understand what Lehi meant both in terms of being "cast off" and of being in "the presence of the Lord." While we

---

Jennifer C. Lane is associate academic vice president for curriculum at Brigham Young University–Hawaii.

do not have the original language of the Book of Mormon to directly compare with the Hebrew of the Old Testament, both "cast off" and "the presence of the Lord" are important terms in the Bible, describing distance from and proximity to God, often directly related to temple imagery.

After exploring this Old Testament background, noting the foundational temple imagery of these terms, I will show how paying attention to the uses of "cast off" and "the presence of the Lord" in the Book of Mormon can deepen our appreciation of the doctrinal insights found in Lehi's dream. These terms show up in critical passages throughout the Book of Mormon that explain the criteria for either being in the presence of God or being cast off. By studying the term "presence of the Lord" in the Old Testament and the Book of Mormon, we can see that it has a broader, more multifaceted scope than any particular specialized meaning such as entering the celestial kingdom or receiving the Second Comforter in mortality.

The choice to come unto Christ and partake of the fruit can be understood both in terms of daily choices and experiences as well as ultimate choices and one's final destiny. When Lehi describes his own experience of partaking of the fruit, he comments: "I beheld that it was most sweet, above all that I ever before tasted. Yea, and I beheld that the fruit thereof was white, to exceed all the whiteness that I had ever seen. And as I partook of the fruit thereof it filled my soul with exceedingly great joy" (1 Nephi 8:11–12). The act of partaking of the sweetness, purity, and joy of coming unto Christ and experiencing his presence does not require waiting until the end of our life or receiving the Second Comforter. It is significant that Helaman writes to Captain Moroni, "And now, my beloved brother, Moroni, may the Lord our God, who has redeemed us and made us free, *keep you continually in his presence*" (Alma 58:41; emphasis added). What it means to be in the presence of the Lord in mortality, as well as in the eternal world, is richly developed in Lehi's dream as well as in the related Old Testament and Book of Mormon references.

Lehi's interpretation of responses to the offer of the fruit combines two overarching themes of the Book of Mormon. First, it captures the invitation to come unto Christ, to enter into his presence and partake of the kind of life that he enjoys. At the same time, this image is coupled with an awareness that not all who are separated will choose to come. This is the awareness that one can choose to be cast off forever—clearly the fear of Lehi for his sons.

While the events in Lehi's dream were more encompassing, his concluding commentary focuses on the state of his sons. Lehi "exceedingly feared for Laman and Lemuel; yea, he feared lest they should be *cast off from the presence of the Lord*" (1 Nephi 8:36; emphasis added). Before looking closely at the uses of the terms "cast off" and "the presence of the Lord," it may be helpful to look narrowly at the things Lehi saw that he described in these terms.

There are two places in the dream where Laman and Lemuel appear. The first is partway through the dream, where Lehi himself is at the tree and looks around for his family. Other family members come and partake of the fruit, but even though Laman and Lemuel are specifically invited, "they would not come unto me and partake of the fruit" (1 Nephi 8:18). Then, at the very end of Lehi's description of his dream, he observes that some who had partaken of the fruit fell away because they heeded the scorn of those in the great and spacious building. The very last line of description that we have from Nephi, however, focuses not on those who chose to leave the tree, but on those who chose not to come: "And Laman and Lemuel partook not of the fruit, said my father" (v. 35). Recognizing individuals' use of agency in responding to the offer to partake of the fruit of the tree is critical to making sense of the foundational theological issues represented by "the presence of the Lord" and being "cast off" by the Lord. These issues include questions of justice, mercy, and agency.

"Presence of the Lord": Insights from the Old Testament

The term "presence" in English versions of the Old Testament is usually a translation of the Hebrew word *pānîm*. It literally means "face," as in one's visage, but its usage has a broader sense.[1] For example, "*pānîm* was used in reference to entering or leaving the presence of a king or a superior"[2] or, by extension, the presence of the Lord. The term appears about four hundred times in the Old Testament, and in over a quarter of those instances it refers to the Lord Jehovah.[3] "In some cases, the term 'face' or 'presence' stands in for naming the individual that is being referred to as the subject of the action."[4]

A key dimension of the term "presence" is the expression of relationships,[5] both among humans and between God and humans. These aspects include "real personal presence, relationship, and meeting (or refusal to meet)."[6] Simian-Yofre notes that "insofar as *pānîm* bespeaks presence, its purpose is to underline the positive aspect of the interpersonal relationship. The negative aspect of the relationship is expressed by separation from *pānîm*."[7]

One example of how one's relationship with the presence of the Lord can change is illustrated in Genesis 3:8, where, after eating of the forbidden fruit, "Adam and his wife hid themselves from the presence [*pānîm*] of the Lord God amongst the trees of the garden." Their disobedience had changed their relationship to the presence of the Lord. They no longer desired to be in his presence. Not only can people remove themselves from God's presence, but we also see a change in relationship expressed in the Old Testament phrase of the Lord "hiding his face," which "is not simply a punishment: it signifies a radical disruption of the relationship with God."[8] The issues of both humans approaching God's presence and the availability or withdrawal of that presence run through the Old Testament in the language related to the temple.

Central to the understanding of the tabernacle or temple in the Old Testament is that this is the place in which the Lord's presence is made available. There are a number of *pānîm*-related expressions in the Old Testament that are almost always associated with the language of worship at the temple. These include being seen before the face of Jehovah, being before Jehovah, and seeking his face.

The commandment for all Israelite men to visit the sanctuary three times a year during the feasts of Passover, Pentecost, and Tabernacles (see Exodus 23:14–17) can literally be read as "to appear (be seen) before the [face of] Yahweh."[9] This expression functions as "a technical term for a cultic encounter with the deity,"[10] meaning that the term "appear before the presence" refers to the setting of temple worship.[11]

The other *pānîm* expression that consistently points to a temple setting is *lipne YHWH*, meaning "before or to Yahweh [Jehovah]." This technical expression of worship appears 225 times in the Old Testament.[12] The term describes not only the worship and sacrifices of the priests in the temple, "but also private religious acts are performed *lipne yhwh*."[13] This phrase emphasizes that actions of sacrifice and worship, as well as private acts of devotion, "are performed in some sense in the presence of Yahweh [Jehovah]."[14]

In addition, the term "seek his face" (*biqqēš pānîm*) can also include a formal act of worship or sacrifice, although this sense is not always required.[15] The spirit of seeking his face in connection with the technical language of temple worship can be seen in Psalm 42:2: "My soul thirsteth for God, for the living God: when shall I come and appear before God?" We see here the desire to be in God's presence.[16]

"Cast Off": Insights from the Old Testament

Because of the various verbs that could be translated "cast off" and the breadth of Old Testament examples of this concept, for the sake of simplicity this study will only briefly consider passages that discuss the fear of being "cast off forever." In each case, the root verb is *zanach*. The term is generally understood to mean "to reject, exclude, or abandon."[17] Cognates to other Semitic languages suggest a possible meaning of "to hate" or "to be angry," but this is debated.[18] Of the nineteen times the verb *zanach* appears in the Old Testament, fourteen of those instances have God as the subject of the verb.[19] Ten of those instances are found in the Book of Psalms, where poetic structures can help enhance our understanding of the term.

Part of the meaning of the term *zanach* can be seen in the parallels with which it is coupled. On many occasions, we see that being cast off is not being given access to God's presence in the context of the temple. Separation from worship can be seen in the parallel use of the questions "Why castest thou off my soul?" and "Why hidest thou thy face [*pānîm*] from me?" (Psalm 88:14).[20] This parallel can be seen in Psalm 74:1, where the Psalmist asks, "O God, why hast thou cast us off for ever? why doth thine anger smoke against the sheep of thy pasture?" Ringgrin observes, "There is a parallel reference to the wrath of God. The psalm deals with destruction of the temple by enemies, which is taken to prove that Yahweh is angry with his people and therefore ignores his temple."[21]

The fear of abandonment can be seen in Psalm 44:23, in which the plea "Cast us not off for ever" suggests that here "*zānach* means that God has totally turned his back on his people."[22] In Psalm 77:7–9, the Psalmist asks, "Will the Lord cast off for ever? and will he be favourable no more? Is his mercy clean gone for ever? doth his promise fail for evermore? Hath God forgotten to be gracious? hath he in anger shut up his tender mercies?" Here we see the parallels to being "cast off" appear to be the opposite of the mercy and compassion we normally associate with the Lord. Here "*zānach* is associated with 'never be favorable (rātsāh),' 'his *chesedh* [mercy] has ceased,' 'forget to be gracious (shākhach channôth),' and 'shut up compassion (qāphats rachᵃmîm).'"[23]

While the thought of being separated and cast off in this manner is truly fearsome, we are given a reason why it occurs. An explanation for the Lord's action in casting off his people is found in 1 Chronicles 28:9, where David gives Solomon his charge concerning the building of the temple. Here the Lord's relationship to humans is set in terms of response to human agency. "And thou, Solomon my son, know thou the God of thy father, and serve him with a perfect heart and with a willing mind: for the Lord searcheth all hearts, and understandeth all the imaginations of the thoughts: *if thou seek him, he will be found of thee; but if thou forsake him, he will cast thee off for ever*" (1 Chronicles 28:9; emphasis added). It is significant that by making the presence of the Lord available with the building of the temple, the terms of access are also presented. The principle taught here has a striking resonance with the message conveyed by Lehi's dream of the tree of life. Those who seek him find his presence, and those who forsake him are separated from his presence.

"Presence of the Lord" in the Book of Mormon

A clear picture that emerges from the Book of Mormon discussion of the presence of the Lord highlights the role of human agency and desire in our relationship to his presence. A consistent theme is that we will not *want* to be in his presence if we are unclean. These comments emphasize the Day of Judgment or the thought of the Day of Judgment as a time when our recognition of our state before God will cause us to recoil from him. Jacob testifies that if we are unclean on the Day of Judgment, we will "shrink with awful fear" because we "remember [our] awful guilt in perfectness, and be constrained to exclaim: Holy, holy are thy judgments, O Lord God Almighty—but I know my guilt; I transgressed thy law, and my transgressions are mine" (2 Nephi 9:46). Alma warns that if we are in that "awful state" of being unclean on the Day of Judgment, we will want "the rocks and the mountains to fall upon us to hide us from his presence" (Alma 12:14). In telling of his conversion, Alma describes how "the very thought of coming into the presence of my God did rack my soul with inexpressible horror" (Alma 36:14). He later warns how justice will be administered on the Day of Judgment and how the unclean will be consigned "forever to be cut off from his presence" (Alma 42:14). The idea that only clean things will be allowed into God's presence seems to be something we will all acknowledge as being right and just.

The overarching message of both the gospel and the Book of Mormon is that God himself does not desire our separation from his presence. The image of Lehi beckoning to his family to come and partake of the fruit emphasizes the central message of the Book of Mormon—that God's arms of mercy are extended to his children (see 2 Nephi 28:32; Jacob 4:47; Jacob 6:4; Mosiah 16:12). Alma expresses the Lord's desire for all his children: "Behold, he sendeth an invitation unto all men, for the arms of mercy are extended towards them, and he saith: Repent, and I will receive you. Yea, he saith: Come unto me and ye shall partake of the fruit of the tree of life" (Alma 5:33). The fruit of the tree is waiting for us if we will trust in the Atonement of Christ and come and partake, rather than choose to perish in our separated and fallen state. The way to be clean and fit for the Lord's presence is prepared for all. Alma invites those not yet in the Church, "Come and be baptized unto repentance, that ye also may be partakers of the fruit of the tree of life" (Alma 5:62). In his very last writing, Mormon reminds us that Christ "hath brought to pass the redemption of the world, whereby he that is found guiltless before him at the judgment day hath it given unto him to dwell in the presence of God in his kingdom" (Mormon 7:7).

The availability of the tree of life suggests that being in God's presence throughout eternity is offered to us, but the options not to come and partake of the fruit or not to stay at the tree are also real. Our choice to receive or not will ultimately determine our fate. Our separation will be an expression of our own desire, not God's desire. The vision of the tree clarifies the reality that agency is the final factor in our eternal status. Mormon's summary reemphasizes this tension between a godly desire for all to enjoy the presence of the Lord and the consequences of agency and human choice. Note how his language echoes that of Lehi: "And I would that all men might be saved. But we read that in the great and last day there are some who shall be cast out, yea, who shall be *cast off from the presence of the Lord*" (Helaman 12:25; emphasis added).

While many of the passages in which the term "presence of the Lord" appears in the Book of Mormon emphasize judgment and the afterlife, some passages seem to focus on our condition in this life. These passages are helpful to note since they show that we need not read being at the tree solely as arriving in the celestial kingdom. When we can see being at the tree and partaking of the fruit as experiencing the presence of the Lord in this life, we get greater insight into how the blessings of the Atonement give us access to the divine presence in mortality.

One critical insight that is frequently repeated in the Book of Mormon is the relationship between being in a state of disobedience and being cut off from the presence of the Lord. Because the English of the Book of Mormon does not give us access to the original terms, it is hard to draw many conclusive findings about why in these places the expression is consistently "cut off" rather than "cast off."[24] The Book of Mormon usage might suggest that the different term ("cut off") represents a temporary condition that can change, because one's rebellion or disobedience may ebb and flow and thus change one's access to the presence of the Lord in mortality.

One of the earliest teachings of Lehi, found in 1 Nephi 2:21, explains the relationship of obedience and access to God's presence: "And inasmuch as thy brethren shall rebel against thee, they shall be cut off from the presence of the Lord." Later in the Book of Mormon we see a fulfillment of this warning, as Alma reminds the people of Ammoniah: "Now I would that ye should remember, that inasmuch as the Lamanites have not kept the commandments of God, they have been cut off from the presence of the Lord. Now we see that the word of the Lord has been verified in this thing, and the Lamanites have been cut off from his presence, from the beginning of their transgressions in the land" (Alma 9:14). Over and over again, our choices are portrayed as affecting our access to the presence of God in this life.

While the negative version of this lesson can seem to be a dominant theme in the Book of Mormon, we do find a beautiful portrayal of the possibility of enjoying God's presence in this life as well. In this epistle from the prophet Helaman to Captain Moroni, the desirability of living in such a way as to always enjoy the presence of the Lord in mortality is captured with a simple prayer for another's well-being: "May the Lord our God . . . keep you continually in his presence" (Alma 58:41).

Again, it is this sense of being in his presence now—of being at the tree and partaking of the fruit now—that we need to read in the message of Lehi's dream, in addition to the ultimate sense of being in his presence forever. But how is it that we are in the presence of the Lord during this life? It may be easier to read the vision of the tree of life in terms of our eternal state, because there we can see ourselves literally in the presence of the Father and the Son in celestial glory forevermore.

Psalm 51 can help us appreciate a central way in which we can enjoy his presence continually in this life. The Psalmist prays, "Cast me not away from thy presence; and take not thy holy spirit from me" (Psalm 51:11). Sometimes we forget the privilege that is ours with the gift of the Holy Ghost. By coming unto Christ with faith, repenting, and partaking of the cleansing power of baptism, we are made fit to be temples of God, to have the presence of the Lord literally within us in the gift of the Holy Ghost (see 1 Corinthians 3:16; 6:19). So while seeking to be in the presence of the Lord can be a quest focusing us on preparing for the next life, it can also focus us on living worthy to be "continually in his presence" in this life as well.

When we understand both the contemporary as well as the future dimensions of reading ourselves into Lehi's vision, we realize that in any time frame we must be clean to be at the tree, to enjoy the presence of the Lord. We also realize that we can have no access to his presence on our own because "all are fallen and are lost" (Alma 34:9). Lehi reminds Jacob, "No flesh . . . can dwell in the presence of God, save it be through the merits, and mercy, and grace of the Holy Messiah" (2 Nephi 2:8). Whether we read being at the tree and partaking of the fruit as enjoying the gift of the Holy Ghost, partaking of the sacrament, entering into holy temples, or being worthy to dwell in celestial realms of glory, access to his presence is made possible only in and through Christ's Atonement.

"Cast Off" in the Book of Mormon

As in the Old Testament, the term "cast off" is also widely used in the Book of Mormon, and a full study would be beyond the scope of this paper. However, it is critical to notice the central place the term holds in framing the message of the Book of Mormon. In the title page of the Book of Mormon, Moroni emphasizes its message of mercy rather than condemnation. He explains that one of the purposes of the Book of Mormon is "to show unto the remnant of the House of Israel what great things the Lord hath done for their fathers; and that they may know the covenants of the Lord, *that they are not cast off forever*" (emphasis added). Just as we focused our examination of "cast off" in the Old Testament on the expression "cast off forever," the introductory sentence of the Book of Mormon suggests the question of our eternal relationship to the presence of the Lord as a major theme of the book.

We started this study with Lehi's expression of concern for Laman and Lemuel, that "he feared lest they should be cast off from the presence of the Lord" (1 Nephi 8:36). We see that concern deepened with Nephi's fear for Laman and Lemuel: "Behold, my soul is rent with anguish because of you, and my heart is pained; *I fear lest ye shall be cast off forever*" (1 Nephi 17:47; emphasis added).

Although a loved one's fear or concern for us may not always be sufficient to change our course of action, it is very important to notice that this is not an idle fear but one that can potentially wake us up to the reality of our situation. The Book of Mormon provides vivid examples of those who experience the fear of being cast off forever. In those who face this reality it brings a realization of the need for mercy and repentance, leading to profound change.

The two clearest examples are also perhaps the most striking instances of deep repentance in the Book of Mormon. They are the examples of the sons of King Mosiah and the father of King Lamoni. We read that the sons of King Mosiah were able to experience mercy, precisely because they began to understand justice. "They were desirous that salvation should be declared to every creature, for they could not bear that any human soul should perish; yea, even the very thoughts that any soul should endure endless torment did cause them to quake and tremble" (Mosiah 28:3). The consequences of sin were very real for them. They knew from personal experience what it was like to be cast off from the presence of God. "And thus did the Spirit of the Lord work upon them, for they were the very vilest of sinners. And the Lord saw fit in his infinite mercy to spare them; nevertheless they suffered much anguish of soul because of their iniquities, suffering much and *fearing that they should be cast off forever*" (Mosiah 28:4; emphasis added). They had experienced being cast off in mortality and did not want to remain in that state forever.

We see the power of the fear of eternal separation from God, or being "cast off forever," also working on the father of King Lamoni to bring him down to repentance. We learn that Ammon had taught him that "if ye will repent ye shall be saved, and if ye will not repent, ye shall be cast off at the last day" (Alma 22:6). As Aaron continued to work with the father of King Lamoni, he taught him the good news of God's mercy, coupled with a message of justice—the reality of where we would be without Christ—"laying the fall of man before him, and their carnal state and also the plan of redemption, which was prepared from the foundation of the world, through Christ, for all whosoever would believe on his name. And since man had fallen he could not merit anything of himself; but the sufferings and death of Christ atone for their sins, through faith and repentance, and so forth" (vv. 13–14).

Aaron's message was a second witness of the reality of justice, of being eternally cast off from God, combined with the mercy of Christ's redemption, which gives us hope of again being restored to God's presence. Only this direct message of choices and consequences could bring about such a mighty change. "And it came to pass that after Aaron had expounded these things unto him, the king said: What shall I do that I may have this eternal life of which thou hast spoken? Yea, what shall I do that I may be born of God, having this wicked spirit rooted out of my breast, and receive his Spirit, that I may be filled with joy, *that I may not be cast off at the last day*? Behold, said he, I will give up all that I possess, yea, I will forsake my kingdom, that I may receive this great joy" (v. 15; emphasis added).

It is striking that the father of King Lamoni understood that through the power of Christ's redemption he could have access to the presence of God not only in the eternities but also right now. Note that the hope of not being "cast off at the last day" is paired with the immediate hope of receiving his Spirit and being filled with joy. Think of the experience of those partaking of the fruit of the tree; Lehi says, "As I partook of the fruit thereof it filled my soul with exceedingly great joy" (1 Nephi 8:12).

As Latter-day Saints, testifying of a loving, merciful Father and a compassionate, self-sacrificing Son of God, we rarely use phrases such as "fear of God" or "wrath of God." As we have seen in Psalms, the terms associated with God's justice in casting people off forever can seem contrary to our understanding of God. "Will the Lord cast off for ever? and will he be favourable no more? Is his mercy clean gone for ever? doth his promise fail for evermore? Hath God forgotten to be gracious? hath he in anger shut up his tender mercies?" (Psalm 77:7–9).

Our fear should be about the right thing—not about God's relation to us, but about ours to him. The Book of Mormon provides a means of understanding the message of mercy and justice taught in the Bible. Again, the title page states that the Book of Mormon is designed "to show unto the remnant of the House of Israel what great things the Lord hath done for their fathers; and that they may know the covenants of the Lord, *that they are not cast off forever*" (emphasis added). Our fear should not be about God's disposition, but about ours.

A striking example that "casting off forever" is the result of our actions and not the Lord's can be seen in an additional line of Isaiah 50, also found in 2 Nephi 7:1: "Yea, for thus saith the Lord: *Have I put thee away, or have I cast thee off forever?* For thus saith the Lord: Where is the bill of your mother's divorcement? To whom have I put thee away, or to which of my creditors have I sold you? Yea, to whom have I sold you? Behold, for your iniquities have ye sold yourselves, and for your transgressions is your mother put away" (emphasis added). It is very significant that the first line does not appear in the biblical manuscripts as they have been preserved. In the King James Version, chapter 50 of Isaiah begins, "Thus saith the Lord: Where is the bill of your mother's divorcement?" The additional Book of Mormon phrase emphasizes the central doctrinal question of whose agency is at work when we find ourselves in a state of separation, of "being cast off." Has *he* cast us off forever?

With this additional sentence the principle taught is still the same—it is human agency, not divine will that has brought about the rupture in our relationship with the Lord—but the additional phrase perfectly captures the central Book of Mormon message we find encapsulated in Lehi's vision. Laman and Lemuel were separated from the presence of the Lord because "*they would not* come unto me and partake of the fruit" (1 Nephi 8:18; emphasis added).

We must be careful in how we read the modal verb "would" in this sentence. It does not talk about their destiny not to come. In modern-day English we use "would" or "will" to express future tense, but *will* also means "what we *want*"; its root is the German verb *willlen*. Laman and Lemuel did not come because they did not *want* to come. Their state of being "cast off from the presence of the Lord" was not because the Lord cast them off, but because they rejected him.

This doctrinal emphasis is perhaps one of the most consistent and important threads of the Book of Mormon. It is our desires that determine our destiny. We are offered the path to the tree of life—faith, repentance, and covenants with the Lord. But it is our choice to accept or refuse that covenant path that determines our status—whether we are "cast off" or we enter into the "presence of the Lord."

This principle, that choosing faith in Christ and repenting is the only means of getting access to his presence, is clearly taught by Nephi, who explained "that as many of the Gentiles as *will* repent are the covenant people of the Lord; and as many of the Jews as *will not* repent shall be cast off; for the Lord covenanteth with none save it be with them that repent and believe in his Son, who is the Holy One of Israel" (2 Nephi 30:2; emphasis added). The Lord wants "the remnant of the House of Israel" to know "that they are *not cast off forever*" on his part. But the choice to accept his gift of mercy remains on our part. Just as in Lehi's dream, where only following the path will lead to the tree, at the end, only faith and repentance will determine our access to the presence of the Lord.

Conclusion

The soberness of this reality appears often in the writings of Book of Mormon prophets. They repeatedly warn that if we do not choose to come unto Christ and become clean through him, then not only *shall* we be cast off, but we *must* be cast off. Nephi testifies, "If ye have sought to do wickedly in the days of your probation, then ye are found unclean before the judgment-seat of God; and no unclean thing can dwell with God; wherefore, ye *must be* cast off forever" (1 Nephi 10:21; emphasis added). Nephi explains to his brothers that "if they should die in their wickedness they *must be* cast off also, as to the things which are spiritual, which are pertaining to righteousness; wherefore, they must be brought to stand before God, to be judged of their works; and if their works have been filthiness they *must needs be* filthy; and if they be filthy it *must needs be* that they cannot dwell in the kingdom of God; if so, the kingdom of God *must be* filthy also" (1 Nephi 15:33; emphasis added).

Alma the Younger learned for himself that his eternal access to God's presence was in his own hands when the angel warned him, "Go thy way, and seek to destroy the church no more, that their prayers may be answered, and this even *if thou wilt* of thyself be cast off" (Mosiah 27:16; emphasis added). When Alma awoke from his conversion experience, he testified that escape from eternal banishment was possible only through being born again: "Marvel not that all mankind, yea, men and women, all nations, kindreds, tongues and people, must be born again; yea, born of God, changed from their carnal and fallen state, to a state of righteousness, being redeemed of God, becoming his sons and daughters; and thus they become new creatures; and unless they do this, they can in nowise inherit the kingdom of God. I say unto you, unless this be the case, they *must be* cast off; and this I know, because I was like to be cast off" (vv. 25–26; emphasis added).

These passages send a clear and consistent message about choices and consequences. But the sharp dichotomy of the Book of Mormon worldview can sometimes sound harsh in the context of the restored gospel and might end up sounding like a message of heaven or hell. What sense are we to make of this stark Book of Mormon division of the "presence of the Lord" and being "cast off," given the Restoration nuances of postmortal life found in sections 76 and 88 of the Doctrine and Covenants? We learn from these scriptures that, in a sense, all who inherit a degree of glory *will* enjoy a degree of the presence of God, whether it be the presence of the Son in the terrestrial kingdom or the presence of the Holy Ghost in the telestial kingdom (see D&C 76:77, 86). In this sense, being fully cast off forever would only apply to those in outer darkness.

But choosing to receive less is also choosing to separate oneself from the fullness of God's presence. That outcome is *not* God's goal or plan for any of his children, but allowing us to choose for ourselves is. Mormon wrote, "I would that all men might be saved. But we read that in the great and last day there are some who shall be cast out, yea, who shall be cast off from the presence of the Lord" (Helaman 12:25). Like the temple, Lehi's dream lays out for us a model or template of spiritual reality. Just as Lehi beckoned to his family to come and partake of the fruit, God wishes our salvation and makes it available to us through the gift of his Son. We need to learn about that offer and then choose to come unto Christ and partake of his salvation (see 2 Nephi 26:24, 27; Omni 1:26). "The way is prepared from the fall of man, and salvation is free" (2 Nephi 2:4). But just like those on the path toward the tree, to partake of that gift we must choose to follow the way through our obedience to the principles and ordinances of the gospel—faith, repentance, and making and keeping covenants—allowing ourselves to be made clean and become fit to enter into the presence of the Lord and partake of the kind of life that he enjoys.

The offer is real, and so is our choice. After seeing his family's spiritual state played out in the vision of the tree of life, Lehi feared for Laman and Lemuel "lest they should be cast off from the presence of the Lord" (1 Nephi 8:36). It was a real fear because it was a real possibility. At that point there was no fixed outcome. It was still their choice. Like our loving Father in Heaven, Father Lehi could "call, persuade, direct aright, and bless with wisdom, love, and light, in nameless ways be good and kind," but he could not choose for his sons. Lehi's dream testifies that God "will never force the human mind."[25]

Notes

1. See E. F. Harrison, "Presence of God," in *International Standard Bible Encyclopedia*, ed. Geoffrey W. Bromiley (Grand Rapids, MI: Eerdmans, 1986), 3:956;

and Joel F. Drinkard, "Face," in *The Anchor Bible Dictionary*, ed. David Noel Freedman (New York: Doubleday, 1992), 2:743.

2. Drinkard, "Face," 2:743.

3. Horacio Simian-Yofre, "Pānîm," in *Theological Dictionary of the Old Testament*, ed. G. Johannes Botterweck, Helber Ringgren, and Heinz-Joseph Fabry, trans. David E. Green (Grand Rapids, MI: Eerdmans, 2001), 11:591.

4. "In Exod 33:16 the Lord said that his face (NIV my Presence) would go with Moses. This means that God himself would accompany Moses. The expression is used in the same way in Isa 63:9 and Lam 4:16. In Deut 4:37 Moses said that God led the people from Egypt through his face (NIV his Presence) and his great power. His face is equated with his power as the means through which God did his mighty deeds." Harry F. van Rooy, "Panim," in *New International Dictionary of Old Testament Theology and Exegesis*, ed. Willem A. VanGemeren (Grand Rapids, MI: Zondervan, 1997), 3:638–39.

5. Simian-Yofre, "Pānîm," 11:607.

6. "All the fundamental relationships between God and human beings can be described by *pānîm* and its associated expressions." Simian-Yofre, "Pānîm," 11:607.

7. Simian-Yofre, "Pānîm," 11:607.

8. Simian-Yofre, "Pānîm," 11:603.

9. Drinkard, "Face," 2:743.

10. Simian-Yofre, "Pānîm," 11:604.

11. This can be both with and without bringing a sacrifice. "The expression . . . is used to state that someone is appearing before the Lord. This usually meant in a cultic sense, to appear in the sanctuary during a festival (Exod 34:20, 24; Deut 16:16; 31:11) or when bringing a sacrifice (Isa 1:12). Hannah also used this expression for her son's appearance in the temple (1 Sam 1:22)." Van Rooy, "Pānîm," 3:639.

12. Drinkard, "Face," 2:743. On *lipne* and *panim*, see Simian-Yofre, "Pānîm," 11:608–9. On its role in covenants, see Simian-Yofre, "Pānîm," 11:610.

13. Simian-Yofre, "Pānîm," 11:610.

14. Simian-Yofre, "Pānîm," 11:606, see also 609–10.

15. Simian-Yofre, "Pānîm," 11:598.

16. Psalm 42 "voices an intense yearning, not found in other texts, to behold the face of Yahweh. The cultic aspect is present in the allusion to the temple (v. 5[4]), the assurance of appearing before the altar of God (43:4), and liturgical praise (*ydh*)." Simian-Yofre, "Pānîm," 11:605.

17. See Helmer Ringgren, "Zanach," in *Theological Dictionary of the Old Testament* (Grand Rapids, MI: Eerdmans, 1980), 4:105; and Eugene H. Merrill, "Zanach," in *New International Dictionary of Old Testament Theology and Exegesis*, 1:1126–27.

18. Rueven Yaron argues that in most cases it is best to understand *zanach* in light of the Akkadian cognate, *zenû*, "to be angry," rather than "to abandon." "The Meaning of Zanah," *Vetus Testamentum* 13, no. 2 (April 1963): 237–39. This is not universally agreed upon. Some argue that it is better understood as "reject" or "spurn" and that Assyrian "*zinû*, to be angry" is not connected. Francis Brown, Samuel R. Driver, and Charles A. Briggs, "Zanach," in *A Hebrew English Lexicon of the Old Testament* (Oxford: Clarendon, 1968), 276. Ringgren considers Yaron's suggestion of following the Akkadian reading of 'hate' as a possible meaning "not certain, but likely." "Zanach," 4:105. Merrill notes that

cognates have been suggested in Arabic and Akkadian, but does not suggest any meaning of anger in the Biblical Hebrew period. Merrill, "Zanach," 1:1126–27.

19. Merrill, "Zanach," 1:1126.
20. Ringgren, "Zanach," 4:105.
21. Ringgren, "Zanach," 4:105.
22. Ringgren, "Zanach," 4:106.
23. Ringgren, "Zanach," 4:106.
24. The phrase "cut off from the presence of the Lord" appears in Leviticus 22:2–3, describing the holiness required by the priests and Levites to officiate in the temple and be near the sacred offerings: "Speak unto Aaron and to his sons, that they separate themselves from the holy things of the children of Israel, and that they profane not my holy name in those things which they hallow unto me: I am the Lord. Say unto them, Whosoever he be of all your seed among your generations, that goeth unto the holy things, which the children of Israel hallow unto the Lord, having his uncleanness upon him, that soul shall be cut off from my presence: I am the Lord." The verb here for "cut off" is *karat*, which, in addition to "cut off," can also mean "cut down," as in trees. It is also the verb for cutting used in "cutting or making a covenant." Brown, Driver, and Briggs, *Hebrew English Lexicon of the Old Testament*, 503.

John E. Hartley argues that "defilement of the holy carries the severe cut-off penalty (cf. 7:20–21). Never again could such an offender serve at the altar." "Leviticus," in *Word Biblical Commentary* (Nashville, TN: Thomas Nelson, 1987), 4:355. Jacob Milgrom believes that being "cut off" in this context for priests implies "the end of his line ... or death by divine agency." *Anchor Bible Dictionary*, vol. 3a, *Leviticus 17–22: A New Translation with Introduction and Commentary* (New York: Doubleday, 2000), 1850.

25. "Know This, That Every Soul Is Free," *Hymns* (Salt Lake City: The Church of Jesus Christ of Latter-day Saints, 1985), no. 240.

8

The Strait and Narrow Path: The Covenant Path of Discipleship Leading to the Tree of Life

Aaron Schade

The visions and interpretations of the tree of life constitute some of the greatest didactic, or teaching, chapters in the Book of Mormon. The symbols and images in these chapters inspire us to reflect and ponder the rich messages that lie behind the tree of life's meaning. The theme and timing of this conference are appropriate, as over the last few years, there have been significant statements made by leaders of the Church in relation to the interpretation and application of the tree of life visions.[1] Much can be written about these visions, but this paper will focus on one central theme: the strait and narrow path as the covenant path of discipleship leading to the tree of life. What that means is simply this: God has prepared a way, a path, that can bring us, his children, back into his presence in a state of immortality. That way is through the Atonement of Christ and the covenantal system that he has set up (see Articles of Faith 1:3, 4). Joseph Fielding McConkie and Robert L. Millet state that in the vision of the tree of life, "partaking of the fruit of the tree . . . represent[s] the partaking of the powers of Christ and his atonement: forgiveness of sins, as well as feelings of peace, joy, and gratitude.

Aaron Schade is department chair of Religious Education at Brigham Young University–Hawaii.

Ultimately, through partaking of the powers of the gospel one is qualified to partake of the *greatest fruit* of the Atonement—the blessings associated with eternal life."[2] Thus there is a difference between the immediate and future occurrences of partaking of the fruit associated with the covenantal nature inherent in the process. Elder Bruce R. McConkie elucidates the meaning of the final partaking of the fruit: "To eat thereof is to inherit eternal life in the kingdom of God."[3]

Through the vision of the tree of life, we enter the world of symbolism underlying the necessary discipleship that leads to exaltation. If we carefully examine the vision, the pathway leading to the tree of life seems to reflect the covenant road (which leads to eternal salvation in God's presence) rather than to describe the rough roads of life (where we are to do good and avoid temptations to the best of our ability). Thus, on the path of discipleship, "enduring to the end" has a greater covenantal significance. In discussing Lehi's dream, it should be stated that the covenant path not only symbolizes ordinances and covenants but also represents the lifestyle of one who has entered, and continues to enter, into those ordinances and covenants with God throughout the course of life—one who moves forward on that path and attempts to stay faithful to the end of this mortal journey. The strait and narrow path and the iron rod are components of the dream that make obtaining the fruit of the tree possible. Elder Neal A. Maxwell described the path of discipleship in these terms:

> Deeds, not words—and becoming, not describing—are dominant in true discipleship. Of necessity, of course, we are to teach and learn the doctrines. We would be spiritually stranded without them and, likewise, without the saving and exalting gospel ordinances, because 'in the ordinances thereof, the power of godliness is manifest. And without the ordinances thereof, and the authority of the priesthood, the power of godliness is not manifest unto men in the flesh' (D&C 84:20–21). So it is that discipleship requires all of us to translate doctrines, covenants, ordinances, and teachings into improved personal behavior. Otherwise we may be doctrinally rich but end up developmentally poor. . . . The gospel's rich and true doctrines combine to constitute a call to a new and more abundant life, but this is a lengthy process. It requires much time, experiencing the relevant learning experiences, the keeping of covenants, and the receiving of

the essential ordinances—all in order to spur us along the discipleship path of personal progression.[4]

The necessity of staying on the path of discipleship is highlighted in Lehi's dream as he witnesses individuals partake of the fruit of the tree and then fall away from the path. The people partaking of the fruit of the tree are a representation of individuals who had taken upon themselves all of the ordinances and covenants necessary to qualify for eternal life (thus receiving conditional blessings contingent upon obedience and enduring to the end). Because they fall away, these individuals do not witness the ultimate fulfillment of those blessings (receiving exaltation in the presence of God and entering into the rest of the Lord). President Joseph F. Smith highlighted the meaning of entering into the Lord's rest in both immediate and future contexts:

> What does it mean to enter into the rest of the Lord? Speaking for myself, it means that through the love of God I have been won over to Him, so that I can feel at rest in Christ, that I may no more be disturbed by every wind of doctrine, by the cunning and craftiness of men, whereby they lie in wait to deceive; and that I am established in the knowledge and testimony of Jesus Christ, so that no power can turn me aside from the straight and narrow path that leads back into the presence of God, to enjoy exaltation in His glorious kingdom; that from this time henceforth I shall enjoy that rest until I shall *rest* with Him in the heavens.[5]

Lehi's vision teaches of fidelity to covenants—a topic applicable to all. As President Boyd K. Packer has taught, "You may think that Lehi's dream or vision has no special meaning for you, but it does. You are in it; all of us are in it."[6]

An Overview of the Tree of Life: From Eden to Eternal Life

The tree of life motif permeated ancient societies, including Israel and Egypt.[7] Sacred trees were associated with the dwelling place of deities, and, like the agricultural connections inherent in the motif of the sacred trees' power to rejuvenate each season, so also the tree became a symbol of resurrection after death, rebirth into immortality, and eternity (Representations of these concepts were often portrayed on sarcophagi and epithets).[8] In connection with God's giving and sustaining of life, the tree of life is commonly linked to rituals and cultic objects within temples. An example of this is the Menorah in the Israelite temple, which is frequently viewed as a stylized tree of life. The light that falls on the twelve loaves beneath the Menorah symbolizes God's power sustaining the twelve tribes of Israel (both temporally and spiritually).[9] Rituals, and the keeping of the laws attached to them, enabled individuals to obtain the tree of life. The Jerusalem Targum on Genesis 2:9 states, "For the law is the tree of life; whoever keepeth it in this life liveth and subsisteth as the tree of life. The law is good to keep in this world, as the fruit of the tree of life in the world that cometh."[10] The law required worship associated with the temple, and the law itself was originally housed in the ark of the covenant in the Holy of Holies, thus highlighting its relevance to the temple and demonstrating its place in leading one back to God (the very symbol depicted in the architecture of the temple). New Testament writings, such as Revelation chapter 2, have also linked salvation with sacred ritual and the partaking of the fruit of the tree of life.[11] Furthermore, Reformation theologians including Calvin, Polanus, Wolleb, and Diodati viewed the tree of life as a type of eternal life, a sacrament that would extend immortality to the obedient through Jesus Christ.[12]

The tree of life image also abounds in other religious texts; the sacred nature of this symbolic depiction of eternal life is highlighted in the rituals that underlie temple worship in ancient societies. This literature of the tree of life reflects the fact that ritual is necessary to obtain the tree.[13] Griggs summarizes a few Egyptian iconographic examples of this notion: "Many other Egyptian artifacts show divine beings refreshing the pharaohs with the fruit of the tree of life. A pond or stream of sacred water often lies near or under the tree, with the god of writing, Thoth, inscribing the name of the king on the tree. In all these examples, partaking of the fruit of the tree is a sacramental act, one that symbolizes unity with the gods; hence, the fruit is not available to mortals in the normal course of daily life but can be found only in the rituals relating to eternity."[14] Ritual that would lead the worshipper, or devotee, into the presence of God or the eternities, portrayed by the means of a tree of life, was a concept fairly common in the region.[15]

In the scriptural record, the tree of life is first encountered in the Garden of Eden (see Moses 4:31; Genesis 3:22). There Adam and Eve enjoyed association with God, and the tree of life highlighted their immortal existence with him.[16] Because of the Fall, Adam and Eve were cast out from his presence and could no longer enjoy face-to-face communication with him. Adam and Eve lost access to the tree of life and the blessing of immortality; death would then enter their lives. Their subsequent mortality would become a preparatory state for their eventual return to immortality (the tree of life) and the presence of God (eternal life; see Moses 4:30–31).

In order for Adam and Eve and their posterity, who would inherit this condition of separation, to reenter God's presence, it was necessary to provide a way to overcome and reverse the effects of the Fall (see 2 Nephi 2:21). The gospel of Jesus Christ, which includes both covenants and ordinances, would constitute the path back to the tree of life, and thus the Atonement of Jesus Christ would become the mechanism to open up that way.[17] Through the Atonement of Christ, the obstacles of sin and death could, and would, be removed for all individuals who would claim the Atonement's blessings (see Moses 7:1; D&C 19:16–19). Remembrance of the Atonement became a form of discipleship symbolically manifested in the worship system that required Adam and Eve to participate in "the plan of salvation unto all men, through the blood of mine Only Begotten, who shall come in the meridian of time" (Moses 6:62). Adam and Eve, and subsequently their posterity, offered sacrifices in similitude of the sacrifice of the Son of God (see Moses 5:7–8), were baptized and received the Holy Ghost (see Moses 6:65–66), and entered into the order of the priesthood (see Moses 6:67). All of this was done "by an holy ordinance, and the Gospel preached" (Moses 5:59). Consequently, the Lord commanded "that all men, everywhere, must repent, or they can in nowise inherit the kingdom of God, for no unclean thing can dwell there, or dwell in his presence" (Moses 6:57). The Lord also taught them:

> That by reason of transgression cometh the fall, which fall bringeth death, and inasmuch as ye were born into the world by water, and blood, and the spirit, which I have made, and so became of dust a living soul, even so ye must be born again into the kingdom of heaven, of water, and of the Spirit, and be cleansed by blood, even the blood of mine Only Begotten; that ye might be sanctified from all sin, and enjoy the words of eternal life in this world, and eternal life in the world to come, even immortal glory;
>
> For by the water ye keep the commandment; by the Spirit ye are justified, and by the blood ye are sanctified. (Moses 6:59–60)[18]

The entire gospel plan given to Adam and Eve, and subsequently to all of us, constituted a path that would enable them to claim all of the blessings of the Atonement by allowing them to take upon themselves the candidacy of eternal life through ordinances. They would enjoy the consummation of those promises at the end of life if they endured to the end. As Elder McConkie stated:

> Adam and Eve—our first parents, our common ancestors, the mother and father of all living—had the fulness of the everlasting gospel. They received the plan of salvation from God himself. . . . They saw God, knew his laws, entertained angels, received revelations, beheld visions, and were in tune with the Infinite. They exercised faith in the Lord Jesus Christ; repented of their sins; were baptized in similitude of the death, burial, and resurrection of the Promised Messiah; and received the gift of the Holy Ghost. They were endowed with power from on high, were sealed in the new and everlasting covenant of marriage, and received the fulness of the ordinances of the house of the Lord. . . .
>
> Having charted for themselves a course leading to eternal life, they pressed forward with a steadfastness in Christ—believing, obeying, conforming, consecrating, sacrificing—until their calling and election was made sure and they were sealed up unto eternal life.[19]

From the time Adam and Eve were driven away from the tree of life and the presence of God, the covenant path was established to lead them back again to him in a renewed state of immortality.[20] In the *Vita Adae et Evae*, Adam is told, after partaking of the fruit of the tree of knowledge of good and evil, that he would return to partake of the fruit of the tree of life after his resurrection:

> And the Lord turned and said to Adam, "From now on I will not allow you to be in Paradise." And Adam answered and said, "Lord, give me from the tree of life that I might eat before I am cast out." Then the Lord spoke to Adam, "You shall not now take from it; for it was appointed to the cherubim and the flaming sword which turns to guard it because of you, that you might not taste of it and be immortal forever, but that you might have the strife which the enemy has placed in you. But when you come out of Paradise, if you guard

yourself from all evil, preferring death to it, at the time of the resurrection I will raise you again, and then there shall be given to you from the tree of life, and you shall be immortal forever."[21]

For Adam and Eve, the journey back to the presence of God was (and is for each of us) to take place on the road of discipleship, a road that would lead them to partake of the fruit of the tree in this life and in the life to come.[22]

Getting on the Path Leading to the Tree of Life: Baptism and Pressing Forward

In the Book of Mormon, the dreams and interpretations of partaking of the fruit of the tree of life seem to carry the same ritualistic connotations as they did in other ancient Near Eastern cultures. In 1 Nephi 8:21, Lehi states that he saw "numberless concourses of people, many of whom were pressing forward, that they might obtain the path which led unto the tree by which I stood." This description highlights the fact that not all people were on the path and that significant effort was being exerted by concourses of people pressing forward just to obtain and get on it. Second Nephi 31:9, 15–21 describe the gateway that brings one *onto* the path and underscores the covenant nature underlying the process. Nephi, at the latter end of his life, discusses the essential nature of baptism and specifically draws upon motifs from the dream of the tree of life to incorporate how the Savior's baptism "showeth unto the children of men the straitness of the path, and the narrowness of the gate, by which they should enter, he having set the example before them" and that "the gate by which ye should enter is repentance and baptism by water; and then cometh a remission of your sins by fire and by the Holy Ghost. And *then* are ye in this strait and narrow path which leads to eternal life; yea, ye have entered in by the gate; ye have done according to the commandments of the Father and the Son" (2 Nephi 31:9, 17–18; emphasis added).

Elder L. Tom Perry further clarifies the concept that baptism, both by water and by fire, gets one on the path:

> The ordinance of baptism by *water and fire* is described as a gate by Nephi (see 2 Nephi 31:17). Why is baptism a gate? Because it is an ordinance denoting entry into a sacred and binding covenant between God and man. Men promise to forsake the world, love and serve their fellowmen, visit the fatherless and the widows in their afflictions,

proclaim peace, preach the gospel, serve the Lord, and keep His commandments. The Lord promises to "pour out his Spirit more abundantly upon [us]" (Mosiah 18:10), redeem His Saints both temporally and spiritually, number them with those of the First Resurrection and offer life eternal. Baptism and receiving the Holy Ghost are the prescribed ways to enter the strait and narrow path to eternal life.[23]

This statement describes the path as a covenantal road that leads to the tree of life and makes it clear that it is entered through baptism. Second Nephi 31:19–21 then describes the necessity of traversing the path and enduring to the end by feasting upon the word of Christ (holding the iron rod), as there is no other name or way given to obtain eternal life. In 2 Nephi 33:6–7, 9, Nephi glorifies in Christ, who has redeemed his soul from hell, and describes his charity and hope for others as they also become reconciled unto Christ, enter into the narrow gate, and endure in the strait path leading to eternal life.[24]

Elder McConkie expounded upon the principle of entering and pressing forward on the covenantal path:

> As far as you and I are concerned, at this time, this life is the most important part of all eternity. We have the light and knowledge and revelations of heaven. This life is the time for us to prepare to meet God, to keep the commandments of God, to hearken to the counsels of the living oracles and to press forward in righteousness.
>
> The plan of salvation is to find the truth; and the Latter-day Saints have found it. It is to accept the truth; and we have accepted it in the waters of baptism by covenant, a covenant that we will keep the commandments of God. The remaining step is to endure to the end, in righteousness and in faithfulness. Nephi said that repentance and baptism are the gate to salvation, and that having entered in by the gate, men are then in the straight and narrow path which leads to eternal life. We Latter-day Saints have entered in by the gate. We are now on the path. It remains for us to press forward with a steadfastness in Christ, having a perfect brightness of hope, and a love of God and of all men. It remains for us to press forward, feasting upon the words of Christ, and endure to the end, which if we do, we will gain eternal life.[25]

The dreams of the tree of life in the Book of Mormon seem to reflect the following concept: ordinances, covenants, and living the gospel of Jesus Christ constitute the life of discipleship leading along the strait and narrow path to the tree of life.[26]

Staying on the Path

A major theme of tree of life dreams revolves around staying on the path leading to the tree. Just as Nephi clarified that one gets on the path to eternal life through baptism, he explained that this is only the beginning of the covenant path:

> And now, my beloved brethren, after ye have gotten into this strait and narrow path, I would ask if all is done? Behold, I say unto you, Nay....
>
> Wherefore, ye must press forward with a steadfastness in Christ, having a perfect brightness of hope, and a love of God and of all men. Wherefore, if ye shall press forward, feasting upon the word of Christ,[27] and endure to the end, behold, thus saith the Father: Ye shall have eternal life....
>
> This is the way; and there is none other way nor name given under heaven whereby man can be saved in the kingdom of God. (2 Nephi 31:19–21)

Elder David A. Bednar describes the need to look to future responsibilities that attend entering the covenant at baptism and enduring to the end—these responsibilities involve the temple. He expounded upon the nature of the gathering of Israel and taught the principle of worshipping in the temple using an analogy given in the Book of Mormon:

> This essential relationship between the principle of gathering and the building of temples is highlighted in the Book of Mormon:
>
> "Behold, the field was ripe, and blessed are ye, for ye did thrust in the sickle, and did reap with your might, yea, all the day long did ye labor; and behold the number of your sheaves! And they shall be gathered into the garners, that they are not wasted" (Alma 26:5).
>
> The sheaves in this analogy represent newly baptized members of the Church. The garners are the holy temples. Elder Neal A. Maxwell explained: "Clearly, when we baptize, our eyes should gaze beyond

the baptismal font to the holy temple. The great garner into which the sheaves should be gathered is the holy temple." . . . This instruction clarifies and emphasizes the importance of sacred temple ordinances and covenants. . . .

The baptismal covenant clearly contemplates a future event or events and looks forward to the temple. . . . As we stand in the waters of baptism, we look to the temple. As we partake of the sacrament, we look to the temple. We pledge to always remember the Savior and to keep His commandments as preparation to participate in the sacred ordinances of the temple and receive the highest blessings available through the name and by the authority of the Lord Jesus Christ. Thus, in the ordinances of the holy temple we more completely and fully take upon us the name of Jesus Christ.[28]

Elder McConkie clarifies how we progress along the covenantal path and how entering into more covenants is a part of this process: "As with baptism, so it is with celestial marriage. It opens the door, a second door. It starts one out in the direction of exaltation. It puts one on the path that leads to eternal life. You cannot get on the path without entering the gate, but having entered the gate then you must traverse the length of the path. The process of going up that path is the process of keeping the covenant made in connection with this holy order of matrimony. It is the process of obeying the laws, commandments, principles, and ordinances of the gospel."[29]

It seems evident that the ancients viewed the path leading to the tree as a covenantal road of discipleship that found its consummation in the exaltation of all the obedient who entered into and remained faithful in the kingdom of God throughout their days. This is also consistent with the application of the dream in latter-day prophetic interpretations.[30]

As we witness the context in which Lehi's vision of the tree of life occurs, we see that it fits into the theme of staying on the path and enduring to the end through the hardships he and his family were facing. In 1 Nephi 2:10, in the valley which Lehi named Lemuel, he pleaded with his son to remain faithful, "And he also spake unto Lemuel: O that thou mightest be like unto this valley, firm and steadfast, and immovable in keeping the commandments of the Lord!"

Just before Lehi explains his dream to his family, he states that he has reason to rejoice because of Nephi and Sam but then expresses the concern he has for Laman and Lemuel (see 1 Nephi 8:3–4). After explaining the dream to his family, Lehi expresses concern once again as "he feared lest they should be cast off from the presence of the Lord" (1 Nephi 8:36). Lehi desperately attempted to get Laman and Lemuel to hearken unto his words, both as a loving father and as a prophet (playing the part of a key component of the dream—the iron rod), that they may not be "cast off from the presence of the Lord."[31] This term seems to imply that Laman and Lemuel had access to the Lord; this takes us back to the scene of the Fall, in which Adam and Eve were cast out of Garden of Eden and driven from the presence of the Lord and the tree of life, and thus situates the content of the dream in this light.[32]

A literary device referred to as *framing* highlights the fact that Lehi's dream was, in fact, speaking to his sons and family members who were already in the covenant; this accentuates Lehi's pleas for faithfulness and endurance, lessons that are the very essence of the dream. We get some indication of this as we witness the beginning of Nephi's experience with the dream (which came after his father's experience): "And all these things did my father see, and hear, and speak, as he dwelt in a tent, in the valley of Lemuel, and also a great many more things, which cannot be written upon these plates" (1 Nephi 9:1). The reference to the valley of Lemuel, where Lehi encouraged Lemuel to be diligent in keeping the commandments, acts as the point of reference that helps bring into focus the entire meaning of the tree of life. Nephi is about to come to understand this meaning through a series of visions and dreams. He states, "For behold, it came to pass after my father had made an end of speaking the words of his dream, and also of exhorting them to all diligence, he spake unto them concerning the Jews" (1 Nephi 10:2). Lehi's exhortations to be diligent are followed by results stemming from disobedience. In the heading for chapter 10 we read the following: "Lehi predicts the Babylonian captivity—He tells of the coming among the Jews of a Messiah, a Savior, a Redeemer—He tells also of the coming of the one who should baptize the Lamb of God—Lehi tells of the death and resurrection of the Messiah—He compares the scattering and gathering of Israel to an olive tree—Nephi speaks of the Son of God, of the gift of the Holy Ghost, and of the need for righteousness."

Nephi's experience in coming to understand the dream takes him into the realms of individuals and peoples who wander off the path and are brought back onto it through the process of being gathered into the covenant through the gospel of Jesus Christ. This gives us glimpses into the magnificent nature of the dream: it is about individuals who are provided firsthand information as to *how* to come to the tree of life, get on the path to eternal life (see 1 Nephi 15:14), stay on the path, and avoid temptations; however, it also speaks of nations and peoples who apostatized and are to be restored through the covenant, drawing upon the marvelous image encountered in Jacob 5 and the allegory of the olive tree (see 1 Nephi 10:12). The dream thus includes phases of apostasy and restoration cycles.[33] In the next several chapters, Nephi will have the dream explained to him by angels and visions. These will include episodes of the tree of life, the birth and life of the Son of God, the advent of the Twelve Apostles, the great and abominable church, the Apostasy, the colonization of the Americas, the grafting in of the natural branches of the olive tree (see 1 Nephi 15:16), and the Restoration of the gospel in the latter days. Nephi concludes all of these visions and explanations in the following manner: "Wherefore, the wicked are rejected from the righteous, and also from that tree of life, whose fruit is most precious and most desirable above all other fruits; yea, and it is the greatest of all the gifts of God. And thus I spake unto my brethren. Amen" (1 Nephi 15:36).[34]

After Laman and Lemuel inform Nephi that he has spoken hard things, through the framing device, Nephi draws our attention back to the valley of Lemuel and the message of diligence in keeping the commandments proclaimed there by his father, the prophet: "And it came to pass that I, Nephi, did exhort my brethren, with all diligence, to keep the commandments of the Lord. And it came to pass that they did humble themselves before the Lord; insomuch that I had joy and great hopes of them, that they would *walk in the paths of righteousness*. Now, all these things were said and done as my father dwelt in a tent in the valley which he called Lemuel" (1 Nephi 16:4–6).[35]

The framing device thus seems to help us wrap our minds around the overall meaning of the vision: diligence on the covenant path leading to exaltation. Nephi hopes that his brothers will get back on that path after their murmuring had taken them off of it. This is really the challenge Lehi's family is facing: staying on the covenant road when so many hardships and doubts (manifested as the mists of darkness within the dream) are leading some of them away from it. Lehi and Nephi knew there was still much to be done and many promises to be fulfilled and they refused to stray off the path leading to the tree of life. At this point in the story, the interpretation of the dream is over. Its content, however, will occupy the teachings of Book of Mormon prophets throughout the rest of their history.[36]

The Iron Rod

It is essential for us to stay on the path and endure to the end by making and keeping sacred covenants. This section deals with a component of the dream that explains *how* to stay on the covenant path and avoid getting lost—the iron rod. Nephi explained, "And it came to pass that there arose a mist of darkness; yea, even an exceedingly great mist of darkness, insomuch that they who had commenced in the path did lose their way, that they wandered off and were lost" (1 Nephi 8:23). The mists of darkness posed the greatest threats in preventing individuals from reaching and partaking of the fruit of the tree of life. In their visions, both Lehi and Nephi witnessed what they described as a rod of iron leading to the tree, a rod which, if grasped, would enable those on the path to safely navigate through the mists of darkness. Lehi described this scenario, "And it came to pass that I beheld others pressing forward, and they came forth and caught hold of the end of the rod of iron; and they did press forward through the mist of darkness, clinging to the rod of iron, even until they did come forth and partake of the fruit of the tree" (1 Nephi 8:24). Nephi additionally witnessed this and provided a description of the meaning and purpose of the rod of iron: "And it came to pass that I beheld that the rod of iron, which my father had seen, was the word of God, which led to the fountain of living waters, or to the tree of life; which waters are a representation of the love of God; and I also beheld that the tree of life was a representation of the love of God" (1 Nephi 11:25).

The rod of iron played a critical role in enabling individuals to stay on the path that would lead them to the tree of life. Mists of darkness (teachings, philosophies, trials, and temptations) would arise throughout the course of life, tempt individuals to release the iron rod (the word of God), and cause them to stray onto foreign paths and become lost. Elder David S. Baxter stated, "The truth is that our only safety, our only security, our only hope is to hold fast to that which is good. As the mists of darkness gather around us, we are only lost if we choose to let go of the iron rod, which is the word of God."[37] Elder Neil L. Andersen described the threefold meaning of the "word of God" in these terms: "The word of God contains three very strong elements that intertwine and sustain one another to form an immovable rod. These three elements include, first, the scriptures, or the words of the ancient prophets. . . . The second element of the word of God is the personal revelation and inspiration that comes to us through the Holy Ghost. . . . The third element, a critical addition intertwining with the other two, . . . represents the words of the living prophets. We must also hold fast to the word of God as delivered by the living prophets."[38]

These same elements are found in Nephi's life, and we will see that it is by searching the scriptures, being guided by the light of the Holy Ghost, and following the living prophets, that safety will be found along the path. Nephi demonstrates the necessity of following these components of the word of God.

1. *Ancient scripture.* When Nephi and his brothers were up against insurmountable odds in trying to retrieve the brass plates (the word of God), Laman and Lemuel murmured, doubted, and feared resistance they might encounter. On the other hand, Nephi, appealing to ancient scripture, declared, "Let us go up; let us be strong like unto Moses; for he truly spake unto the waters of the Red Sea and they divided hither and thither, and our fathers came through, out of captivity, on dry ground, and the armies of Pharaoh did follow and were drowned in the waters of the Red Sea. . . . Let us go up; the Lord is able to deliver us, even as our fathers, and to destroy Laban, even as the Egyptians" (1 Nephi 4:2–3). Nephi's experience demonstrates that obedience to the teachings in the scriptures can bring strength and answers to life's difficult questions and help us keep the commandments in the face of adversity.[39] Nephi ultimately explained the reason for obtaining the plates: "And we had obtained the records which the Lord had commanded us, and searched them and found that they were desirable; yea, even of great worth unto us, insomuch that we could preserve the commandments of the Lord unto our children. Wherefore, it was wisdom in the Lord that we should carry them with us, as we journeyed in the wilderness towards the land of promise" (1 Nephi 5:21–22).

In his vision, the sacred nature of the plates was revealed to Nephi, along with the commandment that he and his people keep records of their own. These records would contain the fullness of the truths and covenants of the Lord, which would, at a future date, be removed: "And the angel spake unto me, saying: These last records, which thou hast seen among the Gentiles, shall establish the truth of the first, which are of the twelve apostles of the Lamb, and shall make known the plain and precious things which have been taken away from them; and shall make known to all kindreds, tongues, and people, that the Lamb of God is the Son of the Eternal Father, and the Savior of the world; and that all men must come unto him, or they cannot be saved." (1 Nephi 13:40).[40] Ancient scripture was, and continues to be, a vital component of the word of God that helps keep individuals on the path.[41]

2. *The Holy Ghost.* Nephi also consistently draws attention to the absolute necessity of the Holy Ghost's companionship in remaining faithful and enduring life's challenges (and thus remaining on the path leading to the tree of life). In 1 Nephi 2:16–18, Nephi describes his own conversion to the teachings of a living prophet, his father. While his brothers were hardening their hearts against the prophet, Nephi's heart was being softened, changed, and converted by the power of the Holy Ghost. It was this tractability that enabled Nephi to gain a great treasure of revelation:

> And it came to pass after I, Nephi, having heard all the words of my father, concerning the things which he saw in a vision, and also the things which he spake by the power of the Holy Ghost, which power he received by faith on the Son of God—and the Son of God was the Messiah who should come—I, Nephi, was desirous also that I might see, and hear, and know of these things, by the power of the Holy Ghost, which is the gift of God unto all those who diligently seek him, as well in times of old as in the time that he should manifest himself unto the children of men.
>
> For he that diligently seeketh shall find; and the mysteries of God shall be unfolded unto them, by the power of the Holy Ghost, as well in these times as in times of old, and as well in times of old as in times to come; wherefore, the course of the Lord is one eternal round. (1 Nephi 10:17, 19)

Through a series of visions, Nephi sees future events and realizes that people would need the companionship of the Holy Ghost in order to endure to the end. Seeing into the future events of the Restoration, Nephi writes, "And blessed are they who shall seek to bring forth my Zion at that day, for they shall have the gift and the power of the Holy Ghost; and if they endure unto the end they shall be lifted up at the last day, and shall be saved in the everlasting kingdom of the Lamb; and whoso shall publish peace, yea, tidings of great joy, how beautiful upon the mountains shall they be" (1 Nephi 13:37).⁴² Nephi understood well the necessity of utilizing the gift of the Holy Ghost to stay on the path.

3. *The living prophets.* Nephi repeatedly taught his brothers to follow the living prophets, especially their father, and warned against rejecting those prophets. He describes the consequences of such behavior, "For behold, the Spirit of the Lord ceaseth soon to strive with them; for behold, they have rejected the prophets, and Jeremiah have they cast into prison. And they have sought to take away the life of my father, insomuch that they have driven him out of the land" (1 Nephi 7:14). In this verse we learn that rejecting the prophets leads individuals to lose the Spirit. President Henry B. Eyring echoes this teaching in our day:

> Now our obligation is to remain worthy of the faith necessary for us to fulfill our promise to sustain those who have been called. The Lord was well pleased with the Church at the beginning of the Restoration, as He is today. But He cautioned the members then, as He does now, that He cannot look upon sin with the least degree of allowance. For us to sustain those who have been called today, we must examine our lives, repent as necessary, pledge to keep the Lord's commandments, and follow His servants. The Lord warns us that if we do not do those things, the Holy Ghost will be withdrawn, we will lose the light which we have received, and we will not be able to keep the pledge we have made today to sustain the Lord's servants in His true Church.⁴³

Nephi describes the difficult struggle his brothers were having in following the living prophets, a struggle that was causing them to lose the Spirit and leading them further and further away from the path to the tree of life: "And thus Laman and Lemuel, being the eldest, did murmur against their father. And they did murmur because they knew not the dealings of that God who had created them. Neither did they believe that Jerusalem, that great city, could be destroyed according to the words of the prophets. And they were like unto the Jews who were at Jerusalem, who sought to take away the life of my father" (1 Nephi 2:12–14).⁴⁴ The lives of Lehi and his family are filled with examples of the necessity of receiving modern revelation through living prophets.

Elder Andersen's threefold description of the word of God is confirmed in the course of Nephi's teachings.[45] As it is today, so it was with the Nephites. All three elements of the word of God help individuals to endure through the mists of darkness and avoid deception and falling off the covenant path. Obeying all three components of the word, not just one or two, is the key to staying on the path.[46]

Concluding Observations

When we look at the path that leads to the tree of life in the visions of Lehi and Nephi, we find a path that is entered onto through the waters of baptism, a path accompanied by an iron rod representing the words of the ancient and living prophets, as well as the guidance of the Holy Ghost. We find a covenantal path of discipleship that may only be endured by traversing the mists of darkness and avoiding straying from that path by clinging to the rod. Having entered that path, the journey would be dangerous. President Packer stated, "At your baptism and confirmation, you took hold of the iron rod. But you are never safe. It is *after* you have partaken of that fruit that your test will come."[47] The dreams of the tree of life invite all to get on the path by making covenants, and, once they are on the path, to speak to individuals and encourage them to stay true to the covenants they have entered into. Lehi describes the dangers these people would face but simplifies the response to dangerous situations in our lives: "And after they had tasted of the fruit they were ashamed, because of those that were scoffing at them; and they fell away into forbidden paths and were lost, . . . [and] they did point the finger of scorn at me and those that were partaking of the fruit also *but we heeded them not*" (1 Nephi 8:28, 33; emphasis added).[48]

President Packer stated, "The mist of darkness will cover you at times so much that you will not be able to see your way even a short distance ahead. You will not be able to see clearly. But with the gift of the Holy Ghost, you can *feel* your way ahead through life. Grasp the iron rod, and do not let go."[49] The covenant path to the tree of life marks the way to return to the presence of God to live with Him in immortality and enjoy eternal life; this is the plan of salvation revealed to Adam and Eve after the Fall and made possible only in and through the Atonement of Jesus Christ. The covenant path seen in the dreams truly encompasses and highlights the meaning of the love of God— the very meaning of the tree of life. President Ezra Taft Benson left us this blessing: "God bless all of us that we may follow the course laid out for us by our Heavenly Father and our greatest example—the Lord, Jesus Christ. May we do so regardless of what the world may say or do, that we may hold fast to the iron rod, that we may be true to the faith, that we may maintain the standards set for us and follow this course to safety and exaltation (see 1 Nephi 8:19). The door is open. The plan is here on earth. It is the Lord's plan. The authority and power are here. It is now up to you."[50]

Notes

1. See, for example, Neil L. Andersen, "Hold Fast to the Words of the Prophets" (CES fireside, March 4, 2007); David A. Bednar, "A Reservoir of Living Water" (CES fireside, February 4, 2007), 6; and Boyd K. Packer, "Finding Ourselves in Lehi's Dream," *Ensign*, August 2010, 21–25.

2. Joseph Fielding McConkie and Robert L. Millet, *Doctrinal Commentary on the Book of Mormon* (Salt Lake City: Bookcraft, 1987), 1:56; emphasis added.

3. Bruce R. McConkie, *Doctrinal New Testament Commentary* (Salt Lake City: Bookcraft, 1973), 3:447.

4. Neal A. Maxwell, "Becoming a Disciple," *Ensign*, June 1996, 12.

5. "Finding Rest in Christ," in *Teachings of Presidents of the Church: Joseph F. Smith* (Salt Lake City: The Church of Jesus Christ of Latter-day Saints, 1998), 426; emphasis added.

6. Packer, "Finding Ourselves," 22.

7. The sacred tree motif is also found on garments in Assyria, as well as on numerous objects in various cultures, demonstrating the prominence of this motif in Near Eastern religiosity. See Donald W. Parry, *The Cherubim, the Flaming Sword, the Path and the Tree of Life* (forthcoming), 9–10, and bibliography. He states: "Sacred trees or plants figure prominently in ancient Near Eastern cultures. Not only are they mentioned or described in texts, such as the Epic of Gilgamesh, but there exist numerous art motifs of sacred trees that are displayed on jewelry, seals, sculptures, wall paintings, stelae, cylinder seals, monuments, and garments. The concept of sacred trees also belongs to the ancient Mediterranean communities and Far Eastern cultures. According to Amihai Mazar, these trees 'have been and continue to be one of the most basic features of human religion in many cultures and periods.' These trees have magical or healing powers. The trees may represent a deity, a king, or a queen. Scholars have also associated the tree of life with Jesus's cross of Jesus Christ himself."

8. See E. O. James, "The Tree of Life," *Folklore* 79, no. 4 (1968): 245–46.

9. See Gordon J. Wenham, *Genesis 1–15* in *Word Biblical Commentary* (Dallas, TX: Word Publishing, 1987), 1:62.

10. John M. Steadman, "The 'Tree of Life' Symbolism in *Paradise Regain'd*," *Review of English Studies* 11, no. 44 (1960): 384.

11. Richard D. Draper describes partaking of the fruit of the tree of life in Revelation 2 as follows: "The promises to the faithful individual symbolize exaltation and come loaded with allusions to the temple. The promise is that they shall eat of the tree of life in paradise and of the hidden manna (see 2:7, 17), both considered to be the food of angels, but the former with particular significance. In it was the seed of 'eternal lives' (D&C 132:24) and immunity to death (see D&C 132:19–22; Gen. 3:12–24)." *Opening the Seven Seals: The Visions of John the Revelator* (Salt Lake City: Deseret Book, 1991), 40.

12. Steadman, "The 'Tree of Life' Symbolism," 384–85. The sacred tree's connection with deity and ritual is also displayed in condemned practices in the groves and high places mentioned in the Old Testament. The sacramental rituals of totems within groups in the Sudan have been linked to the concepts of the tree of life and the power and order such practices bring to the group. See James, "Tree of Life," 248–49.

13. C. Wilfred Griggs summarizes the writings in which we find images of the tree of life: "Jewish literature outside the Old Testament also contains tree of life references. The Books of Enoch, the Testaments of the Twelve Patriarchs, and 4 Ezra are the best known of such books. When Enoch journeyed to the Seven Sacred Mountains, he saw a sacred tree similar to a date palm but more beautiful and grand than any he had ever beheld (see 1 Enoch 29). His guide on the visionary journey, Michael, told Enoch that the fruit of the tree could not be eaten by mortals until they were purified after the judgment and that they would have to enter the temple of God to partake of it. (See 1 Enoch 25.) In the Secrets of Enoch 9:1, the seer is shown the heavenly dwelling place of the righteous, where stands the tree of life. In the Testament of Levi 18:9–11, Enoch prophesies that in the last days the Lord 'shall open the gates of paradise, and shall remove the threatening sword against Adam. And he shall give to the saints to eat from the tree of life, and the spirit of holiness shall be on them.' Likewise, 4 Ezra 8:52 promises to the righteous that in the last days 'is opened Paradise, planted the Tree of life; the future Age prepared, plenteousness made ready.' Jewish literature often portrays the tree of life as the seat of an oracle of God, a source of inspiration as well as of nourishment, a sacred sanctuary apart from worldly cares and dangers." "The Tree of Life in Ancient Cultures," *Ensign*, June 1988, 27.

14. Griggs, "Ancient Cultures," 27. The god Thoth, here depicted as inscribing the name of the king on the tree, is also found in final judgment scenes where the deceased is presented at the divine scales awaiting his eternal fate. Thoth was the divine scribe who had recorded the deeds of the individual. If the deceased was declared "justified," access was granted to appear before the throne of Osiris.

15. See T. Stordalen, *Echoes of Eden* (Louvain: Peeters, 2000), 459.

16. Charles W. Penrose describes the immortal state and marriage of Adam and Eve in the Garden; this highlights the significant nature of what the tree of life symbolized, both before and after the Fall, "The first marriage recorded in scripture was the union of immortals. The curse of death had not been pronounced when the ceremony was solemnized. There was no sin then, and therefore there was no death. The man and woman became one as eternal beings, and dominion was given to them over all earthly things, together." *"Mormon" Doctrine, Plain and Simple, or, Leaves from the Tree of Life* (Salt Lake City: Juvenile Instructor Office, 1882), 49.

17. Notice that cherubim and a flaming sword kept *the way of the tree of life* (see Moses 4:31; emphasis added). Thus the *way* could only be accessed and traveled by those who could pass by the cherubic guards.

18. Alvin R. Dyer stated, "Adam and Eve, cut off from the presence of God, were given instruction concerning the necessity of repentance as a means to regain their place in God's presence, there to continue in the way of light and intelligence to the attainment of ultimate perfection. Adam, seeking earnestly to know the will of God, asked this question of the Lord: 'Why is it that men must repent and be baptized in water?' (Moses 6:53). The Lord's answer was clear and distinct, for unto Adam and Eve, who had fallen from God and upon whom darkness had come, came this vital instruction of about the necessity of repentance: 'Wherefore teach it unto your children, that all men, everywhere, must repent, or they can in nowise inherit the kingdom of God' (Moses 6:57)." In Conference Report, October 1969, 54.

19. Bruce R. McConkie, *The Mortal Messiah* (Salt Lake City: Deseret Book, 1981), 1:228–29.

20. "The earth will be renewed and receive its paradisiacal glory" (Articles of Faith 1:10). Much could be said about the covenantal implications of the cherubim guarding the path leading back to the tree of life. This does factor into the visions of the tree of life in the Book of Mormon but cannot be discussed in this short paper. For a good discussion on the topic, see Parry, *The Cherubim*, 26–27, which describes the nature and relationship of the Garden of Eden, temples, and ritual in returning to partake of the tree of life: "The primary mission of the cherubim, together with the flaming sword, was to serve as guardians of the path that leads to the tree of life. . . . All three components—holding to the rod of iron, overcoming the world, and gestures of approach—are obligatory for those who wish to approach the tree of life and partake of its fruits. One may not choose one component and ignore the other two. . . . In sum, God established safeguards to protect the path to his tree of life. Primarily these are the cherubim and the flaming, revolving sword. When one attempts to travel the path without authorization, he or she will be cut down by the sword and/or burned by the sword's flame. To obtain proper authorization to travel the path, one must hold to the rod of iron, or grasp the word of God, overcome the world, and so live to become one who is allowed entry into the sacred temple of the Lord." Subsequently, "it has been suggested by numerous Latter-day Saint scholars that the Garden of Eden was the first temple, inasmuch as it was there that God first revealed himself to man. In addition to this similarity, the Garden of Eden may have possessed a number of other features similar to later temples, thus serving as the great archetype of the House of the Lord." Cobin T. Volluz, "Lehi's Dream of the Tree of Life: Springboard to Prophecy," *Journal of Book of Mormon Studies* 2, no. 2 (1993): 14–38. The earthly temple has also been linked to replicating the Garden of Eden, an archetype of the earthly temple, thus providing a "linkage between the garden in Genesis 2–3 and the spiritual experience of the Temple." T. Stordalen, *Echoes of Eden*, 309. See also Draper, *Opening the Seven Seals*, 241, for a discussion on Revelation 22 and the celestial city, where the throne of God is found, designated as the new Eden and in whose midst the tree of life stands.

21. *The Old Testament Pseudepigrapha*, ed. James H. Charlesworth (Peabody, MA: Hendrickson, 2009), 2:285. In Revelation, John summarizes the general process of

coming to the tree of life, "Blessed are they that do his commandments, that they may have right to the tree of life, and may enter in through the gates into the city" (Revelation 22:14). In *Opening the Seven Seals*, Richard D. Draper writes: "Note that the tree stands alone. It has no competition. The tree of good and evil has ceased to exist because the inhabitants of the city, knowing good from evil, have spurned all evil and eternally choose the good. In consequence the cherubim, placed to guard the tree of life, have been removed, allowing God's people to eat freely of the fruit.... The prophet Nephi stated, 'I beheld that the rod of iron, which my father had seen, was the word of God, which led to the fountain of living waters, or to the tree of life' (1 Ne. 11:25). Note that in Nephi's vision the tree and the water represent the same thing, each image expressing but a different aspect. The same is true in Revelation. The heart of John's city is love—the pure love of Christ. John, as few others, understood the life-power behind that love. 'For God so loved the world,' he testified, 'that he gave his only begotten Son, that whosoever believeth in him should not perish, but have everlasting life' (John 3:16, KJV). Christ was the Lamb slain before the foundation of the world. He became flesh so that 'as many as received him,' he could give the 'power to become the sons of God, even to them that believe on his name' (John 1:12, KJV). In another epistle the Seer had taught the Saints: 'God is love,' and 'love is of God; and every one that loveth is born of God, and knoweth God' (1 Jn. 4:7–8, KJV). In the eternal city, all are free to partake of that love, which flows out of him and sustains and embraces all who have been transformed into his very image." *Opening the Seven Seals*, 241, 245. Robert J. Matthews adds, "those in the meridian of time who were earnest in their hearts partook of the living fruit from the living tree of life offered by Christ and his appointed servants; those who rejected the fruit denied themselves access to God's new covenant with Israel and spurned fellowship with the Mediator of that covenant." *Selected Writings of Robert L. Millet* (Salt Lake City: Deseret Book, 2000), 52.

22. The Prophet Joseph Smith described teaching presiding leaders of the Church in his day: "I spent the day in the upper part of the store, that is in my private office, . . . instructing them in the principles and order of the Priesthood, attending to washings, anointings, endowments and the communication of keys pertaining to the Aaronic Priesthood, and so on to the highest order of the Melchizedek Priesthood, setting forth the order pertaining to the Ancient of Days, and all those plans and principles by which any one is enabled to secure the fullness of those blessings which have been prepared for the Church of the Firstborn, and come up and abide in the presence of the Eloheim in the eternal worlds. In this council was instituted the ancient order of things for the first time in these last days." *Teachings of the Prophet Joseph Smith*, comp. Joseph Fielding Smith (Salt Lake City: Deseret Book, 1976), 237.

23. L. Tom Perry, "The Gospel of Jesus Christ," *Ensign*, May 2008, 44–46; emphasis added. Henry B. Eyring explains, "The book makes plain that we must receive the Holy Ghost as a baptism of fire to help us stay on the strait and narrow path." "The Book of Mormon as a Personal Guide," *Ensign*, September 2010, 4.

24. The distinction is often made between the "straight" path (one without deviation or without curves) and the "strait path" (strict, narrow, or rigorous). See McConkie and Millet, *Doctrinal Commentary*, 1:362; and Stephen E. Robinson and H. Dean Garrett, *A Commentary on the Doctrine and Covenants* (Salt Lake City: Deseret Book,

2000), 1:156. D. Kelly Ogden and Andrew C. Skinner describe the difference in terms of the Savior's path. He was the only sinless individual who never needed course corrections, his path was "straight," versus our path, which is "strait." An important usage of the "strait path" often associates it with the covenant path. *The Four Gospels* (Salt Lake City: Deseret Book, 2006), 221–22. McConkie and Millet describe this as "the emphasis is on the strictness with which all who would be saved must comply with the ordinances of salvation." *Doctrinal Commentary*, 362. Robinson and Garrett add, "A strait or narrow gate must be approached deliberately and at just the right angle. It is restrictive. Only what has originated or been sealed on God's side of the gate, that which is eternal, can be carried with us through the gate into God's kingdom. The saying 'You can't take it with you' is not true of priesthood blessings, ordinances, and sealings." *Commentary on the Doctrine and Covenants*, 156. Nephi seems to use the "strait path" in this covenantal context and later pleads, "O Lord, wilt thou not shut the gates of thy righteousness before me, that I may walk in the path of the low valley, that I may be strict in the plain road!" (2 Nephi 4:32). This highlights the rigorous nature of the path to eternal life. Second Nephi 9:18 also describes this: "But, behold, the righteous, the saints of the Holy One of Israel, they who have believed in the Holy One of Israel, they who have endured the crosses of the world, and despised the shame of it, they shall inherit the kingdom of God, which was prepared for them from the foundation of the world, and their joy shall be full forever."

25. Bruce R. McConkie, in Conference Report, April 1948, 51–52. "It may seem preposterous to many to declare that within the teachings of The Church of Jesus Christ of Latter-day Saints may be found a bulwark to safeguard against the pitfalls, the frustrations, and the wickedness in the world. The plan of salvation formed in the heavens points clearly to the straight and narrow path that leads to eternal life, even though there are many who refuse to follow that way. . . . The mission of this church is to bear witness of the truths of the gospel and put to flight the false teachings on every side that are causing the restlessness and the aimlessness that threaten all who have not found the straight path and that which could be an anchor to their souls." Harold B. Lee, "The Iron Rod," *Ensign*, June 1971, 5.

26. The Prophet Joseph Smith taught, "A man may be saved, after the judgment, in the terrestrial kingdom, or in the telestial kingdom, but he can never see the celestial kingdom of God, without being born of water and the Spirit. He may receive a glory like unto the moon, [i.e. of which the light of the moon is typical], or a star, [i.e. of which the light of the stars is typical], but he can never come unto Mount Zion, and unto the city of the living God, the heavenly Jerusalem, and to an innumerable company of angels; to the general assembly and Church of the Firstborn, which are written in heaven, and to God the judge of all, and to the spirits of just men made perfect, and to Jesus the Mediator of the new covenant, unless he becomes as a little child, and is taught by the Spirit of God." *Teachings of the Prophet Joseph Smith*, 12.

27. Later Book of Mormon prophets adopted the theme of enduring to the end on the covenant path; they identified feasting upon the word as an essential behavior that would help qualify individuals to eventually partake of the fruit of the tree. Additionally, the fruit is compared to virtues that have yielded fruit, as is witnessed in the book of Proverbs. See Alma 32:40–43; Proverbs 3:18; 11:30; 13:12; 15:4.

28. David A. Bednar, "Honorably Hold a Name and Standing," *Ensign*, May 2009, 97–100. In light of the current discussion on the tree of life, this connection with the temple in the Book of Mormon is important. The nature of the tree of life in the Garden of Eden is significant in this regard, as the garden can be viewed as God's temple and the temple as a re-creation of the garden. It is also interesting that the Nephites operated under the Melchizedek Priesthood, as there were no Levites in their group. See Paul Y. Hoskisson, "By What Authority Did Lehi, a Non-Levite Priest, Offer Sacrifices?" *Ensign*, March 1994, 54; and David R. Seely, "Lehi's Altar and Sacrifice in the Wilderness," *Journal of Book of Mormon Studies* 10, no. 1 (2001): 62–69.

29. Bruce R. McConkie, "New and Everlasting Covenant of Marriage," in *BYU Speeches of the Year* (Provo, UT: Brigham Young University Publications, 1960), 6. It is important that in 1 Nephi 16:7–8, Nephi describes the command of the Lord to return and find wives for him and his brothers in these terms: "And it came to pass that I, Nephi, took one of the daughters of Ishmael to wife; and also, my brethren took of the daughters of Ishmael to wife; and also Zoram took the eldest daughter of Ishmael to wife. And thus my father had fulfilled all the commandments of the Lord which had been given unto him. And also, I, Nephi, had been blessed of the Lord exceedingly." Joseph Fielding McConkie, Robert L. Millet, and Brent L. Top also point out the multiple usage of gates within the context of baptism (getting on the path to eternal life) and eternal marriage (exaltation). *Doctrinal Commentary on the Book of Mormon* (Salt Lake City: Deseret Book, 2007), 4:93–94.

30. This concept of partaking of the fruit at baptism, as a condition that would lead to the ultimate partaking of the fruit and exaltation in God's kingdom, is paralleled in a summary of Jacob's dream, in which he sees the Lord standing at the top of a ladder (see Genesis 28:10–19). Marion G. Romney described the rungs of the ladder as covenants that Jacob would have to make, "Jacob realized that the covenants he made with the Lord there were the rungs on the ladder that he himself would have to climb in order to obtain the promised blessings—blessings that would entitle him to enter heaven and associate with the Lord." "Temples—The Gates to Heaven," *Ensign*, March 1971, 16. Andrew C. Skinner writes: "Thanks to Elder Romney's insight, Latter-day Saints can more fully understand that their temple experiences are really the experiences of every Saint in every dispensation. Jacob's faithfulness was rewarded with an opportunity to make eternal temple covenants. But the great promises and blessings proffered to Jacob in Bethel at that time were conditional rather than absolute. Nowhere does the text say they were sealed or ratified with surety at this point, as is sometimes supposed; Jacob would have a long time to prove his loyalty and secure for himself the unconditional guarantee of all the terms of the covenant. Neither does the text say that Jacob's dealings with the Lord at that time constituted the ultimate theophany, or revelation of God, which the scriptures promise to the faithful. This would come later, after years of his righteousness. But Jacob undoubtedly came away from Bethel understanding the order of heaven, the possibilities for exaltation, and the promises of the Abrahamic covenant if he proved faithful. So it is with all of us." "Jacob: Keeper of Covenants," *Ensign*, March 1998, 51.

31. Henry B. Eyring states, "I speak today of young people already within His true Church and so are started on the strait and narrow way to return to their heavenly home. He wants them to gain early the spiritual strength to stay on the path. And He needs

our help to get them back to the path quickly should they begin to wander." "Help Them on Their Way Home," *Ensign*, May 2010, 22–25. Lehi and Nephi seem to be attempting to get Laman and Lemuel back on the path when they are beginning to wander off it. They seem to have some success as Laman and Lemuel repent several times in these early episodes and follow the commands of the Lord. However, Lehi's concerns eventually materialize. President Eyring taught, "All of us feel, in our best moments, a desire to return home to live with God. He gave us all the gift of His Beloved Son as our Savior to provide the path and to teach us how to follow it. He gave us prophets to point the way. The Prophet Joseph Smith was inspired to translate the record of prophets that is the Book of Mormon. It is our sure guide on the way home to God. . . . Each time I read even a few lines in the Book of Mormon, I feel my testimony strengthened that the book is true, that Jesus is the Christ, that we can follow Him home, and that we can take those we love home with us." "Personal Guide," 4–5.

32. As we do not possess the original text, we do not know what word was used here for "cast off." If it is parallel with the word in the garden scene, "drive out, cast out," then the Hebrew text offers another interesting parallel of being "cast out" of the presence of God. See Genesis 4:14 where Cain is cast out from the face of the Lord. Moses 5 contains a more detailed account of Cain's rejection of the covenant and highlights his rebellion against God.

33. For a discussion on the potentially long span and repercussions of Lehi's dream and its interpretation, see Volluz, "Lehi's Dream," 16: "The primary interpretation revealed to Nephi of Lehi's dream of the tree of life was a panoramic view of the future from the advent of the Savior in mortality up until the Second Coming." What is striking, and thus a large part of the warning of the dream to the covenant people, is that Israel is described as part of the host fighting against the Apostles and the Lamb (see 1 Nephi 11:35).

34. Nephi's description of the "righteous" here clearly takes on a covenantal relationship with God. A few examples paralleling this include the following: "And I said unto them that it was an awful gulf, which separated the wicked from the tree of life, and also *from the saints of God*" (1 Nephi 15:28; emphasis added); "He that hath an ear, let him hear what the Spirit saith *unto the churches*; to him that overcometh will I give to eat of the tree of life, which is in the midst of the paradise of God" (Revelation 2:7; emphasis added); "Yea, he saith: Come unto me and ye shall partake of the fruit of the tree of life; yea, ye shall eat and drink of the bread and the waters of life freely" (Alma 5:34); "I speak by way of command unto you that *belong to the church*; and unto those who *do not belong to the church* I speak by way of invitation, saying: Come and be baptized unto repentance, that ye also may be partakers of the fruit of the tree of life" (Alma 5:62; emphasis added). This last verse teaches that the "wicked" Nephi referenced are not all people outside of the covenant. The visions of the tree of life describe many good people pressing forward to get on the path, and Alma 5:62 describes the necessity of missionary work in bolstering those individuals' efforts. See also McConkie and Millet, *Doctrinal Commentary*, 1:360–62, for a discussion on the covenant nature of the "righteous."

35. See 2 Nephi 33, where Nephi, towards the end of his life, glories in Christ, using phraseology from the tree of life vision. In 2 Nephi 4, Lehi offers patriarchal blessings to his grandchildren. As he describes the tree of life within the context of his vision, Lehi

expresses concern that the seed of Laman and Lemuel will be "cut off" from the presence of the Lord and discusses the need to be "brought up in the *way* ye should go" (2 Nephi 4:4–5; emphasis added).

36. For a few other passages relevant to the tree of life, see 1 Nephi 8:24–25, 28; Alma 5:21–24, 26–27, 33–38 (39), 53–57, 62; and Alma 6:3. Also see Helaman 3:24–30, which uses similar language to describe entering the covenant through baptism, laying hold upon the word of God, and being led in a strait and narrow course to the presence of God. Noel B. Reynolds offers a summary of the process of getting and staying on the path: "Alma teaches Zeezrom and others at Ammonihah that God 'has all power to save every man that believeth on his name and bringeth forth fruit meet for repentance' (Alma 12:15, cf. 12:33; 13:13; 34:30). Mormon writes to his son, Moroni, that "the first fruits of repentance is baptism" (Moroni 8:25). We have seen that baptism is tightly linked to repentance because it serves as a public witness to the Father of the private, internal covenant the repentant sinner makes to turn from evil and keep all of the Father's commandments. Repentance is incomplete without baptism, and baptism is meaningless without repentance. Thus the person who has come to believe in Christ and trust in his power of deliverance must enter the strait gate of repentance and baptism, which starts him on the road to eternal life. The straitness or narrowness of the gate indicates that people must go through one at a time by an act of their own and that only the prescribed acts or choices are adequate for this gate. It also shows that the gate leads precisely to the entrance to one path, not the myriad of paths that lead to other destinations. The path to eternal life has one starting place and hence needs only one narrow gate to admit those who will walk it. Rich and poor enter on the same terms, as unaccompanied pedestrians, leaving all burdens and possessions behind. They all walk with God or with the guidance of his Spirit (the iron rod) as long as they wish to progress to the tree of life and partake of its fruit." "The True Points of My Doctrine," *Journal of Book of Mormon Studies* 5, no. 2 (1996): 26–56.

37. David S. Baxter, "Faith, Service, Constancy," in Conference Report, October 2006.

38. Neil L. Andersen, "Hold Fast to the Words of the Prophets" (CES fireside, March 4, 2007), 3.

39. A. Theodore Tuttle, "Developing Faith," *Ensign*, November 1986, 73, taught that "[Nephi] was trying to do what you and I as parents need to do with our families today—to develop faith in the Lord. And the way to do it is to recount the examples of faith that have happened in our history and in our heritage and with our people. That's the value of history. It contains accounts of faith of our own blood and ancestry and of our own people and our children."

40. See also 1 Nephi 13:23–27. Subsequently, the Lord stated, "Search the scriptures; for in them ye think ye have eternal life: and they are they which testify of me" (John 5:39).

41. To highlight the essential nature of the scriptures, Omni 1:17 states that the Mulekites, a group of people who had left Jerusalem around the time of Lehi and his family, had lost their language and "denied the being of their Creator" because "they had brought no records with them."

42. The reference to mountains here may be linked to the temple (see Isaiah 2 and 2 Nephi 12). Mountain experiences are often linked with theophonies and divine

manifestations. For a few examples, see Moses 1:1; 7:3–4, 17; Exodus 3:1; Matthew 17:1–2; 1 Nephi 11:1; and 2 Nephi 4:25.

43. Henry B. Eyring, "The True and Living Church," *Ensign*, May 2008, 20–24.

44. A significant challenge faced in Jerusalem during Lehi's day was the presence of false prophets who were proclaiming false ideologies (see, for example, Jeremiah 28). These teachings split the kingdom of Judah and would eventually lead to its downfall. For a discussion on this topic, see Aaron P. Schade, "The Kingdom of Judah: Politics, Prophets, and Scribes in the Late Preexilic Period," in *Glimpses of Lehi's Jerusalem*, ed. David R. Seely, JoAnn H. Seely, and John W. Welch (Salt Lake City: Covenant Communications, 2004).

45. Andersen, "Hold Fast," 3. Elder Andersen subsequently quoted George Q. Cannon, then a member of the First Presidency, in a summary of the interrelatedness of these constituents: "We have the Bible, the Book of Mormon and the Book of Doctrine and Covenants; but all these books, without the living oracles and a constant stream of revelation from the Lord, would not lead any people into the Celestial Kingdom of God. This may seem a strange declaration to make, but strange as it may sound, it is nevertheless true. Of course, these records are all of infinite value. They cannot be too highly prized, nor can they be too closely studied. But in and of themselves, with all the light that they give, they are insufficient to guide the children of men and to lead them into the presence of God. To be thus led requires a living Priesthood and constant revelation from God to the people according to the circumstances in which they may be placed."

46. Elder Claudio D. Zivic states, "I testify that we can avoid the mists of darkness that lead to personal apostasy by repenting of our sins, overcoming offense, eliminating faultfinding, and following our Church leaders. We can also avoid those mists by humbling ourselves, forgiving others, keeping our covenants, partaking of the sacrament worthily each week, and strengthening our testimonies through prayer, daily scripture study, temple attendance where possible, magnifying our Church callings, and serving our fellowmen." "Avoiding Personal Apostasy," *Ensign*, June 2009, 27. This statement highlights the covenant road of discipleship leading to the tree of life.

47. Packer, "Finding Ourselves," 23.

48. Elder Dennis B. Neuenschwander stated, "In reality these stories are not about crowds but individuals among those crowds. They are really about you and me. All of us are among the crowds of this world. Almost all of us are like the woman who, despite the crowd, comes to the Savior. We all have faith that just a touch will bring healing to our aching souls and relief to our innermost needs. New members of the Church in many lands are often like Alma. They hear the words of life when no one else in their family or circle of friends does. Yet they still have the courage to accept the gospel and chart a course through the crowds. I think each one of us understands what it means to partake of the fulfilling fruit of the tree of life within sight and sound of those who mock and what it means to exert every courageous effort to pay them no heed." "One among the Crowd," *Ensign*, May 2008, 101–3.

49. Packer, "Finding Ourselves," 23; emphasis added.

50. *The Teachings of Ezra Taft Benson* (Salt Lake City: Bookcraft, 1988), 26.

9

The Doctrine of Christ in 2 Nephi 31–32 as an Approach to the Vision of the Tree of Life

Jared T. Parker

The vision of the tree of life in 1 Nephi 8 and 11–14 and the doctrine of Christ in 2 Nephi 31–32 are two familiar subjects in the Book of Mormon. What may not be well recognized is that Nephi apparently drew upon elements of the vision of the tree of life to teach the doctrine of Christ.[1] Recognition of this connection sets the stage for us to appreciate how the vision of the tree of life portrays the fundamental doctrine of Christ—the way to return to God's presence and partake of eternal life as described in 2 Nephi 31–32.

Structure and Setting

Nephi's exposition of the doctrine of Christ can be divided into two parts, both of which provide insight into the vision of the tree of life. The first part is found in 2 Nephi 31 and is a complete, self-contained unit. Nephi indicates that he feels compelled to address the doctrine of Christ before concluding his portion of the record. "The things which I have written sufficeth me, save it be a few words which I must speak concerning the doctrine of Christ" (2 Nephi

---

Jared T. Parker received a PhD in chemical engineering from Brigham Young University and is a medical device specialist in Flagstaff, Arizona.

31:2). By the end of the chapter, it is clear that Nephi believes he has said all that is needed: "And now, behold, this is the doctrine of Christ, and the only and true doctrine of the Father, and of the Son, and of the Holy Ghost, which is one God, without end. Amen" (v. 21).

The second part of the doctrine of Christ is found in 2 Nephi 32. Here Nephi continues to write about the doctrine of Christ because he anticipates his readers will not fully understand 2 Nephi 31. Nephi did not originally intend to say more, but he perceives by the Spirit it is necessary to do so. Still, he is only allowed to say so much: "Behold, this is the doctrine of Christ, and there will be no more doctrine given until after he shall manifest himself unto you in the flesh. . . . And now I, Nephi, cannot say more; the Spirit stoppeth mine utterance" (vv. 6–7). Though Nephi was restrained from saying more, the content of chapter 32 provides important clues for a more complete understanding of the doctrine of Christ.

It is also important to recognize the setting of 2 Nephi 31–32. Nephi writes about the doctrine of Christ at the end of a long, prophetic life. His incredible vision of Lehi's dream occurred over thirty years before,[2] when Nephi was very young and had limited life experience. In contrast, Nephi concludes his sacred record with the doctrine of Christ after he had married and had children, built a ship to cross the ocean, led a colony away from his murderous brothers, constructed a temple, experienced war and bloodshed, and served as a prophet and king for many years. Thus 2 Nephi 31–32 was written by an extremely experienced and inspired Nephi, a prophet who had spent his entire life studying, pondering, and teaching the things of God. Near the end of his life, Nephi provides his readers greater insight and understanding by drawing upon the visions he and his father had so many years before.

The Doctrine of Christ and the Vision of the Tree of Life

It has been observed by others that Nephi's prophecies in 2 Nephi 25–30 correlate to topics from his vision of the tree of life in 1 Nephi 11–14.[3] However, it may not be generally recognized that Nephi seems to continue this approach in 2 Nephi 31–32. He introduces the doctrine of Christ by directing his readers back to a specific part of his earlier vision. "I would that ye should remember that I have spoken unto you concerning that prophet which the Lord showed unto me, that should baptize the Lamb of God" (2 Nephi 31:4). In his vision of the tree of life, Nephi saw John baptize Christ (see 1 Nephi 11:27), and Nephi turns to this event to begin his great doctrinal exposition.

Having oriented his readers back to his vision of the tree of life, Nephi refers to several things that are clearly from his father's dream or his own vision: Christ's baptism (compare 1 Nephi 11:27 with 2 Nephi 31:4–8),[4] the strait[5] and narrow path (compare 1 Nephi 8:20–23 with 2 Nephi 31:9, 18–19), the rod of iron or word of God/Christ (compare 1 Nephi 8:19–20, 24, 30; 11:25; 15:23–25 with 2 Nephi 31:19–20; 32:3), pressing forward on the path (compare 1 Nephi 8:21, 24, 30 with 2 Nephi 31:20), and the fruit of the tree of life, or eternal life (compare 1 Nephi 8:10; 15:21–22, 36 with 2 Nephi 31:18, 20). Certainly Nephi does not accidentally mention these dream or vision elements. Rather, he intentionally draws upon them to teach the doctrine of Christ. In other words, the vision of the tree of life is the setting for the doctrine of Christ.

What is fascinating is that Nephi includes many other things not mentioned explicitly in either his or his father's visions but that relate within the framework of the vision's original imagery. Consider the following: Christ set the example in that he was baptized by water, received the Holy Ghost, and endured to the end (see 2 Nephi 31:6–9, 12–13, 16–17); there is a gate to the strait and narrow path which is repentance and baptism by water (see vv. 9, 17–18); the Holy Ghost will baptize with fire those who enter the gate and show them all things they should do on the path to eternal life (see vv. 13–14; 32:5); those who fail to endure to the end on the path cannot be saved (see 2 Nephi 31:14–16); faith, hope, and love are how one presses forward on the path (see vv. 19–20); holding fast to the iron rod means feasting on the words of Christ, which will tell all things one should do on the strait and narrow path (see vv. 20; 32:3); while on the path, one must pray always in the name of Christ (see v. 9); those who press forward and endure to the end will receive eternal life (see 2 Nephi 31:20); and there is only one name and one way for man to be saved (see v. 21).

By including new concepts along with previous ones from the vision of the tree of life, Nephi is providing another approach to his father's dream and to his own vision. This is not to say that Nephi is revising or correcting his earlier record of the visions but rather that he is synthesizing various concepts and creating another perspective using key elements of the vision of the tree of life. While Lehi's dream centers on his family and Nephi's vision contemplates future events, the doctrine of Christ appears to be another approach focused on the individual requirements to obtain eternal life.

Second Nephi 31: The Doctrine of Christ

Christ set the example. One principle we may explore is Nephi's thought-provoking suggestion that Christ's example may be seen within the symbolism of the vision of the tree of life. Lehi saw various groups interact with the tree (see 1 Nephi 8:21–25, 30) and Nephi saw Christ's birth and ministry as the interpretation of the tree (see 1 Nephi 11:10–31), but now Nephi gives another perspective. Not only is Christ the manifestation of the love of God, or the tree of life, but he is also the perfect example for all because he traversed the path himself. "And he said unto the children of men: Follow thou me. . . . Follow me, and do the things which ye have seen me do" (2 Nephi 31:10, 12). In essence, the Savior says to all, "Follow me to the tree of life." Christ set the example because he got on the path and pressed forward to the tree himself.

Nephi also explains that Christ did not set the example just because an example was needed. Even though he was holy, Christ needed to enter by the gate of baptism "to fulfill all righteousness" (v. 6). In demonstrating obedience to the Father's commandment to be baptized, Christ himself was holding fast to the iron rod of his Father's word. Nephi describes Christ's baptismal covenant as that he "witnesseth unto the Father that he would be obedient unto him in keeping his commandments" (v. 7). Christ also needed to receive the Holy Ghost, press forward on the strait and narrow path, resist every mist of darkness of Satan's temptations, and endure to the end to partake of eternal life.

Gate of repentance and baptism by water. An innovation found in the doctrine of Christ is Nephi's inclusion of a gate to the strait and narrow path. There was no hint of a gate to the path in Lehi's dream or in Nephi's vision. Nephi's brother Jacob first mentions a gate to the strait and narrow way (see 2 Nephi 9:41), but it is Nephi who expands this idea and identifies the gate as repentance and baptism by water.

Why did Nephi identify repentance and baptism as the gate to the path? Lehi's dream gave the impression that anyone could commence in the path without meeting a specific requirement (see 1 Nephi 8:21–22). However, it seems Nephi adds the imagery of a gate to the path because of Christ's example and the Father's commandment. Christ's baptism "showeth unto the children of men the straitness of the path, and the narrowness of the gate, by which they should enter, he having set the example before them.... And the Father said: Repent ye, repent ye, and be baptized in the name of my Beloved Son" (2 Nephi 31:9, 11). Nephi understood that he was shown Christ's example so he could tell others the universal requirement to get on the path. "Wherefore, do the things which I have told you I have seen that your Lord and your Redeemer should do; for, for this cause have they been shown unto me, that ye might know the gate by which ye should enter. For the gate by which ye should enter is repentance and baptism by water.... And then are ye in this strait and narrow path which leads to eternal life" (vv. 17–18). Nephi knew that the only way to get on the path is to be baptized as Christ would be, and so he added a gate to the strait and narrow path.

Receiving the Holy Ghost and baptism by fire. Another principle not found in either Lehi's or Nephi's vision is the reception of the Holy Ghost when one is on the strait and narrow path. Nephi spoke of the Holy Ghost in his earlier vision (see 1 Nephi 11:27; 12:7, 18; 13:37), but not as related to the path to the tree. Also, neither Lehi nor Nephi mentioned the baptism of fire and of the Holy Ghost. Now, as with baptism by water, Christ's example of receiving the Holy Ghost becomes a critical part of reaching the tree of life. The Savior says, "He that is baptized in my name, to him will the Father give the Holy Ghost, like unto me; wherefore, follow me, and do the things which ye have seen me do" (2 Nephi 31:12). A person who receives the Holy Ghost is baptized with fire and with the Holy Ghost, speaks "with the tongue of angels" (v. 13), and receives a remission of sins (see v. 17). Moreover, the Holy Ghost is one source of the iron rod, the word of God, because he "witnesses of the Father and the Son" (v. 18). All these things come to those who get on the path to eternal life and receive the Holy Ghost.

Failing to endure to the end. In Lehi's dream, many commenced on the path but later "wandered off" or "fell away into forbidden paths and were lost" (1 Nephi 8:23, 28). Now in the doctrine of Christ, we learn the gravity of what it means to be lost. Nephi receives a revelation from the Son explaining the seriousness of entering the covenant and then turning away: "After ye have repented of your sins, and witnessed unto the Father that ye are willing to keep my commandments, by the baptism of water, and have received the baptism of fire and of the Holy Ghost ... and after this should deny me, it would have been better for you that ye had not known me" (2 Nephi 31:14).

Nephi testifies that this means such persons cannot be saved: "And now, my beloved brethren, I know by this that unless a man shall endure to the end, in following the example of the Son of the living God, he cannot be saved" (v. 16). Enduring to the end is the only way anyone will be able to partake of the tree of life in eternity.

Press forward with faith, hope, and love. Nephi gives new insight into the way a person actually presses forward on the path to the tree. "Wherefore, ye must press forward with a steadfastness in Christ, having a perfect brightness of hope, and a love of God and of all men" (v. 20). What was previously a general description of pressing forward on the path has now become specific. The triad describing a true Christian—faith, hope, and love—summarizes what is required to successfully press forward on the path. And as Christ set the example, each is to exercise faith as he did, hope as he did, and love as he did. All of this makes the person more like him, which is one goal of pressing forward to the tree of life.

Feast on the word of Christ. In Lehi's dream, those who reached the tree were "clinging" or "continually holding fast" (1 Nephi 8:24, 30) to the rod of iron. Now Nephi describes this differently. He says that one must be "feasting upon the word of Christ" (2 Nephi 31:20) on the path to eternal life. It is as if Nephi wants those on the path to internalize the word of God and make it a part of them. He seems to portray this by changing the imagery from "clinging" or "continually holding fast" to "feasting" on the word.

Ye shall have eternal life. The fruit of the tree of life symbolizes eternal life as it is "most precious and most desirable above all other fruits" and represents "the greatest of all the gifts of God" (1 Nephi 15:36; compare D&C 14:7). Taking his readers all the way to partaking of the tree of life, Nephi includes a revealed promise to those who press forward on the path and endure to the end. "Thus saith the Father: Ye shall have eternal life" (2 Nephi 31:20). This promise appears to be that of being sealed up to eternal life. In other words, Nephi feels he has given enough instruction for his readers to know how to make their calling and election sure. It is actually quite simple: get on the path and press forward until you obtain the promise of eternal life. Elder Bruce R. McConkie explained similarly: "The way it operates is this: you get on the path that's named the 'straight and narrow.' You do it by entering the gate of repentance and baptism. The straight and narrow path leads from the gate of repentance and baptism, a very great distance, to a reward that's called eternal life.... If you're on the path when death comes—because this is the time and the day appointed, this is the probationary estate—you'll never fall off from it, and, for all practical purposes, your calling and election is made sure."⁶

No other name, no other way. Nephi punctuates the doctrine of Christ with the final statement that there is no other name nor way man can reach the tree of life. Even though there was no mention of the importance of the name of Christ in the earlier visions, Nephi includes it in the doctrine of Christ with the Father's commandment, "Be baptized in the name of my Beloved Son" (2 Nephi 31:11). All must be baptized in the name of Christ, and those who are baptized witness that they are "willing to take upon [them] the name of Christ" (v. 13). And so it becomes clear that only those who have taken upon themselves the name of Christ will be allowed to partake of the tree of life because there is "none other . . . name given under heaven whereby man can be saved in the kingdom of God" (v. 21).

In Lehi's dream, there was no specific path to get to the great and spacious building; apparently it was open to all, however they came. In stark contrast, 2 Nephi 31 emphasizes that there is only one way to reach the tree of life, the one way that all must follow, without exception. Nephi knows he has taught the only way to return to God, which is the fundamental doctrine of Christ. "And now, behold, my beloved brethren, this is the way; and there is none other way.... And now, behold, this is the doctrine of Christ, and the only and true doctrine of the Father, and of the Son, and of the Holy Ghost, which is one God, without end. Amen" (v. 21).

Second Nephi 32: Nephi's Commentary

Like chapter 31, chapter 32 is about the doctrine of Christ, but here Nephi anticipates his readers' questions that may arise from his description of the doctrine, specifically what to do while on the path. It is important to study these two chapters together, or we might miss the greater insights Nephi wants us to gain about the doctrine of Christ.

With prophetic sensitivity to the Spirit, Nephi realizes that his readers may not fully comprehend what they should do after baptism to obtain eternal life. He feels he has explained it sufficiently because he asks them why they ponder this. "And now, behold, my beloved brethren, I suppose that ye ponder somewhat in your hearts concerning that which ye should do after ye have entered in by the way. But, behold, why do ye ponder these things in your hearts?" (2 Nephi 32:1).

To help explain what one should do while on the path to eternal life, Nephi returns to the concept of speaking with the tongue of angels. "Do ye not remember that I said unto you that after ye had received the Holy Ghost ye could speak with the tongue of angels? And now, how could ye speak with the tongue of angels save it were by the Holy Ghost?" (v. 2). Nephi mentioned this idea only briefly in 2 Nephi 31, but now he explains the connection more directly: "Angels speak by the power of the Holy Ghost; wherefore, they speak the words of Christ" (v. 3). Therefore, words spoken by the power of the Holy Ghost, such as those spoken by angels, are the words of Christ. Nephi further elucidates this point by quoting what he previously said and identifying why it is so important to feast on the words of Christ. "Wherefore, I said unto you, feast upon the words of Christ; for behold, the words of Christ will tell you all things what ye should do."

Clearly, the words of Christ will tell those who have been baptized all things they should do to partake of the tree of life. Nevertheless, Nephi follows this point with an interesting statement: "Wherefore, now after I have spoken these words, if ye cannot understand them it will be because ye ask not, neither do ye knock; wherefore, ye are not brought into the light, but must perish in the dark" (v. 4). Nephi still seems concerned that his readers may not fully comprehend his words. It also appears that he wants his readers to pray to obtain a greater understanding of what he has said.

Verse 5 continues Nephi's efforts to help his readers understand: "For behold, again I say unto you that if ye will . . . receive the Holy Ghost, it will show unto you all things what ye should do." Even though he has already mentioned this before, Nephi emphasizes the role of the Holy Ghost again. Not only is the Holy Ghost the source of the words of Christ that will "tell . . . all things" one should do on the path, he will also "show . . . all things" that should be done. Truly receiving the Holy Ghost is absolutely critical for each person on the path to be able to reach the tree of life.

More than once now, Nephi has referred to "things" to be done after baptism, but he has not identified anything in particular. Why is this? Is it that Nephi does not have anything specific in mind or are there additional things required of every person on the path to eternal life that he chooses not to mention? Unfortunately, Nephi does not answer this question but instead continues rather cryptically: "Behold, this is the doctrine of Christ, and there will be no more doctrine given until after he shall manifest himself unto you in the flesh. And when he shall manifest himself unto you in the flesh, the things which he shall say unto you shall ye observe to do" (v. 6). While it is ambiguous what Nephi means here by Christ manifesting himself "unto you in the flesh," it is clear that when this happens, Christ himself will provide additional doctrine and tell what things should be done.

Whatever it is that Nephi will not write about explicitly, he makes it plain that he has taken the topic as far as he can. "And now I, Nephi, cannot say more; the Spirit stoppeth mine utterance, and I am left to mourn because of the unbelief, and the wickedness, and the ignorance, and the stiffneckedness of men; for they will not search knowledge, nor understand great knowledge, when it is given unto them in plainness, even as plain as word can be" (v. 7). We can almost feel Nephi's grief at this point. He wants his readers to understand more, but the Spirit stops him. What could be so important that Nephi would mourn? It seems he mourns because men will not value sacred knowledge enough to search until they find it themselves. Men will not seek to understand greater knowledge even when they are told plainly such knowledge exists and is available.

In a sad conclusion to Nephi's mourning, we can sense his feelings as he perceives that his readers still will not comprehend what they should do to reach the tree of life, even though he briefly alluded to additional revelation that may result from the doctrine of Christ: "And now, my beloved brethren, I perceive that ye ponder still in your hearts; and it grieveth me that I must speak concerning this thing. For if ye would hearken unto the Spirit which teacheth a man to pray, ye would know that ye must pray; for the evil spirit teacheth not a man to pray, but teacheth him that he must not pray" (v. 8). He already told his readers that if they do not understand what they should do after baptism, it is because they do not ask or knock. He also said that his readers must receive the Holy Ghost, which if they did, would teach them to pray.

It must have seemed obvious to Nephi that prayer would bring the revelation of what he wanted his readers to understand. "But behold, I say unto you that ye must pray always, and not faint; that ye must not perform any thing unto the Lord save in the first place ye shall pray unto the Father in the name of Christ, that he will consecrate thy performance unto thee, that thy performance may be for the welfare of thy soul" (v. 9). With this statement

Nephi ends his explanation of the doctrine of Christ, leaving his readers with an implicit invitation to seek additional knowledge that he has gained for himself but was not allowed to share, such as the greater doctrine that awaits one at the end of the strait and narrow path.

Nephi's commentary in chapter 32 is ultimately an exhortation to endure to the end while on the strait and narrow path, which is accomplished by being worthy of and heeding to the whispering of the Holy Ghost, symbolically represented in the voice of angels. Though mention of the words of angels in chapter 32 may refer back to the explicit words of Christ in 2 Nephi 31 (promising that those who had been baptized by fire and by the Holy Ghost could speak with the tongue of angels), it may also hearken back to the role of angels in both Nephi's visionary experience and his father's dream.

The Words of Angels[7]

In 1 Nephi 8 and 11–14, an important, though subtle, gospel principle is revealed—the role of angelic ministry in the plan of salvation. In both Lehi's dream and Nephi's subsequent vision, angelic ministration plays a fundamental role in the revelatory experience. For Lehi, an angel guides him through the "dark and dreary waste" (1 Nephi 8:7), functioning in the same manner as the iron rod. For Nephi, an angel guides him through his vision, teaching him about Christ, who will also appear and function like angels in delivering the word of God. In light of the role of angelic ministration in Lehi's dream and Nephi's vision, perhaps it is not surprising to find angelic function described in connection with the doctrine of Christ. Certainly, angelic ministration has played and continues to play a fundamental role in bringing about the salvation of mankind. As such, it may be useful to review how angels function as deliverers of the words of Christ, both explicitly and implicitly.

Words of angels in the scriptures. Explicit angelic ministration can be found throughout the scriptures. Consider how often the words of angels are recorded in the Book of Mormon: Lehi was taught by angels (see 1 Nephi 1:8–15); Nephi recorded the words of angels (see 1 Nephi 3:29–31; 11–14; 19:8, 10; 2 Nephi 25:19); Jacob learned many things, including Christ's name, from an angel (see 2 Nephi 6:9, 11; 10:3); King Benjamin taught the words of an angel to his people (see Mosiah 3:2–27); Alma and the sons of Mosiah were rebuked by an angel (see Mosiah 27:11–17); Alma was instructed by and delivered the message of angels (see Alma 8:14–18; 9:25, 29); Amulek was called and prepared for his ministry by an angel (see Alma 10:7–10); an angel taught Alma the state of the soul between death and resurrection (see Alma 40:11); and an angel taught Samuel the Lamanite what to preach to the wicked Nephites (see Helaman 13:7; 14:9, 26–28). Certainly the Book of Mormon contains the ministration and teachings of angels. We could also add many examples from the other standard works,[8] but the point is clear: ministering angels speak the words of Christ to tell mortals what they need to do on the strait and narrow path. Thus angels are a key source of the iron rod, the word of God in the vision of the tree of life, and all can feast on their words in the scriptures.

Words of angels not found in the scriptures. Interestingly, not all angelic ministration is explicitly retold in the scriptures. Again just looking in the Book of Mormon, consider how many experienced the ministering of angels, but we do not have a record of what was communicated: Nephi (see 1 Nephi 14:25–28; 2 Nephi 4:24); Jacob (see Jacob 7:5); many among the Nephites (see Alma 13:22–26); many converted Lamanites (see Alma 19:34; 24:14); various men and women (see Alma 32:23); Nephi, Lehi, and about three hundred Lamanites (see Helaman 5:38–39, 48–49); wise men (see Helaman 16:14); Nephi (see 3 Nephi 7:18); the Nephites and their children (see 3 Nephi 17:24; 19:14–15); and Mormon and Moroni visited by the three translated Nephites (see 3 Nephi 28:25–26, 30; Mormon 8:11).

Apparently some things angels say are to be shared with all who will listen while other things are not for the world to know. In either case, it seems that feasting on the words of Christ spoken by angels can prepare one eventually to feast on the words of Christ directly from him. This is consistent with what Nephi said in 2 Nephi 32:3 and 6, that his readers should feast on the words of Christ, recognized and understood through the ministration of the Holy Ghost, but that no more doctrine would be given until Christ manifests himself "unto you in the flesh." One possible fulfillment of this promise may have been Christ's ministry among the Nephites after his resurrection.[9] Christ ministered to the Nephites as the ultimate angel, the messenger of the Father, and all of them obtained eternal life (see 3 Nephi 27:30–31). The Nephite golden years occurred because all of them feasted on the words of Christ until they were at the tree of life partaking of its fruit. Nevertheless, we currently have less than "a hundredth part" (3 Nephi 26:6) of what Christ taught the Nephites. Possibly similar to Nephi being stopped from saying more, Mormon was forbidden from including all that Christ taught the Nephites (see 3 Nephi 26:11).[10]

Though the injunction against saying more suggests some knowledge that cannot be discussed in a more public forum, it also encourages the reader to contemplate that which has been given more closely. As Lehi did not interpret his dream for his family (see 1 Nephi 15:2–3), Nephi left his readers to seek more light and knowledge about the doctrine of Christ on their own (compare Alma 12:9). In essence, it seems Nephi wanted his readers to do what he had done throughout his life—feast on the words of Christ, including those spoken by angels, to learn more—which takes us back to the invitation he provides in chapter 32.

Yet the role of angelic ministration in both Lehi's and Nephi's revelatory experiences and in Nephi's description of the doctrine of Christ may have another symbolic meaning, one that points to another approach that can be taken to understand the relationship between Lehi's dream and the doctrine of Christ—that of the temple.

The Doctrine of Christ, the Dream, and the Temple

The primary relationship between the vision of the tree of life, the doctrine of Christ, and the ancient temple is that they all portray the way man may return to God's presence and partake of eternal life. As temple allusions may be noted in Lehi's dream[11] and Nephi's vision,[12] such allusions in 2 Nephi 31–32 would be consistent with seeing the doctrine of Christ as an approach to the vision of the tree of life. Even so, this perspective is not explicit in the text and must be approached with care. Identifying parallels should not be considered conclusive, but solely as observations for consideration.

The tree of life is closely associated with the ancient temple. When Adam and Eve were cast out of God's presence and the Garden of Eden, cherubim and a flaming sword blocked them from "the way of the tree of life" (Genesis 3:24). "Perhaps it would not be too much to assume that the way spoken of could have been a strait and narrow path. Thus it seems possible that when Lehi saw the tree of life in his dream, he was in reality seeing a representation of that same tree which existed in the midst of the Garden of Eden."[13] Ever since the Fall, man has sought to return to the tree of life, and the revealed pattern of the ancient temple modeled the Garden of Eden and how man could return to God's presence.[14] In other words, the way to the tree of life may be seen as the path through the ancient temple. This suggests a connection between the ancient temple and the way to the tree of life as portrayed in the Garden of Eden, Lehi's dream, Nephi's vision, and the doctrine of Christ.

Nephi taught the doctrine of Christ in such a manner that it is possible to see parallels to the ancient temple.[15] In fact, it is only with all the elements Nephi emphasized in 2 Nephi 31–32 that the two models correlate to each other. Consider how the doctrine of Christ corresponds to the symbolism of the ancient temple.[16]

Ancient Temple	Strait and Narrow Path
Outer Court	
Altar of sacrifice	Obedience and sacrifice/Faith and repentance
Laver of water/Brazen sea	Gate of repentance and baptism by water
Holy Place	
Shewbread	Feasting on word of Christ
Candlestick(s)	Holy Ghost shows the way
Altar of incense	Prayer in Christ's name
Holy of Holies	
Cherubim	Angels
Ark of covenant/Mercy seat	Presence of God/Eternal life
High priest	Christ the example

The Outer Court. In the outer court of the ancient temple, the altar of sacrifice and laver of water/brazen sea were used regularly for animal sacrifices and ritual washings. These symbolized obedience and sacrifice, as well as faith, repentance, and baptism by water.[17] Likewise, Nephi emphasized obedience, repentance, and baptism by water in the doctrine of Christ (see 2 Nephi 31:10–13). Perhaps the gate of repentance and baptism is akin to the requirement that the ancient priests be cleansed by sacrifice and washed with water before entering the Holy Place (see Exodus 30:18–21).

The Holy Place. It is interesting that when Nephi sought to help his readers understand what to do after baptism in 2 Nephi 32, he emphasized three things that may be compared to the three items in the Holy Place: the word of Christ, the Holy Ghost, and prayer. First, Nephi's description of "feasting upon the word of Christ" (2 Nephi 31:20) might be likened to the shewbread the priests ate each week (see Exodus 25:30; Leviticus 24:5–9). Second, the oil in the candlestick(s), which was to "burn always" (Exodus 27:20), literally showed the way inside the otherwise dark Holy Place. This may be compared to Nephi's statement that the Holy Ghost "will show unto you all things what ye should do" (2 Nephi 32:5). Third, incense was associated with prayer anciently (see Psalm 141:2) and was to be offered on the altar in the Holy Place twice daily (see Exodus 30:7–8). Perhaps this is related to the fact that Nephi "did pray oft" in a Temple setting (1 Nephi 18:3) and corresponds to his exhortation to "pray always, and not faint . . . in the name of Christ" (2 Nephi 32:9).

Cherubim and angels. In the ancient temple, the cherubim on the mercy seat (see Exodus 25:18–22) and overshadowing the ark of the covenant (see 1 Kings 6:23–28) guarded the throne or dwelling place of God.[18] In addition, cherubim were found on the veils (see Exodus 26:32) and curtains or walls (see 1 Kings 6:29) of the temple, all representing the guardians of the way to the tree of life. To enter the Holy Place and the Holy of Holies, one had to be ritually clean and pass by the cherubim.

Angels may be compared to the cherubim because they "call men unto repentance . . . to prepare the way among the children of men, by declaring the word of Christ unto the chosen vessels of the Lord" (Moroni 7:31). As Nephi said, they teach those on the strait and narrow path "all things [they] should do" (2 Nephi 32:3) to reach the tree of life. "And by so doing, the Lord God prepareth the way that the residue of men may have faith in Christ, that the Holy Ghost may have place in their hearts" (Moroni 7:32). Thus cherubim guard the way and angels prepare the way for mankind to obtain the strait and narrow path and press forward to eternal life.

The Holy of Holies. The culminating symbol in the ancient temple was entering the Holy of Holies to be in God's presence and partake of eternal life.[19] This may be compared to the doctrine of Christ where those who get on the path and press forward eventually hear the Father say, "Ye shall have eternal life" (2 Nephi 31:20), and are thus prepared to enter his presence.[20] In the doctrine of Christ, Nephi taught how to prepare for God's presence and was an example of this himself in that he saw the Lord (see 2 Nephi 11:2).

High priest, Christ the example. As a final potential parallel between the doctrine of Christ and the ancient temple, Nephi portrayed Christ as setting the example by entering through the gate and pressing forward on the path to obtain eternal life. Like the high priest in ancient Israel, Christ, the great high priest, offered himself as a sacrifice and entered into God's presence (see Hebrews 9), symbolically passing through the ancient temple himself. When Christ said to Nephi, "Follow me, and do the things which ye have seen me do" (2 Nephi 31:12), we could imagine him saying, "Follow me through the temple to the presence of my Father." Both in the ancient temple ritual and the doctrine of Christ, Jesus is the model for all who want to return to God's presence and partake of the tree of eternal life.

Having identified some possible allusions to the ancient temple in the doctrine of Christ, we must ask, did Nephi have these things in mind when he wrote 2 Nephi 31–32? Was he trying to point his readers to the ancient temple to help them better understand the doctrine of Christ? We do not and cannot know the answers to these questions. The comparisons between the ancient temple and 2 Nephi 31–32 are consistent with seeing the doctrine of Christ as an approach to the vision of the tree of life, but without more information from Nephi himself, allusions to the ancient temple in the doctrine of Christ must be only considered possible, not certain or sure. Yet in terms of application, recognizing that the temple could be depicted in the doctrine of Christ may help us understand even better the role of the temple in our own journey along the strait and narrow path.

Conclusion

Nephi used the vision of the tree of life as the model for teaching the doctrine of Christ. In doing this, he included many new elements along with imagery from the original vision, creating another approach that describes what one must do to reach the tree of life. Even so, Nephi mourned because he could not say more and his readers would not seek to know more about the doctrine of Christ. Yet he also invited us to find out more, just as he did, and in that invitation he becomes our angel and our guide like his father before him. Through the Holy Ghost such ministration can become our iron rod to lead us to the tree. That the temple can be symbolically represented in the dream is not really surprising because the temple, like angelic ministration and the Holy Ghost, functions to lead us back to God and the gift of eternal life. This complex symbolism is one of the primary reasons Lehi's dream is such a powerful discourse on the doctrine of Christ.

Notes

1. Others have noted that Nephi referred to elements of the vision of the tree of life later in his record (see Daniel B. McKinlay, "Strait and Narrow," in *Encyclopedia of Mormonism*, ed. Daniel H. Ludlow (New York: Macmillan, 1992), 3:1419), but a survey of Latter-day Saint literature suggests that an in-depth study of 2 Nephi 31–32 and the vision of the tree of life is lacking.

2. Lehi's family left Jerusalem in 600 BC and camped in a valley they called Lemuel (see 1 Nephi 2:4–6, 14). Here Lehi and Nephi received their visions of the tree of life (see 1 Nephi 16:6), which appears to have been early on in the eight year journey from Jerusalem to Bountiful (see 1 Nephi 16:13–17, 33; 17:1–5). Nephi wrote about the doctrine of Christ sometime after 559 BC (see 2 Nephi 5:34) and probably closer to 544 BC when he gave Jacob charge concerning the small plates (see Jacob 1:1). This means more than thirty years, and at most fifty-five years, had passed between Nephi's vision and his writing of the doctrine of Christ in 2 Nephi 31–32.

3. See a comparison in Frederick W. Axelgard, "1 and 2 Nephi: An Inspiring Whole," *BYU Studies* 26, no. 4 (1986): 58. Also, Nephi's prophecies "referred to events revealed not only to Isaiah but to Nephi himself in his vision of the tree of life: the birth, crucifixion, and resurrection of the Messiah (2 Ne. 25); the ministry of Christ to the Nephites and the condition of the Gentiles in the last days (2 Ne. 26); the coming forth of the Book of Mormon (2 Ne. 27); the workings of the devil and his abominable church in the last days (2 Ne. 28); the Gentiles' rejection of the Book of Mormon (2 Ne. 29); and the conversion of Gentiles, Jews, and Lehi's seed (2 Ne. 30:1–8) before the millennial day. . . . Thus Nephi's prophecies in 2 Nephi 25–30 correlate to both passages in Isaiah and to Nephi's vision of the tree of life." John Sears Tanner, "Nephi$_1$," in *Book of Mormon Reference Companion*, ed. Dennis L. Largey (Salt Lake City: Deseret Book, 2003), 585.

4. Though not explicit in the text, it appears Lehi also learned this and other information recorded in 1 Nephi 10 from his vision of the tree of life (see vv. 7–10, 17). The content is similar to what Nephi saw in vision when he said, "I saw the things which my father saw" (1 Nephi 14:29).

5. Even though the two words "strait" and "straight" are pronounced the same, they have quite different meanings. "Strait" means narrow, while "straight" means not crooked. "In the 1829 printer's manuscript of the Book of Mormon, the word 'straight' was never used. When Joseph Smith said the word 'strai[gh]t,' Oliver Cowdery apparently always preferred to spell it 's-t-r-a-i-t,' which was, in the early nineteenth century, an acceptable spelling for either meaning. Indeed, spellings varied from one early edition of the Book of Mormon to the next; thus, one must consider the word in context to determine its meaning." John W. Welch, "Strait, straight," in *Book of Mormon Reference Companion*, 746. Regarding the path leading to the tree of life, all earlier editions of the Book of Mormon read "straight and narrow," while the current (1981) edition reads "strait and narrow." Careful analysis had led some to favor the earlier reading (Noel B. Reynolds and Royal Skousen, "Was the Path Nephi Saw 'Strait and Narrow' or 'Straight and Narrow'?," *Journal of Book of Mormon Studies* 10, no. 2 [2001], 30–33; John W. Welch, "Straight (Not Strait) and Narrow," *Journal of Book of Mormon Studies* 16, no. 1 [2007],

18–25) or the current reading. See Paul Y. Hoskisson, "Straightening Things Out: The Use of *Strait* and *Straight* in the Book of Mormon," *Journal of Book of Mormon Studies* 12, no. 2 (2003): 58–71.

6. Bruce R. McConkie, "The Probationary Test of Mortality," address given at the University of Utah Institute, January 10, 1982, 8–9.

7. I take the term "angel" in Nephi's writings to mean a heavenly messenger. This is based on its use in the Book of Mormon, which is consistent with the King James translation of the Bible. The Hebrew *mal'ak* and the Greek *aggelos*, both meaning "messenger," can refer to earthly or heavenly beings, but Jerome's Latin translation of the Bible (almost a thousand years after Nephi) used different words to distinguish between human and heavenly messengers. See Carol A. Newsom, "Angels (Old Testament)," in *The Anchor Bible Dictionary*, ed. David Noel Freedman (New York: Doubleday, 1992), 1:248–49. The King James translators maintained this distinction by rendering *mal'ak* and *aggelos* as "angel" when they believed a heavenly being was intended. Likewise, the use of "angel" in the Book of Mormon appears to refer to heavenly messengers (see Book of Mormon Index, "Angel" and "Angels, ministering of"). Nephi's statement that those who receive the Holy Ghost can speak "with the tongue of angels" (2 Nephi 31:13, 14; 32:2) indicates that mortals can speak the words of Christ as angels do, but not that they are angels themselves (see likewise D&C 42:6). Angels in Nephi's day would have included unembodied spirits, disembodied spirits, or translated beings, but not resurrected beings since none were yet resurrected, and only those who belong to this earth minister to it (see D&C 130:5; see also Oscar W. McConkie, "Angels," in *Encyclopedia of Mormonism*, 1:40–41).

8. Note that some form of the word "angel" is found 543 times in the standard works, according to a search of the English text of The Church of Jesus Christ of Latter-day Saints, *The Scriptures: CD-ROM Resource Edition* 1.0 (Salt Lake City: Intellectual Reserve, Inc., 2002).

9. This is based on the similarity between 2 Nephi 32:6 and Nephi's earlier statement in 2 Nephi 26:1: "And after Christ shall have risen from the dead he shall show himself unto you, my children, and my beloved brethren; and the words which he shall speak unto you shall be the law which ye shall do."

10. The brother of Jared had a similar experience and restriction (see Ether 3:21). The things he saw were made known to the Nephites after Christ's ministry among them, but we do not have them today (see Ether 4:1–7).

11. See Corbin T. Volluz, "Lehi's Dream of the Tree of Life: Springboard to Prophecy," *Journal of Book of Mormon Studies* 2, no. 2 (1993): 34–8.

12. For his vision, Nephi was "caught away in the Spirit of the Lord, yea, into an exceedingly high mountain" (1 Nephi 11:1). As mountains were associated anciently with sacred space and Temples (see Isaiah 2:2–3; 56:7), Nephi was in a temple setting when he saw his vision of the tree of life.

13. Volluz, "Lehi's Dream of the Tree of Life: Springboard to Prophecy," 35.

14. An excellent visual portrayal of this may be found in Donald W. Parry, "Garden of Eden: Prototype Sanctuary," in *Temples of the Ancient World*, ed. Donald W. Parry (Salt Lake City: Deseret Book; Provo, UT: FARMS, 1994), 134–5.

15. It should be noted that Nephi built a temple and kept the law of Moses, which centered around temple worship (see John W. Welch, "The Temple in the Book of

Mormon: The Temples at the Cities of Nephi, Zarahemla, and Bountiful," in *Temples of the Ancient World*, 297–387). "And we did observe to keep the judgments, and the statutes, and the commandments of the Lord in all things, according to the law of Moses.... And I, Nephi, did build a temple; and I did construct it after the manner of the temple of Solomon" (2 Nephi 5:10, 16). Certainly Nephi would have regularly participated in the performances and ordinances of the law of Moses at the temple he built. Moreover, the Nephites had the Melchizedek Priesthood (see Joseph Fielding McConkie, "Priesthood among the Nephites," in *Book of Mormon Reference Companion*, 656–58) and, unlike ancient Israel, were not restricted from entering into the rest of the Lord (see Jacob 1:7). This suggests the righteous among the Nephites had access to the blessings of the temple that were available before Christ's resurrection by virtue of the Holy Order of God among them (see 2 Nephi 6:2; Alma 13:1–16). Thus it seems Nephi was thoroughly informed on the critical role of the temple and its symbolism, including the higher ordinances that were originally offered to ancient Israel to bring them into God's presence (see D&C 84:19–25).

16. The symbolism of the ancient temple is adapted from Church Educational System, *Old Testament Student Manual: Genesis–2 Samuel*, 2nd ed. (Salt Lake City: The Church of Jesus Christ of Latter-day Saints, 1981), 155–56. I appreciate Robert J. Norman of the Church Educational System for introducing me to the idea that the strait and narrow path may be seen in the ancient temple.

17. There is no scriptural indication that the laver of water/brazen sea was used for baptisms anciently. Perhaps the brazen sea of Solomon's Temple was used for baptisms for the living and reference to this has been removed from the record we have. Bruce R. McConkie, *Mormon Doctrine*, 2nd ed. (Salt Lake City: Bookcraft, 1966), 103–4. Whatever the case, the laver of water/brazen sea symbolized baptism, which was part of the law of Moses (see D&C 84:26–27).

18. See Numbers 7:89; 1 Samuel 4:4; 2 Samuel 6:2; Psalm 80:1; 99:1; Isaiah 37:16.

19. Since some fell away after partaking of the fruit of the tree of life, it seems that Lehi's dream portrayed a symbolic entering into God's presence, as in entering the Holy of Holies in the ancient temple, not actually entering God's presence and partaking of eternal life.

20. Notice how the Prophet Joseph Smith's description of this process is similar to Nephi's: "After a person has faith in Christ, repents of his sins, and is baptized for the remission of sins and receives the Holy Ghost, ... then let him continue to humble himself before God, hungering and thirsting after righteousness, and living by every word of God, and the Lord will soon say unto him, Son, thou shalt be exalted. When the Lord has thoroughly proved him ... then the man will find his calling and election made sure. Then it will be his privilege to receive the other Comforter.... When any man obtains this last Comforter, he will have the personage of Jesus Christ to attend him, ... and even He will manifest the Father unto him." *Teachings of the Prophet Joseph Smith*, comp. Joseph Fielding Smith (Salt Lake City: Deseret Book, 1938), 150–51.

10

Lehi's Dream as a Template for Understanding Each Act of Nephi's Vision

Amy Easton-Flake

Elder Jeffrey R. Holland, in his work *Christ and the New Covenant*, suggests an important way to study the scriptures when he writes, "The Spirit made explicit that the Tree of Life and its precious fruit are symbols of Christ's redemption."[1] Because neither the Spirit nor Nephi ever vocalizes this connection between the tree and Christ (Nephi gives two direct interpretations of the tree and its fruit: to the angel he identifies it as "the love of God" [1 Nephi 11:22], and to his brethren he identifies it as "a representation of the tree of life" [1 Nephi 15:22]), Elder Holland teaches us through his reading how to uncover doctrine and messages within the scriptures that are not explicitly stated. He explains how the Spirit first links the tree to Christ when he tells Nephi he will show him the tree and then the Son of God descending out of heaven. After this occurs and Nephi asks to know the interpretation of the tree, the Spirit immediately shows him Christ's nativity—the virgin Mary with an infant in her arms. Then the angel, who replaces the Spirit of the Lord and becomes Nephi's guide for the duration of the vision, concludes this image by declaring, "Behold the Lamb of God, yea, even the Son

---

Amy Easton-Flake has a PhD in American literature from Brandeis University and specializes in nineteenth-century women writers and narrative theory.

of the Eternal Father!" (1 Nephi 11:21). To ensure Nephi understands the connection, the angel follows the image and the declaration with a question for Nephi: "Knowest thou the meaning of the tree which thy father saw?" (v. 21).[2] Elder Holland reaches his conclusion by looking closely at how the Spirit frames the images, the sequence in which Nephi's guides show him the images, and the dialogue or interactions between Nephi and his guides.

Elder Holland's interpretation illustrates the additional layers of meaning we will find within the dream when we give credence to what is seen as well as spoken and when we link images to statements. The dream has been called "one of the richest, most flexible, and far-reaching pieces of symbolic prophecy contained in the standard works,"[3] and "a literary masterpiece and a doctrinal gem."[4] Yet, when we as readers hold to the one interpretation directly stated by Nephi or his guides and never seek out the multiplicity of meanings contained within Nephi's vision, we miss much of the vision's majesty. To begin the excavation of these meanings, I employ a methodology of literary analysis similar to Elder Holland's in which I analyze Nephi's authorial choices, the interactions between Nephi and his guides, the established narrative logic, and the repetition, overlapping, and conjoining of words and images in 1 Nephi 11 through 14.

Such an analysis reveals that the connections between Lehi's dream and Nephi's vision do not cease after 1 Nephi 12, as most readers believe, but instead continue until the end of Nephi's vision in chapter 14. As neither 1 Nephi 13 nor 14 contains any explicitly vocalized interpretations of the symbols in Lehi's dream, readers most often see these chapters as unrelated bonus material in which Nephi is shown the future inhabitants of the American continent and the period before the Second Coming.[5] However, close analysis reveals that these chapters contain further interpretations of different aspects of Lehi's dream played out in specific temporal and historical moments. Nephi's vision may be better understood as a four-act play: act 1, Christ's earthly ministry (1 Nephi 11); act 2, the Nephites and Lamanites in the land of promise (1 Nephi 12); act 3, the Gentiles and house of Israel in America (1 Nephi 13); and act 4, the period immediately preceding Christ's Second Coming (1 Nephi 14). Nephi's vision repeats the imagery of Lehi's original dream, but in different contexts, each subsequent chapter building on the meaning of the imagery in the previous chapters. Although the angel appears to provide Nephi with fewer interpretations of the symbols as the dream proceeds, the layering of images from

1 Nephi 11 through 14 allows Nephi, and readers along with him, to see how the imagery of Lehi's dream is still at work and how each act contains distinct prophetic interpretations.

At the end of his vision, Nephi informs the reader, "I have written but a small part of the things which I saw" (1 Nephi 14:28). While this refers in part to the portion of the vision the angel forbids him to record, such a statement also signals Nephi's crucial role in reconstructing his vision for future readers. Nephi has the difficult task of taking a multisensory experience and relating it through words only. He must choose when to let the images speak for themselves and when to offer commentary—when to record the words of his guide and when to offer his own interpretation. Multiple moments within the text indicate that Nephi at times sees images that he does not describe or hears interpretations that he does not recount.[6] Ultimately, we can base our analysis only on what Nephi wrote, but we drastically undervalue Nephi's authorial role when we do not recognize his hand in the intricate retelling of his vision. He is constantly helping the reader to understand and see connections between the acts of his vision and his father's dream and revealing new layers of meaning for each of the symbols.[7]

Act 1: Christ's Earthly Ministry (1 Nephi 11)

General Authorities, scholars, and various readers have previously recognized many of the connections between Nephi's vision of Christ's birth, baptism, ministry, and crucifixion and the elements of Lehi's dream. I will touch on them briefly and offer a few new insights in order to make explicit the implicit narrative patterns and phrases that Nephi and his guides use to link Nephi's vision to Lehi's dream. When Nephi is first "caught away in the Spirit of the Lord," he asks to "behold the things which [his] father saw" (1 Nephi 11:1, 3). In response to this request, the Spirit links the tree to Christ, telling Nephi he will show him first the tree and then the Son of God descending out of heaven. After showing Nephi the tree, however, he does not immediately show him the Son of God. Instead he pauses and asks Nephi, "What desirest thou?" (v. 10). Nephi's response, "to know the interpretation thereof" (v. 11), appears to alter the intended vision because rather than seeing the Son of God descending out of heaven he sees first the virgin Mary and then later "the Son of the Eternal Father" in her arms (v. 21). Such change in the dream's direction should cause us as readers to reflect on how seeing Mary and Christ as a newborn baby helps Nephi, and by extension ourselves, to understand the interpretation of the tree as the love of God (made manifest through the gift of his Son) better than simply seeing the Son descending out of heaven.[8] One answer could be that each image illustrates the magnitude of God's condescension: God the Father's condescension in having a mortal child, and God the Son's condescension in coming down as a helpless infant.[9]

The change in the vision's direction, coupled with the angel testing Nephi to make sure he comprehends what he sees, underscores the fact that his understanding of the condescension of God is critical to knowing the interpretation of the tree. Recognizing this first explicit connection between an element in Lehi's dream and in Nephi's vision is essential on the structural level because it establishes the basic pattern the angel will use to provide Nephi with interpretations of his father's dream: the angel shows Nephi a symbol followed by a vision sequence that is an interpretation of that symbol. With this first symbol, the angel explicitly tells Nephi to make the connection; hereafter, the angel relies on the narrative pattern to signal to Nephi, as well as to the modern reader, that he is providing an interpretation.

The next vision sequence illustrates this pattern at work and establishes Nephi's common interpretive strategy of stating clearly the general interpretation of a symbol and leaving the reader to recognize the specific interpretation through the vision sequence. The sequence begins with Nephi informing the reader that he beheld "the rod of iron," which is the "word of God"; "the fountain of living waters," which is "a representation of the love of God"; and "the tree of life," which is also "a representation of the love of God" (v. 25). Immediately after, he sees Christ's baptism and ministry. Following the established logic of the vision, Nephi receives the specific interpretation of each of these symbols within this vision of Christ's life. Christ becomes a living iron rod, showing and teaching through his baptism and ministry how to return to God's presence. Nephi expands upon this connection near the end of his ministry when he explains to his people that to commence on the "path which leads to eternal life," they must follow Christ's example and be baptized (see 2 Nephi 31:18; see v. 17). Significantly in this context, "the word of God" is one of the titles for Jesus Christ—Christ is God's word made flesh (see John 1:1, 14). As Christ himself explained, "I am the way, the truth, and the life: no man cometh unto the Father, but by me" (John 14:6). In this statement, as in the vision, Christ simultaneously performs multiple functions.

Along with being the rod of iron, he continues to represent the fountain of living water and the tree of life as he heals the sick and afflicted, providing another example of what occurs as people come unto Christ and partake of the fruit. Likewise, Christ's crucifixion is another manifestation of the condescension of God and his great love.

The final image sequence of act 1, in which the great and spacious building moves to the forefront, is particularly important from a narrative viewpoint because it illustrates multiple strategies that the angel and Nephi use to build connections between symbols and historical moments. While in previous sequences the symbol is shown and then the interpretation is shown, here the two are intertwined as Nephi beholds the large and spacious building filled with multitudes gathered together "to fight against the twelve apostles of the Lamb" (v. 35). In this sequence, the angel emphasizes that both general and (multiple) specific interpretations exist for each symbol by vocalizing the general meaning—"the world and the wisdom thereof"—and a specific meaning—"the house of Israel hath gathered together to fight against the twelve apostles of the Lamb" (v. 35). Remaining true to the narrative pattern he has established, Nephi then offers further commentary on the general interpretation—"the great and spacious building was the pride of the world" (v. 36)—but leaves the reader to gain his or her own understanding of the specific interpretation.

Another rhetorical tool in this sequence is the linking of phrases to symbols; such linking allows the phrase to stand in later for the symbol. Three times within two short verses, Nephi uses the phrase "gathered together" to describe the inhabitants of the great and spacious building. Repetition creates a solid connection in the mind of the reader that allows Nephi to evoke the image of the "large and spacious building" with simply the phrase "gathered together" (vv. 34–35).[10] As Nephi and the angel explicitly link phrases and concise general interpretations with elements from Lehi's dream, they mention the elements less frequently and adopt a shorthand of sorts. For instance, the angel unequivocally links the tree and Christ in act 1; consequently, throughout the rest of the vision Christ's appearance calls up the image of the tree as well.

One last narrative strategy that merits attention in act 1 is Nephi's and the angel's repetition of similar words and actions to recall an earlier moment in the dream or vision. For instance, once the angel establishes Christ as the meaning of the tree, he shows Nephi an image of the Son of God as the children of men "fall down at his feet and worship him" (v. 24). The repetition of words and actions signals this as a historical echo to the individuals in Lehi's dream who "fell down and partook of the fruit of the tree" (1 Nephi 8:30).

Lehi's Dream (1 Nephi 8)

Before proceeding with the connection between Lehi's dream and Nephi's vision, a brief review of the kaleidoscope[11] of elements shown to Lehi is critical. Although the major elements are clear in most readers' minds—a rod of iron leading to the tree of life set in opposition to a great and spacious building and a mist of darkness arising to lead people from the path if they do not hold firmly to the rod—other elements are more prone to become hazy or to merge together in both our personal interpretations and artists' renditions. The river and fountain of water are two such elements. Most depictions of Lehi's dream include only one body of water; however, the text clearly states there are two: a river of filthy water that represents the depths of hell and a fountain of living waters that represents the love of God (see 1 Nephi 11:25; 12:16). The confusion likely stems from Nephi and the angel using *river* and *fountain* as interchangeable terms throughout the dream to describe both the pure and impure bodies of water.[12]

Another element that is often hazy in our minds and left out of artistic renditions is the large and spacious field. After spending hours in the "dark and dreary waste" (1 Nephi 8:7), Lehi prays and then beholds "a large and spacious field" (v. 9). Significantly, Lehi does not say he is in the field, rather that he beholds the field and then beholds the tree. Lehi's sense of relief is evident as he now has something to look to and move toward—the field and the fruit of the tree. Later in his dream, Lehi explains that the strait and narrow path and rod of iron lead first to the tree and then on to the head of the fountain and a large and spacious field: "And I also beheld a strait and narrow path, which came along by the rod of iron, even to the tree by which I stood; *and it also led* by the head of the fountain, unto a large and spacious field, as if it had been a world" (v. 20; emphasis added). Visual representations of the dream often have the tree as the end point of the rod and either leave out the large and spacious field or conflate it with the space where concourses of people are trying to obtain the path. While this may not seem like an important oversight in the context of Lehi's dream, such conflation obscures our ability to see the connections between Lehi's dream and Nephi's vision.

Many textual details make it clear that the large and spacious field is not where the concourses of people currently are but what they are pressing toward. First, Lehi is not in the field but rather moves toward the field; second, the mists of darkness that cover the concourses of people recall Lehi's experience of being in darkness for many hours in the dark and dreary waste, not the relief and joy he feels at seeing the field and the tree; and third, Lehi tells his family the rod of iron *leads* to the large and spacious field. If we imagine, as readers often do, that the concourses of people are located in the large and spacious field at one end of the rod and the tree of life is located at the opposite end of the rod, then Lehi's description of the rod of iron as *leading* to the large and spacious world would be inappropriate for the word of God, as the rod would not lead individuals to a place God does not want them to go. A look at the 1828 edition of Webster's dictionary makes it clear that at the time Joseph Smith translated the Book of Mormon, the term *lead* meant to guide or conduct to a purposeful place. The dictionary cited examples such as the following: "The Israelites were *led* by a pillar of a cloud by day, and by a pillar of fire by night," and "He *leadeth* me beside the still waters Ps. 23."[13]

Lehi seeing the word of God leading to a field, or as he redefines it "a world" (v. 20), is unsurprising because running throughout ancient and modern scripture—most notably in part of the Abrahamic covenant—is God's promise to his chosen people that they will receive a land for their inheritance if they are faithful.[14] Both Lehi and Nephi, before seeing their respective visions, receive a promise from the Lord that they "shall be led to a land of promise" (1 Nephi 2:20; see 1 Nephi 5:5). In Lehi's dream, he sees a large and spacious field—a symbol of the promised land his family is currently journeying toward. As Daniel L. Belnap argues convincingly, this dream becomes a new cultural narrative for the family of Lehi as they leave Jerusalem behind and seek a new land of inheritance.[15] Significantly, this world in the dream can only be reached by holding firm to the word of God, and Lehi is told that all those who come to this promised land "should be *led* out of other countries by the hand of the Lord" (2 Nephi 1:5). Nephi sees the historical fulfillments of this prophecy in acts 1 and 3 of his vision. Recognizing that the rod of iron leads to a new world as well as the tree of life helps us apprehend how intimately connected to Lehi's dream are acts 2, 3, and 4 of Nephi's vision—in essence, they show what happens to individuals as they obtain and live in this new world.

Lehi's reference to the large and spacious field as "a world" (1 Nephi 8:20) deserves further discussion. In the context of what Nephi will soon see in his vision, both words are significant. First, it is *a* world, not *the* world, indicating the existence of multiple worlds. Second, Lehi's choice of the word *world* to describe what he sees connects the promised land to the "New World," as it will be called at the time of Columbus's discovery of the Americas.[16] With these elements of the dream in the forefront rather than the backdrop of our dream landscape, the sequence in Nephi's vision from Christ's ministry to the inhabitants of the promised land becomes the next logical step rather than a disconnect.

Act 2: The Nephites and Lamanites in the Land of Promise (1 Nephi 12)

Act 1 closes in the Old World, and act 2 opens in the New World, where Nephi see his descendants, their cities and wars, their visitation from Christ, and their eventual destruction. The symbol of the great and spacious building provides the unifying transition from one scene to the next. Without mentioning the building explicitly, Nephi relies on the connection he has established a few verses earlier between the building and the phrase "gathered together" to signal that the great and spacious building takes on a new historical interpretation in the New World: Nephites and Lamanites "gathered together to battle, one against another" (1 Nephi 12:2). That the Nephite and Lamanite civilizations have become another incarnation of the great and spacious building is reinforced by the elements associated with "the pride of the world" (1 Nephi 11:36)—wars, contentions, and cities—that dominate this vision sequence (see 1 Nephi 12:1–3).

Soon another element from Lehi's dream enters the scene: "a mist of darkness" (v. 4). The mist of darkness, like the other symbols, has more than one interpretation; in this case, it has a physical manifestation as well as a metaphorical meaning. Later in this chapter, we learn that "the mists of darkness" represent "the temptations of the devil, which blindeth the eyes, and hardeneth the hearts of the children of men" (v. 17). Here the specific temptation facing the Nephites and Lamanites is war, which most likely springs from the temptations of power, greed, pride, and hatred. Because the people succumb to these temptations and associate with the large and spacious building, an actual mist of darkness covers the earth and many are lost during the time prior to Christ's appearance in the New World. Although this physical mist of darkness is not actually the temptations of the devil, it does relate to the Nephites' spiritual reality and is a result of their succumbing to Satan's temptations. The mist performs a similar function in real life to what it does in Lehi's dream: it covers and confuses those individuals who are not standing firm in their commitment to Christ and symbolically holding to the iron rod. The presence of the rod of iron, although not mentioned specifically, is felt when its function is fulfilled and those who are not lost in the mist of darkness qualify to see the Lord.

Nephi next beholds a prophetic interpretation of individuals partaking of the fruit and accessing the Atonement as he witnesses his people being in the presence of the Lamb of God and having their garments made white "in his blood" (v. 10). The angel repeats this interpretation of their garments being made white in the blood of the Lamb for both the twelve disciples and the people collectively (see vv. 10–11). Such imagery reinforces the fruit of the tree as being Christ and his Atonement, and it reiterates the connection between whiteness and the fruit. The books of 3 Nephi and 4 Nephi recount the fulfillment of this prophecy in the coming of the Savior to the New World and the three generations who pass away in righteousness "because of the love of God which did dwell in the hearts of the people" (4 Nephi 1:15).

In a kaleidoscope of overlapping images, Nephi next beholds his people battling against the Lamanites until their eventual destruction; this event is overlaid with the symbolic images of the filthy river, the mist of darkness, and the large and spacious building. As Nephi sees these image sequences simultaneously, the angel voices the ahistorical and atemporal interpretation of each element. "The fountain of filthy water [is] . . . the depths of hell," "the mists of darkness are the temptations of the devil," and "the large and spacious building" is the "vain imaginations and the pride of the children of men" (1 Nephi 12:16–18). Nephi displays his ability to connect the symbols to the visionary history when he attributes the destruction of his people to their "pride" and the "temptations of the devil" (v. 19). Having each of the three elements—the filthy river, the mist of darkness, and the large and spacious building—together emphasizes that the destruction of the Nephites will be the result of their choosing to follow Satan and the ways of the world rather than God. The Lamanites remain after the Nephites are gone, but Nephi makes it clear that their fate is not pleasant. By calling the people a "dark, and loathsome, and a filthy people" (v. 23), Nephi connects them to symbols of hell—the filthy water and the dark mist. God may not have literally destroyed the Lamanites, but by dwindling in unbelief they have become a part of hell.

Act 3: The Gentiles and House of Israel in America (1 Nephi 13–14:6)

In act 3 the scene shifts again to show "the nations and kingdoms of the Gentiles" (1 Nephi 13:3). A new symbol, "this great and abominable church" (v. 6), displays striking similarities to the great and spacious building—so much so that this church should be seen as a historical analogue of the building.[17] In both function and characteristics, the great and abominable church mirrors the great and spacious building. In the two previous historical explanations of the great and abominable church, multitudes gathered together to first war against the Apostles of the Lamb and then against the Nephites—God's once chosen people (see 1 Nephi 11:34; 1 Nephi 12:13–15). In act 3 of his vision, Nephi learns that the church "slayeth the saints of God, yea, and tortureth them and bindeth them down, and yoketh them with a yoke of iron, and bringeth them down into captivity" (1 Nephi 13:5). This description connects the church to both the historical function of the great and spacious building, as individuals in the building literally slay the saints of God, and the ahistorical, metaphorical function, as people become captive and yoked once they allow the pride and vanity of the world to consume them. The angel further cements this connection between the two elements when he explains that the church, "for the praise of the world, . . . destroy[s] the saints of God" (v. 9). Thus pride and worldly praise motivate individuals within both the building and the church. The two groups are also the same in character: the materiality of the great and abominable church—described as a love of "gold, and silver, and silks, and scarlets, and fine-twined linen" (v. 7)—is simply a historical representation of the "exceedingly fine" dress and "mocking" attitude that characterized the inhabitants of the great and spacious building (1 Nephi 8:27).

After seeing the latest manifestation of the great and spacious building, the vision shifts to show Nephi God's plan for helping individuals escape Satan's influence, as represented in the great and abominable church, and again Lehi's dream becomes the template for understanding this historical moment. In essence, act 3 is the societal equivalent to Lehi's individual experience. The actors in this vision begin at a place similar to Lehi's dark and dreary wasteland, as Nephi repeats multiple times they are in "captivity" in the Old World (see 1 Nephi 13:13, 16). The waters that separate the Gentiles from the New World are a historical interpretation of the waters that separate the great and spacious building from the tree and the field in Lehi's dream. As the angel has explained to Nephi, the gulf that separates the great and spacious field and tree of life from the great and spacious building is "the word of the justice of the Eternal God, and the Messiah who is the Lamb of God" (1 Nephi 12:18). The two remain separated because of the justice of God.

This ahistorical interpretation fits precisely with the historical interpretation in 1 Nephi 13, in which the Old World inhabitants are kept separated from the New World inhabitants until Lehi's posterity through their wickedness lose their right to the land and bring upon themselves "the wrath of God" (1 Nephi 13:14).[18] Lehi's dream teaches that only the iron rod, meaning the word of God, leads people to the tree and the field; the Spirit of God performs this function in act 3 as he leads individuals out of captivity and to the New World (vv. 12–16). Worth noting is the manifestation of the word of God in each of its major forms over the course of this vision.[19] In act 1 Jesus Christ embodies the word of God, here in act 3 the Holy Ghost becomes the iron rod that leads individuals to the New World, and later in act 3 the scriptures hold the word of God that leads God's children to Christ and eternal life. Consequently, Nephi's vision also helps the reader understand the different ways God makes known his word and leads his children to eternal life.

When one looks at this prophetic revelation through the lens of Lehi's dream, it also becomes apparent that the individuals who possess this New World have partaken of the fruit of the tree in the course of their journey. The description of the New World inhabitants as "white, and exceedingly fair and beautiful" is one indication of this (v. 15). By this point in Nephi's vision, the angel and Nephi have established through repetition that the color white is synonymous with partaking of the fruit: the fruit is white, the tree is white, and individuals who partake of the fruit are made white through the blood of the Lamb. The fact that the Saints have "the power of the Lord" implies that they have partaken of the fruit because they can merit his power only as they "humble themselves before the Lord" (v. 16). The act of humbling themselves before Christ recalls the image of those who kneel before the tree in Lehi's dream. In both instance, individuals recognize their dependence on the Lord: he alone has delivered them out of captivity, whether temporally or spiritually.

Although Christ does not physically appear in this sequence, his presence is felt through "the power of the Lord" (a term layered with connections to Christ and the fruit), that is with the Gentiles as they battle against "their mother Gentiles" (vv. 16–17). By using the term "gathered together" to mark the mother Gentiles as another iteration of the great and spacious building, Nephi indicates to the reader that this battle is a historical analogue to the symbolic opposition between the inhabitants of the great and spacious building and the individuals at the tree.

"Knowest thou the meaning of the book?" the angel asks (v. 21). With this question, the angel connects the book that the Gentiles carry with them to the New World with the two most significant elements of Lehi's dream and Nephi's vision—the tree of life and the condescension of God. Only three times does the angel engage Nephi in dialogue and test his understanding by asking him, "Knowest thou . . ." (1 Nephi 11:16, 21; 13:21). Such limited questioning underscores the importance of these three elements and ties them together. One might be tempted because of the overt connection among the three to see if the book—which we recognize to be the Bible—fulfills the same function as the condescension of God and is therefore another manifestation of the tree of life. This is an intriguing idea; however, close analysis of the book reveals its function to be analogous to that of Jesus Christ in his baptism and ministry and of the Holy Ghost in leading individuals to the New World, as the book brings people to accept Christ as their Savior. Consequently, it is another manifestation of the iron rod. However, the book clearly has some other significance than being another manifestation of the word of God.

The book's importance is underscored first by the company it keeps with the tree and the condescension of God—it is an instrument of salvation—and second by the strikingly different presentation it occasions from Nephi. Nephi's staging of the book's vision sequence is unlike any other because he quotes the angel's explanation of the book for twenty-two verses rather than sharing what he saw—a marked shift from the rest of the vision in which descriptions of what he saw dominate. Comments from the angel, such as "thou hast beheld" and "thou seest" (1 Nephi 13:24–26, 28–30), indicate irrefutably that Nephi sees what the angel describes and possibly more since at other times in the vision Nephi sees multiple sequences simultaneously, yet Nephi chooses to record the words rather than the images. This shift in narrative strategy reveals the high value Nephi places on the angel's precise interpretation and his desire to pass it on undiluted to his readers.

In a similar rhetorical move, the angel turns to a higher authority, the Lamb of God, to explain the future role of the books: the angel introduces another book midway through the vision sequence (which we recognize as the Book of Mormon), so the singular *book* becomes the plural *books*. The angel quotes the Lamb of God, bearing record that the Book of Mormon will contain the gospel, his word, and will be the instrument through which individuals will be brought to him (vv. 24–36). Nephi later expands on this idea in 2 Nephi 25–28 when he illustrates how the Jews, Lamanites, and Gentiles reject Christ. The solution to their problem is an acceptance of Christ through the Book of Mormon and its teachings. Notably, Christ's words are only heard in Nephi's vision, testifying of the book and the great and marvelous work Christ will perform among the children of men at the last day. The significance of the Book of Mormon in the time preceding Christ's Second Coming cannot be overstated.

Within Nephi's vision sequence of the book lies another expansive historical interpretation of Lehi's dream. Though the symbols from Lehi's dream are not mentioned overtly, the connections become clear through specific interpretations that have become analogous to the symbols. For instance, the great and abominable church continues to fulfill the function of the great and spacious building as it seeks to destroy the word of God by taking away the "plain and most precious" parts from the Bible (1 Nephi 13:26). The result of such tampering with the Bible is a mist of darkness that settles over it. Without explicitly using the phrase "mist of darkness," the angel evokes its presence through the phrases he uses to describe what happens to individuals when truth is missing from the Bible: they are in an "awful state of blindness" (v. 32), and "an exceedingly great many do stumble, yea, insomuch that Satan hath great power over them" (v. 29). Such consequences are the result of wandering in darkness and recall the image in Lehi's dream of the multitudes wandering in this mist. In both instances, an individual may still hold firm to the rod, or the truths contained within the book, and come unto Christ. However, the mists—or lack of truth that "blind[s] the eyes" (v. 27)—make the process much more difficult.

Each interpretation of the mist of darkness expands our understanding of what constitutes the temptations of the devil. From the Lamanites and Nephites, we see how wars and contentions tempt us away from the word of God. In this sequence, the mist of darkness both creates temptations and was created by Satan's temptations. Elder Bruce R. McConkie explains this phenomenon: "The devil wages war against the scriptures. He hates them, perverts their plain meanings, and destroys them when he can. He entices those who heed his temptings to delete and discard, to change and corrupt, to alter and amend, thus taking away the key which will aid in making men, 'wise unto salvation.'"[20] In this vision sequence, the angel makes known Satan's plan to cover the word of God with a mist of darkness.

Standing in opposition to this mist and the great and spacious building in this sequence are the rod of iron and the tree of life. In each expanded interpretation of Lehi's vision, the word of God is available to lead individuals to Christ. With the following statement, the angel establishes how the Book of Mormon and Bible will fulfill the function of the rod: "These last records ... shall make known to all kindreds, tongues, and people, that the Lamb of God is the Son of the Eternal Father, and the Savior of the world; and that all men must come unto him, or they cannot be saved" (v. 40).[21] In his final recorded sermon given near the end of his life, Nephi reinforces the necessity of partaking of the word of God to reach the tree and confirms that readers should have recognized the dream symbols in his historical vision by using language from the dream: "If ye shall press forward, feasting upon the word of Christ, and endure to the end, behold, thus saith the Father: Ye shall have eternal life" (2 Nephi 31:20).[22] The word *feasting* appropriately describes how the word of God must become a part of us, changing us and qualifying us for the blessings of eternal life. As is often the case, the elements in Nephi's vision function on both the spiritual and temporal level. Spiritually, the Book of Mormon and the Bible, which contain "the words of the Lamb" (1 Nephi 13:41), will lead individuals to Christ. Temporally, the Book of Mormon and the Bible will prepare the world for the literal appearance of Christ at the Second Coming.

The high point of Nephi's vision occurs when the tree of life (a representation of the Lamb of God) and the great and spacious field (a representation of the promised land) are brought together as the culminating promise. Those who partake of the fruit, referred to here as those who "hearken unto the Lamb of God," shall have the Lamb of God "manifest himself unto them in word, and also in power . . . [and] shall be numbered among the seed of thy father; yea, they shall be numbered among the house of Israel; and they shall be a blessed people upon the promised land forever" (1 Nephi 14:1–2). Individuals who press forward and hold fast to the rod will come into the presence of the Savior and receive the promised land; however, the connection to the earlier image in Lehi's dream of individuals partaking of the fruit and falling away reminds the reader that steadfastness is required even after the destination is reached.

At the end of act 3, after the illustration of this beautiful promise, a new element from Lehi's dream comes briefly to the forefront. Thus far, the angel has shown Nephi prophetic, expansive interpretations of the tree and its fruit, the iron rod, the large and spacious field, the great and spacious building, and the mist of darkness. Now the angel focuses his attention on the terrible gulf, filthy water, and the many individuals wandering off the path. Similar to how the angel incorporates the other elements of Lehi's dream into act 3, he does not explicitly mention the filthy river and corresponding gulf but instead relies on preestablished layers and connections to evoke their presence. First, the imagery of a great pit and a gulf align closely. Second, the angel explains that the pit, like the river and gulf, is a representation of hell (v. 3). Third, the pit, like the river and gulf, is in the interesting position of being the devil's creation but also upholding the justice of God (see 1 Nephi 12:18; 14:4)—thus the common function of the two establishes their connection. Recognizing how the symbols build upon one another increases our comprehension of each symbol. In this particular instance, the angel's explanation of how the pit will be "digged" and "filled" by "the devil and his children" answers the question of who will create the gulf of hell that Nephi tells his brothers is "prepared for the wicked" (1 Nephi 14:3; 15:29).

Act 4: Time before Christ's Second Coming (1 Nephi 14:7–30)

Act 4 of Nephi's vision, which begins in 1 Nephi 14:7, offers the last prophetic interpretation of Lehi's vision and fittingly commences with the angel quoting the Lamb of God's announcement that "a great and a marvelous work" is about to come forth that will lead individuals to "peace and life eternal" or to "the captivity of the devil" (v. 7). Several aspects of the Lord's statement evoke Lehi's dream. First, the basic divide between peace and life eternal and the captivity of the devil is simply another way of illustrating the divide between the tree of life and the great and spacious building that has governed each vision sequence. Second, in terms of word choice, Christ uses key terms—blindness, captivity, and destruction—that Nephi and the angel have connected to each element associated with Satan in Lehi's dream—the mist of darkness, the great and spacious building, and the gulf of water. By this point in the vision, each symbol has become dense with meaning; consequently, Christ's statement possesses greater richness and power than it would have if placed at the beginning of the vision because here it draws on everything that precedes it.

Following the established narrative pattern, the angel then proceeds to show Nephi the explanation of the Savior's prophecy. Nephi beholds what we now understand to be the analogue for the great and spacious building, the great and abominable church, which has "dominion over all the earth" (v. 11). The number of the righteous are small in comparison—just as Lehi's dream has indicated they would be: "Great was the multitude that did enter into that strange building" (1 Nephi 8:33). Soon the great and abominable church fulfills its narrative function when it "gather[s] together multitudes . . . to fight against the Lamb of God" (1 Nephi 14:13), just as the great and spacious building has "gathered together" (1 Nephi 11:35) multitudes to fight against the Twelve Apostles of the Lamb, the Nephites, the Saints of God, and the Gentiles in America.[23]

Similar to what he does in act 3, the Lord manifests his presence through the power of the Lamb of God that descends upon the covenant people of the Lord. Nephi underscores the connection between obtaining the power of God and partaking of the fruit by using phrases that signify an individual has partaken of the fruit: "saints," "covenant people," and "righteousness" (v. 14). In this final iteration of the battle between the great and spacious building and the tree of life—here referred to as the church of the Lamb of God and the church of the devil—the great gulf has become unsurpassable. The either-or language that dominates this sequence indicates a polarization so strict that individuals no longer switch sides or sit on the fence but rather belong to God or the devil (see vv. 7, 10).[24] The ending of Nephi's recorded vision parallels the ending of Lehi's dream—both finish in midstride with individuals pressing towards God and partaking of the fruit of the tree or "feeling their way towards that great and spacious building" (1 Nephi 8:31; see v. 30).

Conclusion

A literary analysis of Lehi's dream and Nephi's vision makes clear the sincerity with which Nephi penned the words, "I bear record that I saw the things which my father saw, and the angel of the Lord did make them known unto me" (1 Nephi 14:29). By paying close attention to the established narrative logic, the repetition, overlapping, conjoining of words and images, and Nephi's role in the retelling process, we recognize that although Nephi did not experience the elements in the same manner as his father did (Nephi's vision was collective and historic, while his father's was intimate and symbolic), he did see the same symbols and comprehend how his father's dream acted as a template for understanding the future of his posterity, the Gentile inhabitants of the New World, and all people before Christ's Second Coming. He then sought to make these connections known to his reader in his reconstruction of his vision.

After Nephi's vision concludes, his brethren ask him to explain the things their "father saw in a dream" (1 Nephi 15:21). In light of the immense interpretation Nephi has just received, the recorded insight he provides to his brethren is staggering in its brevity. He offers them only the meaning of the symbols in their most general terms, keeping to himself all the specific and layered insights he now possesses. What is Nephi's reason for this? Likely he recognizes they will benefit most from hearing the basics: an "awful gulf," which is hell, has been prepared for those individuals who "die in their wickedness" (vv. 28, 33); the fruit of the tree of life "is most precious and most desirable above all other fruits; yea, and it is the greatest of all the gifts of God" (v. 36); and they must "hearken unto the word of God" in order to withstand "the temptations and the fiery darts of the adversary" (v. 24). The information that Nephi sets forth simply and clearly is what we must know and understand to finish successfully our mortal sojourn and return to God, yet more knowledge exists if we are willing to seek it.

When comparing the examples of Nephi and his brethren, it is significant to note how much information beyond the basics the Lord desires to make known to his children. As Nephi chastises his brethren, "Do ye not remember the things which the Lord hath said?—If ye will not harden your hearts, and ask me in faith, believing that ye shall receive, with diligence in keeping my commandments, surely these things shall be made known unto you" (v. 11). Nephi's experience of receiving his vision illustrates the reality of

God's promise: he saw not only the interpretation of the dream his father had seen but also a vision of the whole history of the world, similar to that seen by John the Beloved and the brother of Jared. Our personal experience of reading Lehi's dream and Nephi's vision may parallel either Nephi's or his brethren's: we may accept the essential doctrine that Nephi and his guides explicitly state and move on, or we may choose to look closer and use narrative tools to excavate the layers of meaning and connections set out by Nephi and his guides.

Notes

1. Jeffrey R. Holland, *Christ and the New Covenant* (Salt Lake City: Deseret Book, 1997), 160.

2. Holland, *Christ and the New Covenant*, 160.

3. Corbin T. Volluz, "Lehi's Dream of the Tree of Life: Springboard to Prophecy," *Journal of Book of Mormon Studies* 2, no. 2 (1993): 38.

4. Robert L. Millet, "Another Testament of Jesus Christ," in *The Book of Mormon: First Nephi, the Doctrinal Foundation*, ed. Monte S. Nyman and Charles D. Tate Jr. (Provo, UT: Religious Studies Center, Brigham Young University, 1988), 163.

5. Although the standard reading is to see no connection between 1 Nephi 8 and 1 Nephi 13 and 14, Corbin T. Volluz has provided an insightful interpretation of 1 Nephi 12, 13, and 14 as an extended prophetic vision of the three separate multitudes that attempt to make their way to the tree of life. See Volluz, "Lehi's Dream of the Tree of Life," 20–29. While I find Volluz's reading convincing, our readings overlap on very few points.

6. For instance, in 1 Nephi 13:23–30 Nephi cites the angel's explanation of what he is seeing rather than describing it himself, and in 1 Nephi 14:5 the angel mentions showing Nephi things that Nephi has not described.

7. As seen in his quotations of and expansions on Isaiah's words, Nephi delighted in the multiplicity of meanings that could be contained in a single image or prophecy (see for example 2 Nephi 26–27). He rejoiced to show his people and his future readers that Isaiah's prophecies could speak simultaneously of Isaiah's time, the meridian of time, and the Second Coming. Therefore, we should not be surprised to find Nephi recounting his vision in a manner that helps his reader see how the elements in Lehi's dream take on different meanings at various points in his vision.

8. "The tree of life . . . is the love of God. The love of God for His children is most profoundly expressed in His gift of Jesus as our Redeemer." Neal A. Maxwell, "Lessons from Laman and Lemuel," *Ensign*, November 1999, 8.

9. For further explanation of the condescension of God in 1 Nephi 11, see Bruce R. McConkie, "Behold the Condescension of God," *New Era*, December 1984, 35–39.

10. Volluz too noted that whenever Nephi uses the phrase "multitudes gathered together," it seems to refer to the great and spacious building. "Lehi's Dream of the Tree of Life," 19.

11. Charles L. Swift, "Lehi's Vision of the Tree of Life: Understanding the Dream as Visionary Literature," *Journal of Book of Mormon Studies* 14, no. 2 (2005): 58–61, explains how Lehi's dream follows the kaleidoscopic structure of visionary literature as explained by Lelend Ryken in *How to Read the Bible as Literature* (Grand Rapids, MI: Zondervan, 1984), 170.

12. The fountain is negative in 1 Nephi 8:32 and 12:16; the fountain is positive in 1 Nephi 8:20 and 11:25; the river is ambiguous in 1 Nephi 8:13, 17, 19, 26 because it has not yet been identified as filthy; the river is negative in 1 Nephi 12:16 and 15:26–27.

13. *Webster's Revised Unabridged Dictionary* (1828), "lead."

14. Abraham 2:5 and Genesis 12:7 and 17:8 contain the Lord's promise to Abraham that he and his seed are given the land of Canaan for an everlasting possession. Much of the Old Testament recounts his posterity's ability to obtain and keep or lose this promised land according to their righteousness. In the early history of the Church, the saints moved from place to place in search of the land of Zion promised to them by the Lord. In the Doctrine and Covenants we are promised that if we are faithful in keeping the new and everlasting covenant, we "shall inherit thrones, kingdoms, principalities, and powers, dominions" (D&C 132:19).

15. For more information, see Daniel L. Belnap, "'There Arose a Mist of Darkness': The Narrative of Lehi's Dream in Christ's Theophany" (paper presented at the Scholars Focus Conference on Third Nephi, Laura F. Willes Center for Book of Mormon Studies, Provo, UT, September 2008), 4–5.

16. The term "New World" is believed to have been coined in 1492 by a Spanish scholar named Peter Martyr d'Anghiera in a letter discussing Columbus's first voyage to the Americas. Edmundo O'Gorman, *The Invention of America* (Bloomington: Indiana University Press, 1961), 84–85.

17. John W. Welch suggests that "the great and spacious building was the same as the great and abominable church" but offers very little to back up the assertion. "Connections between the Visions of Lehi and Nephi," in *Pressing Forward with the Book of Mormon: The FARMS Updates of the 1990s*, ed. Melvin J. Thorne and John W. Welch (Provo, UT: FARMS, 1999). Such a reading confirms my argument that readers intrinsically want to link the great and abominable church to the great and spacious building, although they cannot or do not precisely explain why. The object of my article is to make explicit those implicit connections that Nephi and the angel provide to help readers make the intuitive connections.

18. Similarly, the Nephites were earlier protected and kept separate from the Lamanites until their wickedness no longer merited the "justice of the Eternal God" to keep them separate (1 Nephi 12:18; see v. 19).

19. Terry B. Ball defines the word of God as "that which is given of God to lead one to eternal life. It includes Jesus Christ and his plan of redemption, scriptures, and truths revealed by the Holy Ghost." *Book of Mormon Reference Companion*, ed. Dennis L. Largey (Salt Lake City: Deseret Book, 2003), "word of God," 792.

20. Bruce R. McConkie, *Doctrinal New Testament Commentary* (Salt Lake City: Bookcraft, 1965–73), 1:624–25.

21. The Book of Mormon and the Bible are not the only last records. First Nephi 13:39 makes it clear that there are multiple "other books" that will assist in this work.

Robert J. Matthews has identified the Joseph Smith Translation of the Bible, the Pearl of Great Price, and the Doctrine and Covenants as three of these other books. Robert J. Matthews, "A Study of the Text of Joseph Smith's Inspired Version of the Bible," *BYU Studies* 9, no. 1 (1968): 3.

22. For more information on this idea, see Belnap, "Narrative of Lehi's Dream in Christ's Theophany," 13–14.

23. For an excellent discussion on the great and abominable church and how it is used historically in chapter 13 and typologically in chapter 14, see Stephen E. Robinson, "Warring against the Saints of God," *Ensign*, January 1988, 34–40. Robinson also notes that the church of the devil should be seen as the equivalent to the great and spacious building because they share many characteristics.

24. This strict divide could be attributed to the apocalyptic nature of this vision. Since, as Robinson reminds us, "Apocalyptic literature is dualistic. . . . There are no gray areas in apocalyptic writing." Robinson, "Warring against the Saints," 34.

11

Prophetic Perspectives: How Lehi and Nephi Applied the Lessons of Lehi's Dream

Grant Hardy

Occasionally in history and in scripture we have multiple eyewitness accounts of the same revelatory event. These can help us understand the nature of revelation and the intersection of the human and the divine that takes place during such moments. This was the case with Lehi's dream and Nephi's vision. Nephi reported, "I bear record that I saw the things which my father saw" (1 Nephi 14:29), though his own version exhibits a few significant differences from his father's account. While Nephi's testimony certainly confirms his father's experience, according to the familiar law of witnesses (see Deuteronomy 17:6; 19:15; cf. 2 Nephi 11:3), the places where their accounts seem to diverge can also be instructive.

We can begin, however, with another example a bit closer to home—with the last few pages of the current edition of the Pearl of Great Price. Joseph's 1839 account of the visit of John the Baptist describes how he appeared to Joseph and Oliver Cowdery on May 15, 1829, while they were praying in the woods and ordained them, saying, "Upon you my fellow servants, in the name of Messiah, I confer *the* Priesthood *of* Aaron, which holds the keys of

---

Grant Hardy is a professor of history and religious studies at the University of North Carolina at Asheville.

the ministering of angels, and of the gospel of repentance, and of baptism by immersion for the remission of sins; and this shall never be taken again from the earth *until* the sons of Levi *do* offer *again* an offering unto the Lord in righteousness" (Joseph Smith—History 1:69; italics used to show variations between quotations).[1]

And then on the next page is a long footnote containing Oliver Cowdery's 1834 record of the same visionary experience, with a few differences. According to Oliver, John the Baptist's words were more along the lines of: "Upon you my fellow-servants, in the name of Messiah, I confer *this* Priesthood *and this authority, which shall remain upon* earth, *that* the Sons of Levi *may yet* offer an offering unto the Lord in righteousness!"

Basically, the two accounts are in harmony, yet Joseph's provides more details, and there is at least one puzzling variant. Would the Aaronic Priesthood remain on the earth *until* the sons of Levi offered an offering? Or was it bestowed *so that* the sons of Levi could again resume their ancient responsibilities?

In addition to the divergent wording, the experience itself seems to have held different meanings for the two men. For Joseph, the main issue was the authority to baptize—this was the subject of his and Oliver's prayer, and immediately after they received the priesthood they went to the river and baptized each other, as John had commanded. Oliver, by contrast, saw the visitation of John as a tangible example of new revelation. He mentions in passing that they had questions about who had authority to administer the ordinances of the gospel, but when he describes his reaction, it is all about religious certainty: "'Twas the voice of an angel from glory, 'twas a message from the Most High! . . . Where was room for doubt? Nowhere; uncertainty had fled, doubt had sunk no more to rise, while fiction and deception had fled forever!" And the next paragraph goes on at some length about how deceit and falsehood were struck into insignificance by their shared vision, which brought assurance, certainty, and truth.

So, was the visit of John the Baptist more about ecclesiastical authority or about religious certainty? It is not hard to imagine why the two men, reflecting on the same experience, may have focused on different aspects. Conflict within the Church in 1838–39 could have made Joseph particularly sensitive to the issue of authority. On the other hand, we might note that this was Oliver's first experience with an angelic visitation, while Joseph had seen heavenly beings on numerous occasions previously. Historians often give more credence to the earlier of two divergent accounts, but in this case Latter-day Saints have canonized Joseph's version—even though it followed Oliver's by five years—because Joseph was the prophet. But what if two prophets, with equal spiritual authority, each offered their own version of the same spiritual experience? This is exactly what we find in 1 Nephi, and, as with Joseph and Oliver, Lehi and Nephi seem to have discovered different meanings in their shared vision.[2] The historiographical issues are somewhat more complicated since Nephi is ultimately the source for both his own and his father's experiences (though he tells us that he is adapting Lehi's personal record; see 1 Nephi 1:17), yet a close reading can reveal some intriguing distinctions in their prophetic perspectives.

Lehi's Dream: Family Matters

In 1 Nephi 8, Lehi relates a recent dream to his sons, and then in chapter 10 he adds additional information on the destiny of the Jews and the coming Messiah. Nephi, describing himself as "desirous also that I might see, and hear, and know of these things" (1 Nephi 10:17), received his own visionary experience as he was pondering Lehi's words. When Nephi is taken to a high mountain and asked by the Spirit what he desires, he replies, "I desire to behold the things which my father saw" (1 Nephi 11:3). His request is granted and, as we have seen, he ends the account of his vision with the assertion, "I bear record that I saw the things which my father saw, and the angel of the Lord did make them known unto me" (1 Nephi 14:29). The report of Nephi's vision is more extensive than Lehi's (or at least Nephi's retelling is more extensive—it is always worth a sigh when we remember how much was lost in the book of Lehi, in the 116 pages that disappeared with Martin Harris), but they saw the same imagery, more or less. Even so, they seem to have perceived things slightly differently.

Nephi tells his brothers at one point that "the water which my father saw was filthiness; and so much was his mind swallowed up in other things that he beheld not the filthiness of the water" (1 Nephi 15:27). Apparently, even prophets sometimes notice things they are looking for, while missing other details. Nephi's observation naturally leads to two questions: (1) what else might Lehi have overlooked that Nephi later perceived (or vice versa), and (2) what had so preoccupied Lehi? It is impossible to answer the first question without more information from Lehi and Nephi themselves, but the current text of the Book of Mormon gives some indication of what was on Lehi's mind at the time.

Lehi's dream followed on the heels of his sons' second journey to Jerusalem, when they brought back Ishmael's family and when the older brothers nearly killed Nephi in the wilderness.[3] Lehi would have been worried about his two older sons, and his dream only increased that anxiety.[4] He begins his account with the admission, "Behold, because of the thing which I have seen, I have reason to rejoice in the Lord because of Nephi and also of Sam. . . . But behold, Laman and Lemuel, I fear exceedingly because of you" (1 Nephi 8:3–4; note that he is speaking directly to the older sons by the beginning of the next sentence).

Lehi then retells the well-known story of how, in his dream, he saw a great open field with a beautiful tree on one side and a large, tall building on the other. In between were crowds of people trying to get to the tree. Many could not see the path, and their confusion became more acute when a mist of darkness rolled in. The solution was an iron rod that ran along the path, which they could grasp and then follow to the tree. Numerous individuals did just that, though some later left when they saw the jeering of the well-dressed, haughty inhabitants of the building. Other people were more interested in the large building in the first place, but in making their way there they got lost or even drowned in a nearby river. When Lehi tells his family of his dream, he notes that Sariah, Nephi, and Sam joined him at the tree, while Laman and Lemuel ignored his shouts and gestures of encouragement.

As Lehi ends his dream narrative, his mind is in exactly the same place as when he began: "And it came to pass after my father had spoken all the words of his dream or vision, which were many, he said unto us, because of these things which he saw in a vision, he exceedingly feared for Laman and Lemuel; yea, he feared lest they should be cast off from the presence of the Lord. And he did exhort them then with all the feeling of a tender parent, that they would hearken to his words, that perhaps the Lord would be merciful to them, and not cast them off; yea, my father did preach unto them" (1 Nephi 8:36–37). Apparently, Lehi felt that the point of his dream was obvious. He does not offer allegorical interpretations or universalizing commentary; instead, he goes straight to exhortation, pleading, and preaching. For Lehi, the dream of the tree is about his own family.

Nephi's Vision: Allegory and Prophecy

Nephi wanted to see and know for himself the things which his father had spoken of, and accordingly, he was granted an apocalypse-style vision—complete with a spirit journey, an angelic guide, and a tour of the end times—that cleverly combined elements of his father's dream with a vision of future events, thus transforming a family drama into an allegory of Everyman and an outline of the future history of the world.[5] Lehi may have originally seen more than just the vision of the tree; in fact, 1 Nephi 8 concludes by noting that Lehi "prophesied unto them [Nephi's brothers] of many things." But whatever Lehi's additional explanations and prophecies may have been, he does not seem to have explained his dream as an allegory; Nephi needs an angel to provide the key interpretive identifications.

Lehi, according to Nephi's account, had presented a simple contrast. He said that after he had tasted the sweet fruit of the tree, he looked around for his family and saw Sariah, Sam, and Nephi. When he beckoned to them and shouted, they joined him, but Laman and Lemuel, a little farther off, did not. Nephi, with some guidance from an angel, discerns larger significance in the particular elements of the dream. In his new allegorical interpretation, the tree represents the "love of God" (particularly as manifest in Jesus), the great and spacious building is the "vain imaginations and pride of the children of men" (later the persecutors of the faithful), and the iron rod is the "word of God" (exemplified in the still-to-be-written Christian Bible). The allegorical keys in 1 Nephi 11–12 are matched by visions of future events in world history. I would line them up in this way.

Dream	Allegory	Future Events	Verses
Tree (and fountain)	Love of God	Life of Jesus	11:21–32
Rod of Iron	Word of God	Bible and Book of Mormon	11:25; 13:38–41
Great Building	Pride of the world	Persecutors of the Apostles; great and abominable church	11:34–36; 12:18; 13:4–6
Mists of Darkness	Temptations of the devil	Literal mists of darkness at Jesus' coming to the Americas; missing scriptures and covenants	12:4–5, 17; 13:26–29

Dream	Allegory	Future Events	Verses
River (filthy water)	Depths of hell	Wars between the Nephites and Lamanites; wars among the Gentile nations	12:13–16; 14:16

Nephi goes on to give specific prophecies about the coming of Jesus to the Nephites, the fate of the descendants of Lehi in the promised land, the restoration of the gospel, and the interactions of Jews and Gentiles in the last days.[6]

Obviously, Nephi's vision is much more extensive than Lehi's dream, at least as presented in the small plates, but several times Nephi informs his readers that he has greatly abridged Lehi's words (see 1 Nephi 8:29, 36–38; 9:1; 10:15). There is also a hint that Lehi may have seen more than what was reported in 1 Nephi 8 and 10. When he began his discourse, he observed that "because of the thing which I have seen . . . I have reason to believe that they [Nephi and Sam], *and also many of their seed*, will be saved" (1 Nephi 8:3; emphasis added). Neither chapter 8 nor chapter 10 explicitly mentions the descendants of Nephi and Sam, but Lehi seems to have been aware of some of the righteous generations that would follow. (Though if he also witnessed the seed of Laman and Lemuel eventually destroying the descendants of Nephi, he did not mention it.)

So Lehi and Nephi apparently saw much the same thing, though perhaps in slightly different contexts (i.e., with or without angelic commentary) or with different emphases (immediate family with some prophecy vs. universal meaning, descendants, and future world events). What is perhaps more striking, however, are the different ways in which the two men apply what they have learned through revelation.

Divergent Applications and Understandings

As we noted earlier, Lehi follows up his retelling of his dream with urgent preaching aimed at Laman and Lemuel. In Nephi's words, he was "exhorting them to all diligence" (1 Nephi 10:2). Given the fact that Lehi's beckoning and shouting had succeeded in bringing Sam and Nephi to the tree, he may have wondered whether he might have been partly to blame for Laman and Lemuel's failure. Could he have called out more loudly or gesticulated more emphatically to them? This is probably the reason he concludes his dream narrative with impassioned pleas, "exhort[ing] them with all the feeling of a tender parent." Lehi has not given up on them (as we will later see in 2 Nephi 1 and 4). But Nephi treats his older brothers in a very different fashion.

Nephi picked up the story of sibling interactions after he had returned from his visionary experience: "And it came to pass that after I, Nephi, had been carried away in the spirit, and seen all these things, I returned to the tent of my father. And it came to pass that I beheld my brethren, and they were disputing one with another concerning the things which my father had spoken unto them" (1 Nephi 15:1–2). There were some sharp words about inquiring of the Lord and hardness of hearts, but it is sometimes surprising to modern readers that the brothers' first question was not about the dream of the tree, but rather about their father's description of the olive tree and the Gentiles, that is, the information from 1 Nephi 10. Nephi had skimmed over those things quickly, giving much more attention in his edited account to Lehi's dream, but for some reason, the brothers are mostly interested in those other prophecies. Nephi gives them an explanation, along with supporting scriptural references from Isaiah, and then they are finally ready to ask about the dream.

Yet what Nephi does not say speaks almost as loudly as his actual words: "And it came to pass that they did speak unto me again, saying: What meaneth this thing which our father saw in a dream? What meaneth the tree which he saw? And I said unto them: It was a representation of the tree of life" (1 Nephi 15:21–22). Then they ask about the images of the rod and the river (apparently, they already have a good idea of what the great and spacious building might be). Notice that Nephi never mentions the "love of God," a concept that played such a prominent role in his own perception of the meaning of the tree (1 Nephi 11:17, 22, 25). Instead, he introduces a much harsher, more judgmental reading of the allegory. In his defense, we might observe that Nephi was devastated by his discovery that his descendants would be destroyed by the Lamanites (something else he apparently did not tell his brothers): "I was overcome because of my afflictions, for I considered that mine afflictions were great above all, because of the destructions of my people, for I had beheld their fall" (1 Nephi 15:5). Evidently, the prophecies of the future were grimmer than Lehi had led him to believe, and that does not instill in him a feeling of generosity toward his stubborn, rebellious brothers.

Latter-day Saints usually refer to 1 Nephi 8 as Lehi's dream of the tree of life, but it is striking (and significant) that Lehi himself never uses that term from the Garden of Eden story.[7] Rather, it is Nephi who first introduces the label at 1 Nephi 11:25, and the identification does not fit exactly. Lehi's tree is not in a garden, there is no angel guarding it, and it does not confer eternal life (according to 1 Nephi 8:25–28, it is possible to eat of its fruit and then fall away), but Nephi is reminded of the Genesis account of a tree kept off limits from the unrighteous by a "flaming sword which turned every way" (Genesis 3:24). As he explains to his brothers the meaning of their father's dream, it becomes clear that the two prophets interpreted the same imagery somewhat differently. Nephi generally emphasizes the connotations of judgment and justice that might be associated with the "tree of life." Note the way that he interprets for them the meaning of the river (and how he adds more details on the eternal nature of the consequences, which expand upon the family significance of Lehi's telling and the historical implications of Nephi's vision):

> And they said unto me: What meaneth the river of water which our father saw? And I said unto them that the water which my father saw was filthiness; and so much was his mind swallowed up in other things that he beheld not the filthiness of the water. And I said unto them that it was an awful gulf, which separated the wicked from the tree of life, and also from the saints of God.
>
> And I said unto them that it was a representation of that awful hell, which the angel said unto me was prepared for the wicked.
>
> And I said unto them that our father also saw that the justice of God did also divide the wicked from the righteous; and the brightness thereof was like unto the brightness of a flaming fire, which ascendeth up unto God forever and ever, and hath no end. (1 Nephi 15:27–30)

Royal Skousen's recent work on the text of the Book of Mormon highlights the connection between this passage and the tree of life in Genesis. In all printed editions of the Book of Mormon, the angel's explanation at 1 Nephi 12:18 has read, "a great and a terrible gulf divideth them, yea, even the word of the justice of the Eternal God." The original manuscript, however, clearly has "the *sword* of the justice of the Eternal God"—an image more reminiscent of the "flaming sword" of Genesis 3:24.[8]

Nephi is not exactly improvising here, some of his description is derived from the narration provided by his angel guide (see 1 Nephi 12:16–18). Yet this is apparently the first time the brothers have heard their father's dream portrayed with words such as *hell, gulf,* and *justice*. It is an open question as to whether people are more motivated by promised rewards or by the threat of punishment. Perhaps it depends on the person, but Nephi obviously feels that the latter approach is the right one to take with Laman and Lemuel.

In Lehi's gentle account, the invitation was open to all to come and partake of the fruit of the tree, and the only thing hindering anyone was his or her inability to find the path or a refusal to grasp the iron rod. The water was a hazard, but it seemed more of a danger for those trying to get to the spacious building (see 1 Nephi 8:31–33), and in any event, the iron rod was there to guide wanderers safely through the mists. By contrast, when Nephi offers his interpretation of the dream imagery, the river becomes a barrier set up to keep the wicked away from the tree. It sternly separates the occupants of the spacious building from the saints of God, and there is a brightness associated with it "like the brightness of a flaming fire." Lehi was concerned about how the building might entice people away from the tree; Nephi apparently worries that the tree might attract people from the building who are not worthy to eat of its fruit.

For Lehi, the wicked tragically refuse what is freely offered by God; Nephi reverses this and has God refuse the wicked. He elaborates for his brothers the eternal consequences implied by the allegory, how those people whose "works have been filthiness . . . cannot dwell in the kingdom of God," and how "the final state of the souls of men is to dwell in the kingdom of God, or to be cast out because of that justice of which I have spoken." And then he concludes with a stark warning: "Wherefore, the wicked are rejected from the righteous, and also from the tree of life, whose fruit is most precious and most desirable above all other fruits; yea, and it is the greatest of all the gifts of God" (1 Nephi 15:33–36).[9]

Of course, God is both merciful and just, and some prophets may stress one aspect of his character while others emphasize different features. Lehi spoke as a concerned father, Nephi as a frustrated, reproving younger brother. Both men loved Laman and Lemuel, and both feared that the two brothers would ultimately be "cast off from the presence of the Lord" (Lehi's words at 1 Nephi 8:36), or be numbered among those who "if they should die in their wickedness . . . must be cast off also, as to the things which are spiritual, which are pertaining to righteousness" (Nephi's phrasing at 1 Nephi 15:33). So Nephi joins his father in exhorting, perhaps even cajoling, his brothers: "Wherefore, I, Nephi, did exhort them to give heed unto the word of the Lord; yea, I did exhort them with all the energies of my soul, and with all the faculty which I possessed, that they would give heed to the word of God and remember to keep his commandments in all things" (1 Nephi 15:25). Yet the tone the two prophets use is so strikingly different! No wonder Laman and Lemuel's response was to complain that Nephi had "declared unto us hard things, more than we are able to bear" (1 Nephi 16:1).

Prophetic Perspectives

Prophets, as we are often reminded, are *forthtellers* as well as *foretellers*. That is to say, they do not just predict the future, but they speak for God generally and mediate his words to people at large. They certainly tailor their message to different audiences at different times; yet in this case, Lehi and Nephi are both speaking to the same people—Laman and Lemuel—within days of each other. Why does Lehi interpret his dream as an expression of God's mercy, while Nephi, who also understands the "condescension of God" implicit in its imagery, nevertheless explains its meaning in terms of divine judgment and the separation of the wicked from the righteous? Let me suggest some possibilities.

As I mentioned at the beginning, it seems that prophets bring their own personalities, questions, and preoccupations to any encounter with the divine. It appears from Lehi's and Nephi's visionary experiences that revelation is not simply a matter of opening one's mind to be passively filled; they look here and there, they ask questions, they perceive some elements of the dream/vision, while others may escape their notice. In this particular instance, one of the crucial factors seems to be that Lehi and Nephi have quite different relationships with Laman and Lemuel.

As long as Lehi was alive, he always held out hope that his older sons might eventually see the light (or taste the fruit in this case). He was not blind to their weaknesses and follies, but he never gave up on them either. He continues to respect the significance of birth order; when the family entered the ship, they did so in order, "every one according to his age" (1 Nephi 18:6), perhaps signaling to Laman and Lemuel that their precedence in the family was not irretrievably lost (they had just recently "humble[d] themselves again before the Lord"; 1 Nephi 18:4).[10] Lehi's final blessings also appear to have been given in order, from oldest to youngest and then to the next generation (with the sons of Ishmael and Zoram inserted in Nephi's place, between Sam and Joseph). Even on his deathbed Lehi continues to exhort his sons to unify in righteousness: "And now, that my soul might have joy in you, . . . arise from the dust, my sons, and be men, and be determined in one mind and in one heart, united in all things," specifically telling Laman and Lemuel, "If ye will hearken unto the voice of Nephi ye shall not perish" (2 Nephi 1:21–28). He urges them to "choose eternal life," as if this were still a real possibility (2 Nephi 2:28).

At this point in the small plates, we tend to see Lehi's hope for a change of heart in his older sons as wishful thinking, while we see Nephi writing as a disappointed, reviled-against younger brother, not as a "tender parent." Years of unpleasant interactions had led Nephi to a more judgmental, harsher view. While Lehi held out a hope for repentance, Nephi had a much more realistic assessment of Laman and Lemuel's spiritual state. He was frustrated with their murmuring, their rebellions, the times they had rejected his father's pleas and had even lightly dismissed the words of an angel, although there was a moment, not long after his explanation of Lehi's dream, when Nephi tells us that he believed that Laman and Lemuel might have a chance: "It came to pass that they did humble themselves before the Lord; insomuch that I had joy and great hopes of them, that they would walk in the paths of righteousness" (1 Nephi 16:5; apparently Nephi's strong criticisms had the desired effect). When they threaten him again, shortly after Lehi's death, he takes them at their word and flees with whoever will follow him; in fact, just as with Lehi's flight from Jerusalem, God himself warned Nephi to leave (see 2 Nephi 5:5).

Because we are working from a single account, that is, Nephi's second version of his family history written some thirty to forty years after Lehi's dream (see 2 Nephi 5:28–34), the historiographical chronology is not as clear as it was with Joseph Smith, Oliver Cowdery, and John the Baptist. In that earlier example, the date of the angelic visitation was 1829 and the two separate documents were composed in 1834 and 1839. We know who wrote what, and we have a good idea of the situations in all three time periods. First Nephi, by contrast, is related by a single narrator, and we do not have much background information. (The historical details virtually stop after Lehi's family arrives in the promised land; after 1 Nephi 19 we get sermons, prophecies, and scriptural exegesis, but we know next to nothing about Nephi's immediate family, his settlements and building projects, or his reign as king.)[11]

Nevertheless, Nephi chooses to tell the story with a great deal of direct quotation. Lehi's dream is recounted in 1 Nephi 8, mostly in Lehi's own words, which Nephi probably took, to some extent, from Lehi's own first-person account (1 Nephi 1:17).[12] The record of his own vision and subsequent conversation with Laman and Lemuel includes quite a bit of direct quotation and even dialogue, perhaps recalled a couple of decades later but also derived from an earlier written version. Stories, even true stories, are often reshaped over time as they are told and retold, written and rewritten for different audiences and under different circumstances. For instance, in 1 Nephi 15, Nephi's explanation of the dream imagery to his brothers can be read aloud in three or four minutes; in my experience, family discussions generally take somewhat longer. Nephi is radically editing, as he so often reminds us (see 1 Nephi 9:1, 4; 10:15; 14:28; 19:2; 2 Nephi 4:14; 5:33). In addition, he is writing his final version—the small plates—for the benefit of his posterity and, as he eventually realizes, for generations far in the future; that is, for us. All this can make it difficult to determine whether Nephi's attitudes towards his brothers from chapter to chapter reflect his feelings when he was a teenager or when he was middle-aged, yet it is certainly possible to discern the contours of Lehi's and Nephi's different perspectives on Laman and Lemuel.

Lehi was speaking to his still living, still redeemable sons. By contrast, although Nephi may be reporting old conversations accurately, at the time he composed this particular account he knew that his family had irrevocably split and the two sides had gone to war with each other, and that perspective may have colored the way he tells his story.[13] He was also thinking of the needs of future readers. Thus Nephi offers a double meaning as he explicates the details of his father's dream: for those of us who still are in a position to choose life and come to Christ, he includes his own perceptions of the tree as "the love of God, which sheddeth itself abroad in the hearts of the children of men" (1 Nephi 11:22); yet his remembrances of how he explained things to his brothers stress the consequences of rejecting that love: "And there is a place prepared, yea, even that awful hell of which I have spoken, and the devil is the proprietor of it. Wherefore the final state of the soul of man is to dwell in the kingdom of God or to be cast out because of that justice of which

I have spoken. Wherefore the wicked are separated from the righteous, and also from that tree of life, whose fruit is most precious and most desirable of all other fruits; yea, and it is the greatest of all the gifts of God. And thus I spake unto my brethren. Amen" (1 Nephi 15:35–36).[14] In speaking to Laman and Lemuel, this was a rather harsh note to end on. Latter-day readers will have access to more information about God's plan, both in previous and later chapters, yet this passage still presents an ominous warning.

Prophetic Prerogative

It is a prophetic prerogative for those called by God to choose how best to express the truths they have received through revelation: to decide when it might be appropriate to highlight the open-ended nature of God's invitation to come unto him and enjoy the blessings that he has prepared; or when a harsher, more judgmental voice of warning is required. Both are probably necessary in different circumstances, though the personalities and histories of particular prophets may incline them to take one approach more often than the other. In relating to Laman and Lemuel what was essentially the same visionary experience, Lehi urgently emphasized the rewards for righteousness and the possibility for change, while Nephi offered a stern reminder of the fate that awaits the wicked.

In similar fashion, in our own callings as leaders, and especially as parents, there are times when it is best to hold out hope, to offer second (and third and fourth) chances, and not to give up on the wayward and weak. Yet there are also situations in which stern admonitions and imposing strict consequences may be the better course. It is undoubtedly a blessing that different bishops and relief society presidents and mission presidents bring their own particular sensibilities to their callings; some may be able to touch the hearts of some members, while a different style of leadership may work better for others. Indeed, it is probably a good thing that such positions are rotated regularly.

Mothers and fathers may also balance the principles of mercy and justice in slightly different ways, depending on the child and the circumstances (though the two principles are not, in themselves, gendered—there are plenty of strict mothers and kindhearted fathers and vice versa). Finding the right balance is one of the great challenges in life, one that requires us to seek personal revelation. Fortunately, we have the examples of both Lehi and Nephi, who demonstrate how prophets are able to take the lessons they need from their encounters with the divine. Lehi shows what it means to express wholehearted love and concern, while Nephi may give us the courage to articulate sometimes difficult truths with boldness. Yet both men, despite their different approaches, speak for God sincerely and authoritatively.

It is also worth noting how Nephi, in recording many years later the experiences of both his father and himself, does not entirely rewrite the former. It is still possible to recover Lehi's original words and perspective from Nephi's record. This is significant because it highlights the process by which Nephi's history was written—based on prior accounts, exhibiting unfolding understanding, and responding to different stages of life. (In my opinion, coming to see Nephi as a narrator or an author is a crucial step in recognizing him as a real, historical person.) Rather than an abstract discussion of the contrasting principles of justice and mercy, which might only be reconciled by ranking one above the other, 1 Nephi offers a narrative in which gospel values are applied by different prophets, in different circumstances, and within different sorts of relationships. This narrative perspective—of true principles in action—makes the Book of Mormon a rich source not only of truth but also of wisdom.

Notes

1. See *The Papers of Joseph Smith: Autobiographical and Historical Writings*, ed. Dean C. Jessee (Salt Lake City: Shadow Mountain, 1989), 1:265–67, for an explanation of the dating and manuscript history.

2. Much of this paper is based on material from my *Understanding the Book of Mormon: A Reader's Guide* (New York: Oxford University Press, 2010), 49–55.

3. S. Kent Brown has suggested that Lehi's burnt offerings of 1 Nephi 7:22 may have been Lehi's attempt to make propitiation for Laman and Lemuel's sins. See S. Kent Brown, "What Were Those Sacrifices Offered by Lehi?" in *From Jerusalem to Zarahemla: Literary and Historical Studies of the Book of Mormon* (Provo, UT: Religious Studies Center, Brigham Young University, 1998), 1–8.

4. It is odd that Ishmael's family does not figure at all in Lehi's dream, even though according to Nephi's account they would have just arrived. Is it possible that Nephi has inserted an earlier dream—from a time when Lehi's concerns were limited to his own family—into this point in his narrative to make certain points clearer? In any event, by this time in the story we know that Lehi has good reason to worry about Laman and Lemuel.

5. Note how well 1 Nephi 11–14 fits John Collins's classic definition of an apocalypse:

"'Apocalypse' is a genre of revelatory literature with a narrative framework, in which a revelation is mediated by an otherworldly being to a human recipient, disclosing a transcendent reality which is both temporal, insofar as it envisages eschatological salvation, and spatial insofar as it involves another, supernatural world." John J. Collins, ed., "Introduction: Towards the Morphology of a Genre," *Semeia* 14 (1979): 9. The part of this definition that does not fit is the absence in 1 Nephi 11–14 of a cosmic journey through the heavens to "another, supernatural world." That would have to wait until Joseph Smith's vision in 1832 of the three degrees of glory in Doctrine and Covenants, section 76.

6. For other attempts to connect the specific symbols of Lehi's dream with the events foreseen in Nephi's vision, see Corbin T. Volluz, "Lehi's Dream of the Tree of Life: Springboard to Prophecy," *Journal of Book of Mormon Studies* 2, no. 2 (1993): 14–38; John W. Welch and J. Gregory Welch, "A Comparison of Lehi's Dream and Nephi's Vision," in *Charting the Book of Mormon: Visual Aids for Personal Study and Teaching* (Provo, UT: FARMS, 1999), chart 92; and John W. Welch, "Connections between the Visions of Lehi and Nephi" in *Pressing Forward with the Book of Mormon*, ed. John W. Welch and Melvin J. Thorne (Provo, UT: FARMS, 1999), 49–53. My approach is most similar to the last of these articles.

7. Brant Gardner has also noted this fact in his *Second Witness: Analytical and Contextual Commentary on the Book of Mormon* (Draper, UT: Greg Kofford Books, 2007), 172.

8. Royal Skousen, *Analysis of Textual Variants of the Book of Mormon, Part One* (Provo, UT: FARMS, 2004), 257–58.

9. However, in Royal Skousen's reconstruction of the original text, the verse should read "the wicked are *separated* from the righteous and also from that tree of life." Skousen, *Analysis of Textual Variants*, 334.

10. See S. Kent Brown, *Voices From the Dust: Book of Mormon Insights* (American Fork, UT: Covenant, 2004), 54–55.

11. The only exception from 1 Nephi 19 to the end of 2 Nephi is 2 Nephi 5, which sketches out a few historical events.

12. The most careful reconstruction of Lehi's own writings is S. Kent Brown's "Recovering the Missing Record of Lehi," in *From Jerusalem to Zarahemla*, 28–54. Note that 1 Nephi 8:2–28 consists of a single extended quotation from Lehi; Nephi shifts to third-person paraphrase at v. 29 with the explanation, "And now I, Nephi, do not speak all the words of my father. But to be short in writing . . ."

13. Gardner offers a similar reminder that Nephi's account was written later and was undoubtedly influenced by his strained relationship with his now alienated brothers. See Gardner, *Second Witness*, 260–62.

14. The reading here is from Royal Skousen's reconstructed version, based on the original manuscript, as found in Royal Skousen, ed., *The Book of Mormon: The Earliest Text* (New Haven: Yale University Press, 2009), 45. The key differences from the 1981 text are "proprietor" instead of "preparator," "soul of man" rather than "souls of men," "separated from the righteous," as opposed to "rejected from the righteous," and "most desirable of all other fruits" for "most desirable above all other fruits." For full discussions of these variants, see Skousen, *Analysis of Textual Variants*, 330–36.

12

"Even as Our Father Lehi Saw": Lehi's Dream as Nephite Cultural Narrative

Daniel L. Belnap

Though Lehi received his dream in a tent near the Red Sea years before his family ever reached the promised land, the images and symbols impacted later generations of Nephites, providing meaning to the events and experiences of their lives. Like a subtle yet crucial weave in the fabric that is the Book of Mormon, elements of the dream can be found in personal narratives such as Alma's but perhaps are most evident in the description of Christ's theophany. From the darkness to his voice to his appearance at the temple, the terminology and symbolism of Lehi's dream is utilized to recount Christ's climatic visit. All of these textual passages suggest that to later Nephites the dream was much more than simply an interesting story from a long-deceased ancestor. The dream defined these people, acting as a cultural narrative that provided meaning and context to the entire Nephite experience.[1]

Cultural Narratives

All societies and cultures have some narrative by which they define themselves and their place in the greater cosmos; these narratives often incorporate

---

Daniel L. Belnap is an assistant professor of ancient scripture at Brigham Young University.

creation imagery.² Of course, their content depends upon the values and understandings of the given culture. Sometimes the narratives may be fictive, containing principles or ethics that reflect the unique nature of the community; sometimes they include actual historical events. Oftentimes these narratives are accompanied with ritual behavior that reinforces the narrative, allows the participant to become a part of the narrative, and creates solidarity among the community.³

For ancient Israel, the cultural narrative was the Exodus narrative, which recounted how God delivered his chosen people from captivity in Egypt by spectacularly parting the Red Sea. Though the event is completely historical, the biblical writers saw in it the same type of process that was performed at the Creation.⁴ Thus creation language and imagery were used in texts recounting the event. For example, in Deuteronomy 32:10, the beginning of Israel's covenant relationship with God is situated in "the waste howling wilderness." The Hebrew term translated as "waste howling wilderness" is *tohu*, the same term used to describe the primeval chaos found in Genesis 1:2. Thus Israel was in a state of "chaos" prior to their covenantal relationship with God, and with the establishment of that relationship Israel became a cosmos. This state included a unique definition of the differences between Israel and the world around them.⁵

But the Exodus narrative was more than simply a re-creation. Because Israel had existed before the entrance into Egypt, the Exodus narrative suggested a restoration or return home as much as it did a new creation. The Israelites were not so much going to enter into a new creation as they were going to return to their old lands of inheritance. In other words, the Israelites were not going anywhere new; they were going back home. Israel relied on God not to create a new world but to restore them to the one they had already possessed. This sense of return, one of the primary characteristics of Israel's distinctive cultural narrative, is the power behind the enduring nature of that narrative.⁶

Lehi's Dream Narrative

Many have noted the role of the Exodus narrative in certain Book of Mormon events, particularly the original journey from Jerusalem to the promised land.⁷ However, the Exodus narrative does not fully encompass the Nephite experience, for, unlike the Israelites in the Exodus narrative, the

Nephites were never going to return to their original lands of inheritance. Instead, they were to leave their home and attempt to establish another somewhere else in the wilderness, a pattern that was repeated over and over again in Nephite history. Some thirty to fifty years after arriving in the promised land, they had to leave the lands of first inheritance and travel into the unknown, eventually settling a land they called the land of Nephi. Approximately four hundred years later, they again had to leave their lands of inheritance and journey into the wilderness, ultimately settling in the land of Zarahemla, a territory already inhabited by the Mulekites. These periodic migrations (without returns to the original territories) differ fundamentally from the Israelite Exodus narrative, a difference not lost on the Nephites. One of the biggest challenges the Book of Mormon prophets had to deal with was the overall communal sense of being scattered, abandoned, and lost, without any promise of returning home. To recognize this ongoing fear, one need only look at Nephi's message in 1 Nephi 19–21, Jacob's speech in 2 Nephi 6–10, and Zeniff's eventual failure to return and reclaim.[8]

At first glance, Lehi's dream does not necessarily appear to be an alternative cultural narrative. There is no historical background to the dream; unlike the Exodus narrative, Lehi's dream is not concerned with where he was before the dream. Moreover, the dream is just that—a dream and therefore fiction. It does not describe an actual historical event or series of events. Yet, paradoxically, these elements are also the means by which the dream could become a cultural narrative, and a powerful one at that.

The dream itself is made up of two sequences, each containing three general scenes differentiated by their emphasis on a microcosmic or macrocosmic scale. The first sequence depicts a personalized scene with a small-scale landscape. We begin with Lehi and follow him through the dark and dreary waste, where he encounters a divine guide who helps Lehi to enter into a large and spacious field dominated by a tree of light. Upon partaking of the fruit of the tree, Lehi seeks to bring the rest of his immediate family (or at least his wife and sons), to the tree so that they may eat of the fruit as well. Running alongside the path leading to the tree is a river. This is the setting of the first sequence.

The second sequence of the dream begins in 1 Nephi 8:19 with "numberless concourses of people" (v. 21) seeking to get to the tree. Not only have the participants expanded in scale, the large and spacious field has also done so, becoming the world. According to the text, mists of darkness cover the path and are destructive to those seeking to get to the tree. An iron rod can overcome the power of the darkness and must be used to reach the tree. Though these last elements are not found in the first sequence, they do have their analogues, as the chart below demonstrates. Symbolically, the mists of darkness perform the same function as the dark and dreary waste/wilderness, and the iron rod, as explained in greater detail later, is analogous to the divine guide.

First Sequence	Second Sequence
Dark and dreary waste/wilderness	Mists of darkness
Angelic guide	Iron rod
Large and spacious field	World
Tree of life	Tree of life
Lehi and his family	Numberless concourses of people
River	Endless gulf

In light of the correspondence between the two sequences, Lehi's dream basically retells the same story. In both sequences, the symbolic elements reflect the cosmological understanding of the ancient Near East in Lehi's day, particularly the tension between the elements that may represent chaos and those that represent the cosmos. Below is a quick review of the cosmological nature of the symbolism in the three scenes that make up each sequence.

Scene 1: Journey through the darkness. The first element in the first sequence is that of the dark and dreary wilderness, later described as the dark and dreary waste, which may be seen as analogous to the pre-cosmic chaos found in the Creation narrative. Though we do not have the original text of the Book of Mormon, the terms "wilderness" and "waste" and their descriptions (dark and dreary) describe something akin to the chaos described in the Old Testament.[9] As we have seen already, the terms "waste" and "wilderness" were used in Deuteronomy 32:10 to translate *tohu*, the Hebrew term for "chaos." Job 12:24 uses the term "wilderness" to designate *tohu*, or *chaos*. This verse also associates darkness with the wilderness: "He taketh away the heart of the chief of the people of the earth, and causeth them to wander in a wilderness [*tohu*], where there is no way." Similarly, Jeremiah 4:23 associates the *tohu* with darkness: "I beheld the earth, and, lo, it was without form, and void [*tohu*]; and the heavens, and they had no light."

This dark and dreary wasteland is represented in the second sequence by the mists of darkness. Though the two are not exactly the same, they perform the same function in the narrative, acting as obstacles to be overcome before reaching the cosmos. The description of the darkness as a mist encapsulates its chaotic nature, for, as mentioned earlier, Genesis 1:2 depicts the primal chaos as the abyss, a dark, fathomless sea: "And the earth was without form, and void [*tohu*]; and darkness was upon the face of the *deep*. And the Spirit of God moved upon the face of the *waters*" (emphasis added).

The river, too, can be understood in this same continuum as the chaotic ocean. Often the terms "sea" and "river" are used interchangeably in the Old Testament to represent chaos such as that described in Psalm 24:2, which speaks of the Creation in the following manner: "For he hath founded it upon the seas, and established it upon the floods [rivers]." As we shall see, Nephi, in his version of the dream imagery, also connects the mists of darkness to the river. Thus, in both sequences, the individuals have some type of experience with the dark chaos.

While in the darkness, Lehi meets a guide who leads him through the wilderness.[10] Though Lehi's dream is not the Exodus narrative, there are similarities, no doubt because both stories share elements with the Creation narrative. One such commonality is that of the divine guide, sent to lead participants through the chaos. Again, referring back to Deuteronomy 32:10, we find a description of the Exodus in which God found his people: "He found him [Jacob] in a desert land, and in the waste howling wilderness; he led him about, he instructed him." Historically, the Israelites were led through the wilderness by a divine guide. Later, Joshua also encountered a divine guide, a pattern experienced in visionary encounters as well.

In the second sequence, the counterpart to the guide is the iron rod. Though they differ in form, these two symbols perform the same function—that of helping individuals to reach the cosmic state. We are first introduced to the iron rod in 1 Nephi 8:19, which explains that the iron rod "extended along the bank of the river," suggesting to our modern senses that the rod ran along the river like a handrail. Yet some have suggested that the iron rod was not a handrail but a weapon like that found in the Old Testament, where it is associated with kingship and power.[11] As we shall see, in the book of Helaman it is used in the latter sense.

Scene 2: Obtaining the tree. Following Lehi's encounter with the guide, the prophet begins to pray for mercy, whereupon he is brought to a large and spacious field with a tree that is later revealed to be the tree of life. The transition from the dark and dreary wasteland into a field possessing the tree of life is ultimately a cosmic one. It corresponds to the Creation narrative, in which the physical cosmos emerged from the watery chaos (see Genesis 1:1–8). In Isaiah 32:15, a similar transformation is described: "Until the spirit be poured upon us from on high, and the wilderness be a fruitful field." The transformation of the waste into a cosmos also lies behind the powerful imagery recorded in Isaiah 51:3: "For the Lord shall comfort Zion: he will comfort all her waste places; and he will make her wilderness like Eden, and her desert like the garden of the Lord." This latter reference in particular demonstrates the manner in which the Creation narrative could be used outside of the actual Creation event. Though we do not have the original text, the term "field" is used elsewhere in the Book of Mormon to designate cultivated land (as opposed to the wilderness). Thus the chaos/cosmos dichotomy includes the uncultivated/cultivated dichotomy.

The image of the tree of life itself is an iconic representation of the cosmos. Like the cosmic mountain, the tree of life is a symbol of the axis mundi, or the connection between heaven, earth, and the underworld.[12] Its presence in the field is suggestive of the Garden of Eden, which has been recognized as the template for a temple, which is, in turn, the architectural expression of the finished cosmic state. Like the tree in the Garden of Eden, Lehi's tree is the source of the living waters, suggesting that the tree is elevated to some degree.[13] Yet the tree is more than just a symbol of the physical cosmos. The tree also represents Jesus Christ and therefore acts as a symbol of the individual transformation into deity, the true cosmic state of which all other states are merely types.

Just as the tree is symbolic of the whole cosmos, so the fruit becomes symbolic of the tree in its entirety. According to Lehi, the fruit of the tree "was white, to exceed all the whiteness that [he] had ever seen" (1 Nephi 8:11). Later, in Nephi's vision, the entire tree is described as white: "The beauty thereof was far beyond, yea, exceeding of all beauty; and the whiteness thereof did exceed the whiteness of the driven snow" (1 Nephi 11:8). In both versions, the brightness is as significant as the color itself, suggesting that the fruit gave off light. Thus the journey is not only from a wilderness state to the garden, but also from darkness into light. Lehi, then, has experienced an abbreviated version of the Creation with himself as a type of Adam. This interpretation is strengthened in the second sequence when one realizes that, unlike other elements of the dream, the tree has no analogue. It is integral to both.

Scene 3: Partaking of the fruit and the transformation. The final cosmic transformation is found in 1 Nephi 8:12: "As I partook of the fruit thereof it filled my soul with exceedingly great joy; wherefore, I began to be desirous that my family should partake of it also." As Lehi partakes of the fruit of the tree of life, he too is transformed, symbolically becoming one with the divine. The ritual of the meal is used universally as a social function to denote place within a given society for both host and guest.[14] In the Bible, the meal is an important event that binds individuals and groups together.[15] The most important, of course, are those relationships between mortals and God.[16]

The act of eating is fundamental to the Garden of Eden pericope, but eating was also the ritual that bound Israel to God in the wilderness. The power of meal imagery to signify the mortal/divine relationship may explain why at least one biblical reference uses it to describe the entire Sinai experience: "He [Jehovah] made him [Israel] ride on the high places of the earth, that he might eat the increase of the fields; and he made him to suck honey out of the rock, and oil out of the flinty rock; butter of kine, and milk of sheep, with fat of lambs, and rams of the breed of Bashan, and goats, with the fat of kidneys of wheat; and thou didst drink the pure blood of the grape" (Deuteronomy 32:13–14).

Earlier, in Exodus 24, the covenant-making experience is, in fact, a literal meal: "And Moses came and told the people all the words of the Lord, and all the judgments: and all the people answered with one voice, and said, All the words which the Lord hath said will we do. And Moses wrote all the words of the Lord. . . . And he sent young men of the children of Israel, which offered burnt offerings and sacrificed peace offerings. . . . And Moses took the blood, and sprinkled it on the people, and said, Behold the blood of the covenant. . . . Then went Moses, and Aaron, Nadab, and Abihu, and seventy of the elders of Israel: and they saw the God of Israel . . . and did eat and drink" (Exodus 24:3–5, 8–11).

Both of these references use imagery from the peace offering, the one form of sacrifice in which the offerer literally ate of the flesh and God partook symbolically. Lehi's dream was received following the offering of such sacrifices.

Yet more than communion is expressed in Lehi's partaking of the fruit. Just as the guest who partakes of a meal becomes a member of the community, so also is the one who partakes of the divine meal accepted into the divine world. Thus not only has Lehi become one with the divine, he also symbolically becomes divine, a transformation that Alma emphasizes in his discourse on the tree of life. This assimilation into the true cosmos is revealed in Lehi's desire for and attempts to help others taste of the fruit; through this action, Lehi becomes a creator himself. This progression does not seem to be explicitly repeated in the second sequence, but that does not necessarily mean it should not be implied. The similarities between each scene and the symbols within each scene can lead us to conclude that those who got to the tree and remained there in the second sequence also sought to help others reach the tree. Thus the dream tells of a creation in an ascending series of transformations: the physical state organized from chaotic matter, civilization from wilderness, and the ultimate transformation—that of the fallen, chaotic man into a fully realized, divine being.

The One and the Many

Though the reception and presentation of the dream fits into a specific, historical context and describes a certain worldview, the atemporal and ahistorical nature of the dream gives it significance beyond the immediate placement. In other words, the events transcend a specific time and place. While Lehi is the one who experiences the Creation, the symbolism is such that he is completely replaceable: anyone can be put into his situation and reenact the scene.[17] In other words, since there is no specific time and space to the dream, the elements of the dream may be used in any space and time.[18] The Exodus narrative, on the other hand, though it may share imagery with other narratives, is very much a historical incident; its power to define Israel is bound by the space and time of the event. Though others may borrow the Exodus narrative, because of its historicity it is primarily the narrative of a specific, chosen people.

Like the Exodus narrative, the dream narrative creates a group identity. However, because of its universal nature, the identity of the group it applies to is not necessarily bound by genetic or cultural affinities. Instead, the group is bound by the spiritual transformation described in the dream. It includes the group of people who have reached the tree, whoever they may be; thus the dream can be used to define disparate groups connected only by their journey through the dark wasteland. Moreover, the transformation and the coinciding new identity it affords are greater than those provided by any historical/

temporal narrative. This is because the individuals in the dream are not merely passive agents but also creative beings who bring about cosmos, no matter what chaos they may experience.[19]

The Dream Narrative in Later Book of Mormon Writings

The dream narrative was first used to define the Nephite experience in Nephi's own writings: "Having heard all the words of my father, concerning the things which he saw in a vision, . . . I, Nephi, was desirous also that I might see, and hear, and know of these things" (1 Nephi 10:17). Though Nephi will gain an understanding of his Father's dream and will see the same symbols, this does not mean he will experience it in the same manner. Unlike his father's version, Nephi's vision is very much temporally oriented. Relating the symbolic elements of the dream to the future history of his people and their relationship with Christ, it commences with Christ's birth, shows his theophany in the promised land, and concludes with the people's eventual apostasy and restoration. This is accomplished by providing a two-sequence structure in which instead of seeing one sequence followed by another, as in the case of Lehi, Nephi experiences both at the same time. In other words, while he interacts with the angel concerning the symbols of the first sequence, he sees the second sequence. For instance, the guide is present in the form of the angel, and Christ is connected with the iron rod in the historical parts of the vision.[20] In this manner, the dream becomes a historical narrative concerning Nephi's future descendants.

Yet, by the end of his writings, Nephi uses the dream narrative in its universal context (as it was used in his father's dream) rather than his own historical context as he discusses the doctrine of Christ. In 2 Nephi 31, he writes of entering the strait and narrow path, which, if followed, leads one to the Father's proclamation, "Ye shall have eternal life." Along the way, one must "press forward with a steadfastness in Christ, having a perfect brightness of hope." The journey is a progressive one: "Wherefore, you must press forward, . . . feasting upon the word of Christ" (v. 20). In each of these stages, the dream narrative can be discerned. The path reflects the journey through mortality in which one endures to the end. One encounters the mists of darkness on this path, which would require a perfect brightness to be traversed. Finally, the iron rod, or the word of Christ, will lead to eventual communion with God, who will provide eternal life—the fruit of the tree of life.

The dream narrative continues in the writings of Nephi's brother Jacob, who describes the actual, physical state of the Nephites as one like a dream in which they, like Lehi, were "wanderers . . . in a wilderness" (Jacob 7:26).

By the book of Mosiah, the dream narrative has become the primary narrative used to describe personal and social Nephite transformation. Alma the Younger, in particular, utilized the dream narrative to describe his personal transformation. In Mosiah 27, upon emerging from his comalike sleep, Alma speaks of being cast off and "wading through much tribulation . . . in the darkest abyss" until being brought to "the marvelous light of God" (vv. 28–9). Though the term "abyss" is not found in the dream narrative itself, its analogue (the river) is. Though Lehi does tell us that the river acts as a separating agent between the righteous and the wicked, Nephi's account reveals that the river is a gulf representing the depths of hell. The association of depths and water are found in the Hebrew term *tehom* that is most often translated as "deep" and that is the primary term used for the precosmic ocean.[21] The term "gulf" is an English word that originally meant a large body of water,[22] and the term "abyss" is a Greek word denoting the cosmic sea. Thus Alma's abyss is an analogue for the precosmic chaos represented also as the dark and dreary waste and the mists of darkness. Later, to his son Helaman, he again recounts the event, emphasizing the role of Christ in obtaining the light: "I remembered also to have heard my father prophesy unto the people concerning the coming of one Jesus Christ. . . . Now as my mind caught hold upon this thought, I cried within my heart: O Jesus, thou Son of God, have mercy on me, who am in the gall of bitterness. . . . And oh, what joy, and marvelous light I did behold. . . . Yea, and from that time even until now, I have labored without ceasing, . . . that I might bring them to taste of the exceeding joy of which I did taste" (Alma 36:17–18, 20, 24). One can readily notice the elements of the dream in both references, as demonstrated in the chart:

Lehi's Dream	Alma's Conversion
Dark and dreary waste/mists of darkness	"wading . . . in the darkest abyss"
Angelic guide/iron rod	"I remembered . . . the coming of one Jesus Christ"
	"as my mind caught hold upon this thought"

Lehi's Dream	Alma's Conversion
Lehi cries for God's mercy	"O Jesus, thou Son of God, have mercy on me"
Lehi partakes of the fruit of the tree of life	"taste of the exceeding joy of which I did taste"

The dream narrative also appears in Alma's missionary discourses. Beginning with his discourse to those in Zarahelma, Alma states, "My brethren, that belong to this church, have you sufficiently retained in remembrance the captivity of your fathers? . . . Have ye sufficiently retained in remembrance that he has delivered their souls from hell?" (Alma 5:6). Though the terminology is reminiscent of that expected in the Exodus narrative, Alma continues by answering these rhetorical questions using imagery from the dream narrative: "Behold, he changed their hearts. . . . Behold, they were in the midst of darkness; nevertheless their souls were illuminated by the light of the everlasting word" (v. 7). Later in the chapter, Alma invites them to come unto Christ and partake of the fruit of the tree of life, and he ends his discourse by reiterating the invitation, "Come and be baptized unto repentance, that ye also may be partakers of the fruit of the tree of life" (v. 62).[23] While it is clear that the dream narrative is being utilized, it may be even more important to note the manner in which the Exodus narrative is folded into the dream narrative, which now defines the Nephite experience.

Perhaps most familiar to the Book of Mormon reader is Alma's use of the dream in his message to the Zoramites. In Alma 32, while explaining to the inhabitants of Antionum the transforming power of the word of God, Alma compares the word to a seed that, if planted and nourished, will "take root; and behold it shall be a tree springing up unto everlasting life. . . . By and by, ye shall pluck the fruit thereof, which is most precious, which is sweet above all that is sweet, and which is white above all that is white; . . . and ye shall feast" (vv. 41–42).

Clearly, the language used to describe the fruit and tree reflects the imagery recorded in the dream as well as the ability for any and all to be able to eat of the fruit, an important message considering his audience. But Alma goes further. In his description of the narrative, the transformation is especially vivid—eating the fruit leads to becoming a tree of life: "Plant this word in your hearts. . . . And behold it will become a tree, springing up in you unto everlasting life" (Alma 33:23). Though this image is not one found in the original narrative, it does fit the overall scheme of the narrative and suggests that the narrative changed from time to time to fit specific needs.

Both Alma and Ammon tie the Nephite experience of lacking a true land of inheritance to dream narrative imagery. Speaking to the Ammonihahites, Alma stated, "The voice of the Lord, by the mouth of angels doth declare it [the gospel] . . . because of our being wanderers in a strange land" (Alma 13:22–23), which is the same pattern established in the narrative with the wandering Lehi and the angelic guidance. While among the Lamanites, Ammon declared that God "is my life and light, my joy and my salvation, and my redemption from everlasting wo. . . . Blessed is the name of my God, . . . who has been mindful of us, wanderers in a strange land" (Alma 26:36), thereby recalling the same type of experience that Alma had iterated.[24]

The sons of Mosiah use terminology from Lehi's dream to describe their own transformation and the work they had been performing. In Alma 26, Ammon describes his conversion in the following manner: "Behold, he did not exercise his justice upon us, but in his great mercy hath brought us over that everlasting gulf of death and misery, even to the salvation of our souls" (v. 20). Earlier in Alma 26, Ammon, speaking to his brother Aaron, uses the same type of language to describe the Lamanites before their conversion: "Our brethren, the Lamanites, were in darkness, yea, even in the darkest abyss, but behold, how many of them are brought to behold the marvelous light of God! . . . Yea, they were encircled about with everlasting darkness and destruction; but behold he has brought them into his everlasting light" (Alma 26:3, 15). Ammon suggests that he and his brethren acted as the guides, or the iron rod: "Behold, how many thousands of our brethren has he loosed from the pains of hell; . . .and this because of the power of his word which is in us. . . . And we have been instruments in his hands of doing this great and marvelous work" (vv. 13, 15)

Ammon's use of Lehi's dream may explain why Mormon, while editing the account, also used dream imagery to describe Lamoni's conversion: "The cloud of darkness [was] dispelled, and . . . the light of everlasting life was lit up in his soul" (Alma 19:6).

Mormon also uses Lehi's dream imagery to describe the missionary labors of Helaman and his two sons, Lehi and Nephi, about seventy years later: "Yea, we see that whosoever will may lay hold upon the word of God, which is quick and powerful, which shall divide asunder all the cunning and the snares and the wiles of the devil, and lead the man of Christ in a strait and narrow course across that everlasting gulf of misery" (Helaman 3:29).[25]

Like Alma's use of the dream narrative when speaking to the Zoramites, this reference also suggests that the narrative was changed at times to fit certain events. Though the iron rod in the original dream narrative may imply the concept of the divine warrior (as found in the older Creation narrative), this reading is not explicit. However, here in Helaman 3, Mormon describes the dream narrative in terms that reflect martial behavior. The word of God is explicitly a weapon, and the mists of darkness are now the tools of an adversary who seeks one's destruction.

Yet perhaps one of the most explicit uses of Lehi's dream narrative is in the conversion of the Lamanites as recorded in Helaman 5. There, according to the text, following the imprisonment of Nephi and Lehi, the Lamanites were "overshadowed with a cloud of darkness" (v. 28). In the darkness, a voice provided the way for deliverance. Following his instruction, the Lamanites prayed and were "filled with that joy which is unspeakable and full of glory" (v. 44). On a historical level, having achieved this state of cosmos, the Lamanites ceased aggression against the Nephites, the converted went out and transformed other Lamanites, and eventually the whole society was changed. At this point point they ended hostilities and gave back all conquered territories still in their possession. Moreover, from this point on, there was no more Nephite-Lamanite aggression; for the next 260 years, all conflict centered on secret societies versus everyone else. Thus one of the most important historical turning points for both the Nephites and the Lamanites is described using Lehi's dream narrative.

Christ's Theophany

In light of the manner in which the dream narrative is found throughout the Book of Mormon, it is not surprising to find the narrative hinted at in the texts describing the events leading up to and including Christ's theophany to the New World, especially as the promise of his visit defines the Nephite experience as much as the dream. From as early as Lehi to just a few years preceding the event, the future visitation by Christ had been prophesied of by almost every prophet in the Book of Mormon. It was the focal point of Nephite spirituality and provided a cultural identity for the Nephites, acting as an anchor to the general Nephite malaise of feeling cut off, isolated, and abandoned. As the table demonstrates, the overall atmosphere of the dream and the actual Nephite experience culminate in the theophany of Christ.

Element of Lehi's Dream Narrative	Events of Christ's Theophany
Dark and dreary wasteland/mists of darkness	Earth completely redone; mists of darkness
Iron rod/angelic guide	Christ's arm is stretched out still
	Christ is the Word of God
	"They saw a Man . . . and he was clothed in a white robe"
	Voice of God
Tree of life	Glorious arrival of Christ at temple
	His declaration as "the light and life of the world"
Partaking of the fruit/experiencing true cosmos	All touch Christ one by one
	All partake of the sacrament
Become a guide for others	Spend the night finding and delivering message to others

Scene 1: The destruction. This synthesis begins with a wasted landscape. According to 3 Nephi 8, "there arose a great storm, such an one as never had been known in all the land" (v. 5). The storm prefigured an entire list of physical phenomena—earthquakes, tempests, fire, and raging seas, which completely reconfigured the landscape. Immediately following the storm, the text describes a "thick darkness upon all the face of the land," adding that "the inhabitants thereof who had not fallen could feel the vapor of darkness; and there could be no light, because of the darkness, neither candles, neither torches; neither could their be fire kindled with their fine and exceedingly dry wood, so that there could not be any light at all" (vv. 20–21).

While many have provided scientific, geological explanations of the nature of the darkness, Mormon simply describes the phenomenon in the following manner: "There was not any light seen, neither fire, nor glimmer, neither the sun, nor the moon, nor the stars, for so great were the mists of darkness, which were upon the land" (v. 22).[26] This description is similar to that which Nephi himself wrote to describe the same event: "I saw a mist of darkness on the face of the land of promise" (1 Nephi 12:4), and the presence of these physical mists was related to the spiritual state of the Nephites.

In 3 Nephi 9:2, Christ laments the destruction of the Nephites and relates their destruction to their spiritual state: "Because of their iniquity and abominations . . . they are fallen!" This same relationship between their spiritual state and their experience with the mists of darkness was emphasized at least twice in Nephi's vision. First, in 1 Nephi 12:2 the description of physical devastation is preceded by a description of the Nephite sinful state in which "the multitudes gathered together to battle." The wars, rumors of wars, and "great slaughters with the sword" (v. 2) represent on a cultural level the chaos that the mists of darkness and other phenomena represent on physical level.[27] Later, when witnessing the destruction of his people following Christ's arrival, the angel defines the mists for Nephi as "the temptations of the devil, which blindeth the eyes, and hardeneth the hearts of the children of men and leadeth them away into broad roads, that they perish and are lost" (v. 17), suggesting that the result of the Nephites' getting lost in the mists of darkness is their final destruction.[28]

Christ continues to associate the actual mists with the spiritual state of the Nephites. According to 3 Nephi 9:7, 12, the cities were destroyed "to hide their wickedness and abominations from before my face, that the blood of the prophets and the saints shall not come up any more unto me against them. . . . And many great destructions have I caused to come upon this land, and upon this people, because of their wickedness and their abominations." Even those who were spared in the destruction were in a sinful place: "O all ye that are spared because ye were more righteous than they, will ye not now return unto me, and repent of your sins?" (v. 13). Of course, the physical darkness is not actually sin and temptation, but the literal manifestation of precosmic chaos. Physical darkness is the Nephite symbol for the chaotic nature of sin that restrains us from becoming the creation we are meant to be.[29] Yet, because the mists are also associated with chaos, their presence hints at restoration, at a new creation. In other words, those things that are lost can be found and made anew.

Scene 2: "Mine arm of mercy is extended towards you." According to the text, the central feature experienced by those who were encompassed by the darkness, besides the ongoing destruction, was the manifestation of Christ's voice. In this, the symbolism inherent in the iron rod and its analogue, the divine guide, is exemplified by Christ himself. To understand how comforting the voice would have been, we must recognize the soundscape that surrounded the people. According to the text, for the three days in which the darkness was present, the earth continued to be torn apart, creating "groanings" and "tumultuous noises" (3 Nephi 10:9). These, coupled with the wailing of the survivors, would have created an eerie, frightening experience for everyone. Thus the voice of Christ would have acted as a lifeline, something by which the people could retain their sanity. Among the messages the voice delivered was the following invitation: "Yea, verily I say unto you, if ye will come unto me ye shall have eternal life. Behold mine arm of mercy is extended towards you, and whosoever will come, him will I receive" (3 Nephi 9:14).

The image of the extended arm of God is one found throughout the Old Testament; it is most commonly associated with the power of God to deliver Israel from Egypt and is thus a symbol of the Exodus narrative.[30] This image does show up in the Book of Mormon, but the martial elements of it are nonexistent. Instead the qualifier "of mercy" is added, changing the image from a violent one to one reflecting the dream narrative.[31] Alma's invitation at the end of Alma 5 is a good example of this: "Behold, he sendeth an invitation unto all men, for the arms of mercy are extended towards them, and he saith: Repent, and I will receive you. Yea, he saith: Come unto me and ye shall partake of the fruit of the tree of life" (Alma 5:33–34). Use of the term *extended* here and in Christ's invitation of 3 Nephi 9 echoes use of the verb *extended* in relation to the iron rod (see 1 Nephi 8:19). In the dream, the purpose of the rod and its analogue, the divine messenger, was to act as a guide to reaching the tree. In the invitations above, it is Christ's arms that represent the guide leading to the tree. The image of the extended arm can be found in Lehi's dream as well.

According to 1 Nephi 8:15, after partaking of the fruit, Lehi sees his family and beckons to them, saying "that they should come unto me, and partake of the fruit." Though technically this reference falls with the third scene of the dream rather than the second, the imagery is still relevant because in this third scene transformation the guided becomes a guide. Thus the angelic guide leads Lehi to the tree, and Lehi in turn becomes a guide, extending his arm to others so that they can come unto the tree. Back in 3 Nephi, the image of God's extended arms of mercy is reinforced when he actually appears: "And it came to pass that he stretched forth his hand and spake unto the people ..." (3 Nephi 11:9). In both cases, Christ is the iron rod that leads to the tree.

There in the darkness, Christ also declares that he is "Jesus Christ the Son of God. I created the heavens and the earth ..." With this statement, the chaotic environment, characterized by the darkness itself, is put into a context of a coming creation. Thus, like the angelic guide, Christ's voice leads the people to a new creation, thereby giving the whole experience meaning by replacing the fear with the knowledge that Christ, the Creator, was at work. This in turn would have provided an assurance that they would survive this and in fact become something more than what they were before. This declaration, coupled with his earlier invitation, depicts Christ holding out the iron rod—a creative action. Coming unto Christ is a creative endeavor; one enters into his presence and experiences a cosmos.

Following these declarations, Christ then relates his invitation to a group that had accepted it earlier: "And whoso cometh unto me with a broken heart and a contrite spirit, him will I baptize with fire and the Holy Ghost, even as the Lamanites because of their faith in me at the time of their conversion" (v. 20). Of course, this conversion is the Lamanite experience described in Helaman 5, which followed the dream narrative. According to the Helaman text, the Lamanites experienced physical upheaval (a symbolic return to the pre-creation state) in the form of earthquakes leading to an overwhelming cloud of darkness that paralyzed them. In this state, they received divine assistance in the form of the guide Aminadab and experienced the indescribable joy of union with God. So far this is the exact same pattern the survivors follow. Christ's allusion to the Lamanite experience not only gives the survivors further assurances as to how everything will play out, but also suggests that Christ himself is well aware of the narrative and is using it accordingly to provide peace to the frightened, isolated people in the dark. In the process, he demonstrates why Nephi can insist that the iron rod is the Word of God.[32]

Scene 3: "Hold up your light." The final scene of the dream narrative is of union with the tree of life and becoming a force of creation ourselves. In 3 Nephi this culminates in the descriptions of Christ prior to his arrival (his actual arrival) and in the ordinance he establishes at the end of the first day. The setting of Christ's theophany at the temple in Bountiful suggests that he is to be understood as the tree of life. As we saw above, there was an association between the images of the dream and the Garden of Eden, which is where the final organizing events of the creation took place and a completed cosmos was finished. The Garden of Eden has been recognized as a temple prototype, the tree of life playing an integral role in both the spatial meaning of the temple and in the ritualized behavior of those attending.[33] Christ (as a tree of life) appearing at the temple would have corresponded to the tree of life residing in the field (the representation of the Garden of Eden).

The association is highlighted in Christ's own description of himself as "the light and the life of the world" (3 Nephi 9:18). Christ will make this same declaration again in 3 Nephi 11 as part of his physical introduction to the people: "I am the light and life of the world" (v. 11).[34] The association of the light emerging from the darkness and the tree of life was discussed earlier. The tree must be understood as the source of light, yet in Christ's theophany this understanding is enhanced by recognizing the relationship between the dream and the condescension of God as taught to Nephi.

In 1 Nephi 11, a series of images connecting the tree to Christ begins in verse 8 as the tree of life is described as exceedingly white, followed by a description of Mary as "exceedingly fair and white" (v. 13).[35] At this point, Nephi's divine guide begins to ask him a series of questions that will connect the image of the tree of life to the doctrine of the condescension of God. This series of exchanges between Nephi and the angel suggests that Nephi is to understand that the tree is a symbol of the condescension of God and that the condescension is represented in Christ as the Redeemer; thus the tree represents Christ. This meaning is then reiterated in the historical portion of the vision recorded in chapter 12, as Nephi observes the multitude of Nephites experiencing the mists of darkness and then witnessing the literal condescension of Christ: "And I saw the heavens open, and the Lamb of God descending out of heaven" (1 Nephi 12:6). Later, Alma explicitly ties the clause "light of the world" to Christ. Recounting to his second son his experience in the "darkest abyss" and his subsequent redemption, Alma declares, "Behold, he is the life and the light of the world" (Alma 38:9).

The connection of Christ to the tree of life finds its ultimate meaning in the ordinances that open and close Christ's first-day ministry. Following his arrival and introduction, Christ invites all present, "Arise and come forth unto me, that ye may thrust your hands into my side, and also that ye may feel the prints of the nails in my hands and in my feet" (3 Nephi 11:14). The tactile experience, which probably lasted for hours, would have left an indelible impression on those present and would have been seen as the fulfillment of his invitation made earlier in the darkness, "If ye will come unto me ye shall have eternal life."[36] This would have been reinforced by the institution of and partaking of the sacrament established at the end of the day, in which the people literally partook of a meal provided by the tree of life. Just as one eats the fruit of the tree, so in the sacrament one partakes of the flesh and blood of Christ.[37]

Yet perhaps one of the most important elements of the dream narrative is the transformation following the partaking of the fruit, in which partakers become a source of the fruit themselves. This is demonstrated powerfully in 3 Nephi 17 and 18. According to the text, following Christ's ministrations to all the sick and then the children, the multitude experiences the joy associated with the fruit of the tree of life: "And no one can conceive of the joy which filled our souls at the time we heard him pray for us unto the father" (3 Nephi 17:17). This is followed by the blessing and encircling of their children with angels: "And he spake unto the multitude, and said unto them: Behold your little ones. . . . And they saw the heavens open, and they saw angels descending out of heaven . . . ; and they came down and encircled those little ones about, and they were encircled about with fire" (vv. 23–24).[38] Following this miraculous event, Christ then exhorts the multitude to reflect on their own transformation: "I am the light; I have set an example for you. . . . Therefore, hold up your light that it may shine unto the world. Behold I am the light which ye shall hold up. . . . And ye see that I have commanded that none of you should away, but rather have commanded that ye should come unto me, that ye might feel and see; even so shall ye do unto the world" (3 Nephi 18:16, 24–25).

That this exhortation follows the giving of the sacrament and alludes back to the earlier ordinance only strengthens the final scene of the dream narrative—by partaking of the tree we too can become sources of transformation by extending our arms and holding up the light so that others may attain the tree as well.

The people immediately act on this lesson by doing exactly what Lehi did after partaking of the tree: "And it was noised abroad among the people immediately, before it was yet dark. . . . Yea, and even all the night it was noised abroad concerning Jesus; and insomuch did they send forth unto the people that there were many, yea, an exceedingly great number, did labor exceedingly all that night, that they might be on the morrow in the place where Jesus should show himself to the multitude" (3 Nephi 19:2–3). In this, the narrative is once again used to describe the Nephite experience: the journey through the darkness, the divine guide (this time represented by the people themselves) and the communion with the tree of life when Christ miraculously provides the sacrament for those who have gathered the next day.[39]

Conclusion

The three scenes that make up Lehi's dream, used again and again in the Book of Mormon to describe the Nephite experience, become in 3 Nephi a template to help the lost Israelites to understand and relate to Christ's theophany. Lehi's dream, as the Nephite cultural narrative, defined in a symbolic manner their unique experience. Recognizing the use of Lehi's dream and how it was referred to elsewhere in the Book of Mormon is a valuable exercise. On one level, it gives us a better understanding of the culture and context of the Book of Mormon people. Yet, because the book was edited with our contemporary experience in mind, Lehi's dream becomes more than a Nephite cultural narrative; it becomes one that can be utilized by anyone. Its message to those who feel lost and alone is as applicable today as it was then. The transformation promised in the narrative is as real today as it was for the Nephites, and it is in this recognition of the power of Lehi's dream narrative that it reaches full bloom, and, like the tree of life itself, "sheddeth itself abroad in the hearts of the children of men" (1 Nephi 11:22), even for readers 2,600 years removed.

Notes

This is a reworking of a paper presented at 2008 Neal A. Maxwell Institute for Religious Scholarship conference, in Provo, UT, "The Savior's Three-day Ministry among the Nephites," and will be published in a forthcoming volume of the same conference.

1. Credit must be given to Bruce W. Jorgensen, who approached the dream as a narrative from a literary perspective rather than a sociological/cultural one. See Bruce W. Jorgensen, "Reading the Book of Mormon as Typological Narrative," in the *Second Annual Church Educational System Religious Educators' Symposium on the Book of Mormon* (Salt Lake City: The Church of Jesus Christ of Latter-day Saints, 1978), 64–70; see also Bruce W. Jorgensen, "The Dark Way to the Tree: Typological Unity in the Book of Mormon," in *Literature of Belief: Sacred Scripture and Religious Experience*, ed. Neal A. Lambert (Provo, UT: Religious Studies Center, Brigham Young University, 1981), 217–31. More recently, Richard Dilworth Rust has used similar literary approaches

to explore themes within the Book of Mormon in *Feasting on the Word: the Literary Testimony of the Book of Mormon* (Salt Lake City: Deseret Book; Provo, UT: FARMS, 1997).

2. Paul G Hiebert, *Transforming Worldviews: An Anthropological Understanding of How People Change* (Grand Rapids, MI: BakerAcademic, 2008), 67: "[Narratives] tell people about the community to which they belong, their place in it, and the moral order of the society. To be a part of a people is to be a part of their story."

3. For more on narrative as form of social identity, see Stephen Cornell, "That's the Story of Our Life," in *We Are a People: Narrative and Multiplicity in Constructing Ethnic Identity*, ed. Paul Spickard and W. Jeffrey Burroughs (Philadelphia: Temple University Press, 2000), 41–53, 42: "When people take on, create, or assign an ethnic identity, part of what they do—intentionally or not—is to take on, create, or assign a story, a narrative of some sort that captures central understandings about what it means to be a member of the group." For a study on the US narrative as reflected in its art, see Michael Kammen, *Meadows of Memory: Images of Time and Tradition in American Art and Culture* (Austin: University of Texas Press, 1992), xx, quoting Joshua Taylor: "The emphatic protestation [by artists] of being purely American is the proclamation of a social attitude, not a description of style. That the artist wished to feel himself different from his European colleagues is of sociological importance." See also *From Generation to Generation: Maintaining Cultural Identity Over Time*, ed. Wendy Leeds-Hurwitz (Cresskill, NJ: Hampton Press, 2006), which describes ways in which different cultures have sought to maintain their identity through their native narratives while integrating into the greater US narrative.

4. The biblical creation narrative describes a creation process in which God took unorganized matter, which the Greeks called *chaos*, symbolically represented as a watery abyss or sea, and organized it (shaped or formed it) into the physical cosmos. Building upon this imagery, many biblical writers personified these waters, thus making the creation narrative a battle between God the Creator and the chaos monster. Because the basic theme of the Creation narrative describes a transformation from a chaotic state to a cosmic one, it can be used to describe specific historical or cultural events. Concepts such as death, the enemy, and the wilderness can all be on a continuum representing chaos, while the city, your people, and your land can represent a state of cosmos or organization. One's emergence into a new territory then can be a creation event. In this manner, the dichotomy provided in the narrative becomes a paradigm in which not only history but contemporary events can be understood. For more on the Exodus narrative as a representation of the cosmic battle between God and chaos, see Bernard F. Batto, *Slaying the Dragon: Mythmaking in the Biblical Tradition* (Louisville, KY: Westminster/John Knox Press, 1992), 113, 119: "In a series of spectacular battles Yahweh overwhelms and finally defeats Pharaoh-Egypt in the midst of the sea. Through this same battle Israel emerges from out of the midst of the defeated enemy as God's newly fashioned people, the final 'work' of the Creator who brings forth life out of the midst of the unruly sea. . . . In the second act of creation Yahweh went on to found his people Israel as his covenanted people and establish his 'resting place'—the place from which he rules the cosmos—in their midst. . . . The exodus, no less than the creation in Genesis, is an 'event' of cosmic proportions, a story of origins through which the cosmic order is established

and actualized." The relationship between the creation account and the deliverance of Israel is also explored in Frank Moore Cross, *Canaanite Myth and Hebrew Epic: Essays in the History of the Religion of Israel*, (Cambridge, MA: Harvard University Press, 1973), 87–88: "The overthrow of the Egyptian host in the sea is singled out to symbolize Israel's deliverance, Yahweh's victory. Later, an equation is fully drawn between the 'drying up of the sea' and the Creator's defeat of Rahab or Yamm (Isaiah 51:9–11); the historical event is thereby given cosmic or primordial meaning.... It is highly likely that the role of the sea in the Exodus story was singled out and stressed precisely because of the ubiquitous motif of the cosmogonic battle between the creator god and the sea."

5. Hiebert, *Transforming Worldviews*, 67: "The exodus in the Old Testament is both history and myth. Historically it happened. Mythologically it became the story the Israelites used to interpret history. Whenever they were in trouble, they looked back to the exodus."

6. See E. Theodore Mullen Jr., *Ethnic Myths and Pentateuchal Foundations: A New Approach to the Formation of the Pentateuch* (Atlanta, GA: Scholars Press, 1997). The continuity of this narrative across millennia can be seen in mediums as diverse as *Seinfeld* and the Passover. For an excellent example of the narrative still contributing to the way in which contemporary Jewish experience is perceived, see Liora Gubkin, *You Shall Tell Your Children: Holocaust Memory in American Passover Ritual* (New Brunswick, NJ: Rutgers University Press, 2007).

7. Bruce J. Boehm, "Wanderers in the Promised Land: A Study of the Exodus Motif in the Book of Mormon and the Bible," *Journal of Book of Mormon Studies* 3, no. 1 (Spring 1994): 186–202; Mark J. Johnson, "The Exodus of Lehi Revisited," *Journal of Book of Mormon Studies* 3, no. 2 (Fall 1994): 123–26; George S. Tate, "The Typology of the Exodus Pattern in the Book of Mormon," in *Literature of Belief*, ed. Neal E. Lambert (Provo, UT: Religious Studies Center, Brigham Young University, 1978); Terrence L. Szink, "Nephi and the Exodus," in *Rediscovering the Book of Mormon*, ed. John L. Sorenson and Melvin J. Thorne (Salt Lake City: Deseret Book; Provo, UT: FARMS, 1991), 38–51; S. Kent Brown, "The Exodus: Seeing It as a Test, a Testimony, and a Type," *Ensign*, February 1990, 54–57; S. Kent Brown, "The Exodus Pattern in the Book of Mormon," *BYU Studies* 30, no. 3 (1990): 111–26; and "Nephi and the Exodus," *Ensign*, April 1987, 64–65.

8. The Book of Mormon does record at least one attempt at returning and restoring an older land of inheritance, but the experiment failed spectacularly. In the book of Mosiah, the reader is told of two attempts made by a group of Nephites to reclaim the land of Nephi. The first fails before they even get there. The second accomplishes a temporary establishment, but by the third generation the descendants are forced to return to the land of Zarahemla. Thus it would seem that any Exodus-like tradition cannot be found in the Book of Mormon.

9. The English terms *wilderness* and *waste* were used to describe that which was uncultivated. This is reflected in Joseph Smith's translation of Genesis 1:2, "without form and void" as "empty and desolate." See "wilderness" and "waste" in *Oxford English Dictionary*, vol. XX and XIX respectively (Oxford: Claredon Press, 1989), 335 and 959.

10. We are not told who this guide is. Similarly, we do not know who Nephi's divine mentor was either. With that said, some have suggested that it was the Holy

Ghost, perhaps even Christ himself. See Sidney B. Sperry, *Answers to Book of Mormon Questions* (Salt Lake City: Bookcraft, 1964), 29–30.

11. See Hugh Nibley, "Ezekiel 37:15–23 as Evidence for the Book of Mormon," in *An Approach to the Book of Mormon*, ed. John W. Welch, 3rd ed. (Salt Lake City: Deseret Book; Provo, UT: FARMS, 1988), 311–28; John A. Tvedtnes, "Rod and Sword as the Word of God," *Journal of Book of Mormon Studies* 5, no. 2 (1996): 148–55. Both Nibley and Tvedtnes discuss the rod as staff/weapon.

12. The tree of life as a symbol of the unified cosmos has long been recognized. See E. O. James, *The Tree of Life: An Archaeological Study*, vol. 11, *Studies in the History of Religions* (Leiden: Brill, 1966). For a pictorial study on the universal belief of the tree of life, see Roger Cook, *The Tree of Life: Image for the Cosmos* (New York: Thames and Hudson, 1974). For more on the menorah as a symbol for the tree of life, see Carol L. Meyers, *The Tabernacle Menorah*, vol. 2, *American Schools of Oriental Research Dissertation Series* (Missoula, MT: Scholars Press, 1976), 143–44.

13. According to Nephi, the tree is associated with the "fountain of the living waters." Contrary to the modern conception of *fountain*, the term has the primary meaning of "a source of water." See *Oxford English Dictionary*, "fountain." Both the tree of life and the source of living waters are found in the Garden of Eden, which, according to Ezekiel 28:13–14, is itself understood to be "the holy mountain of God."

14. E. N. Anderson, *Everyone Eats: Understanding Food and Culture* (New York and London: New York University Press, 2005), 124: "Food as communication finds most of its applications in the process of defining one's individuality and one's place in society." See also Susan Pollock, "Feast, Funerals, and Fast Food in Early Mesopotamian States," in *The Archaeology and Politics of Food and Feasting in Early States and Empires*, ed. Tamara L. Bray (New York: Kluwer Academic/Plenum Publishers), 17–19: "The ways that food and drink are prepared, presented, and consumed contribute to the construction and communication of social relations, ranging from the most intimate and egalitarian to the socially distant and hierarchical." See also Michael Dietler, "Feasts and Commensal Politics in the Political Economy," in *Food and the Status Quest*, ed. Polly Wiessner and Wulf Schiefenhövel (Providence, Oxford: Berghahn Books), 87–126, 89: "Feasts are, in fact, ritualized social events in which food and drink constitute the medium of expression in the performance of what Cohen has called 'politico-symbolic drama.' As public ritual events, in contrast to daily activity, feasts provide an arena for the highly condensed symbolic representation of social relations."

15. Joan M. Gero, "The Practice of Stately Manners," in *Archaeology and Politics of Food and Feasting*, 285–87: "Feasts present a unique occasion to celebrate together and experience a commonality, all the while asserting the distinctions of social identity that are increasingly dividing the commonality. Feasts provide common social experiential references in time and space for an increasingly dispersed, segmented, and hierarchically arranged social body. Feasts create and intensify the microcosm of social and political and economic complexity that agriculturalists, producers, kin, and neighbors must grow accustomed to under conditions of intensifying social complexity and power consolidations. One gets used to what it means to be a citizen."

16. See Hallvard Hagelia, "Meal on Mount Zion—Does Isa 25:6–8 Describe a Covenant Meal?," *Svensk exegetisk arskbok* 68 (2003), 73–95; David Elgavish,

"The Encounter of Abram and Melchizedek King of Salem: a covenant establishing ceremony," in *Studies in the Book of Genesis: Literature, Redaction, and History*, ed. A. Wénin (Leuven: Uitgeverij Peeters; Sterling, VA: University Press, 2001), 495–508; also Kathryn L. Roberts, "God, Prophet, and King: Eating and Drinking on the Mountain in First Kings 18:41," *Catholic Biblical Quarterly* 62, no. 4 (2000), 632–44. Henrietta Lovejoy Wiley, "Gather to My Feast: YHWH as Sacrificer in the Biblical Prophets" (PhD diss., Harvard University, 2004); Robert C. Stallman, "Divine Hospitality in the Pentateuch: A Metaphorical Perspective on God as Host" (PhD diss., Westminster Theological Seminary, 1999).

17. This has been recognized most thoroughly by Charles L. Swift in his dissertation, "'I Have Dreamed a Dream': Typological Images of Teaching and Learning In the Vision of the Tree of Life" (PhD diss., Brigham Young University, 2003), in which the archetypal nature of the dream's symbols are discussed. For a study that approaches the archetypal nature from Joseph Campbell's hero paradigm, see Tod R. Harris, "The Journey of the Hero: Archetypes of Earthly Adventure and Spiritual Passage in 1 Nephi," *Journal of Book of Mormon Studies* 6, no. 2 (1997): 43–66.

18. See Charles L. Swift, "Lehi's Vision of the Tree of Life: Understanding the Dream as Visionary Literature," *Journal of Book of Mormon Studies* 14, no. 2 (2005), 53–63, for more on the atemporal, ahistorical nature of the dream; see also Mark Thomas, "Lehi's Dream: An American Apocalypse," in *Fourth Annual Symposium of the Association for Mormon Letters* (Provo, UT: Brigham Young University, 1979).

19. It is possible that this dream provides a missionary opportunity among non-Israelites when the family of Lehi establish themselves in the promised land. The dream's inclusive nature allows for those not of Lehi's own cultural or biological upbringing to become a part of the chosen. Whether or not this is the case cannot be established firmly from the Book of Mormon.

20. The vision itself appears to be made up of four sections. The first is a previsionary interaction, which includes Nephi's worthiness interview and the instructions, comprising verses 1–7 of chapter 11. In the second section, Nephi is shown symbolic images of the dream and given an explanation. He then is shown the history of his people and more symbolism is explained, but only after the historical content has been seen. Finally, he is shown the apocalyptic vision including the last days. In this section, no dream symbolism is overtly explained, though dream terminology is still utilized. Following these four stages, we can see that Nephi is repeating the dream in three successive stages of the visionary history and that by the end he is expected to find the connections between history and the symbolism. The dream as template to the sections of the vision is overt in the beginning but becomes more subtle as the vision progresses. Thus Nephi is taught how to apply the elements of the dream to the history. For more on the relationship between Nephi's vision and Lehi's dream, see Corbin T. Volluz, "Lehi's Dream of the Tree of Life: Springboard to Prophecy," in *Journal of Book of Mormon Studies* 2, no. 2 (1993): 14–38.

21. E. J. Waschke, "מותח," in *Theological Dictionary of the Old Testament*, 15:574–81.

22. *Oxford English Dictionary*, "gulf."

23. Interestingly, this group apparently was made up of converts: "And behold, he [Alma the Elder] preached the word unto your fathers, and a mighty change was also

wrought in their hearts," which would demonstrate the universality of the dream for all and any who would become "Nephite."

24. This declaration may also be referring to his experiences among the Lamanites. But whether he is speaking to the overall Nephite experience, like Alma, or his own personal journey among the Lamanites, the meaning is the same. As Ammon suggested earlier in the book, he is not planning on going home. That he and his brothers do so is beside the point. According to his own words, he was not expecting to do so and thus his words in this particular text reflect more closely the larger Nephite theme of creation, not restoration.

25. Interestingly, in this text the preposition *across* creates a different imaginative landscape for the dream's setting. Instead of lying next to the path, the gulf is placed in front of the travelers and they must go across the gulf to get to the destination. Thus the description of the path as the "strait" fits in this particular instance with the setting and fits the overall creation landscape, with the cosmos in the center and the chaos surrounding.

26. See John Gee, "Another Note on the Three Days of Darkness," *Journal of Book of Mormon Studies* 6, no. 2 (1997), 235–44, for the most recent discussion on this topic and for a list of related studies prior to his own.

27. The first six verses of 1 Nephi 12, as a whole, reflect the dream narrative in its historical context. Beginning in verse 1, Nephi sees "multitudes of people, yea, even as it were in number as many as the sands of the sea," which correspond to the numberless concourses of people that open up the second sequence of the original dream. Nephi then sees the multitude experience both the spiritual mists of darkness, as noted in the continual warfare and the actual mists: "a mist of darkness, the vapor of darkness" (vv. 4–5). This is followed in verse 6 by the condescension of Christ: "And I saw the heavens open, and the Lamb of God descending out of heaven," which, in the earlier part of the vision, is equated with the tree of life.

28. At least two references by Moroni suggest the dream narrative was at work even after the final destruction. In Mormon 8:16, speaking of the coming forth of the Book of Mormon, Moroni writes, "And blessed be he that shall bring this thing to light; for it shall be brought out of darkness unto light, according to the word of God; . . . and it shall shine forth out of the darkness." In Mormon 9:6, Mormon speaks of the transformation made possible through Christ to a state in which one is "pure, fair, and white," reminiscent of the terms used to describe the tree of life, Mary, and those who were transformed following Christ's arrival in the New World.

29. It appears that the physical mists themselves were also among the causes of death and loss: "And they were spared and were not sunk and buried up in earth; and they were not drowned in the depths of the sea; and they were not burned by fire, neither were they fallen upon and crushed to death; and they were not carried away in the whirlwind; neither were they overpowered by the vapor of smoke and darkness" (3 Nephi 10:13).

30. For example, see Exodus 3:20; 6:6; 7:5; Deuteronomy 4:34; 5:15; 7:19; 9:29; 1 Kings 8:42; 2 Kings 17:36; Jeremiah 32:21; Ezekiel 20:34. Other references use the term to refer to God's destroying power over the nations, including Israel (see Isaiah 5:25; 9:17, 21; Jeremiah 6:12; 51:25; Ezekiel 25:7; 13, 16).

31. Jacob 6:5: "Repent, and come with full purpose of heart. . . . His arm is extended towards you"; Mosiah 16:12: "having never called upon the Lord while the arms of mercy

were extended towards them"; and Alma 19:36: "his arm is extended to all people who will repent and believe on his name."

32. See Matthew L. Bowen, "What Meaneth the Iron Rod?" *Insights* 25, no. 2 (2005): 2–3, in which he compares the Hebrew term for rod with the Egyptian term for word.

33. For more on the Garden of Eden, see Donald W. Parry, "Garden of Eden: Prototype Sanctuary," in *Temples of the Ancient World: Ritual and Symbolism*, ed. Donald W. Parry (Salt Lake City: Deseret Book; Provo, UT: FARMS, 1994), 126–48.

34. Christ's two statements, and their placement within the sequence of events described in 3 Nephi, seem to highlight the atemporal nature of the dream narrative. No time frame is provided by Mormon between the lifting of the darkness and the arrival of Christ, though this has not stopped many from trying to establish the chronology. Yet it may be that the omission is deliberate. It is clear that Mormon can provide very specific information on times and dates, but he chooses not to do so here, perhaps highlighting the symbolic nature of the events rather than the literal, sequential elements. Thus the text emphasizes that Christ's coming is to be associated with the emergence of light into the New World (the chaos giving way to a new cosmos) and is not so concerned with the details of when. In this case, the symbolic represents the reality better than the actual, literal history does.

35. For more on the relationship between the Marian scene and the image of the tree of life, see Daniel C. Peterson, "Nephi and his Asherah: A Note of 1 Nephi 11:8–23," in *Mormons, Scripture, and the Ancient World: Studies in Honor of John L. Sorenson*, ed. Davis Bitton (Provo, UT: FARMS, 1989), 191–243.

36. See *The Words of Joseph Smith: The Contemporary Accounts of the Nauvoo Discourses of the Prophet Joseph*, ed. Andrew F. Ehat and Lyndon W. Cook (Salt Lake City: Grandin, 1991), 120: "No one can truly say he knows God until he has handled something, and this can only be in the Holiest of Holies."

37. This relationship may have been intimated in 1 Nephi 11, when Nephi learns that the tree of life is "the love of God that sheddeth itself . . ." The similarity between this language and that of the sacramental prayer: "and ye shall do it in remembrance of my blood, which was shed for you . . ." is striking.

38. This scene seems to be an instruction to the meaning of Christ's earlier words, in which he stated that we need to be like little children. See M. Gawain Wells, "The Savior and the Children in 3 Nephi 17," *Journal of Book of Mormon Studies* 14, no. 1 (2005): 62–73.

39. Interestingly, in the account of the second day is the following description of the transformation of the disciples: "They did pray unto him; . . . and behold they were as white as the countenance and also the garments of Jesus; and behold the whiteness thereof did exceed all the whiteness, yea, even there could be nothing on earth so white as the whiteness thereof" (3 Nephi 19:25).

13

Not Partaking of the Fruit: Its Generational Consequences and Its Remedy

Matthew L. Bowen

Adam and Eve's choice to partake of the fruit of the tree of the knowledge of good and evil had enduring consequences for themselves and their posterity. Similarly, Laman and Lemuel's choice *not* to partake of the tree of life resulted in long-lasting bitter consequences for themselves and their posterity. In both instances, the consequence of the decision was being "cut off"[1] or "cast off"[2] from the presence of the Lord. Adam and Eve subjected their posterity to physical death; Laman and Lemuel subjected generations of their posterity to spiritual death.

The generational consequences of Laman and Lemuel's unwillingness to partake seem to have been uppermost in Lehi's mind when he related his vision of the tree of life to his family. Nephi prefaces the account with his father's statement, "But behold, Laman and Lemuel, I fear exceedingly because of you" (1 Nephi 8:4). Nephi punctuates the account with two summative comments: "And Laman and Lemuel *partook not* of the fruit, said my father," (v. 35; emphasis in all scriptural citations is mine) and "he exceedingly feared

---

Matthew L. Bowen is a teaching fellow at The Catholic University of America.

for Laman and Lemuel; yea, he feared lest *they should be cast off from the presence of the Lord*" (v. 36).

The statements "Laman and Lemuel, I fear exceedingly because of you" (v. 4) and "he exceedingly feared for Laman and Lemuel" (v. 36) constitute a framing device known as an *inclusio*, or envelope figure.[3] This framing repetition places the entire dream in the context of Lehi's fear for his sons, their families, and their families' posterity: Laman and Lemuel were choosing not to partake of the fruit of the tree of life, which would inevitably lead to their being cut off from the Lord's presence. As Lehi knew, this was the "curse" that would—like the consequences of the Fall—be passed on to their posterity and perpetuated for generations (see Alma 3:19; 2 Nephi 4:3–9, especially vv. 5–6).

Nephi's twofold declaration that he saw "the things which [his] father saw" (1 Nephi 11:3; 14:29) provides a similar *inclusio* for his own vision, a framework which recommends 1 Nephi 11–14 as a reliable guide for interpreting Lehi's vision and his exceeding fear for Laman and Lemuel. Nephi explicitly states that he saw his posterity and the posterity of his brothers, who eventually overpowered his own descendants (1 Nephi 12:19). He was then told by his angelic guide that "these [would] dwindle in unbelief" (v. 22), and he saw the far-reaching cultural and spiritual consequences of this unbelief on his brothers' posterity (v. 23; see also 2 Nephi 5).

In this essay, I will examine how the term *unbelief*, as used among the Nephites, alluded back to Laman and Lemuel's choice *not* to partake of the fruit of the tree and to its spiritual impact on their posterity (see Alma 56:4). I will also show how prophets who were critical of Nephite pride—the "pride of the world" which eventually falls[4]—exercised great faith in the Lord, secured promises regarding Laman and Lemuel's posterity, and eventually wrought a miraculous change among them. Through their prayers and faithful efforts, many of those who "dwindl[ed] in unbelief" (1 Nephi 12:22) became the unshakable faithful.

The Book of Mormon is not only a chronicle of the tragic consequences of choosing unbelief,[5] but also powerful evidence of the fruits of faith. *Faithfulness*—enduring and unshakeable faith in Jesus Christ—emerges as the only means of remedying the generational consequences of unbelief, a remedy which sometimes has its desired effect only after long periods of time. The faithfulness of Lehi, Nephi, Jacob, Enos, and the holy men who followed (whose faith was typical of the faith of the patriarchs and ultimately of the

Savior himself) eventually helped reverse the consequences of Laman and Lemuel's choice. Their examples emerge as ones fully worthy of our emulation. Although the tragic final chapters of Mormon's history suggest that he constructed his story to show the final and complete fulfillment of Lehi's and Nephi's visions, his record and the record on the small plates show how the Lord's people are to help remedy the almost universal sin of unbelief, so that "faith . . . might increase in the earth" (D&C 1:21) and eventually prevail (see Jacob 5:66, 75).

"Children in Whom Is No Faith"

Nephi's account of his family's departure from Jerusalem depicts his oldest brothers struggling to have faith and to be faithful: "And thus Laman and Lemuel . . . did murmur because they knew not the dealings of that God who had created them, *neither did they believe* that Jerusalem, that great city, could be destroyed" (1 Nephi 2:12–13). Despite Nephi's having "exhort[ed his] brethren to *faithfulness* and diligence" (1 Nephi 17:15), he reports that when he undertook to build a ship in which to cross the great waters, they complained against him, "for *they did not believe* that I could build a ship; *neither would they believe* that I was instructed of the Lord" (1 Nephi 17:18). He repeatedly exhorts them to faithfulness (1 Nephi 3:16–21; 7:8–12), with little success. Nephi, on the other hand, is blessed for his faith (1 Nephi 2:18–19; 11:6). Such scenes illustrate Laman's and Lemuel's ongoing lack of faith, represented in Lehi's dream by their refusal to partake of the fruit of the tree, which is literally demonstrated with the departure of Nephi (and those who followed him) from Laman and Lemuel and their followers (see 2 Nephi 5).

When Nephi is granted his own vision of the tree of life, his angelic guide says in 1 Nephi 12:22 that Laman and his posterity will "dwindle in unbelief." The unique phrase "dwindle in unbelief" occurs numerous times in the Book of Mormon with reference to groups of people but overwhelmingly with direct or indirect reference to "Lamanites."[6]

The angel's words in 1 Nephi 12:22 may have had reference to Deuteronomy 32:20, part of a Hebrew poetic text called the Song of Moses. Rebellious Israelites are there characterized as "children in whom is *no faith*" [Hebrew *bānîm lōʾ-ʾēmun bām*], or, rendered differently, "children in whom there is *unbelief*," from whom the Lord would "hide [his] face," that is, cut off from his presence (Deuteronomy 32:30).[7] The phrase *lōʾ-ʾēmun* (unvowelled *lʾ ʾmn*) may have been the basis of, or catalyzed the formation of, a negative pun on the name "Laman" among the early Nephites. If so, this pun may have imbued the term "Lamanites" with the meaning of "unfaithful" or "unbelieving ones." In any case, as Mormon reported centuries later, the term *unbelief* was part of an unflattering description of the Lamanites that originated in Nephi's account of his vision and was "ever among" the Nephites (Mormon 5:15; see also 1 Nephi 12:23 and 2 Nephi 5:21–24).[8]

"They Would Not Come unto [Us] and Partake of the Fruit"

Lehi foresaw the division of his family in his dream. When he looked around to find his family, he saw Sariah, Sam, and Nephi at the head of the river, but he did not at first see Laman and Lemuel (see 1 Nephi 8:13–14). Sariah, Sam, and Nephi responded to his calling to them to come to him and partake of the fruit of the tree of life (see vv. 15–16). Not until after these three had partaken of the fruit of the tree did Lehi look again for Laman and Lemuel, at which time he saw them at the head of the river, separated from the rest of the family and unwilling to come to their father and partake of the fruit of the tree of life (see vv. 17–18, 35). It is evident throughout Nephi's account that Laman and Lemuel were already making choices that were leading them away from the rod of iron and the tree of life. Sadly, Lehi's spurned invitations to his eldest sons augured generations of failed attempts by his righteous posterity to reclaim and restore his eldest sons' posterity to the true faith.

At the time of their separation from the Lamanites, Nephi describes his people as "those who *believed* in the warnings and revelations of God" (2 Nephi 5:6), in contrast to "the people who were now called *Lamanites*" (v. 14). Based on Nephi's designation of his people as those who believed, it stands to reason that the Lamanites included those who did *not* believe warnings and revelations of God and who could be distinguished by "their hatred towards [Nephi] and [his] children and those who were called [his] people" (v. 14). Thus, we are presented with a people who are not just defined by their genetic affiliations, but by their animosity to a set of believers. The reason for their unfaithfulness was revealed years earlier when Nephi asked his brothers a simple but poignant question about their willingness to seek revelation from the Lord through faith: "Have ye inquired of the Lord?" (1 Nephi 15:8). Their response—"We have not; for the Lord maketh no such thing known unto us"

(v. 9)—became one of the saddest self-fulfilling non-prophecies ever uttered. Because Laman and Lemuel hardened their hearts and would not "ask [the Lord] in faith, believing that [they would] receive" (v. 11), they, their families, and many thousands of their posterity perished (cf. v. 10), that is, "dwindle[d] in unbelief" (1 Nephi 12:22–23; compare 1 Nephi 4:13).

Nevertheless, Nephite missionary efforts had begun or had been conceived even within that first generation, as indicated by Nephi's remark: "For *we labor diligently* to write, to persuade our children, *and also our brethren, to believe in Christ,* and to be reconciled to God; for we know that it is by grace that we are saved, after all we can do" (2 Nephi 25:23). This passage, often cited in discussions of Latter-day Saint views on saving grace, is usually cut loose from its contextual moorings. The diligent labor of writing (that is, record keeping on plates) and persuasion (i.e., preaching, missionary work) that Nephi speaks of was directed toward the rising generation of Nephites *and* Lamanites. They were still inviting the Lamanites to come and partake of the tree of life.

Jacob, perhaps recapitulating Nephi's earlier remark, puts it similarly: "And *we labor diligently* to engraven these words upon plates, *hoping that our beloved brethren and our children will receive them* with thankful hearts" (Jacob 4:3). Jacob's words show his faith and hope that his "beloved brethren" (the Lamanites) would receive his words at some future time and also suggest that the missionary labor of which Nephi spoke was ongoing, though unsuccessful. That this was the case is confirmed by Jacob late in his life: "And it came to pass that *many means were devised to reclaim and restore the Lamanites to the knowledge of the truth*; but it all was vain, for they delighted in wars and bloodshed, and they had an eternal hatred against us, their brethren. And they sought . . . to destroy us continually" (Jacob 7:24). Jacob came to realize that no change would be effected among the Lamanites during his lifetime. His frustration is evident as he evokes Nephi's unflattering description of Lamanite culture (1 Nephi 12:23; 2 Nephi 5:14, 22–24) to explain why their diligent labors and many means had failed. The Lamanites' delight in wars and bloodshed and their eternal hatred were among the worst of the consequences of their ancestors' decision not to partake of the tree of life.

Still, Jacob, unlike many of his Nephite contemporaries, could see what was commendable in Lamanite culture—and this was a basis for hope. When many of the Nephites were seeking to skirt the Lord's commandments on monogamy and chastity, Jacob declared to the Nephites: "The Lamanites . . . are more righteous than you; for they have not forgotten the commandment of the Lord, which was given unto our father—that they should have one wife, and concubines they should have none, and there should not be whoredoms committed among them" (Jacob 3:5). Jacob notes that because of this obedience the Lamanites would one day become a "blessed people" (v. 6). Then he criticizes the Nephites' pride and self-perception as "good ones" or "fair ones,"[9] declaring, "their *unbelief* and their hatred towards you is because of the iniquity of their fathers; wherefore, how much *better* [literally, good[10]] are you than they in the sight of your great Creator?" (v. 7). Just as his father, Lehi, was unwilling to give up on his eldest sons, until the end of his life Jacob was unwilling to give up on the Lamanites, and he continued to invite his "beloved brethren" to come and partake of the tree of life.

Enos's record shows that the Nephites continued to try to "restore the Lamanites unto the true faith" throughout his lifetime as well:

> And I bear record that the people of Nephi did *seek diligently* to restore *the Lamanites* unto the *true faith* in God. But *our labors were vain*; their hatred was fixed, and they were led by their evil nature that they became wild, and ferocious, and a blood-thirsty people, full of idolatry and filthiness; feeding upon beasts of prey; dwelling in tents, and wandering about in the wilderness with a short skin girdle about their loins and their heads shaven; and their skill was in the bow, and in the cimeter, and the ax. And many of them did eat nothing save it was raw meat; and they were continually seeking to destroy us. (Enos 1:20)

After faithfully wrestling (Hebrew: *yē'ābēq*) (v. 2; see also Genesis 32:24) or "struggling" (vv. 10–11, 14) on behalf of the Lamanites,[11] Enos, like Jacob,[12] is downhearted about the prospects of such efforts succeeding immediately. He, like Jacob, uses an unflattering description of the Lamanites reminiscent of what Nephi said he saw in his tree of life vision (1 Nephi 12:23; 2 Nephi 5:24). This description conveyed in concrete terms the aggregate spiritual effects of Laman and Lemuel's not partaking of the tree of life on their posterity.

Yet, like his own story of repentance, Enos's vision regarding the Lamanites is ultimately one of faith (see Enos 1:8, 11–12, 15–16, 18). His faithfulness secures the blessing he desires most: a covenant that the records of his people—their scriptures—would be brought forth to the Lamanites in a future day (vv. 13, 16). Here we learn that Lehi and Jacob had also besought the Lord for this blessing: "Thy fathers have also required of me this thing; and it shall be done unto them according to their *faith*; for their *faith* was like unto thine" (v. 18). The Lord promised that their faithfulness would bear the desired fruit among the Lamanites "in his own due time" (v. 16).

When Enos's son Jarom writes, he does not mention any active Nephite missionary efforts among the Lamanites, though he explicitly states that the small plates were being written and kept "for the intent of the benefit of our brethren the *Lamanites*" (Jarom 1:2). He too, however, gives an unflattering description of the Lamanites that evokes Nephi's tree of life vision, "they loved murder and would drink the blood of beasts" (v. 6), thus illustrating the persistence of the awful spiritual and cultural consequences of Laman and Lemuel's choice not to partake of the fruit of the tree of life (see 1 Nephi 12:23, 2 Nephi 5:24).

The laconic accounts of Omni, Amaron, Chemish, and Abinadom present an even grimmer picture. The Nephites' desperate struggle for self-preservation precluded any missionary activity. No longer were righteous men with the gift of prophecy keeping the small plates, but battle-hardened warriors (see Omni 1:2, 10). Many of the Nephites themselves had ceased to partake of the tree of life. Amaron notes that "the Lord did visit [the Nephites] in great judgment" (v. 7), such that "the more wicked part of the Nephites were destroyed" (v. 5), while a righteous remnant were spared (v. 7). Amaleki notes that these Nephites were "warned of the Lord [to] flee out of the land of Nephi" into the wilderness (v. 12), a picture eerily reminiscent of the initial Nephite departure from the Lamanites (2 Nephi 5). This is the first intimation that many Nephites had been dissenting to the Lamanites (see Alma 47:35).[13] The consequences of Laman and Lemuel's choosing unbelief were having an increasingly direct and catastrophic effect on Nephi's own descendants. They were becoming subject to the same kind of "spiritual death" that their less enlightened brethren were suffering.

"But When I Saw That Which Was *Good* among Them"

Though the scriptures above suggest that the Lamanites were doomed to an existence of spiritual ignorance, Nephi, in his later revelation, envisioned the descendants of his brother eventually coming to the tree. We often associate Nephi's prophecy with Lamanite restoration in this dispensation, but the Book of Mormon recounts Lamanite spiritual transformation beginning in the Nephite–Lamanite interaction described near the end of the book of Mosiah. Although he could not have appreciated it at the time, Zeniff's self-described "over-zealous" (Mosiah 7:21; 9:1) attempts to reinherit the land of Nephi would eventually lead to the "language of Nephi [being] taught among all the people of the Lamanites" (Mosiah 24:4).[14] Unlike other Nephites in his recolonization party, Zeniff's humanity would not allow him to participate in a preemptive slaughter of Lamanites. Zeniff was even willing to contend with his own people rather than launch a preemptive attack on the Lamanites (see Mosiah 9:2; contrast Omni 1:28). In the self-introduction that prefaces his record, he declares: "I, Zeniff, having been taught in all the language of the *Nephites*, and having had a knowledge of the land of *Nephi*, or the land of our fathers' first inheritance, and having been sent as a spy among the Lamanites that I might spy out their forces, that our army might come upon them and destroy them—*but when I saw that which was good among them* I was desirous that they should not be destroyed" (Mosiah 9:1). Zeniff's recognition of the good among the Lamanites would eventually allow them to learn the language of Nephi, which would prepare them for later Nephite ministration and the opportunity to partake of the goodness of God[15]—the tree of life.

Unfortunately, as it had Jacob and Enos, frustration overtook Zeniff after years of bloody war with the Lamanites precipitated by a hatred rooted in tradition—hatred that was the fruit of Laman and Lemuel's refusal to partake of the fruit of the tree of life, manifest in trenchant unbelief. Although Zeniff had once seen and appreciated "that which was *good* among [the Lamanites]," at the end of his life he would report:

> They were a wild, and ferocious, and a blood-thirsty people, *believing in the tradition of their fathers, which is this—Believing* that they were driven out of the land of Jerusalem because of the iniquities of their fathers, and that they were wronged in the wilderness by their brethren, and they were also wronged while crossing the sea;
>
> And again, that they were wronged while in the land of their first inheritance, after they had crossed the sea, and all this because that *Nephi was more faithful* in keeping the commandments of the Lord— therefore he was favored of the Lord, for the Lord heard his prayers

and answered them, and he took the lead of their journey in the wilderness. . . .

And again, they were wroth with him because he departed into the wilderness as the Lord had commanded him, and took the records which were engraven on the plates of brass, for they said that he robbed them.

And thus *they have taught their children that they should hate them*, and that they should murder them, and that they should rob and plunder them, and do all they could to destroy them; therefore they have *an eternal hatred towards the children of Nephi*. (Mosiah 10:12–13; 17)

Zeniff, like earlier Nephite writers, adapts Nephi's description of the Lamanites as "a dark, and loathsome, and a filthy people, full of idleness and all manner of abominations" and their "dwindl[ing] in unbelief" (1 Nephi 12:23), characterizing Lamanite unbelief as a firm *belief* in false traditions, as opposed to Nephite faithfulness.[16]

In bearing the brunt of the Lamanites' tradition-rooted, "eternal" hatred, Zeniff experienced something akin to what the Prophet Joseph Smith would later describe as "creeds of the fathers" (traditions) being "so strongly riveted . . . upon the hearts of the children" (D&C 123:7). Zeniff had learned through painful experience that a *belief* in incorrect traditions could be the worst kind of *unbelief* in which a nation might dwindle. What Nephi foresaw in 1 Nephi 12:22–23 must have seemed bitterly true to Zeniff, but he himself had witnessed a basis for hope. Zeniff's compassion for the Lamanites (Mosiah 9:1) eventuated in the Lamanite's being taught the language of Nephi (24:4). This charity would have eternal consequences.

"So Great a Miracle"!

When Ammon and his brothers announced their intention to undertake a mission to the Lamanites, their fellow Nephites "laughed [them] to scorn" (Alma 26:23). Every previous invitation to the Lamanites to come and partake of the tree of life had been a miserable failure. The resistance from fellow Nephites that Ammon recalls receiving was hardly surprising (see Alma 26:24). The argument against this mission recalled the worst aspects of Lamanite culture (Alma 26:24). More disturbing, however, were the arguments of some Nephites that a mission of genocide be undertaken instead (v. 25).

Fortunately, Ammon was the right man to preside over this mission.[17] Ammon himself (as one of the unbelievers who had worked to destroy the Nephite church) knew what it was like to be captive to unbelief (Mosiah 27:8–10). He could thus empathize with the Lamanites in ways that perhaps previous missionaries could not. Just as an angel had been sent to turn him and his brethren from their iniquities (vv. 11–18), he was now being sent by the Lord as an angel to the Lamanites (see Alma 27:4). He became the servant of a Lamanite king named Lamoni and immediately sought for opportunities to, in his words, "win the hearts of these my fellow-servants, that I may lead them to *believe* my words" (Alma 17:29). He immediately impressed Lamoni with his faithful acts of service, who when "he had learned of the *faithfulness of Ammon* in preserving his flocks, and also of his great power . . . was astonished exceedingly, and said: *Surely* this is more than a man. Behold, is not this the Great Spirit" (Alma 18:2). Ammon's fellow-servants asserted that they did *"not believe* that a man has such great power" (v. 3). They believed Ammon's power was divine.

Mormon here pauses to make an important comment on Lamanite (un)belief and tradition: "Now this was the tradition of Lamoni, which he had received from his father, that there was a Great Spirit. Notwithstanding *they believed* in a Great Spirit, they supposed that whatsoever they did was right" (Alma 18:5). Lamoni believed that Ammon was "the Great Spirit" and yet was still faithfully serving Lamoni: "Now when king Lamoni heard that Ammon was preparing his horses and his chariots he was more astonished, because of the *faithfulness* of Ammon, saying: Surely there has not been any servant among all my servants that has been *so faithful* as this man" (v. 10).

Faithfulness begat faith as Lamoni allowed Ammon to teach him the gospel according to Nephite traditions, declaring, "Yea, *I will believe* all thy words" (Alma 18:23). At this point in the narrative, the reader witnesses a proliferation of the word *belief*, as the verb *believe* occurs no less than thirteen times throughout Alma 18–19, together with other potentially related words, *faith* (used at least four times) and *true* (used once).[18] Ammon is moved to exclaim to Lamoni's wife, who so readily believed what she was taught: "Blessed art thou because of thy *exceeding faith*; . . . there has not been *such great faith* among all the people of the Nephites" (Alma 19:10).

At this important moment in the narrative history, Lamanite "unbelief" and tradition give way to faith and faithfulness as Lamoni "believe[s] all

[Ammon's] words" (Alma 18:40), cries unto the Lord for mercy, and falls to the earth (18:41) like those in Lehi's vision who "came forth and fell down and partook of the fruit of the tree" (1 Nephi 8:30). Lamoni then partook of the fruit. "Now, this was what Ammon desired, for he knew that king Lamoni was under the power of God; he knew that *the dark veil of unbelief* was being cast away from his mind, and the light which did light up his mind, which was the light of the glory of God, which was a marvelous light of his goodness—yea, this light had infused such joy into his soul, the cloud of darkness having been dispelled, and that the light of everlasting life was lit up in his soul, yea, he knew that . . . he was carried away in God" (Alma 19:6).

The "dark veil of unbelief" mentioned here is analogous to the mist of darkness in Lehi's vision that had to be overcome through faithfulness (see 1 Nephi 8:23–24; 12:17). Thus, the removal of the "dark veil of unbelief" suggests that Lamoni had, in a sense, come into the presence of God and partaken of the fruit of the tree of life—"the light of everlasting life." The joy that had been infused into his soul was the same that Lehi and Nephi both describe. Key to this transformation was Ammon's use of the scriptures:

> [Ammon] began at the creation of the world, and also the creation of Adam, and told him all the things concerning the fall of man, and rehearsed and laid before him the records and the holy scriptures of the people. . . .
>
> And he also rehearsed unto them (for it was unto the king and to his servants) all the journeyings of their fathers in the wilderness. . . .
>
> And he also rehearsed unto them concerning the rebellions of Laman and Lemuel, and the sons of Ishmael, yea, all their rebellions did he relate unto them; and he expounded unto them all the records and scriptures from the time that Lehi left Jerusalem down to the present time. (Alma 18:36–38)[19]

Both Lehi's and Nephi's visions make it clear that without a rod of iron to hold fast to, there is no access to the tree of life. When Nephi was compelled to depart with the plates of brass and the other records (see 2 Nephi 5:12), "robbing" Laman and Lemuel according to Lamanite tradition (Mosiah 10:16), the two oldest brothers had, in fact, deprived their own posterity of direct access to the words of eternal life—the scriptures. In losing access to the word of

God, they had been "cut off from the presence of the Lord" as foretold (see 2 Nephi 5:20).

When Nephi later speaks of "press[ing] forward *with a steadfastness in Christ,*" that is, "press[ing] forward, *feasting* upon the word of Christ" (2 Nephi 31:20; 32:3), he is addressing himself to people who have access to scriptures and revelation—a rod of iron (1 Nephi 11:25; 13:23–24).[20] Without a rod like Moses's rod of God (Exodus 4:20, 17:9)[21] to stave off or "divide asunder all the cunning and snares of the devil, and lead the man [or woman] of Christ in a strait and narrow course across that everlasting gulf of misery" (Helaman 3:29; compare D&C 8:1–3),[22] the posterity of Laman and Lemuel could hardly exhibit any "*steadfastness* in Christ" (2 Nephi 31:20; see also 25:24; 26:8) and stood no chance of "feasting upon the word of Christ" (2 Nephi 31:20) or partaking of the fruit of the tree of life. It was as the Spirit had stated to Nephi when he slew Laban: a nation had "dwindle[d] . . . in unbelief" without scriptures (1 Nephi 4:13).[23]

King Benjamin was keenly aware of the value of scriptures. He and his father, Mosiah, had experienced the difficulties of integrating a scripture-less society (the Mulekites of Zarahemla) into their own. He understood that access to the scriptures had given his fathers the opportunity to partake of the tree of life—an opportunity that Laman and Lemuel had denied their children:

> Were it not for [these records], . . . even our fathers would have dwindled in *unbelief* [see especially 1 Nephi 4:13 and 12:22–23], and we should have been like unto our brethren, the Lamanites, who know nothing concerning these things, or even do *not believe* them when they are taught them, because of the traditions of their fathers, which are *not correct.*
>
> O my sons, . . . remember that these sayings are *true,* and also that these records are *true.* And behold, also the plates of Nephi, . . . they are *true,* and we can know of their *surety* because we have them before our eyes. (Mosiah 1:5–6)

Benjamin's words to his sons also demonstrate how ensconced the description of Lamanites as those who dwindled in unbelief had become by his time. Benjamin places strong emphasis on the unbelief of the Lamanites and the incorrectness of their traditions, while pointing at the truth or surety of the Nephite records.[24] In light of this, it is no surprise to find that the conversions of Lamoni and Lamoni's father (as well as those who were within hearing), from states of unbelief to believing, are the result of the Nephite missionaries' efforts and their application of the scriptures (the iron rod).

Because of Ammon's and his brothers' faithfulness and Lamoni's faithful response to their teaching, many of the Lamanites partake of the fruit of the tree: "And as *sure* as the Lord liveth, so *sure* as many as *believed*, or as many as were brought to the knowledge of the *truth*, through the preaching of Ammon and his brethren, according to the spirit of revelation and of prophecy, and the power of God working miracles in them—yea, I say unto you, as the Lord liveth, *as many of the Lamanites as believed* in their preaching, and were converted unto the Lord, *never did fall away*" (Alma 23:6). Not even persecution could shake the faithfulness of these Lamanites: "And thus we see that, when these Lamanites were brought to *believe* and to know the *truth*, they were *firm*, and would suffer even unto death rather than commit sin" (Alma 24:19). "Many of [these] *Lamanites* should perish by fire because of their *belief*" (Alma 25:5), even "all those that *believed*" (Alma 25:7). Nevertheless, many Lamanites "began to *disbelieve* the traditions of their fathers, and to *believe* in the Lord" (Alma 25:6). They partook of the fruit of the tree of life and neither became ashamed nor fell away.[25]

Mormon further notes that these Lamanites became known as the "people of Ammon," and that "they were distinguished by that name ever after" (Alma 27:26), and that they "were also distinguished for their zeal towards God, and also towards men; for they were perfectly honest and upright in all things; and *they were firm in the faith of Christ*, even unto the end" (v. 27). At this time, the faithfulness of earlier Nephite holy men was realized in Ammon and his brethren, whose faithfulness in turn begot unsurpassed faithfulness in the Lamanites.

Mormon illustrates how this faithfulness only increased among the next generation of these Lamanites. When called upon to defend the Nephites whose faith they shared, more than two thousand of their sons saved the day. Helaman states that they were "*firm* and undaunted. Yea, and they did obey and observe to perform every word of command with exactness; yea, and even *according to their faith* it was done unto them" (Alma 57:20–21). These young men ascribed their faithfulness to the teaching of their mothers (see Alma 57:21; 56:47–48). Miraculously, not one of these young men was killed in battle, a fact to which Helaman appends this remarkable comment: "And we do justly ascribe it to the miraculous power of God, because of *their exceeding faith* in that which *they had been taught to believe*—that there was a just God, and whosoever did *not doubt*, that they should be preserved by his marvelous power. Now this was the *faith* of these of whom I have spoken; they are young, and their minds are *firm*, and *they do put their trust in God continually*" (Alma 57:26–27). Mormon includes this firsthand account in his history to show that just as unbelief is taught and perpetuated generationally, so too are faith and faithfulness. The mothers of these young men had helped them come to the tree of life and to partake of its fruit. The faithfulness of Lamanite mothers again showed that Lamanites could be the *most faithful* of all people. This faithfulness was the fruit of Ammon's faithfulness a generation earlier. As Moroni noted long after regarding these events, "Behold, it was the *faith* of Ammon and his brethren which wrought so great a miracle among the Lamanites" (Ether 12:15). Many Lamanites were now partakers of the fruit of the tree of life, in pleasing contrast to what Lehi (see 1 Nephi 8:13, 35) and Nephi (see 1 Nephi 12:22–23) had seen in vision.

"They Are More Righteous Than You"

Given the history presented up to this point, Mormon makes another truly remarkable observation when he notes that, not too many years later, "*the Nephites did begin to dwindle in unbelief*, and grow in wickedness and abominations, while the *Lamanites* began to grow exceedingly in the knowledge of their God; yea, they did begin to keep his statutes and commandments, and to walk in *truth* and uprightness before him" (Helaman 6:34). Where "the Spirit of the Lord began to withdraw from the Nephites, . . . the Lord began to pour out his spirit upon the Lamanites, because of their easiness and *willingness to believe* in his words" (Helaman vv. 35–36). Mormon's point is clear: the Lamanites were no longer the unfaithful who had dwindled in unbelief; they were the *very* faithful. The Lamanites were partaking freely of the fruit of the tree of life, while the Nephites were refusing it (compare 1 Nephi 8:13, 35).

Samuel the Lamanite's prophetic address to the Nephites of Zarahemla further illustrates this development. The content of Samuel's speech recommends it as one of the best prophetic speeches in the Book of Mormon.[26] Samuel seems to play off of traditional notions of Nephite goodness and Lamanite unbelief to emphasize that the reverse had become true:

And behold, ye do know of yourselves . . . that *as many of them as are brought to the knowledge of the truth, and to know of the wicked and abominable traditions of their fathers, and are led to believe the holy scriptures*, yea, the prophecies of the holy prophets, which are written, *which leadeth them to faith on the Lord*, and unto repentance, *which faith and repentance bringeth a change of heart unto them*—

Therefore, *as many as have come to this . . . are firm and steadfast in the faith*, and in the thing wherewith they have been made free.

And ye know also that they have buried their weapons of war, and they fear to take them up lest by any means they should sin; yea, ye can see that they fear to sin—for behold they will suffer themselves that they be trodden down and slain by their enemies, and will not lift their swords against them, and *this because of their faith in Christ*.

And now, *because of their steadfastness when they do believe in that thing which they do believe, for because of their firmness when they are once enlightened, behold, the Lord shall bless them and prolong their days*, notwithstanding their iniquity—

Yea, *even if they should dwindle in unbelief the Lord shall prolong their days*, until the time shall come which hath been spoken of by our fathers, and also by the prophet Zenos, and many other prophets, concerning the restoration of our brethren, the *Lamanite*s, again to the knowledge of the *truth*—

Yea, I say unto you, that in the latter times *the promises of the Lord have been extended to our brethren, the Lamanites . . .*

And this is according to the prophecy, that they shall again be brought to the *true* knowledge, which is the knowledge of their Redeemer, and their great and true shepherd, and be numbered among his sheep.

Therefore I say unto you, it shall be better [see Jacob 3:5; Helaman 7:23] for them than for you except ye repent.

For behold, had the mighty works been shown unto them which have been shown unto you, *yea, unto them who have dwindled in unbelief because of the traditions of their fathers, ye can see of yourselves that they never would again have dwindled in unbelief.*

Therefore, saith the Lord: I will not utterly destroy them, but I will cause that in the day of my wisdom they shall return again unto me, saith the Lord.

And now behold, saith the Lord, concerning the people of the Nephites: If they will not repent, and observe to do my will, I will utterly destroy them, saith the Lord, *because of their unbelief notwithstanding the many mighty works which I have done among them;* and as surely as the Lord liveth shall these things be, saith the Lord (Helaman 15:7–17)

S. Kent Brown has identified elements of ancient Israelite lamentation in Samuel's speech,[27] and Donald W. Parry has demonstrated that Samuel made extensive use of Israelite prophetic speech forms.[28] David Bokovoy has shown that Samuel's use of *love* and *hate* in Helaman 15:1–4 conforms to the meaning of these terms in ancient Near Eastern vassal treaties (as evident in Hosea 9:15 and elsewhere).[29] Samuel's familiarity with Israelite prophetic tradition probably suggests a thorough knowledge of the corpus of Nephite prophetic tradition, including Lehi's and Nephi's visions of the tree of life. Samuel evidently refers to the stereotype of Lamanite unbelief from Nephi's vision (1 Nephi 12:22–23, familiar to his Nephite audience) in order to show that converted Lamanites had become the most steadfast of believers and that the state of Nephite spirituality had become very precarious.

When descendants of Laman and Lemuel were able to overcome the mists of darkness (the dark veil of unbelief, the traditions of their fathers), they—unlike those apostate Nephites who "tasted of the fruit [and] were ashamed" (1 Nephi 8:28)—"never did fall away" (Alma 23:6; compare Mormon 6:17–19). On the contrary, the Nephites (the "fair ones" or "goodly ones"[30]) who supposed themselves better than the Lamanites would be utterly destroyed because of their unbelief—a lack of faith in spite of centuries of miraculous deliverances in fulfillment of Alma's prophecy to Helaman (Alma 45:9–14).

During this period and at other times of widespread apostasy, Nephites believed that their "goodness" or "chosenness" was inherent,[31] but such beliefs were a sure sign of pride and an imminent fall. They were now choosing unbelief and refusing to partake of the fruit of the tree of life. The Nephites had, in large measure, become the kind of unbelievers that exemplified the worst aspects of what they—in their own pride—had always detested about Lamanite unbelief and culture. For a time, this trend would only get worse. Mormon reports that amid a general fracturing of society, "the church began to be broken up; yea, insomuch that in the thirtieth year the church was broken up in all the land *save it were among a few of the Lamanites* who were converted unto the *true faith; and they would not depart from it*, for they were *firm*, and *steadfast*, and *immovable, willing with all diligence* to keep the commandments of the Lord" (3 Nephi 6:14).[32] The Lamanites, not the Nephites, were the very faithful. It was as Nephi had said to the wicked Nephites not many years earlier: "For behold, they [the Lamanites] are more righteous than you, for they have not sinned against that great knowledge which ye have received" (Helaman 7:24; see especially Jacob 3:5). Fortunately for the righteous, the Savior would come "with healing in his wings" (2 Nephi 25:13) just four years later. At that time, all the children of Lehi would have access to the fruit of the tree of life in an unprecedented way.

They All "Came Forth and Fell Down and Partook of the Fruit of the Tree"

The account of the Savior's ministry in 3 Nephi is, among many things, a chronicle of how "the people of Nephi . . . and also those who had been called Lamanites" (3 Nephi 10:18) together "came forth and fell down and partook of the fruit of the tree [of life]" (1 Nephi 8:30; see also 3 Nephi 11:12–19; 17:9–10). This account offers the best picture of what having full access to the tree of life would mean for a people.

Mormon reports that "they had all things common among them" and that "there were not rich and poor, bond and free, but they were all made free, and *partakers of the heavenly gift*" (4 Nephi 1:3)—the Second Comforter, even the Savior himself (see Ether 12:8–9; John 14:16–18). In other words, all were *partakers* of the tree of life—the full measure of the blessings of the Atonement. He also notes that "there was no contention in the land because of the love of God which did dwell in the hearts of the people" (4 Nephi 1:15). This is what Nephi envisioned when he saw that the tree of life signified "the love of God, which sheddeth itself abroad in the hearts of the children of men" (1 Nephi 11:22). Mormon even declares that "surely there could not be a happier people" (4 Nephi 1:16), because there were no "Lamanites, nor any manner of -ites" (v. 17).

The "first generation from Christ" of righteous Lamanites and Nephites (4 Nephi 1:18) fits Lehi's description of those who had passed through "a mist of darkness" (1 Nephi 8:23; see also 12:4), or a "vapor of darkness" (3 Nephi 8:10; see also 8:3–10:14), and "press[ed] their way forward, continually holding fast to the rod of iron, until they came forth and fell down and partook of the fruit of the tree" (1 Nephi 8:30). Moroni states that "it was *by faith* that Christ showed himself unto [the Lamanites and Nephites], after he had risen from the dead; and he showed not himself *until after they had faith in him*" (Ether 12:7). This statement suggests an equivalence between having faith and pressing one's way forward, holding fast to the rod or (as Nephi put it) "press[ing] forward with a steadfastness in Christ" and "press[ing] forward, feasting upon the word" (2 Nephi 31:20).

Most of the second generation was heir to their great faithfulness (see 4 Nephi 1:19–22). Sadly, at the end of that generation, many entered into the great and spacious building (1 Nephi 8:31–33) and indulged themselves in its desires (4 Nephi 1:24; see also 1 Nephi 8:27; 13:7–8).

"They Did Willfully Rebel"

Mormon suggests that the splintering of this unified Zion society and the reemergence of the old ethnic and religious divisions among the descendants of Lehi was a lasting consequence of Laman and Lemuel's initial choice. It was a reenactment of the scene in Lehi's dream that caused him such exceeding fear. Mormon, however, describes the situation as being worse than when Laman and Lemuel initially refused the blessings of the gospel: "And it came to pass that they who rejected the gospel were called *Lamanites*, and Lemuelites, and Ishmaelites; and *they did not dwindle in unbelief*, but they did wilfully rebel against the gospel of Christ; and *they did teach their children that they should not believe, even as their fathers, from the beginning, did dwindle. And it was because of the wickedness and abomination of their fathers*, even as it was in the beginning. And they were taught to hate the children of God, even as the Lamanites were taught to hate the children of Nephi from the beginning" (4 Nephi 1:38–39). Mormon seems to imply that if Laman and Lemuel had not chosen unbelief from the beginning, events would not have come to pass as they did at this much later time, fulfilling anew the angel's and Nephi's words in 1 Nephi 12:22–23. The Lamanites hatred of the Nephites had strong, deep roots. It was the worst of the consequences of Laman and Lemuel's choice, resulting in the loss of countless lives and the misery of many souls.

Unfortunately, this extreme manifestation of unfaithfulness and rebellion "against the gospel of Christ" was surpassed almost immediately by Nephite pride (4 Nephi 1:24; see also 1 Nephi 11:36), leading to the rapid deterioration of society (see Mormon 8:27). Alma had foreseen that the Nephites themselves would "dwindle in unbelief" (Alma 45:12) and would, by and large, become like the Lamanites with the exception of "a few who [would] be called the disciples of the Lord" (Alma 45:14). Those who were pressing forward to partake of the fruit of the tree were few by that time. Yet the remedy then was the same as it had always been: faith and faithfulness in Christ.

Faithfulness amid Deteriorating Faith

When Mormon and Moroni stated the need to have faith, hope, and charity (see Moroni 7) they knew what they spoke of. Like Nephi, they saw the final consequences of Laman and Lemuel's unbelief; they witnessed the genocide (the final fall) of their own people, yet they could write about the promises that were still extended to the Lamanites if they would repent (see Alma 17:15; see also Enos 1:16; Alma 9:16; Helaman 15:12). Until the end of his life, Moroni continued to refer to the Lamanites as his brethren (see Moroni 1:4, 10:1), even his "beloved brethren" (see Moroni 10:18–19).

Ranging from hope and joy (see Mormon 2:12) to hopelessness (see Mormon 2:13; 5:2), Mormon and Moroni knew that they had "a labor to perform whilst in this tabernacle of clay" (Moroni 9:6). Even though their faithful efforts seemed to bear little or no fruit in their time, those efforts are bearing plentiful fruit today. The entire Book of Mormon can be said to be the fruit of their faithfulness, as well as the millions of lives their record has touched and the Christ-centered faithfulness that record continues to inspire. They have afforded millions a rod of iron—a means of accessing the tree of life that would be otherwise unavailable.

We too are living in what appear to be times of deteriorating faith and faithfulness, and it may seem to us that our best efforts to bring our brothers and sisters to Christ are in vain. We need only, however, to look to such examples as Lehi, Nephi, Jacob, Enos, Ammon, the sons of Mosiah, the Lamanite converts, Mormon, and Moroni to see that our faithful efforts will bear fruit in the Lord's own due time (see Enos 1:16). Their faithfulness is similar to the Savior's, who wrought an infinite atonement—the full effects of which still have yet to be realized. We are living in the times of the prophesied "gather[ing] together in one" (see Ephesians 1:10; Jacob 5:74; John 11:52). Although the harvest is truly great and the laborers are few (see Jacob 5:70), each faithful act of service helps to prepare or clear the way (see Jacob 5:61, 65–66) so that eventually "the good shall overcome the bad" (Jacob 5:66). Though the reverse may seem true at the moment, the Atonement of Jesus Christ will one day have its intended effect (see Jacob 5:75).

"Ye Know Not but What They Will Return and Repent" (3 Nephi 18:32)

Like Mormon and Moroni, we too "have a labor to perform whilst in this tabernacle of clay" (Moroni 9:6). First, as the "peaceable followers of Christ" ours must be a "peaceable walk with the children of men" (Moroni 7:3–4), even as the mists of darkness and wickedness grow thicker all around us. Second, we have the responsibility to "invite all to come unto Christ" (D&C 20:59) and "partake of his goodness" (2 Nephi 26:28, 33) even as he invites all to come and partake. Third, we (like Lehi and others) are not to give up on people or write people off (especially our own family), even when they seem to spurn every invitation to partake of the fruit of the tree of life. Elder Robert D. Hales, alluding to the scene in Lehi's vision, noted the following: "*The greatest rescue, the greatest activation will be in our homes.* If someone in your family is *wandering in strange paths*, you are a rescuer, engaged in the greatest rescue effort the Church has ever known. I testify from personal experience: There is no failure except in giving up. It is never too early or too late to begin. Do not worry about what has happened in the past."[33] Our faithfulness will beget faith in those around us, but so will our unfaithfulness beget unfaithfulness. Our immediate responsibility is, through our faithfulness in Jesus Christ, to beget faith in the rising generation (D&C 123:11), our own families, and especially our posterity.

The Book of Mormon's lesson about the long-term consequences of unbelief on posterity is indeed a lesson for us today. Even Mormon and Moroni, who as the record's editors and compilers were well situated to appreciate the historical significance of the Lamanites again dwindling in unbelief in the manner that Nephi had seen (1 Nephi 12:22–23), had hope for their brethren (Mormon 9:35–37). We are living in the days of the complete fulfillment of the Lord's promises to the Lamanites. They (and all so-called unbelievers) can still become the *exceedingly faithful* by repenting and choosing to experience (taste) the love of God as manifest in the Savior. As the Savior himself said, "Ye know not but what they will return and repent" (3 Nephi 18:32) and partake of the fruit of the tree of life. The promises of the Lord, like the rod of iron[34] and (more importantly) the arms of the Savior, remain extended.[35] In the Lord's own due time, his Atonement, in no small part through our faithfulness, will eventually reach all with its full intended embrace.

Notes

This paper is dedicated to my wife, Suzy, and to the memory of our son Nathan Lon Bowen. Nathan has given his mother, father, and brother (Zachariah) all the more reason to press forward in faith and endure to the end. We look forward with hope to the day when we shall partake of the fruit of the tree of life with him and all the faithful.

1. "Cut off from the presence of the Lord": varieties of this collocation (combination of terms) describe the condition of the Lamanites in 2 Nephi 5:20 and Alma 9:13–14. It is first used in 1 Nephi 2:21; 2 Nephi 1:20; 4:4, warning of the Lamanites' future condition. The original form of the Lord's promise to Lehi is evidently preserved in Alma 50:20: "Blessed art thou and thy children; and they shall be blessed, inasmuch as they shall keep my commandments they shall prosper in the land. But remember, inasmuch as they will not keep my commandments they shall be cut off from the presence of the Lord." Originally, this promise was directed toward Lehi's posterity generally and not towards the Lamanites in particular. Alma understood the implications of this, as is evident in his counsel to each of his sons (see Alma 36:30; 37:13; and 38:1). This collocation is also used to describe Adam and Eve (and their posterity) in 2 Nephi 9:6 and Alma 42:7–11 (see also Ether 2:15).

2. For examples of "cast off" and "cast out," see 1 Nephi 8:36; 2 Nephi 25:29; and Helaman 12:25.

3. For a survey of the varieties of *inclusio* in Hebrew poetry and prose, see *Dictionary of the Old Testament: Wisdom, Poetry, and Writings*, ed. Tremper Longman III and Peter Enns (Downers Grove, IL: InterVarsity Press, 2008), 323–25.

4. See 1 Nephi 12:18–19. Nephite pride was the pride of "the great and spacious building." Compare 1 Nephi 11:36; Alma 5:53, 7:6; 3 Nephi 6:15; 4 Nephi 1:24.

5. N. Eldon Tanner framed the issue of unbelief as a matter of choice. See N. Eldon Tanner, "The Consequences of Choosing Unbelief," *Ensign*, December 1979, 2.

6. See especially 1 Nephi 13:35; 15:13; 2 Nephi 1:10; 26:15; Mosiah 1:5; Alma 46:10–14; 50:22; Helaman 6:34; 15:11; 3 Nephi 25:5; 4 Nephi 1:34–38; Mormon 9:20; Ether 4:3.

7. The Hebrew *pānîm* (literally *faces*) denotes both an individual's physical face and his or her presence.

8. Similar descriptions of the Lamanites based on Nephi's characterization can be found in Enos 1:20; Jacob 7:24; Jarom 1:6; Mosiah 9:12. Mormon 5:15 indicates that the Nephites had characterized the Lamanites this way for much of their shared history.

9. See Matthew L. Bowen, "'O Ye Fair Ones': An Additional Note on the Meaning of the Name *Nephi*," *Insights* 23, no. 6 (2003): 2; "Wordplay on the Name 'Enos,'" *Insights* 26, no. 3 (2006): 2; "'And He Was a Young Man': The Literary Preservation of Alma's Autobiographical Wordplay," *Insights* 30, no. 4 (2010): 2–3n8.

10. A possible wordplay on (or play on the meaning of) Nephi. Hebrew and Egyptian both create a two-member comparative construction using a regular adjective with a preposition (*m-* or *min* in Hebrew, *r* in Egyptian). See Paul Joüon, *A Grammar of Biblical Hebrew*, trans. T. Muraoka (Rome: Editrice Pontificio Istituto Biblico, 2005), 2:522–23; Alan Gardiner, *Egyptian Grammar*, 3rd ed. rev. (Oxford: Griffith Institute, 1957), 47.

11. There is good evidence that Enos saw this struggle in terms of the Jacob–Esau conflict. See John A. Tvedtnes and Matthew Roper, "Jacob and Enos: Wrestling before God," *Insights* 21, no. 5 (2001): 2–3.

12. Enos's use of the term *wrestle* in Enos 1:2 is a deliberate paronomasia on the name of his own father, Jacob, and his ancestor, Jacob, borrowed from the interplay of the river Jabbok *yabbōq* (Genesis 32:23), Jacob (*yaʿaqōb*), the verb "to wrestle" (*yēʾābēq* / *bᵉhēʾābᵉqô*, Genesis 32:25–26), and the verb "embrace" (*wayᵉḥabēqēhû*, Genesis 33:4). Enos must have taken heart in the fact that Jacob and Esau's broken brotherly relationship was ultimately reconciled—"at-one-ed."

13. Commenting on Amalickiah's rise to power among the Lamanites, Mormon notes that "the people of the Lamanites . . . were composed of the Lamanites and the Lemuelites and the Ishmaelites, and *all the dissenters of Nephites, from the reign of Nephi down to the present time*" (Alma 47:35).

14. Although Zeniff may not have appreciated the significance of these events, Mormon did. When Mormon reports that because of Noah's ex-priest Amulon and his henchmen, "the language of Nephi began to be taught among all the people of the Lamanites" (Mosiah 24:4), he may have been alluding to Zeniff's own explanation of why he was in the party that went up to reinherit the land of Nephi: "I, Zeniff, having been taught in all the language of the Nephites" (Mosiah 9:1).

15. See Alma 24:7; 2 Nephi 26:28, 33; 33:14; Jacob 1:7.

16. Zeniff's description suggests a thorough familiarity with the contents of the small plates.

17. Interestingly, Ammon's name could have meant—or was thought to mean—"faithful." "Ammon" could be an alternative spelling of the Hebrew name Amon (אמון), which Martin Noth thought meant "faithful" or "trustworthy," that is, "[The Lord is] faithful" or "[The Lord is] trustworthy." See Martin Noth, *Die israelitischen Personennamen im Rahmen der gemeinsemitischen Namengebung* (Hildesheim: Georg Olms Veragsbuchhandlung, 1966), 228. See also Ludwig Koehler and Walter Baumgartner, *The Hebrew and Aramaic Lexicon of the Old Testament* (Boston: Brill: 2001), 1:62. Another, although less likely, possibility is that it is a biform of Amnon (אמנון or אמנן), which also means "faithful" (Noth, *Israelitischen Personennamen*, 38, 228). See *Hebrew and Aramaic Lexicon*, 1:65. Still less likely is that it is *Ammon* with an initial *ayin* (עמון), since that gentilic name was not traditionally held in high esteem by the Israelites. See Genesis 19:30–38, where it is associated with incest.

18. This would imply that the Nephite language of Ammon's time (and still later, Mormon's—see Mormon 9:32–33) was still Hebrew at its base (which is possible, but far from certain). The words *believe*, *faith*, and *true* might then still derive from Hebrew *'mn.

19. Similarly, Aaron's success among the Lamanites may also be attributed to his familiarity with and use of the scriptures (see Alma 22:12–14).

20. For more on the word of God as a rod or sword, see Hugh W. Nibley "Ezekiel 37:15–23 as Evidence for the Book of Mormon," in *An Approach to the Book of Mormon*, ed. John W. Welch, 3rd ed. (Salt Lake City: Deseret Book; Provo, UT: FARMS, 1988), 311–28; John A. Tvedtnes, "*Rod* and *Sword* as the Word of God," *JBMS* 5, no. 2 (1996): 148–55. Matthew L. Bowen, "What Meaneth the Rod?," *Insights* 25, no. 2 (2005): 2–3.

21. "Rod of God"—Hebrew, *maṭṭeh ha-'elōhîm*. Compare Egyptian *mdw*, "rod," "word." See also 1 Nephi 17:26, 29. For "word of God," compare Egyptian *mdw-nṯr*, literally "word of God," or "sacred writings," "scripture." The meaning of *mdw-nṯr* ranges from "word of God [or] divine decree" to "sacred writings" (scriptures), and even to the "written characters [and] script" in which such "sacred writings" and "divine decrees" were written. Raymond O. Faulkner, *A Concise Dictionary of Middle Egyptian* (Oxford: Griffith Institute, 1999), 122.

22. Mormon's description of the word of God in Helaman 3:29–30 is a creative blending of imagery from Lehi's vision and the Exodus.

23. Nephi's inclusion of the Spirit's statement, "It is better that one man should perish than that a nation should dwindle and perish in unbelief" (1 Nephi 4:13), is probably meant to be understood in the wider context of Lamanite dwindling in unbelief without the scriptures. In Nephi's mind, the Lamanites had proven that a nation does dwindle in unbelief without the scriptures, thus further justifying his actions against Laban on that occasion.

24. The root *'mn has the basic meaning "to be firm, trustworthy," with related meanings "reliable," "faithful," "to believe," "to have trust in," "surety," "faithfulness," "steadfastness," and "truth" ('mt < *'mnt). See *Hebrew and Aramaic Lexicon*, 1:62–65.

25. In contrast to apostate Nephites (see 1 Nephi 8:25).

26. See S. Kent Brown, "The Prophetic Laments of Samuel the Lamanite," *Journal of Book of Mormon Studies* 1, no. 1 (1992): 163–80; Donald W. Parry, "'Thus Saith the Lord': Prophetic Language in Samuel's Speech," *Journal of Book of Mormon Studies* 1, no. 1 (1992) 181–83. David E. Bokovoy, "Love vs. Hate: An Analysis of Helaman 15:1–4," *Insights* 22, no. 2 (2002): 2–3.

27. Brown, "The Prophetic Laments of Samuel the Lamanite," 163–80.

28. Parry, "Thus Saith the Lord," 181–83.

29. Bokovoy, "Love vs. Hate," 2–3.

30. Bowen, "'O Ye Fair Ones,'" 2.

31. It is hardly surprising that the Nephites were so enraged by Samuel's turning things upside down that they immediately set about trying to kill him. The emphasis on Lamanite faithfulness and Nephite unbelief continues in Mormon's description of the aftermath of Samuel's speech: after his speech some Nephites "*believed* on his word" and sought baptism (Helaman 16:1). Amid the attempts of the many Nephites who did *not* believe Samuel's words to kill him, a few others *did believe* on his words and also sought

Nephi for baptism. However, "the more part of [the Nephites] *did not believe* the words of Samuel," even after witnessing these miracles (v. 6).

32. "Firm, and steadfast, and immovable." The only other place where this phrase occurs is in Lehi's counsel to his son Lemuel (see 1 Nephi 2:10). It would seem, then, that Mormon's allusion is deliberate. The descendants of Laman and Lemuel were now fully living up to Lehi's counsel to Laman and Lemuel: "continually running into the fountain of all righteousness" like an *'êtān* (a perennial stream). And, like a valley (*'ēmeq*), they were "firm and steadfast, and immovable in keeping the commandments of the Lord" (1 Nephi 2:9–10). For the possibility of wordplay in Lehi's counsel, see John Tvedtnes, "I Have a Question," *Ensign*, October 1986, 64–67.

33. Robert D. Hales, "Our Duty to God: The Mission of Parents and Leaders to the Rising Generation," *Ensign*, May 2010: 95–98. He continues, "Pick up the phone. Write a note. Make a visit. Extend the invitation to come home. Don't be afraid or embarrassed. Your child is Heavenly Father's child. You are about His work. He has promised to gather His children, and He is with you."

34. 1 Nephi 8:19: "And I beheld a rod [Hebrew *matteh*] of iron, and it *extended* [Hebrew *nāṭāh*] along the bank of the river, and led to the tree by which I stood." Lehi's statement may contain a play on words. In any case, a rod is a beautiful metaphor for an ever-extended blessing, as is the extended or outstretched arm.

35. Compare Jacob 6:5; Mosiah 16:12; 29:20; Alma 5:33; 19:36; 29:10; 3 Nephi 9:14.

14

"Delivered by the Power of God": Nephi's Vision of America's Birth

Kenneth L. Alford

In contrast to Lehi's tree of life vision, which is not tied to specific historical events, Nephi's vision in 1 Nephi 11–14 is brimming with historical details, references, and prophetic insights. In 1 Nephi 13, Nephi was probably shown the successful struggle surrounding the birth of the United States[1] and the fact that the Lord would use his power to influence the outcome.

Nephi wrote "that the Gentiles who had gone forth out of captivity" would "humble themselves before the Lord" so they could be "delivered by the power of God out of the hands of all other nations" (1 Nephi 13:16, 19). Nephi foresaw "the restoration of the gospel six hundred years before the Savior's birth, and the events leading up to it were shown him in considerable detail,"[2] namely concerning the colonization of North America and the American Revolution.

The sheer improbability of an American victory in the Revolutionary War is staggering. By all the standard measures of military contests—population, power, wealth, size and experience of the respective armies and navies, depth and experience of each country's military leadership, diplomatic

---

Kenneth L. Alford is an associate professor of Church history and doctrine at Brigham Young University.

power and connections, and political organization—Great Britain should easily have been victorious. To face the most professional army and navy in the world, the American colonists could field only an army of volunteer militia and a few undergunned ships. As the historian Robert Thompson noted: "Especially great were the difficulties of America from the lack of the manufactures [sic] needed to equip and support an army. They had no cloths to make uniforms, no canvas for tents, no shoes and no leather to make them, no cannon save such as they could borrow or buy in Europe, no gunpowder for either large or small arms, no bunting for flags. Twice the patriotic women of Philadelphia searched their household stores, and sent every blanket they could spare to Washington's forces; and the awnings from the shops, the sails from the ships, and the contents of the sail-lofts went to make tents."[3]

Never before had colonies militarily defeated their mother country and established themselves as an independent republic. Early Americans recognized the Lord's hand in their unlikely victory over Great Britain. On July 2, 1776, when the Continental Congress signed the Declaration of Independence and pledged to each other their lives, fortunes, and sacred honor, they did so "with a firm reliance on the protection of divine Providence."[4] Throughout the Revolutionary War and the decades that followed, Americans openly acknowledged God's intervention on their behalf.

During 1976, the American bicentennial year, President Ezra Taft Benson commented, "Secular scholarship, though useful, provides an incomplete and sometimes inaccurate view of our history. The real story of America is one which shows the hand of God in our nation's beginning."[5] It is fair to ask, then, what evidence exists to demonstrate that the power of God was with the American cause during the fight for independence? And how widely recognized was that assistance?

To prove absolutely to a skeptical world that God influenced the outcome of the American War for Independence will probably remain elusive. Through his prophets, though, God has declared that it was so. Elder L. Tom Perry has pointed out that the "evidence is overwhelming of God's hand in the establishment of this nation."[6] If we look at events through the eyes of faith, we will find numerous instances of divine assistance. As the Reverend John F. Bigelow stated in a Civil War–era sermon, "My purpose is simply to verify, by a few brief references, the presence of God's hand."[7] In the interest of space and time, we will examine just three of the many possible instances of Divine

Providence, "the power of God," coming to the aid of the fledgling colonies: George Washington and the Founding Fathers, the wartime weather, and the great chain across the Hudson River in New York at West Point.

Washington and the Founding Fathers

In addressing the events of the Revolutionary War, Nephi referred to the American colonists as "the Gentiles who had gone forth out of captivity," and he noted that they "did humble themselves before the Lord; and the power of the Lord was with them" (1 Nephi 13:16). As if to stress the recognition that God would be on their side, in the following three verses Nephi again clearly states that he "beheld that the power of God was with them" (v. 18) and that they would be "delivered by the power of God" (v. 19).

It is truly inspiring to study the humility, character, competence, and integrity of the great men God assembled to give birth to the American republic. As Bigelow noted, the "same Providence which gave us Washington, gave us others also, who were worthy to be his brothers, if not his peers in the common cause of the country."[8] At a White House dinner on April 29, 1962, President John F. Kennedy, not entirely in jest, acknowledged how unique the Founding Fathers were when he told a distinguished gathering of Nobel Prize winners, "I think this is the most extraordinary collection of talent, of human knowledge, that has ever been gathered together at the White House, with the possible exception of when Thomas Jefferson dined alone."[9] In latter-day scripture, the Lord announced the very personal interest that he had taken regarding the birth of the United States. The Founding Fathers, he declared in section 101 of the Doctrine and Covenants, were "wise men whom I raised up unto this very purpose" (D&C 101:80). Bigelow also stated: "The American cause needed men of far-sighted sagacity, of regulative talent, of constitutive ideas, of able statesmanship. It needed men of diplomatic abilities, those who would be faithful at home, and just abroad. It needed men of incorruptible patriotism, those who would fill the offices of Government, not in the interest of self, but in that of the country. How adequately God supplied the men to meet these demands, our constitutional history leaves us in no doubt."[10]

The Founding Fathers were truly men "furnished by Providence."[11] During the April 1898 general conference, President Wilford Woodruff said, "I am going to bear my testimony to this assembly, if I never do it again in my life, that those men who laid the foundation of this American government...

were the best spirits the God of heaven could find on the face of the earth. These were choice spirits, not wicked men. General Washington and all the men that labored for the purpose were inspired of the Lord."[12] Interestingly, it was to President Woodruff that those men appeared at the St. George Temple in 1877 requesting that their temple work be completed. President Benson shared his conviction regarding America's Founding Fathers that "when one casts doubt about the character of these noble sons of God, I believe he or she will have to answer to the God of heaven for it."[13]

While all of the Founding Fathers contributed significantly, in their own way, to the establishment of the United States of America, one man was absolutely essential—George Washington. Referring to Washington in an 1841 nationally published sermon, the Reverend George Cheever stated that "Divine Providence had, for years, been giving him special training for his work.... I cannot but think that the hand of God was signally manifest, and in nothing more so than in giving us just such a man as our Washington.... It is not too much to say that, had he been a different man, in the slightest essential degree, ... he would have failed ... and the American cause would have been lost."[14]

God's protection and intervention to bring about an American victory in the Revolutionary War, as foretold in Nephi's vision, was demonstrated many times during George Washington's life. There are several historical accounts when Washington—like Samuel, the Lamanite—had his life miraculously preserved. One early incident occurred in the summer of 1755 during the French and Indian War. As a twenty-three-year-old aide-de-camp, Washington accompanied General Edward Braddock's regiments into the Ohio region, where they were attacked on July 9, 1755, by French and Indian forces at the Battle of the Monongahela. Braddock and over half of the approximately 1,300 British regulars were killed or wounded. Colonel Washington, although not officially in the chain of command, organized survivors and helped the army retire from the field. In a letter to his brother John, written from Fort Cumberland a few days following the battle, Washington acknowledged his miraculous escape. "As I have heard since my arriv'l at this place, a circumstantial acct. of my death and dying speech," he wrote, "I take this early oppertunity of contradicting both, and of assuring you that I now exist and appear in the land of the living by the miraculous care of Providence, that protected me beyond all human expectation; I had four Bullets through my Coat, and two Horses shot under me, and yet escaped unhurt."[15]

In his 1843 book *The Life of George Washington*, historian Jared Sparks related an incident told by Dr. James Craik, a boyhood and lifelong friend of Washington's who was with him at the Battle of the Monongahela. Craik was also one of the three doctors who attended to Washington on his deathbed at Mount Vernon in 1799. Craik reported that fifteen years after the Battle of the Monongahela, he and Washington

> travelled together on an expedition to the western country, with a party of woodsmen, for the purpose of exploring wild lands. While near the junction of the Great Kenhawa and Ohio Rivers, a company of Indians came to them with an interpreter, at the head of whom was an aged and venerable chief. This personage made known to them by the interpreter, that, hearing Colonel Washington was in that region, he had come a long way to visit him, adding, that, during the battle of the Monongahela, he had singled him out as a conspicuous object, fired his rifle at him many times, and directed his young warriors to do the same, but to his utter astonishment none of their balls took effect. He was then persuaded, that the youthful hero was under the special guardianship of the Great Spirit, and immediately ceased to fire at him. He was now come to pay homage to the man, who was the particular favorite of Heaven, and who could never die in battle.[16]

Similar incidents happened to Washington during the course of the Revolutionary War. In January 1777, for example, in an effort to halt a possible American retreat at the Battle of Princeton, General Washington rode into the thick of the battle and positioned himself directly between the fighting American and British soldiers. Although he was mounted on a horse and sitting just a few dozen yards from the nearest British riflemen with "a thousand deaths flying around him,"[17] he again miraculously escaped unharmed.

Recognizing George Washington as the "Father of His Country" is not simply an honorific title; it is also a statement of fact. Over a century ago, the historian Robert Thompson called Washington "God's unique gift to America."[18] Contemporaries and historians alike have long noted that George Washington, more than any other individual, was responsible for the success of the American Revolutionary cause. His character, temperament, experience, and faith were uniquely suited to the heavy and almost impossible demands placed upon him; he was "called to perform a particular work, a work allowing him to be nothing other than just what he was. His destiny ... was, with the scanty resources furnished to his hands, and with fearful odds against him, to lay the foundations of this great American Republic."[19] Truly, "the power of God was with [him]" (1 Nephi 13:18).

Following the conclusion of the Revolutionary War, King George III of Great Britain asked Benjamin West, an American-born artist living in London, if he had heard any information regarding what George Washington might do after the war. West replied, "Oh, they say he will return to his farm." "If he does that," said the king, referring to the fact that Washington would voluntarily be giving up a position of great power, "he will be the greatest man in the world."[20] Many generations of Americans would concur with the king's assessment.

Wartime Weather

Nephi was shown in vision that "the wrath of God was upon all those that were gathered together against them [the American colonists] to battle" (1 Nephi 13:18). Interestingly, the first time the phrase "the wrath of God" appears in the Book of Mormon is just a few verses earlier in that same chapter when Nephi discusses the fate of his brother's descendants (see 1 Nephi 13:11). "Wrath of God" is a thought-provoking phrase—one of the meanings of which is "divine chastisement"[21]—and it appears frequently throughout the scriptures. Echoing the words of Nephi, Elder Bruce R. McConkie observed, "In the American Revolution the Lord was with the colonists and poured out his wrath upon Great Britain and those who opposed the Americans. (1 Nephi 13:17–19)."[22] One way God's wrath was displayed was through providing difficult and challenging weather conditions when American military forces most needed them.

God controls the elements and can use them to further his purposes. Weather played a decisive and supportive role several times during the Revolutionary War, as British and Hessian forces found themselves on the receiving end of divine chastisement. Following "the shot heard 'round the world," the first major engagements of the war took place on the hills surrounding Boston Harbor. In January 1776, General Knox decided to use sleds to transport almost fifty artillery pieces from Fort Ticonderoga in New York, where they had been captured from the British, to Boston, and it snowed sufficiently to speed the journey. Once the artillery pieces reached Boston, Washington placed them on Dorchester Heights overlooking Boston Harbor and the British ships at anchor there. During the night of March 4, 1776, while the Americans worked feverishly on fortifications, a "ground mist completely covered their operations" from the British "while the weather was perfectly clear on the top of the hill" where they were working. At the same time, an inland breeze carried noise of the American's actions away from the British forces.[23]

Upon seeing the finished fortifications the next morning, British general Sir William Howe is quoted as having said, "The rebels have done more in one night than my whole army would have done in a month."[24] Howe ordered an immediate attack upon the Heights, but a severe snowstorm arose and canceled his plans. One British soldier wrote that the storm was "more violent than any I had ever heard."[25] Regarding the storm, General Washington wrote that the British made great preparations "for attacking us; but not being ready before the afternoon" the weather became "very tempestuous," which resulted in "much Blood" being saved, "and a very important blow (to one side or the other) prevented. That this remarkable interposition of Providence is for some wise purpose, I have no doubt."[26]

The bid for American independence would have ended near New York City in August 1776 with the capture of the Continental Army if favorable weather had not intervened and created the means for their escape. In the summer of 1776, British forces landed on Long Island in overwhelming numbers and sought to end the rebellion quickly by capturing General Washington and his army. Washington's forces were pushed across Long Island and into Brooklyn with their backs against the river. Rather than risk losing his entire army, Washington decided to evacuate his forces across the mile-wide East River. Colonel Benjamin Tallmadge, an American officer, explained that by ten o'clock on the night of August 29, 1776,

> the troops began to retire from the lines in such a manner that no chasm was made in the lines, but as one regiment left their station on guard, the remaining troops moved to the right and left and filled up the vacancies, while Gen. Washington took his station at the ferry, and superintended the embarkation of the troops. It was one of the most anxious, busy nights that I ever recollect, and being the third in which hardly any of us had closed our eyes to sleep, we were all greatly fatigued. As the dawn of the next day approached, those of us who

> remained in the trenches became very anxious for our own safety, and when the dawn appeared there were several regiments still on duty. At this time a very dense fog began to rise, and it seemed to settle in a peculiar manner over both encampments. I recollect this peculiar providential occurrence perfectly well; and so very dense was the atmosphere that I could scarcely discern a man at six yards' distance.
>
> When the sun rose we had just received orders to leave the lines, but before we reached the ferry, the Commander-in-Chief sent one of his Aids [sic] to order the regiment to repair again to their former station on the lines. . . . [B]ut the fog remained as dense as ever. Finally, the second order arrived for the regiment to retire, and we very joyfully bid those trenches a long adieu.[27]

Colonel Tallmadge noted that he was one of the last soldiers to be evacuated. As he was leaving, he remembered that he had left his horse tied to a post at the ferry. His account of that morning continues:

> The troops having now all safely reached New York, and the fog continuing as thick as ever, I began to think of my favorite horse, and requested leave to return and bring him off. Having obtained permission, I called for a crew of volunteers to go with me, and guiding the boat myself, I obtained my horse and got off some distance into the river before the enemy appeared in Brooklyn.
>
> As soon as they reached the ferry we were saluted merrily from their musketry, and finally by their field pieces; but we returned in safety. In the history of warfare I do not recollect a more fortunate retreat. After all, the providential appearance of the fog saved a part of our army from being captured. . . .
>
> When the enemy had taken possession of the heights opposite the city, they commenced firing from their artillery, and the fleet were in motion to take possession of those waters, which, had it been done a little earlier, this division of our army must inevitably have fallen into their hands.[28]

Samuel DeForest, a six-term Connecticut militiaman, reported that during the evacuation of Brooklyn Heights "a most wonderful thunderstorm took place. It commenced about one o'clock in the day. The thunder and the lightning were dreadful. The clouds run so low. . . . The darkness was so great that the two armies could not see each other, although within one hundred rods of each other."²⁹ The heavy northeastern winds, rain, and fog combined to create three significant results. First, it stopped the British Navy from blocking Washington's evacuation; second, it halted attempts by the British Army to attack and capture Washington's forces; and third, it facilitated the escape of the American Army.

The oft-told story of Washington crossing the Delaware River on December 25, 1776, to attack Trenton, New Jersey, often ignores the vital role that weather played in that battle's success. The blinding snowstorm that began on Christmas Day not only convinced the British and Hessians that Washington would not attack, but also concealed noise of Washington's movement and provided frozen roads that quickened the army's approach to Trenton. The Battle of Trenton was a complete American victory.

The Battle of Princeton, a few days later, provided Washington with weather perfect for his purposes. For four consecutive nights in early January 1777, the temperature remained above freezing, which left muddy roads far too soft to move the Continental Army into position to attack the British. The fourth night, though, a hard freeze turned the roads solid, "enabling the Americans, who began to move out after midnight, to proceed with greater dispatch. Thick clouds piled high, adding to the darkness, and a cold wind blew from the northwest, carrying sounds away from the British lines."³⁰ The cold weather enabled Washington's forces to march sixteen miles in the dark in less time than it had taken the British to march just ten miles in daylight the previous day.

Weather intervened to save American forces in the southern colonies as well. On January 17, 1781, at the Battle of Cowpens in South Carolina, General Daniel Morgan's soldiers soundly defeated a larger and more experienced British force commanded by the infamous Colonel Banastre Tarleton. Following the defeat, General Charles Cornwallis pursued Morgan's men in a vigorous chase. Cornwallis, after destroying his excess baggage in order to increase the speed of their march, believed that he had cornered Morgan at the Catawba River. Morgan's forces crossed the Catawba just two hours before Cornwallis arrived. Heavy rain that morning and during the next two days made the river impassable and allowed Morgan's soldiers to escape. A few days later, a similar series of events occurred when American forces under General Nathanael Greene were protected because the British Army could not cross the swollen Yadkin River.³¹

Individually, any one of these extremely fortunate bouts of weather so favorable to the American cause might be explained away as coincidence or extremely good luck. Collectively, though, they demonstrate divine interest and influence.[32] The Book of Mormon includes other instances, such as the visit of the resurrected Christ to the Americas, when God has used weather—in that instance, "the thunderings, and the lightnings, and the storm, and the tempest" (3 Nephi 8:19)—to further his purposes. Several times during the American Revolution, favorable weather conditions meant the difference between victory and defeat, and the final result, being "delivered by the power of God" (1 Nephi 13:19), was exactly as Nephi prophesied.

West Point Chain

God, who knows "the end from the beginning" (Abraham 2:8), knew exactly what the American colonists would need to secure victory in the Revolutionary War in order to provide a suitable environment for the Restoration a few decades later. The final evidence discussed here of God's prophesied hand in America's Revolutionary victory, as recorded by Nephi in the Book of Mormon, involves a river, iron ore, a very large chain, and God's inspiration to bring them together.

The important role that the Hudson River played in America's Revolutionary War victory can hardly be overstated. As General Washington wrote to General Israel Putnam, the American commander in the Hudson Highlands, on December 2, 1777, "The importance of the Hudson river in the present contest and the necessity of defending it, are subjects which have been so frequently and so fully discussed and are so well understood, that it is unnecessary to enlarge upon them."[33] If the British had retained possession of the river throughout the war, they would have effectively cut the American colonies in half. Just one month after shots were fired in Massachusetts at Lexington and Concord, the Continental Congress passed its first resolution addressing the strategic importance of American forces controlling the river.[34] From 1776 to early 1778, the colonists failed several times to retain command of the river (using booms, chevaux-de-frise, sunken vessels, firerafts, and other obstacles). One of those attempts, in 1777, involved placing a heavy metal chain with links 1½ inches thick across the river between Fort Montgomery on the west and Anthony's Nose on the east. On October 6, 1777, British forces attacked and soundly defeated the chain's defenders.

The idea of using a chain to block the Hudson was sound, but the initial execution was flawed. At the insistence of General Washington, who was at Valley Forge, and the New York Fortifications Commission, plans were made to retry placing a chain across the river approximately fifty miles north of New York City at West Point. On February 2, 1778, a government contract was executed to forge a new chain that would stretch across the Hudson a few miles upriver from the site of the original chain. The contract was signed late Saturday night and by "daylight on Sunday morning the forges were in operation."[35] West Point, the "keystone of the country,"[36] was the perfect location for the new chain. A double bend in the river there required sailing ships to stop and tack not once but twice as they passed West Point and nearby Constitution Island. In an engineering feat that would be difficult to duplicate even today, the chain was manufactured from start to finish in just six weeks. Creation of the chain was so important that the government's contract specified that workmen were exempted from military duty throughout the period of its construction. When finished on April 1, 1778, the chain weighed an estimated 186 tons and was over five hundred yards long. The hundreds of individual chain links ranged from 2¼ to 3½ inches thick and from two to three feet in length; there were also eight swivels and 80 clevises.[37] When stretched across the river, sections of chain floated on pitch-covered logs a few feet beneath the surface of the water.

The chain was deployed on April 30, 1778. With several forts, numerous redoubts, artillery, and soldiers effectively placed on both sides of the river, the installation of the great chain at West Point ensured American control of the Hudson River until the end of the war. During the remaining years of conflict, the chain was removed from the river each winter and replaced each spring on dates chosen by General Washington. West Point became so strategically and tactically important that it was the West Point fortification plans that General Benedict Arnold gave to Major John Andre when he infamously betrayed his country. The American chain that stretched across the Hudson denied British forces access to the river north of West Point throughout the duration of the war.

While the significance of the great chain at West Point is often recognized by historians, the circumstances behind the chain's actual construction are less widely known. How could such a massive construction project be completed by a fledgling country in such a brief period during wartime?

Simply stated, the creation of the chain at West Point was another example of Divine Providence. It was an act of Providence that one of the largest and richest iron deposits in the world is located just a few miles from West Point.[38] The Sterling iron works near West Point were established a few decades before the Revolutionary War.[39] The New York Fortifications Committee insisted that "the chain should be immediately made of the very best iron the Country afforded,"[40] and the Sterling iron works were widely recognized as producing some of the highest grade iron in the world. The government's February 1778 contract specifically required that the chain be made of "the best Sterling iron."[41] As a New Englander noted shortly before the war, "Of all the other countries of the world, Nature has best fitted the Northern [American] Colonies for the iron manufacture."[42] The rich, black magnetite ore at Sterling was 60 to 70 percent pure, which meant that it was "easily broken into chunks sufficiently pure to bypass customary and time-consuming 18th century washing and drying procedures,"[43] enabling the chain to be completed and emplaced in record time. Seven forges and ten welding fires were kept in operation around the clock. The famously cold winter of 1777–78 that severely tested soldiers at Valley Forge proved to be a blessing at the Sterling Forge, where it alleviated the intense heat of the forges,[44] and the great chain that stretched across the Hudson contributed significantly to the ultimate American victory.

Recognizing God's Hand

How exciting it is to be able to recognize the hand of God in the events of history and to understand the truthfulness of his words. Contemporary statements acknowledging God's hand in the outcome of the American Revolution are too numerous to include here; a few samples will suffice. Washington was especially aware of God's role in his victories. In May 1778, after learning that Benjamin Franklin had successfully negotiated an alliance with France, General Washington, from his headquarters at Valley Forge, noted in a general order to his soldiers that it had "pleased the Almighty ruler of the Universe propitiously to defend the Cause of the United American-States."[45] In an August 20, 1778, letter, Washington wrote, "The hand of Providence has been so conspicuous in all this, that he must be worse than an infidel that lacks faith, and more than wicked, that has not gratitude enough to acknowledge his obligations."[46] On October 20, 1781, George Washington urged his soldiers to attend a special public meeting to show "gratitude of Heart" for the "astonishing interpositions of Providence."[47] Throughout the course of the war, Washington commented a dozen times regarding the "smiles of Heaven"[48] upon the American cause. He also frequently acknowledged "the support of the Supreme power" and "the patronage of Heaven."[49] In his Farewell Orders to the Continental Army, dated November 2, 1783, Washington wrote, "A contemplation of the complete attainment (at a period earlier than could be expected) of the object for which we contended against so formidable a power, cannot but inspire us with astonishment and gratitude. The disadvantageous circumstances on our part, under which the war was undertaken, can never be forgotten. The singular interpositions of Providence in our feeble condition were such, as could scarcely escape the attention of the most unobserving."[50]

During the Constitutional Convention of 1787, Benjamin Franklin noted that, "In the beginning of the contest with Great Britain, when we were sensible of danger, we had daily prayer in this room for the divine protection. Our prayers, sir, were heard, and they were graciously answered. All of us who were engaged in the struggle must have observed frequent instances of a superintending Providence in our favor."[51] Numerous other participants expressed their belief regarding God's direct hand in their astonishing and highly unlikely victory. Charles Pinckney, a signer of the Constitution from South Carolina, acknowledged, "Nothing less than the superintending hand of Providence . . . miraculously carried us through the war."[52] James Madison, often referred to as the father of the Constitution, declared, "It is impossible for the man of pious reflection not to perceive in it [the Constitution] a finger of that Almighty hand which has been so frequently and signally extended to our relief in the critical stages of the revolution."[53] Church leaders across the nation frequently reminded their congregations of the Lord's hand in their affairs. During the War of 1812, a Christian minister named John Dunlap insisted:

> Without presumption we may assert, that the Lord appeared in behalf of America, during the arduous struggle with her parent state, Great Britain, before her independence. . . . America was destitute of armies, munitions of war and foreign connections: she had only God and the goodness of her cause to rely upon; but these were sufficient. . . . In the short space of seven years, the most powerful and warlike nation in the world, relinquished all authority over a number of her provinces, which she had treated as rebels, and acknowledged them

sovereign independent states. This was the work of the Lord, and glorious in our eyes.[54]

History bears witness to the fulfillment of the vision of the American Revolution that Nephi received and recorded two thousand years earlier.

America a Safe Haven for the Restoration

Latter-day Saint history is full of confirming testimony regarding the Lord's hand in the establishment of the United States. As recorded in prophecy and illuminated by prophetic commentary, we understand that the "destiny of America was divinely decreed."[55] President Brigham Young explained that the leaders of the American Revolution "were inspired by the Almighty, to throw off the shackles of the mother government, with her established religion."[56] Elder Perry taught that "the establishment of the United States was a part of God's plan and was brought about by men who were inspired and guided by God." He also claimed, "One must merely study history to know that to defeat the world's most powerful country by a group of fledgling colonies was a result of a force greater than man."[57]

For what purpose, then, did the Lord consciously intervene in the affairs of men in order to secure an American victory in the Revolutionary War? Elder Mark E. Petersen boldly proclaimed that "there was only one reason why the United States came into being—only one reason. It is a different reason from anything that we know in any other nation. There is a United States only because God planned to restore the gospel in the last days and he had to have a free country in which to do it."[58] The establishment of the United States was "a prologue to the restoration of the gospel and the church of Jesus Christ,"[59] and the Constitution was established to maintain "the rights and protection of all flesh" (D&C 101:77). As the Reverend John Bigelow pointed out in 1861, "God's Providence comes in among [us], disturbing and arranging to suit its own ends."[60]

Summary

Following his Resurrection, the Savior declared that "it is wisdom in the Father that they [the Gentiles] should be established in this land, and set up as a free people by the power of the Father" (3 Nephi 21:4). The American Revolutionary War "redeemed the land by the shedding of blood" (D&C

101:80) and prepared the way for the Restoration of the gospel that began in upstate New York during the spring of 1820.

In the book of Ether, Moroni briefly summarized the conditions for retaining possession of this land, "Behold, this is a choice land, and whatsoever nation shall possess it shall be free from bondage, and from captivity, and from all other nations under heaven, if they will but serve the God of the land, who is Jesus Christ" (Ether 2:12). Nephi emphasized those responsibilities when he wrote, "Wherefore, this land is consecrated unto him whom he shall bring. And if it so be that they shall serve him according to the commandments which he hath given, it shall be a land of liberty unto them; wherefore, they shall never be brought down into captivity; if so, it shall be because of iniquity; for if iniquity shall abound cursed shall be the land for their sakes, but unto the righteous it shall be blessed forever" (2 Nephi 1:7).

God's influence and intervention in the birth of the American Republic is not discussed today as frequently or as openly as it once was. We would do well to consider and privately answer three questions that Reverend Bigelow asked his listeners in July 1861, "To what other nation has God given such a history? To none. Then are we adequately conscious of, and adequately grateful for, the signal distinction which has been vouchsafed to us? Do we appreciate the peculiarities of our past history and our present condition?"[61]

The United States of America was established so that the Lord would have a suitable place to restore his gospel. In 1841, George B. Cheever, an American minister, pointed out that in "every respect our origin imposes upon us vast obligations."[62] It is our responsibility to live worthy of our political and religious heritage and to reverence and protect what we have received.

The more we study Nephi's vision in the Book of Mormon and compare it with the history of the American Revolution, the more we will appreciate and recognize God's hand in assisting the American colonists to bring about their ultimate and highly improbable victory. The birth of the United States of America was truly a miracle wrought by the power of God, just as Nephi saw in vision over twenty-three centuries earlier.

Notes

1. While additional prophetic commentary may yet be added in the future, Elders Ezra Taft Benson and Marion G. Romney identified "the Gentiles" (1 Nephi 13:15) with

the American colonies, "their mother Gentiles" (1 Nephi 13:17) with the British, the "battle against them" (1 Nephi 13:17) with the American Revolutionary War, and being "delivered by the power of God out of the hands of all other nations" (1 Nephi 13:19) with the American colonies winning their freedom as a result of the Revolutionary War. See Ezra Taft Benson, "God's Hand in Our Nation's History," in *1976 Devotional Speeches of the Year: BYU Bicentennial Devotional and Fireside Addresses* (Provo, UT: Brigham Young University Press, 1977), 299, and Marion G. Romney, "America's Fate and Ultimate Destiny," same volume, 322–23.

2. Mark E. Petersen, *The Great Prologue* (Salt Lake City: Deseret Book, 1975), 23.

3. Robert Ellis Thompson, *The Hand of God in American History: A Study of National Politics* (New York: Thomas Y. Crowell & Co., 1902), 53.

4. The United States Declaration of Independence.

5. Benson, "God's Hand in Our Nation's History," 301.

6. L. Tom Perry, "The Church and the American Bicentennial," in *1976 Devotional Speeches of the Year: BYU Bicentennial Devotional and Fireside Addresses* (Provo, UT: Brigham Young University Press, 1977), 63.

7. Rev. John F. Bigelow, *The Hand of God in American History: A Discourse Delivered in the Baptist Church, Reeseville, N. Y., July 7, 1861* (Burlington, VT: W. H. & C. A. Hoyt, 1861), 24.

8. Bigelow, *Hand of God in American History*, 23.

9. Quotations of John F. Kennedy, John F. Kennedy Presidential Library and Museum. http://www.jfklibrary.org/Historical+Resources/Archives/Reference+Desk/Quotations+of+John+F+Kennedy.htm.

10. Bigelow, *Hand of God in American History*, 24.

11. Bigelow, *Hand of God in American History*, 26.

12. Wilford Woodruff, in Conference Report, April 1898, 89.

13. Ezra Taft Benson, *The Teachings of Ezra Taft Benson* (Salt Lake City: Bookcraft, 1988), 604.

14. In Bigelow, *Hand of God in American History*, 21.

15. George Washington to John Augustine Washington, July 18, 1755, in *The George Washington Papers at the Library of Congress, 1741–1799*. http://lcweb2.loc.gov/ammem/mgwquery.html.

16. Jared Sparks, *The Life of George Washington* (Boston: Tappan and Dennet, 1843), 66n.

17. Michael Stephenson, *Patriot Battles: How the War of Independence Was Fought* (New York: HarperCollins, 2007), 265–66.

18. Thompson, *Hand of God in American History*, 57.

19. Bigelow, *Hand of God in American History*, 21.

20. Paul Johnson, *George Washington: The Founding Father* (New York: HarperCollins, 2005), 78.

21. *Merriam Webster's Collegiate Dictionary*, 10th ed., "wrath."

22. Bruce R. McConkie, *Mormon Doctrine*, 2nd ed. (Salt Lake City: Bookcraft, 1966), 827.

23. Peter Marshall and David Manuel, *The Light and the Glory* (Grand Rapids, MI: Fleming H. Revell, 1977), 299.

24. General Henry B. Carrington, *Washington the Soldier* (New York: Charles Scribner's Sons, 1899), 77.

25. Marshall and Manuel, *The Light and the Glory*, 300.

26. George Washington to Landon Carter, March 25, 1776, in *The George Washington Papers at the Library of Congress, 1741–1799*.

27. Benjamin Tallmadge, *Memoir of Col. Benjamin Tallmadge* (New York: Thomas Holman, 1858), 10–11.

28. Tallmadge, *Memoir of Col. Benjamin Tallmadge*, 11–12.

29. Statement of Samuel DeForest in John C. Dann, ed., *The Revolution Remembered: Eyewitness Accounts of the War for Independence* (Chicago: The University of Chicago Press, 1980), 43.

30. John Ferling, *Almost a Miracle: The American Victory in the War of Independence* (New York: Oxford University Press, 2007), 184.

31. Regarding the crossing of the Catawba River, Henry Watson wrote, "Thus was Morgan's division saved, as if by the interposition of Providence. This circumstance was generally regarded by the Americans as an evidence of the justice of their cause." Regarding the incident at the Yadkin, he said, "This was regarded by the Americans as a second interposition of Providence in their behalf." See Henry C. Watson, *History of the United States of America, from the Discovery to the Present Time* (Philadelphia: Thomas, Cowperthwait & Co., 1854), 520–23.

32. It should be noted that the Revolutionary War was not the first time that timely weather conditions had come to the military aid of American colonists. In 1746, for example, a fleet of forty French ships of war was sailing to attack New England. Upon learning of the impending danger, many inhabitants of Boston called for a season of fasting and prayer. It is reported that while pastors were praying in Boston, "a tempest ensued, in which the greater part of the French fleet was wrecked on the coast of Nova Scotia" ending the French attempt at conquest. See E. A. Park and S. H. Taylor, eds., *The Bibliotheca Sacra and American Biblical Repository* (Andover, MA: Warren F. Draper, 1855), 12:187.

33. George Washington to Israel Putnam, December 2, 1777, in *The George Washington Papers at the Library of Congress, 1741–1799*.

34. See MacGrane Coxe, "The Sterling Furnace and the West Point Chain: An Historical Address" (New York: privately printed, 1906), 3.

35. Benson J. Lossing, *The Pictorial Field-Book of the Revolution* (New York: Harper Brothers, 1860), 1:706n1.

36. Lossing, *The Pictorial Field-Book of the Revolution*, 1:706.

37. A clevise is a U-shaped metal fastener connected by a bolt that allows portions of a chain to rotate and move freely. For additional physical details regarding the great chain at West Point, see Lincoln Diamant, *Chaining the Hudson: The Fight for the River in the American Revolution* (New York: Citadel Press, 1994), 142.

38. Coxe, "The Sterling Furnace," 51n2.

39. "Sterling" is also spelled "Stirling" in some early accounts.

40. Diamant, *Chaining the Hudson*, 141.

41. Coxe, "The Sterling Furnace," 19.

42. Quoted in Diamant, *Chaining the Hudson*, 145.

43. Diamant, *Chaining the Husdon*, 142. Sterling's igneous magnetite ore (Fe_3O_4) was much richer than the standard sedimentary hematite (Fe_3O_3) found in many other iron deposits. See Diamant, *Chaining the Hudson*, 151.

44. Diamant, *Chaining the Husdson*, 152.

45. George Washington, May 5, 1778, General Orders, in *The George Washington Papers at the Library of Congress, 1741–1799*.

46. George Washington to Thomas Nelson Jr., August 20, 1778, in *The George Washington Papers at the Library of Congress, 1741–1799*.

47. George Washington, October 20, 1781, General Orders, in *The George Washington Papers at the Library of Congress, 1741–1799*.

48. See, for example, George Washington to Continental Congress, August 22, 1776, and George Washington to Israel Putnam, September 10, 1777, in *The George Washington Papers at the Library of Congress, 1741–1799*. To view all instances, visit http://memory.loc.gov/ammem/mgwquery.html and enter "smiles of Providence" as the search text.

49. George Washington, December 23, 1783, Resignation Address, in *The George Washington Papers at the Library of Congress, 1741–1799*.

50. George Washington to Continental Army, November 2, 1783, Farewell Orders, in *The George Washington Papers at the Library of Congress, 1741–1799*.

51. In Henry D. Gilpin, ed., *The Papers of James Madison* (Mobile, AL: Allston Mygatt, 1842), 2:984–85.

52. Charles Pinckney, *The State Gazette of South Carolina*, May 5, 1788, in E. H. Scott, ed., *The Federalist and Other Contemporary Papers on the Constitution of the United States* (New York: Scott, Foresman, and Company, 1894), 710.

53. Benson, "God's Hand in Our Nation's History," 304.

54. John Dunlap, *The Power, Justice and Mercy of Jehovah, Exercised upon his Enemies and his People: A Sermon Delivered on Board the Fleet, at Whitehall, December 12, 1814* (Albany: Websters and Skinners, 1815), 25–26.

55. Benson, "God's Hand in Our Nation's History," 298.

56. John A. Widtsoe, ed., *Discourses of Brigham Young* (Salt Lake City: Deseret Book, 1954), 359.

57. L. Tom Perry, "The Church and the American Bicentennial," in *1976 Devotional Speeches of the Year: BYU Bicentennial Devotional and Fireside Addresses* (Provo, UT: Brigham Young University Press, 1977), 61, 64.

58. Mark E. Petersen, "America—World Leader," in *1976 Devotional Speeches of the Year: BYU Bicentennial Devotional and Fireside Addresses* (Provo, UT: Brigham Young University Press, 1977), 348.

59. Benson, "God's Hand in Our Nation's History," 315.

60. Bigelow, *Hand of God in American History*, 11.

61. Bigelow, *Hand of God in American History*, 26.

62. George B. Cheever, *God's Hand in America* (New York: M. W. Dodd, 1841), 87.

15

What Nephi's Vision Teaches about the Bible and the Book of Mormon

Frank F. Judd Jr.

When Nephi's brothers were having a difficult time understanding their father's dream, Nephi pointedly asked them, "Have ye inquired of the Lord?" (1 Nephi 15:8). Nephi himself exemplified the process by which disciples of the Lord seek after and obtain personal revelation. After Lehi related his dream to his family, this righteous son declared, "I, Nephi, was desirous also that I might see, and hear, and know of these things" (1 Nephi 10:17). Nephi knew that "he that diligently seeketh shall find; and the mysteries of God shall be unfolded unto them" (1 Nephi 10:19). As Nephi sought for this greater understanding, he "was caught away in the Spirit of the Lord" (1 Nephi 11:1) and was shown marvelous things.

Both the process and the content of the revelation in Nephi's vision help the reader understand many things about the scriptures. Nephi's vision makes numerous references to the Bible (i.e., the book that would proceed forth out of the mouth of a Jew) as well as to the Book of Mormon (i.e., the record of the seed of Nephi). These important teachings fall into three basic categories. First, Nephi's vision mentions elements of stories found in the Bible and acts

---

Frank F. Judd Jr. is an associate professor of ancient scripture at Brigham Young University.

as a confirming witness that the Bible is true. Second, Nephi's vision provides essential details that shed light on the nature of the Bible and the process by which it was transmitted over the centuries. Third, Nephi's vision teaches important truths concerning the role of the Bible and the Book of Mormon in the restoration of the gospel. Book of Mormon writers repeatedly testified that they wrote for future generations under the inspiration of God (see 1 Nephi 6:3–6; 19:6; 2 Nephi 33:10–15; Jacob 7:27; Mormon 8:35; Mormon 9:30–31; and Ether 8:26). It is therefore vital that Latter-day Saints understand what Nephi's vision teaches about the witness of the Bible, the nature of the Bible, and the role of both the Bible and Book of Mormon in the latter days.

Confirming Witness of the Bible

In a revelation given through the Prophet Joseph Smith in April 1830, the Lord testified that one of the important purposes of the Book of Mormon was to "prov[e] to the world that the holy scriptures are true" (D&C 20:11).[1] Therefore, one of the important reasons for the Book of Mormon is that it corroborates the events and teachings contained in the Bible.[2] This process is particularly true of the life and mission of the Savior Jesus Christ, which Nephi's vision clearly and repeatedly confirms. Before his family fled into the wilderness, Nephi had already heard his father preach to the inhabitants of Jerusalem concerning "the coming of a Messiah, and also the redemption of the world" (1 Nephi 1:19). Nephi's account of Lehi's vision, however, provides important details not included in his abridgment of his father's record and therefore confirms the veracity of these items mentioned in the Bible.

After relating the account of Lehi's dream, Nephi prophesied that "six hundred years from the time that my father left Jerusalem, a prophet would the Lord God raise up among the Jews—even a Messiah, or in other words, a Savior of the world" (1 Nephi 10:4).[3] The word *Messiah* comes from the Hebrew language and means "anointed one."[4] An equivalent word from the Greek language is *Christ*.[5] During the time of the Old Testament, prophets, priests, and kings were anointed with oil and understood to be messiahs.[6] These important figures, however, were symbolic of the one true Messiah who was to come and who would be the ultimate Prophet, Priest, and King.

During his mortal ministry, the Savior declared on special occasions that he was indeed the promised Messiah. One such instance was when a woman at Jacob's well in Samaria told Jesus, "I know that Messias cometh, which is called Christ: when he is come, he will tell us all things" (John 4:25). The Savior responded to her simply, "I that speak unto thee am he" (John 4:26).[7] Nephi's vision therefore confirms one of the primary purposes of the Book of Mormon, which is "to the convincing of the Jew and the Gentile that JESUS is the CHRIST" (title page), or in other words, that Jesus is the Messiah.

Nephi's vision also confirms essential details concerning the nature of the Savior's mortal birth. The Spirit of the Lord explained to Nephi that he would "behold a man descending out of heaven, and him shall ye witness; and after ye have witnessed him ye shall bear record that it is the Son of God" (1 Nephi 11:7). The birth of the Savior was no ordinary birth. Jesus was not literally the son of Joseph the carpenter, but rather he was "the Son of the most high God" (1 Nephi 11:6). Nephi saw that the mother of the Savior was "a virgin, most beautiful and fair above all other virgins" (1 Nephi 11:15) who lived "in the city of Nazareth" (1 Nephi 11:13).[8] This young woman became "the mother of the Son of God, after the manner of the flesh" (1 Nephi 11:18) after she had been "carried away in the Spirit for the space of a time" (1 Nephi 11:19).[9]

The beginning of Nephi's vision confirms these sacred elements as they are recorded in the New Testament. Luke's Gospel testifies that Jesus would not be the paternal offspring of Joseph but that Mary's son "shall be called the Son of the Highest" (Luke 1:32).[10] We are told in Luke's account that Mary was "a virgin espoused to a man whose name was Joseph" (Luke 1:27) and that she lived in "a city of Galilee, named Nazareth" (Luke 1:26). Before the conception and birth of Jesus, the angel Gabriel instructed her, "The Holy Ghost shall come upon thee, and the power of the Highest shall overshadow thee: therefore also that holy thing which shall be born of thee shall be called the Son of God" (Luke 1:35).[11] The vision of Nephi confirms the reality of the Savior's identity as the son of God.

Just before Nephi received his vision, Lehi prophesied in detail concerning John the Baptist, "a prophet who should come before the Messiah, to prepare the way of the Lord" (1 Nephi 10:7). Following this, Nephi saw the Messiah in vision and also "beheld the prophet who should prepare the way before him" (1 Nephi 11:27). The details shared by both Lehi and Nephi confirm many important teachings from the New Testament Gospels about John the Baptist and the baptism of the Savior. For example, John was the fulfillment of Isaiah's prophecy, "the voice of him that crieth in the wilderness, Prepare ye the way of the Lord, make straight in the desert a highway for our God" (Isaiah 40:3).[12] John's testimony to his audience was that, unbeknownst to them, the Savior was standing among them and that because of the Savior's virtue the Baptist felt unworthy to even unlatch the Messiah's sandals.[13] Nephi clearly saw in his vision that John baptized "the Redeemer of the world" (1 Nephi 11:27). Lehi prophesied that John would "baptize in Bethabara, beyond Jordan" (1 Nephi 10:9).[14] Even though it is uncertain precisely where the ancient site of Bethabara is located today, Lehi's prophecy nonetheless confirms the location mentioned in John 1:28.[15]

Lehi also declared that after John baptized the Savior, he would then "bear record that he had baptized the Lamb of God, who should take away the sins of the world" (1 Nephi 10:10).[16] This postbaptismal testimony is recorded in John 1:29.[17] Nephi saw in vision that following the baptism, the Holy Ghost would come down out of heaven "and abide upon him in the form of a dove" (1 Nephi 11:27). Although the word *form* can mean "shape or external appearance," when Joseph Smith translated the Book of Mormon it could also mean other things, such as "pattern" as well as "beauty; elegance, splendor; dignity."[18] These meanings of *form* would correspond better with the language and intent of the Gospel accounts: the Spirit descended "like a dove."[19]

The Prophet Joseph Smith taught the following about the dove's appearance at the baptism of Jesus:

> Whoever led the Son of God into the waters of baptism, and had the privilege of beholding the Holy Ghost descend in the form of a dove, or rather in the *sign* of the dove, in witness of that administration? The sign of the dove was instituted before the creation of the world, a witness for the Holy Ghost, and the devil cannot come in the sign of a dove. The Holy Ghost is a personage, and is in the form of a personage. It does not confine itself to the *form* of the dove, but in *sign* of the dove. The Holy Ghost cannot be transformed into a dove; but the sign of a dove was given to John to signify the truth of the deed, as the dove is an emblem or token of truth and innocence.[20]

Thus, according to the Prophet, an actual dove was present at the Savior's baptism, but the Holy Ghost was not transformed to look like a dove, nor was the Holy Ghost inside the dove. Rather, the dove at the baptism was a sign to John the Baptist that the Spirit was present and that John had indeed baptized the Lamb of God. Nephi's vision confirms the truth of the New

Testament accounts that the Holy Ghost descended like a dove and thereafter remained with the Savior.

Nephi also learned many things in his vision concerning the mortal ministry of Jesus. He saw "multitudes of people who were sick, and who were afflicted with all manner of diseases, and with devils and unclean spirits. . . . And they were healed by the power of the Lamb of God; and the devils and the unclean spirits were cast out" (1 Nephi 11:31).[21] The New Testament is replete with examples of the Savior's miracles, both "healing all manner of sickness and all manner of disease among the people" (Matthew 4:23) and also exorcising devils and unclean spirits.[22] In addition, Nephi saw that the Savior taught his gospel as "the multitudes were gathered together to hear him" (1 Nephi 11:28). The popularity of Jesus as a master teacher is clearly illustrated in the Gospels as "great multitudes were gathered together unto him" (Matthew 13:2) on numerous occasions in order to listen to his teachings.[23] Further, Nephi saw that many who came in contact with the Savior would "fall down at his feet and worship him" (1 Nephi 11:24), a response that was repeated multiple times during the Savior's life (see, for example, Matthew 2:11, 8:2, 9:18, 14:33, 15:25, 20:20, and 28:9).

The vision also provided Nephi with valuable information about the disciples of Christ. Nephi saw "twelve others following" the Savior (1 Nephi 11:29). The angel of the Lord called these twelve other followers by the name of "apostles" (1 Nephi 11:34). The English term *Apostle* comes from a Greek word that means "messenger" or "envoy."[24] The Gospel accounts consistently relate that the Savior called his twelve special messengers by the name Apostle.[25] The angel also explained to Nephi that these Apostles "shall judge the twelve tribes of Israel" (1 Nephi 12:9), a sacred stewardship confirmed by the Savior during his mortal ministry.[26]

Nephi was given specific information about one of these Apostles. He saw someone who was "dressed in a white robe" (1 Nephi 14:19). The angel of the Lord explained that this man was "one of the twelve apostles of the Lamb" (1 Nephi 14:20) and that his name was John.[27] The angel further explained that John would see the same things that Nephi had beheld in his vision and that "he shall see and write the remainder of these things, . . . and he shall also write concerning the end of the world" (1 Nephi 14:21–22; see also 1 Nephi 14:24–25). This is a very important identification for Latter-day Saints. The author of the book of Revelation identifies himself simply as

John (see Revelation 1:1, 4, 9). Many non-Latter-day Saint scholars, however, are unwilling to identify the author of the book of Revelation with John the Beloved, the Apostle of the Lord.[28] The Book of Mormon confirms that this special Apostle was indeed the author of the book of Revelation.[29]

Most importantly, Nephi's vision provides a confirming witness to the rejection, atonement, death, and resurrection of Jesus Christ. Nephi saw that after the Redeemer "went forth ministering unto the people, in power and great glory; . . . they cast him out from among them" (1 Nephi 11:28). Nephi seems to have been shown in detail the events surrounding the death of the Messiah: "And I looked and beheld the Lamb of God, that he was taken by the people; yea, the Son of the everlasting God was judged of the world; and I saw and bear record. And I, Nephi, saw that he was lifted up upon the cross and slain for the sins of the world" (1 Nephi 11:32–33). Before this vision, Father Lehi had already testified to his sons that "after [the Messiah] had been slain he should rise from the dead, and should make himself manifest, by the Holy Ghost, unto the Gentiles" (1 Nephi 10:11).

These sacred events are at the heart of the New Testament. The Savior was rejected many times by those who heard him teach (see, for example, Luke 4:16–30). This rejection culminated in being betrayed by his Apostle Judas Iscariot and taken by an armed guard to stand trial. Accounts of the arrest and trials—first before the Sanhedrin and then before Pontius Pilate the Roman governor—as well as the crucifixion itself are contained in the Gospels.[30] Importantly, however, Nephi understood from his vision that the purpose of the crucifixion of the Savior was expiatory: "for the sins of the world" (1 Nephi 11:33). The crucial testimony declared by early Christian missionaries like the Apostle Paul, was precisely this: "Christ died for our sins" (1 Corinthians 15:3; see also Romans 5:19; 2 Corinthians 5:21; Galatians 1:4; Ephesians 1:7; Colossians 1:14; Hebrews 9:28 and 10:12; 1 Peter 2:24). Additionally, the narratives contained in the Gospels and the book of Acts amply testify that the Messiah was raised from the dead and appeared to his chosen disciples (see Matthew 27; Mark 16; Luke 24; John 20–21; and Acts 1:1–9; 9:1–9).

Again, however, Nephi taught an important detail from his vision, that the resurrected Savior would "make himself manifest, by the Holy Ghost, unto the Gentiles" (1 Nephi 10:11). When Christ appeared to the Nephites, he taught concerning the Gentiles, "I should not manifest myself unto them save it were by the Holy Ghost" (3 Nephi 15:23). He further explained concerning his Jewish disciples that "the Gentiles should be converted through their preaching" (3 Nephi 15:22).[31] The example of Cornelius, the Roman centurion, confirms this process: a heavenly messenger appeared to Cornelius "in a vision" (Acts 10:3) and led him to the Apostle Peter. After being taught by the chief Apostle, "the Holy Ghost fell on all them which heard the word" (Acts 10:44), including the Gentile Cornelius. Following this, Jewish members of the Church were amazed "because that on the Gentiles also was poured out the gift of the Holy Ghost" (Acts 10:45). The account of Nephi's vision beautifully fulfills the purpose set forth by the Lord in Doctrine and Covenants 20: it demonstrates that the Bible is true, particularly the Gospels.

The Nature of the Bible

The Bible as we know it today has undergone a long and complicated process of transmission.[32] Nephi's vision teaches many important truths concerning this process and the nature of our Bible. Once Lehi's family fled into the wilderness and camped in the valley of Lemuel, Nephi and his brothers were commanded to return to Jerusalem to obtain the brass plates of Laban (see 1 Nephi 3:1–12). After Nephi brought the brass plates back to their camp in the wilderness, Lehi discovered that they contained "a genealogy of his fathers" (1 Nephi 5:14), as well as "the five books of Moses" (1 Nephi 5:11). They also contained "a record of the Jews" and "the prophecies of the holy prophets" from the time of Father Adam down to time of King Zedekiah of Judah, including many of the prophecies of Jeremiah (see 1 Nephi 5:12–13).

Nephi saw in his vision another book—the Bible—which also was "a record of the Jews" (1 Nephi 13:23). The angel told Nephi that this other book was "a record like unto the engravings which are upon the plates of brass" (1 Nephi 13:23). The angel also explained that the primary difference between the two records was that the Bible did not contain as many "prophecies of the holy prophets" (1 Nephi 13:23). Examples of prophets whose prophecies are on the brass plates but not in the Bible are Zenos, Zenock, Neum, and Ezias.[33] It is possible that the brass plates were a Northern Kingdom version of the scriptures—as opposed to the Bible, which was a Southern Kingdom version—and were brought south into the Kingdom of Judah by the ancestors of Laban and Lehi who fled from the invading Assyrian army around 722 BC.[34] Additional material would have continued to be added to the brass plates, in particular many of the prophecies of Jeremiah, until Nephi obtained them.

Regardless of exactly how the brass plates came into Laban's possession, they contained more pronouncements from the prophets of old than the Bible.

Even though the Bible which Nephi saw in vision included fewer prophetic books than the brass plates, the information it contained was nonetheless accurate and true. The angel of the Lord testified to Nephi that the Bible originally "contained the fulness of the gospel of the Lord" (1 Nephi 13:24) and that when this record went from the Jews to the Gentiles—meaning from the original Jewish Apostles to the early Gentile members of the Church—it did so "in purity" (1 Nephi 13:25).[35] The angel later instructed Nephi, "At the time the book proceeded out of the mouth of the Jew, the things which were written were plain and pure, and most precious and easy to the understanding of all men" (1 Nephi 14:23). Unfortunately, after Nephi saw the early Christian Gentiles receive the Bible from the Apostles, he then saw the formation an organization that was "most abominable" (1 Nephi 13:26).[36] Nephi saw "many plain and precious things taken away" from the Bible by this group (1 Nephi 13:28).

The Prophet Joseph Smith also taught concerning the original pure condition of the Bible and its subsequent corruption. On one occasion the Prophet testified, "I believe the Bible as it read when it came from the pen of the original writers."[37] In addition, the Prophet also observed, "From sundry revelations which had been received, it was apparent that many important points touching the salvation of men, had been taken from the Bible, or lost before it was compiled."[38] It is important to note that Joseph Smith taught that the various corruptions of the Bible included both intentional (i.e., "taken from") as well as unintentional (i.e., "lost"). In an in-depth study of the differences in the manuscripts of the New Testament, Bart D. Ehrman concluded that "most of the changes were accidental, the result of scribal ineptitude, carelessness, or fatigue. Others were intentional, and reflect the controversial milieux within which they were produced."[39] Nephi's vision emphasizes the deliberate kinds of changes: "And all this have they done that they might pervert the right ways of the Lord, that they might blind the eyes and harden the hearts of the children of men" (1 Nephi 13:27). Whether intentional or unintentional, however, the changes certainly had a detrimental effect upon people, as the angel foresaw: "Because of these things which are taken away out of the gospel of the Lamb, an exceedingly great many do stumble, yea, insomuch that Satan hath great power over them" (1 Nephi 13:29).

The process of removing "plain and precious things" (1 Nephi 13:28) was probably more complicated than one might suppose. Nephi was taught by the angel of the Lord that "there are many plain and precious things taken away *from the book*" (1 Nephi 13:28; emphasis added) or "taken out *of the book*" (1 Nephi 13:29; emphasis added). Certainly there is ample evidence for this when one compares the early manuscripts of the New Testament, as Professor Ehrman has concluded: "Scribes sometimes changed their scriptural texts to make them *say* what they were already known to *mean*."[40] But for Latter-day Saints, the idea that scribes made changes to manuscripts in order to fit their theological views presupposes that these scribes were already functioning under some level of doctrinal corruption themselves before they actually corrupted the manuscripts of the Bible.

Nephi's heavenly guide may have had this phenomenon in mind when he taught Nephi concerning that great and abominable group: "they have taken away *from the gospel* of the Lamb many parts which are plain and most precious; and also *many covenants* of the Lord have they taken away" (1 Nephi 13:26; emphasis added). Further, the angel testified that "because of these things which are taken away *out of the gospel* of the Lamb, an exceedingly great many do stumble" (1 Nephi 13:29; emphasis added).[41] Concerning what it may mean to take away plain and precious truths *from the gospel*, rather than merely *from the manuscripts*, Richard L. Anderson has written: "In recent centuries, rationalism rather than changes in manuscripts has led the attack on Christ's gospel and divinity. Although there certainly were changes in documents, as Nephi pointed out in his prophecy (see 1 Nephi 13:28), the greater losses came as the gospel and its ceremonies were changed. By ignoring major parts of the scriptures, various Christian theologies have either explained away or changed vital covenants and rites still mentioned in the Bible."[42] Thus original doctrinal corruption may have eventually led to ceremonial and covenantal corruption, as well as changes in manuscripts. The various processes may have, over time, fed off one another in a vicious cycle. Regardless of the precise process of events, however, Nephi's vision testifies that the Bible as we know it today is not in its original pristine condition. In addition, it is important to note, as I will demonstrate below, that the Lord has provided Latter-day Saints with abundant testimony concerning the great worth of the Bible despite its current imperfect state.

The Role of the Book of Mormon and the Bible

Nephi's vision reveals important truths concerning the sacred role of the Bible and the Book of Mormon in the latter days. When originally written, the Bible contained "the covenants of the Lord, which he hath made unto the house of Israel" (1 Nephi 13:23). As mentioned above, the great and abominable group tampered with the Bible and the gospel, removing "many covenants of the Lord" (1 Nephi 13:26), and as a result "an exceedingly great many do stumble" (1 Nephi 13:29).[43] But the angel testified to Nephi that the Lord would not "suffer that the Gentiles shall forever remain in that awful state of blindness" (1 Nephi 13:32). He would mercifully provide a way to overcome the stumbling blocks of a corrupted Bible and an incomplete gospel. This would be part of "a great and a marvelous work" (1 Nephi 14:7) which the Lord designed to accomplish in the latter days. The Lord testified through his heavenly messenger to Nephi, "I will be merciful unto the Gentiles in that day, insomuch that I will bring forth unto them, in mine own power, much of my gospel, which shall be plain and precious" (1 Nephi 13:34; see also Moses 1:41).

The Lord, through the angelic guide, explained to Nephi the process by which this restoration of truth would be accomplished: "I will manifest myself unto thy seed, that they shall write many things which I shall minister unto them, which shall be plain and precious" (1 Nephi 13:35). After Nephi's descendants recorded these sacred items, "these things shall be hid up, to come forth unto the Gentiles, by the gift and power of God" (1 Nephi 13:35). This record is the Book of Mormon, which contains a number of statements declaring the inspiration by which it was written, preserved, and brought forth.[44] For example, the title page of the Book of Mormon testifies that this record was "written by way of commandment, and also by the spirit of prophecy and of revelation—written and sealed up, and hid up unto the Lord, that they might not be destroyed—To come forth by the hand of Moroni, and hid up unto the Lord, to come forth in due time by way of the Gentile—The interpretation thereof by the gift of God."[45] Similarly, the Prophet Joseph Smith declared concerning his role in bringing forth the Book of Mormon, "I translated the record by the gift and power of God."[46]

Nephi was told by the angel that these two scriptural records—the Bible and the Book of Mormon—would "be established in one," and as a result "the words of the Lamb shall be made known" (1 Nephi 13:41). The record of the

Jews and the record of the Nephites were to work together in sacred partnership in order to further the work of God.[47] This association of two books of scripture was to serve important purposes. First, as Nephi saw, the "other books" of scripture came forth in order to testify of the Bible, specifically to convince people "that the records of the prophets and of the twelve apostles of the Lamb are true" (1 Nephi 13:39).[48] In his final testimony to the future readers of the Book of Mormon, the prophet Mormon testified that this special relationship was intended to flow both ways: "This [Book of Mormon] is written for the intent that ye may believe that [the Bible]; and if ye believe that [the Bible] ye will believe this [the Book of Mormon] also" (Mormon 7:8). Second, the angel of the Lord declared to Nephi that a primary purpose for the Book of Mormon was to "make known the plain and precious things which have been taken away" (1 Nephi 13:40). The angel further specified important truths that the Book of Mormon would restore to the world, "that the Lamb of God is the Son of the Eternal Father, and the Savior of the world; and that all men must come unto him, or they cannot be saved" (1 Nephi 13:40).[49] Nephi's vision gives Latter-day Saints hope that through the instrumentality of modern prophets and scripture, the corruptions of the Bible will not stand as a stumbling block to the work of God.

Conclusion

The details of Nephi's vision have been preserved for us so that we might learn from them. Modern prophets have emphasized this reality. For example, Ezra Taft Benson testified: "The Book of Mormon . . . was written for our day. The Nephites never had the book; neither did the Lamanites of ancient times. It was meant for us. . . . Under the inspiration of God, who sees all things from the beginning, [Mormon] abridged centuries of records, choosing the stories, speeches, and events that would be most helpful to us. . . . We should constantly ask ourselves, 'Why did the Lord inspire Mormon (or Moroni or Alma) to include that in his record? What lesson can I learn from that to help me live in this day and age?'"[50] When we ask those important questions of the Book of Mormon's account of Nephi's vision, several answers beautifully testify of God's love for his children.

First, Latter-day Saints not only need to have a testimony of modern prophets and latter-day scripture but should also appreciate the truth of the Bible. The Lord prophesied to Joseph of Egypt that one of the gifts of the future seer, Joseph Smith, would be not only to "bring forth my word unto the seed of thy loins"—referring to the Book of Mormon—but also "to the convincing of them of my word, which shall have already gone forth among them" (2 Nephi 3:11). As our fourth Article of Faith teaches, "We believe the Bible to be the word of God as far as it is translated correctly" (Articles of Faith 1:8). More specifically, we should have a greater appreciation of the Bible precisely because the Book of Mormon, the latter-day word of God, testifies of its truthfulness.

Second, Latter-day Saints understand that the Bible does not currently contain all the truths that it did when it was originally written. This highlights not only the need for additional revealed truth to supplement and correct that which was incomplete or incorrect but also the love God has for his children by providing these things in the latter days. The word *translated* in the Article of Faith phrase "as far as it is translated correctly" implies more than merely transforming from one language to another. As Robert J. Matthews explained, "Joseph Smith often used the words 'translated' and 'translation,' not in the narrow sense alone of rendering a text from one language into another, but in the wider senses of 'transmission,' having reference to copying, editing, adding to, taking from, rephrasing, and interpreting. This is substantially beyond the usual meaning of 'translation.'"[51] Thus Latter-day Saints also believe the Bible to be the word of God as far as it has been transmitted over time correctly.

These two latter-day perspectives on the Bible are not incompatible. In spite of having been transmitted to us in an incomplete and corrupted state, the Bible is still true—it is the word of God. For example, President J. Reuben Clark Jr. taught: "Notwithstanding the corruptions themselves, the Good Old Book stands as a record of God's dealings with and commandments and promises to his children, in their days of righteousness and in their generations of sin. It still, though corrupted, points out the way of righteousness to the man of faith seeking to serve God. It contains some of God's counsel to his children."[52] Latter-day Saints should be a Bible-believing and a Bible-loving people.

Finally, just as people more fully value the Atonement of Christ once they realize the reality of their fallen condition, so also acknowledgement of the limitations of the Bible should help Latter-day Saints more fully appreciate the need for the Restoration of the gospel, specifically the need for modern prophets and latter-day scripture, such as the Book of Mormon. Elder M. Russell Ballard taught, "While we accept the Bible as the word of God as far as it is translated correctly, we believe that this generation has as much, if not more, of a need for God's guidance and direction than generations of former times. Our belief that our Heavenly Father has sent prophets and apostles and has given us additional scripture for our day and time is a manifestation of His great love and concern for His children."[53] This love, which God has demonstrated toward us by providing additional revelation and scripture, is the central feature of Nephi's vision, represented by the tree of life. In the words of Nephi, "it is the love of God, which sheddeth itself abroad in the hearts of the children of men; wherefore, it is the most desirable above all things" (1 Nephi 11:22).

Notes

1. The phrase "holy scriptures" is clearly a reference to the Bible. See, for example, D&C 20:35 and 33:16.

2. See Monte S. Nyman, "Restoring 'Plain and Precious Parts': The Role of Latter-day Scriptures in Helping us Understand the Bible," *Ensign*, December 1981, 19–25.

3. Lehi also called the Messiah "the Lamb of God" (1 Nephi 10:10). This identification of the Lamb of God as the Messiah is repeated by the angel in 1 Nephi 12:18.

4. Francis Brown, S. R. Driver, and Charles A. Briggs, *A Hebrew and English Lexicon of the Old Testament* (Oxford: Clarendon Press, 1952), 603.

5. Frederick William Danker, *A Greek-English Lexicon of the New Testament and Other Early Christian Literature*, 3rd ed. (Chicago: University of Chicago Press, 2000), 122.

6. For references from the Old Testament, see Richard Neitzel Holzapfel, "I Have a Question," *Ensign*, April 1991, 53.

7. For other New Testament references in which Jesus confirmed his identity as Messiah, see Matthew 16:13–20 and Mark 14:60–62.

8. King Benjamin later prophesied that "his mother shall be called Mary" (Mosiah 3:8; see also Alma 7:10).

9. Four times in Nephi's vision, Jesus was originally identified as "God" (1 Nephi 11:18), "the Eternal Father" (1 Nephi 11:21 and 13:40), and "the everlasting God" (1 Nephi 11:32). The Prophet Joseph Smith later added the phrase "the son of" to each of those four references so readers would not mistakenly identify Jesus as God the Father. Nephi and the Spirit of the Lord clearly identify Jesus as "the son of God" earlier in the section (1 Nephi 10:17; 11:7). See Royal Skousen, *Analysis of Textual Variants of the Book of Mormon*, Part One (Provo, UT: Foundation for Ancient Research and Mormon Studies, 2004), 220. Jesus, of course, was Jehovah, the God of the Old Testament (see 3 Nephi 15:4–5). This is likely the understanding that was originally intended in the previous references. Abinadi was eventually executed for similarly claiming that "God

himself should come down among the children of men" (Mosiah 17:8). On these issues, see Jared T. Parker, "Abinadi on the Father and the Son: Interpretation and Application," in *Living the Book of Mormon: Abiding by Its Precepts*, ed. Gaye Strathearn and Charles Swift (Salt Lake City: Deseret Book, 2007), 136–50.

10. The original wording of 1 Nephi 11:6 identified the Savior as "the Son of the Most High," omitting the word "God." See Skousen, *Analysis of Textual Variants*, 220. This wording corresponds even more closely with the King James Version rendering of Luke 1:32: "the Son of the Highest."

11. Similarly, Matthew's Gospel testifies that before she married Joseph, Mary "was found with child of the Holy Ghost" (Matthew 1:18).

12. Compare 1 Nephi 10:7–8 with Matthew 3:1–3, Mark 1:2–4, Luke 3:3–6, and John 1:23.

13. Compare 1 Nephi 10:8 with John 1:26–27; see also Matthew 3:11, Mark 1:7, and Luke 3:16.

14. The phrase "beyond Jordan" normally refers to the east side of the Jordan River (see John 10:40). The earliest extant manuscripts containing John 1:28 actually read "Bethany" rather than "Bethabara." The early Church fathers Origen and John Chrysostom, however, claimed that most early and accurate manuscripts, which apparently have not survived to the present day, contained the reading "Bethabara." On this, see Bruce M. Metzger, *A Textual Commentary on the Greek New Testament*, 2nd ed. (Stuttgart: Deutsche Bibelgesellschaft, 1994), 171. It is possible that Origen and Chrysostom were correct and that the Book of Mormon confirms that "Bethabara" is the original reading. Or it is possible that the original reading is "Bethany" and that, because the two names are spelled so similarly in Greek, the word "Bethabara" was eventually written by mistake as a corruption of the name "Bethany." If this is the case, it may be that Joseph Smith simply relied upon his knowledge of the wording in the King James Version of the Bible when translating 1 Nephi 10:9. In the end, whether one prefers the name Bethany or Bethabara, Lehi's prophecy confirms John's account of the location where John the Baptist performed baptisms, *even though it is uncertain precisely where that location is today*. For a recent study of a possible location for the place where John baptized on the east side of the Jordan River, see Rami Khouri, "Where Jesus Baptized: Bethany Beyond the Jordan," *Biblical Archaeology Review* 31, no. 1 (January/February 2005): 34–43.

15. Although John 3:23 indicates that John "was baptizing in Aenon, near to Salim," John clearly states concerning the baptism of Jesus that "these things were done in Bethabara beyond Jordan, where John was baptizing" (John 1:28). The reference to Salim is simply an alternative location in which John was also performing baptisms after he baptized the Savior (see John 10:40: "beyond the Jordan into the place where John *at first* baptized" [emphasis added]). On this, see Raymond E. Brown, *The Gospel According to John* (New York: Doubleday, 1966), 1:151. The Joseph Smith Translation (JST) confirms the location of Bethabara, but moves the reference to the end of John 1:34. For a comprehensive collection of the JST in the New Testament, see Thomas A. Wayment, ed., *The Complete Joseph Smith Translation of the New Testament* (Salt Lake City: Deseret Book, 2005).

16. Similarly, Nephi was instructed by the Spirit of the Lord that when he witnessed the Savior in vision, he was to "bear record that it is the Son of God" (1 Nephi 11:7).

17. The Joseph Smith Translation confirms that John the Baptist bore testimony of the Savior multiple times and more explicitly than is recorded in the preserved text of the Gospels, both before (see JST, Matthew 3:11–12, JST, Mark 1:11, and JST, John 1:27) and following the baptism (see JST, John 1:30).

18. Noah Webster, *An American Dictionary of the English Language* (New York: S. Converse, 1828), "form."

19. See Matthew 3:16, Mark 1:10 and John 1:32. The King James translation of Luke's account reads, somewhat ambiguously, "The Holy Ghost descended in a bodily shape like a dove" (Luke 3:22). The phrase "in a bodily shape" could technically, in the Greek, refer to the body of the dove or the visible shape or appearance of the personage of the Holy Ghost. On this, see François Bovon, *Luke 1* (Minneapolis: Fortress Press, 2002), 129. It is more likely, however, that the phrase "in a bodily form" refers to the visible shape or appearance of the Holy Ghost. In my view, the JST confirms this interpretation by removing the indefinite article "a" before the phrase "bodily shape." Thus "the Holy Ghost descended in bodily form like a dove" (JST, Luke 3:22). Wayment, *Complete Joseph Smith Translation*. Joseph Smith taught that "the Holy Ghost has not a body of flesh and bones, but is a personage of Sprit" (D&C 130:22). Further, the Book of Mormon clearly teaches that spirits have a bodily shape and look like physical bodies (see Ether 3:16–17).

20. *Teachings of the Prophet Joseph Smith*, comp. Joseph Fielding Smith (Salt Lake City: Deseret Book, 1976), 275–76; emphasis in original. See also Larry E. Dahl and Donald Q. Cannon, eds., *Encyclopedia of Joseph Smith's Teachings* (Salt Lake City: Deseret Book, 2000), 202.

21. Compare King Benjamin's prophecy that the Son of God would "go forth amongst men, working mighty miracles, such as healing the sick, raising the dead, causing the lame to walk, the blind to receive their sight, and the deaf to hear, and curing all manner of diseases" (Mosiah 3:5).

22. See, for example, Matthew 8:16 and 10:1. For a collection of the miracles of the Savior, see E. Keith Howick, *The Miracles of Jesus the Messiah* (Salt Lake City: Bookcraft, 1985).

23. See also Mark 4:1 and Luke 12:1. For collections of the teachings of the Savior, see E. Keith Howick, *The Parables of Jesus the Messiah* (Salt Lake City: Bookcraft, 1986) and E. Keith Howick, *The Sermons of Jesus the Messiah* (Salt Lake City: Bookcraft, 1987).

24. Danker, *A Greek-English Lexicon*, 1091.

25. See, for example, Matthew 10:2, Mark 6:30, and Luke 6:13.

26. See, for example, Matthew 19:28 and Luke 22:30. For more information about the Apostles, see S. Kent Brown, "The Twelve," in *The Life and Teachings of Jesus Christ: From the Transfiguration through the Triumphal Entry*, ed. Richard Neitzel Holzapfel and Thomas A. Wayment (Salt Lake City: Deseret Book, 2006), 98–124.

27. See 1 Nephi 14:27. There are two men by the name of John in the New Testament. One is John the Baptist. The other is known by a number of nicknames: John the Beloved, John the Disciple, John the Apostle, John the Revelator, John the Evangelist, John the brother of James, and so forth. Nephi saw the second of these two

men. For more information about this John, see Jonn D. Claybaugh, "What the Latter-day Scriptures Teach about John the Beloved," in *The Testimony of John the Beloved*, ed. Daniel K. Judd, Craig J. Ostler, and Richard D. Draper (Salt Lake City: Deseret Book, 1998), 16–35.

28. See, for example, Brian K. Blount, *Revelation: A Commentary* (Louisville: Westminster John Knox Press, 2009), 5–8.

29. On the complex issues of the authorship of the New Testament books, see Frank F. Judd Jr., "Who Really Wrote the Gospels? A Study of Traditional Authorship," in *How the New Testament Came to Be*, ed. Kent P. Jackson and Frank F. Judd Jr. (Salt Lake City: Deseret Book, 2006), 123–40, and Lincoln H. Blumell, "Scribes and Ancient Letters: Implications for the Pauline Epistles," in *How the New Testament Came to Be*, 208–26.

30. See Matthew 26:47 through 27:24; Mark 14:43 through 15:15; Luke 22:47 through 23:25; and John 18:2 through 19:16.

31. Jesus may have been alluding to the role the disciples would play in this process when he testified to them, "Ye shall receive power, after that the Holy Ghost is come upon you: and ye shall be witnesses unto me both in Jerusalem, and in all Judea, and in Samaria, and unto the uttermost part of the earth" (Acts 1:8).

32. For more information, see the studies of Ellis R. Brotzman, *Old Testament Textual Criticism: A Practical Introduction* (Grand Rapids, MI: Baker Book House, 1994), and Bruce M. Metzger and Bart D. Ehrman, *The Text of the New Testament: Its Transmission, Corruption, and Restoration*, 4th ed. (New York: Oxford University Press, 2005).

33. We know about these prophets because they are mentioned elsewhere in the Book of Mormon (see 1 Nephi 19:10 and Helaman 8:19–20). There also seems to have been more information on the brass plates about Jacob's prophecy concerning the garment of his son Joseph (see Alma 46:24 and 3 Nephi 10:17).

34. On this issue, see Robert L. Millet, "Plates of brass," in *Book of Mormon Reference Companion*, ed. Dennis L. Largey (Salt Lake City: Deseret Book, 2003), 643. Laban and Lehi were both descendants of Joseph (see 1 Nephi 5:14–16).

35. The angel said that the Bible went "forth by the hand of the twelve apostles of the Lamb, from the Jews unto the Gentiles" (1 Nephi 13:26).

36. The parameters of this paper do not permit a comprehensive study in order to identify the "great and abominable church." For more information on this, see Stephen E. Robinson, "Nephi's 'Great and Abominable Church,'" *Journal of Book of Mormon Studies*, no. 1 (1998): 32–39.

37. *Teachings of the Prophet Joseph Smith*, 327. Although Joseph Smith certainly taught concerning the corruption of the Bible, the statement "Ignorant translators, careless transcribers, or designing and corrupt priests have committed many errors" seems to have been added by an editor. Compare the original quote in Andrew F. Ehat and Lyndon W. Cook, eds., *The Words of Joseph Smith* (Provo, UT: Religious Studies Center, Brigham Young University, 1980), 256.

38. *Teachings of the Prophet Joseph Smith*, 9–11. See also Dahl and Cannon, *Encyclopedia of Joseph Smith's Teachings*, 74.

39. Bart D. Ehrman, *The Orthodox Corruption of Scripture: The Effect of Early Christological Controversies on the Text of the New Testament* (Oxford: Oxford University Press, 1993), 275.

40. Ehrman, *The Orthodox Corruption of Scripture*, xii; emphasis in original. Whether one accepts Ehrman's proposals concerning the most likely original reading or the reasons for the changes, the fact that there are alternative readings among the manuscripts demonstrates the reality of these corruptions.

41. Similarly, the angel later clarified that the Lord would be merciful to his children "because of the plain and most precious parts *of the gospel* of the Lamb which have been *kept back*" (1 Nephi 13:32; emphasis added).

42. Richard Lloyd Anderson, "The Restoration of the Sacrament, Part 1: Loss and Christian Reformations," *Ensign*, January 1992, 40.

43. The angel later intensified that assessment, declaring that "the Gentiles do stumble *exceedingly*" (1 Nephi 13:34; emphasis added).

44. See, for example, 2 Nephi 27:6–12; 30:3–5, and Mormon 5:12–13. When Nephi saw the Bible coming forth to his descendants, he also saw "other books, which came forth by the power of the Lamb" (1 Nephi 13:39). Certainly these "other books" include the Book of Mormon as well as other latter-day books of scripture.

45. On the authorship of the Title Page of the Book of Mormon, see Daniel H. Ludlow, "The Title Page," in *The Book of Mormon: First Nephi, The Doctrinal Foundation*, ed. Monte S. Nyman and Charles D. Tate Jr. (Provo, UT: Religious Studies Center, Brigham Young University, 1988), 19–33.

46. *History of the Church of Jesus Christ of Latter-day Saints*, ed. B. H. Roberts, 2nd ed. rev. (Salt Lake City: Deseret Book, 1971), 4:537.

47. The Lord had earlier declared to Joseph of Egypt that these two books of scripture "shall grow together" (2 Nephi 3:12). Later, the Lord told Ezekiel that these two records "shall become one in thine hand" (Ezekiel 37:17). When the new edition of the scriptures were published, Elder Boyd K. Packer testified: "The stick or record of Judah—the Old Testament and the New Testament—and the stick or record of Ephraim—the Book of Mormon, which is another testament of Jesus Christ—are now woven together in such a way that as you pore over one you are drawn to the other; as you learn from one you are enlightened by the other. They are indeed one in our hands." See Boyd K. Packer, in Conference Report, October 1982, 75.

48. The angel also said that the record of the Nephites "shall establish the truth of the first [i.e. the Bible], which are of the twelve apostles of the Lamb" (1 Nephi 13:40). Compare the statement of Spencer W. Kimball: "We declare that the Book of Mormon was brought forth by the gift and power of God and that it stands beside the Bible as another witness of Jesus the Christ, the Savior and Redeemer of mankind. Together they testify of his divine sonship." See First Presidency and the Quorum of the Twelve Apostles of The Church of Jesus Christ of Latter-day Saints, "Proclamation," *Ensign*, May 1980, 52.

49. Similarly, when Nephi later explained the meaning of his father's dream to his brothers, he taught them in detail that when "the fulness of the gospel of the Messiah" (1 Nephi 15:13) would be restored in the latter-days to their descendants through the Nephite record, these descendants would "know that they are of the house of Israel,

and that they are the covenant people of the Lord; and then shall they know and come to the knowledge of their forefathers, and also to the knowledge of the gospel of their Redeemer, which was ministered unto their fathers by him; wherefore, they shall come to the knowledge of their Redeemer and the very points of his doctrine, that they may know how to come unto him and be saved" (1 Nephi 15:14).

50. Ezra Taft Benson, *A Witness and a Warning* (Salt Lake City: Deseret Book, 1988), 19–20.

51. Robert J. Matthews, "Joseph Smith Translation of the Bible (JST)," in *Encyclopedia of Mormonism*, ed. Daniel H. Ludlow (New York: Macmillan, 1992), 2:764. Professor Matthews further concluded: "Of course, Joseph Smith also stated that the Bible had not been preserved in its original purity: 'We believe the Bible to be the word of God as far as it is translated correctly' (Articles of Faith 8). The word *translated* as it is used here must be understood to include the idea of *transmission* (italics in orginal). That is, error has occurred not only in the translation from one language to another, but also in the transcription of the text from manuscript to manuscript, even in the same language." Robert J. Matthews, "The Bible and Its Role in the Restoration," *Ensign* (July 1979): 41.

52. J. Reuben Clark, *On the Way to Immortality and Eternal Life* (Salt Lake City: Deseret Book, 1961), 210. Note also the statement of Elder Joseph B. Wirthlin: "The fragmentary nature of the biblical record and the errors in it, resulting from multiple transcriptions, translations, and interpretations, do not diminish our belief in it as the word of God 'as far as it is translated correctly.' We read and study the Bible, we teach and preach from it, and we strive to live according to the eternal truths it contains. We love this collection of holy writ." Joseph B. Wirthlin, "Christians in Belief and Action," *Ensign*, November 1996, 71.

53. M. Russell Ballard, "Building Bridges of Understanding," *Ensign*, June 1998, 64.

16

Illuminating a Darkened World

Seth J. King

It is no mystery that we live in a dark and troubled world of lewdness, deceit, and selfishness; a time when "every man walketh in his own way, and after the image of his own god" (D&C 1:16); a time when many "put darkness for light, and light for darkness" (Isaiah 5:20; 2 Nephi 15:20); even a time when light shines in darkness and the "darkness comprehendeth it not" (D&C 45:7). The Lord has declared that "darkness covereth the earth, and gross darkness the minds of the people" (D&C 112:23), so in such darkness of mind and sight, how will one fully acquire gospel light? President Boyd K. Packer suggests that an answer may be found in Lehi's dream. Said he, "Lehi's dream or vision . . . has in it everything a Latter-day Saint needs to understand the test of life."[1] In studying Lehi's dream and his son Nephi's subsequent vision, it appears that what they *experienced* in the revelation process was as enlightening as what they *saw*. These vision experiences present the disciple of Christ with a parabolic guide that highlights how mankind may illuminate a dark and dreary waste into a sensible world of purpose and pitfall. The objective of this paper is to help the reader gain new insights into the symbolism of events

---

Seth J. King is a teacher at Desert Hills Seminary in St. George, Utah.

(not just items) experienced in Lehi's dream and Nephi's vision, thereby encouraging renewed desire to follow the prophets in tasting and remaining at the fruit-bearing tree.

Illuminating a Darkened World

Lehi was a man of faith, love, and obedience. When he heard prophets preach concerning the destruction of his city, he lovingly prayed for the people with "all his heart" (1 Nephi 1:5). His affectionate prayer for others yielded revelation wherein he read and saw marvelous things that further witnessed the destruction coming upon Jerusalem (see 1 Nephi 1:13). Despite their mocking, he testified to his people of the things he had seen and heard until their anger led them to seek his life (see 1 Nephi 1:20). Then, recognizing the tender mercies of the Lord, Lehi obeyed revelatory commands to take his family and flee into the wilderness (see 1 Nephi 2:3–4). In the wilderness he tenderly pled, "being filled with the Spirit," for his sons to be faithful and obedient to the commands of God (1 Nephi 2:14). Twice he would heed revelations from the Lord commanding his sons to return to Jerusalem. All throughout his life, and even on his deathbed, he taught, begged, and pleaded with his children to listen to the Lord and hearken to their prophetic brother, Nephi (see 2 Nephi 2:28). There is no doubt that he loved his children, his people, and the Lord. Such love, faithfulness, and obedience were clearly evident in all his actions and invited revelations—revelations that illuminated his understanding.

While encamped along the borders of the Red Sea and not long after the return of his sons with Ishmael's family, Lehi received the glorious vision of the tree of life. Whether it occurred in a night dream, during prayer, or after offering sacrifice, the record does not say, but this much is known: a dream was dreamed; or, in other words, a vision was beheld (see 1 Nephi 8:2). The revelatory experience begins with Lehi seeing a man dressed in a white robe (see 1 Nephi 8:4–5). It is significant that the man came and stood before him, inviting him to follow (see 1 Nephi 8:6). Upon fulfilling this request, Lehi found himself in a dark and dreary wasteland. Hours went by as Lehi experienced traveling in darkness, perhaps feeling abandoned, confused, and alone. Strange it is that the white-robed man he dutifully chose to follow is seemingly lost from his view. Discouraged, desperate, and lost in darkness, Lehi began an emphatic prayer to God for mercy (see 1 Nephi 8:8). The record makes clear that *after* Lehi prayed, he "beheld a large and spacious field" (1 Nephi 8:9). The dark and dreary wasteland he was wandering through was never spoken of again. It is as if his prayer enlightened him to see that the waste he was trudging through was, in fact, a large and spacious field, even a world (see 1 Nephi 8:9, 20).

The beginning of Lehi's dream experience is symbolically significant and parallels our own journey to mortality. Like Lehi, all people on this earth once chose to follow the invitations of a white-robed man (see Daniel 10:2–12). This man stood before us in the premortal world and bade us follow him. Those who did so found themselves born into a place that may seem dark and dreary, even purposeless. Memories of the world before and the man followed there were wiped clean, and many wandered in darkness, some for numerous hours and others for a lifetime. Mercifully, some in darkness eventually come to the same resolution as Lehi, or young Joseph Smith Jr., who concluded, "I must either remain in darkness and confusion, or . . . ask of God" (Joseph Smith—History 1:13). Only after sincere prayer and pleading to the Lord for mercy do we begin to see clearly and have the cloud of darkness dispelled from our minds.[2] Experiencing such enlightenment makes us aware of our true surroundings and blessings; suddenly the dreary wasteland we have been wandering illuminates, and we behold, as did Lehi, a spacious field that is, in fact, a world! (see 1 Nephi 8:20; see also Matthew 13:38). Perhaps the words of a well-known hymn are appropriate: "So when life gets dark and dreary, don't forget to pray. . . . Prayer will change the night to day"![3]

Consider the children of Lehi, who followed their father's commands to leave the comforts of home and embark on a twelve- to fourteen-day journey through the treacherous, hot, barren wasteland between Jerusalem and the Red Sea.[4] Could you imagine this dark and dreary trip? The record makes clear that Nephi, Lehi's fourth son, is in his youth, even "exceedingly young" (1 Nephi 2:16). Because Nephi's older brethren were unmarried, they were likely also fairly young and perhaps still in their teens or early twenties.[5] Parents with youth this age could rightly imagine the fights, complaining, questions, and conversations that would erupt during such an arduous journey. Are we there yet? Where are we going? Why are we going? Can we rest? When are we coming back? Laman's throwing rocks! My camel stinks! and so forth. The record verifies that Laman and Lemuel murmured about many things and did not believe Lehi's teachings that Jerusalem "could be destroyed" (1 Nephi 2:13; see vv. 11–12). Their minds were darkened to the prophet's words.

Nephi gives additional insight into Laman's and Lemuel's spiritually dark minds when he writes that "they knew not the dealings that of God who had created them" and were like those at Jerusalem who were seeking to "take away the life of my father" (1 Nephi 2:12–13). Their spiritually closed minds were so dark to the workings of the Lord that they could not understand the words of Lehi, even when he spoke so powerfully by the Spirit that it confounded them (see 1 Nephi 2:14; 15:1–7). Nephi would later comment that they were "past feeling" and could not feel the words of the Spirit, just as none of the wicked could "understand great knowledge, when it [was] given unto them in plainness" (1 Nephi 17:45; 2 Nephi 32:7).

Though Nephi wrote his scriptural account of leaving Jerusalem some twenty years after the fact, it appears he personally had no complaints at his father's requests but was completely faithful to the prophet's commands (see 1 Nephi 19).[6] However, the record does hint that perhaps Nephi was not always cheery and excited about abruptly leaving his comfortable life in Jerusalem. A close look at Nephi's own words reveals that his heart at one time was slightly hardened. Wrote Nephi, "He . . . did *soften* my heart that I did believe" (1 Nephi 2:16; emphasis added). Perhaps in typical teenage fashion, even Nephi may have first experienced hardness of heart and feelings of doubt about the journey they were to make. For how could his heart be softened if it was not hard? Perhaps initially his mind was dark to the things which the Lord had revealed to his father, yet his reaction to his doubting is simply profound: "Having great *desires to know* of the mysteries of God, wherefore, *I did cry unto the Lord*; and behold he did visit me, and did *soften* my heart that I did believe all the words which had been spoken by my father; wherefore, I did not rebel against him like unto my brothers" (1 Nephi 2:16; emphasis added).

Nephi's reaction to hard-hearted, dark feelings was sincere prayer to God. Such a choice, though incredibly simple and plain, is key to illuminating understanding, for "he that receiveth light, and continueth in God, receiveth more light; and that light groweth brighter and brighter until the perfect day," and then cometh the time that "there shall be no darkness in you; and that body which is filled with light comprehendeth all things" (D&C 50:24; 88:67). After having his own personal revelatory experience, Nephi would happen upon his unbelieving, arguing, and darkened brothers who still could not understand the words of their father's dream. Perhaps in frustration, Nephi asked, "Have ye inquired of the Lord?" (1 Nephi 15:8).

Nephi knew the keys to understanding and gaining spiritual light. From his wilderness experience, he learned that God answers prayers. He was visited of the Lord and knew that if people desire to know the things of God, they must diligently seek him out, which seeking would allow them to be taught the mysteries of God by the power of the Holy Ghost (see 1 Nephi 10:17–19). Because he knew that God was the same "yesterday, today, and forever" and believed that he could make all things known, Nephi was quick to seek personal revelation (1 Nephi 10:18; see 1 Nephi 10:19; 11:1). When Father Lehi finished relating his vision, Nephi immediately commented on his desire to see, hear, and know the things his father had seen (see 1 Nephi 10:17). Such desires led to diligent seeking that allowed Nephi to not only see all his father saw, but even to have explanations from the Spirit of God of all the things he desired (see 1 Nephi 11:6).

In the repetitive nature of the gospel of Jesus Christ, have Saints forgotten the simple power of prayer, the power that dispels darkness? Many General Authorities, including Elder Neal A. Maxwell, have reiterated President Brigham Young's assertion that "we live far beneath our privileges" in terms of receiving revelation from God for guidance.[7] It seems that too often many seek God out only when they are desperate, and, like Lehi, they pray, recognizing that they have wandered many hours in darkness. But what of spiritual darkness that is harder to recognize because it does not fall into the categories of trial, despair, or need? What of darkness that is felt but not initially perceived as destructive? What of the hard, inconvenient truths taught by prophets? Do those who call themselves Saints ask God to soften their hearts towards prophetic commands that do not conveniently harmonize with personal views and lifestyles? Do we pray for enlightenment about perceived burdens of home and visiting teaching, Church callings, Scouting, Sabbath observance, or Saturday sessions of conference? What of offending words, hearts that hold grudges, and unforgiving feelings that make us lash out in belittling gossip or silent treatment? Do we seek darkness-dispelling light through prayer in *these* times?

The power of sincere prayer is the ultimate act of faith and invites the Spirit of the Lord to drive out darkness of mind and hardness of heart. It is the first step toward cognitive clarity and heart-softening light. Perhaps we would do well to remember that King Lamoni's conversion began with heartfelt pleadings to God for mercy, pleadings that caused him to fall to the earth in a spiritual coma (see Alma 18:41–42). Like Lehi, Lamoni began to experience the enlightening effect of a sincere petition to God. His perspective changed as light chased away the darkness of unbelief. Ammon knew this was happening; "he knew that the dark veil of unbelief was being cast away from his mind, and the light which did light up his mind, which was the light of the glory of God, which was a marvelous light of his goodness—yea, this light had infused such joy into his soul, the cloud of darkness having been dispelled, and that the light of everlasting life was lit up in his soul, yea, . . . this had overcome his natural frame, and he was carried away in God" (Alma 19:6). Immediately after experiencing this light of God and witnessing a vision of his Redeemer's birth and mission, Lamoni would joyfully testify of God's blessedness (see Alma 19:13).

These light-increasing prayers of Lehi and Lamoni are two of many scriptural accounts that affirm the power of prayer in inviting and receiving God's light in dark times. Nearly 510 years after the death of Nephi, approximately three hundred Lamanites struggled to flee a prison overshadowed with a thick cloud of darkness (see Helaman 5:49). Four times the earth had shaken, three times the voice of God was heard commanding repentance and speaking marvelous things, yet all the while they remained in darkness (see Helaman 5:27–33). In desperation, the Lamanites cried out, "What shall we do, that this cloud of darkness may be removed from overshadowing us?" (Helaman 5:40). A Church member who had dissented replied, "Cry unto the voice, even until ye shall have faith in Christ" (Helaman 5:41).

These Lamanites heeded the counsel and began to pray to the voice until the cloud of darkness was dispersed (see Helaman 5:42). Looking around, they found their vision illuminated and all saw that they were each encircled by a pillar of fire (see Helaman 5:43). This light filled their souls with unspeakable joy as the Holy Ghost entered into their hearts, giving them revelations that allowed them to speak marvelous words (see Helaman 5:43–45). Could there be any doubt that prayer brings illumination and understanding? It was faithful, consistent prayer that brought light to these Lamanites, joy to Lamoni, clarity to Lehi, softening to Nephi, and visions to all four. It is prayer that illuminates our darkened world.

Learning by Faith: Our Path to Illumination

Lehi's prayer for mercy brought a world into view. His new, illuminated perspective allowed him to see not only a spacious field but also a glorious tree whose fruit is desirable to make one happy. With little or no recorded struggle, Lehi immediately went forth and partook of the fruit thereof (see 1 Nephi 8:11). After tasting the fruit, his vision increased, for he "beheld that it was most sweet" and white beyond anything he had ever before seen (1 Nephi 8:11). Though at first glance the tree's fruit appeared desirable, his awareness of the true quality thereof came only *after* partaking of it (see 1 Nephi 8:9–11).

It is evident that Lehi's faithful actions (following the invitation of the white-robed man, praying for mercy, going forth to the tree, partaking of the fruit) illuminate his understanding and allow him to see his surroundings more clearly. In his dream experience, the prophet Lehi learns *after* he righteously acts upon scenes presented before him. Elder David A. Bednar teaches that such learning is what the scriptures deem "learning by faith," a type of true spiritual learning that "involves the exercise of moral agency to act," bringing confirming instruction from the Spirit of the Lord.[8] The Spirit is the true teacher of gospel truth. When people teach by the Spirit, the "Holy Ghost carrieth it *unto* the hearts of the children of men" (2 Nephi 33:1; emphasis added), but only personal action (like the prayers of the Lamanities, Lehi, and Nephi) allows the Spirit to enter *into* the learner's heart (see Helaman 5:42–45; see also 2 Nephi 2:16).[9]

Lehi exemplifies such faith-inspired action all throughout his dream. He follows, prays, looks, goes forth, partakes, and ponders. Each action brings light to the next scene of the revelatory dream as it allows the Holy Ghost to speak to Lehi's *heart* and *mind* (see D&C 8:2–3). These actions are the *symbolic* events of the dream that give insights into making sense of this world. It is our faith-inspired action that yields "light that quickeneth [our] understandings" (D&C 88:11). Had Lehi not faithfully acted, he would have never comprehended the joy of the fruit or testified that he knew it was "desirable above all other fruit" (1 Nephi 8:12). Faithful action yields illumination by the Spirit of the Lord. Prayer is one basic form of that action and the starting point for all who remain in darkness, but there are many acts of faith required for full enlightenment.

Nephi's experience gives further insight into the principle of action in illuminating revelation. His desires, prayers, ponderings, beliefs, and asking were actions that allowed him to be taught. Elder Bednar invited religious educators to "recall how Nephi desired to know about the things his father, Lehi, had seen in the vision of the tree of life. Interestingly, the Spirit of the Lord begins the tutorial with Nephi by asking the following question: 'Behold, what desirest thou?' (1 Nephi 11:2). Clearly the Spirit knew what Nephi desired. So why ask the question? The Holy Ghost was helping Nephi to act in the learning process and not simply be acted upon. Notice in 1 Nephi 11–14 how the Spirit both asked questions and encouraged Nephi to 'look' as active elements in the learning process."[10]

Learning by the Spirit comes after we begin to act. Even Nephi's simple action of looking invited the spirit into his heart to instruct him further. We learn in the Lectures on Faith that faith is "the first principle in revealed religion, and the foundation of all righteousness" and "the principle of action in all intelligent beings."[11] Moroni testified that seekers received spiritual witnesses after they had faith, or, in other words, after they acted (see Ether 12:6). Seven times he referenced spiritual manifestations that resulted after faith, concluding with his testimony that God "workest *after* men have faith" (Ether 12:30; see also 12:6, 7, 12, 17, 18, 31). Lehi's dream provides additional insights to the type of faith-inspired action that illuminates our view of the world, illumination that comes *after* acting.

Following his tasting of the fruit, Lehi straightway desires his family to partake. He begins searching the field to find them (see 1 Nephi 8:13). In his search he sees things he had not seen before as again his perspective broadens. First, he sees a river running by the tree where he stands. He discovers some of his family downriver, standing at the river's head as if they "knew not whither they should go" (1 Nephi 8:14). How can it be that Sariah, Sam, and Nephi know not whither to go? Does not the brightness of the tree illuminate the darkness? Can they not see Lehi standing by it? Clearly he sees them! Perhaps their inability to see the tree lingers because they have yet to act in faith, while their father, even their prophet, sees them and desires that they behold and partake as he has.

In a loud beckoning voice Lehi calls to them, inviting them to come and eat the glorious fruit (see 1 Nephi 8:15). Sariah, Sam, and Nephi hearken to Lehi and come and partake. It appears that their view of the tree did not come until after they followed the prophet; an action providing them with illumination (see 1 Nephi 8:14–16). Laman and Lemuel, however, are not with them. Looking more fervently at the head of the river, Lehi sees and calls to them, but they will not come. His earnest efforts to find and invite Laman and Lemuel seem fruitless, but such loving action is the very catalyst that allows the scene to illuminate further. It is after Lehi lovingly looks, finds, and invites Laman and Lemuel that he beholds a rod of iron and a strait and narrow path leading to the tree by which he stands (see 1 Nephi 8:20). The act of looking for others brings Lehi greater understanding of the world around him. We know that Lehi enjoyed savoring the fruit and its happiness before noticing that there was a river, a rod of iron, or a strait path leading to where he was. So did he arrive at the tree without any guiding aids? Was he completely devoid of the fear of slipping into a filthy river? Obviously no one would doubt Lehi's ability to walk the strait path or hold to the word of God, but perhaps full understanding of such guiding aids only illuminates *after* tasting the fruit and then looking back to help others arrive.

Elder David A. Bednar and others have taught that during scripture reading or commandment keeping, people rarely comprehend the personal spiritual growth occurring.[12] Similarly, the Lord referenced the Lamanites, who during their conversion were "baptized with fire and with the Holy Ghost, and *they knew it not*" (3 Nephi 9:20; emphasis added). However, after consistent faith, holding to the words of God, and keeping the commandments, many believers experienced tender mercies that showed how guided and blessed they really were. Consider the missionary who bears witness to his beliefs without complete testimony of their surety; this act of faith allows the missionary to experience President Packer's promise that a testimony is found in bearing it.[13] Does not the act of bearing testimony bring the Spirit *into* the heart of the bearer although it may only convey the Spirit *unto* the heart of the listener? (see 2 Nephi 33:1; Helaman 5:45). President Brigham Young commented, "More people have obtained a testimony while standing up trying to bear it than down on their knees praying for it."[14] President Dieter F. Uchtdorf testified, "We must learn that in the Lord's plan, our understanding comes 'line upon line, precept upon precept' [2 Nephi 28:30]. In short, knowledge and understanding come at the price of patience. Often the deep valleys of our present will be understood only by looking back on them from the mountains of our future experience."[15] The idiom "Hindsight is 20/20" surely applies to understanding the guidance of the Lord after we have acted.

Lehi followed the prophets, prayed fervently, kept the commandments of God, and searched the scriptures, all before experiencing his dream (see 1 Nephi 1:5, 18; 2:3; 5:10, 21). He held to the rod and walked the path. These faithful actions made it possible for Lehi to taste the fruit and have a revelatory experience, but the action of seeking to help others come and partake appears to be the faith-inspired action that illuminates the rest of the scene in his dream. For as Lehi was looking to guide others, he clearly beheld "a world" with numberless concourses of people "pressing forward, that they might obtain the path" (1 Nephi 8:20–21).

These multitudes came and began to walk in the path that led to the tree (see 1 Nephi 8:22). The record does not indicate whether they saw the tree clearly or only hoped the path was taking them somewhere they would want to be. However, it does mention them "pressing forward, that they might obtain the path which led unto the tree" (1 Nephi 8:21). Perhaps they were told about the tree and had been invited to walk in a path that led to it. It could also be that they recognized this path as one leading to light. Even if they could behold the tree at first, it is significant that there is no mention of these multitudes grasping the iron rod. Could they not see the rod even though it was only a few feet or even inches away from the path? Or did they choose not to see and hold to it? Possibly Lehi wondered the same thing as a mist of darkness overshadowed them and they blindly wandered off and were lost, having failed to anchor themselves tangibly to the path (see 1 Nephi 8:22–23).

Like many people in the world, these multitudes did not recognize the importance of the word of God, symbolized by the iron rod. Though it lay distinctly before them, they would not so much as reach out their hand in faith to grasp the stable guide. Instead, these concourses of people were content to wander off. It seems that they did not notice or feel the dark mist, for would not any human beings in their right minds reach out for help when suddenly bombarded by misty darkness? Lehi's illuminated perspective allowed him to see their surroundings (mist, guiding rod, and path), but the multitude may not have fully recognized these things. In many ways Lehi can sympathize with parents like Elder Henry B. Eyring who, seeing the mists of darkness, feel "the anxiety of sensing danger [their] children cannot yet see."[16]

Continuing to look, Lehi beheld others pressing forward who not only found the path, but "caught hold of the end of the rod of iron" (1 Nephi 8:24). When mists of darkness accumulated, this multitude continued to press forward through the dark haze, clinging to the rod for guidance and support (see 1 Nephi 8:24). These came forth and partook of the fruit, but the immense joy of tasting was short-lived. Shortly after these people reached the tree, Lehi saw them looking around, ashamed (see 1 Nephi 8:24–25). He "cast [his] eyes round about," looking to see why anyone would be ashamed to taste of such joy (1 Nephi 8:26). Again the world of his dream was illuminated, and Lehi saw for the first time what had symbolically always been there. Perceiving the vista on "the other side of the river," Lehi beheld a great and spacious, foundationless building standing "high above the earth" (1 Nephi 8:26). Inside this mighty edifice, people of all ages and genders had the "attitude of mocking and pointing their fingers towards those who had come at and were partaking of the fruit" (1 Nephi 8:27). Such ridicule shamed these individuals, and though they had been enlightened by the tree and tasted its fruit, they fell away into "forbidden paths and were lost" (1 Nephi 8:28).

How could this be? These people had experienced guidance by the rod and walked the strait path. They had tasted of that which was most joyous to the soul! Undoubtedly, Lehi knew the pressures these at the tree may have experienced at the hands of worldly scoffing and ridicule. He had already endured the mockery of the Jews when he proclaimed to them the revelation wherein his "whole heart was filled" and "his soul did rejoice" (1 Nephi 1:15). Yet the world's mocking, anger, and threats did not push Lehi away from the glory of the tree. He remained there, obediently looking to help others arrive.

As he was looking for and perhaps calling others to come to the tree, Lehi saw "other multitudes" (1 Nephi 8:30). Some made it to the tree and partook, "continually holding fast" (v. 30) to the rod of iron. We have no record of these falling away from the tree—it seems that their continual holding exemplified stronger faith and commitment than the aforementioned ashamed individuals who were clinging to the rod. Elder Bednar offers this enlightening insight: "Clinging to the rod of iron suggests . . . only occasional 'bursts' of study or irregular dipping rather than consistent, ongoing immersion in the word of God. . . . People who pressed forward continually holding fast to the rod of iron . . . *consistently* read *and* studied *and* searched the words of Christ. Perhaps it was the constant flow of living water that saved the third group from perishing."[17] So are Saints today *clingers* or *continual holders*?

True it is that many experience clinging instants of religious zeal when life becomes dark or dreary. They recognize the feelings of misty darkness surrounding them and make new resolutions to seek the Lord. The question is, how long do these resolution efforts last? Are they merely moments in a lifetime when people cling strongly to the rod and strive to faithfully walk the path, or are they genuine, long-lasting efforts of repentance and continual grasping of the iron rod? When life gets easy and clear again, do they slacken their grip on the very thing that has stabilized them? Much like the pride cycle, which rotates from ease and blessings to pride, suffering, and repentance, the cling cycle seems to rotate from clinging in firm determination to slackened commitment, darkness, and recommitted clinging. Often it is the attitude of "when it is convenient" or "when I need it" that typifies the clinging multitude. Hence many fall away when perceived gospel needs do not match what the world considers essential to happiness. Others will fall onto forbidden paths when gospel living is not conveniently allowing them to shine in worldly eyes.

It is interesting to note that these clingers were quick to "cast their eyes about" after eating the fruit, as if looking to see if those in the spacious building approved of their actions (1 Nephi 8:25). Although their eyes were what the Savior deemed "the light of the body," as the Savior later mentions, "if thine eye be evil, thy whole body shall be full of darkness. If, therefore, the light that is in thee be darkness, how great is that darkness!" (3 Nephi 13:22–23). This multitude's eyes seemed to testify of the darkness within, as they cared more about the "world and the wisdom thereof" than they did of the glorious fruit of the tree (1 Nephi 11:35). This worldly focus darkened their minds, and they treated lightly the things they had received, wandered off in a dark-minded stupor, followed forbidden paths, and were lost (see 1 Nephi 8:28).

When Saints seek worldly direction from the great and spacious building, they leave the tree and walk back into the darkness. As he sought to know the meaning of his father's symbolically rich dream, Nephi's mind was illuminated and he was able to understand the true significance of the tree (see 1 Nephi 11). Elder Bednar summarizes Nephi's tutelage, stating, "The tree of life is the central feature in the dream and is identified in 1 Nephi 11 as a representation of Jesus Christ. The fruit on the tree is a symbol for the blessings of the Savior's Atonement."[18] No wonder darkness envelops those who leave the tree, for it is not just any tree they are leaving—it is the Light of the World! Only those who remain in that light can see clearly the guides and pitfalls of the world around them. A view from any other location is a perspective darkly misconstrued, tainted, and nonsensical.

Consider the last multitudes to come into Lehi's view; these were "feeling their way towards that great and spacious building" (1 Nephi 8:31). Why were they feeling their way? Could they not see its location in relation to themselves? What of the paths that led to it? Away from the Light of the World, these were in darkness; why else would they purposely fall into and drown in watery depths or wander in strange roads if they were able to see and knew how to get to the worldly building they desired? (see 1 Nephi 8:32). Clearly their vision was not clear. Though many perished in feeling their way toward worldly acceptance, there were great multitudes that successfully found and entered that strange building (see 1 Nephi 8:31, 33). Upon arrival, these begin to point a scorning finger of mockery towards Lehi and others at the tree (see 1 Nephi 8:33). It appears that the perspective of those in the building allowed them to see the tree, but what they saw it as remains a mystery. Was it light? Was it glorious? Surely their mocking attitude suggests a tainted view and understanding, but is that not how the world has always seen and treated the tree? Unquestionably, Nephi would argue that their perception of the tree was tainted, for in his vision he saw the Lamb of God lifted up, crucified, and slain, and multitudes gathered against his apostles; then, when the vision changed, he saw the same multitudes gathered in the great and spacious building (see 1 Nephi 11:31–35).

After seeing these last multitudes, Lehi's dream concluded and he was left to worry about his sons Laman and Lemuel. With all the "feeling of a tender parent," he begged them to hearken to him that they might not be "cast off from the presence of the Lord" (1 Nephi 8:36–37). His vision had impressed upon him the importance of guiding aides that led to the tree and its fruit. He had clearly seen the struggles involved in arriving and remaining at the tree. The magnitude of his vision was vast. The symbolism of the scenes before him was rich, but how intimately did this prophet's dream apply to all humankind? President Packer answered this question in his direct and loving way when he stated, "You may think that Lehi's dream or vision has no special meaning for you, but it does. You are in it; all of us are in it."[19] Such an apostolic insight begs all people to ask whether they are in light or darkness.

Illuminating Where We Stand

President Packer insightfully counseled, "One word in this dream or vision should have special meaning to young Latter-day Saints. The word is *after*.

. . . It is *after* you have partaken of that fruit that your test will come."[20] Lehi also experienced illumination and testing after acting in faith, for after partaking of the fruit he too was mocked by the world (see 1 Nephi 8:33). However, his ability to see clearly gave him the strength to remain at the tree and give no heed to the mocking crowd (see 1 Nephi 8:33). So what faithful actions performed after partaking of the fruit brought this clarity of vision? We can correctly assume that he never was looking to selfishly fill his belly with fruit or gain praise from those around him; rather, he was always engaged in looking to see what halted, shamed, or stopped people from staying in the light of the tree. Elder Dallin H. Oaks reminds us of Christ's words: "He taught that each of us should follow Him by denying ourselves of selfish interests in order to serve others. 'If any man will come after me [He said], let him deny himself, and take up his cross, and follow me. For whosoever will save his life shall lose it: and whosoever will lose his life for my sake shall find it' (Matthew 16:24–25; see also Matthew 10:39). . . . Those who are caught up in trying to save their lives by seeking the praise of the world are actually rejecting the Savior's teaching that the only way to save our eternal life is to love one another and lose our lives in service."[21] Only selfless seeking to help others arrive allowed Lehi to see the world clearly. That act of continued faith illuminated all the pitfalls, dangers, and temptations aimed to stop mankind from arriving at and remaining with Christ the Lord, symbolized in the dream as a glorious tree. Hence, we can gauge where we are in Lehi's dream by determining whether we serve others or selfishly seek to satisfy our own desires.

The moment Latter-day Saints start focusing on selfish worldly accolades rather than looking to help others arrive is the moment their minds begin to darken and they wander from the tree. President Brigham Young once expressed his worst fear: that converted Saints would "get rich in this country, forget God and his people, wax fat, and kick themselves out of the Church and go to hell."[22] Though wealth may lead some away from the tree and onto forbidden paths, there are more subtle worldly influences that sway Saints toward the great and spacious building. President Packer asserted, "Largely because of television, instead of looking over into that spacious building, we are, in effect, living inside of it. That is your fate in this generation. You are living in that great and spacious building."[23] Because of this, the real question becomes, are we just living inside of the spacious building, or have we become a part of it?

Christ prayed to his Father, pleading for his disciples who were "*in* the world," recognizing that "the world hath hated them, because they are not *of* the world" (see John 17:11, 14 emphasis added). He knew that these disciples would have the filth of worldliness all around but that they would neither join in nor seek the acceptance of those who did. They literally would be *in* the world, but not partakers *of* it. Though disciples today should follow these first apostolic stalwarts, there seem to be too many who acknowledge worldly wickedness but still live for worldly value and acceptance. These have unknowingly and slowly become part of the world they are living in.

Parents may stand inside the great and spacious building, unaware that their hearts are more concerned about what others think than what God feels. They may be trying to point their mission-aged son or struggling daughter to the tree of life and teach the need to serve the Lord, when in reality their blindness has led them to care more about what the ward and community might think than about the actual salvation of their child. What about the family who leaves church meetings for a sporting event or an early break-the-fast meal? Are parents still genuinely looking to help children and others arrive at the tree, or do selfish desires opaquely taint parental vision and cause them to justify gospel living according to worldly standards of the strange building? Even more blinded are those who adopt worldly definitions of family, morality, good media, and career success in the place of revealed counsel. Addressing this problem, Elder Robert D. Hales declared, "I caution all of us to avoid looking to the great and spacious building for answers to questions about our future pursuits, our companions, and our lifestyles. Instead, let us kneel and talk with our Heavenly Father, learn about our gifts and talents, find ways to develop them, make choices based on who we are and what we have been given."[24]

Individuals too often become mentally clouded when their actions unknowingly give too much value to popularity, careers, relationships, entertainment, beauty, talents, sports, or academia. Soon they fall victim to Elder Oaks's warnings to not allow "good" to become the robber of "best."[25] Victims of this plight usually become clingers who find that convenience and perceived good endeavors are outweighing exact commandment keeping. These individuals stop looking to help others come to Christ and start drifting away from the radiance of the tree. Losing this radiance and light, their minds are darkened and perceptions tainted. No matter where they may stand in the geography of Lehi's dream, they do not see the world for what it really is, but rather they see it "through a glass, darkly" (1 Corinthians 13:12).

Conclusion

Satan is ever persistent in lulling the Church "away into carnal security" and thinking that "all is well in Zion" (2 Nephi 28:21). This deceptive lullaby stops many members from looking to help others arrive as they themselves slip away into a sleep of darkness. Suddenly these once faithful members do not see their children wandering off on strange roads. They do not see bad habits creeping into their own lives and the lives of their children. They fail to recognize truth and are offended easily. They do not see their growing pride and all of its destructive reactions and behaviors. In short, their minds are darkened and they lose sight of the reality that the building wherein they stand is foundationless!

Those who stand away from the tree do not fully see, but those who, like Lehi, remain at the tree are wholeheartedly engaged in looking to help others arrive. Lehi's complete understanding and perspective of his dream did not come all at once. It came by degrees as he prayed for mercy and learned by faith. Multiple times the events in Lehi's dream brought new light to the world he was in. These events were simply his actions of heartfelt prayer, obedience, and constant looking to help others arrive at the tree. His faithful actions allowed him to clearly see the pitfalls, temptations, darkness, and dangers that stand between mankind and the fruit of the Lord Jesus Christ. As Latter-day Saints, we might proclaim that we have tasted the fruit, but will we remain at the tree? Will we be like Lehi? Have we prayed to see clearly? Are we still consistently trying to help others arrive at the tree?

When John and Peter Whitmer were wondering what would be of greatest worth to them personally, God responded, "Declare repentance unto this people, that you may bring souls unto me, that *you may rest with them* in the kingdom of my Father; . . . [this] will be of the most worth unto you" (D&C 15:6; 16:6; emphasis added). When Saints seek to help others arrive, they will learn by faith, sincerely pray, and consistently hold to the word of God. They will always remain in the light of Christ, and even when this world is covered in thick darkness, their eyes will be illuminated, for where light is, darkness cannot be; and unless light diminishes, darkness cannot intrude, for "darkness cannot conquer light."[26]

Notes

1. Boyd K. Packer, "Finding Ourselves in Lehi's Dream," *Ensign*, August 2010, 22.

2. Lamoni prayed mightily to God, exclaiming, "O Lord, have mercy; according to thy abundant mercy which thou hast had upon the people of Nephi, have upon me, and my people" (Alma 18:41). This prayer caused his strength to fail, and he lay helpless for two days and nights (see Alma 19:1). Mormon commented on the situation, saying that Ammon "knew that king Lamoni was under the power of God; he knew that the *dark veil* of unbelief was being cast away from his mind, and the light which did light up his mind, which was the light of the glory of God, which was a marvelous light of his goodness—yea, this light had infused such joy into his soul, the *cloud of darkness* having been dispelled, and that the light of everlasting life was lit up in his soul, yea, he knew that this had overcome his natural frame, and he was carried away in God" (Alma 19:6; emphasis added). Prayer to God for mercy does seem to have rending effects on the dark, veiled cloud of darkness caused by sin, unbelief, and ignorance.

3. Mary A. Pepper Kidder, "Did You Think to Pray?" *Hymns* (Salt Lake City: The Church of Jesus Christ of Latter-day Saints, 1985), no. 140.

4. The Book of Mormon institute study manual for students and other sources teach that the approximately 180-mile journey was infested anciently by many marauders. Lehi and his family would have traveled at least twelve to fourteen days to make such a journey by camel or horse. It could have taken even longer, as livestock, tents, and other necessities (e.g., water and food) may have slowed their journey. *Book of Mormon Student Manual: Religion 121–122* (Salt Lake City: The Church of Jesus Christ of Latter-day Saints, 2009), 14.

5. "Nephi's Life Inspires Many in Times of Old and in Present," *Church News*, February 8, 1992. See also George Reynolds and Janne M. Sjodahl, *Commentary on the Book of Mormon*, 7 vols. (Salt Lake City: Deseret Book: 1973).

6. Immediately after making it to the promised land, Nephi was commanded to make plates. However, he was not commanded to create the small plates (the set our text is from) until twelve to thirty years after leaving Jerusalem.

7. "Priesthood Leaders Worldwide Receive Training via Satellite," *Ensign*, April 2003, 76; see also Sheri L. Dew, "We Are Not Alone," *Ensign*, November 1998, 94; and Joe J. Christensen, "Toward Greater Spirituality: Ten Important Steps," *Tambuli*, August 1983, 23.

8. David A. Bednar, "Seek Learning by Faith," *Ensign*, September 2007, 63; see also D&C 88:118.

9. Note that the Lamanites in the darkened prison (Helaman 5) heard the voice of God, saw prophets' faces illuminated, felt earthquakes when the Lord spoke, and recognized a spiritual cloud of darkness. But, however powerful the Spirit of the Lord was, it did not enter *into* their hearts until they acted and cried unto the voice themselves (see Helaman 5:42–45).

10. Bednar, "Seek Learning by Faith," 63–64.

11. Joseph Smith, comp., *Lectures on Faith* (Salt Lake City: Deseret Book, 1985), 1, 6.

12. David A. Bednar, "More Diligent and Concerned at Home," *Ensign*, November 2009, 17–20. President Packer tells the story of his son in the mission field. "Several years ago I met one of our sons in the mission field in a distant part of the world. He had been there for a year. His first question was this: 'Dad, what can I do to grow spiritually? I have tried so hard to grow spiritually and I just haven't made any progress.' That was his perception: to me it was otherwise. I could hardly believe the maturity, the spiritual growth that he had gained in just one year. He 'knew it not' for it had come as growth, not as a startling spiritual experience." Boyd K. Packer, "The Candle of the Lord," *Ensign*, January 1983, 54.

13. Boyd K. Packer, "The Candle of the Lord," *Ensign*, January 1983, 54.

14. Junius F. Wells, "Historic Sketch of the YMMIA," *Improvement Era*, June 1925, 715.

15. Dieter F. Uchtdorf, "Continue in Patience," *Ensign*, May 2010, 58.

16. Henry B. Eyring, "Let Us Raise Our Voice of Warning," *Ensign*, January 2009, 5.

17. David A. Bednar, "A Reservoir of Living Water" (address delivered at Church Educational System fireside, February 4, 2007), 9.

18. Bednar, " A Reservoir of Living Water," 8.

19. Packer, "Finding Ourselves in Lehi's Dream," 22.

20. Packer, "Finding Ourselves in Lehi's Dream," 22–23.

21. Dallin H. Oaks, "Unselfish Service," *Ensign*, May 2009, 93, 95.

22. Preston Nibley, *Brigham Young: The Man and His Work* (Salt Lake City: Deseret News, 1965), 128.

23. Packer, "Finding Ourselves in Lehi's Dream," 23.

24. Robert D. Hales, "Our Essential Spiritual Agency," *Brigham Young University Speeches, 2010–2011* (Provo, UT: Brigham Young University, 2010), 4–5.

25. Dallin H. Oaks, "Good, Better, Best," *Ensign*, November 2007, 104–8.

26. Robert D. Hales, "Out of Darkness into His Marvelous Light," *Ensign*, May 2002, 69.

17

Bitter and Sweet: Dual Dimensions of the Tree of Life

C. Robert Line

Doth a fountain send forth at the same place sweet water and bitter? (James 3:11)

Many readers of the Book of Mormon are familiar with the text in 1 Nephi 8, often referred to simply as "Lehi's dream," as well as the associated symbolism and interpretation revealed in Nephi's vision in chapters 11 through 14. The centerpiece of the dream seems to focus on the tree of life (see 1 Nephi 11:2–10), whose fruit is described by Lehi as being "most sweet, above all that I ever before tasted. Yea, and I beheld that the fruit thereof was white, to exceed all the whiteness that I had ever seen. And as I partook of the fruit thereof it filled my soul with exceedingly great joy." Additionally, he states that "it was desirable above all other fruit" (1 Nephi 8:11–12). This symbolic tree and its associated fruit appear to be not only the same tree described in the Garden of Eden story but also the same described in Alma's discourse: "the fruit thereof, which is most precious, which is sweet above all that is sweet, and which is white above all that is white, yea, and pure above all that is pure" (Alma 32:42).

C. Robert Line is an instructor at the Salt Lake City Utah University Institute of Religion.

Regarding the fruit of the tree of life, a peculiar verse of scripture in 2 Nephi 2 may go unnoticed at first glance. But a closer look reveals a phrase that seems a bit confusing and almost contradictory. This verse lies between two powerful and succinct concepts—one teaching the doctrine of the Atonement (vv. 3–10) and the other the doctrine of the Fall (vv. 16–25). In 2 Nephi 2:15 we read, "And to bring about his eternal purposes in the end of man, after he had created our first parents, and the beasts of the field and the fowls of the air, and in fine, all things which are created, it must needs be that there was an opposition; *even the forbidden fruit in opposition to the tree of life; the one being sweet and the other bitter*" (emphasis added).

The items of interest here are the different fruits. One is the forbidden fruit, obviously from the tree of knowledge of good and evil; the other, though not explicitly stated, is the fruit of the tree of life. At least two points of view become apparent when one seeks to make an interpretation of each type of fruit. First, a textual logic seems to indicate that the forbidden fruit is the one that is "sweet" because it is mentioned first and then so described in the latter part of the sentence. Similarly, the fruit of the tree of life appears to be the one that is "bitter" for the reasons described previously. However, there is a second possible meaning. When viewed from a chiastic perspective, the fruit of tree of life could be the one that is sweet, while the forbidden fruit would be bitter.[1] In light of these two possibilities, it is interesting to note President Harold B. Lee's commentary: "[God] set the tree of the knowledge of good and evil in opposition to the tree of life. The fruit of the one which was 'bitter' was the tree of life, and the forbidden fruit was the one which was 'sweet to the taste.'"[2] President Lee's interpretation of this scriptural verse clearly coincides with the first point of view.

What is the predicament then? Simply stated, one would think that the fruit of the tree of life is the fruit that is sweet, as Lehi explicitly states in 1 Nephi 8, not bitter as Lehi seems to later indicate in 2 Nephi 2. The question that this paper will seek to answer is this: Is the fruit of the tree of life bitter, sweet, or both? What are the implications for understanding this scriptural and doctrinal concept?

Two Trees and Two Fruits

It might be asked how the fruit of the tree of life can be both sweet and bitter? Yet, this problem begs a similar question regarding the forbidden fruit:

is it bitter or sweet? Interestingly, the scriptural account of the Garden of Eden in Genesis 3:6 seems to concur with Lehi's assessment that the forbidden fruit is actually the one that is sweet: "And when the woman saw that *the tree was good* for food, and that *it was pleasant* to the eyes, and a *tree to be desired* to *make one wise*, she took of the fruit thereof, and did eat, and gave also unto her husband with her; and he did eat." Logic seems to indicate that if the fruit of the tree of life in Lehi's vision is sweet, then the forbidden fruit must therefore be bitter. It should be noted that the partaking of the forbidden fruit could be considered a "sweet" thing (i.e., good) in a certain sense. Later on in 2 Nephi 2 (which, again, seems to be referring to the forbidden fruit as the "sweet" fruit), we read the following: "Adam fell that men might be and men are that they might have joy" (v. 25). The action of partaking the forbidden fruit is perhaps bitter, but the long-term ramifications are sweet. That is to say, the partaking of the forbidden fruit was tactically a fault but strategically a success! Or, as Elder Dallin H. Oaks has declared, the Fall "was formally a transgression but eternally a glorious necessity to open the doorway toward eternal life."[3] Said Eve to Adam, "Were it not for our transgression we never should have had seed, and never should have known good and evil, and the joy of our redemption" (Moses 5:11). Elder Orson F. Whitney explained, "The Fall had a two-fold direction—downward, yet forward. It brought man into the world and set his feet upon progression's highway."[4] Despite these observations, there is still the dilemma of the description of the fruit of the tree of life in Lehi's dream, wherein the fruit of the tree of life is described as sweet. How might this be so?

Perspectives and Implications

Perhaps the answer to this simple dilemma can be found in the scriptural account of the Garden of Eden as found in the Pearl of Great Price, specifically, the verse in Moses 4:12; this verse reads almost identical to its counterpart in Genesis 3:6, but it has two very interesting, albeit small, changes: "And when the woman saw that the tree was good for food, and *that it became pleasant* to the eyes, and a tree to be desired *to make her wise*, she took of the fruit thereof, and did eat, and also gave unto her husband with her, and he did eat."

The phrase from Genesis "was pleasant" is changed to "became pleasant," perhaps suggesting that the forbidden fruit really isn't sweet at all—the serpent just made it appear that way. In the end, sin is never sweet, or, as Alma would say, "wickedness never was happiness" (Alma 41:10). The chart below can serve as a model for what is being suggested. On the surface, Satan makes sin and transgression appealing through enticements, but in reality these things are bitter. Such is the assessment of King Benjamin, where he equates the forbidden fruit with the bitter realities of guilt, misery, and endless torment (Mosiah 3:25–26). Likewise, Alma equates partaking of the forbidden fruit with being "a lost and fallen people" (Alma 12:22).

	On the surface	Reality
Forbidden fruit	Sweet (by deception)	Bitter
Fruit of tree of life	Bitter (by deception)	Sweet

There may be times when the initial taste of sin is sweet or desirable to an individual. But once wickedness and perversion are swallowed and processed by our eternal spirits, we sadly discover the bitter reality of our choice. Although sin is and always will be bitter, one can experience (just as Eve did) a momentary pleasure or rush of seeming happiness or fun. These disguised delights and fleeting flashes of excitement might even last more than a few moments—perhaps a day, a week, or even longer. "But if it be not built upon my gospel, and is built upon the works of men, or upon the works of the devil, verily I say unto you *they have joy in their works for a season,* and by and by the end cometh, and they are hewn down and cast into the fire, from whence there is no return" (3 Nephi 27:11). It might sound strange that God would permit a person to "have joy" in sinning, albeit for a short season. One might think that an immediate divine punishment would be the best response to sin and to sinners.

President Spencer W. Kimball once gave this wise counsel:

> Now, we find many people critical when a righteous person is killed, a young father or mother is taken from a family, or when violent deaths occur. Some become bitter when oft-repeated prayers seem unanswered. Some lose faith and turn sour when solemn administrations by holy men seem to be ignored and no restoration seems to come from repeated prayer. . . . But if all the sick were healed, if all the righteous were protected and the wicked destroyed, the whole program of the Father would be annulled and the basic principle of

the Gospel, free agency, would be ended. *If pain and sorrow and total punishment immediately followed the doing of evil, no soul would repeat a misdeed. If joy and peace and rewards were instantaneously given the doer of good, there could be no evil—all would do good and not because of the rightness of doing good.* There would be no test of strength, no development of character, no growth of powers, no free agency, no Satanic controls. Should all prayers be immediately answered according to our selfish desires and our limited understanding, then there would be little or no suffering, sorrow, disappointment, or even death; and if these were not, there would also be an absence of joy, success, resurrection, eternal life, and godhood.[5]

Conversely, Satan would have us believe that the fruit of the tree of life is bitter, not sweet. Although the fruit of the tree is ultimately eternal life, all sons and daughters of God can taste small portions of this precious fruit as they adhere to principles of righteous living throughout their lives. Scripture study, prayer, tithes and offerings, service, Sabbath worship—these are all activities that the adversary would have us believe are bitter, unwanted, profitless, boring, and meaningless pursuits. Perhaps to the spiritually dead, such is the case. But "to the hungry soul every bitter thing is sweet" (Proverbs 27:7).

Obviously it is one of Satan's tactics to blur the lines and meaning of good and evil. In his book *The Great Divorce*, C. S. Lewis asserts that the adversary's sophistry portrays Christ as "the tyrant of the universe."[6] Likewise, the parable of the talents highlights a servant who receives but one talent and was unfaithful therewith. Then he complains to the Lord and even engages in name calling: "I knew thee that thou art an hard man" (Matthew 25:24). Elder James E. Talmage's commentary is notable:

> The unfaithful servant prefaced his report with a grumbling excuse, which involved the imputation of unrighteousness in the Master. The honest, diligent, faithful servants saw and reverenced in their Lord the perfection of the good qualities which they possessed in measured degree; the lazy and unprofitable serf, afflicted by distorted vision, professed to see in the Master his own base defects. The story in this particular, as in the other features relating to human acts and tendencies, is psychologically true; in a peculiar sense men are prone

to conceive of the attributes of God as comprising in augmented degree the dominant traits of their own nature.[7]

After all is said and done, "we see the end of him who perverteth the ways of the Lord; and thus we see that the devil will not support his children at the last day, but doth speedily drag them down to hell" (Alma 30:60). Thus, depending on one's perspective, the fruit from either tree can be perceived as both bitter and sweet. The important thing, then, is to have the proper perspective. Perhaps this is what Isaiah was alluding to when he emphatically declared: "Woe unto them that call evil good, and good evil; that put darkness for light, and light for darkness; that put *bitter for sweet*, and *sweet for bitter!*" (Isaiah 5:20; emphasis added; compare 2 Nephi 15:20).

The Close Proximity of the Bitter and Sweet

Although we should never mistake *sweet* for *bitter*, we should understand that these two adjectives are nonetheless intertwined and closely related to each other. It is interesting to note the nearness of the symbolic *tree of life* in Lehi's dream to another symbol in his dream, mainly, the *river of water*: "And as I cast my eyes round about, that perhaps I might discover my family also, I beheld a river of water; and it ran along, and *it was near* the tree of which I was partaking the fruit" (1 Nephi 8:13, emphasis added). In Nephi's subsequent vision, the river of water is a representation of the depths of hell and is described as containing "filthy water" that proceeds from a fountain (1 Nephi 12:16).

Also interesting in Lehi's dream is the nearness of the filthy river to the iron rod that leads to the tree of life and its associated fruit: "And I beheld a rod of iron, and it extended along the bank of the river, and led to the tree by which I stood" (1 Nephi 8:19). Later, in Nephi's vision, we learn the symbolism of the iron rod as Nephi answers questions from his brothers: "And they said unto me: What meaneth the rod of iron which our father saw, that led to the tree? And I said unto them that it was the word of God; and whoso would hearken unto the word of God, and would hold fast unto it, they would never perish; neither could the temptations and the fiery darts of the adversary overpower them unto blindness, to lead them away to destruction" (1 Nephi 15:23–24).

Thus it is apparent from Lehi's symbolic dream that the river of filthy water runs alongside the iron rod, all the way to the tree of life. The point in this analysis is to highlight the proximity of the *sweet* to that which is *bitter*.

These two are always near to each other, that is, they run alongside each other from beginning to end! (see 1 Nephi 8:13). This geographical and symbolic occurrence points to a literal and sobering reality here in mortality. Although one might be holding to the iron rod and safely walking the strait and narrow path, sin is only a step away; or, as is the case with modern media and technology, it is sometimes only a "click" away! The same is true with any form of bitterness, whether it be sin or natural trials and adversity—there always seems to be a divine deference that allows joy and misery to seemingly be on the heels of each other incessantly. Elder Neal A. Maxwell once said: "So often in life a deserved blessing is quickly followed by a needed stretching. Spiritual exhilaration may be quickly followed by a vexation or temptation. Were it otherwise, extended spiritual reveries or immunities from adversity might induce in us a regrettable forgetfulness of others in deep need. *The sharp, side-by-side contrast of the sweet and the bitter is essential* until the very end of this brief, mortal experience."[8]

Similarly, President Brigham Young taught: "Will sin be perfectly destroyed? No, it will not, for it is not so designed in the economy of Heaven. . . . Do not suppose that we shall ever in the flesh be free from temptations to sin. . . . We shall more or less feel the effects of sin so long as we live, and finally have to pass the ordeals of death."[9]

We see this pattern repeated so often in the scriptures, especially with the tutoring and training of prophets, the "sharp, side-by-side" contrast of good and evil, that is, Joseph Smith and the First Vision, Moses in the Pearl of Great Price (see Moses 1), and even the vision of God and Christ in section 76, where the vision is immediately followed by the vision of Lucifer and the one third—the list of pedagogical foils goes on. Elder John A. Widtsoe declared: "Truth and untruth travel together side by side. Light and darkness both offer themselves to the seeker after truth, one to bless, the other to destroy mankind. Whenever a man sets out to seek truth, he will for a time be overtaken by evil. No seeker after truth is, therefore, ever free from temptation, from evil powers."[10] This perplexing truth is declared and described beautifully in a poem by William Blake:

> Joy & Woe are woven fine
> A Clothing for the Soul divine
> Under every grief & pine
> Runs a joy with silken twine

It is right it should be so
Man was made for Joy and Woe
And when this we rightly know
Through the World we safely go[11]

With such close proximity between the sweet and bitter, we must be ever-vigilant. How do we avoid the filthy water? True it is that we cannot escape this world of sin. We can perhaps avoid sinning to some degree, but, as President Young states, we cannot ever avoid the temptation to sin. We must be in the world but not of the world. A wonderful principle found at the conclusion of Nephi's vision gives us a clue as to how this can be accomplished. While explaining to Laman and Lemuel the symbols of his vision (and his father's dream), Nephi gives the following instruction regarding the meaning of the river of water: "And I said unto them that the water which my father saw was filthiness; *and so much was his mind swallowed up in other things that he beheld not the filthiness of the water*" (1 Nephi 15:27). One of the key's to avoiding the ever-encroaching river of sin in our lives is to have our minds and actions focused on many other good and uplifting *things*—to the point where there is no time or interest in sin itself. It can be as though sin is not even there. Cognitively we may know it is there, but we are not perplexed or filled with undue anxiety over its existence. As Elder David A. Bednar taught, being "endowed with agency, we are agents, and we primarily are to act and not merely be acted upon."[12]

How Bitter Is Bitter?

Having established that we should never mistake sweet for bitter or bitter for sweet, we thus face an interesting dilemma here in mortality wherein we cannot avoid tasting the bitter, while likewise experiencing the sweet. Both of these realities, as has been stated, appear intertwined and inextricably linked together: "And the Lord spake unto Adam, saying: Inasmuch as thy children are conceived in sin, even so when they begin to grow up, sin conceiveth in their hearts, and they taste the bitter, that they may know to prize the good. And it is given unto them to know good from evil; wherefore they are agents unto themselves" (Moses 6:55–56). In this verse, sin is definitely equated with bitterness. But it is interesting to note that apparently we are to taste the bitter here in mortality in order "to prize the good," i.e., to taste the sweet. A passage from the Doctrine and Covenants seems to concur with Moses: "And it must needs be that the devil should tempt the children of men, or they could not be agents unto themselves; for if they never should have bitter they could not know the sweet—wherefore, it came to pass that the devil tempted Adam, and he partook of the forbidden fruit and transgressed the commandment, wherein he became subject to the will of the devil, because he yielded unto temptation" (D&C 29:39–40).

Although it is a scriptural truth, that "all have sinned, and come short of the glory of God" (Romans 3:23), are we to infer that to know and achieve righteousness we first must experience sin? Paul seems to clarify that such might not be case: "What shall we say then? Shall we continue in sin, that grace may abound? God forbid." (Romans 6:1–2) President Kimball's words are instructive. He teaches that resistance to sin is better than repentance:

> Another error into which some transgressors fall, because of the availability of God's forgiveness, is the illusion that they are somehow stronger for having committed sin and then lived through the period of repentance. This simply is not true. That man who resists temptation and lives without sin is far better off than the man who has fallen, no matter how repentant the latter may be. The reformed transgressor, it is true, may be more understanding of one who falls into the same sin, and to that extent perhaps more helpful in the latter's regeneration. But his sin and repentance have certainly not made him stronger than the consistently righteous person.[13]

Obviously, since we all sin, Christ is the spiritually strongest of all of Father's spirit children; he is the only really consistently righteous person who has or ever will live (1 Nephi 10:6; D&C 82:2, 6; Romans 3:10–12, 23). However, this is not to say that he is unacquainted with the bitterness of trials, grief, affliction and temptation. Interestingly, it is because of His perfect righteousness that he understands the bitterness of sin so much more than the rest of humanity. C. S. Lewis' words are memorable: "A silly idea is current that good people do not know what temptation means. This is an obvious lie. Only those who try to resist temptation know how strong it is. After all, you find out the strength of the [opposing] army by fighting against it, not by giving in. You find out the strength of a wind by trying to walk against it, not by lying down. A man who gives in to temptation after five minutes simply does not know what it would have been like an hour later. That is why bad people, in one sense, know very little about badness. They have lived a sheltered life by always giving in."[14]

To be sure, sin is bitter. But is bitterness always the same thing as sin? Trials are definitely part of our mortal probation, and we must experience "opposition in all things" in order to grow towards eternal life. Therefore, we must experience the bitter in order to prize the sweet. But, once again, must we experience the bitterness of sin? Elder Bruce C. Hafen once observed, "As part of an eternal plan, our Father placed us in this world subject to death, sin, sorrow, and misery—ALL of which serve the eternal purpose of letting us taste the bitter that we may learn to prize the sweet."[15] On another occasion he remarked, "We might think of the degree of our personal fault for the bad things that happen in our lives as a continuum ranging from sin to adversity, with the degree of our fault dropping from high at one end of the spectrum to zero at the other. . . . Along this fault-level continuum, between the poles of sin and adversity, lie such intermediate points as unwise choices and hasty judgments. . . . Bitterness may taste the same, whatever its source, and it can destroy our peace, break our hearts, and separate us from God. Could it be that the great 'at-one-ment' of Christ could put back together the broken parts and give beauty to the ashes of experience such as this? I believe that it does, because *tasting the bitter in all its forms* is a deliberate part of the great plan of life."[16]

We might ask if our bitter moments in life, whether through sin or adversity, have helped us to become humble. Have our fiery trials served the purpose of softening our hearts? We know we can either be humble because we so choose or because we are compelled to be so (see Alma 32:13–14). Elder Maxwell once said: "The returning prodigals are never numerous enough, but regularly some come back from 'a far country' (Luke 15:13). Of course, it is better if we are humbled 'because of the word' rather than being compelled by circumstances, yet the latter may do! (see Alma 32:13–14). Famine can induce spiritual hunger."[17] Whether the bitter fruit is through sin or adversity or a combination of both, it should be sufficient to help us appreciate the sweet fruits of virtue, benevolence, and righteous living.

Conclusion

Lehi's dream is an entrancing narrative that, although symbolic, can teach many powerful life lessons, including the necessity of learning through the experience of the sweet and the bitter. It could be said that this mortal probation is an experiential escalator. It is a realm of rigorous reality, tempering trials, and tough learning. The school of hard knocks is always in session. Our divine dean has given the demanding directive: "And we will prove them herewith, to see if they will do all things whatsoever the Lord their God shall command them" (Abraham 3:25). Although we might seek to skip class at times, we eventually discover the eternal truth that "it must needs be, that there is an opposition in all things" (2 Nephi 2:11). Although some lessons are bitter, we rejoice in those moments that are sweet. We soon realize, if we are willing, that these two existing realities (the bitter and the sweet) are not mutually exclusive courses that can be taken through independent study; they are, rather, reinforcing and complementary classes that must be taken simultaneously, for *"all these things* shall give [us] experience, and shall be for [our] good" (D&C 122:7; emphasis added). Elder Maxwell perceptively observed that "God [is not] a kindly grandfather who would indulge mankind in whatever they wish to do. . . . Ours is a loving Father who will, if necessary, let come to each of us some harsh life experiences, that we might learn that his love for us is so great and so profound that he will let us suffer, as he did his Only Begotten Son in the flesh, that his and our triumph and learning might be complete and full."[18] May we learn our lessons well and always hold to the iron rod, seeking constantly for the fruit of that sacred knowledge and experience that is "most precious, which is sweet above all that is sweet, and which is white above all that is white, yea, and pure above all that is pure" (Alma 32:42).

Notes

1. Chiasmus is a form of writing or speech in which various words or clauses are related to each other through a reversal of structure (i.e., inverted parallelism).
2. Harold B. Lee, *Stand Ye in Holy Places* (Salt Lake City: Deseret Book, 1974), 364.
3. Dallin H. Oaks, "The Great Plan of Happiness," *Ensign*, November 1993, 73.
4. Orson F. Whitney, in *Cowley and Whitney on Doctrine*, comp. Forace Green (Salt Lake City: Bookcraft, 1963), 287.
5. Spencer W. Kimball, "Tragedy or Destiny," *Improvement Era*, March 1966, 180, 210; emphasis added.
6. C. S. Lewis, *The Great Divorce* (San Francisco: HarperSanFrancisco, 1946), 136.
7. James E. Talmage, *Jesus the Christ* (Salt Lake City: The Church of Jesus Christ of Latter-day Saints, 1981), 582.
8. Neal A. Maxwell, "Enduring Well," *Ensign*, April 1997, 7.

9. Brigham Young, in *Journal of Discourses* (London: Latter-day Saints' Book Depot, 1854–86), 10:173.

10. John A. Widtsoe, "The Significance of the First Vision," Fourth Annual Joseph Smith Memorial Sermon, Logan Institute of Religion, December 8, 1946, 2.

11. *The Complete Poetry and Prose of William Blake*, ed. David V. Erdman (Berkeley: University of California Press, 1982), 494–95.

12. David A. Bednar, "Watching with All Perseverance," *Ensign*, May 2010, 43; see also 2 Nephi 2:14.

13. Spencer W. Kimball, *The Miracle of Forgiveness* (Salt Lake City: Deseret Book, 1969), 357.

14. C. S. Lewis, *Mere Christianity* (San Francisco: HarperSanFrancisco, 2001), 142.

15. Bruce C. Hafen, "Elder Bruce C. Hafen Speaks on Same-Sex Attraction," address at Evergreen International Nineteenth Annual Conference, September 19, 2009, 2.

16. Hafen, *"Beauty for Ashes" and the Restored Doctrine of the Atonement* (Salt Lake City: Deseret Book, 1998), 12–15.

17. Neal A. Maxwell, "The Tugs and Pulls of the World," *Ensign*, November 2000, 36.

18. Neal A. Maxwell, "The Gospel Gives Answers to Life's Problems," *Liahona*, February 1978, 36.

18

Sacrifice and Condescension: Types and Shadows for Latter-day Living

D. Mick Smith

Almost any reader of the Book of Mormon is aware of the greatness of Lehi's dream of the tree of life and Nephi's subsequent vision. Yet how many have truly pondered the extent of doctrinal teaching available from an in-depth study of these spiritual experiences? Do we see the Atonement of Christ spelled out in magnificent clarity? Do we grasp the complex yet simple narrative of how the Son would sacrifice and condescend as part of his mission to save us? Do we comprehend how this dream and vision set an example for us to follow as part of our daily personal covenants for latter-day living? Our purposes must be to discover what doctrine is taught through these experiences and how the lessons learned have application in our lives.

The Book of Mormon is a treasure trove of doctrine and understanding for the true seeker of the things of God. Lehi's dream and Nephi's interpretive vision rival Old and New Testament revelations such as Nebuchadnezzar's dream of the great image and latter-day Restoration (see Daniel 2:19–45), Jacob's dream of the ladder connecting earth and heaven (see Genesis 28:12–15; John 1:51), and Peter's vision of the gospel going to all nations (see Acts 10).

D. Mick Smith is a teacher at Maple Mountain Seminary in Spanish Fork, Utah, and an adjunct instructor of religion at Brigham Young University.

Nebuchadnezzar's dream helps us understand how the Restoration of the gospel will roll forth and encompass the earth. Jacob's dream helps us better comprehend the ascension of the souls of men to God, and Christ's role as the pathway by which we ascend and descend from God's presence. Peter's vision communicates the importance of carrying the gospel to all of the nations of the earth. In comparison, Lehi's dream and Nephi's vision may teach us the sweetness and joy that can come from partaking of the fruit of the gospel, especially as we gain a greater appreciation of the condescension of the Father and the Son. In other words, each of these great dreams or visions assists us in understanding the relationship our Heavenly Father has with his children and his desires to see his work progress here upon the earth.

The vision of the tree of life provides hidden nuggets of truth that elucidate such basic gospel principles as holding fast to the word of God, staying on the strait and narrow path, avoiding the temptations that seek to cloud our view of eternity, and receiving the consummate reward and joy if we endure to the end and taste of the fruit offered by the Savior. It is this sacred fruit that we all desire and have desired to partake of since the Fall of Adam and Eve brought about our earthly separation from the Father and the Son (see Genesis 3:17–24).[1]

In addition to these principles comes the awe-inspiring central theme of all scripture, which is that the Father has sent his Son to ransom and redeem mankind from our lost and fallen state. The depth and majesty of this sacrifice is magnificently expressed in Nephi's portion of the vision when he is asked about "the condescension of God" and the associated principles of sacrifice and service that are so movingly taught as we learn of the Father's and Son's example for each of us (see 1 Nephi 11:16–33). While some may question the "majesty" or "beauty" of sacrifice, those who benefit from the sacrificial offering stand in awe of what was offered, especially by our Heavenly Father and Elder Brother.

Understanding the Law of Sacrifice and Condescension

To understand the interrelationship between sacrifice and condescension, it may be beneficial to briefly define each word and then apply their meanings to what is discovered from Nephi's vision. The word *sacrifice* comes from the Latin *sacra-* (sacred rites) combined with *facere* (to do, perform), meaning to perform sacred rites or to make something sacred.[2] To condescend is "to behave as if one is conscious of descending from a superior position, rank, or dignity, or to put aside one's dignity or superiority voluntarily and assume equality with one regarded as inferior."[3] President Ezra Taft Benson taught that condescension "means to descend or come down from an exalted position to a place of inferior station."[4] We may condescend from positions of wealth, knowledge, good health, or any other of life's blessings in order to serve our fellowmen. Parents may condescend as they teach and work with their children on a level that the child will understand or as they sacrifice something they have in order to teach and bless the life of the child. A brother or sister may condescend by helping a younger sibling learn a skill, or by sacrificing something for the benefit of the younger sibling.

The importance of condescension is exemplified by the idea of voluntarily giving up a position of superiority in an act of service to those who may be considered to be in a lower position. Essentially, any act of selflessness that blesses others' lives may be considered a form of condescension.[5] The Father and the Son provide the ideals of condescension by which we learn and follow.

Thus the relationship between condescension and sacrifice is a sacred offering wherein one who is superior does something on behalf of someone else who could not, or may not, have been able to do that thing. This may occur when one condescends to help make someone sacred or sanctified who cannot achieve that level of purity on their own. An excellent example of this is when "the Lamb of God [descended] out of heaven and showed himself unto them," and "because of their faith in the Lamb of God their garments are made white in his blood" (see 1 Nephi 12:6, 10). In other words, an exalted being voluntarily came down from heaven, manifested himself unto his people, and then sanctified them with his blood. This is the essence of sacrifice and condescension.

Condescension as Sacrifice

The law of sacrifice was instituted with the Fall of Adam and Eve. Upon being sent forth from the garden, they were commanded to offer sacrifice (see Moses 5:5), and although they initially did not fully understand the meaning or symbolism of the law, they were obedient to its demands.[6] This relationship of sacrifice and condescension was taught when the angel asked Adam, "Why dost thou offer sacrifices?" and then instructed, "This thing is a similitude of the sacrifice of the Only Begotten of the Father, which is full of grace and truth. Wherefore, thou shalt do all that thou doest in the name of the Son, and thou shalt repent and call upon God in the name of the Son forevermore" (Moses 5:7–8). Although the angel never spoke the word *condescend*, the act he described would be the condescension of the great Creator Jehovah as Jesus Christ roughly four thousand years later.

This symbolic law of sacrifice (which utilized other items such as animals or harvest fruit as tokens wherein something was substituted in behalf of or as a reminder for another) and consecration was taught to Adam and Eve's children, who were commanded to take the firstlings of their flocks or the first fruits of their fields to make an offering unto the Lord (see Genesis 4:3–4). This same law of sacrifice was then passed from generation to generation (as Noah took seven of each of the clean animals on the ark and subsequently used them to offer sacrifices once they were safely upon the earth again) and continued through Abraham, Isaac, Jacob, and the children of Israel.[7]

The token is a physical reminder of something significant in one's life, and so the sacrifice was a type of Christ, a similitude (the likeness, representation, or imitation) of that which would come, and a shadow representing the actual offering that would be performed in the meridian of time. This idea of a burnt offering is presented to Nephi when the angel says, "Behold the Lamb of God, yea, even the Son of the Eternal Father!" (1 Nephi 11:21). As Nephi is instructed, and as we understand, "the characteristic rite was the burning of the *whole* animal on the altar (Lev. 1:9; Deut. 33:10)," representing Israel's "obligation to surrender" themselves to God.[8] Thus God's Only Begotten Son, his Lamb, would be the Father's offering on behalf of each of us.

This doctrine is especially significant because it manifests that the Father will condescend and comply with the law he has instituted upon the earth by providing a sacrifice. The Son, as the Lamb, voluntarily submitted himself to be offered upon the cross and overcame death so that he could bring all men unto him. This supreme condescension is that Jesus descended below all things by sacrificing his life so that each of us can overcome the effects of the Fall.

The only time in scriptural passages when it appeared that someone would be required to follow the Father's example in offering his own son was the command that came to Abraham to offer Isaac upon the altar, yet even there deliverance was provided (see Genesis 22:1–14). Although Adam and his posterity offered animals or first fruits in similitude of Jesus Christ, they were not required to offer their own children. This was not the case in the Father's sacrifice, or in the Son's offering in Gethsemane and Golgotha. There was no ram in the thicket for their deliverance, yet in each of our cases the Lamb has already been offered and redemption is available.

The law of sacrifice was also a significant part of the lives of Lehi and his posterity both during their time in Jerusalem and during their travels to and arrival in the promised land. This law continued to be handed down from generation to generation and was practiced here in the Americas until the time of the coming of Jesus Christ shortly after his ascension in Jerusalem.[9]

The sacrifice of Jesus Christ fulfilled the law of Moses and halted the shedding of blood but did not put an end to the requirements associated with the law of sacrifice; it just altered the manner by which sacrifice was to be rendered. The resurrected Christ taught this change during his visit to the Americas when he instructed: "And ye shall offer up unto me no more the shedding of blood; yea, your sacrifices and your burnt offerings shall be done away, for I will accept none of your sacrifices and your burnt offerings. And ye shall offer for a sacrifice unto me a broken heart and a contrite spirit. And whoso cometh unto me with a broken heart and a contrite spirit, him will I baptize with fire and with the Holy Ghost, even as the Lamanites, because of their faith in me at the time of their conversion, were baptized with fire and with the Holy Ghost, and they knew it not" (3 Nephi 9:19–20).

The infinite and atoning sacrifice had been completed. The Father had offered his Only Begotten as his Lamb upon the altar. The Savior had willingly submitted to the will of the Father by allowing himself to be taken and offered as the Lamb. The bloodshed of animals would not be required "until the sons of Levi do offer again an offering unto the Lord in righteousness" (D&C 13) as part of the dispensation of the fulness of times. The Prophet Joseph Smith taught that this latter-day offering would include an animal sacrifice, and some people also believe that the sacrifice is conversion to the gospel and acceptance of God's ordinances as found in the temple.[10] In place of animal sacrifice, all who would now be willing to make a sacrificial offering before the Lord would be expected to do so with a broken heart and a contrite spirit.

Appreciating Sacrifice and Condescension through Nephi's Vision

Many have taught how the law of sacrifice is associated with the condescension of God by emphasizing the Son's mortal ministry and experience as he descended below all things as a willing sacrifice for each of us.[11] For example, Jesus suffered "pains and afflictions and temptations of every kind, ... sicknesses, ... death, ... their infirmities, ... [and] the sins of his people" so "that his bowels may be filled with mercy" and "that he might blot out [our] transgressions according to the power of his deliverance" (Alma 7:11–13). Many have also pondered the Father's condescension and willingness to create with the chosen Mary to bring forth the Only Begotten Son.[12] Yet, even in considering these two realities, some may have never considered how the lessons taught through Nephi's vision of the condescension of the Father and the Son provide examples for us to follow in making the law of sacrifice and condescension an active and vibrant part of our daily lives.

Nephi's vision shows us that Jehovah would become the Only Begotten by being born of a mortal mother and would dwell here among the sons and daughters of God (see 1 Nephi 11:15, 20–21). The Creator of all things is one of us. In so becoming, he set an example of sacrifice and condescension that each of us could emulate during our mortal experiences. Although his capacity to overcome was greater than ours due to his immortal parentage, more was required and expected of him in his mortal sojourn. He was baptized and the Holy Ghost came upon him, but he also suffered pain, afflictions, and temptations (see 1 Nephi 11:18, 27) above that which we can suffer. Nevertheless, we can follow his example by receiving the ordinances as he did and taking upon ourselves his name. We can then do as he did in going among those who are less fortunate, and we can "bear one another's burdens, ... mourn with those that mourn, ... and comfort those that stand in need of comfort" (Mosiah 18:8–9).

Nephi learned that the Lamb of God was the Father's sacrifice. Under the Mosaic law that Nephi obeyed, the lamb was supposed to be an offering of the firstling of the flock. The sacrifice was also a type or shadow of the Atonement of the Lamb that would be offered for each of us. Nephi's vision helps us see a union of the Mosaic law of Old Testament times with the law of Christ that we would be bound by today. The Lord "offereth himself a sacrifice for sin, to answer the ends of the law" (see 2 Nephi 2:7). Consequently, we are no longer required to offer an animal sacrifice but are expected to "offer a sacrifice unto the Lord" (D&C 59:8), namely "a broken heart and a contrite spirit" (3 Nephi 9:20). We should understand that the principle of being willing to condescend in servitude and consecration is perfectly exemplified in the sacrifice and condescension of the Father's Only Begotten Son.

The sacrifice of the Son was in no way self-serving but rather self-sacrificing. Therein we are taught that in following Christ, we must be willing to do as he did and submit our wills to that of the Father. Moreover, as we gain a greater understanding of sacrifice and condescension, the clarity and beauty of the angel's seemingly simple question, "Knowest thou the condescension of God?" (1 Nephi 11:16), will enlighten our hearts with the fruits of the gospel and fill our souls with the joy spoken of by Lehi (see 1 Nephi 8:10–12). As the Spirit reveals these truths to our heart and mind, we begin to realize that much of what Nephi saw was a visual depiction of ways that Jesus's exemplary sacrifice was a pattern for us to follow by condescending and sacrificing.

Although Nephi's vision highlighted the significant points in the life of Christ (see 1 Nephi 11:13–31), the focus was on a particular event. Nephi records that he witnessed that the "Son of the everlasting God was judged of the world" and that "he was lifted up upon the cross and slain for the sins of the world" (see 1 Nephi 11:32–33). He was our offering, and his voluntary willingness to sacrifice himself was the fulfillment of the Father's plan of salvation for each of us. Therefore, we must also be willing to offer up all that we have to further the Father's work upon the earth.

Immediately after Nephi's view of "a virgin, most beautiful and fair" (1 Nephi 11:15), the angel asks, "Knowest thou the condescension of God?" (v. 16). In this question, Nephi's subsequent answer, and the follow-up instructions, we gain our first lesson of the importance of this sacrifice. Nephi states, "I know that he loveth his children; nevertheless, I do not know the meaning of all things" (v. 17). Nephi understands that God loves us, but he does not quite understand what the "condescension of God" implies. Would we answer any differently? The angel then shows and instructs Nephi about multiple facets of the condescension of God: "Behold, the virgin whom thou seest is the mother of the Son of God, after the manner of the flesh" (v. 18).

Here we find our first understanding of the condescension of God the Father, and Jehovah, his Firstborn. Elder Bruce R. McConkie of the Quorum of the Twelve Apostles elaborates, "'The condescension of God,' of which the scriptures speak, means that the Immortal Father—the glorified, exalted, enthroned ruler of the universe—came down from his station of dominion and power to become the Father of a Son who would be born of Mary, 'after the manner of the flesh' (1 Nephi 11:16–18)."[13] We also understand the condescension of Jehovah. As President Benson instructed, "When the great God of the universe condescended to be born of mortal woman, He submitted Himself to the infirmities of mortality to 'suffer temptations, and pain of body, hunger, thirst, and fatigue, even more than man can suffer, except it be unto death' (Mosiah 3:7)."[14] This special parentage would allow him to experience all of the pains and suffering associated with mortality and to voluntarily lay down his life and then take it up again in the Resurrection.

The Father's act of bringing his Son into mortality sets in place the ultimate sacrifice of the Father offering his Lamb upon the altar. The Father teaches us a very important principle regarding obedience to the law of sacrifice as he willingly offers his Son to redeem all mankind from the Fall. This Son was "the Lamb of God, yea, even the Son of the Eternal Father!" (1 Nephi 11:21). Our Heavenly Father would not expect our obedience to the law of sacrifice unless he first demonstrated his own willingness to obey the same law that he initiated.

We might be inclined to ask if this is merely a doctrine without an accompanying expectation of adherence. Would we ever be asked to sacrifice our own child as the Father has shown us? Is this example something we may be expected to follow?[15] In this mortal existence we do not have the capacity to pay for sins or redeem our fellow men through some sacrifice of our own, but we may sacrifice our time and become saviors on Mount Zion by doing temple work for those who are in need on the other side of the veil. Similarly, it would seem unrealistic to think that the Father would require any of us to sacrifice one of our children as a redemptive offering for others, first because it is impossible for us, but second because that is not part of his plan. Nevertheless, we may be required to offer all that we have for the gospel's sake.

The great plan of happiness will only require one infinite and atoning sacrifice. This is especially poignant to consider when we contemplate that "the Lamb of God . . . was taken by the people; yea, the Son of the everlasting God was judged of the world; and . . . he was lifted up upon the cross and slain for the sins of the world" (see 1 Nephi 11:32–33). The ultimate sacrifice of the Savior became evident as the Creator and Judge of the world was taken, judged, and crucified by those who were lower than him—without question a supreme act of condescension.

The Father's sacrificial offering of his Lamb upon the altar is a beautiful manifestation of his love for us and his willing condescension to submit his sacrifice as payment for our sins and transgressions. It is an impossible sacrifice that we are unable to duplicate or imitate. Not only had the Father brought his pure and sinless Son to the earth, but he also knew that this Son would be sacrificed in a most cruel and inhumane manner.

This sacrifice of the Father allows us to better understand the condescension and sacrifice of the Son. Whereas the Father created a Son to be born upon the earth, the Son would be that being who would fulfill the will of the Father, "to bring to pass the immortality and eternal life of man" (Moses 1:39). Nephi introduces us to the Savior's condescension when he sees in vision the "child" in the arms of Mary (see 1 Nephi 11:20), followed by his "going forth among the children of men" (1 Nephi 11:24), and then we see that the "Redeemer of the world . . . went forth and was baptized" (1 Nephi 11:27) and then "went forth ministering unto the people, . . . and they cast him out from among them" (1 Nephi 11:28). This brief treatise on the life of Christ beautifully describes how his condescension into mortality provides him with the understanding and compassion necessary to fulfill his role as our Righteous Judge.[16] He has lived a mortal life, was obedient to gospel law by being baptized, and then went about for the rest of his life fulfilling the will of his Father.

A secondary feature of Jesus Christ's condescension is explained in the following verses as Nephi observed: "I beheld the Lamb of God going forth among the children of men. And I beheld multitudes of people who were sick, and who were afflicted with all manner of diseases, and with devils and unclean spirits; and the angel spake and showed all these things unto me. And they were healed by the power of the Lamb of God; and the devils and the unclean spirits were cast out" (1 Nephi 11:31). The Savior went among those who were the cast off and afflicted of the earth; he ministered unto them, thereby setting an example for us to follow. Yet, even in providing this example, the depth of his offering was beyond that which we can comprehend.

Amulek, a great testator in the Book of Mormon, explains, "For it is expedient that an atonement should be made; for according to the great plan of the Eternal God there must be an atonement made, or else all mankind must unavoidably perish; yea, all are hardened; yea, all are fallen and are lost, and must perish except it be through the atonement which it is expedient should be made. For it is expedient that there should be a great and last sacrifice; yea, not a sacrifice of man, neither of beast, neither of any manner of fowl; for it shall not be a human sacrifice; but it must be an infinite and eternal sacrifice" (Alma 34:9–10).

Bishop Richard C. Edgley expounded upon Amulek's words as he clarified: "It had to be infinite, covering all transgression, all suffering, and it had to be eternal—applying to all mankind from the infinite beginning to the endless end. No, it could not be a sacrifice of man, beast, or fowl. It had to be a sacrifice of a God, even God the Creator, God the Redeemer. He had to condescend from godhood to mortality, and in mortality to sacrificial lamb. His gift of redemption, through His condescension, necessitated His suffering, exquisite pain, and humiliation."[17] All that he did was in subjection to the will of the Father, not out of requirement but out of obedience, love, and humility. The Son desired that the Father's will would become his own and the glory would be his Father's.

The Son of God condescended from his throne on high to come to the earth in order to serve all mankind, but even more to sacrifice and consecrate all that he had to his Father and to each of us in need of spiritual and physical deliverance. Jesus went to the sick, afflicted, diseased, and possessed, and he delivered them from their various forms of suffering. He delivers us from the sting of the grave and from the pains of sin, affliction, temptation, and sickness (see Alma 7:11–13). His example establishes that if he who is our Lord and our King would descend from his place of glory and honor and would condescend to be judged and crucified by us, all in order to serve and save us, we should be willing to do the same for our fellowmen. Part of the mark of discipleship is that we look beyond the outward appearance and serve in a similar manner as the Savior served us.

Prophetic instruction helps us to gain a partial understanding of the depth of the sacrifice and condescension that was made on our behalf. In *Lectures on Faith*, the Prophet Joseph Smith taught that one reason Jesus Christ is called the Son of God is because he "descended in suffering below that which man can suffer; or, in other words, suffered greater sufferings, and was exposed to more powerful contradictions than any man can be."[18] Isaiah further explained: "He is despised and rejected of men; a man of sorrows, and acquainted with grief: and we hid as it were our faces from him; he was despised, and we esteemed him not. Surely he hath borne our griefs, and carried our sorrows: yet we did esteem him stricken, smitten of God, and afflicted. But he was wounded for our transgressions, he was bruised for our iniquities: the chastisement of our peace was upon him; and with his stripes we are healed" (Isaiah 53:3–5). We may be smitten, bruised, or wounded for the cause of Christ, but we are not suffering for someone else's sins. We still have the Savior and the Father on our side, whereas Christ suffered alone for us and because of us.

Bishop Richard C. Edgley helps us realize that Jesus' offering for us was born of his love for us:

> His condescension is an integral, necessary, and inseparable part of the Atonement. The Atonement itself was predicated upon His willingness to descend and suffer. His condescension, as part of the Atonement, is probably as essential to the redemption of mankind as was His suffering in the Garden of Gethsemane or on the cross. His Atonement was a free gift to all mankind—a gift that could be obtained no other way. It resulted from His willingness to descend. He descended not because of obligation, nor for glory, but only for love. His condescension to redeem us through the Atonement was the price He paid to provide salvation and exaltation.[19]

Nephi's vision of the tree of life, more especially of the Savior's life, helps us to see and understand what it means to condescend and sacrifice in fulfillment of a covenant. The Father's plan provided for a Redeemer, and fulfillment of the covenant in that plan comes in the form of Jesus Christ. The sick, afflicted, diseased, and possessed "were healed by the power of the Lamb of God" (1 Nephi 11:31). Jesus ministered to those we might be inclined to shun because of their afflicted state. We then see that even after blessing these infirmed "he was taken by the people; yea, the Son of the everlasting God was judged of the world" and was then "lifted up upon the cross and slain for the sins of the world" (vv. 32–33). He was not guilty. He had not committed any sin. He was perfect, pure, and undefiled, yet in the very act of serving and saving he was judged as a thing of naught, cast aside, and crucified.

Applying Christ's Example of Sacrifice and Condescension

The preceding perspectives of the condescension of Christ are masterful examples that each of us can strive to follow, except for taking upon ourselves the sins and suffering of others. Everything we have comes from God, so we are all equally dependent upon the mercy and grace of the Father and the

Son. We are not their equals; they obviously are superior to each of us. Yet they serve us! And now, as disciples of the Lord Jesus Christ, we must learn to serve others as Christ served us.

Jesus' example of serving others is one everyone can follow to some degree. We can sacrifice the things of the world for the things of God and we can submit our will to his, but it must be voluntary on our part. King Lamoni's father expressed part of our offering quite succinctly when he said, "I will give away all my sins to know thee" (Alma 22:18). Elder Neal A. Maxwell similarly taught, "The submission of one's will is really the only uniquely personal thing we have to place on God's altar."[20]

We may sacrifice one to two years of time with our children as they (or we) serve missions. We may give up family relationships as we accept the gospel of Jesus Christ and choose to leave families behind. Leaders of the Church have sacrificed their lives in the service of this latter-day work. Someone may even give up their life to save the life of another, as exemplified by "greater love hath no man than this, that a man lay down his life for his friends" (John 15:13). As we willingly sacrifice for others, our insights increase and we better comprehend the sacrifice of Christ.

Elder Quentin L. Cook taught, "The Savior also emphasized love and unity and declared that we would be known as His disciples if we have love one to another. In the face of the eternity-shaping Atonement He was about to undertake, such a commandment requires our obedience." He further explained, "We manifest our love for God when we keep His commandments and serve His children. We don't fully comprehend the Atonement, but we can spend our lives trying to be more loving and kind, regardless of the adversity we face."[21] We see that there is an expectation that if we are true disciples of the Savior, we will serve Father's children, even in the face of our own personal adversity and challenges. In striving to be more loving and kind, our very actions manifest that we are trying to emulate the Savior as much as is humanly possible. Elder Maxwell taught, "The only true veneration of Jesus is emulation of Him."[22] To venerate is to worship, revere, respect, and admire, and to emulate is to imitate, follow, or copy. In other words, as disciples of Christ, our daily actions indicate the depth of our admiration for him.

When we consider the Savior's life while applying the lessons of sacrifice and condescension in our life, we see that in his invitation to become his disciples and to take his name upon ourselves, we are then expected to act as he would act. When we become his disciples, we must then be willing to "bear one another's burdens," "mourn with those that mourn," "comfort those that stand in need of comfort," and "stand as witnesses of God at all times and in all things, and in all places that ye may be in, even until death" (see Mosiah 18:8–10). As disciples of Jesus Christ, even in our weakest conditions, we too may offer all that we have in the service of others because of our love for our Father and for his children.

Elder Maxwell further helped us to understand the principles of sacrifice, condescension, and consecration when he taught: "Consecration is thus both a principle and a process, and it is not tied to a single moment. Instead, it is freely given, drop by drop, until the cup of consecration brims and finally runs over. Long before that, however, as Jesus declared, we must 'settle this in [our] hearts' that we will do what He asks of us (JST, Luke 14:28)."[23] Our willingness to follow the Savior is a process, and during the course of our lives what we do on a daily basis is the manifestation of the level of consecration and sacrifice we maintain. In our service to others, we also manifest our own willingness to condescend to whatever level may be required by the Father or the Son.

Elder Cook continued this explanation of discipleship:

> The Savior's charge to His disciples to love one another—and the dramatic and powerful way He taught this principle at the Last Supper—is one of the most poignant and beautiful episodes from the last days of His mortal life.
>
> He was not teaching a simple class in ethical behavior. This was the Son of God pleading with His Apostles and all disciples who would come after them to remember and follow this most central of His teachings. How we relate and interact with each other is a measure of our willingness to follow Jesus Christ.[24]

We should notice by now that if we are true disciples of Christ, our willingness to follow him in all that we do is a manifestation of our offering our wills upon the altar. We may not be able to offer ourselves as an offering for sin but we can surely provide relief and succor to those who are facing the challenges of life, even at the peril of our own life.

For example, the Apostle Peter taught us of servitude and discipleship by saying, "For even hereunto were ye called: because Christ also suffered for us, *leaving us an example, that ye should follow his steps*" (1 Peter 2:21; emphasis added). Mormon similarly taught, "If it so be that ye believe in Christ, and are baptized, first with water, then with fire and with the Holy Ghost, *following the example of our Savior*, according to that which he hath commanded us, it shall be well with you in the day of judgment" (Mormon 7:10; emphasis added). In each of these examples, there is an expectation that discipleship will lead to obeying and following the example of Christ, not merely expressing lip service.

Latter-day Lives of Consecration and Sacrifice

Although we are incapable of literally placing ourselves on the altar as an offering for sin, we can present ourselves before the Lord by voluntarily offering our will to him. Elder Neal A. Maxwell explained: "The submission of one's will is really the only uniquely personal thing we have to place on God's altar. The many other things we 'give,' brothers and sisters, are actually the things He has already given or loaned to us. However, when you and I finally submit ourselves, by letting our individual wills be swallowed up in God's will, then we are really giving something to Him! It is the only possession which is truly ours to give! Consecration thus constitutes the only unconditional surrender which is also a total victory!"[25] The sacrifice of self is manifested by following his example and by becoming as he is (see 3 Nephi 27:27).

It is in the act of consecration, by which we dedicate all that we have, or are, to the Lord and to furthering his work here upon the earth, where we display how devoted we are to doing what the Lord requires of us. Interestingly enough, to consecrate is to give to,[26] yet in the giving we often receive a stewardship over what we have just given and what we are now using. If I have given my life to Christ, I understand my stewardship in doing all that I can to further his work here upon the earth. In other words, I do as he did and submit my will to his. In contrast, to sacrifice is to give up,[27] and generally we will no longer have the thing we have sacrificed. The Lord truly expects us to be willing to enter into covenants to do both, sacrifice and consecrate.

It may be necessary for us to sacrifice all that we possess (see 1 Nephi 2:2, 4), even our families (see Matthew 10:37; see also D&C 122:6) or our lives (see Mosiah 18:10; see also D&C 122:7) in pursuit, or defense, of the cause of Christ. Or, we may be required to consecrate our lives in furthering the cause of Christ against those who may fight against "the twelve apostles of the Lamb" (1 Nephi 11:34–36), "Zion and the covenant people of the Lord" (2 Nephi 6:13), or "God and the people of his church" (2 Nephi 25:14). Whether it be sacrificing or consecrating, we may even find ourselves condescending into circumstances of poverty, pestilence, or plague where we normally would never think to pass (as missionaries in the mission field do on occasion) in order to demonstrate our devotion to emulating the example of our Savior Jesus Christ.

Consider this powerful promise from President Lorenzo Snow: "Our future is glorious. We could not desire more for our happiness than has been prepared for us. Those who endure unto the end shall sit upon thrones, as Jesus hath overcome and sat down upon His Father's throne. All things shall be given unto such men and women, so we are told in the revelations we have received. In view of these prospects, what should we not be willing to sacrifice when duty requires?"[28] Bishop Keith B. McMullin similarly taught, "As the literal offspring of God and being born of a mortal mother, the premortal Christ became the Only Begotten of the Father in the flesh. Though the fulness of His majesty, messiahship, and godhood came not at first, He 'continued from grace to grace, until he received a fulness,' and so can we."[29] As these quotes suggest, we are to follow the example of Jesus Christ, and in doing so we may be "joint-heirs with Christ; if so be that we suffer with *him*, that we may be also glorified together" (Romans 8:17). It is through this process of learning about his sacrifice and condescension and following his example that we may receive all that the Father has, even as Jesus Christ has done.

Essentially, Nephi's vision of the tree of life teaches us important truths that pertain to our desire to become disciples of Jesus Christ. We must be willing to do all that the Lord would ask of us. We must voluntarily walk in whatever paths Jesus would have us go. And we must be willing to condescend and sacrifice to whatever levels he would ask of us in order to manifest that we truly desire to follow him. We must ultimately strive to be "perfect, even as [he], or your Father who is in heaven is perfect" (3 Nephi 12:48). This is possible because he who "descended below all things" (D&C 88:6) has also made it possible to ascend above all things and to become even as He is.

Notes

1. For Adam and Eve's partaking of the fruit, see Moses 4:23–31; for the consequences of partaking of the fruit, see Moses 4:28–31; 1 Nephi 15:22–36; 2 Nephi 2:18–25; Alma 12:21–26; 42:2–6; Revelation 2:7; 22:2, 14; for our renewed partaking of the fruit, see Alma 5:62 along with our understanding in 1 Nephi 11:25 that the tree of life was a representation of the love of God.
2. http://www.etymonline.com/index.php?search=sacrifice&searchmode=none.
3. http://dictionary.reference.com/browse/condescend.
4. Ezra Taft Benson, "Five Marks of the Divinity of Jesus Christ," *New Era*, December 1980, 45.
5. The United Nations, World Health Organization, International Red Cross, Catholic Relief Services, Mormon Helping Hands, and Amnesty International are a small sampling of worldwide organizations that help relieve suffering.
6. Moses 5:4–7 helps us understand that Adam and Eve were separated from God's presence and the subsequent offering that they made was a test of their obedience to what they had now been commanded to do, especially in view of the fact that they had previously received commands in the garden and had chosen to transgress the law of God.
7. For a few of the many times the people offered sacrifice, see Genesis 7:2–3 and Hebrews 11:4 (Abel and Cain); Moses 6:3 (Seth); Genesis 8:20 (Noah); Genesis 12:7–8; 15:8–17; 22:2–13; and Hebrews 11:17 (Abraham and Isaac); see also Abraham 2:17–18 for Abraham's offering that the famine could be taken from his people and the land; Genesis 31:54; 35:1, 7 (Jacob), 46:1 (Israel); Exodus 10:25; 20:24–26 (Moses and the children of Israel); Leviticus 1; 1 Chronicles 6:49 (Aaron and his sons); Joshua 8:30 (Joshua); 1 Samuel 14:35 (Saul); 1 Kings 9:25 (Solomon); Numbers 23:1–2 (Balak and Balaam).
8. See LDS Bible Dictionary, "Sacrifices," 766.
9. See 1 Nephi 5:9 (Lehi upon the safe return of his sons from Jerusalem); 1 Nephi 7:22 (Lehi and Ishmael and their families upon joining together on the journey); Mosiah 2:3 (King Benjamin).
10. See *Teachings of the Prophet Joseph Smith*, comp. Joseph Fielding Smith (Salt Lake City: Deseret Book, 1976), 172–73; Joseph Fielding McConkie and Craig J. Ostler, *Revelations on the Restoration* (Salt Lake City: Deseret Book, 2000), 120; Joseph Fielding Smith, "Restoration of Blood Sacrifices" (Salt Lake City: Deseret Book, 1957–63), 3:94.
11. See Jeffrey R. Holland, "Broken Things to Mend," *Ensign*, May 2006, 69–71; Neal A. Maxwell, "'Plow in Hope,'" *Ensign*, May 2001, 59; David B. Haight, "The Sacrament—and the Sacrifice," *Ensign*, November 1989, 59.
12. See Richard C. Edgley, "'The Condescension of God,'" *Ensign*, December 2001, 16; Bruce R. McConkie, "Behold the Condescension of God," *New Era*, December 1984, 35; Richard D. Draper, "The Book of Mormon on Christ's Role as Redeemer," *Ensign*, January 2000, 7; Robert D. Hales, "In Remembrance of Jesus," *Ensign*, November 1997, 24; Merrill J. Bateman, "A Season for Angels," *Ensign*, December 2007, 10–15; and D&C 88:6.

13. Bruce R. McConkie, *A New Witness for the Articles of Faith* (Salt Lake City: Deseret Book, 1985), 111.

14. Benson, "Five Marks," 45.

15. Jesus set an example by being baptized by John and then taught that all men must be baptized in order to enter the kingdom of God (see John 3:5). He also instructed his disciples that they should go into all the world and preach his gospel as he had done (see Mark 16:15; see also Mormon 9:22). The expectation was that they would follow his example.

16. See Alma 7:11–13 for further scriptural evidence of how the mortal life of Christ endowed him with power over and comprehension of the trials, temptations, and adversity we would each face as part of our own mortal experience.

17. Richard C. Edgley, "'The Condescension of God,'" *Ensign*, December 2001, 16.

18. Joseph Smith, comp., *Lectures on Faith* (Salt Lake City: Deseret Book, 1985), 59.

19. Edgley, "'Condescension of God,'" 16.

20. Neal A. Maxwell, "Insights from My Life," *Ensign*, August 2000, 9.

21. Quentin L. Cook, "We Follow Jesus Christ," *Ensign*, May 2010, 84.

22. Quoted in "Elder Neal Ash Maxwell: A Promise Fulfilled," *Ensign*, September 2004, 12.

23. Neal A. Maxwell, "'Swallowed Up in the Will of the Father,'" *Ensign*, November 1995, 22.

24. Cook, "We Follow Jesus Christ," 84.

25. Maxwell, "'Swallowed Up in the Will of the Father,'" 22.

26. "Consecrate: *dedicated to* a sacred purpose," http://mw4.merriam-webster.com/dictionary/consecrate; emphasis added.

27. "Sacrifice: an act of *offering to* a deity something precious; . . . something offered in sacrifice; . . . something *given up* or lost," http://mw4.merriam-webster.com/dictionary/sacrifice; emphasis added.

28. Lorenzo Snow, in Conference Report, October 1898, 55–56.

29. Keith B. McMullin, "Jesus, the Very Thought of Thee," *Ensign*, May 2004, 33.

19

"It Filled My Soul with Exceedingly Great Joy": Lehi's Vision of Teaching and Learning

Charles Swift

There is much discussion about education these days, ranging from "What is the best way to teach?" to something even more fundamental: "What is education itself? What does it mean to teach, and what does it mean to learn?" This paper will explore Lehi's vision of the tree of life as a model of teaching and learning. In studying this vision with such a purpose in mind, I will explore a pattern of ritualistic initiation in the vision and how it relates to the idea of teaching and learning as experiential acts. Taking a close look at some of the symbolic elements of the initiatory experiences in the vision can help us better understand the teaching and learning that occurs and apply that understanding to education today. When applying this knowledge, I will primarily rely on the writings of Parker Palmer, one of the most well respected scholars writing about teaching and learning today.[1] His emphasis on the spiritual elements of teaching and learning will help us understand the implications the tree of life vision may have for education.

Author and anthropologist Joan Halifax notes that the Western approach to teaching and learning holds that "the word *education* means 'to be

---

Charles Swift is an associate professor of ancient scripture at Brigham Young University.

led out of ignorance into knowing and knowledge.' Learning is described in terms of the accumulation of facts."[2] There is another way to view teaching and learning, however: the idea of education as rooted in experience, particularly ritual experience. As Halifax points out, there is a "wide variety of forms and styles" of ritual learning in cultures that practice it, but "the most important context of learning occurs in the ritual process of initiation, known as *rites of passage*." She continues by discussing three stages associated with initiation, as formulated by Arnold Van Gennep: (1) separation, in which an individual moves away from the familiar social landscape into something or somewhere unknown; (2) "the threshold experience," in which the individual experiences liminality,[3] a transformative time when "myth and story unfold and where love and death become amplified for the initiate," and "when the initiate learns to bear witness, to be present for all dimensions of reality"; and (3) incorporation, "the movement back into the everyday world, a time of healing, of making whole again," in which the individual is brought back into normal society as a changed, transformed person, ready to accept the new duties or responsibilities such transformation has brought about.[4] Richard Dilworth Rust, a scholar who writes about the Book of Mormon as a literary testimony, sees a similar phenomenon in God's interaction with man as described in the Book of Mormon: "Many of the characteristics of God's ways pertain to thresholds—or, to use a word derived from *limen*, the Latin word for *threshold*, they are *liminal*."[5] As we shall see, Lehi participates in such a process of experiential learning in his vision of the tree of life.

It is essential to this discussion to remember that we are talking about a ritual experience *as it occurs in a vision or dream*. If we wished to explore the vision within the context of Lehi's actual, physical life at that time, we could argue that the rite of separation occurs when he and his family flee Jerusalem and enter the wilderness, that the threshold experience is the vision itself, and that the incorporation is when he comes back from the vision and tries to spiritually heal his family. However, since we are discussing this initiation ritual as experienced in a vision or dream, we need to remember that each stage—separation, threshold experience, and incorporation—occur through Lehi's role as a receiver of the vision. If we were to claim, for example, that Lehi never actually experienced the separation stage because, most likely, he was with his family in their camp while he was having the vision, we would miss the point that this discussion is about what symbolically happens in the vision, not in the physical world.

Lehi's Separation Stage

Lehi's separation stage is at the beginning of the vision, when he moves away from the known world and is separated, finding himself in a dark and dreary wilderness. Here Lehi is faced with the "unfamiliar, the unknown." He is confronted by what he does not know and is eventually left alone to find his way toward the meaning of his experience.

The wilderness and the man in the white robe. The Book of Mormon portrays Lehi as a caring, loving father. We also know him to be a good husband, leader, and prophet of God.[6] But he also plays another role in the Book of Mormon that we do not often speak of: he is a model teacher who is constantly learning and teaching. In his vision of the tree of life, he is a humble learner, listening to the man in the white robe and following him, and a bold teacher, sharing what he has learned rather than merely keeping the benefit to himself.

The first image Lehi sees in his vision is one of darkness: "For behold, methought I saw in my dream, a dark and dreary wilderness" (1 Nephi 8:4). In a religious context, darkness symbolizes "a silencing of prophetic revelation" and "the state of the human mind unilluminated by God's revelation."[7] In our context of teaching and learning, darkness represents "ignorance"[8] and "the unknown."[9] It is significant that it is not just any place that is dark and dreary, but a wilderness. In scripture, such wilderness is a "spiritual as much as a physical testing ground,"[10] "any place in which the people are tested, tried, proven, refined by trials, taught grace, and prepared to meet the Lord."[11] Since Lehi and his family have not yet made their journey to the New World, it is highly likely that the wilderness he sees in his vision is a desert.[12]

This dark and dreary wilderness becomes a classroom of sorts for Lehi. At this point, he is symbolically alone with his awareness of his own ignorance—of his need to learn. In his vision, he is separated from others and beginning his initiation, confronted with how much he does not know.

Next, Lehi sees a man dressed in a white robe. Significantly, in biblical symbolism, white is not set opposite to black but rather to darkness,[13] making it the perfect symbolic color for the man in the robe to wear. The color symbolizes "purity, chastity, innocence, spotlessness, and . . . peace,"[14] as well as "timelessness."[15] More than any other color, white "has been associated with religious devotion since the days of ancient Egypt." The reason white has been used in devotion so much is because it represents "spiritual purity and chastity of thought."[16] "White" is not the only word in this verse that carries symbolic importance. The term "robe" is also symbolic, representing a "godly, upright character,"[17] and a white robe can symbolize "innocence, virtue."[18] The fact that Lehi's guide appears dressed in a white robe is of tremendous symbolic importance.[19]

The man in the white robe can be a symbol of a number of things. He can be seen as representing the Holy Spirit in that he acts as a guide to the prophet. He may be considered a type of Christ in that he redeems him from the fallen dark and dreary world by taking him to a place that can offer salvation.[20] There is yet another individual that the man in the white robe represents: the teacher. "The most important thing a teacher can do," writes Elder Gene R. Cook, "is to help the student feel the Spirit of the Lord. If the Spirit is there, true teaching and true learning will take place, and lives will begin to be changed."[21] Often the role of the teacher is to speak, to teach through words, but sometimes the role requires little speaking at all. Whether the man in the white robe said much or not, however, what he did was the act of a great teacher. The man was a guide for Lehi, and, as BYU professor (and current Sunday School general president for the Church) Russell T. Osguthorpe writes, to be "an effective guide one must possess two attributes: (1) knowledge of the terrain, and (2) knowledge of the traveler."[22] He did not simply tell Lehi where he needed to go, nor did he go for him, but he guided the prophet to the place he needed to be. The fact that he knew where Lehi needed to go implies that he had "knowledge of the traveler" and not just the terrain.

Counterintuitively, this teacher in the white robe does not deliver Lehi from the dark and dreary wilderness to the open field; after following the man, Lehi finds himself in "a dark and dreary waste."[23] In effect, the man does not take Lehi to where Lehi would probably want to go, but instead takes him to the place the prophet needed to be to continue his journey.

Teachers who guide their students develop the trust necessary for true teaching and learning to happen. "Because our guide accompanies us on our journey, we develop a trust in one another that always comes when we are seeking truth. Our guide is not there to dispense truth but to show us the way to find it—knowing all the while that because truth is intimate, we shall each come to know it in our own way."[24] If we accept the fact that it is the Spirit who teaches, then an important part of the guide's job is to bring us to a point where we can be taught by the Spirit, who will then help us to come to know in our own way. As Elder Cook teaches: "I suspect we sometimes think that if we don't convey all the information we have on a subject, those we teach won't learn what they need to know. But I would suggest a different perspective. As we develop greater trust in the Lord, we will know that if we can bring the Spirit into a teaching situation, that Spirit will help the other person to learn and know what is most essential."[25]

The man in the white robe taught Lehi more by teaching less.[26] So far as we know, he did not lecture Lehi about the Savior, nor did he even talk to him about the symbol of the tree of life. In fact, he did not even do so much as take him to the tree. He simply helped Lehi get to a point, as a student, where he could do what he needed to do in order to learn. What Lehi is about to learn in this vision is at the very core of what he needs to know—it is the single truth by which he will understand the universe. It is the gospel of Jesus Christ at its most simple and sublime: the Savior, his Atonement, and the life we must lead to come unto him.

Solitude. Since there is no longer any mention of the man in the white robe, it is reasonable to conclude that Lehi traveled for many hours in darkness alone and is alone when he begins to pray. The man in the white robe does not abandon his student but purposefully leaves him in solitude—a state that is significant to learning. This scene from Lehi's vision is not a random occurrence without importance. "Scriptural *journeys* often symbolize man's earthly walk from birth through the spiritual wildernesses of a fallen world (see Ether 6:4–7 for the ocean allegory of man's journey; see also 1 Nephi 8 for the *path* leading to the tree of life)."[27] The image of "the lone wanderer lost in the darkness" is the most common one to "haunt the early Arab poets" and "is the standard nightmare of the Arab." In fact, "it is the supreme boast of every poet that he has traveled long distances through dark and dreary wastes all alone."[28] It is clear why this experience in the dark wilderness, alone, would be sufficient to cause Lehi to turn to the Lord in prayer.

Lehi's finding himself in several hours of solitude in his vision contributes significantly to this rite of separation. This experience can often contribute to one's learning; as Palmer notes, "If knowledge allows us to receive the world as it is, solitude allows us to receive ourselves as we are. If silence gives us knowledge of the world, solitude gives us knowledge of ourselves."[29]

This image of Lehi traveling alone for many hours presents a number of questions: Why did the man in the white robe leave—or, did Lehi leave him? Why did Lehi travel in darkness for so long? What did Lehi do during all those hours? The answer to each of these questions may lie in the meaning of such a pilgrimage. This journey, consisting of only thirteen words, serves as a necessary preparation for his prayer. "The point of requiring people to undertake the journeys in the Book of Mormon is to make it possible for them to have experiences that drive them to their extremity, at which point they discover the delivering power of God."[30] Lehi's experience in the dark waste helps prepare him not only for his prayer but ultimately for his coming to the tree of life.

Lehi's Threshold Experience Stage

Lehi's threshold stage, when he undergoes a liminal experience that transforms him, occurs when he partakes of the fruit of the tree of life. If we keep in mind what we learn from Nephi's vision about what Lehi saw, this is definitely a time in which Lehi sees the "myth and story unfold" as "love and death become amplified" through his partaking of the fruit and witnessing the life and death of the Son of God (see 1 Nephi 10:11). During this stage the prophet "learns to bear witness, to be present for all dimensions of reality" represented in the following symbolic principles incorporated in the dream.

The tree of life. Lehi sees the tree of life, "whose fruit was desirable to make one happy" (1 Nephi 8:10). The tree is a significant archetype in literature and culture. "The sacredness of trees and plants is so firmly and deeply rooted in almost every phase and aspect of religious and magico-religious phenomena that it has become an integral and a recurrent feature in one form or another at all times and in most states of culture, ranging from the Tree of Life to the May-pole."[31] The tree has played an important symbolic role in many cultures throughout the world.[32]

We can see another dimension of the meaning of the tree of life by looking at part of the vision Nephi experienced when he wanted to see what his father saw. When Nephi wonders about the meaning of the tree of life, he is immediately shown Mary and the birth of the Son of God (see 1 Nephi 11:9–22). Nephi understands by what he sees that the tree represents the love of God, but it is also clear that the love of God is personified in the Savior. "We need to read this in connection with other statements made by the prophets, e.g., 'God is love; and he that dwelleth in love dwelleth in God, and God in him' (1 John 4:16). That is to say, 'the love of God' spoken of by Nephi relates readily to Jesus Christ, the great exemplar of love, and thus we may think of the tree as a symbol of the Savior."[33]

Truth. Understanding the tree of life as a symbol of the Lord is crucial to understanding the idea of teaching and learning in ritual that can be conveyed through this vision. The Savior is "the way, the truth, and the life" (John 14:6), and education is the pursuit of truth. If the Savior is truth, and the tree of life is a symbol for the Savior, then the tree of life can also be a symbol for truth. The way in which Lehi interacts with the tree of life teaches us how to teach and learn—how to interact with truth. We come to know the Savior as truth not by objectifying him but by entering a relationship with him.[34] Lehi does not objectify the tree of life but enters into a relationship with it—first by seeing it and admiring its fruit and then by partaking of the fruit. It is easy to become so familiar with the vision of the tree of life and with what people would actually do in "real life" if they were to come upon a tree bearing fruit that looks delicious that we assume that what happened in the vision is the only thing that could have happened. The point, though, is that this is a vision—*it is not real life*. We may eat fruit because we are hungry or because the fruit looks good; there is usually no deeper meaning to the act. In a vision full of symbolism, however, we need to ask ourselves if even the most common of acts is intended to teach us something more deeply. Considering what *could have* happened illuminates the importance of what *did* happen. Lehi does not make the tree the object of his analytical study. He does not break off a leaf or piece of fruit and dissect it. He does not pull out a knife and scrape away at the bark to study it or analyze what is underneath it. Nor does he cut the tree down in an attempt to construct something out of it. It would have made an interesting, highly symbolic story if Lehi had crafted the tree into an altar on which he could offer sacrifices to God. Or he could have incorporated the tree's lumber into the boat he and his family would sail in during their journey to the promised land. Perhaps the tree could have even remained intact as the mast. In each of these scenarios, Lehi would have been objectifying the tree. Instead, however, he becomes one with it—just as we are to become one with the Lord and not try to objectify him.

If we are to learn about learning from the vision of the tree of life, we must appreciate the personal nature of the experience Lehi had with it. Lehi had a deep, intimate experience with truth, and it filled his soul with joy. It was a paradoxical moment of solitude (not even his wife or children were present) and ultimate communion. Just as in the physical world, where people enter into a type of relationship with their food when they partake of it, Lehi enters into a relationship with the tree and its fruit when he partakes of the fruit. The fruit, and by extension the tree, becomes a part of Lehi. Spiritually speaking, this act helps Lehi and the Lord become one. Lehi's partaking of the tree of life becomes a type of sacramental act—the sacrament being the ultimate experience of partaking of food and becoming one: "He that eateth my flesh, and drinketh my blood," the Savior said, "dwelleth in me, and I in him" (John 6:56).

Palmer offers us an approach to education that is spiritual in nature: "*To teach is to create a space in which obedience to truth is practiced.*"[35] Teaching and learning involve a relationship—a covenantal relationship. Palmer explains that the English word "truth" comes from a Germanic root that also gives us the word "troth." When you pledge your troth (as in *betrothed*), you enter into a covenantal relationship of mutual trust and faith: "Truthful knowing weds the knower and the known."[36] While this relationship with truth may make sense to a religious person who might see the Savior as truth, it is not limited to that perspective. The ultimate relationship is with the ultimate truth, naturally, but teaching and learning are about relationships with truth at all levels. Such relationships grow and develop naturally; they are not coerced.

Lehi's Incorporation Stage

Lehi's incorporation stage, in which there is "the movement back into the everyday world," begins when Lehi sees his family and beckons them to partake of the fruit. This is a "time of healing, of making whole again." He is no longer separated but is once again part of the society of his family.

After Lehi partakes of the fruit, he sees his family and asks them to come to him and partake of the fruit as well.[37] The righteous members of his family—Sariah, Nephi, and Sam—come and partake, while Laman and Lemuel, his unrighteous sons, do not. When he invites his family to partake of the fruit, Lehi is entering into the incorporation stage of his initiation. He is returning to society as a transformed person. It is important to keep in mind, as I mentioned earlier, that we are discussing a vision and that he returns to society in the context of his vision. He is not returning to the society of the Arab world in which his family exists historically; he is returning in his vision to the society of his family after the separation stage of having followed the man in the white robe and then being by himself for a number of hours. Lehi is still on his journey, but this journey has changed significantly. He has transformed from learner to teacher/learner. He teaches his family by inviting them to partake of the fruit, but he continues to learn as he observes who in his family accepts his invitation and who rejects it.

One of the amazing aspects of Lehi's calling to his family is how little is said.[38] According to the record that we have, Lehi simply invited his family to come and partake of the fruit. He may have told them that it was desirable above all other fruit, or that may have just been his repeated description of the fruit in his narrative. In any case, he says very little, inviting but not commanding or requiring. "He could not and would not force them."[39] He does not describe the tree, nor does he explain why the fruit is so good—he just asks them to come to him and eat the fruit. Interestingly, this is also the way in which the man in the white robe taught Lehi: there was no lecture; he just asked Lehi to follow him. Lehi allows his family to enter into a relationship with the tree of life instead of making himself the gate they must enter through to gain what he has gained.

This is a mark of a good teacher. Lehi does not make himself the subject of what is to be learned, nor does he draw attention to himself rather than to the subject. True, he invites his family to come to him—not to listen to him but to partake of the fruit. He is standing right next to the tree (as far as we know), but it is the fruit he wants to get into those he loves, not his words or observations. Palmer speaks of this difference. In an academic culture that frames the debate as between being teacher-centered or student-centered, he argues for being centered on the subject, as Lehi was. "Passion for the subject propels that subject," he writes, "not the teacher, into the center of the learning circle—and when a great thing is in their midst, students have direct access to the energy of learning and of life."[40] The issue at hand is not what technique is used but how the teacher views the act of teaching. A teacher-centered teacher can still divide the class into groups, just as a student-centered teacher might lecture. A subject-centered teacher, however, will focus on how to help the students gather around the subject and learn, allowing the best technique for any given time to flow from the subject. Such a teacher lectures when that is what will best help everyone learn from the subject and does group work when that is best.

This marks the end of Lehi's incorporation stage. He has returned to the society of his family. It is a time of being made whole, since the family is together again, and a time of healing, since some of his family partake of the fruit. However, it is not without pain, since Laman and Lemuel refuse to partake. Lehi is a transformed person because of his liminal experience of partaking of the fruit, and he is ready to live his life in harmony with that experience. Yet the dream is not over with Lehi's personal transformation. Instead the dream now reveals the same pattern but on a larger scale, where instead of just Lehi, it is now every man who will go through the pattern.

Transition

The next two verses of the vision (1 Nephi 8:19–20) comprise what I consider to be a transition. Though there are different ways of viewing this part of the vision, I see this point as being between the end of the Lehi's incorporation stage and the beginning of the multitudes' separation stage. These transition verses introduce two key elements of the vision: the rod of iron and the path. They become significant components of the separation stage for the multitudes.

The rod of iron. After his experience with his family, Lehi sees the rod of iron that "extended along the bank of the river" and "led to the tree by which [he] stood" (1 Nephi 8:19). This rod is an important symbol in the vision and can have a number of different interpretations. Even Nephi's idea that the rod of iron represents the word of God (see 1 Nephi 15:23–24) can be interpreted on different levels. Taken at the most apparent level, the rod of iron represents the scriptures and other words from God: "The rod of iron is a representation of the 'word of God' (1 Ne. 15:23–24). During the millennial era, Jesus will rule the nations with an iron rod, or with the word of God (Rev. 19:15)."[41] However, I think a more meaningful interpretation of the rod of iron is that it is a type of Christ, who is *the* Word of God (see John 1:1–5). It is significant that Nephi understands that the rod of iron is the word of God when he observes, in vision, the Lord in his mortal ministry (see 1 Nephi 11:24–25).

Because the rod of iron is one of the most prevalent and easily remembered symbols in Lehi's vision, it is easy to forget that he had not seen any rod until much later in his vision. Lehi follows the man in the white robe, wanders in the wilderness, sees the field, approaches the tree, partakes of the fruit, sees his family, invites them to partake, and watches some of his family partake while others do not—all without his seeing the rod of iron in the vision. It is not until we are leaving Lehi's incorporation stage and are moving forward to the multitudes' separation stage that Lehi sees the rod. This fact makes sense if we use the ritual paradigm to study the vision. Lehi does not need the rod of iron in the separation and threshold stages because he is directly relying on the Lord. He prays to the Lord after he has traveled alone in darkness for many hours (see 1 Nephi 8:8) during the separation, and he communes with the Lord when he partakes of the fruit of the tree of life in the threshold experience. And, in his incorporation stage, his family has the word of God when he, the prophet, beckons them to partake of the fruit. The prophetic word is, after all, the word of God.

The rod of iron is needed at this very specific point in preparing for the multitudes' separation stage, when the larger society, represented by the various multitudes that appear, becomes a part of Lehi's vision. The rod of iron is one of the things Lehi brings back with him from the threshold stage of his initiation—not the rod of iron *per se* but the idea of the word of God that is represented by the rod. Lehi interacts with the man in the white robe and with his family but never with the greater society represented by the multitudes. This greater society, then, will have the word of God in their world by virtue of the rod of iron.

If we see the rod of iron as representing the Savior as the Word of God, to hold to the rod is not only studying the scriptures but also entering into a meaningful relationship with the Savior and letting him be our guide throughout life. We hold to the rod, and, in a sense, the rod holds to us, protecting us and guiding us. Palmer speaks of this phenomenon: "By this understanding, I not only pursue truth but truth pursues me. I not only grasp truth but truth grasps me. I not only know truth but truth knows me. Ultimately, I do not master truth but truth masters me. Here, the one-way movement of objectivism, in which the active knower tracks down the inert object of knowledge, becomes the two-way movement of persons in search of each other. Here, we know even as we are known."[42]

Through our holding to the rod of iron, we can know as we are known. It is a relationship with the Lord that takes us to the tree of life, not the mere reading or hearing of words. Of course, studying the scriptures is part of that relationship, as is participating in ordinances and making covenants. They are, in fact, a large part of how we come to know him. Seeing the rod of iron as symbolic of the Savior includes all that seeing it as the word of God would entail, plus much more. What has been written about the rod of iron could apply equally to living a life in which we follow the Savior: "It followed each turn, guided over each stumbling rock, and beckoned around each precipice of the deadly river. It led with secured, enduring strength through the spacious field to the tree."[43] But it is important to remember that symbols often represent different ideas that are not mutually exclusive. Many are inclined to make a list of each symbol in the dream and what each one represents, as though they were making a list of mathematical formulas. Symbolism rarely works that way, however. Often symbols can have multiple interpretations. So the rod of iron could represent the Savior, and the tree of life could represent his Atonement. Or the rod could represent the commandments of God, and the tree of life, the Savior. There are other interpretations as well, and they can each be correct so long as each is in harmony with doctrine and is supported by the text. By saying that the rod of iron symbolizes the Savior, I am not saying that it does not symbolize the word of God as scripture or as guidance through the Holy Spirit. The symbol is simply not limited to the single interpretation of the rod as the written or spoken word of God.

As we consider the rod of iron as a symbol for the Savior, we can accept the message of the vision as including his role throughout our lives. He is not simply the tree—the end product of our journey through life. We are not required to make our way through the dangers along the path with only the scriptures at our side. Instead, the Lord can be with us throughout our lives; we can rely on him and all that he has to offer—grace, the Atonement, his personal guidance, the Holy Spirit, our knowledge of the Father, commandments, scripture, covenants, ordinances—to help us make it back to him and partake of the fruit of eternal life. Just as the fruit is "desirable above all other fruit" (1 Nephi 8:12), so is eternal life "the greatest of all the gifts of God" (D&C 14:7).

Jesus Christ, as we have seen, is Truth. If the rod of iron symbolizes the Savior, then to hold to the rod can mean to establish a relationship with the Savior. And, to establish a relationship with him is to relate with Truth. If true education is to *create a space in which obedience to truth is practiced*," then the vision of the tree of life is the ultimate education because it is the image of practicing obedience to the ultimate Truth—the Savior. Truth is throughout the vision, both as the tree of life and as the rod of iron. To enter into a loving relationship with the Savior requires obedience: "If ye love me, keep my commandments" (John 14:15). Obedience does not mean "slavish adherence to authority, but careful listening and responding in a conversation of free selves."[44] The Lord does not ask of us blind obedience but rather visionary obedience. We follow him because we see who he is, we love him, and we want to be like him.

This type of obedience is key to teaching and learning. It requires humility and a willingness to submit ourselves to another—a teacher, a student, a subject, a truth, *the* Truth. The vision of the tree of life is the prototypical educational experience. It teaches us how to come to *all* truth by showing us how to come to *the* Truth. It teaches us how to learn calculus or literature or history by submitting ourselves to the truth that is in them, showing us how to learn through submitting ourselves to the Savior.

The path. In addition to seeing the rod of iron, Lehi also sees a path that leads to the tree. A path can represent "life, experience, learning."[45] There is an element of choice involved with a path, as it is usually assumed that it is "the route or way which a person chooses to travel. His choice may be to journey on the 'path of the wicked' (Prov. 4:14), which is the way of darkness; or he may choose to walk the 'path of the just,' which is 'as the shining light' (Prov. 4:18–19)."[46] Paths are part of the typological world in scripture and secular literature. As the literary critic Northrop Frye notes, the "human use of the inorganic world involves the highway or road as well as the city with its streets, and the metaphor of the 'way' is inseparable from all quest-literature, whether explicitly Christian as in *The Pilgrim's Progress* or not."[47] Though many do not succeed, the people on the path in Lehi's dream are on a quest for the tree of life.

This combination of the tree of life and the path is also archetypally significant. As historian and philosopher Mircea Eliade notes, the center is the "zone of the sacred," and "the road leading to the center is a 'difficult road.'" Similarly, the tree of life is at the center of Lehi's dream, if not geographically, then, without a doubt, thematically and symbolically. And the path leading to that tree is made more difficult, even dangerous, because of the mists of darkness. According to Eliade, there is a reason the path is difficult: "The road is arduous, fraught with perils, because it is, in fact, a rite of the passage from the profane to the sacred, . . . from man to the divinity. Attaining the center is equivalent to a consecration, an initiation; yesterday's profane and illusory existence gives place to a new, to a life that is real, enduring, and effective."[48] The path is important in this moving toward the multitudes' separation stage because it acts as part of this "rite of the passage from the profane to the sacred." While the path was not a part of Lehi's approaching the tree of life, nor was it part of his family's, it is the very way by which the multitudes will try to progress toward the tree. It is how the multitudes can attain the center of this vision.

The Multitudes' Ritual of Initiation

While it could be argued that the multitudes are part of the greater society to which Lehi returns as part of his incorporation stage, I consider them not to be part of that stage for Lehi because they have no interaction with him. He does not return to them as he does to his family; he is not incorporate back into their society. He sees them from a distance and notes what they do and what happens to them, but the multitudes are a new part of the vision and have their own rite of initiation.

The multitudes of people. Lehi saw a number of people who commenced on the path. The very act of beginning the journey along the path was a sign of the people's willingness to follow God to some extent. Later in the vision there will be people who do not even attempt to follow the path, but the ones who do attempt have some desire to follow it, even for a short period of time. The path becomes a symbol, too, for dependence on the Lord. According to Book of Mormon scholar Hugh Nibley, Nephi generally sees the journey in the desert as "the most compelling image of man's dependence on God."[49] People who choose to follow the path acknowledge that this is the way to the tree of life, that they must depend on the path the Lord has set if they wish to partake of the fruit.

These people who start along the path are important to the symbolism in the vision. "The elements of wandering, deliverance, and coming unto Christ are all in the tree of life complex of symbolism."[50] It is especially clear later in the Book of Mormon that the Nephites see themselves as wanderers, searching for the promised land that is beyond this life.[51] In this vision, the tree of life is the promised land, and those who seek it become pilgrims on a religious quest. From a symbolic perspective, there is no need for Lehi to see multitudes of people. He could have seen one person in each situation and that would have sufficed in terms of conveying the particular meaning. However, using the image of huge numbers of people adds at least two dimensions to the symbol. First, it reinforces the idea and feeling that this is indeed the world we are looking at, that everybody is part of this vision in one way or another (see 1 Nephi 8:20), that it applies to us. And second, what is going on in the vision at this point is a communal activity. This is not something people do alone.

Teaching and learning are communal acts. The community may consist of the family in informal settings, the classroom in formal education, or the community of the reader, author, and the people who inhabit the text in the case of an individual reading a book.[52] As a psycholinguist who has focused on the nature of teaching and learning, author and education scholar Frank Smith explains, "Learning is social rather than solitary. It can be summarized in seven familiar words: *We learn from the company we keep.*"[53] He calls these communal groups of learning "clubs" and writes of the importance of these clubs to our efforts to teach and learn:

> These may sometimes be the formal organizations that we join and maintain membership in by paying a fee—the political clubs, sports clubs, and social clubs with which we might be affiliated. But clubs may often be the informal associations that we belong to just by sharing an interest and a sense of community—the metaphorical clubs of teachers, parents, students, book readers, gardeners, joggers, or cyclists—all of the different groups with which we identify ourselves.
>
> The way we identify ourselves is at the core of it all. We don't join a club, or stay in it, if we can't identify with the other members. We are uncomfortable if we feel the other members are not the kind of people we see ourselves as being.[54]

The relationship between learning and ritual, being established in Lehi's dream, is even stronger when one realizes that, like learning, ritual is social in function. Ritual, even when practiced in solitude, is a communal event. It is a community that decides upon a ritual—deciding not only what the ritual elements are but also their meaning. The initiate is separated from community, and, once the initiation is complete, the initiated returns to community. Yet, as becomes clear in verse 30, Lehi does not just see one generic mass, but "multitudes." Though the makeup of the groups is homogeneous (making them somewhat surrealistic), the groups may be distinguished by a characteristic or characteristics that define themselves along with the other members of the specific grouping.

The distinction between "numberless concourses of people" and "multitudes" can be found in the separation stage, where they are truly separated from one another into three primary groupings. Everyone in the first group does the exact same thing: they start on the path and then lose their way after the mist of darkness arises. The people in the second group make their way to the tree and partake of the fruit, then fall away because of the people in the great and spacious building. And, while the people in the third group actually comprise two subgroups, each of the subgroups is homogeneous—the first group partakes of the fruit and remains true, while everyone in the second group does not even try to make it to the tree and falls away in various ways. Though it would be unrealistic in the actual, physical world, in this visionary world there is absolutely no overlapping.

At first, it may seem surprising to consider the groups to be learning communities when it does not appear that they are organized for the purpose of learning, but it is important to remember that many of the clubs Smith writes about are not primarily organized for learning purposes either. (People usually organize a soccer team to play soccer, not to learn about soccer—though the players will naturally learn about soccer while they play it.) The central image of learning in the vision is the tree of life, so it is important to see how these learning communities relate to that image. Most of the groups never make it to the tree. In fact, several of the groups do not even seem to have the partaking of the fruit as their purpose. However, despite the fact that most of the groups never participate in the full learning experience made possible by the tree of life, they are still learning communities.

Though we often speak of one influence or another impeding learning, what we more accurately mean is that the influence is impeding learning the skill or idea that we wish to be learned. People learn all of the time; it is virtually impossible to stop a person from learning something, even if the only thing he or she is learning is that there is not much worth learning at the moment. Students who are frustrated over the multiplication tables may not be learning the multiplication tables, but they are learning something: memorizing the multiplication tables is frustrating, difficult work. "If there is interest and comprehension, then learning is inevitable and effortless. If there is no interest or comprehension, learning may still take place but with more difficulty and what is also inevitably learned is that the task or subject matter is uninteresting, incomprehensible, and not something anyone would normally do."[55] The groups in Lehi's dream are learning communities because they are grouped together for common purposes that center on the tree of life—either going to it or staying away from it. Though they may not be organized for the sole purpose of learning—or even for the primary purpose of learning—they cannot avoid learning as a community.

The first multitude. If we study the first group as a learning community we quickly see a fundamental quality to their experience as a group: despite the dangers of the mist of darkness, they do not even attempt to hold to the rod of iron. The mist would pose no danger to their progression along the path if they would hold to the rod, but they do not touch it. Perhaps they do not see the rod or they see it but do not believe it can help them. Perhaps they consider it too much work to hold to the rod. Though we do not know the specific reason they do not touch the rod, it is possible that the underlying principle could be lack of faith. Just as someone who has faith in Christ turns to him and relies on him, if this group had had sufficient faith they would have seen the rod and known its importance.

One of the elements of their experience that could have easily prevented or destroyed the group's faith is the fear that the mist of darkness probably created in them.[56] It makes sense that a group of people traveling along a path would feel intense fear if suddenly a mist of darkness arose and they could no longer see where they were going. Such fear would have a devastating effect on their ability to learn.[57] Fear is often a daunting enemy to teaching and learning. Teachers may be fearful that they will not be liked, that they will look foolish for not knowing some answer, that students will be disruptive, that their jobs are in jeopardy for one reason or another. Students' fears may often be similar to those of their teachers: they will not be liked, they will look foolish for not knowing some answer, the learning environment will be disruptive rather than safe, or their status may be in jeopardy for one reason or another.[58] Because of these fears, there is the danger that less teaching and less learning will take place. Teachers may be more prone to rely on old notes—and methods—that seemed to work last time, and students may find safety in not answering a question or answering in a safe way that the textbook supports despite their own thoughts.

The initiation of this first multitude ends with the separation stage. They do not have a threshold experience, as they never even make it to the tree of life. And they do not have an incorporation stage because they never return to society. They simply wander off and are lost.

The second multitude. While the first multitude never holds the rod of iron, this second group does take hold of the rod and makes it to the tree of life. They successfully complete their separation stage and do not get lost. And, since they partake of the fruit, they successfully complete their threshold experience as well—at least, at first it appears that way. Quickly they become ashamed and fall away because of the mocking of the people in the great and spacious building.[59] This second multitude apparently cares more about what others think of them than they do about the fruit of the tree of life. Unfortunately, they have not learned what these people about whom Palmer writes understand: "These are people who have come to understand that no punishment anyone might lay on us could possibly be worse than the punishment we lay on ourselves by conspiring in our own diminishment, by living a divided life, by failing to make that fundamental decision to act and speak on the outside in ways consonant with the truth we know on the inside. As soon as we make that decision, amazing things happen. For one thing, the enemy stops being the enemy."[60]

And who is the enemy of this second group? It is yet another group—a group not on the path but rather in the great and spacious building. Like the others, this group in the building represents another club, another communal learning group. Their "exceedingly fine" (1 Nephi 8:27) clothes and their relative seclusion up in the building are barriers to others knowing them for who they really are. As Elder Cook notes, "We want people to know us and love us for being ourselves, not for external adornments used to attract attention or perhaps even motivate some unrighteous feelings in those who might be influenced by us."[61] These people are learning things while in that building, but they are not things of the heart. The people in the building have learned the power they may have through being critical of others, through mocking them. Perhaps these people secretly envy those who have partaken of the fruit of the tree of life, but they are determined to keep such a feeling a secret. "Fashionably dressed beautiful people," Nibley writes, "partying in the top-priced upper apartments and penthouses of a splendid high-rise, have fun looking down and commenting on a bedraggled little band of transients eagerly eating fruit from a tree in a field."[62]

Why do the people in the building persecute those who partake of the fruit? What difference does it make to them that there are those who have gone to the tree of life? The people who have been to the tree are not preaching against those in the building. They are not preaching against anything. So far as we know, they are not even speaking. Perhaps they are being persecuted for the same reason that prophets often are. Nibley writes that "a prophet is a witness, not a reformer. Criticism of the world is always implicit in a prophet's message of repentance, but he is *not* sent for the purpose of criticizing the world." The Lord and his Apostles were not persecuted for their ideas, but it "was as witnesses endowed with power from on high that they earned the hatred of the world." The Prophet Joseph Smith was likewise persecuted for his witness.[63] The people who have partaken of the tree do not have to say anything to be a threat to the people in the building; their simple existence stands as a witness against the flashier group up high. They show the world that there is a way other than that of the great and spacious building. They have learned what needed to be learned and have done what needed to be done. Despite their experience, however, those in the second group fall because of the persecution they receive.

The persecution the partakers of the fruit receive from the people in the building is relatively mild, especially compared to any kind of physical, violent persecution. We would like to believe that the experience of partaking of the fruit would be such an exquisite, life-changing moment that no amount of persecution would deter them from living righteously. But such is not always the case. Those who teach may wish to believe that if their students are exposed to truth they will embrace it and choose to live in harmony with it. However, the act of teaching and learning does not guarantee the integrity of the soul. Teachers may teach truth with power and authority, and students may even learn that truth, but living up to that truth is sometimes a different matter.

Though the second multitude completes its separation stage, it does not complete its initiation. The members of this group partake of the fruit but deny themselves the complete life-changing, threshold experience by feeling ashamed and falling into "forbidden paths"—lost. Like the first multitude, this second group fails their initiation.

The third multitude. The third group consists of two subgroups. This portion of the vision "appears to depict a polarization between the wicked and the righteous."[64] The righteous subgroup partakes of the tree and remains faithful to the experience. The wicked subgroup has three smaller groups within it: the first feels their way to the building, creating the image of people groping in the dark, not being able to rely on vision because they are blind; the second drowns in the depths of the fountain; and the third wanders on strange roads, lost from Lehi's view.

Interestingly, this first subgroup completes the separation and threshold experience stages of the ritual, but we are not given an account of their incorporation phase. We can assume they return to society as transformed individuals, ready to live up to their knowledge and experience, but the record ends with their threshold experience. In a way, this account is similar to the experience that many teachers have with their very best students. They see them successfully complete their separation stage as they grow more independent, and their threshold experience stage as they gain new knowledge and experiences that transform them for the better, but the teachers often do not get to see what their former students do with what they have learned.

The second subgroup barely begins their separation stage before they end up lost, without even trying to progress toward the threshold experience. Unfortunately, this story reminds teachers of the students they have often agonized over—the ones who, for whatever unseen reason, do not seem to try to learn and often give up, lost.

From an educational viewpoint, the nature of these three multitudes is fascinating. The fact that no group ever intermingles with another group, that each appears as a discreet unit with no variances within it, supports what Smith writes about learning clubs and Palmer about learning communities. There is nothing in the vision to indicate that the people are assigned to their respective groups, or that they are forced into them in any way. The people in the groups seem to be together because they choose to be together. And they learn from those within their group—for better or worse. Except for the one subgroup in the third multitude, the experiences of each of the groups and of Laman and Lemuel teach us that, unfortunately, there are students who fail—sometimes not because of being poorly taught, but because they choose not to experience what they could through wholly participating in the initiation process.

Conclusion

Lehi's vision of the tree of life is a powerful passage of scripture on many different levels. Among its many lessons is what the careful reader can learn about how a great teacher may teach and how diligent students may learn through what can be called a ritual of initiation. The vision also shows us how students who refuse to embrace this kind of experiential learning can, as a result, end up failing. By reading the vision of the tree of life with the question of teaching and learning in mind, we can see it as a model of teaching and learning that reveres the importance of the spirit and not just the mind. "These terms would describe the roots of teaching and learning, not just the branches—words like *faith, love, joy, reverence, discernment, and humility, or inspire, ponder, and edify*," Osguthorpe writes. "These terms were once central to teaching and learning but have long since lost their place in our conversation about education."[65]

Notes

1. I rely upon Parker Palmer's writings because he is recognized as one of the leaders in the movement to consider the spiritual qualities of teaching and learning. Rather than just focusing on how the vision might help us learn more about teaching and learning the gospel, this paper is also concerned with how it helps with teaching and learning in general. Palmer helps us to see that these principles do not just apply to teaching the scriptures in a religious setting; they are helpful in any educational environment.

2. Joan Halifax, "Learning as Initiation: Not-Knowing, Bearing Witness, and Healing," in *The Heart of Learning: Spirituality in Education*, ed. Steven Glazer (New York: Jeremy P. Tarcher/Putnam, 1999), 173.

3. In fact, Van Gennep writes of these three stages as centered around the concept of thresholds, or *liminality*. The rites of separation are preliminal, the rites of transition are liminal, and the rites of incorporation are postliminal. See Arnold van Gennep, *The Rites of Passage*, trans. Monika B. Vizedom and Gabrielle L. Caffee (London: Routledge & Kegan Paul, 1960), 11.

4. Halifax, "Learning as Initiation," 174. Halifax also correlates the rites of passage with phases of a particular Zen Buddhist order. "The first tenet of the order is 'not-knowing' and denotes separation from the familiar, conditioned world of knowing, the opening of the spontaneous mind of the beginning. The second tenet is 'bearing witness,' and emphasizes being fully present to the suffering and joy in oneself and the world. The third tenet is 'healing oneself and others' through returning to the world with the aspiration of liberating oneself and others from suffering."

5. Richard Dilworth Rust, *Feasting on the Word: The Literary Testimony of the Book of Mormon* (Salt Lake City: Deseret Book; Provo, UT: FARMS, 1997), 221. For more on this topic, see pages 221–28.

6. For an informative discussion of Lehi, see H. Donl Peterson, "Father Lehi," in *The Book of Mormon: First Nephi, the Doctrinal Foundation*, ed. Monte S. Nyman and Charles D. Tate Jr. (Provo, UT: Religious Studies Center, Brigham Young University, 1988).

7. Leland Ryken, James C. Wilhoit, and Tremper Longman III, eds., *Dictionary of Biblical Imagery* (Downers Grove, IL: InterVarsity Press, 1998), 192.

8. Ad de Vries, *Dictionary of Symbols and Imagery* (Amsterdam: North-Holland, 1974), 129. It also symbolizes "mythic nothingness" and "the Great Void."

9. Wilfred L. Guerin and others, eds., *A Handbook of Critical Approaches to Literature*, 4th ed. (New York: Oxford University Press, 1999), 161.

10. Richard Dilworth Rust, "Book of Mormon Imagery," in *Rediscovering the Book of Mormon*, ed. John L. Sorenson and Melvin J. Thorne (Salt Lake City: Deseret Book; Provo, UT FARMS, 1991), 137.

11. M. Catherine Thomas, "The Provocation in the Wilderness and the Rejection of Grace," in *Thy People Shall Be My People and Thy God My God*, ed. Paul Y. Hoskisson (Salt Lake City: Deseret Book, 1994), 169.

12. "Certainly there is no doubt at all that the Book of Mormon is speaking of desert most of the time when it talks about wildernesses." Hugh Nibley, *An Approach to the Book of Mormon*, 3rd ed. (Salt Lake City: Deseret Book; Provo, UT: FARMS, 1988), 135. Nibley later observes that the "desert has two faces: it is a place both of death and of refuge, of defeat and victory, a grim coming down from Eden and yet a sure escape from the wicked world, the asylum alike of the righteous and the rascal. The pilgrims' way leads through sand and desolation, but it is the way back to paradise; in the desert we lose ourselves to find ourselves" (148).

13. Ryken, Wilhoit, and Longman, *Dictionary*, 944.

14. Arnold Whittick, *Symbols, Signs, and Their Meaning and Uses in Design*, 2nd ed. (London: Leonard Hill, 1971), 349.

15. Guerin and others, *Handbook of Critical Approaches*, 161.

16. Whittick, *Symbols, Signs, and Their Meaning*, 349.

17. Walter Lewis Wilson, *Wilson's Dictionary of Bible Types* (Grand Rapids, MI: Eerdmans Publishing, 1957), 382.

18. de Vries, *Dictionary of Symbols and Imagery*, 388.

19. "The Book of Mormon has a good deal to say about messengers in white. Lehi's desert vision opens with 'a man, and he was dressed in a white robe,' who becomes his guide (1 Nephi 8:5). Lehi is shown 'twelve ministers, . . . their garments . . . made white' (1 Nephi 12:10), followed by three generations of men whose 'garments were white, even like unto the Lamb of God' (1 Nephi 12:11). Soon after, Nephi also in a vision 'beheld a man, and he was dressed in a white robe,' this being John who was to come (1 Nephi 14:19).

"'There can no man be saved,' says Alma, 'except his garments are washed white' (Alma 5:21). He tells how the ancient priesthood 'were called after this holy order, and were sanctified, and their garments were washed white through the blood of the Lamb. Now they . . . [have] their garments made white, being pure and spotless before God' (Alma 13:11–12).

But the most moving and significant passage is his formal prayer for the city of Gideon: 'May the Lord bless you, and keep your garments spotless, that ye may at last be brought to sit down with Abraham Isaac, and Jacob, and the holy prophets, . . . having your garments spotless even as their garments are spotless, in the kingdom of heaven to go no more out' (Alma 7:25)." Hugh Nibley, *Since Cumorah*, 2nd ed. (Salt Lake City: Deseret Book; Provo, UT: FARMS, 1988), 156.

20. I have written elsewhere about another possible identity for the man in the white robe:

"One more future historical event is part of the vision of the tree of life but is not included in either account: the end of the world. In his vision, Nephi sees John the Revelator and is told that John 'shall see and write the remainder of these things; yea, and also many things which have been. And he shall also write concerning the end of the world' (1 Nephi 14:21–22). In other words, Nephi is stopped from giving a complete account of his vision because it includes the end of the world, and the Savior has chosen John to write about that in the book of Revelation.

"The presence of John the Revelator in Nephi's vision adds another element of historical reality to the vision. The way in which Nephi describes his vision of John is significant to the beginning of Lehi's vision: 'I looked and beheld a man, and he was dressed in a white robe' (1 Nephi 14:19). Nephi's prophetic vision, which forms an interpretation of his father's dream, drawing out its apocalyptic nature, now comes full circle, ending where his father's dream began (see 1 Nephi 8:5). Though there have been other interpretations of whom the man in the white robe represents in Lehi's dream, from a messenger to a Christ-figure to Moses, I believe that John the Revelator is one important possibility.

"Pursuing this idea, we find John greeting Lehi at the beginning of his vision and serving as his guide, taking him to the point when Lehi can turn directly to the Lord and see a vision that can be understood to concern not just his family, or even his descendants, but also the entire world and its ultimate destiny. Thus, when reading 1 Nephi 14:25—'The Lord God hath ordained the apostle of the Lamb of God [John] that he should write [of the apocalypse]'—we are not surprised that the Lord would appoint the man he ordained for that purpose to begin and end the vision of the tree of life in the Book of Mormon. Lehi and Nephi may have experienced more in their visions than they recorded. For example, perhaps they both saw the man in the white robe at the beginning and end of their respective visions. However, if we consider what we do know from the record the Book of Mormon offers, it becomes significant that the man who appears at the beginning of Lehi's account could also be the one appearing at the end of Nephi's, thus emphasizing the relatedness of the two accounts." Charles Swift, "Lehi's Vision of the Tree of Life: Understanding the Dream as Visionary Literature," *Journal of Book of Mormon Studies* 14, no. 2 (2005): 63.

21. Gene R. Cook, *Teaching by the Spirit* (Salt Lake City: Deseret Book, 2000), 15.

22. Russell T. Osguthorpe, *The Education of the Heart: Rediscovering the Spiritual Roots of Learning* (American Fork, UT: Covenant Communications, 1996), 84.

23. If we turn to an American dictionary in use at the time that the Book of Mormon was translated we find that *waste* has as its third definition a meaning that is remarkably appropriate for this vision: "A desolate or uncultivated country. The plains of Arabia are mostly a wide waste." *Waste* can be another word for wilderness, so this waste could either

be a part of the previously mentioned wilderness or a different one entirely. See Noah Webster, *American Dictionary of the English Language, 1828, Facsimile Edition*, 6th ed. (San Francisco: Foundation for American Christian Education, 1989).

24. Osguthorpe, *Education of the Heart*, 84–85.

25. Cook, *Teaching by the Spirit*, 15–16.

26. Palmer explains the notion that "covering the field" may mean teaching less. "In every great novel, there is a passage that when deeply understood, reveals how the author develops character, establishes tension, creates dramatic movement. With that understanding, the student can read the rest of the novel more insightfully. In every period of history, there is an event that when deeply understood, reveals not only how historians do their work but also illumines the general dynamics of that epoch. In the work of every philosopher, there is a pivotal idea that when deeply understood, reveals the foundations of his or her system or nonsystem of thought.

"By teaching this way, we do not abandon the ethic that drives us to cover the field—we honor it more deeply. Teaching from the microcosm, we exercise responsibility toward both the subject and our students by refusing merely to send data 'bites' down the intellectual food chain but by helping our students understand where the information comes from and what it means. We honor both the discipline and our students by teaching them how to think like historians or biologists or literary critics rather than merely how to lip-sync the conclusions others have reached." Parker J. Palmer, *The Courage to Teach: Exploring the Inner Landscape of a Teacher's Life* (San Francisco: Jossey-Bass, 1998), 123.

27. Thomas, "Provocation," 169.

28. Nibley, *Approach to the Book of Mormon*, 253–54.

29. Parker J. Palmer, *To Know As We Are Known* (New York: HarperCollins, 1983), 121.

30. M. Catherine Thomas, "Types and Shadows of Deliverance in the Book of Mormon," in *Doctrines of the Book of Mormon: The 1991 Sperry Symposium*, ed. Bruce A. Van Orden and Brent L. Top (Salt Lake City: Deseret Book, 1992), 186.

31. E. O. James, *The Tree of Life: An Archaeological Study* (Leiden: E. J. Brill, 1966), 1.

32. A number of scholars have discussed the tree as a symbol of the sacred in various cultures, such as Thomas Barns, "Trees and Plants," in *Encyclopaedia of Religion and Ethics*, ed. James Hastings (New York: Charles Scribner's Sons, 1928), 12:448–57; John L. Sorenson, *An Ancient American Setting for the Book of Mormon* (Salt Lake City: Deseret Book; Provo, UT: FARMS, 1985), 47; John M. Lundquist, "The Common Temple Ideology of the Ancient Near East," in *The Temple in Antiquity: Ancient Records and Modern Perspectives*, ed. Truman G. Madsen (Provo, UT: Religious Studies Center, Brigham Young University, 1984), 53–76; C. Wilfred Griggs, "The Tree of Life in Ancient Cultures," *Ensign*, June 1988, 26–31; John W. Welch, "The Narrative of Zosimus (History of the Rechabites) and the Book of Mormon," in *Book of Mormon Authorship Revisited: The Evidence for Ancient Origins*, ed. Noel B. Reynolds (Provo, UT: FARMS, 1997), 323–74; Irene M. Briggs, "The Tree of Life Symbol: Its Significance in Ancient American Religion" (master's thesis, Brigham Young University, 1950); Allen J. Christenson, "The Sacred Tree of the Ancient Maya," *Journal of Book of Mormon Studies* 6, no. 1 (1997): 1–23; Donald W. Parry, "Garden of Eden: Prototype Sanctuary," in *Temples of the Ancient World: Ritual*

and Symbolism, ed. Donald W. Parry (Salt Lake City: Deseret Book; Provo, UT: FARMS, 1994), 126–57; Arnold Whittick, *Symbols, Signs, and Their Meaning* (cited above).

33. Joseph Fielding McConkie and Donald W. Parry, *A Guide to Scriptural Symbols* (Salt Lake City: Bookcraft, 1990), 104.

34. "From the outset of their encounter Pilate tries to objectify Jesus by forcing him into the category of 'king.' He is trying to make Jesus a comprehensible and dispensable entity in the political terms of the time. But Jesus, the person, resists Pilate's categories. He asks, 'Do you say this of your own accord, or did others say it to you about me?' suggesting that Pilate's opening question comes from impersonal caricature, not personal understanding. He says that his 'kingdom' is not of this world, that it cannot be comprehended in objective political terms. He puts forward a personal claim related to his very birth about his reason for being. But Pilate is incapable of knowing this personal truth because he holds the person at arm's length, treating him as an object, a thing, a 'what.' By reducing truth to objective terms Pilate puts himself beyond truth's reach. Eventually, he assents to murdering a personal truth that calls for conversion in favor of an objectivism that leaves him in control.

"The story suggests that in Christian understanding truth is neither an object 'out there' nor a proposition about such objects. Instead, truth is personal, and all truth is known in personal relationships. Jesus is a paradigm, a model of this personal truth. In him, truth, once understood as abstract, principled, propositional, suddenly takes on a human face and a human frame. In Jesus, the disembodied 'word' takes flesh and walks among us. Jesus calls us to truth, but not in the form of creeds or theologies or world-views. His call to truth is a call to community—with him, with each other, with creation and its Creator. If what we know is an abstract, impersonal, apart from us, it cannot be truth, for truth involves a vulnerable, faithful, and risk-filled interpenetration of the knower and the known. Jesus calls Pilate out from behind his objectivism into a living relationship of truth. Pilate, taking refuge behind the impersonal objectivist 'what,' is unable to respond." Palmer, *To Know As We Are Known*, 48–49.

35. Palmer, *To Know As We Are Known*, 69.

36. Palmer, *To Know As We Are Known*, 31.

37. Lehi's desire to share what he has discovered with his family is not only a powerful illustration of a father and husband's love for his family, but is also indicative of the feeling of a people. "Perhaps the most common and most touching theme in the vast corpus of Arabic desert inscriptions is the theme of longing and looking for one's family. When the writer comes to water and rests, he wishes for his family, and is usually smitten with terrible longing to see them." Nibley, *Approach to the Book of Mormon*, 255.

38. One might argue that it is possible Lehi said quite a bit, but that it was simply not recorded. Perhaps Lehi, in telling his family about his vision, said that he had lectured them but Nephi just left if out of his account. Or, perhaps, Lehi did have more to say in the actual vision but did not relate that to his family. In any case, we are studying the account of Lehi's vision as found in 1 Nephi 8. If more were said in the vision but the account does not include that, then that in itself is significant. Whether the lack of speaking can be attributed to what happened in the vision or to how it was recorded in the Book of Mormon, the fact remains that the text we have has Lehi saying very little—regardless of the cause, that fact is symbolically significant. This principle of interpretation holds true throughout

our discussion of Lehi's vision—we are discussing the text itself, not all of the possibilities we can imagine surrounding the events that actually occurred. Indeed, the only access we have to those events is through the text.

39. Susan Easton Black, "'Behold, I Have Dreamed a Dream,'" in *The Book of Mormon: First Nephi, the Doctrinal Foundation*, 118.

40. Palmer, *Courage to Teach*, 120.

41. McConkie and Parry, *Guide to Scriptural Symbols*, 94. Though I quote this passage from Revelation, I do not imply that the Greek word translated into *iron rod* means the same thing as *iron rod* in the Book of Mormon. One of the unique qualities of the Book of Mormon is that it is an ancient text that was translated by the inspiration of God directly into nineteenth-century American English. Regardless of original Greek meanings, the Lord knew when he inspired the translation of the Book of Mormon that the term *iron rod* was also used in the English version of Revelation. That fact alone warrants a comparison regardless of what the Greek word originally meant.

42. Palmer, *To Know As We Are Known*, 59.

43. Black, "'Behold, I Have Dreamed a Dream,'" 118.

44. Palmer, *To Know As We Are Known*, 65.

45. de Vries, *Dictionary of Symbols and Imagery*, 359.

46. McConkie and Parry, *Guide to Scriptural Symbols*, 89.

47. Northrop Frye, *Anatomy of Criticism* (Princeton: Princeton University Press, 1957), 144.

48. Mircea Eliade, *The Myth of the Eternal Return*, trans. Willard R. Trask (London: Routledge & Kegan Paul, 1955), 17–18.

49. Nibley, *Since Cumorah*, 157.

50. Rust, *Feasting on the Word*, 209.

51. Bruce J. Boehm, "Wanderers in the Promised Land: A Study of the Exodus Motif in the Book of Mormon and Holy Bible," *Journal of Book of Mormon Studies* 3, no. 1 (1994): 187–203.

52. Reading "is not a solitary activity. Readers are never alone. Readers can join the company of the characters they read about—that is the reason we read stories of people with whom we can identify or of situations in which we would like to be." We do not only join the company of the characters, but also of the authors. "We can share ideas and experiences with them, often in considerably more comfort and security than the authors were in when they had their ideas and experiences or wrote their books. We can also employ authors as guides to help us to learn new words, to sharpen our skills of reading and writing, and to augment our abilities in the expression of ideas, in argument, and in thinking creatively." Frank Smith, *The Book of Learning and Forgetting* (New York: Teachers College Press, 1998), 24.

53. Frank Smith, *Between Hope and Havoc: Essays into Human Learning and Education* (Portsmouth, NH: Heinemann, 1995), 40.

54. Smith, *Book of Learning and Forgetting*, 11.

55. Smith, *Book of Learning and Forgetting*, 54.

56. After the disciples on the boat awoke the Savior because they feared the storm, he drew a relationship between fear and faith: "And he saith unto them, Why are ye fearful, O ye of little faith?" (Matthew 8:26).

57. Palmer, *Courage to Teach*, 36–38. Palmer identifies four particular fears that hurt us in education: fear of diversity, fear of conflict, fear of losing identity, and fear of changing our lives. Each of these fears is part of what he calls the "fear of the live encounter."

58. "Space itself is often frightening. Students are threatened by an open invitation to learn for themselves and to help each other learn; they would much rather have their education packaged and sold by the teacher. They are threatened by the strangeness of what they do not know, by the thought of having to expose their ignorance, by having to relate to their peers in ways that would hardly occur to them outside the classroom, and by the possibility of a failure that will mar their self-esteem and careers. Students come into a classroom with these fears close to the surface. If they are not acknowledged and addressed they will close down the space for learning.

"But teachers, too, enter the classroom with fears; at least I do. I am afraid of being inadequately prepared, of having my own ignorance exposed, of meeting the glazed eyes and bored expressions of some of my students. Behind my role and my expertise, I wonder what they think about me as a person. They may be afraid of my power over their lives, the power of the grade and credential, but I am afraid of the negative or ambivalent feelings my power creates in them. I need their affirmation as much as they need mine; I need a sense of community with them that our roles make tenuous." Palmer, *To Know As We Are Known*, 84.

59. Hugh Nibley discusses an historical account of a similar situation in which someone in that area of the world felt extreme distress over public humiliation. "If this seems an extreme reaction to a little loss of face, we need only contemplate a touching inscription cut in the rocks by one who 'encamped at this place . . . and he rushed forth in the year in which he was grieved by the scoffing of the people: he drove together and lost the camels. . . . Rest to him who leaves (this inscription) untouched!'" *Approach to the Book of Mormon*, 260.

60. Parker J. Palmer, "The Grace of Great Things: Reclaiming the Sacred in Knowing, Teaching, and Learning," in *The Heart of Learning*, 32.

61. Cook, *Teaching by the Spirit*, 168–69.

62. Hugh Nibley, *The Prophetic Book of Mormon* (Salt Lake City: Deseret Book; Provo, UT: FARMS, 1989), 503.

63. Hugh Nibley, *The World and the Prophets* (Salt Lake City: Deseret Book; Provo, UT: FARMS, 1987), 13, 14, 15–16.

64. Corbin T. Volluz, "Lehi's Dream of the Tree of Life: Springboard to Prophecy," *Journal of Book of Mormon Studies* 2, no. 2 (1993): 27.

65. Osguthorpe, *Education of the Heart*, xxiv.

20

Lehi's Dream and Nephi's Vision as Used by Church Leaders

*Mary Jane Woodger
and Michelle Vanegas Brodrick*

One time I (Woodger) was babysitting my four-year-old nephew and went into the other room as he was taking a bath. After a few minutes, he ran into the front room stark naked, holding a little plastic sword and yelling, "Look, Aunt Mary Jane. I am a stripling warrior!" Though my four-year-old nephew was unfamiliar with the meaning of *stripling*, he was well acquainted with the Book of Mormon story of the stripling warriors. In many ways we are all like my nephew; we have a basic but incomplete knowledge of certain scriptural symbols. For the Church, this may be especially true of the symbols found in 1 Nephi 8–14.

Former Primary general president Cheryl C. Lant agreed with this premise when she spoke to Brigham Young University students in January 2010. Referring to the symbols found in 1 Nephi 8, she said, "Now these images that I have suggested to you today may seem very common. You have heard about them since you were in Primary. But they are basic. They are essential for us not only to know but to understand."[1] Sister Lant took it as a given that BYU students knew and understood the symbols presented in this scripture block.

Mary Jane Woodger is a professor of Church history and doctrine at Brigham Young University. Michelle Vanegas Brodrick is a senior in advertising at Brigham Young University.

Lehi's Dream and Nephi's Vision as Used by Church Leaders

For the current generation of Latter-day Saints, Lehi's dream is commonplace. The usage of Lehi's dream and Nephi's subsequent vision as recorded in 1 Nephi 8–14 has become one of the most oft-quoted scriptural blocks in general conference addresses. Yet this does not mean that the dream has been used the same way from era to era. This study will identify who has referenced the dream-vision; in what context it is used; and the interpretations, analysis, and application that are shared among these addresses. This paper is divided into three sections, each corresponding to a period of Church history. The first period covers Joseph Smith's day until the turn of the twentieth century, when the images were used to describe the political, religious, and social separation between the Church and the world as well as the importance of following the Brethren. The second period covers 1901 to 1985, when the dream was used to counter the rise of secular, academic humanism and when it expanded to include the growing importance of missionary work and the importance of holding to gospel standards. In the final period, from 1985 to the present, greater emphasis was given to individual challenges resulting from the relativism of modern society and the significance of family relationships in our spiritual progress.

Joseph Smith's Day to 1900

Use of Lehi's dream begins with an inauspicious start. The Prophet Joseph Smith made some very definitive statements in reference to the Book of Mormon. He once declared, "Take away the Book of Mormon and the revelations, and where is our religion? We have none."[2] He also stated that the volume is "the most correct of any book on earth . . . and a man would get nearer to God by abiding by its precepts, than by any other book" (introduction of the Book of Mormon). Though the Book of Mormon certainly was powerful in the early Church as a catalyst for conversion, Joseph Smith never quoted 1 Nephi 8 in any of his recorded sermons, teachings, writings, or journals, and "when Joseph Smith outlined the Church's doctrine and undertook to expound in detail his personal 'religious principles' in an 1835 'Letter to the Elders of the Church,' he quoted at great length from Luke, Acts, Revelation, Matthew, Isaiah, and Hebrews to teach the fundamentals" rather than turning to Book of Mormon prophets like Lehi and Nephi.[3] The reason for this is unclear, though historian Alex Smith, who has done extensive work on the *Joseph Smith Papers*, suggests that Joseph considered his translation of the text of the Book of Mormon a finished task. It was a missionary text, and he had finished his responsibility.[4]

At first glance, it would appear that those who led the Church after the Prophet's martyrdom continued to refer mostly to the Old and New Testaments when applying scripture. Terryl L. Givens reminds us that as Brigham Young brought the Saints west, "pioneers referred to themselves as a modern-day Israel, being led across the plains by a modern Moses. . . . And that identification has been thorough and continuous to the present day. True enough, Utah would eventually found her Lehi and her Bountiful . . . [but] it was the Camp of Israel, not the Clans of Lehi, that moved across the plains. Old Testament names and places occur some fifteen to twenty times on Utah maps. Book of Mormon sources are confined to three prophets, one city, and a honeybee."[5] Yet allusions to the dream in the *Journal of Discourses* suggest that the dream was known and had become, or at least was becoming, a part of the Church's scriptural awareness. As early as 1853, Brigham Young alluded to the dream, in particular to the "finger of scorn" pointed by those in the large and spacious building. In fact, five times from 1853 to 1870 President Young references this term, using it to describe the derision the world had concerning the Church, the missionaries, and even the clothing made by the members. In all of these examples, President Young appears to use the image as a means to build Church solidarity, though in one particular address he encouraged listeners to make sure they did not wander into "forbidden paths," that they stay true to the narrow path that led to eternal life. Though the term *iron rod* is not mentioned in this reference, President Young did say that the Holy Ghost would guide them so they did not lose their way.[6]

The imagery of people becoming lost without the iron rod is a common one in the *Journal of Discourses*. In 1879, Elder Erastus Snow focused on the fact that those who retained hold of the iron rod successfully negotiated the mists and clouds of darkness, while those that did not became lost.[7] President Joseph F. Smith warned that those who turned from the truth and wandered into "forbidden paths" could not claim the blessings of the gospel, and President George Q. Cannon wondered how long it would take for Church members to stray into the "forbidden paths" if it were not for the "knowledge of God and the ordinances."[8] In 1859, Elder George A. Smith declared that those who did not follow the Holy Spirit were "blinded by the mists of darkness."[9]

In 1863, President John Taylor made passing reference to the importance of grasping the iron rod. Like President Young, he taught that continually holding on represented having God's Spirit with us always.[10] Elder Orson Hyde in 1873 mentioned the peace that one may gain by holding on to the iron rod.[11] Significantly, both he and President Taylor compared holding the iron rod to engaging in regular prayer. President Daniel H. Wells stated that holding the rod kept one from swerving to the right or to the left, with the rod being the promise of exaltation. Elder Orson Pratt associated the surety of the iron rod with the Holy Spirit of Promise.[12] Perhaps the most detailed text alluding to the dream was a discourse by Orson Pratt in 1872, in which he used the dream to describe that at times, like Lehi, we are left on our own to experience the challenges of our own journeys in the darkness. Though he suggests that in those times the Spirit may not be directly with us, he did say that Lehi was not left alone but had the iron rod to lead him to the tree of life.[13]

In all of these references, we see similar usages, through three main scenes. Though the tree of life is mentioned in all of them, of particular interest for the early Apostles was the importance of the iron rod. In most cases, the iron rod was understood to be the word of God, which included an understanding of the Spirit as a guide. Concern was expressed about losing one's way and becoming lost, and a distinction was made between the Saints on the path and the world that mocked them and pointed the finger of scorn. This last element is of interest because at the time these talks were given the Church's relationship with the outside world could be described as one of antagonism, or at least opposition.

Near the end of the century, the dream was used by the Brethren to describe specific scenarios challenging the Saints. For instance, in April 1888, Elder Franklin D. Richards taught: "This vision that was here seen, though it applied to the people who received it, and to the new land to which they were going, still the circumstances attendant upon them were in some respects so analogous to the circumstances of the present day, that it seems to me that from this lesson we may derive profit and be strengthened in our work and induced to hold firmly to this rod of iron, . . . which is the word of God."[14] In his discourse, Elder Richards equated the situation of Latter-day Saint fathers and husbands who were imprisoned because of persecution to that of walking in the mists of darkness. Closing his talk, he declared, "There will come to those who are true and faithful, these manifestations, from time to time, that will show them from one step to the next the way to the Tree of Life."¹⁵ A year later, Elder John W. Taylor referenced Lehi's vision as he spoke about the Saints' morals and ethics—which he felt were lacking, due in part to the youth of the Church being too caught up into the things of the world. He warned that immorality led one into paths of darkness.¹⁶ The next year, Elder Anthon H. Lund paraphrased the entire dream and used the law of tithing and obedience as a metaphor for holding to the rod of iron.¹⁷

1901 to 1985

General Authorities' use of the dream in the twentieth century continued to relate the importance of grasping the iron rod, or heeding the words of the prophets.¹⁸ For example, the iron rod was used to represent revealed, scriptural authority, as opposed to secular, academic humanism. This application began as early as 1897, when President George Q. Cannon of the First Presidency admonished Saints to grasp the rod of iron by accepting revelation concerning the divine nature of man rather than getting caught up by the theory of evolution.¹⁹

In 1909, Elder Rulon S. Wells warned about so-called "new religion," alluding to a publication written by Harvard university president and professor emeritus Charles Eliot earlier that summer. Eliot had expressed the need for a "new religion," one not based on authority or eschatological promises. In his talk, Elder Wells reminded the Saints that following the iron rod would get them to the tree of life, where they could partake of the fruit and feel the love of God. He also warned the Saints that they should fear God and not just rely on His love. Elder Wells explained that a fear of the penalties associated with disobedience should serve as a driving force for obedience; in other words, Church members could use fear to drive them to the fruit of the tree.²⁰

That same year, Elder Stephen L. Chipman repeated almost verbatim the admonition Elder Wells had given: "If we will do so, clinging to the word of God, remembering the penalties that come from transgressing and going against it, we will eventually arrive at the tree and partake of that love of God."²¹ Eight years later, Elder Chipman, concerned with an apparent growing skepticism and "reason" among the youth, again referred to Lehi's dream, promising that if Latter-day Saints study the scriptures, they "will cling to the iron rod, and will not be led astray by the wisdom and by the cunning craftiness of men."²²

In October 1916, Elder James E. Talmage contrasted the "theories and conceptions of men" with the "the rod of certainty, the rod of revealed truth" of the restored gospel.[23] Likewise, Anthony W. Ivins, referencing again the concept of evolution versus the divine nature of man, talked about holding on to the iron rod, the scriptures, and revealed revelation, promising that "it will bear us safely through, until we find our way back into the presence of our Creator."[24] A year later, Elder Anthon H. Lund mentioned the iron rod with a warning: "There is a great danger before our young people in modern ideas that are being taught them, and we want to be on our guard that they take the word of God, the iron rod, and cling to it." Elder Lund warned Latter-day Saints about letting youth fall into the trap of thinking that the world is a "self-running machine" and that God is not needed.[25]

As the century progressed, the dream continued to be used to confirm the importance of following the Brethren, though it also began to be used in two new applications, the first of which was missionary work. In 1918, Elder Charles A. Callis, then mission president of the Southern States Mission, spoke of inviting, like Lehi of old, those who did not possess the gospel: "I invite you, my fellow-beings, who are not in the Church 'to come and be baptized unto repentance, that ye also may be partakers of the fruit of the tree of life.'"[26] Similarly, in 1924, Elder James E. Talmage compared missionaries to Lehi, who beckoned to his own family after he partook of the fruit.[27]

In April 1929, Elder Talmage used the dream to distinguish between revelation and secular knowledge, tailoring the dream to those who were engaged in academics. In his address he portrayed the iron rod as being important for those who were exploring academic research. He encouraged scholars be true to their testimony so they would not be led away by the "lack of physical evidences [of the gospel] in the eyes of the academic/scientific community." In his analogy Elder Talmage used a particularly interesting approach to holding to the iron rod. Whereas most references speak of grasping the rod, he spoke of tying one's guide rope to the rod: "To those of you who want to explore I say, in all earnestness, tie fast your guide rope to the rod of iron, which is defined as the Word of God. Hold to it firmly, and you may venture out into the region of the unexplored in search of truth if you will; but do not loosen your hold on the rope; and remember that there is very little safety in holding to a rope that is loose at both ends."[28]

We see a new focus in 1943, when Elder Harold B. Lee compared individuals near the tree of life to Saints who had stored food during World War II. He compared those who were accusing Church members of being hoarders to those "who sat in the house of Lehi's dreams, and pointed fingers of scorn."[29] During the same year, Elder Marion G. Romney used the dream as an example of the necessity of studying the word of God in order to develop unity among the members, an important principle stressed during the war.[30] In both cases, the dream was used to help solidify the specific welfare plan espoused by the Church leadership.

In April conference in 1957, Elder Marion D. Hanks associated his experience traversing a cave with the dream to emphasize to the youth that they need not abandon the gospel truth merely because the answers were not as satisfactory as they would wish. He warned the youth against using secular or worldly views to govern their thinking by comparing the mists of darkness to a factory fire in which many died because smoke and fear kept them from finding an exit door. Similarly, said Elder Hanks, those who got caught up in academic institutions and abandon their testimony could also become lost and unable to find an emergency exit door which leads to the Savior.[31]

In 1961, Elder Harold B. Lee addressed the concern among the Brethren about the science and philosophies of man attempting to discredit the gospel of Jesus Christ. Elder Lee identified four groups of people represented in the dream: "Those who partook of the fruit . . . and remained steadfast; those who did partake and then were blinded by mists of darkness which arose from the river and lost their way; those who went so far as to taste the fruit and then fell away because they were ridiculed by those living in spacious dwellings, representing the riches of the world; and finally those who refused to partake of the delicious fruit of the tree." Elder Lee also spoke of the necessity of good works. He stated that the "good fruits of the Church" come from the "good works of its members."[32]

Later that decade, in 1966, Elder Delbert L. Stapley's conference address focused on an interpretation of Lehi's dream. Elder Stapley's thorough discussion of Nephi's reaction to his father's dream gave various modern interpretations of each symbol.[33]

In 1971, President Harold B. Lee compared the mists of darkness to "the numerous institutions of secular and theological learning" and the great and spacious building to "the mockery and ridicule of the world." President Lee declared, "If there is any one thing most needed in this time of tumult and frustration, when men and women and youth and young adults are desperately seeking for answers to the problems which afflict mankind, it is an 'iron rod.'"[34] He quoted an article from the *Wall Street Journal* that stated, "Religion represents the accumulation of man's insight over thousands of years into such questions [of life] . . . [which are] at the root of man's restlessness."[35] He then stated, "Wouldn't it be a great thing if all who are well schooled in secular learning could hold fast to the 'iron rod,' or the word of God, which could lead them, through faith, to an understanding, rather than to have them stray away into strange paths of man-made theories and be plunged into the murky waters of disbelief and apostasy?" He also said that man is hungry for a knowledge of who they are, where they come from, and what their purpose is. His address encouraged Latter-day Saints not to let go of the rod or get lost in the mists of darkness that were being created by the theories of man.[36]

In April 1975, Elder Ezra Taft Benson, then President of the Quorum of the Twelve, spoke of the iron rod as being the Book of Mormon, warning, "Every Latter-day Saint should make the study of this book a lifetime pursuit. Otherwise he is placing his soul in jeopardy and neglecting that which could give spiritual and intellectual unity to his whole life. There is a difference between a convert who is built on the rock of Christ through the Book of Mormon and stays hold of that iron rod, and one who is not."[37]

The theme of missionary work emerged again when Elder Carlos E. Asay associated the missionary's zeal with Lehi's desire to have his family come to the tree[38] and when Elder Robert L. Backman, a former mission president, urged would-be missionaries to retain a hold on the iron rod.[39] One particularly interesting application associated with missionary work is found in Elder David B. Haight's April 1979 talk, in which he spoke about the responsibility of members to make sure new converts retained a hold on the iron rod of the restored gospel.[40]

In 1984, Elder William Grant Bangerter said, "All you who have read 1 Nephi, chapter 8, will recall the scene. If you have not read it, I wish you would do so and get the feeling and the vision of this picture."[41] In his address, Elder Bangerter referred to a painting that depicted the dream that a young man in prison had produced. After narrating the dream, Elder Bangerter stated, "I know of no more graphic description of the condition of those who call themselves Latter-day Saints in relation to the influences of the world than this great vision. This story is reality. It is a great prophecy. It is a vivid warning." He stated that those people who wandered into forbidden paths of destruction could represent modern day Latter-day Saints who were easily influenced by the thoughts of the world.[42]

In many of these talks one can discern concerns of Church leadership about the ever-increasing threat of secular, humanistic approaches to mankind's problems. Recognizing that these philosophies could lead members astray, the Brethren found a divine model in Lehi's dream that could be applied to this challenge. Yet at the same time the dream was used to emphasize the unique power of the gospel of Christ as an instrument of change and the dream could thus be applied to missionary work.

1985 to the Present

The year 1985 marked a renewed emphasis on the dream, no doubt a result of the teachings of President Benson. John W. Welch declared, "A person would need to be both deaf and blind not to have noticed that President Benson has made [the Book of Mormon] a main theme of paramount importance."[43] With a renewed emphasis on the Book of Mormon in general, the Brethren began to speak of new personal applications of the dream. For instance, Elder Joseph B. Wirthlin often used the dream in his talks concerning enduring to the end.[44] Yet even as the dream began to be associated with various new principles, some approaches emerged as important themes. One of these was the use of the dream to speak about permissive social morals and ethics. To some degree, this may have been a natural offshoot of earlier concerns about secular humanism, but here it is differentiated by social concerns rather than academic ones, and it reflects an increasing concern about new media formats and their influence on the Saints.

This new theme is explicit in President Benson's April 1986 address entitled "The Power of the Word," in which he used the dream to describe the growing threat of immorality: "When we read of the spreading curse of drugs, or read of the pernicious flood of pornography and immorality, do any of us doubt that these are the forbidden paths and rivers of filthiness Lehi described?" Further he adds, "Not only will the word of God lead us to the fruit which is desirable above all others, but in the word of God and through it we can find the power to resist temptation, the power to thwart the work of Satan and his emissaries."[45]

A major concern was the social pressure exerted against the Saints. Elder Neal A. Maxwell addressed concerns about both humanistic and moral laxness in his April 1987 address, speaking of the great and spacious building as a "spacious but third-class hotel."[46] Then, in May 1996, he warned of the influence of those in the great and spacious building, which can lead others into forbidden paths:

> [A] few eager individuals . . . lecture the rest of us about Church doctrines in which they no longer believe. They criticize the use of Church resources to which they no longer contribute. They condescendingly seek to counsel the Brethren whom they no longer sustain. Confrontive, except of themselves of course, they leave the Church, but they cannot leave the Church alone. Like the throng on the ramparts of the "great and spacious building," they are intensely and busily preoccupied, pointing fingers of scorn at the steadfast iron-rodders (1 Ne. 8:26–28, 33). Considering their ceaseless preoccupation, one wonders, "Is there no diversionary activity available to them, especially in such a large building—like a bowling alley?" Perhaps in their mockings and beneath the stir are repressed doubts of their doubts.[47]

Years later, Elder Maxwell used this imagery again when he asked Latter-day Saints to place themselves figuratively in the dream. He encouraged Latter-day Saints to "bear the pointing fingers which, ironically, belong to those finally who, being bored, find the 'great and spacious building' to be a stale and cramped third-class hotel."[48] Elder W. Craig Zwick made a similar observation when he exhorted youth to remember that those who made it to the tree did so by not heeding the mocking of those in the large and spacious building, and Elder Robert S. Wood challenged the Saints, and youth in particular, to avoid the cynicism and mockery that is so common in society and thereby bypass entrance into the large and spacious building.[49]

In 1985, Elder Boyd K. Packer suggested that the Saints "would do well to read very thoughtfully the parable of the tree of life in the eighth chapter of 1 Nephi, and to ponder very soberly verse twenty-eight," which describes those who fell away from the tree and were ashamed "because of those that were scoffing at them." Elder Packer mentioned this scripture as a warning to individuals who were easily persuaded by the world. Later in the talk he referred to those who fell away into forbidden paths and were lost. He asked Saints to be cautious of letting the world influence their faith.⁵⁰ Seven years later, Elder Packer was even more explicit in his talk "Our Moral Environment," where he identified the increasing moral pollution as the mists of darkness.⁵¹

Reacting to the ever-increasing influence of the media and its promotion of a way of life that is alien to the gospel, Elder M. Russell Ballard stressed the importance of parents teaching their children to hold to the iron rod against the encroaching pervasiveness of television.⁵² In April 2002, Elder Jeffrey R. Holland said, "We are bombarded with the message that on the *world's* scale of things we have been weighed in the balance and found wanting. Some days it is as if we have been locked in a cubicle of a great and spacious building where the only thing on the TV is a never-ending soap opera entitled *Vain Imaginations*."⁵³

Elder William R. Bradford spoke of the "clutter" of modern life and suggested that great benefit would come from a renewed emphasis on holding to the rod through scripture study,⁵⁴ a solution that Elder Merrill J. Bateman offered as well.⁵⁵ Elder Yoshihiko Kikuchi reiterated the promise when he said, "We can partake of 'the love of God,' 'the tree of life,' and drink from 'the fountain of living waters' daily by communing with our Holy Father, immersing ourselves in the scriptures, and meditation."⁵⁶

Another common yet specific application of the mists of darkness was to pornography, a medium that spread virally with new media forms. In 2002, President Thomas S. Monson, in reference to the mists of darkness, declared, "In the interpretation of Lehi's dream, we find a rather apt description of the destructiveness of pornography."⁵⁷

The increasing nature of materialism also fits within this category. Elder L. Tom Perry in particular used the dream more than once to teach the importance of gospel integrity rather than the desire for material possessions. In his address "If Ye are Prepared Ye Shall Not Fear," we read:

> The current cries we hear coming from the great and spacious building tempt us to compete for ownership in the things of this world. We think we need a larger home, with a three-car garage, a recreational vehicle parked next to it. We long for designer clothes, extra TV sets, all with VCRs, the latest model computers, and the newest car. Often these items are purchased with borrowed money, without giving any thought to providing for our future needs. The result of all

this instant gratification is overloaded bankruptcy courts and families that are far too preoccupied with their financial burdens.[58]

In another context, he stated:

> Many of you are trying too hard to be unique in your dress and grooming to attract what the Lord would consider the wrong kind of attention. In the Book of Mormon story of the tree of life, it was the people whose "manner of dress was exceedingly fine" who mocked those who partook of the fruit of the tree. It is sobering to realize that the fashion-conscious mockers in the great and spacious building were responsible for embarrassing many, and those who were ashamed "fell away into forbidden paths and were lost" (1 Nephi 8:27–28).[59]

This interpretation was reiterated in April 2009 by Elder Dallin H. Oaks, who warned the "me" generation to avoid the desire to enter the great and spacious building of worldly acclaim and possessions.[60]

As the Church's stance on various social issues such as gay rights became more publicized and ridiculed in the press, Latter-day Saints were instructed to not focus their energy on verbally attacking those who mocked their faith. Instead, General Authorities urged Latter-day Saints to avoid the temptations of Satan as symbolized in the dream-vision.

Elder Robert D. Hales specifically used the dream to describe the manner by which Saints could overcome the world: "Nephi gives a clear and compelling account of the process, which includes desiring, believing, having faith, pondering, and then following the Spirit."[61] In 2006, Elder Hales asked Church members to picture themselves in the dream. He asked, "Are we holding onto the iron rod, or are we going another way? I testify that how we choose to *feel* and *think* and *act* every day is the way we get on the path, and stay on it, until we reach our eternal destination."[62]

The power of the dream as a metaphor for the increasing moral and social concerns were summed up by Elder Holland in 2008 when he spoke of the trials Saints were then dealing with:

> In the course of life all of us spend time in "dark and dreary" places, wildernesses, circumstances of sorrow or fear or discouragement. Our present day is filled with global distress over financial crises,

energy problems, terrorist attacks, and natural calamities. These translate into individual and family concerns not only about homes in which to live and food available to eat but also about the ultimate safety and well-being of our children and the latter-day prophecies about our planet. More serious than these—and sometimes related to them—are matters of ethical, moral, and spiritual decay seen in populations large and small, at home and abroad.[63]

Another theme from this period is that of family relationships and obligations. As early as 1985, Elder Perry emphasized that Latter-day Saints should strive to save their families just as Lehi had encouraged his family to partake of the tree.[64]

Elder Richard G. Scott emphasized the fact that when "Lehi partook of the fruit of the tree of life and was filled with joy, his first thought was to share it with each member of his family, including the disobedient," illustrating the importance of loving "without limitations" instead of judging or giving up on loved ones that need help.[65] Though Elder Scott did not focus solely on Laman and Lemuel, others did; this was an innovation not found at any other time in this dispensation. For example, Elder Glenn L. Pace said that even after Lehi saw in his vision that Laman and Lemuel would not partake of the fruit of the tree, "he never gave up but labored with them and loved them even with his dying breath."[66] Elder William Grant Bangerter said that Laman and Lemuel "turned their back on the tree of life. They joined the world and lost the promise."[67]

Elder Maxwell similarly analyzed Laman and Lemuel's actions: "Laman and Lemuel also displayed little lasting spiritual curiosity. Once true, they asked straightforward questions about the meaning of a vision of the tree, the river, and the rod of iron. Yet their questions were really more like trying to connect doctrinal dots rather than connecting themselves with God and His purposes for them. . . . As to their spiritual significance, Laman and Lemuel were sad ciphers."[68] Addressing the need to liken all scriptures to ourselves, Elder Maxwell used Laman and Lemuel as examples of individuals who did not see their full potential because they could not see Godlike qualities, nor did they express the desire to do so. Later, relating the dream to the relativism of the day, Elder Maxwell taught that the desire to know truth is essential to salvation, noting that Laman and Lemuel never partook of the fruit of the tree of life because they did not seek to understand God.[69]

Speaking of the challenges of parenting, President Boyd K. Packer acknowledged, "It is a great challenge to raise a family in the darkening mists of our moral environment,"[70] while in April 1999 Elder Ballard used the dream to stress the importance of setting the right example in parenting to counteract the prevailing mists of immorality: "As parents, teachers, and leaders, it is our solemn duty to set a powerful, personal example of righteous strength, courage, sacrifice, unselfish service, and self-control. These are the traits that will help our youth hold on to the iron rod of the gospel and remain on the straight and narrow path."[71]

Elder Rex D. Pinegar also built upon the analogy between Lehi and Latter-day Saint fathers, emphasizing "the importance of a father, as patriarch to his family and as its chief priesthood officer, setting a righteous example by making the gospel lifeline operative and effective in his own life and then extending it to his family."[72] In the same vein, in October 2001, Elder Russell M. Nelson spoke of the importance of parents, and fathers specifically, holding on to the iron rod and teaching their children to do the same.[73]

The dream was increasingly used in speeches directed specifically to youth. During the priesthood session in October 1987, Elder Vaughn J. Featherstone referred to the time period as "the most trying time in history." He taught that "the rod of iron leading to the tree of life for you, our young men, may well be the implementation of the complete and full work of the Aaronic Priesthood."[74] Sharon G. Larsen of the Young Women general presidency suggested that the light symbolized in the Young Women torch logo was to help Young Women through their own mists of darkness.[75] In 2009, Ann M. Dibb, also of the Young Women general presidency, built her entire talk to the youth around the powerful imagery of Lehi's dream, concluding with the promise that true joy comes from being obedient and keeping both hands on the rod of iron.[76]

Sister Larsen and Sister Dibb are not the only sisters to use the dream in their talks. In general conference in October 1995, Aileen H. Clyde of the Relief Society general presidency used the iron rod as a general term but then went on to speak of a South African sister who she saw as an example of one who had clung to the rod.[77] Describing the manner in which the Relief Society had led this African Saint to bless her community, particularly through the family organization, Sister Clyde revealed how one could be like Lehi by holding on to the rod. Recently, Mary N. Cook of the Young Women general presidency also spoke of teaching children through example by grasping the iron rod through challenging life experiences. Barbara Thompson of the Relief Society general presidency told of experiences where she observed her niece and her husband teaching their young children about the importance of grasping to the iron rod, suggesting that it is never too early to start teaching children about staying on the path through the simple symbols used in the vision.[78]

As one can see, Lehi's dream continues to play a fundamental role in the teachings of Church leaders, just as it did in earlier generations. Yet, reflecting changes in society and culture, the dream has been adapted to address specific challenges for the Saints. Since President Benson's reemphasis on the Book of Mormon in 1985, the dream has become even more common in the speeches and talks of our leaders, particularly as a means of understanding the fundamental and foundational role of families as well as the challenges of modern life.

Conclusion: You Are in the Dream

Since 2008, when President Monson became President of the Church, the dream has continued to be one of the most often discussed scriptural texts. In the October 2010 conference alone there were at least six allusions to the dream, reflecting the contexts used above.[79] President Monson himself has used the dream twice in one general conference setting, asking the members to recall Lehi's vision of the tree of life[80] and suggesting that the dream continues to grow in importance for Latter-day Saints.

President Boyd K. Packer has described this importance through his own experience. Admitting that earlier in his life the dream "did not mean all that much to me,"[81] he gave Brigham Young University students the current and future view of the dream-vision. His address gives us the answer to why the dream-vision has come of age. President Packer informed Church members that they might find themselves in the dream figuratively, due to the greater influence of the media and the political involvement in individual lives. He observed:

> Largely because of television, instead of looking over into that spacious building, we are, in effect, living inside of it. That is your fate in this generation. You are living in that great and spacious building. . . .

> The mist of darkness will cover you at times so much that you will not be able to see your way even a short distance ahead. You will not be able to see clearly....
>
> Atheists and agnostics make nonbelief their religion and today organize in unprecedented ways to attack faith and belief. They are now organized, and they pursue political power....
>
> You live in an interesting generation where trials will be constant in your life.[82]

President Packer suggested that the dream could be more than simply an allegory or story but a template or guide that one could pattern one's life by. Expressing the need for us to be more than simply passive readers, President Packer challenged Saints to find themselves in the dream: "You may think that Lehi's dream or vision has no special meaning for you, but it does. You are in it; all of us are in it.... As we think... of the dream or vision that Lehi had we see that there are prophecies in there that can be specifically applied to your life. Read it again.... All of the things that you need to know are there. Read it. And make it a part of your life."[83]

When Elder Kevin W. Pearson was called as a General Authority, he exemplified this challenge when he proclaimed the importance of the dream in his life: "I see the entire world through that dream.... That is the prism through which I've seen life."[84] Like Elder Pearson, we too can use the dream as a prism through which much of the plan of salvation can be understood.

Yet for all the specific modern challenges, it is comforting to realize that the applicability of the dream is, in essence, no different for us than it was for the early Brethren in this dispensation. Though the mists of darkness are different in type, they are not different in effect. Whether one is led away by apostates, secular humanism, or permissive moral values, one ends up lost in forbidden territory. And regardless of whether one views the iron rod as the scriptures, the prophet, the Holy Ghost, or one's testimony, it is the rod that will safely lead one back. And with that we can rest assured that whatever new challenges may arise, as President Packer taught, we can continue to "find ourselves" in Lehi's dream.

Notes

1. Cheryl C. Lant, "Hold Tight to the Iron Rod," *Brigham Young University Speeches, 2009–2010* (Provo, UT: Brigham Young University, 2010), 321.
2. Joseph Smith, *History of The Church of Jesus Christ of Latter-day Saints*, B. H. Roberts, ed., 7 vols., 2d ed. rev. (Salt Lake City: The Church of Jesus Christ of Latter-day Saints, 1932–51), 2:52.
3. Givens, *The Book of Mormon: A Very Short Introduction* (New York: Oxford University Press, 2009), 108.
4. Alex Smith, phone conversation with Mary Jane Woodger, July 13, 2011.
5. Givens, *The Book of Mormon: A Very Short Introduction*, 109.
6. Brigham Young, in *Journal of Discourses* (London: Latter-day Saints' Book Depot, 1854–86), 1:236, 323; 3:362; 12:163, 170; 13:93–94).
7. Erastus Snow, in *Journal of Discourses*, 20:374.
8. Joseph F. Smith, in *Journal of Discourses*, 24:76–77; George Q. Cannon, in *Journal of Discourses*, 18:84.
9. George A. Smith, in *Journal of Discourses*, 10:67.
10. John Taylor, in *Journal of Discourses*, 10:261.
11. Orson Hyde, in *Journal of Discourses*, 16:14.
12. Daniel H. Wells, in *Journal of Discourses*, 16:128; Orson Pratt, in *Journal of Discourses*, 8:106.
13. Pratt, in *Journal of Discourses*, 15: 234.
14. Franklin D. Richards, "Holding Fast to the Iron Rod," in *Collected Discourses, 1886–1898* (Sandy, UT: B.H.S., 1987), 1:104.
15. Richards, "Holding Fast," in *Collected Discourses*, 1:107.
16. John W. Taylor, "Morality and Chastity," in Conference Report, October 7, 1898.
17. Anthon H. Lund, in Conference Report, October 1899, 14.
18. Hyrum M. Smith, in Conference Report, October 1905, 23; Charles W. Penrose, in Conference Report, 1906, 85; J. N. Lambert, in Conference Report, April 1921, 54; Nephi Jensen, in Conference Report, April 1922, 43–44; Anthony W. Ivins, in Conference Report, April 1922, 43–44; George Albert Smith, in Conference Report, April 1937, 35–36; Rulon S. Wells, in Conference Report, April 1935, 25, 28.
19. George Q. Cannon, "Sustaining the Authorities," in *Collected Discourses*,1:293.
20. Rulon S. Wells, in Conference Report, October 1909, 113–14.
21. Stephen L. Chipman, in Conference Report, April 1909, 114.
22. Chipman, in Conference Report, April 1917, 132.
23. James E. Talmage, in Conference Report, October 1916, 75.
24. Anthony W. Ivins, in Conference Report, October 1917, 68.
25. Anthon H. Lund, in Conference Report, April 1918, 9.
26. Charles A. Callis, in Conference Report, April 1918, 107.
27. James E. Talmage, in Conference Report, October 1924, 141.
28. Talmage, in Conference Report, October 1929, 48.
29. Harold B. Lee, in Conference Report, April 1943, 127.
30. Marion G. Romney, in Conference Report, October 1943, 39–41.

31. Marion D. Hanks, in Conference Report, April 1957, 129; Marion D. Hanks, in Conference Report, April 1959, 76–77.

32. Harold B. Lee, in Conference Report, April 1964, 23.

33. Delbert L. Stapley, in Conference Report, April 1966, 23–27.

34. Harold B. Lee, "The Iron Rod," *Ensign*, June 1971, 7.

35. Lee, "Iron Rod," 6.

36. Lee, "Iron Rod," 8.

37. Ezra Taft Benson, "The Book of Mormon Is the Word of God," *Ensign*, May 1975, 65.

38. Carlos E. Asay, "The Spirit of Missionary Work," *Ensign*, November 1976, 41–42.

39. Robert L. Backman, "To the Young Men of the Church," *Ensign*, November 1980, 42.

40. David B. Haight, "'Feed My Sheep,'" *Ensign*, May 1979, 62.

41. William Grant Bangerter, "Coming through the Mists," *Ensign*, May 1984, 28.

42. Bangerter, "Coming through the Mists," 28.

43. John W. Welch, "Study, Faith, and the Book of Mormon," *Brigham Young University Speeches, 1987–1988* (Provo, UT: Brigham Young University, 1988), 140.

44. See, for example, Joseph B. Wirthlin, "Running Your Marathon," *Ensign*, November 1989, 74; Joseph B. Wirthlin, "One Step After Another," *Ensign* November 2001, 25-27; Joseph B. Wirthlin, "The Straight and Narrow Way," *Ensign*, November 1990, 65–66.

45. Ezra Taft Benson, "The Power of the Word," *Ensign*, May 1986, 79, 80.

46. Neal A. Maxwell, "Overcome . . . Even As I Also Overcame," *Ensign*, May 1987, 72.

47. Neal A. Maxwell, "'Becometh As a Child,'" *Ensign*, May 1996, 68.

48. Neal A. Maxwell, "How Choice a Seer!" *Ensign*, November 2003, 102.

49. W. Craig Zwick, "We Will Not Yield, We Cannot Yield," *Ensign*, May 2008, 98; Robert S. Wood, "Instruments of the Lord's Peace," *Ensign*, May 2006, 94–95.

50. Boyd K. Packer, "'From Such Turn Away,'" *Ensign*, May 1985, 35.

51. Boyd K. Packer, "Our Moral Environment," *Ensign*, May 1992, 66.

52. M. Russell Ballard, "The Effects of Television," *Ensign*, May 1989, 80.

53. Jeffrey R. Holland, "The Other Prodigal," *Ensign*, May 2002, 63.

54. William R. Bradford, "Unclutter Your Life," *Ensign*, May 1992, 29.

55. Merrill J. Bateman, "Coming unto Christ by Searching the Scriptures," *Ensign*, November 1992, 28.

56. Yoshihiko Kikuchi, "Heavenly Father Has a Special Plan," *Ensign*, May 2000, 79.

57. Thomas S. Monson, "Peace, Be Still," *Ensign*, November 2002, 54.

58. L. Tom Perry, "'If Ye Are Prepared Ye Shall Not Fear," *Ensign*, November 1995, 35.

59. L. Tom Perry, "Let Him Do It with Simplicity," *Ensign*, November 2008, 10.

60. Dallin H. Oaks, "Unselfish Service," *Ensign*, May 2009, 95.

61. Robert D. Hales, "Receiving a Testimony of the Restored Gospel of Jesus Christ," *Ensign*, November 2003, 30.

62. Robert D. Hales, "To Act for Ourselves: The Gift and Blessings of Agency," *Ensign*, May 2006, 6.

63. Jeffrey R. Holland, "The Ministry of Angels," *Ensign*, November 2008, 29.
64. L. Tom Perry, "'Born of Goodly Parents,'" *Ensign*, May 1985, 22.
65. Richard G. Scott, "To Help a Loved One in Need," *Ensign*, May 1988, 60.
66. Glenn L. Pace, "A Thousand Times," *Ensign*, November 1990, 8.
67. William Grant Bangerter, "The Quality of Eternal Life," *Ensign*, November 1988, 82.
68. Neal A. Maxwell, "Lessons from Laman and Lemuel," *Ensign*, November 1999, 8.
69. Maxwell, "Lessons from Laman and Lemuel," 9.
70. Boyd K. Packer, "Our Moral Environment," 68.
71. M. Russell Ballard, "Like a Flame Unquenchable," *Ensign*, May 1999, 87.
72. Rex D. Pinegar, "The Gospel Lifeline," *Ensign*, November 1985, 40.
73. Russell M. Nelson, "Set in Order Thy House," *Ensign*, November 2001, 69.
74. Vaughn J. Featherstone, "A Champion of Youth," *Ensign*, November 1987, 29–30.
75. Sharon G. Larsen, "Your Light in the Wilderness," *Ensign*, May 1999, 90.
76. Ann M. Dibb, "Hold On," *Ensign*, November 2009, 80–81.
77. Aileen H. Clyde, "What Is Relief Society For?," *Ensign*, November 1995, 97.
78. Mary N. Cook, "A Virtuous Life—Step by Step," *Ensign*, May 2009, 118–19; Barbara Thompson, "His Arm Is Sufficient," *Ensign*, May 2009, 84; see also Mary N. Cook, "Be an Example of the Believers," *Ensign*, November 2010, 80–81.
79. Mary N. Cook, "Be an Example of the Believers," 80–81; Jairo Mazzagardi, "Avoiding the Trap of Sin," *Ensign*, November 2010, 103–5; Neil L. Anderson, "Never Leave Him," *Ensign*, November 2010, 40; Rosemary M. Wixom, "Stay on the Path," *Ensign*, November 2010, 9; Richard G. Scott, "The Transforming Power of Faith and Character," *Ensign*, November 2010, 45–46; Patrick Kearon, "'Come unto Me with Full Purpose of Heart, and I Shall Heal You,'" *Ensign*, November 2010, 51.
80. Thomas S. Monson, "May You Have Courage," *Ensign*, May 2009, 126.
81. Boyd K. Packer, "The Book of Mormon: Another Testament of Jesus Christ—Plain and Precious Things," *Ensign*, May 2005, 7.
82. Boyd K. Packer, "Lehi's Dream and You," *Brigham Young University Speeches, 2006–2007* (Provo, UT: Brigham Young University, 2007), 5.
83. Packer, "Lehi's Dream and You," 6.
84. Julie Dockstader Heaps, "Lehi's Dream Provides a Guiding View of Life," *Church News*, June 14, 2008.

Index

Aaron, 128–29
Aaronic Priesthood, 199–201, 387
Abandonment, 123
Abyss, 223
Academia, 265, 379, 380
Action, faith and, 306–12
Adam and Eve: presence of the Lord and, 122, 153n18; tree of life and, 138–41; marriage of, 153n16; ancient temple and, 172–73; Fall and, 320–21; sacrifice and, 332–33
Addiction, 4
Agency: invitations and, 1–2, 3, 4; to come unto Christ, 120–21; presence of the Lord and, 124–26, 129–31, 132; Spencer W. Kimball on, 321–22; David A. Bednar on, 325; temptation and, 325–26
Allegories: of Lehi, 16–17, 20; prophecy and, 203–4
Alma the Younger, 131, 223–25
American Revolution: introduction to, 264–66; Founding Fathers and, 266–69; weather during, 269–73; West Point chain and, 273–75; hand of God in, 275–77; conclusions on, 277–78
Ammon, 225, 248–50, 252, 253, 261n17
Ancient Near Eastern dream reports, 96–100, 113nn16, 18, 114n25
Ancient scripture, 148–49
Ancient temple, 172–75
Andersen, Neil L., 147–48, 160n45
Anderson, Richard L., 290
Angels: tongue of, 168; words of, 170–72; ancient temple and, 174; defined, 177n7

Apocalyptic eschatology, 59–61
Apocalyptic literature: Nephi's vision as, 39; Lehi's vision as, 53–54; history and, 54–56; description of, 56–57, 212n5; spatial versus temporal dimensions in, 58–59; prophetic versus apocalyptic eschatology in, 59–61; dualism and, 61–64; book of Revelation and, 64–65; application of, 65–67
Apostasy, 74–75, 146
Apostles, 74, 286–87
Application of Lehi's vision: introduction to, 199–201; according to Lehi, 201–2; Nephi's vision and, 203–4; divergent, of Nephi and Lehi, 204–8; prophetic perspective and, 208–11; prophetic prerogative and, 211–12
Asay, Carlos E., 381
Atonement: double nature of salvation and, 29–31; loss of truth concerning, 84; partaking of, 125; path of discipleship through, 135–36, 139–40; in Nephi's vision, 187; as sacrifice, 338–39
Augustine, 76

Backman, Robert L., 381
Ballard, M. Russell, 294, 384, 387
Bangerter, William Grant, 381–82, 386
Baptism: of Jesus Christ, 31–32, 163, 164, 285–86, 295–96nn14, 15, 19; presence of the Lord and, 125; path of discipleship and, 141–44; by fire, 155n23, 165; repentance and, 159n36; as gate to strait and narrow path, 164–65; necessary actions after, 167–70, 178n20

Bateman, Merrill J., 384
Baxter, David S., 147
Beast, in Revelation, 65
Bednar, David A.: on gathering and temple-building, 143; on learning by faith, 306; on spiritual growth, 308; on iron rod, 310; on tree of life, 311; on agency, 325
"Beheld," 106
"Behold," 103, 106
Belnap, Daniel L., 185
Benjamin, King, 251–52
Benson, Ezra Taft: on strait and narrow path, 151–52; on American history, 265; on Founding Fathers, 267; on Book of Mormon, 292, 381; on condescension of God, 332, 336–37; on immorality, 382
Bethabara, 285, 295nn14, 15
Bible: in Nephi's vision, 190–92, 282–83; Book of Mormon as witness of, 283–88; nature of, 288–91; role of, 291–92; conclusions on, 292–94. *See also* Corruption, of biblical texts
Biblical context of dreams: introduction to, 92–93; Lehi's vision and, 93–95, 104–10; ancient Near Eastern dream reports and, 96–100; biblical dream reports and, 100–104; conclusions on, 110–11
Bid, 2
Bigelow, John F., 265, 266, 277, 278
Bitterness, 323–27
Blake, William, 324–25
Blessings: inspired invitations and, 11; proximity of trials and, 324–25
Book of Mormon: human error in, 77; as testament of Jesus Christ, 80–81; as restoration of lost truths, 86–87; presence of the Lord in, 124–27; "cast off" in, 127–31; in Nephi's vision, 191–92, 282–83; dream narrative in, 222–26, 237n20, 238nn27, 28; Exodus narrative in, 235n8; as Bible witness, 283–88; role of, 291–92; conclusions on, 292–94; Joseph Smith on, 375; Ezra Taft Benson on, 381; renewed emphasis on, 382
Book(s), in Nephi's vision, 190–91
Bradford, William R., 384
Brass plates, 148–49, 288–89
Brazen sea, 173, 178n17
Brooklyn Heights, evacuation of, 270–72
Buddhist order, 367n4

Building, great and spacious, 56, 183, 186–87, 312–14, 364–65

Callings, 1–2, 7–8
Callis, Charles A., 379
Candlesticks, 174
Cannon, George Q., 43–44, 160n45, 376, 378
"Cast off": introduction to, 119–21; Old Testament and, 123–24; in Book of Mormon, 127–31; conclusions on, 131–32
Catawba River, 272, 280n31
Chain, West Point, 273–75
Chaos, 215, 217–19, 223, 228, 234n4
Cheever, Rev. George, 267, 278
Cherubim, 140, 154n20, 172–73, 174
Chester Beatty "Dream Book," 96–97
Children: teaching, 314; sacrificing, 333–34, 337
Chipman, Stephen L., 378
Choice: coming unto Christ as, 120; presence of the Lord and, 124–26, 129–31, 132. *See also* Agency
Christianity, theological differences within, 74–76, 88–89n15, 290
Christology, 76, 79
Chrysostom, John, 295n14
Church, great and abominable, 188, 194
Church of Jesus Christ of Latter-day Saints, The: reactivation in, 11–12, 13; as church of Lamb of God, 39–41; growth and membership of, 41–43; righteousness of, 43–44; in last days, 46–47
Church of the devil, 45, 63–65, 194
Church of the Lamb of God: introduction to, 37–38; use and description of, 38–39; historical context of, 39–44; typological context of, 45–47; triumph of, 47–49; conclusions on, 49–50; dualism and, 63–64; book of Revelation and, 64–65; church of the devil and, 194
Church welfare, 380
Clark, J. Reuben Jr., 293
Clubs, 361–63, 366
Clyde, Aileen H., 387
Cognate objects, 95
Collins, John J., 57, 212n5
Community, learning, 361–63, 366

Condescension of God: Nephi's vision and, 181–82, 183, 231, 334–40; Bible and, 190–91; introduction to, 330–31; overview of, 331–32; as sacrifice, 332–34; applying, 340–43
Consecration, 342, 343–44
Cook, Gene R., 350, 351, 364
Cook, Mary N., 387–88
Cook, Quentin L., 341, 342
Copyists, early, 73–74, 88nn13, 15, 290
Cornelius, 288
Cornwallis, Charles, 272
Corporate salvation, 20–21
Corruption, of biblical texts: introduction to, 70–71; defined, 71–72; causes of, 72–81; 88nn13, 15; 90n29; Nephi's vision and, 81–85, 289–90; conclusions on, 85–87
Cosmos, 214–15, 217, 219, 234n4
Covenants: keeping, 8; Boyd K. Packer on, 40; as plain and precious truths, 82–83; path of discipleship and, 136–37, 144, 151; Adam and Eve and, 139–40; meal imagery and, 220
Cowdery, Oliver, 199–201
Cowpens, Battle of, 272
Craik, James, 268
Creation, 215, 217–19, 221, 234n4
Cultural narrative: introduction to, 214–15; Lehi's vision and, 215–22; dream narrative and, 222–26; coming of Christ and, 226–33; conclusions on, 233
"Cut off," 126, 134n24, 260n1

Daniel, 104
Dark and dreary wilderness, 217–18, 349, 369n23
Darkness: at coming of Christ, 227–28; symbolism of, 349. See also Mists of darkness
Day of Judgment, 124
DeForest, Samuel, 271–72
Degrees of glory, 132, 156n26
Desert, 360, 368n12
Desires, 130
Devil, church of, 45, 63–65, 194
Dibb, Ann M., 387
Discipleship, 339, 341–44. See also Path of discipleship

Disobedience, 122, 125–26, 145–46
Divination, 96–97, 99, 113n21
Divine, transformation into, 220–21
Divine guide, 218, 228–30, 292
Doctrine of Christ: introduction to, 161–62; and tree of life vision, 162–64; elements of, 164–67; additional information on, 167–70; angelic ministration and, 170–72; ancient temple and, 172–75; conclusions on, 175
Dove, sign of, 285–86, 296n19
Draper, Richard D., 152n11, 154n21
Dream books, 96–97
Dream narrative, 222–26, 237n20, 238nn27, 28
Dreams, biblical context of: introduction to, 92–93; Lehi's vision and, 93–95, 104–10; ancient Near Eastern dream reports and, 96–100; biblical dream reports and, 100–104; conclusions on, 110–11
Dualism, 61–64
Dunlap, John, 276–77
Dyer, Alvin R., 154n18

Early copyists and scribes, 73–74, 88nn13, 15, 290
Early manuscripts, 73, 78–81, 88nn13, 15, 90n29, 290
Eating, 220–21, 354
Eden. See Garden of Eden
Edgley, Richard C., 339, 340
Education. See Learning and teaching, in Lehi's vision
Ehrman, Bart D., 76, 79, 289, 290
Eliade, Mircea, 359–60
Eliot, Charles, 378
Enduring to the end: covenant path and, 136; Adam and Eve and, 140; feasting on word of Christ and, 142–46, 156n27; salvation through, 163; failure in, 165–66
Enlightenment. See Illumination
Entreat, 2
Eternal life, 135–36, 163, 166–67. See also Immortality
Example, set by Jesus Christ, 31–32, 141, 163–65, 174–75
Exodus narrative, 215–16, 218, 221, 224, 234n4

Experience, education and, 348
Eyring, Henry B., 150, 155n23, 157n31, 309

Faith: developing, 159n39; compared to seed, 224–25; as remedy for unbelief, 241–42; of Laman and Lemuel, 242–46; of Lamanites, 252–53; of Nephites and Lamanites, 256–57; deteriorating, 258–59; of Lehi's children, 303; illumination through, 306–12; of first multitude, 363
Fall, 138–39, 320–23
False prophets, 102, 116n52
Family, 201–2, 259, 386–87
Farrar, Frederic, 69n25
Father of King Lamoni, 128–29
Fathers, 387
Fear, 127–29, 363, 373nn57–59, 378
Featherstone, Vaughn J., 387
Field, large and spacious, 184–86, 193, 216–18, 302
Filthy water, 184
"Finger of scorn," 376
Fire, baptism by, 141, 155n23, 163, 165, 170
Flaming sword, 140, 154n20, 172–73
Fog, 271–72
Food: eating, 220–21, 354; hoarding, 380
Forbidden fruit: introduction to, 318–19; flavor of, 319–20; perspectives on, 320–23; proximity of bitter and sweet, 323–25
Founding Fathers, 266–69, 277
Fountain of water, 184, 187
Framing, 145–46
Franklin, Benjamin, 275, 276
French and Indian War, 267
Fruit: use of term, 106–7; symbolism of, 219–21; introduction to, 318–19; flavor of, 319–20; perspectives on, 320–23; proximity of bitter and sweet, 323–25
Frye, Northrup, 359
Fulness of the Gospel, 33–34

Garden of Eden: presence of the Lord and, 122, 153–54nn16, 18, 20; tree of life and, 138–41; as temple, 156n28, 231; ancient temple and, 172–73; Fall and, 320–21
Garrett, H. Dean, 156n24
Gate, of repentance and baptism, 164–65
Gathering, 143–44

Generational consequences of unbelief: introduction to, 240–42; faith of Laman and Lemuel and, 242–46; compassion for Lamanites and, 246–48; Lamanite conversion and, 248–53; faith of Lamanites and Nephites and, 253–57; rebelliousness and, 257–58; deteriorating faith and, 258–59; conclusions on, 259–60
Gentiles: salvation of, 23; manifestation of Jesus Christ to, 30, 287–88; in America, 188–93
George III, King, 269
Gilgamesh, 98–99
Givens, Terry L., 376
Glory, degrees of, 132, 156n26
God: rest of the Lord and, 137; love of, 196n8, 294, 352–53; wrath of, 269; Jesus Christ as, 294n9; nature of, 328. *See also* Condescension of God; Presence of the Lord; Word of God
Good works, 380
Gospel, fulness of, 33–34. *See also* Church of Jesus Christ of Latter-day Saints, The
Great and abominable church, 188
Great and spacious building, 56, 183, 186–87, 312–14, 364–65
Griggs, C. Wilfred, 138, 153n13
Groups, salvation of: introduction to, 15; Lehi's wilderness address and, 16–21; Nephi's vision and, 21–23; additional development of, 23–33; conclusions on, 33–34
Growth, spiritual, 308, 316n12
Guide, divine, 218, 228–30, 292
Gulf, 193, 223

Hafen, Bruce C., 327
Haight, David B., 381
Hales, Robert D., 259, 314, 385
Halifax, Joan, 347
Hanks, Marion D., 380
Hell, 193, 223
Hexapla, 88n13
High priest, 174–75
Hinckley, Gordon B., 44
Hinneh, 103, 106, 116n55
History, Lehi's vision as, 54–56
Hoarding, 380

Holland, Jeffrey R., 111n1, 179–80, 384, 385–86
Holy Ghost: presence of the Lord and, 126–27; path of discipleship and, 141–42, 149; as doctrine of Christ, 165; tongue of angels and, 168; in form of dove, 285–86, 296n19; Gentiles and, 287–88; learning through, 306–7, 350–51
Holy of Holies, 174
Holy Place, 173–74
Home teaching, 7–3
Hope, 258–59
Howe, Sir William, 270
Hudson River, 273–74
Humility, 327, 335–36
Huntsman, Eric D., 67n7
Hyde, Orson, 377

Ignorance, 349
Illumination: introduction to, 300–301; through prayer, 301–5; through faith and action, 306–12; worldliness and, 312–15; conclusions on, 315. *See also* Revelation
Immorality, 382–87
Immortality, 135–35, 153n16. *See also* Eternal life
Inactive members, reactivating, 11–12, 13
Incense, 174
Inclusio, 241
Incorporation, 348, 354–56, 360
Incubation, 114n38
Individuals, salvation of: introduction to, 15; Lehi's wilderness address and, 16–21; Nephi's vision and, 21–23; additional development of, 23–33; conclusions on, 33–34
Initiation, 347, 348, 360–66, 367
Interpretation: of dreams, 96–97, 99–100, 104, 109–10; of Nephi's vision, 179–81; divergent, of Nephi and Lehi, 204–8
Invitations: introduction to, 1–2; in Lehi's vision, 2–3; temptation and, 3–6; power in giving and receiving, 7–10; Restoration and, 9–11; accepting and extending, 11–14; in dream reports, 103, 106; to come unto Christ, 120; missionary work and, 379
Iron, 275

Iron rod: symbolism of, 56, 356–59; path of discipleship and, 147–51; description of, 184; as divine guide, 218; importance of, 309–10; river of filthy water and, 323–24; in LDS history, 376–88. *See also* Word of God
Israel: salvation of, 16–18, 20–21; scattering of, 23, 83; prophecies on, 24–26; dreams and, 100–102; gathering, 143–44; in America, 188–93; cultural narrative of, 215–16. *See also* Exodus narrative
Ivins, Anthony W., 379

Jacob, dream of, 99, 157n30, 330–31
Jehovah, dreams and, 101–2
Jerusalem, destruction of, 27–28, 301
Jesus Christ: coming of, 28, 81–82, 83, 226–33, 239n34; salvation through, 29–31, 32–33, 167; baptism of, 31–32, 141, 295–96nn14, 15, 19; triumph of, 47–49; coming unto, 66–67; Christology and, 75–76, 79; witnesses of, 80–81; plan of salvation and, 84; rest of the Lord and, 137; example set by, 163–65, 174–75, 342–43; word of, 166, 168, 171; redemption of, 179–80; earthly ministry of, 181–84; sacrifice of, 196n8; as Messiah, 283–86; ministry and disciples of, 286–87; death and resurrection of, 287–88; as God, 294n9; love of God and, 352–53; truth and, 353, 371n34; iron rod and, 357–59. *See also* Atonement; Condescension of God; Doctrine of Christ; Presence of the Lord
Jewish literature, 153n13
Jewish scribes, 90n29
John the Baptist, 31, 199–201, 284–86, 295nn14, 15
John the Beloved, 286–87, 369n20
Jorgensen, Bruce W., 35n11
Joseph of Egypt, 78, 99, 102–3
Journey, 351–52, 360–61
Joy, 324–25
Judgment, 28, 124
Justice, 128–29, 189, 206–7, 321–22

Kennedy, John F., 266
Keret, 97–98
Kikuchi, Yoshihiko, 384

Kimball, Spencer W., 298n48, 321–22, 326
Korihor, 118n75

Laman and Lemuel: differing perspectives on, 204–5, 207–10; faith of, 242–46, 303; Church leaders on, 386. *See also* Generational consequences of unbelief
Lamanites: fate of, 188; conversion of, 225–26, 230, 248–53; unbelief of, 243–45; compassion for, 246–48; faith of, 253–57; rebelliousness of, 257–58; hope for, 258–59
Lamb of God, 31. *See also* Church of the Lamb of God
Lamoni, King, 249–50, 305, 316n2
Lamoni, King, father of, 128–29
Land of promise, 186–93, 197n14, 225
Lant, Cheryl C., 374–75
Large and spacious field, 184–86, 193, 216–18, 302
Larsen, Sharon G., 387
Last days, 46–49
Laver of water, 173, 178n17
Learning and teaching, in Lehi's vision: introduction to, 347–49; separation stage in, 349–52; threshold experience in, 352–54; incorporation stage in, 354–56; transition in, 356–60; initiation of multitudes in, 360–66; conclusions on, 367
Learning by faith, 306–7
Lee, Harold B., 156n25, 319, 380–81
Lehi's vision, application of: introduction to, 199–201; according to Lehi, 201–2; Nephi's vision and, 203–4; divergent, of Nephi and Lehi, 204–8; prophetic perspective and, 208–11; prophetic prerogative and, 211–12
Lehi's vision and Nephi's vision, Church leaders' use of: introduction to, 374–75; during nineteenth century, 375–78; during twentieth century, 378–82; from 1985 to present, 382–88; conclusions on, 388–89
Lewis, C. S., 48, 322, 326–27
Liminality, 348, 352
Linking phrases and symbols, 183
Lipne YHWH, 122

Love: inspired invitation and, 4, 5; of God, 196n8, 294, 352–53
Lund, Anthon H., 378, 379

Madison, James, 276
Manuscripts, early, 73, 78–81, 88nn13, 15, 90n29, 290
Marcion, 88–89n15
Marriage, 144, 153n16, 157n29
Masoretes, 90n29
Masoretic Text, 90n29
Materialism, 64, 66, 384
Matthews, Robert J., 155n21, 293, 299n51
Maxwell, Neal A.: on correction, 9; on path of discipleship. 136–37; on baptism, 143–44; on love of God, 196n8; on revelation, 304; on blessings and trials, 324; on humility, 327; on God's nature, 328; on submission of will, 341, 343; on veneration of Jesus, 341; on consecration, 342; on great and spacious building, 383; on Laman and Lemuel, 386
McConkie, Bruce R.: on church of devil, 45; on persecution of Saints, 49; on temples, 49; on dreams and visions, 112n11; on Adam and Eve, 140; on path of discipleship. 142; on obtaining eternal life, 166–67; on Satan and scriptures, 192; on American Revolution, 269; on condescension of God, 336
McConkie, Joseph Fielding, 135–36, 155n24
McMullen, Keith B., 344
Meal imagery, 220–21
Media, 313, 314, 324, 382, 384, 388
Menorah, 138
Mercy, 124–25, 127–29, 228–30
Message dreams, 97–98, 100
Messiah, 283–84
Millennium, 49–50, 52n27
Millet, Robert L., 135–36, 155n24
Missionary work: as invitation, 5–6, 9, 10–11, 379, 381; Nephites as, 243–46
Mists of darkness, 56, 186–87, 191–92, 217–18, 227–28
Monongahela, Battle of the, 267–68
Monson, Thomas S.: extends call to Russell Osguthorpe, 1; invitation of, 11–12; on reactivating members, 13; on pornography, 384; on Lehi's vision, 388

Morals, social, 382–87
Morgan, Daniel, 272, 280n31
Mortality: presence of the Lord in, 125–27; Lehi's vision as parallel to, 302; opposition in, 325–27
Moses, 78, 133n4
Mosiah, sons of, 128, 225
Multitudes, initiation of, 360–66

Narrative structure, of dream reports, 104–5
Nations, salvation of: introduction to, 15; Lehi's wilderness address and, 16–21; Nephi's vision and, 21–23; additional development of, 23–33; conclusions on, 33–34
Natural disasters, 227, 230, 269–73, 280n32
Near Eastern dream reports, 96–100, 113nn16, 18, 114n25
Nebuchadnezzar, 104, 330–31
Nelson, Russell M., 387
Nephi, land of, 216, 235n8, 246–47, 261n14
Nephi's vision: introduction to, 179–81; Christ's earthly ministry and, 181–84; Lehi's vision and, 184–86; land of promise and, 186–88; Gentiles and Israel in America, 188–93; time before Second Coming in, 193–94; conclusions on, 195–96, 292–94; allegory and prophecy and, 203–4; dream narrative and, 237n20, 238n27; as Bible witness, 283–88; nature of Bible and, 288–91; role of Bible and Book of Mormon and, 291–92; sacrifice and condescension in, 334–40. *See also* Lehi's vision and Nephi's vision, Church leaders' use of
Nephites: destruction of, 187–88, 205, 228, 238n28; Exodus narrative and, 215–16; missionary efforts of, 243–53; unbelief of, 253–56; faith of, 256–57; rebelliousness of, 258
Neuenschwander, Dennis B., 160n48
New Jerusalem, 48–49
"New religion," 378
New World. *See* Land of promise
New York Fortifications Committee, 274, 275
Nibley, Hugh, 360, 364–65, 368n12, 373n59

Oaks, Dallin H., 313, 320, 385
Obedience: presence of the Lord and, 122, 125–26; path of discipleship and, 145–46; to law of sacrifice, 337; to Jesus Christ, 358–59; fear and, 378
Old Testament, 121–24
Olive tree allegory, 16–17, 20
Olsen, Steven L., 35n11, 67n3
Omission, in early biblical texts, 78, 88–89n15, 290
Oppenheim, A. Leo, 113n16, 114n25
Opposition, 325–27. *See also* Temptation; Trials
Ordinances: Boyd K. Packer on, 40; path of discipleship and, 136–37, 144; Adam and Eve and, 139–40
Origen, 88n13, 295n14
Osguthorpe, Russell T., 350, 367
Outer court, of ancient temple, 173

Pace, Glenn L., 386
Packer, Boyd K.: on Lehi's vision, vii, 65–66, 137, 300, 312–13, 383–84, 388–89; on Church doctrine, 40; on priesthood, 44; on path of discipleship, 151; on scriptures, 298n47; on great and spacious building, 313; on spiritual growth, 316n12; on parenting, 387
Palmer, Parker, 347, 351–52, 354–55, 357, 364, 370n26
Pānîm, 121–22
Parables, 54–55, 67n4, 68n8
Parenting, 314, 387
Parry, Donald W., 152n7
Path: straight versus strait, 155n24; leading to tree of life, 359–60
Path of discipleship: introduction to, 135–37; tree of life motif and, 137–41; baptism and, 141–43; staying on, 143–46; iron rod and, 147–51; conclusions on, 151–52; gate to, 164–65; pressing forward on, 166; Joseph Smith on, 178n20
Pearson, Kevin W., 389
Penrose, Charles W., 153n16
Perry, L. Tom: on tree of life vision, viii; on baptism, 141–42; on establishment of United States, 265, 277; on materialism, 384–85; on family, 386

Persecution, 49, 364–65, 377
Perspective, 320–23
Peter, vision of, 330–31
Petersen, Mark E., 277
Pilate, 287, 371n34
Pilgrimage, 351–52, 360–61
Pinckney, Charles, 276
Pinegar, Rex D., 387
Pit, 193
Plain and precious truths, loss of: introduction to, 70–71; defined, 71–72; causes of, 72–81, 88nn13, 15; Nephi's vision and, 81–85, 289–90; conclusions on, 85–87
Plainness, 72
Plan of salvation: Lehi teaches, 18–20; in small plates, 25–26; salvation history and, 27–31; as plain and precious truth, 83–84; Adam and Eve and, 139–40; Harold B. Lee on, 156n25; angelic ministration and, 170–72; agency and, 321–22
Pontius Pilate, 287, 371n34
Pornography, 382, 384
Pratt, Orson, 377
Prayer, 169–70, 174, 301–5, 321–22
Premortal existence, 302
Presence of the Lord: introduction to, 119–21; Old Testament and, 119–21; in Book of Mormon, 124–27; conclusions on, 131–32
Pressing forward, 166. *See also* Enduring to the end
Prete, Roy A., 69n24
Pride, 188, 255–56
Priesthood, 44, 199–201
Princeton, Battle of, 272
Promise, land of, 186–88, 197n14, 225
Prophecy, 39, 69n25, 78, 109, 203–4
Prophetic eschatology, 59–61
Prophets: Nephi and Lehi cite, 24; false, 102, 116n52; word of God and, 150–51; scriptures and, 160n45; differing perspectives of, 208–11; prerogative of, 211–12; following, 304; persecution of, 365
Punctuation, ancient, 79–80
Punning, in dream reports, 99, 103

Rationalism, 290
Redemption, 128–29, 179–80
Repentance: presence of the Lord and, 128–29, 130–31; Adam and Eve and, 153n18; baptism and, 159n36; as gate to strait and narrow path, 164–65; resisting temptation and, 326
Repetition of words, 183–84
Rest of the Lord, 137
Restoration: invitations and, 9–11; parables and, 68n8; establishment of United States and, 277
Resurrection, 29, 287–88
Revelation: loss of, 74–75; through dreams, 99, 100–102, 109; through prophets, 150–51; scriptures and, 160n45; prayer and, 169–70, 303–4; eyewitness accounts of, 199–201; through faith and action, 306–12. *See also* Illumination
Revelation, book of, 57–58, 64–65, 154–55n21, 286–87
Revolutionary War. *See* American Revolution
Reynolds, Noel B., 159n36
Rhetorical value, of dream reports, 108–9
Richards, Franklin D., 377–78
Richardson, Matthew O., 9
Righteousness: of Church, 43–44; before second coming, 46–47; in tree of life vision, 158n34; resisting temptation and, 326
Ringgren, Helber, 123
Rites of passage, 348, 367n4
Ritual, 138, 348, 361
River of filthy water, 56, 184, 206–7, 218, 323–24
Robe, 350. *See also* White robe, man in
Robinson, Stephen E., 38, 39, 156n24
Rod of iron. *See* Iron rod
Romney, Marion G., 157n30, 380
Rust, Richard Dilworth, 348

Sacrament, 354
Sacred trees and plants, 137, 152n7, 153nn12, 13
Sacrifice: *lipne YHWH* and, 122; introduction to, 330–31; overview of, 331–32; condescension as, 332–34; Nephi's vision and, 334–40; applying

Christ's example of, 340–43; conclusions on, 343–44
Salvation, double nature of: introduction to, 15; Lehi's wilderness address and, 16–21; Nephi's vision and, 21–23; additional development of, 23–33; in small plates, 25–26; conclusions on, 33–34; apocalyptic literature and, 59
Salvation history, 20–21, 23–33
Samuel the Lamanite, 253–55, 262n31
Satan, 4, 69n28, 325–27
Scott, Richard G., 386
Scribes, early, 73–74, 88nn13, 15, 90n29, 290
Scriptoriums, 73–74
Scripture(s): ancient, 148–49; revelation and, 160n45; angelic ministration and, 170–71; Bruce R. McConkie on Satan and, 192; importance of, 250–52. *See also* Bible; Book of Mormon; Word of God
Sealing, 144
Second coming, 46, 193–94
Seed, 107, 117n66, 224
Selfishness, 4, 312–15
Separation stage, 348, 349–52, 362
Septuagint, 76, 88n13
Service, 312–14, 339, 341–42
Shared revelation, 199–201
Shewbread, 173, 174
Sin, 321–22, 324–25
Skinner, Andrew C., 157n30
Skousen, Royal, 205
Smith, Alex, 375–76
Smith, Frank, 361
Smith, George A., 376
Smith, George Albert, 39
Smith, Joseph: Restoration and, 9; on Church growth, 43; on latter days, 46; on Millennium, 52n27; parables and, 68n8; on teaching Church leaders, 155n22; on degrees of glory, 156n26; on path of discipleship, 178n20; Aaronic Priesthood and, 199–201; on sign of dove, 285; on Bible, 289; on translating Book of Mormon, 291; gifts of, 293; on latter-day sacrifice, 334; on Jesus as Son of God, 339
Smith, Joseph F., 137, 376
Smith, Joseph Fielding, 42, 49, 52n27
Snow, Erastus, 376
Snow, Lorenzo, 344

Social concerns, 382–83, 385–86
Solitude, 351–52
Solomon, dream of, 98
Sons of Mosiah, 128, 225
Spiritual growth, 308, 316n12
Stapley, Delbert L., 380
Stark, Rodney, 41
Sterling Forge, 275
Straight path, 155n24, 176n5
Strait path, 155n24, 176n5
Stripling warriors, 252–53
Subject-centered teaching, 355–56
Sweetness, 323–25
Sword, flaming, 140, 154n20, 172–73
Symbolic dreams, 98–101, 104–5, 109–10

Tallmadge, Benjamin, 270–71
Talmage, James E., 80, 322–23, 379
Taylor, John, 377
Taylor, John W., 378
Teaching. *See* Learning and teaching, in Lehi's vision
Television, 313, 384, 388. *See also* Media
Temple(s): construction of, 43–44, 49; presence of the Lord and, 122, 124; tree of life and, 138; gathering and, 143–44; Garden of Eden and, 154n20, 156n28, 231; doctrine of Christ and ancient, 172–75; built by Nephi, 177–78n15
Temple work, 337
Temptation: as invitation, 3–6; scriptural examples of, 69n28; of Nephites and Lamanites, 186–87, 192; bitterness of, 321–22; purpose of, 325–27; overcoming, 385–86
Testimony, 308
Theological changes, to early biblical texts, 79, 88–89n15, 290
Theological differences, within Christianity, 74–76, 88–89n15, 290
Thompson, Barbara, 388
Thompson, Robert, 265, 268
Thoth, 138, 153n14
Threshold experience, 348, 352–54
Thunderstorm, 271–72
Tongue of angels, 168, 177n7
Translation, 76–77, 89n22, 293, 299n51
Tree of life: symbolism of, 56, 137–41; Adam and Eve and, 117n70; temple

and, 152n11; rituals and, 153n12; in Jewish literature, 153n13; coming to, 154n21; ancient temple and, 172–75; as symbol of Christ's redemption, 179–80; divergent interpretations of, 206; Jesus Christ as, 230–32; introduction to, 318–19; flavor of fruit from, 319–20; in threshold experience stage, 352–54

Tree of the knowledge of good and evil, 319

Tree(s): use of term, 106–7; symbolism of, 109–10, 117n70, 137–41, 352; sacred, 137, 152n7, 153nn12, 13

Trenton, Battle of, 272

Trials, 324, 325–27, 385–86

Truth, 353–54, 357, 358–59, 371n34

Tuttle, A. Theodore, 159n39

Two thousand stripling warriors, 252–53

Typology, 39, 45–47

Uchtdorf, Dieter F., 11, 308

Unbelief, generational consequences of: introduction to, 240–42; faith of Laman and Lemuel and, 242–46; compassion for Lamanites and, 246–48; Lamanite conversion and, 248–53; faith of Lamanites and Nephites and, 253–57; rebelliousness and, 257–58; deteriorating faith and, 258–59; conclusions on, 259–60

United States, Restoration and, 277. *See also* American Revolution

Van Gennep, Arnold, 348

Violence, in last days, 46, 49

Visions, dreams and, 94–95, 112n11

Vita Adae et Evae, 140–41

Voice, of Jesus Christ, 228–30

Wandering, 225, 360–61

War, 47–48, 55–56, 186–87, 192, 228, 244

Washington, George, 267–73, 275–76

Waste, dark and dreary, 217–18, 369n23

Weather, 269–73, 280n32

Welch, John W., 382

Welfare, 380

Wells, Daniel H., 377

Wells, Rulon S., 378

West Point chain, 273–75

White, 349–50, 368n19

White robe, man in, 349–50, 369n20

Whitney, Orson F., 320

Wicked: during Millennium, 52n27; in tree of life vision, 158n34, 207; punishment of, 321–22

Widtsoe, John A., 324

Wilcox, S. Michael, 62

Wilderness, dark and dreary, 217–18, 349, 369n23

Will, submission of, 341, 343

Wirthlin, Joseph B., 299n52, 382

Witnesses: law of, 25–26; of Jesus Christ, 82; of revelatory experiences, 199–201

Wood, Robert S., 383

Woodruff, Wilford, 266–67

Word clusters, 103, 106–8

Word of Christ, 166, 168, 171

Word of God: coming unto Christ through, 72; iron rod as, 147–51; Jesus Christ as, 182; attack on, 192; importance of, 309–10. *See also* Iron rod; Scripture(s)

Wordplay: of Jacob, 28–29; in dream reports, 99, 103, 106–8

Word repetition, 183–84

Words of angels, 170–72

Works, 380

World, in Lehi's vision, 185–86

Worldliness, 64, 313–15, 382–85

World War II, 380

Worship, 122

Worthiness, 124, 125–26, 131

Wrath of God, 269

Writing style, ancient, 79–80

Young, Brigham: on Millennium, 49; on Founding Fathers, 277; on revelation, 304; on testimonies, 308; on selfishness, 313; on sin, 324; Lehi's vision and, 376

Youth, 387

Zanach, 123, 133n18

Zen Buddhist order, 367n4

Zeniff, 247–48

Zion, 256–57

Zivic, Claudio D., 160n46

Zwick, W. Craig, 383